本书由中央高校基本科研业务费专项资金资助出版

国际法模拟法庭实践教学指南

书状范本·问题研究·技巧分析

宋 岩◎编著

世界知识出版社

图书在版编目（CIP）数据

国际法模拟法庭实践教学指南：书状范本·问题研究·技巧分析 / 宋岩编著. — 北京：世界知识出版社，2022.6

ISBN 978-7-5012-6439-1

Ⅰ. ①国… Ⅱ. ①宋… Ⅲ. ①国际法院—案例—指南 Ⅳ. ① D99-62

中国版本图书馆 CIP 数据核字（2021）第 229740 号

责任编辑	王瑞晴
文字编辑	蔡金娣　张　璐
责任出版	赵　玥
责任校对	张　琨

书　　名	**国际法模拟法庭实践教学指南：书状范本·问题研究·技巧分析** Guojifa Moni Fating Shijian Jiaoxue Zhinan: Shuzhuang Fanben • Wenti Yanjiu • Jiqiao Fenxi
编　　著	宋　岩

出版发行	世界知识出版社
地址邮编	北京市东城区干面胡同 51 号（100010）
电　　话	010-85112689（编辑部） 010-65265923（发行部） 010-85119023（邮购电话）
网　　址	www.ishizhi.cn
印　　刷	北京虎彩文化传播有限公司
经　　销	新华书店
开本印张	710 毫米 ×1000 毫米　1/16　35¼ 印张
字　　数	616 千字
版次印次	2022 年 6 月第一版　2022 年 6 月第一次印刷
标准书号	ISBN 978-7-5012-6439-1
定　　价	120.00 元

序 言

杰赛普国际法模拟法庭竞赛（Phillip C. Jessup）自 1959 年开始，迄今已经举办了 60 多届，是目前国际上规模最大、历史最悠久的专业性国际法模拟法庭比赛，被誉为国际法学界的“奥林匹克竞赛”。自该项赛事引入中国后不久，外交学院持续参与了这项赛事。外交学院代表队的师生们通过多年的不懈努力，在这项赛事中取得了优异的成绩：2017 年获得杰赛普国际法模拟法庭竞赛中国赛区季军、国际赛最佳书状、全球优胜队伍（32 强）、全球百强辩手，2018 年再次夺得中国赛区季军，2019 年获得中国赛区一等奖，2020 年获得中国赛区一等奖（书状赛）。本书的主要目的是总结外交学院参加该项比赛的成果，反映外交学院国际法模拟法庭实践教学成绩，以及分享备赛技巧与经验。

本书由三部分组成：第一，2017 年至 2020 年外交学院代表队参加比赛的书状，书状直接反映了外交学院代表队的竞赛水平；第二，参赛同学在教练老师指导下研究赛题争议问题完成的学术论文，研究涉及环境影响评价、核裁军、国家同意原则、国际野生动物保护、人权条约的域外适用、遗传资源相关的传统知识利用、自主武器系统、豁免等国际法最前沿问题，这些研究反映了外交学院代表队的研究能力和教学水平；第三，外交学院代表队备赛和参赛的经验总结，包括比赛指导、法律研究、事实分析、口头陈述、引注格式等多个重要环节的经验。

国际法模拟法庭竞赛通常围绕两个虚构国家之间的法律争端展开，结合给定事实提出若干争议问题，要求参赛同学模拟请求国和被告国的律师分析案件事实，研究国际法规则，以英语为比赛语言撰写书状，并向法庭口头陈述主张，是一种非常典型的实践教学形式。模拟法庭竞赛对于国际法教学的重要作用主要体现在如下方面：高标准和高水平的竞赛提高了参赛同学的英语水平、专业基础、事实分析能力、团队精神和心理素质；参赛同学通常会选择与比赛相关的主题完成毕业论文，因为有了之前的研究，论文选题具体且新颖，完成质量较高；而比赛的经历通常能够帮助同学们收获心仪的升学和工作机会，达到了“一次比赛，终身受益”的效果。

自2016年进入外交学院工作以来，每年我都指导同学们参加国际法模拟法庭竞赛，这个过程从9月开学一直持续到来年的3月或者4月，每周的讨论、汇报，假期的模拟训练已经融入我的工作和生活。无论是对于参赛同学还是老师来说，杰赛普国际法模拟法庭竞赛确实都是非常具有挑战性的任务。面对纷繁复杂的事实、冲突甚至是空白的国际法规则和案例、漫长的备赛期、各种刁钻古怪的问题、每年不重样的突发情况，没有坚强的意志、乐观的精神和崇高的荣誉感，真的很难坚持到底。值得庆幸的是，我总是能遇到许多可爱的同学，他们愿意为比赛付出努力。我们共同经历过最后期限前的挑灯夜战，经历过赛场上的激烈对抗，经历过“黑八奇迹”后的喜极而泣，经历过赛后樱花林中的闲庭信步，当然也曾有过遗憾出局的不甘与失落……在准备和参加比赛的过程中，我们共同进步，逐渐成熟，收获了珍贵的友谊，我非常有幸能成为其中的一员。

整理和总结比赛资料，为日后的比赛提供经验和借鉴，帮助更多对国际法模拟法庭竞赛感兴趣的同学准备比赛，是我一直以来的心愿。近四届外交学院代表队的同学们（详见文后名单）与我一起实现了这个心愿，大家非常配合并积极投入这项艰巨的工作。很多同学重新整理了几年前的书状和论文，提交了非常用心的备赛总结，并按照我的意见一遍又一遍修改了多次。受疫情影响，在网课之余，我这学期大部分时间都在组稿、审稿和修改，本书的完成经历非常烦琐，大到选题提纲，小到字体标点，基本每一份书状、论文和总结都经历了至少五遍的反复修改，这个过程不亚于我自己写论文，使我充分意识到耐心和热情在教学工作中的重要性。尽管如此，看到每一份稿件最终“旧貌换新颜”，想到我能够发动多届分布在世界各地从事各行各业工作的同学们一起完成这项工作，令我感到无比自豪和骄傲，这是对过去几年教学工作的最好总结。

外交学院“中央高校基本科研业务费专项基金”为本书的出版提供了资助，外交学院国际法系、教务处和研究生部长期以来支持和资助同学们参加国际法模拟法庭竞赛，在此表示特别感谢。外交学院李朗润、严帅东和李冰清几位同学协助我校对了书稿，在此一并表示感谢。感谢世界知识出版社的编辑老师们认真耐心的工作。此外，衷心感谢所有关心和帮助过我们的老师、同学及朋友们！

宋岩

2020年7月于山东烟台

2017—2020 年外交学院杰赛普代表队名单

2016—2017 年

陆晨（队长），外交学院国际法系 2012 级本科生、2016 级硕士研究生，现就职于上海方达（北京）律师事务所。

区炜妍，外交学院国际法系 2012 级本科生、2016 级硕士研究生，哥伦比亚大学法律硕士，现就职于美国世达律师事务所。

刘燕彬，外交学院国际法系 2014 级本科生，复旦大学法学院 2018 级硕士研究生，现就职于上海方达律师事务所。

秦辕东，外交学院国际经济学院 2013 级本科生，墨尔本大学法律博士。

左一彤，外交学院国际法系 2014 级本科生，乔治城大学法律硕士，现就职于亚洲基础建设银行。

2017—2018 年

李子钰（队长），外交学院国际法系 2014 级本科生，中国政法大学 2018 级硕士研究生，现就职于北京汇仲律师事务所。

李泽坤，外交学院国际法系 2017 级硕士研究生，现就职于北京竞天公诚律师事务所。

廉雅雯，外交学院国际法系 2013 级本科生、2017 级硕士研究生，现就职于北京汉坤律师事务所。

罗诗静，外交学院国际法系 2015 级本科生，乔治城大学法律硕士，现就职于上海方达律师事务所。

周睿哲，外交学院国际法系 2015 级本科生，纽约大学法律硕士，现就职于北京金杜律师事务所。

2018—2019 年

杨一梁（队长），外交学院国际法系 2016 级本科生，乔治城大学法律硕士，曾就职于博鳌亚洲论坛。

李冰清，外交学院国际法系 2014 级本科生、2018 级硕士研究生，中国政法大学 2020 级博士研究生。

钟青萌，外交学院国际法系 2015 级本科生，北京大学国际法学院 2019 级硕士研究生。

叶欧仪，外交学院国际法系 2016 级本科生，美国西北大学法律硕士，现就职于（英国）年利达律师事务所。

陈然，外交学院外交学与外事管理系 2016 级本科生，中国人民大学国际关系学院外交学专业 2021 级硕士研究生。

2019—2020 年

叶欧仪（队长），外交学院国际法系 2016 级本科生，美国西北大学法律硕士，现就职于（英国）年利达律师事务所。

林泽宇，外交学院国际法系 2017 级本科生，中国政法大学中欧法学院 2021 级硕士研究生。

余施语，外交学院国际法系 2017 级本科生，中国政法大学国际法学院 2021 级硕士研究生。

李奕慧，外交学院国际法系 2017 级本科生、2021 级硕士研究生。

王姿月，外交学院国际法系 2017 级本科生、2021 级硕士研究生。

支持备赛和比赛的场下研究员：

周振科，外交学院国际法系 2014 级本科生、2018 级硕士研究生，现就职于中铁十八局集团有限公司。

曹超，外交学院国际法系 2015 级本科生，纽约大学法律硕士，现就职于北京金杜律师事务所。

高正霖，外交学院国际法系 2016 级本科生。

严帅东，外交学院国际法系 2017 级本科生、2021 级硕士研究生。

秦子棋，外交学院国际法系 2016 级本科生、2020 级硕士研究生。

此外，卢思琦、郭旭阳、吴雨臻、杜鑫时、周梦迪、王一凡、刘致丽、李玉惠子、李哲茜、姜昕彤、吴宇萱、汪亚蓝、王劲松、吴姝琦等曾参与研究。

目 录

—— 第一部分 ——

书状范本

对书状范本部分的说明

本书的第一部分“书状范本”收录了外交学院代表队 2017 年到 2020 年参加杰赛普国际法模拟法庭竞赛的书状。每年的竞赛都会围绕虚构的案件事实展开，双方认可的事实都被包括在赛题（*compromis*/facts）中，赛题的最后会结合事实提出 4 个法律问题。每支参赛队伍要分别代表请求国（一般是一个首字母为 A 的虚构国家）和被告国（一般是一个首字母为 R 的虚构国家）用英文撰写两份书状（Memorial）和进行口头陈述。

本书所收录书状的各部分内容依据竞赛主办方的要求，包括：目录（Table of Contents）、管辖权说明（Statement of Jurisdiction）、陈述问题（Questions Presented）、事实说明（Statement of Facts）、书状总结（Summary of Pleadings）、书状正文（Pleadings）以及救济请求（Conclusion/Prayer for Relief）。为了图书编辑需要，每份书状删除了比赛书状的封面（Cover Page）、目录中的页码以及文献索引（Index of Authorities）。

书状的各级标题采取了 I. A. i. *a.* (i) 的形式。

书状的脚注参考了《牛津法律依据引注标准》（*Oxford Standard for the Citation of Legal Authorities, OSCOLA*）和《牛津法律依据引注标准：国际法分节》（*OSCOLA: Citing International Law Sources Section*），具体格式可参见本书第三部分中《国际法模拟法庭书状的引注格式及注意问题》一文。

“太阳姐妹案”

Case Concerning the Sisters of the Sun (The Federation of the Clans of the Atan v The Kingdom of Rahad)

陆晨　区炜妍　刘燕彬　秦辕东　左一彤

请求国书状

Memorials for the Federation of the Clans of the Atan

TABLE OF CONTENTS

B. ALTERNATIVELY, RAHAD BREACHED THE OBLIGATION TO TAKE APPROPRIATE MEASURES TO PREVENT DESTRUCTION OF THE HERITAGE.

C. THE SAVALI PIPELINE OPERATIONS VIOLATE RAHAD'S OBLIGATION OF RESPECTING HUMAN RIGHTS.

i. Rahad has the obligation to respect human rights.

ii. The Savali Pipeline operations violate Atanian people's right to participate in cultural life.

III. RAHAD MUST IMMEDIATELY RETURN THE RUBY SIPAR TO ATANIA, ITS LAWFUL OWNER.

A. ATANIA IS THE LAWFUL OWNER OF THE RUBY SIPAR.

i. The Ruby Sipar is a cultural property under the 1970 Convention.

ii. As the State of origin, Atania has the ownership of the Ruby Sipar.

B. RAHAD MUST IMMEDIATELY RETURN THE RUBY SIPAR TO ATANIA.

i. Rahad has an obligation to return the Ruby Sipar to Atania under the 1970 Convention.

ii. Rahad violated the obligation not to defeat the object and purpose of the 1970 Convention and therefore should return the Ruby Sipar to Atania.

iii. Rahad has an obligation to return the Ruby Sipar to Atania under customary international law.

IV. ATANIA OWES NO COMPENSATION TO RAHAD FOR ANY COSTS INCURRED RELATED TO THE KIN MIGRANTS.

A. ATANIA DOES NOT VIOLATE ITS HUMAN RIGHTS OBLIGATIONS BY ITS CONDUCTS TOWARDS CLAN KIN.

i. Atania did not violate Atanian people's right to adequate food and water.

ii. Atania did not violate the right of peaceful assembly of the members of Clan Kin.

iii. The arrest and detention of the protesters were in conformity with Article 9 of ICCPR.

B. IN ANY EVENT, THERE IS NO STANDING FOR RAHAD TO CLAIM COMPENSATION IN ACCORDANCE WITH CLEAN HANDS DOCTRINE.

C. ALTERNATIVELY, RAHAD IS NOT ENTITLED TO CLAIM COMPENSATION SINCE IT IS ITS OBLIGATION TO ACCOMMODATE THE KIN MIGRANTS.

i. The Sisters of the Sun and their family members in Rahad are not refugees under the 1951 Refugee Convention and its Protocol.

ii. It is the international obligation of Rahad to provide non-conventional protection to Kin migrants.

CONCLUSION AND PRAYER FOR RELIEF

STATEMENT OF JURISDICTION

The Federation of the Clans of the Atan (Atania) and the Kingdom of Rahad (Rahad) hereby submit the present dispute to the International Court of Justice (the Court) pursuant to Article 40(1) of the Court's Statute, in accordance with the *Compromis* for submission to the Court of the differences concerning the Sisters of the Sun and other issues, signed in The Hague, The Netherlands, on the twelfth day of September in the year two thousand sixteen. Both States have accepted the jurisdiction of this Court pursuant to Article 36(1) of its Statute.

QUESTIONS PRESENTED

The Federation of the Clans of the Atan respectfully requests the Court to adjudge:

I.

1. Whether Rahad violates the obligation of equitable use of shared natural resources;

2. Whether Rahad violates the obligation to conduct environmental impact assessment;

3. Whether Rahad violates the obligation of cooperation through notification and negotiation.

II.

1. Whether the Savali Pipeline operations violate Rahad's obligation under Article 6 of the 1972 World Heritage Convention (WHC);

2. Whether the Savali Pipeline operations violate Rahad's obligation to take all appropriate measures to prevent destruction of cultural heritage on the territory of other States;

3. Whether Rahad violates the obligation to respect the human right to take part in cultural life.

III.

1. Whether Atania is the lawful owner of the Ruby Sipar;

2. Whether Rahad must immediately return the Ruby Sipar to Atania.

IV.

1. Whether Atania has conducted any internationally wrongful acts with respect to the Kin which will entail its international responsibility;

2. Whether Rahad loses its standing for claiming compensation from Atania in accordance with clean hands doctrine;

3. *Whether* the Kin migrants are conventional refugees or non-conventional refugees;

4. *Whether* all the costs of Rahad related to the Kin migrants are to perform its own obligations.

STATEMENT OF FACTS

The Federation of the Clans of the Atan (Atania) and the Kingdom of Rahad (Rahad), are neighboring countries on the Nomad Coast, an arid and semi-arid area. The Greater Inata Aquifer (the Aquifer) is a transboundary fossil aquifer, the largest source of groundwater in Nomad Coast and one of the largest aquifers in the world.

The Kin Canyon Complex (the Complex) consists of three canyons. Two canyons and the 'Stronghold', a walled fortress, are in Atania; the third canyon and the Sunrise Mesa, a freestanding sandstone, are in Rahad. The ancestors of both countries are the Atan, the original inhabitants of the Complex, which first divided into 17 clans and then two States in 1863.

The Ruby Sipar, named after a legend of a warrior of Clan Kin, was used as a symbol of 'the Sisters of the Sun' (the Sisters), an order of women to protect culture and traditions of the Kin. In 1903, the original Ruby Sipar was discovered by an archaeologist from the University of Atanagrad, founded and predominantly funded by the Atanian Government. In 1996, the Sipar identified as 'on loan from the University of Atanagrad', was moved to the Cultural Center in Atania for public display.

From 1983 to 1988, both Atania and Rahad suffered from sustained drought conditions, and were forced to import water. In 1988, Rahad hired a team of hydrologists to map the sources of fresh water in the Aquifer. The map indicated that 65% of the Aquifer was located in Rahad and 35% was in Atania.

In 1990, as parties to the 1972 World Heritage Convention, Atania and Rahad jointly proposed to include the Complex as a cultural and natural heritage into the World Heritage List, which was accepted on 2 May 1994.

On the first UN World Water Day in 1993, Rahadi Minister of Water and Agriculture promised to protect and preserve the shared fresh water resources and ensure their equitable use. The Atanian counterpart responded with appreciation for the cooperation. From 1999 to present, the area experienced record of low rainfall.

In 2002, Queen Teresa of Rahad stated the government's desire to improve access to the water of the Aquifer, described the Aquifer as resources of her country, and formally directed the Inata Logistic and Scientific Association (ILSA) to study the feasibility and effect of tapping the Aquifer. The report stated the total extractable period of 30 years at a rate of ending reliance on imported water.

On 2 February 2003, Queen Teresa addressed her plans to deal with the water crisis. Subsequently, President Vhen expressed his concern about the equitable division of the waters. On 30 September 2004, Rahad submitted the Savali Pipeline plan (Pipeline) to the World Heritage Committee concerning the impact on the Complex. On 12 June 2005, the Committee published its decision requiring Rahad to ensure the Pipeline targeted for improving the conservation of the Complex.

On 20 February 2006, pumping from the Aquifer started. Since 1 January 2007, Rahad has not imported water. In 2009, Atanian farmers reported that the land in the south of the Complex was becoming dry and difficult to farm. Atania commissioned an international panel of scholars to assess the impact and release a study, which concluded that the Pipeline had caused permanent lowering of water table in the region, 20% of loss of farmland in Atania and an additional 30% if continued.

A panel of geologists, ordered by President Vhen, investigated and found that there had been clear structural degradation of the Canyons and the Stronghold within Atania due to depletion of the Aquifer. Later the sections of the Complex were closed to visitors to ensure their safety. On 7 July 2011, Atania President requested the Complex be added to the List of World Heritage in Danger, which was granted in June 2012.

Faced with continued loss of farmable land due to the absence of water seepage from the Aquifer, the Atanian Parliament enacted the 2012 Water Resource Allocation Program Act (WRAP Act) setting a quota on water in Atania. All farming operations were required to purchase licenses to utilize public water, nearly 86% of which qualified for license exemptions. Few Kin farmers applied for licenses and many Kin households and farms used water in excess of their quotas. All the violators were sent notification for failure to comply with the WRAP Act.

Two Kin farmers did not pay the fine for over-quota water use and failedto obtain a license, so they were thereafter sentenced to prison according to the applicable Criminal Code. The warning flyers distributed across Kin lands did not help the situation. In October 2013, the Atanian Parliament amended the WRAP Act providing that farms in violation of the WRAP Act would be subject to the termination of their state-controlled water supply.

On 17 July 2014, Carla Dugo, one of the elders of the Sisters, engaged in a hunger strike in protest. Over 5,000 Sisters, hundreds of Kin, and their supporters, who wore or carried the replicas of the Ruby Sipar, congregated. They blocked roads, interfered with local businesses, and disrupted regular social activities, rendering the conditions in the city chaotic and entirely unsustainable.

On 5 August 2014, considering the Ruby Sipar had come to ‘provoke disruptive elements within Atania’, President Vhen issued an order to remove the Ruby Sipar from public display and seize the Sipar Pendants. Atanian police arrested some of the protesters and drove the others away with no deaths or serious injuries reported. Those arrested were provided with court-appointed counsel, each of which had an initial appearance and was remanded to custody pending trial under Atanian domestic law.

In September 2014, with the Kin crossing into Rahad, the Rahadi Parliament enacted the Kin Humanitarian Assistance Act (KHAA), which provided that Kin identified as Sisters and their family members were immediately granted refugee status. All other Kin entering Rahad were permitted to apply for refugee status, to be determined on a case-by-case basis, but these applications have been pending until now.

On 3 October 2014, Carla Dugo turned over the Ruby Sipar that she had removed from the Cultural Center to Rahad, without providing more details. Sophia Casa, the Rahadi Minister of Culture, notified her counterpart in Atania that she was in possession of the Ruby Sipar and formally rejected the request for repatriation of the Ruby Sipar on 3 November 2014. The Atanian Minister stated that this demonstrated 'a blatant disregard for the cooperative relationship' and 'a clear violation of international law'.

By August 2015, the International Rescue Committee monitored the conditions at three temporary camps for the Kin. They reported that the number of Kin exceeded the capacity of the facilities created to receive them. While the members of the Rahadi Parliament urged the repeal of the KHAA, the government spokesman dismissed it as 'xenophobic exaggeration'.

On 18 January 2016, the Rahadi Ambassador to Atania submitted to the Atanian Foreign Ministry a memorandum demanding compensation for the costs caused by the Kin as well as expenses continuing to accrue. Atania dismissed the memorandum as 'unprecedented, inconsistent with international law, and unworthy of a reply'. In April 2016, Atania and Rahad agreed to submit the dispute to the jurisdiction of the International Court of Justice.

SUMMARY OF PLEADINGS

FIRST PLEADING

The extraction of water violates the obligation of equitable use and not to cause transboundary damage undertaken by Rahad. Rahad has the obligation of equitable use of shared resources as imposed by its unilateral declaration, or under the principle of estoppel. In any event, such obligation is established under customary international law. Rahad's extraction of water from the Aquifer violates the obligation of equitable use considering: the population relying on the Aquifer, the need of future generations, the effect on Atania and the availability of alternative measures. Rahad has breached the procedural obligation to conduct environmental impact assessment and the obligation to notify and consult.

SECOND PLEADING

Rahad violates the obligation not to take deliberate measures which may cause direct or indirect damage to the Complex under Article 6(3) of the 1972 World Heritage Convention. Even if no deliberate measures have been taken, it is an obligation *erga omnes* to take all appropriate measures to prevent destruction of the cultural heritage. Rahad has breached such obligation by initiating the Savali Pipeline project which is at the risk of causing significant harm. Besides, Rahad has breached the obligation to respect people's right to take part in cultural life. Thus, Rahad must cease the wrongful act.

THIRD PLEADING

Rahad must immediately return the Ruby Sipar to Atania. Since the Ruby Sipar is a cultural property under the Convention on the Means of Prohibiting and Preventing the Illicit Import, Export and Transfer of Ownership of Cultural Property (1970 Convention), Atania, as the State of origin has the ownership of the Ruby Sipar. Rahad therefore has the obligation to return the Ruby Sipar to Atania. *First*, under Article 13 of the 1970 Convention, Rahad should cooperate with Atania to facilitate the earliest return of the Ruby Sipar which was illicitly exported. *Second*, even if the obligation of Article 13 is not established, Rahad still has the responsibility to return the Ruby Sipar, because it violated the obligation under Article 18 of the Vienna Convention on the Law of Treaties (VCLT). *Third*, with the protection for the State of origin of the cultural property, the obligation of Rahad to return the Ruby Sipar is consistent with customary international law.

FOURTH PLEADING

Atania owes no compensation to Rahad for any costs incurred related to the Kin migrants. There is no internationally wrongful act of Atania since it has not breached any of its human rights obligations required by Article 11 of the International Covenant on Economic, Social and Cultural Rights (ICESCR), Articles 21 and 9 of the International Covenant on Civil and Political Rights (ICCPR). Therefore, no responsibility can be entailed and Rahad has no grounds for claiming any kind of reparation. In any event, there is no standing for Rahad to claim compensation since it comes to the Court with unclean hands. Alternatively, according to customary international law, it is an obligation for a State to provide complementary protection to non-conventional refugees. Since the Kin migrants are non-conventional refugees, Rahad has the obligation to accommodate them and should not ask for any compensation for the costs of performing its own obligation.

PLEADINGS

I. EXTRACTION OF WATER FROM THE AQUIFER VIOLATES INTERNATIONAL OBLIGATIONS UNDERTAKEN BY RAHAD AND CONSTITUTES AN INEQUITABLE USE OF A SHARED RESOURCE.

A. RAHAD VIOLATES THE OBLIGATION OF EQUITABLE USE OVER SHARED NATURAL RESOURCES.

i. Rahad has the obligation of equitable use over shared natural resources imposed by its unilateral declaration.

According to the jurisprudence of this Court, to constitute a unilateral declaration, the act should *first* be public or generally known,[1] and *second* be made by persons with the capacity to represent the State.[2] Additionally, for the unilateral act to have legal consequences, it should show the intention of the State to be bound.[3] The content and reaction of interested States should be taken into account.[4] However, there is no requirement as to the form,[5] acceptance,[6] or a process of negotiation.[7]

a. The speech made by the Minister of Rahad constitutes a unilateral declaration.

First, the declaration was made publicly by the Minister of Rahad in a nationally-televised address. [8]*Second,* the power in signing a treaty[9] is 'fully transferable'[10] to the

---

1 *North Sea Continental Shelf cases* (Federal Republic of Germany/Denmark; Federal Republic of Germany/Netherlands) (Judgment) [1969] ICJ Rep 3 [27].

2 *Armed Activities on the Territory of the Congo* (New Application: 2002) (Democratic Republic of the Congo v Rwanda) (Jurisdiction and Admissibility Judgment) [2006] ICJ Rep 6 [46]-[47].

3 *Nuclear Tests case* (New Zealand v France) (Judgment) [1974] ICJ Rep 457 [46].

4 International Law Commission (ILC) 'Guiding Principles Applicable to Unilateral Declarations of States Capable of Creating Legal Obligations, with Commentaries Thereto' (2006) UN Doc A/61/10 art 3.

5 *Case Concerning the Temple of Preah Vihear* (Cambodia v Thailand) (Merits) [1962] ICJ Rep 6, 31.

6 *Nuclear Tests case* (n 3) [46].

7 *Nuclear Tests case* (n 3) [46].

8 *Compromis* [16].

9 Vienna Convention on the Law of Treaties (adopted 22 May 1969, entered into force 27 January 1980) 1155 UNTS 331 (VCLT) art 7(1)(b).

10 ILC 'Eighth Report on Unilateral Acts of States' (2005) UN Doc A/CN4/557, 172.

capacity of addressing a unilateral declaration. Without evidence to the contrary, the Minister of Water and Agriculture of Rahad should be deemed as having *prima facie* capacity[11] to create an obligation by representing Rahad in the specific field of water utilization and protection.[12]

b. The declaration is legally binding on Rahad.

First, from the content[13] of the Minister's declaration, it is 'clear and specific in nature'[14] to impose an obligation. The declaration which the Minister of Rahad gave was unconditional and definite[15]: 'Rahad promises to ... preserve and protect the shared fresh water resources and to ensure their equitable use.'[16]

Promise[17] establishes 'a new rule binding the promising State towards one or more other States'[18] and is also considered as a 'legal transaction giving rise to obligations'.[19] Thus, by expressly declaring 'promise', Rahad has the intention to be legally bound by it.[20]

Second, such declaration is legally binding considering the reaction of Atania and the international community. Under the principle of good faith, interested States and the international community may take trust and cognizance of the unilateral declaration, and thus are entitled to require that the obligation created be respected.[21] Atania has

11 *Armed Activities on the Territory of the Congo* (n 2) [47].

12 *Compromis* [16].

13 ILC Unilateral Declaration (n 4) arts 3, 6, 7.

14 *Nuclear Tests case* (n 3) [43] [51] [46] [53]; *Armed Activities on the Territory of the Congo* (n 2) [50] [52].

15 *Legal Status of Eastern Greenland* (Denmark v Norway) (Judgment) PCIJ Rep Series A/B No. 53, 73.

16 *Compromis* [16].

17 *Nuclear Tests case* (Australia v France) (Judgment) [1974] ICJ Rep 253 [51]; *Case Concerning the Frontier Dispute* (Burkina Faso v Republic of Mali) (Judgment) [1986] ICJ Rep 554 [39]-[40].

18 *Nuclear Tests case* (n 17) [51]; *Frontier Dispute* (n 17) [39]-[40]; Antonio Cassese, *International Law* (2nd edn, OUP 2005) 185.

19 *Military and Paramilitary activities in and against Nicaragua* (Nicaragua v United States of America) (Merits) [1986] ICJ Rep14 [261].

20 *Compromis* [16].

21 *Nuclear Tests case* (n 3) [46] [49].

taken trust in Rahad, so it has not competed to drain the aquifer before Rahad can.[22] Besides, the UN Secretary General Kofi Annan also recalled the Rahadi Minister's statement as 'a commitment to preserve and protect the water resources'.[23] Thus, such declaration is binding on Rahad.

ii. Alternatively, Rahad undertakes the obligation of equitable use under the principle of estoppel.

Rahad has the obligation under the principle of estoppel, as the legitimate expectation of Atania should be respected.[24] As concluded in the *Chagos* case, estoppel may be invoked where four elements are concluded.[25] For the case at hand, the element of clear representation, authorization and reliance have been established above. The only element left to be established is the action to its detriment. Atania was induced by such representations to act to its detriment, refraining from large-scale extraction of water from the Aquifer.[26] Hence, Rahad undertakes the obligation of equitable use.

iii. In any event, Rahad has the obligation of equitable use established in customary international law.

The concept of equity is described as a 'general principle directly applicable as law'.[27] The obligation of equitable use derives from such principle and is generally regarded as a rule of customary international law,[28] qualifying the elements of state practice and *opinio juris*.[29] The state practice of equitable use of shared natural

22 Renee Martin-Nagle, 'Fossil Aquifers: A Common Heritage of Mankind' (2011) 2 *Geo. Wash. J. Energy & Envtl. L.* 39, 51.

23 *Compromis* [17].

24 *Chagos Marine Protection Area Arbitration* (Mauritius v United Kingdom) [2015] PCA Case No. 2011-03 [435].

25 *Chagos Marine Protection Area Arbitration* (n 24) [439].

26 *Clarifications* [9].

27 *Continental Shelf case* (Tunisia/Libyan Arab Jamahiriya) (Judgment) [1982] ICJ Rep 18 [60].

28 'Dissenting Opinion-Water Resources Committee Report' in International Law Association Report of the Seventy-First Conference (Berlin 2004); UNECE 'Model Provisions on Transboundary Groundwaters' (February 2014) UN Doc ECE/MP.WAT/40, 3.

29 Statute of the International Court of Justice (adopted 26 June 1945, entered into force 24 October 1945) 33 UNTS 993 art 38(2); *Continental Shelf* (Libyan Arab Jamahiriya/Malta) (Judgment) [1985] ICJ Rep 13 [27].

resources is reflected in international legal instruments,[30] bilateral agreements[31] and other numerous examples.[32] As suggested in the *Nicaragua* case, *opinio juris* can be 'deduced from ... the attitudes of ... States towards certain Assembly resolutions',[33] and statements made by representatives of States.[34] Equitable use of shared natural resources is widely supported in the United Nations General Assembly (UNGA) Resolutions,[35] and this principle 'had not been objected to and had received some support during the discussions of the International Law Commission (ILC) and the Sixth Committee'.[36]

---

30 ILC 'Draft Articles on the Law of Transboundary Aquifers, with Commentaries' (2008) UN Doc A/63/10 (ILC Aquifers) art 4; Robert D Hayton, Albert Utton, 'Transboundary Groundwaters: The Bellagio Draft Treaty' (1989) 29 *Natural Resources Journal* 668 arts 2, 6; Convention on the Protection and Use of Transboundary Watercourses and International Lakes (entered into force 6 October 1996) 1936 UNTS 269 art 2; Convention on the Law of the Non-navigational Uses of International Watercourses (adopted 21 May 1997, entered into force 17 August 2014) 36 ILM 700 (Watercourses Convention) art 7; Berlin Rules on Water Resources (7 August 2004) 71 ILA 337 arts 12, 42; Helsinki Rules on the Uses of the Waters of International Rivers (with comments) (adopted 20 August 1966) 52 ILA 484 art 4; The Treaty of Peace 1994 (Israel, Jordan and Palestine Liberation Organization) 36 ILM (1997) 763; The Guarani Aquifer Agreement (Argentina-Brazil-Paraguay-Uruguay) (2 August 2010) art 3.

31 *The Indus Water Treaty* (India-Pakistan) (19 September 1960); Convention on Cooperation for the Protection and Sustainable Use of the Danube River (signed 29 June 1994, entered into force October 1998) art 2.

32 *Case concerning the Gabčíkovo-Nagymaros Project* (Hungary/Slovakia) (Judgment) [1997] ICJ Rep 7 [78] [85] [147] [150]; *Case Concerning the Diversion of Water from the Meuse* (Netherlands v Belgium) (Judgment) PCIJ Series A/B No 70, 187-188; *Kansas v Colorado,* 206 US 46 (1907) 44-118; *New Jersey v New York,* 283 US 336 (1931) 1104-1109; *Württemberg & Prussia v The Baden*, German Staatsgerichtshof (18 June 1927).

33 *Nicaragua case* (n 19) [188].

34 *Nottebohm case* (Liechtenstein v Guatemala) (Second Phrase, Judgment) [1955] ICJ Rep 22 [3].

35 'The Law of Transboundary Aquifers' (15 January 2009) UNGA Res 63/124; 'The Law of Transboundary Aquifers' (13 January 2012) UNGA Res 66/104; 'The Law of Transboundary Aquifers-Report of the Sixth Committee' (19 November 2013) UN Doc A/68/470; 'The Law of Transboundary Aquifers' (20 December 2016) UNGA Res 71/150.

36 ILC 'Third Report on Shared Natural Resources: Transboundary Groundwaters by Mr Chusei Yamada, Special Rapporteur' (11 February and 9 March 2005) UN Doc A/CN4/551 and Add 1 [20].

iv. Rahad's extraction of water from the aquifer violates such obligation and constitutes an inequitable use of natural resources.

Since 1900s, groundwater has emerged as a chief source of fresh water and is of fundamental importance to human survival.[37] The principle of equitable use of shared resources requires a balance between the Parties' 'rights and needs',[38] in other words, an equitable share of concerned States[39] and inter-generation equity.[40]

Despite the non-binding nature of the Draft Articles on Transboundary Aquifers, governments are in general favorable and supportive on the first reading of the Draft Articles.[41] Other instruments such as International Law Association (ILA) Berlin Rules on Water Resources, and United Nations Economic Commission for Europe (UNECE) Model Provisions on Transboundary Groundwaters, which to some extent, mirror the factors in the ILC Draft Articles, also reflect the consensus of governments and thus can provide a concrete guidance on relevant factors to be taken into account.[42] The most relevant factors[43] include: *first*, the population dependent on the aquifer; *second*, the future need of the State; *third*, the effect on Atania; and *fourth*, the availability of alternative measures.[44]

a. The extraction of water from the Aquifer is inequitable considering the population dependent on the Aquifer.

Both Atania and Rahad have relied on the discharge from the Aquifer for generations.[45] The population of the concerned States should be a relevant factor to

37 G Eckstein, 'Protecting A Hidden Treasure: The UN International Law Commission and the International Law of Transboundary Ground Water Resources' (2005) 5 *American University Sustainable Development Law & Policy* 5, 5; UNECE 'Task Force on Monitoring and Assessment, Inventory of Transboundary Groundwaters' (September 1999) 21.

38 *Pulp Mills on the River Uruguay* (Argentina v Uruguay) (Judgment) [2010] ICJ Rep 14 [175].

39 *Gabčíkovo-Nagymaros* (n 32) [85].

40 ILC Aquifers (n 30) arts 4, 5.

41 ILC Aquifers (n 30) 28.

42 ILC Aquifers (n 30) art 5; Berlin Rules (n 30) art 13; Helsinki Rules (n 30) art 5.

43 ILC Aquifers (n 30) art 5; Berlin Rules (n 30) art 13.

44 ILC Aquifers (n 30) art 5; *Chagos Marine Protection Area Arbitration* (n 24) [519].

45 *Compromis* [4].

assess equitable use.[46] A rough comparison between Atania and Rahad is 22 million[47] to 3.5 million,[48] which is around 7 to 1. From the viewpoint of the need of 22 million Atanian people, Rahad's extraction of the water is not proportionate and thus inequitable.

b. The extraction of the Aquifer is inequitable considering the need of future generation.

Article 4(b)of the Draft Articles on Transboundary Aquifer emphasizes on maximizing the long-term benefits of the Aquifer. Considering the Aquifer is the largest source of underground water and the region is arid and semi-arid area, with little rainfall,[49] access to the water in the Aquifer is extremely important for future generations to sustain life. However, Rahad has utilized the Aquifer in a way that will exhaust the Aquifer in 30 years,[50] which is contrary to the principle of inter-generation equity and thus constitutes inequitable use.

c. The extraction of water from the Aquifer is inequitable considering its effect on Atania and interest of Atania.

Rahad, by unilaterally assuming that it has absolute sovereignty over the transboundary Aquifer,[51] extracted water from the Aquifer in a large scale,[52] and thereby deprived Atania of its right to an equitable and reasonable share of the natural freshwater resources. Such utilization failed to respect the proportionality required by international law.[53] Besides, Rahad's extraction of water from the aquifer caused 20%

---

46 ILC Aquifers (n 30) art 5; Berlin Rules (n 30) art 13; see B R Chauhan, 'Settlement of International and Inter-state Water Disputes in India' (1993) 30 *Canadian Yearbook of International Law* 443: the allocation of water is 80% to 20% considering Pakistan's huge population relying on the water.

47 *Compromis* [2].

48 *Compromis* [4].

49 *Compromis* [1] [4] [14] [19].

50 *Compromis* [21].

51 *Compromis* [33].

52 *Compromis* [21].

53 *Gabčíkovo-Nagymaros* (n 32) [85].

loss of Atania's farmland and US$300,000,000 annually.[54] Considering such damage on Atania, Rahad's extraction of the water is inequitable.

Rahad's extraction of water from the aquifer ignored the interest of Atania. The concern and proposal of Atania's President received no reply from Rahad.[55] As in the *Pulp Mills* case, failing to consider the interest of riparian State is considered inequitable,[56] the same is with the present case.

d. The extraction of water from the Aquifer is inequitable considering the availability of alternatives to the utilization of the Aquifer.

Alternatives are available to Rahad as it used to import water to solve the problem of low rainfall.[57] There is no evidence showing that the availability of such alternatives has changed. Therefore, relying on the extraction of the Aquifer to meet the need of entire Rahad is inequitable.

B. EXTRACTION OF WATER FROM THE AQUIFER VIOLATES THE PROCEDURAL OBLIGATION UNDERTAKEN BY RAHAD.

A State is obliged to use all the means at its disposal in order to avoid activities which take place in its territory, or in any area under its jurisdiction, causing significant damage to the environment of another State.[58]

This Court has confirmed that if there is risk of significant transboundary harm, the State applying for the activities has the obligation under customary international law to (i) conduct environmental impact assessment (EIA); and (ii) notify and consult.[59]

---

54 *Compromis* [28] [29].

55 *Compromis* [23].

56 *Pulp Mills case* (n 38) [77].

57 *Compromis* [14].

58 *Pulp Mills case* (n 38) [101]; *Construction of a Road in Costa Rica along the San Juan River* (Nicaragua v Costa Rica) (Judgment) [2015] ICJ Rep 665 [104].

59 *Construction of a Road in Costa Rica* (n 58) [104].

The threshold of obligations to conduct the EIA, notify and negotiate[60] is met in the present case. *First*, 'significant' is something more than 'detectable' but need not be at the level of 'serious' or 'substantial'.[61] *Second,* the scale of the project can be a relevant factor.[62] In the Model Provisions on Transboundary Groundwaters, the abstraction of 10 million cubic meters annually is considered large-scale.[63] By contrast, the annual extraction of water from the Aquifer is 1.2 billion cubic meters. Considering the large-scale extraction, there is substantial risk to cause significant transboundary harm.

i. Rahad breached the obligation of carrying out an EIA under the requirement of due diligence.

a. The minimum content of the EIA is not satisfied.

In *Pulp Mills* case, this Court decides that an EIA should consider the 'nature and magnitude of the development', and 'effects on people, property and environment'.[64] The content of an EIA, should at a minimum, include 'a description of practical alternatives'.[65]

In the present case, the EIA issued by the ILSA is incomplete. *First*, it only considered the impact on the Complex,[66] but failed to take account of the potential impact on the region in general.[67] *Second*, the EIA made no provision for alternative sites of the Pipeline and failed to include any consultation of the potentially affected populations.[68]

b. Rahad failed to monitor the effects of the operation of Savali Pipeline continuously.

In its Judgment in the *Pulp Mills* and *Construction of a Road in Costa Rica* case,

60 *Construction of a Road in Costa Rica* (n 58) [156].

61 ILC 'Draft Articles on Prevention of Transboundary Harm from Hazardous Activities, with Commentaries' (2001) UN Doc A/RES/56/10, 152-153.

62 *Construction of a Road in Costa Rica* (n 58) [155].

63 Model Provisions on Transboundary Groundwaters (n 28) 14.

64 *Pulp Mills case* (n 38) [203].

65 *Pulp Mills case* (n 38) [210].

66 *Compromis* [21].

67 *Compromis* [28].

68 *Compromis* [21].

this Court holds that the obligation to carry out an EIA is a continuous one, and that monitoring the project's effects on the environment should be undertaken throughout the life of the project.[69] There is no evidence showing such studies have been carried out.

ii. Rahad breached the obligation of cooperation through notification and consultation.

Rahad was obliged to cooperate[70] in good faith with Atania about the Savali Pipeline plan[71] through notification, consultation and negotiation. Although this does not oblige the States to reach an agreement,[72] it indeed requires States to negotiate with an attitude towards reaching an agreement so that 'negotiations were meaningful',[73] and it will not be the case if 'either of them insists upon its own position without contemplating any modification of it'.[74] Rahad's insistence of its position[75] has rendered the cooperation meaningless.

Rahad's statement created reasonable expectation[76] for Atania to believe that there would be further opportunities to respond and exchange views. Such expectations were frustrated as the studies Rahad promised to undertake were never available. Rahad has not fulfilled the basic purpose of consulting, given the absence of a reasoned exchange between the States. In the *Chagos* case, even the existence of a meeting between the parties is considered unsatisfactory,[77] let alone the situation with Rahad.

---

69 *Pulp Mills case* (n 38) [205]; *Construction of a Road in Costa Rica* (n 58) [161].

70 *MOX Plant* (Ireland v UK) (2003) 42 ILM 1187 [82].

71 *MOX Plant* (n 70) [82]; *Lake Lanoux case* (Spain v France) [1957] 12 RIAA 281 [101].

72 *Railway Traffic between Lithuania and Poland* (Advisory Opinion) [1931] PCIJ Rep Series A/B No 42 [31]; *Application of the International Convention on the Elimination of All Forms of Racial Discrimination* (Georgia v Russia) (Preliminary Objections) [2011] ICJ Rep 70 [158].

73 *North Sea Continental Shelf* (n 1) [85].

74 *North Sea Continental Shelf* (n 1) [85].

75 *Compromis* [33].

76 *Compromis* [33].

77 *Chagos Marine Protection Area Arbitration* (n 24) [530].

II. THE SAVALI PIPELINE OPERATIONS VIOLATE RAHAD'S INTERNATIONAL OBLIGATIONS WITH RESPECT TO THE KIN CANYON COMPLEX AND THEREFORE MUST CEASE.

The Kin Canyon Complex was jointly proposed by Atania and Rahad into the World Heritage List in 1990.[78] Rahad, as the contracting party of 1972 World Heritage Convention (WHC),[79] breached the obligation under Article 6 of WHC [A]. Even if no deliberate measures were taken, Rahad breached the obligation *erga omnes* to safeguard the Complex [B]. Additionally, Rahad breached the obligation to respect human rights [C]. Thus, Rahad must cease the wrongful act pursuant to Article 30 of the ILC Articles on Responsibility of States for Internationally Wrongful Acts (ARSIWA).[80]

A. RAHAD BREACHED THE OBLIGATION UNDER ARTICLE 6 OF WHC.

Rahad breached the obligation not to take deliberate measures under Article 6 (3) of WHC, qualifying (i) a deliberate measure and (ii) existence and causation of damage.

i. The Savali Pipeline operations are a deliberate measure.

The international legal movement for the protection of cultural heritage has evolved through two parallel but separate contexts, that is, peacetime and armed conflicts.[81] Specifically, WHC is to be applied in peacetime.[82] Therefore, the obligation under WHC should be interpreted in the context of peace time.

Under Article 31 of VCLT, Article 6 should be interpreted according to ordinary meaning in the context and in light of its purpose.[83] The ordinary meaning of 'deliberate' includes 'intentional; premeditated; fully considered'.[84] Besides, the

---

78 *Compromis* [13].

79 *Clarifications* [10].

80 ILC 'Articles on Responsibility of States for Internationally Wrongful Acts' (2001) UN Doc A/56/83 (ARSIWA).

81 Federico Lenzerini, 'The UNESCO Declaration Concerning the Intentional Destruction of Cultural Heritage: One Step Forward and Two Steps Back' (2003) 13 *Italian Y B Int'l L* 131, 132.

82 UNESCO 'Report of the Twenty-fifth Session of the Bureau of the World Heritage Committee, 25-30 June 2001' (17 August 2001) WHC-2001/CONF205/10 para I.9.

83 VCLT art 31.

84 Bryan Garner, *Black's Law Dictionary* (9th edn, West Publishing Company 2009) 520.

purpose of WHC is to secure the peacetime protection of cultural heritage and prevent it from 'social and economic threats'.[85] Thus, in the broader sense, the obligation of not taking deliberate measures to cause direct and indirect damage should be interpreted as not taking measures which will threaten the outstanding value of the heritage for social or economic pursuit, either intentionally or with the knowledge after full consideration.

From the geological perspective, as the Kin Canyons were located near the Aquifer,[86] excessive pumping is likely to cause cone of depression and finally collapse of surface.[87] There is no EIA as evidence to guarantee that moving the drilling areas can prevent such harm. With the conclusion of the EIA released by the ILSA, Rahad actually had the knowledge that the depletion of the Aquifer Waters may harm the structural integrity of the Complex.[88] With such knowledge, Rahad initiated the Savali Pipeline Project that may cause damage to the Complex, which shall be characterized as a deliberate measure.

ii. The integrity of the Complex was damaged due to such measure.

To be deemed of 'Outstanding Universal Value', conditions of the integrity and authenticity must be met.[89] There are different notions of integrity, including structural integrity, functional integrity and visual integrity.[90] Integrity is a measure of the wholeness or intactness of the heritage.[91] In general, the wholeness of the Complex has been damaged.[92]

---

85 Convention for the Protection of the World Cultural and Natural Heritage (adopted 16 November 1972) 1037 UNTS 151 (WHC) Preamble.

86 *Compromis* [26].

87 Gabriel Eckstein, Yoram Eckstein, 'A Hydrogeological Approach to Transboundary Ground Water Resources and International Law' (2003) 19 *American University International Law Review* 201, 220.

88 *Compromis* [21].

89 UNESCO 'Operational Guidelines for the Implementation of the World Heritage Convention' (2015) UN Doc WHC 15/01 [78].

90 UNESCO 'Background Document on the Notion of Integrity Prepared by the World Heritage Centre, ICOMOS, ICCROM and IUCN' (7 March 2012).

91 UNESCO Operational Guidelines (n 89) [88].

92 *Compromis* [30].

a. Rahad caused damage to the structural integrity of the Complex.

The structural integrity of the Complex can be assessed by the physical fabric of the heritage.[93] It was damaged as there had been clear structural degradation of the Canyons and the Stronghold.[94] To prove the linkage between the operation of the Pipeline and the damage, the investigation of the geologists[95] shows the extent of the damage, as a just and reasonable inference is sufficient.[96] Thus, Rahad violates such obligation.

b. Rahad caused damage to the visual integrity of the Complex.

The visual integrity refers to the distinctive character[97] or significant features[98] of the heritage. For example, the visual integrity of the Kakadu National Park is viewed as been threatened considering the holes of the site caused by mining.[99] Similarly, the damage of Stronghold (architecturally and archaeologically significant), the sinkholes and collapse of the busy path,[100] showed Rahad's damage to the visual integrity.

B. ALTERNATIVELY, RAHAD BREACHED THE OBLIGATION TO TAKE APPROPRIATE MEASURES TO PREVENT DESTRUCTION OF THE HERITAGE.

This Court has recognized in the *Barcelona Traction* case that there are 'obligations of a State towards the international community as a whole' which are 'the concern of all States' and for whose protection all States have a 'legal interest'.[101]

---

93 UNESCO Operational Guidelines (n 89) [89].

94 *Compromis* [30].

95 *Compromis* [30].

96 *Trail Smelter case* (US v Canada) [1938/1941] 3 UNRIAA 1906, 1920.

97 Background Document on the Notion of Integrity (n 90); UNESCO 'Expert Meeting on Integrity and Authenticity in the African Context' (26-29 May 2000).

98 UNESCO Operational Guidelines (n 89) [89].

99 Natasha Affolder, 'Mining and the World Heritage Convention: Democratic Legitimacy and Treaty Compliance' (2007) 24(1) *Pace Environmental Law Review* 35, 39; UNESCO 'Reports on the State of Conservation of Specific Properties Inscribed on the World Heritage List' (30 September 1997) UN Doc WHC97/CONF207/2, 3-4.

100 *Compromis* [5].

101 *Case Concerning the Barcelona Traction, Light and Power Company, Limited* (Belgium v Spain) (Judgment) [1970] ICJ Rep 3, 33-34.

In the hierarchy of norms in public international law, the human rights law is a strong international norm since human rights are the 'inherent dignity and the equal and inalienable rights of all members of the human family'.[102] The cultural heritage fits under this norm since it is 'part of the general interest of the international community as a whole'[103] and access to it constitutes fundamental cultural rights, an integral part of human rights.[104] Therefore, the prohibition of destruction of cultural heritage of an outstanding universal value and great relevance for humankind is arguably an obligation *erga omnes*.[105]

Such prohibition imposes on States a duty to safeguard, that is, 'take all appropriate measures' to prevent acts of destruction of cultural property, wherever located.[106] Therefore, States should be deterred from undertaking development projects including the Savali Pipeline Project in the present case, which resulted in the destruction of cultural heritage. Failing such deterrence, Rahad breached its obligation to take all appropriate measures to prevent destruction of the heritage.

C. THE SAVALI PIPELINE OPERATIONS VIOLATE RAHAD'S OBLIGATION OF RESPECTING HUMAN RIGHTS.

i. Rahad has the obligation to respect human rights.

Cultural heritage is important not only in itself, but also in relation to its human dimension, in particular its significance for individuals and communities and their identity and development processes.[107] Rahad, as a State Party to the International Covenant on Economic, Social and Cultural Rights (ICESCR), shall recognize

---

102 'Universal Declaration of Human Rights' (10 December 1948) UNGA Res 217 A (III) Preamble.

103 Francesco Francioni, Federico Lenzerini, 'The Destruction of the Buddhas of Bamiyan and International Law' (2003) 14(4) *EJIL* 619, 633.

104 CESCR 'General Comment No 21: Right of Everyone to Take Part in Cultural Life (art 15 [1] (a) of ICESCR)' (21 December 2009) UN Doc E/C12/GC/21 [1].

105 *Request for Interpretation of the Judgment of 15 June 1962 in the Case concerning the Temple of Preah Vihear* (Cambodia v Thailand) (Separate Opinion of Judge Cançado Trindade) [2011] ICJ Rep 566, 598;*The Destruction of the Buddhas* (n 103) 633-634.

106 WHC Preamble; UNESCO 'Declaration Concerning the Intentional Destruction of Cultural Heritage' (17 October 2003) UNESCO Doc 32C/Res 38.

107 HRC 'Report of the Independent Expert in the Field of Cultural Rights, Farida Shaheed' (21 March 2011) UN Doc A/HR/C/17/38 [77]; UNESCO 'Declaration on the Principles of International Cultural Cooperation' (16 November 1966) UNESCO Doc 28C/Res 5.61 art 1.

the right of everyone to take part in cultural life,[108] and thus should refrain from interfering, directly or indirectly, with the enjoyment of the right to take part in cultural life[109] and respect human's cultural rights, both within their territories[110] and extraterritorially.[111]

ii. The Savali Pipeline operations violate Atanian people's right to participate in cultural life.

To participate in cultural life, humans shall have access to their own cultural and linguistic heritage and to that of others.[112] Due to the damage of the Complex caused by Rahad, sections of the Complex were closed, including the significant Stronghold.[113] So not only visitors, but also Atanian people are barred from entering the Complex. Therefore, Rahad violates its obligation of respecting the rights of people to take part in cultural life.

III. RAHAD MUST IMMEDIATELY RETURN THE RUBY SIPAR TO ATANIA, ITS LAWFUL OWNER.

A. ATANIA IS THE LAWFUL OWNER OF THE RUBY SIPAR.

i. The Ruby Sipar is a cultural property under the 1970 Convention.

The 1970 Convention grants each State Party the right to specify the scope and content of the definition of its own cultural property through a declaration of designation.[114] The Ruby Sipar is of importance in the designation by Atania as one

108 International Covenant on Economic, Social and Cultural Rights (adopted 16 December 1966) 993 UNTS 3 (ICESCR) art 15.

109 General Comment No 21 (n 104) [48].

110 General Comment No 21 (n 104) [40].

111 FIAN International 'Maastricht Principles on Extraterritorial Obligations of States in the Area of Economic, Social and Cultural Rights' (29 February 2012) (Maastricht Principles) [3].

112 General Comment No 21 (n 104) [49 (d)].

113 *Compromis* [30].

114 Convention on the Means of Prohibiting and Preventing the Illicit Import, Export and Transfer of Ownership of Cultural Property (adopted 14 November 1970) 823 UNTS 231 (1970 Convention) art 1; UNESCO Doc SHC/MD/3, 5; Patrick O'Keefe, *Commentary on the 1970 UNESCO Convention on the Means of Prohibiting and Preventing the Illicit Import, Export and Transfer of Ownership of Cultural Property* (2nd edn, Institute of Art and Law 2007) 34.

of the 'Atan archaeological objects regardless of material or value, dating from the year 1900 CE or before',[115] as it was part of the archaeological treasures of the Atan[116] which appeared in 500 CE.[117]

Additionally, the Ruby Sipar belongs to the categories of cultural properties enumerated in Article 1 of the Convention.[118] *First*, the Ruby Sipar was associated with the exploits of warrior Teppa defeating the invaders,[119] which is an event of importance to 17 Atan Clans and Atania in particular.[120] *Second*, the Ruby Sipar was discovered in an archaeological excavation,[121] within another category under Article 1.[122]

ii. As the State of origin, Atania has the ownership of the Ruby Sipar.

a. Atania has the ownership of the Ruby Sipar as part of its national cultural heritage.

Considering that cultural property constitutes one of the basic elements of national culture,[123] Article 4 of the 1970 Convention enumerates categories of cultural property which can form part of the cultural heritage of a State Party.[124] As the Ruby Sipar was found within the territory of Atania,[125] and was considered as a symbol of respect that represented the united cultures of Atania,[126] it forms part of the national cultural heritage of Atania.[127]

The 1970 Convention emphasizes the interests of States in the national cultural

---

115 *Compromis* [60].

116 *Compromis* [6]-[7].

117 *Compromis* [8].

118 O'Keefe (n 114) 34.

119 *Compromis* [8].

120 1970 Convention art 1(b).

121 *Compromis* [12].

122 1970 Convention art 1(c).

123 1970 Convention Preamble.

124 UNESCO Doc SHC/MD/3, 6.

125 *Compromis* [12].

126 *Compromis* [43].

127 1970 Convention art 4.

heritage by linking the cultural property to the territory of States.[128] The national interests, values, and pride,[129] in the form of the national cultural patrimony,[130] enable States of origin to acknowledge their ownership of the cultural property.[131] In other words, the State of origin, which includes the geographic area of the cultural property, and whose people are descendants of that culture, rightfully claim that property.[132] Therefore, Atania, as the State of origin, whose people are the descendants of the united culture of the Atan clans,[133] enjoys the ownership of the Ruby Sipar.

b. The principle of State sovereignty ensures Atania's ownership of the Ruby Sipar.

Under the principle of State sovereignty, all things within the territory of a State fall under its territorial authority,[134] so any State has the right to exercise control or govern the objects within its territorial boundaries.[135] In other words, the State of the territory in which the cultural property was found holds the ownership of such a property.[136] Therefore, Atania has the ownership of the Ruby Sipar which was within its territory.

B. RAHAD MUST IMMEDIATELY RETURN THE RUBY SIPAR TO ATANIA.

Rahad deposited its instrument of ratification with UNESCO on 30 September 2014[137] and the 1970 Convention therefore entered into force with respect to Rahad on 30

128 1970 Convention Preamble art 2; *Beyeler v Italy* (2002) ECHR 462 [113].

129 Carol Roehrenbeck, 'Repatriation of Cultural Property–Who Owns the Past? An Introduction to Approaches and to Selected Statutory Instruments' (2010) 38 (2) *International Journal of Legal Information* 185, 190.

130 Francesco Francioni, James Gordley (eds.), *Enforcing International Cultural Heritage Law* (OUP 2013) 12, 81.

131 UNESCO Doc SHC/MD/3, 6; UNESCO 'The Operational Guidelines for the Implementation of the 1970 Convention' (May 2015) [18].

132 John Merryman *et al*, *Law, Ethics and the Visual Arts* (5th edn, Kluwer Law International 2007) 342.

133 *Compromis* [8] [10].

134 Robert Jennings, Arthur Watts (eds), *Oppenheim's International Law* (Vol. 1, Peace, 9th edn, Longman 1992) 458.

135 Ian Brownlie, James Crawford, *Brownlie's Principles of Public International Law* (7th edn, OUP 2008) 448; Joseph Fishman, 'Locating the International Interest in International Cultural Property Disputes' (2010) 35 *YJIL* 347, 352.

136 John Merryman, 'Two Ways of Thinking about Cultural Property' (1986) 80(4) *AJIL* 831, 845-846.

137 *Corrections* [3].

December 2014.[138] The removal of the Ruby Sipar by Carla Dugo took place before the 1970 Convention entered into force for Rahad,[139] but it did not bar Atania from claiming the return of the Ruby Sipar from Rahad.

i. Rahad has an obligation to return the Ruby Sipar to Atania under the 1970 Convention.

a. The removal of the Ruby Sipar by Carla Dugo from the territory of Atania is an illicit export of cultural property.

Under the 1970 Convention, the export of a cultural property contrary to the provisions adopted by the State Parties shall be illicit.[140] According to the Declaration made by Atania, none of the cultural properties may be removed from the territory of Atania without an export license to be issued by the Ministry of Culture.[141] The removal of the Ruby Sipar from the Kin Canyon Complex Cultural Center in Atania to Rahad[142] violated the export prohibitions in Atania and clearly constituted an illicit export.

b. Rahad should cooperate in facilitating the earliest possible return of the illicitly exported Ruby Sipar to Atania.

Article 13 of the 1970 Convention provides that State Parties undertake to cooperate in facilitating the earliest possible restitution of illicitly exported cultural property to its rightful owner.[143] In light of the context of the 1970 Convention,[144] reading Article 13 in conjunction with Article 3 can lead to the conclusion that the illicit export of the cultural property has no time limitation.[145] In other words, State Parties have an obligation of returning the cultural property illicitly exported before the 1970 Convention entered into force. In addition, State Parties are encouraged to exhaust all

138 1970 Convention art 21.

139 *Compromis* [50].

140 1970 Convention art 3.

141 *Compromis* [60].

142 *Compromis* [50].

143 1970 Convention art 13 (b).

144 VCLT art 31.

145 O'Keefe (n 114) 10.

means at their disposal to provide the fullest cooperation.[146]

As elaborated above, Atania is the lawful owner of the Ruby Sipar. After the illicit export of the Ruby Sipar, Rahad refused to return it to Atania and retained possession of it.[147] The acts of Rahad obviously show that it has not provided fullest cooperation to return the Ruby Sipar yet. Therefore, it follows that Rahad has an obligation to return the Ruby Sipar to Atania as early as possible.

ii. Rahad violated the obligation not to defeat the object and purpose of the 1970 Convention and therefore should return the Ruby Sipar to Atania.

According to Article 18 of VCLT, after a State has expressed its consent to be bound, pending the entry into force of the treaty, it is 'obliged to refrain from acts which would defeat the object and purpose of a treaty', provided that the entry into force is not unduly delayed.[148] Rahad violated this obligation and therefore has the responsibility to return the Ruby Sipar to Atania.

a. Rahad expressed the consent to be bound by the 1970 Convention through ratification and the entry into force of the Convention is not unduly delayed.

The effect of the deposition of ratifications by the parties is to establish their consent to be bound by the treaty vis-à-vis States which also establish their consent.[149] Ratification makes a treaty binding on the ratifying party.[150] So by depositing of the instrument of ratification,[151] Rahad consented to be bound and should be in full knowledge of the object of the 1970 Convention.[152] Additionally, it is clearly provided that the entry into force of the 1970 Convention would not be delayed.[153]

146 UNESCO Operational Guidelines (n 131) [96].

147 *Compromis* [51] [52].

148 VCLT art 18 (2).

149 VCLT art 16.

150 Jennings, Watts (n 134) 1235.

151 *Corrections* [3].

152 *Allgemeine Versicherungsgesellschaft v EK* (1972) BGHZ 59, 82, 86-87; *L v Indictment Chamber of the Canton of Geneva*, First Public Law Division (1997).

153 1970 Convention art 21.

b. Rahad violated the obligation not to defeat the object and purpose of the 1970 Convention before it entered into force.

Under Article 18 of VCLT, the State must not act that would invalidate the basic purpose of the treaty.[154] The violation of Article 18 would occur when a State engages in conduct which would amount to a 'material breach'[155] if the treaty was already in force.

As the illicit import, export or transfer of ownership of cultural property is one of the main causes of the impoverishment of the cultural heritage of the State of origin of such property, the 1970 Convention has an object and purpose to put a stop to such practices, which requires the undertaking of the State Parties to cooperate.[156]

As the removal of the Ruby Sipar already constituted the impoverishment of the cultural heritage of Atania, the acceptance and possession of the Ruby Sipar by Rahad encouraged, instead of 'opposing', this practice and clearly defeated the object and purpose of the 1970 Convention. If the 1970 Convention were already in force, Rahad's conduct would materially breach the Convention. Therefore, Rahad violated the obligation under Article 18 of VCLT.

c. Consequently, Rahad should return the Ruby Sipar to Atania.

With the help of the preparatory work of VCLT for interpretation,[157] Article 18 constituted a legal obligation.[158] The violation of this obligation will entail the international responsibility of a State.[159] In this sense, the responsible State is under an obligation of reparation,[160] including reestablishing the situation which existed before

154 Anthony Aust, *Modern Treaty Law and Practice* (3rd edn, CUP 2013)18.

155 VCLT art 60(3)(b).

156 1970 Convention art 2; O'Keefe (n 114) 33.

157 VCLT art 32.

158 ILC 'Documents of the Fifth Session Including the Report of the Commission to the General Assembly' *Yearbook of International Commission* (Vol. II, 1953) UN Doc A/CN 4/SER A/1953/Add 1, 108; ILC 'Documents of the Eighth Session Including the Report of the Commission to the General Assembly' *Yearbook of International Commission* (Vol. II, 1956) UN Doc A/CN 4/SER A/1956/Add 1, 121.

159 ARSIWA arts 1, 2; Joni Charme, 'Interim Obligation of Article 18 of the Vienna Convention on the Law of Treaties: Making Sense of an Enigma' (1991) 25 *Geo Wash J Int'l L & Econ* 71, 95.

160 ARSIWA art 31.

the wrongful act.[161]

As Atania suffers an ongoing injury caused by its lack of possession of the Ruby Sipar, which is a part of Atania's cultural heritage,[162] it is necessary and possible for Rahad to return the Ruby Sipar to Atania, as a way of restoring the integrity of the cultural heritage of Atania prior to the wrongful acts of Rahad.

iii. *Rahad has an obligation to return the Ruby Sipar to Atania under customary international law.*

In any event, international law provides protection for the State of origin's claims of ownership to cultural properties. Under customary international law, Rahad has an obligation to return the Ruby Sipar to Atania, the State of origin, in which the elements of state practice and *opinio juris* are met.

According to this Court, the state practice can be established when many States engage in the same practice.[163] The practice of returning of the cultural properties to the States of origin gains support from international legal instruments,[164] bilateral agreements[165] and other numerous examples.[166]

---

161 *Case Concerning the Factory at Chorzów* (Germany v Poland)(Merits) PCIJ Rep Series A No 17, 47; Paolo Palchetti, 'Article 18 of the 1969 Vienna Convention: A Vague and Ineffective Obligation or a Useful Means for Strengthening Legal Cooperation?' in Enzo Cannizzaro, Mahnoush Arsanjani (eds.), *The Law of Treaties Beyond the Vienna Convention* (OUP 2011) 32.

162 ARSIWA art 42 (a); *Republic of Turkey v OKS Partners*, 797 F Supp 64 (D Mass 1992).

163 *Fisheries case* (United Kingdom v Norway) [1951] ICJ Rep 116, 131, 138.

164 Convention on Stolen or Illegally Exported Cultural Objects (adopted 26 June 1995) 2421 UNTS 457; Committee of Cultural Heritage Law 'Principles for Cooperation in the Mutual Protection and Transfer of Cultural Material' in *International Law Association Report of the Seventy-Second Conference* (2006).

165 Cambodia-Thai Bilateral Agreement to Combat against Illicit Trafficking and Cross-Border Smuggling of Movable Cultural Property and to Restitute it to the Country of Origin (14 June 2000); US-Cambodia Cultural Property Agreement (19 September 2003); Agreement between the Federal Council of the Swiss Confederation and the Government of the Hellenic Republic on the Import, Transit and Repatriation of Cultural Property (15 May 2007); etc.

166 Lyndel Prott (ed.), *Witnesses to History: A Compendium of Documents and Writings on the Return of Cultural Objects* (UNESCO 2009) 414-415.

A number of cases in this Court utilized General Assembly resolutions as confirming the existence of *opinio juris*.[167] The return of cultural property to State of origin is widely supported by UN General Assembly resolutions,[168] in which the consistent endorsement by States persuasively proves the subjective belief that such a practice is obligatory.

Seen from the evidence above, the obligation to return the cultural property to the State of origin is acknowledged to be customary international law. In conclusion, Rahad must return the Ruby Sipar to Atania.

IV. ATANIA OWES NO COMPENSATION TO RAHAD FOR ANY COSTS INCURRED RELATED TO THE KIN MIGRANTS.

A. ATANIA DOES NOT VIOLATE ITS HUMAN RIGHTS OBLIGATIONS BY ITS CONDUCTS TOWARDS CLAN KIN.

Atania does not breach any international obligations of its own and therefore there is no internationally wrongful act[169] that can entail the international responsibility of Atania.[170] Thus, no State can invoke the responsibility of Atania[171] and claim compensation based on that.[172]

i. Atania did not violate Atanian people's right to adequate food and water.

Article 11 of ICESCR recognizes the enjoyment of right to adequate food[173] and

167 *Legality of the Threat or the Use of Nuclear Weapons* (Advisory Opinion) [1996] ICJ Rep 226, 254-255; *Western Sahara* (Advisory Opinion) [1975] ICJ Rep 12, 31-33; *Legal Consequences of the Construction of a Wall in the Occupied Palestinian Territory* (Advisory Opinion) [2004] ICJ Rep 136, 171-172.

168 'Return or Restitution of Cultural Property to the Countries of Origin' (18 December 1972) UN Doc A/RES/3026A; GA Res 52/24 (25 November 1991) UN Doc A/RES/52/24; GA Res 64/78 (7 December 2009) UN Doc A/RES/64/78; GA Res 70/76 (9 December 2015) UN Doc A/RES/70/76; etc.

169 ARSIWA art 2.

170 ARSIWA art 1.

171 ARSIWA art 42.

172 ARSIWA art 31.

173 ICESCR art 11.

water.[174] However, violation does not occur when a State facing resource constraints has made every effort, as a matter of priority, to satisfy its minimum obligations to the maximum of its available resources at its disposition[175] both within it and from the international community[176] and tries to ensure the widest possible enjoyment of the relevant rights.[177]

Atania is obviously facing serious water resource constraints caused by the record-low rainfall, the long-time drought[178] and the Savali Pipeline,[179] which evidenced by the drying-up wells, springs, streams[180] and the rapid lowering of the water table that has been bringing permanent destruction to a large portion of Atanian farmland at a fast rate.[181]

Facing its resource constraints,[182] with both domestic and expensive[183] imported water,[184] Atania launched the WRAP Act by setting a quota to ensure every household, farm and business, certainly including those in Clan Kin, an equal access to water resource,[185] a license system privileging large agricultural producers[186] to help sustain agricultural production as much as possible and protect the right to adequate food, and punishments[187] that can prohibit any over-consumption and assist the widest

174 CESCR 'General Comment No. 15: The Right to Water' (29 November 2002) UN Doc E/C12/2002/11 [3].

175 CESCR 'General Comment No. 12: The Right to Adequate Food' (5 May 1999) UN Doc E/C12/1999/5 [17].

176 CESCR 'General Comment No. 3: The Nature of State Parties' Obligation' (1 January 1990) UN Doc E/1991/23 [14].

177 General Comment No. 3 (n 176) [11].

178 *Compromis* [19].

179 *Compromis* [28].

180 *Compromis* [27].

181 *Compromis* [28].

182 *Compromis* [34].

183 *Compromis* [14].

184 *Clarifications* [9].

185 *Compromis* [34].

186 *Compromis* [35].

187 *Compromis* [35].

enjoyment of water and food.

ii. Atania did not violate the right of peaceful assembly of the members of Clan Kin.

Article 21 of ICCPR recognizes the right of peaceful assembly while at the same time admitting that restrictions which are necessary in a democratic society in the interests of public order can be placed in conformity with the law.[188]

The interests of public order should be defined the functioning of a society.[189] The widespread demonstrations across the country[190] consisting of thousands of people led by the Sisters of the Sun[191] lasted for a long period.[192] The demonstrators paralyzed traffic systems in many areas of the country,[193] interfered with local business, disrupted regular activities,[194] painted their symbols on politically important and public places,[195] which evidently disturbed the normal functioning of the society and justified restrictions.

In such circumstances, Atania government had no choice but to proportionately restrict the demonstration. The purpose of disbandment was to preserve law and maintain social order.[196] The police dispersed the protesters with tear gas and rubbers,[197] both of which are commonly used to control dangerous chaos, and no death or serious injuries were caused.[198]

---

188 International Covenant on Civil and Political Rights (adopted 16 December 1966, entered into force 23 March 1976) 999 UNTS 171 (ICCPR) art 21.

189 UNCHR 'The Siracusa Principles on the Limitation and Derogation Provisions in the International Covenant on Civil and Political Rights' (28 September 1984) UN Doc E/CN 4/1985/4 [22].

190 *Compromis* [46].

191 *Compromis* [41].

192 *Compromis* [41] [43] [46].

193 *Compromis* [42] [46].

194 *Compromis* [46].

195 *Compromis* [42].

196 *Compromis* [43].

197 *Compromis* [45].

198 *Compromis* [45] [46].

iii. The arrest and detention of the protesters were in conformity with Article 9 of ICCPR.

According to Article 9 of ICCPR, no one shall be subjected to arbitrary arrest or detention.[199] The notion of 'arbitrariness' includes elements such as lack of legal basis,[200] unreasonableness and inappropriateness.[201] Therefore, the arrest of the protesters was not arbitrary since it was based on the relevant Atanian law,[202] for the reason to stop the dangerous chaos created by these protesters,[203] and limited to a very small proportion of the protesters.[204]

Article 9 requires that anyone arrested or detained on a criminal charge shall be brought promptly before a judge and be tried within a reasonable time or to release.[205] They are also entitled to legal assistance.[206] In conformity with these requirements, each detainee as provided with a legal counsel and had an initial appearance.[207] The pretrial detention also complies with Atanian domestic law.[208]

B. IN ANY EVENT, THERE IS NO STANDING FOR RAHAD TO CLAIM COMPENSATION IN ACCORDANCE WITH CLEAN HANDS DOCTRINE.

Rahad is foreclosed from asking for compensation concerning the Kin migrants because it comes to the Court with unclean hands. The PCIJ,[209] the ICJ,[210] jurists,[211]

199 ICCPR art 9(1).

200 CCPR 'General Comment No. 35: Article 9 (Liberty and Security of Person)' (16 December 2014) UN Doc CCPR/C/GC/35 [11].

201 General Comment No. 35 (n 200) [12].

202 *Compromis* [45]; *Clarifications* [7].

203 *Compromis* [42] [43] [46].

204 *Compromis* [41] [42] [45] [46].

205 ICCPR art 9(3).

206 General Comment No. 35 (n 200) [34].

207 *Clarifications* [7].

208 *Clarifications* [7].

209 *Case Concerning the Diversion of Water from the River Meuse* (Netherlands v Belgium) (Separate Opinion by Judge Hudson) PCIJ Rep Series A/B No. 70, 77.

210 *Military and Paramilitary Activities in and against Nicaragua* (Nicaragua v United States of America) (Dissenting Opinion by Judge Schwebel) [1986] ICJ Rep 558 [268].

211 Gerald Fitzmaurice, '*The General Principles of International Law considered from the*

international arbitration[212] and the ILC's Special Rapporteur[213] have affirmed clean hands doctrine as a principle of international law. This principle precludes a State guilty of illegal conduct from making claims with regard to corresponding illegalities by another States which were provoked by its own illegal conduct.[214]

There exists an international obligation for Member States, including Rahad, to ICESCR to respect the human rights of individuals beyond their territory, especially the right to water.[215] The obligation of respect requires the Member States to refrain from any conduct which impairs the ability of another State to comply with its human rights obligations.[216]

Ignoring the oppositions from Atania,[217] the risk of causing long-term shortage of water[218] and the constant drought both countries have been faced with,[219] Rahad depletes the Aquifer unscrupulously, which has led to disastrous and irreversible damages to Atanian water supply and agriculture,[220] therefore fails to respect the basic human rights of Atanian people and impairs the ability of Atan to perform its relevant obligations. In this way, even though there is illegality with respect to Atanian treatment to the members of Clan Kin, it is partly caused by Rahad's own breach of international law and thus Rahad owes no standing to claim any relevant compensation.

Standpoint of the Rule of Law' (1957) 92 *Recueil des Cours de l'Académie de Droit International* 119, 119.

212 *Award in the Arbitration regarding the Delimitation of the Maritime Boundary between Guyana and Suriname* (Guyana v Surinam) (2007) 30 RIAA 1 [418]-[421].

213 ILC 'Report of the International Law Commission on the Work of Its 57th Session' (2 May-3 June and 11 July-5 August 2005) UN Doc A/60/10 [226]; ILC 'Report of the International Law Commission on the Work of Its 51st Session' (3 May-23 July 1999) UN Doc A/54/10 [414].

214 Fitzmaurice (n 211).

215 General Comment No 15 (n 174) [21]; Maastricht Principles (n 111) [19].

216 Maastricht Principles (n 111) [21].

217 *Compromis* [23] [33].

218 *Compromis* [22].

219 *Compromis* [19].

220 *Compromis* [27]-[29].

C. ALTERNATIVELY, RAHAD IS NOT ENTITLED TO CLAIM COMPENSATION SINCE IT IS ITS OBLIGATION TO ACCOMMODATE THE KIN MIGRANTS.

Without well-founded fear of persecution for discriminatory reasons, the Sisters of the Sun and their family members are not eligible to the refugee status set out in the 1951 Refugee Convention and its Protocol.[221] However, Rahad still has the obligation to provide protection to all the Kin migrants as non-Convention refugees in accordance with customary international law. Therefore, it has no standing to claim compensation for the cost of performing of its own obligation.

i. The Sisters of the Sun and their family members in Rahad are not refugees under the 1951 Refugee Convention and its Protocol.

a. There is an absence of persecution for any discriminatory reasons.

Persecution, as implied in Article 33 of the 1951 Refugee Convention, is a threat to life or freedom on account of discriminatory reasons.[222] However, it must be distinguished from a just punishment for a common law offence.[223] As mentioned above, the punishment to the demonstrators is in conformity with Atanian domestic law which itself meets the accepted human rights standards.[224] Further, the application of such punishment[225] is not discriminatory because it is not the membership of a certain social group[226] but their illegal acts that might lead to subsequent punishment. In other words, if a member of Clan Kin did not take part in the demonstration or refuse to disband, he would not be punished. Therefore, the application of such punishment is not discriminatory.

221 Convention Relating to the Status of Refugees (adopted 28 July 1951, entered into force 22 April 1954) 189 UNTS 137 art 1; Protocol Relating to the Status of Refugees (adopted 31 January 1967, entered into force 4 October 1967) 606 UNTS 267 art 1.

222 UNHCR 'Handbook on Procedure and Criteria for Determining Refugee Status under the 1951 Convention and the 1967 Protocol Relating to the Status of Refugees' (2011) UN Doc HCR/1P/4/Eng/REV3 [51].

223 Handbook on Procedure and Criteria for Determining Refugee Status (n 222) [56].

224 Handbook on Procedure and Criteria for Determining Refugee Status (n 222) [59].

225 Handbook on Procedure and Criteria for Determining Refugee Status (n 222) [59].

226 Handbook on Procedure and Criteria for Determining Refugee Status (n 222) [78].

b. There is an absence of well-founded fear for being persecuted.

Since fear is subjective,[227] each person must be assessed on its own merits.[228] However, Rahadi legislation granted the Sisters of the Sun and their family members refugee status without case-by-case assessment.[229] Therefore, it is reasonable to doubt their eligibility to the conventional refugee status.

ii. It is the international obligation of Rahad to provide non-conventional protection to Kin migrants.

UN resolution,[230] regional conventions and documents[231] and State legislative practices[232] have proved the protection of 'non-Convention refugees'[233] as customary international law, either by expanding the definition of refugee in its own legislation[234] or by providing them complementary protection.[235]

The criteria to determine the eligibility of non-Convention refugees are mostly based on the existence of serious events disturbing public orders[236] or other serious harms[237]

227 Handbook on Procedure and Criteria for Determining Refugee Status (n 222) [37].

228 Handbook on Procedure and Criteria for Determining Refugee Status (n 222) [43].

229 *Compromis* [48].

230 UNGA Res 71/1 (19 September 2016) UN Doc A/RES/71/1 [5] [11].

231 OAU Convention Governing the Specific Aspects of Refugee Problems in Africa (adopted 10 September 1969, entered into force 20 June 1974) 1001 UNTS 44 (OAU Convention) art 1; Cartagena Declaration on Refugees (adopted 22 November 1984) in Annual Report of the Inter-American Commission on Human Rights (1984-1985) OAS Doc OEA/Ser L/II 66/doc 10 rev 1 (Cartagena Declaration) conclusion 3; Council of the European Union 'Council Directive 2004/83/EC of 29 April 2004 on Minimum Standards for the Qualification and Status of Third Country Nationals or Stateless Persons as Refugees or as Persons Who Otherwise Need International Protection and the Content of the Protection Granted' (2004) OJ L 304, 30.9.2004/83 (EU Directive) art 2 (e).

232 Canada Immigration and Refugee Protection Act (2002) (IRPA) sections 95-98; Ecuador Presidential Decree 3301/92 (1992) arts 1, 2.

233 UNHCR 'Protection Mechanisms Outside of the 1951 Convention' (June 2005) PPLA/2005/02 ix.

234 OAU Convention (n 231) art 1; Cartagena Declaration (n 231) conclusion 3.

235 EU Directive (n 231) art 2(e).

236 OAU Convention (n 231) art 1; Cartagena Declaration (n 231) conclusion 3; Ecuador Presidential Decree (n 232) arts 1, 2.

237 EU Directive (n 231) art 2(e).

in the country of origin which make the return of these individuals inhumane.

As stated above, in Atania, drought has prolonged for many years and has been aggravated by the Savali Pipeline. It leads to serious starvation and lack of water and poses threat on the life of Atanian people. Such circumstances should be reckoned as serious events disturbing public order and serious harm to citizens' lives. Therefore, all the Kin migrants in Rahad who will continue to suffer the severe environmental disaster if returned to their country of origin should certainly be granted non-Convention refugees status.

The majority of the provisions in ICCPR and ICESCR apply to all individuals in the territory of a State, irrespective of their nationality.[238] Non-nationals who are granted relief from removal are entitled to a core set of rights,[239] which means that non-Convention refugees enjoy the right to an adequate standard of living (i.e. shelter, food and clothing).[240]

As a Party to ICCPR and ICESCR, Rahad is obliged to protect these non-Convention refugees by housing and resettling them,[241] and by spending money and resources, including water, food and power supply,[242] to meet their basic life demands. Thus, Rahad has no standing to ask for any compensation for its costs related to the Kin migrants, because they are the costs of performing its own international obligations.

238 ICESCR art 11; ICCPR art 2; General Comment No 12 (n 175) [15].

239 Complementary Protection (n 233) [73].

240 Complementary Protection (n 233) [74]; ICESCR art 11.

241 *Compromis* [49] [54] [57].

242 *Compromis* [53] [57].

CONCLUSION AND PRAYER FOR RELIEF

In view of the facts set forth in this Memorial and the arguments applying the law to the facts as stated;

May it please the Court, on behalf of the Federation of the Clans of the Atan, Applicant herein, respectfully requests this Honorable Court to adjudge and declare that:

1. Extraction of water from the Aquifer violates international obligations undertaken by Rahad and constitutes an inequitable use of a shared resource;

2. The Savali Pipeline operations violate Rahad's international obligations with respect to the Kin Canyon Complex and therefore must cease;

3. Rahad must immediately return the Ruby Sipar to Atania, its lawful owner; and

4. Atania owes no compensation to Rahad for any costs incurred related to the Kin migrants.

Respectfully submitted,
AGENTS FOR ATANIA

被告国书状

Memorials for the Kingdom of Rahad

TABLE OF CONTENTS

OBLIGATION NOT TO DELIBERATELY CAUSE DAMAGE.

i. The Complex was not damaged under WHC since its Outstanding Universal Value was not impaired.

ii. Even though the Complex was damaged, such damage was not caused by any deliberate measures undertaken by Rahad.

iii. Moreover, the Savali Pipeline operations caused no transboundary damage.

B. THE SAVALI PIPELINE OPERATIONS DID NOT VIOLATE THE LEGAL OBLIGATION TO PROTECT AND CONSERVE THE COMPLEX.

i. Articles 4 and 5 of WHC are not legal obligations.

ii. Peacetime protection of world heritage sites is not a customary legal obligation.

iii. Nevertheless, Rahad has endeavored to the utmost of its resources to protect and conserve the Complex.

C. RAHAD HAS DULY COOPERATED WITH THE INTERNATIONAL COMMUNITY.

i. Rahad has duly cooperated with Atania.

ii. Rahad has duly cooperated with the World Heritage Committee.

III. RAHAD IS ENTITLED TO RETAIN POSSESSION OF THE RUBY SIPAR.

A. RAHAD IS ENTITLED TO POSSESS THE RUBY SIPAR TO PROTECT IT AS A CULTURAL HERITAGE UNDER INTERNATIONAL LAW.

i. The Ruby Sipar is a cultural heritage under international law.

ii. Atania failed to fulfill its international obligations towards the Ruby Sipar.

iii. Rahad is performing its international obligation towards the Ruby Sipar.

B. RAHAD IS ENTITLED TO POSSESS THE RUBY SIPAR TO PROTECT INDIGENOUS CULTURAL RIGHTS OF CLAN KIN.

i. Clan Kin are indigenous people.

ii. The Ruby Sipar is a cultural heritage of Clan Kin.

iii. The return of Ruby Sipar would violate cultural rights of Clan Kin.

C. IN ANY EVENT, RAHAD HAS NO OBLIGATION TO RETURN THE RUBY SIPAR TO ATANIA.

i. Rahad has no obligation to return the Ruby Sipar to Atania under the 1970 Convention.

ii. Rahad has no obligation to return the Ruby Sipar to Atania under customary international law.

IV. ATANIA MUST COMPENSATE RAHAD FOR ALL DIRECT AND INDIRECT EXPENSES INCURRED AND ACCRUING AS A RESULT OF ACCEPTING MEMBERS OF CLAN KIN FLEEING FROM ATANIA.

A. ATANIA VIOLATES ITS INTERNATIONAL OBLIGATIONS BY ITS CONDUCTS TOWARDS CLAN KIN MIGRANTS.

i. Atania violates its international obligation to respect the right to 'water, food and life' of Clan Kin under international law.

ii. Atania violates its international obligation to respect the right of 'peaceful assembly' and 'lawful arrest' under international law.

iii. Atania's conducts violate its obligation to take 'effective remedy' under international law.

iv. The obligations violated by Atania are obligations erga omnes.

B. ATANIA'S VIOLATION SPECIALLY AFFECTS AND CAUSES DAMAGE TO RAHAD.

i. Rahad is a specially affected State of Atania's wrongful acts.

ii. The fleeing of Clan Kin resulted from Atania's wrongful acts causes severe social and economic damage to Rahad.

C. THEREFORE, ATANIA SHOULD COMPENSATE ALL EXPENSES INCURRED AND ACCRUING AS A RESULT OF ITS INTERNATIONALLY WRONGFUL ACTS.

CONCLUSION AND PRAYER FOR RELIEF

STATEMENT OF JURISDICTION

The Federation of the Clans of the Atan (Atania) and the Kingdom of Rahad (Rahad) hereby submit the present dispute to the International Court of Justice (the Court) pursuant to Article 40(1) of the Court's Statute, in accordance with the *Compromis* for submission to the Court of the differences concerning the Sisters of the Sun and other issues, signed in The Hague, The Netherlands, on the twelfth day of September in the year two thousand sixteen. Both States have accepted the jurisdiction of the Court pursuant to Article 36(1) of its Statute.

QUESTIONS PRESENTED

The Kingdom of Rahad respectfully requests the Court to adjudge:

I.

1. Whether Rahad enjoys permanent sovereignty over the Greater Inata Aquifer (the Aquifer);

2. Whether the statement made by the Rahadi Minister of Water and Agriculture created legal obligations upon Rahad as a unilateral declaration;

3. Whether the extraction of water from the Greater Inata Aquifer constituted proper use;

4. Whether Rahad has fulfilled its procedural obligations to cooperate with Atania and prevent significant harm.

II.

1. Whether the Kin Canyon Complex has been damaged;

2. Whether Rahad has taken any deliberately measures which might damage directly or indirectly the Kin Canyon Complex;

3. Whether the peacetime protection of the Kin Canyon Complex is a legal obligation under the World Heritage Convention (WHC) or customary international law, and *whether* Rahad has duly protected the Kin Canyon Complex;

4. Whether Rahad has duly cooperated with Atania and the international community.

III.

1. Whether the Ruby Sipar is cultural property under international law;

2. Whether Atania failed to fulfill its international obligations towards the Ruby Sipar;

3. Whether the Ruby Sipar is the cultural heritage of the indigenous people, Clan Kin;

4. Whether the return of Ruby Sipar would violate cultural rights of Clan Kin.

IV.

1. Whether Atania violates its obligation *erga omnes* by its conducts towards Clan Kin;

2. Whether Atania's wrongful acts specially affected Rahad;

3. Whether Atania's wrongful acts caused damage to Rahad;

4. Whether Rahad is entitled to invoke responsibility violated by Atania for compensation to all direct and indirect expenses incurred and accruing.

STATEMENT OF FACTS

The Federation of the Clans of the Atan (Atania), and the Kingdom of Rahad (Rahad), are neighboring states on the Nomad Coast, an arid and semi-arid area. Atania is a newly-industrializing state, whose major revenue comes from hydrocarbon extraction and grain exports. Rahad is a developing state, whose GDP has been considerably lower than Atania.

The Greater Inata Aquifer is a transboundary fossil aquifer and the largest source of fresh groundwater in the Nomad Coast, which has been used for centuries. Around 65% of the Aquifer was located in Rahad and 35% in Atania.

The Kin Canyon Complex (the Complex) is a group of three canyons, whose value lies mainly in natural scene as the Sunrise Mesa, historic site as the Stronghold and archaeological collections. The Aquifer is not subjacent to the Complex. In 1994, the Complex was included as a mixed heritage site on UNESCO's World Heritage List with a two-kilometer buffer zone.

Both countries originated from the Atan, the original inhabitants of the Complex. Clan Kin remained in the Complex and protected the Canyons, which they venerated as birthplace of their ancestors. In 1863, when Atania and Rahad formed, Clan Kin migrated to Atania and lived through simple agriculture while remained culturally and politically independent.

In memory of Teppa (500 CE), a legendary protector of the Complex, Clan Kin established 'the Sisters of the Sun' to protect its culture and traditions, whose members wear symbolic miniature replicas of the Ruby Sipar. The original Ruby Sipar, lost for centuries, was discovered in the Complex. In 1996, the Ruby Sipar, 'on loan from the University of Atanagrad', was moved to the Cultural Center on the Atanian side of the Complex.

On the first UN World Water Day, 22 March 1993, Rahadi Minister of Water and Agriculture made a nationally-televised statement concerning the importance of water when Queen Teresa of Rahad and Atanian President Alexander Vhen appeared together in Atanagrad.

From 1999 to the present, both states have been in severe drought. In 2002, Queen Teresa publicly expressed desire to improve access to the Aquifer to sustain Rahadi people, and directed the Inata Logistic and Scientific Association (ILSA) to study the feasibility and effect. The ILSA report was released in January 2003, including an environmental impact assessment (EIA) completed under Rahadi domestic law. In the ILSA report, integrity of the Complex was carefully considered.

In February 2003, Queen Teresa publicly announced plans to extract water from the Aquifer since there were no alternatives and extraction was a short-term solution. The Rahadi Bureau of the Interior later prepared the Savali Pipeline, which is a network of 30 pump wells connected by a subterranean pipeline system. Considering its potential impact on the Complex, Rahad submitted the plan and EIA to the World Heritage Committee (Committee) in 2004.

In 2005, the Committee published its decision, noting possible subsidence superjacent to the Aquifer and urging to ensure conservation of the Complex. To comply with the decision, Rahad limited drillings to areas more than 15 kilometers outside of the Complex's buffer zone. In February 2006, the Savali Pipeline was completed and pumping started.

In 2009, Atanian farmers south of the Complex reported loss of farmlands and water. The Atanian panel concluded that there was a lowering of the water table there and President Vhen claimed that there had been monetary loss.

In 2010, online images showed environmental modifications in remote sections of the Complex. In February 2011, Atanian geologists were ordered to investigate the veracity of the images. The geologists took weeks to conclude a structural degradation of the Canyons and the Stronghold in Atania and attributed it to depletion of the Aquifer.

In July 2011, President Vhen requested the World Heritage Committee to add the Complex to the List of World Heritage in Danger with the results of the geologists' investigation. In June 2012, the Committee added the Complex to the List without consultation with Rahad. President Vhen later requested a meeting with Queen Teresa. The Queen replied by issuing a press release committing to undertake regular studies of the region.

In September 2012, the Atanian Parliament enacted the 2012 WRAP Act, setting a quota on Atania's water supply to deal with water shortage. Nearly 86% of farming operations qualified for exemptions, while the rest were required to purchase licenses to utilize public water supply. The Kin farmers were not profitable to get exemption, nor could they afford licenses. The Kin's cultural tradition also prevented them in doing so. Consequently, more than 80% of the Kin households and farms used water in excess of their quotas.

In August 2013, Atanian Department of Justice began the prosecution of two Kin farmers for the use of over-quota and failure to obtain a license. In October 2013, the Atanian Parliament amended the WRAP Act and by the end of 2013, the government cut off water to the majority of farms in Kin lands.

On 17 July 2014, Carla Dugo, one of the elders of the Sisters of the Sun, chained herself to a flagpole in the plaza outside the President's residence in Atanagrad to call for a protest. Within two weeks, over 5,000 Sisters of the Sun, hundreds of Kin, and their supporters had congregated in the plaza. The protesters formed human chains across major roads in Atanagrad.

On 5 August 2014, the Atanian President issued an order to clear the plaza and arrest the protestors. As a result, nearly 2,000 Sisters of the Sun and Kin protesters were arrested. No trial dates have been set as of the date of the Special Agreement.

In early September 2014, nearly 100,000 Kin, 'fear of arrest' or 'fleeing starvation', crossed the boundary into Rahad. On 18 September 2014, the Rahadi Parliament enacted the Kin Humanitarian Assistance Act (KHAA). 21,000 Sisters of the Sun and 134,000 of their family members were granted refugee status.

On 30 September 2014, Rahad deposited its instrument of ratification on the 1970 UNESCO Convention. On 3 October 2014, Carla Dugo turned over the Ruby Sipar she took from the Kin Canyon Complex Cultural Center in Atania to Rahad Border agents. The Rahadi Minister of Culture notified her counterpart in Atania that Rahad was in possession of the Ruby Sipar and it would be 'inappropriate' for it to be returned considering the public display prohibition of the Ruby Sipar in Atania.

By August 2015, the International Rescue Committee reported Rahadi national infrastructure 'was being stretched beyond the breaking point'. There were 85% sporadic power outages in 85% of the country lasting for more than four hours at a time, and reduced clean water for more than 150,000 Rahadi families, as well as the Kin in the camps.

On 13 October 2015, *Rahadi National Times* reported thousands of Kin refugees were engaging in petty crime, or sleeping in the streets, and unable to acclimate to the culture of Rahad. On 18 January 2016, the Rahadi Ambassador submitted the memorandum to Atania, demanding incurred expenses amount to US$ 945,000,000 as well as for expenses continuing to accrue.

Atania and Rahad concluded the Special Agreement concerning the Sisters of the Sun, and jointly submitted the dispute to ICJ – Atania as Applicant, Rahad as Respondent.

SUMMARY OF PLEADINGS

FIRST PLEADING

Rahad enjoys permanent sovereignty over its natural resources including the Greater Inata Aquifer (the Aquifer) to use and extract the water. The statement made by the Rahadi Minister of Water and Agriculture did not create any legal obligations upon Rahad since it did not reveal an intention to be bound considering its unclear and non-specific contents and its factual context and circumstances.

Moreover, Rahad's extraction of water constituted proper use of the Aquifer. The principle of equitable and reasonable use does not apply to fossil aquifers. Even though the principle is applicable, Rahad did not violate it considering all the factors. After all, the water extracted has been properly used since it served Rahad's vital human needs.

Finally, Rahad has fulfilled all the procedural obligations concerning shared resources including cooperation through notification and duly prevent significant harm by exercising due diligence including conducting a legal environmental impact assessment (EIA).

SECOND PLEADING

The Savali Pipeline operations did not violate any legal obligations concerning the Kin Canyon Complex (the Complex). The Complex was not damaged under the 1972 World Heritage Convention (WHC) since its Outstanding Universal Value was not impaired. The Savali Pipeline operations did not cause any transboundary harm to the Complex due to the absence of the required causal link and clear and convincing evidence. Even though the Complex was damaged, the damage was not caused by any deliberate measures undertaken by Rahad.

Moreover, Rahad did not violate the legal obligation to protect the Complex. Articles

4 and 5 of WHC concerning the protection and conservation of world heritage sites are not legal obligations. Peacetime protection of world heritage is also not a legal obligation under customary international law. Nevertheless, Rahad has endeavored to the utmost of its resources to protect the Complex.

Meanwhile, Rahad has duly cooperated with Atania by notification and the World Heritage Committee actively throughout the time though the Committee's decision to add the Complex to the List of World Heritage in Danger violated due process.

THIRD PLEADING

Rahad is entitled to possess the Ruby Sipar to protect it as cultural heritage under international law. The Ruby Sipar is a 'cultural heritage' under WHC, but Atania failed to fulfill its international obligations on the protection of the Ruby Sipar and make appropriate publicity when the Ruby Sipar disappeared. Therefore, Rahad shall be entitled to possess the Ruby Sipar to fulfill its international obligation for all human kind.

Moreover, Rahad is entitled to possess the Ruby Sipar to protect indigenous cultural rights of Clan Kin. With the characteristics of ancestral territories, continuity, self-identification, and distinctiveness, Clan Kin are indigenous people, who have cultural rights in respect of the Ruby Sipar as their cultural heritage. As Atania removed the Ruby Sipar from public display, the cultural rights of Clan Kin were violated without access to their cultural heritage, which makes it inappropriate to return the Ruby Sipar to Atania.

In any event, Rahad has no obligation to return the Ruby Sipar to Atania under the Convention on the Means of Prohibiting and Preventing the Illicit Import, Export and Transfer of Ownership of Cultural Property (1970 Convention) or customary international law.

FOURTH PLEADING

Atania must compensate Rahad for all direct and indirect expenses incurred and accruing as a result of accepting members of Clan Kin fleeing from Atania. Atania violated basic human rights of the people of Clan Kin by failing to respect their right to adequate water and food, right to life, right to peaceful assembly and lawful arrest (liberty and security) and right to effective remedy. Thus, it has breached the obligation owed to the international community and gives Rahad, as a specially-affected State, entitlement to invoke its responsibility and claim the performance of the obligation of reparation. The compensation shall cover all the direct and indirect expenses incurred and accruing in order to wipe out all the consequences of the illegal acts and restore the situation.

PLEADINGS

I. RAHAD'S EXTRACTION OF WATER FROM THE AQUIFER DID NOT VIOLATE RAHAD'S LEGAL OBLIGATIONS GOVERNING THE PROPER USE OF SHARED RESOURCES.

A. RAHAD ENJOYS PERMANENT SOVEREIGNTY OVER THE AQUIFER LOCATED WITHIN ITS TERRITORY TO EXTRACT WATER.

It is well established that a sovereign state enjoys permanent sovereignty over their natural resources in the interest of national development and the well-being of the people.[1] As groundwater emerging as a chief source of fresh water,[2] the sovereign rights of Rahad to possess and use[3] the Aquifer has been affirmed.[4]

B. THE STATEMENT MADE BY THE RAHADI MINISTER OF WATER AND AGRICULTURE DID NOT CREATE LEGAL OBLIGATIONS UPON RAHAD AS IT DID NOT REVEAL AN INTENTION TO BE BOUND.

The statement made by the Rahadi Minister[5] did not create legal obligations[6] on Rahad since an intention to be bound[7] was absent[8] considering its content[9] [i] and

1 'Permanent Sovereignty over Natural Resources' (14 December 1962) UNGA Res 1803 (XVII); 'Declaration on the Establishment of a New Economic Order' (1 May 1974) UNGA Res 3201 (S-VI); International Covenant on Civil and Political Rights (adopted 16 December 1966, entered into force 23 March 1976) 999 UNTS 171 (ICCPR) art 1(2); International Covenant on Economic, Social and Cultural Rights (adopted 16 December 1966, entered into force 3 January 1976) 993 UNTS 3 (ICESCR) art 1(2); *Armed Activities on the Territory of the Congo* (Democratic Republic of Congo v Uganda) (Judgment) [2005] ICJ Rep 168 [244].

2 Gabriel Eckstein, 'Protecting a Hidden Treasure' (2005) 5 *Sustainable Dev L & Pol'y* 5, 5.

3 Nico Schrijver, *Sovereignty over Natural Resources: Balancing Rights and Duties* (CUP 1997) 368.

4 International Law Commission (ILC) 'Draft Articles on the Law of Transboundary Aquifers with Commentaries' (2008) UN Doc A/63/10 Preamble art 3.

5 *Compromis* [16].

6 *Nuclear Tests* (New Zealand v France) (Judgment) [1974] ICJ Rep 457 [46].

7 *Fisheries Jurisdiction* (Spain v Canada) (Jurisdiction of the Court) [1998] ICJ Rep 432 [43]; *Nuclear Tests* (Australia v France) (Judgment) [1974] ICJ Rep 253, 268.

8 *Frontier Dispute* (Burkina Faso/Republic of Mali) (Judgment) [1986] ICJ Rep 554 [39]; *Case Concerning the Temple of Preah Vihear* (Cambodia v Thailand) (Preliminary Objections) [1961] ICJ Rep 17, 31-32.

9 *Armed Activities on the Territory of the Congo* (New Application 2002) (Democratic Republic of Congo v Rwanda) (Jurisdiction and Admissibility, Judgment) [2006] ICJ Rep 6 [49].

factual context[10] [ii].

i. The content of the statement lacked clear and specific terms.

An intention to be bound must be interpreted in a restrictive manner,[11] where the actual content of the statement is crucial and should include clear and specific terms.[12] A precise time-frame,[13] awareness of the nature of potential obligations,[14] or detailed description of boundary concerned[15] may assist in the confirmation of legal undertakings. None of these, however, were included in the statement by Rahadi Minister, which merely raised in general terms the importance of water,[16] without reference to any particular act, and can only be deemed as a political gesture.[17]

Despite the importance of contents, the statement shall not always be interpreted in a purely literal way.[18] Words like 'my government will comply with the decision' were not recognized by the Court as legally binding,[19] proving that interpretation of the statement must not focus solely on its wording.

ii. The context and circumstances of the statement indicated no intention to be bound.

First, a radical distinction should be drawn between *Nuclear Tests* and the present

---

10 ILC 'Guiding Principles Applicable to Unilateral Declarations of States Capable of Creating Legal Obligations, with Commentaries Thereto' (2006) UN Doc A/61/10 art 3.

11 Ian Brownlie, James Crawford, *Brownlie's Principles of Public International Law* (OUP 2008) 636; *North Sea Continental Shelf* (Federal Republic of Germany/Denmark; Federal Republic of Germany/Netherlands)(Judgment) [1969] ICJ Rep 3 [47]-[49].

12 Guiding Principles Applicable to Unilateral Declarations (n 10) art 7.

13 *Nuclear Tests* (n 6) [46]; *Armed Activities* (DRC v Rwanda) (n 9) [50].

14 *Nuclear Tests* (n 6) [53].

15 *Frontier Dispute* (n 8) 573-574.

16 *Compromis* [16].

17 *Military and Paramilitary Activities in and against Nicaragua* (Nicaragua v United States of America) (Merits) [1986] ICJ Rep14 [261]; *Frontier Dispute* (n 8) [27].

18 *Anglo-Iranian Oil Co case* (UK/Iran) (Jurisdiction) [1952] ICJ Rep 93, 104; *Case Concerning the Temple of Preah Vihear* (Cambodia v Thailand) (Merits) [1962] ICJ Rep 6, 32.

19 *Frontier Dispute* (n 8) [36].

case. The Court confirmed the binding character of France's unilateral declarations since there were no other ways to express its intention without 'jeopardizing its contention'.[20] In contrast, the statement of Rahadi Minister was made during a bilateral ceremony where heads of both States attended. There were no obstacles for the Parties to manifest such an intention via a normal method, which is a formal agreement on the basis of reciprocity. Without such agreements, the statement of Rahadi Minister shall not be interpreted with legal implications.

Second, binding declarations are based on bilateral negotiations or diplomatic correspondence.[21] A presentation of a general policy in an international conference was denied legal effects,[22] which is identical to the present case since the statement was generally made 'in honor of this World Water Day'.[23]

Finally, by the time of the statement, it would be impossible for Rahadi Minister to foresee the upcoming drought in 1999.[24] Rahad was by no means intended to prohibit itself from future construction arising from an unexpected situation.[25]

C. RAHAD'S EXTRACTION OF WATER FROM THE AQUIFER CONSTITUTED PROPER USE OF THE SHARED RESOURCES.

i. The principle of equitable and reasonable use does not apply to fossil aquifers.

Arising from international surface water law,[26] the principle of equitable and reasonable use is inapplicable to fossil aquifers[27] including the Aquifer[28] since:

---

20 *Frontier Dispute* (n 8) [40].

21 ILC 'Eighth Report on Unilateral Acts of States' (2005) UN Doc A/CN4/557 Note from Colombia.

22 *Armed Activities* (DRC v Rwanda) (n 9) [53].

23 *Compromis* [16].

24 *Compromis* [20].

25 *Legal Status of Eastern Greenland* (Denmark v Norway) (Judgment) PCIJ Rep Series A/B No 53, 71.

26 Convention on the Law of the Non-Navigational Uses of International Watercourses (adopted 21 May 1997, entered into force 17 August 2014) 36 ILM 700 (Watercourse Convention) art 5; ILC 'Report on the Work of the 46th Session' (1994) UN Doc A/49/10 [222].

27 ILC 'Third Report on Shared Natural Resources' (2005) UN Doc A/CN4/551 [19].

28 *Clarifications* [1].

First, the principle's applicability to groundwater is based on a physical relationship between groundwater and surface water.[29] Fossil aquifers, however, are hydrogeologically isolated[30] and were intentionally excluded from the Watercourse Convention and Helsinki Rules on the Uses of the Waters of International Rivers (Helsinki Rules).[31]

Second, its applicability to groundwater and definitions lacks general recognition in State practices.[32] Evidences include: *first*, regional agreements concerning fossil aquifers do not adopted the principle of equitable use;[33] *second*, the word 'equitable' was intentionally revised to 'proper'[34] in a UNGA resolution concerning aquifers;[35]

29 ILC Aquifer Commentaries (n 4) art 5; Gabriel Ecksteil, 'Application of International Water Law to Transboundary Groundwater Resources, and the Slovak-Hungarian Dispute over *Gabčíkovo-Nagymaros*' (1995) *Suffolk Transnational Law Review* 19, 71.

30 UNESCO 'Preface to Non-renewable Groundwater Resources: A Guidebook on Socially-sustainable Management for Water-policy Makers' (2006) UNESCO Doc SC-2007/WS/4, 14.

31 Watercourse Convention art 2; Helsinki Rules on the Uses of the Waters of International Rivers (with comments) (Helsinki Rules) (adopted 20 August 1966) 52 ILA 484 art 1; Renee Martin-Nagle, 'Fossil Aquifers: A Common Heritage of Mankind' (2011) 2 *Geo Wash J Energy &Envtl L* 39, 43.

32 B Wohlwend, 'An Overview of Groundwater in International Law-A Case Study: The Franco-Swiss Genevese Aquifer' (2002) Workshop III on 'Harmonization of Diverging Interests in the Use of Shared Water Resources' ESCWA, 1.

33 Seoul Rules on International Groundwaters (adopted 30 August 1986) 62 ILA 251 (Seoul) art III; 2000 Agreements concerning the Nubian Sandstone Aquifer System <http://www.fao.org/docrep/008/y5739e/y5739e05.htm#fn4> accessed 8 January 2017; SASS Agreements concerning the North-Western Sahara Aquifer System <http://www.fao.org/docrep/008/y5739e/y5739e05.htm#fn4> accessed 10 December 2017; 1978 Arrangement on the Protection, Utilization and Recharge of the Franco-Swiss Genevese Aquifer, <http://www.internationalwaterlaw.org/documents/regionaldocs/2008Franko-Swiss-Aquifer-English.pdf> accessed 1 January 2017; Agreement on the Guarani Aquifer (adopted 2 August 2010) <http://internationalwaterlaw.org/documents/regionaldocs/Guarani_Aquifer_Agreement-English.pdf> accessed 12 December 2016; Kerstin Mechlem, 'Past, Present and Future of the International Law of Transboundary Qquifers' (2011)13(3) *International Community Law Review* 209, 216.

34 'The Law of Transboundary Aquifers' (13 January 2012) UN Doc A/RES/66/104 art 1; 'Draft Resolution on The Law of Transboundary Aquifers' (3 November 2011) UN Doc A/C6/66/L24 Preamble Second Recital.

35 'Summary Records of the 29th Committee' (7 February 2012) UN Doc A/C6/66/SR 29 [36]; 'Report of the Sixth Committee' (9 November 2011) UN Doc A/66/477, II.

and *third*, the definition of the principle of equitable and reasonable use in Draft Article on the Law of Transboundary Aquifers (ILC Aquifers),[36] together with its inclusion of fossil aquifers, was contested by States in arid areas including Libya, Saudi Arabia and Lebanon.[37]

ii. Even though the principle of equitable and reasonable use is applicable, Rahad's extraction of water does not violate the principle considering all the factors.

In determining equitable use, relevant factors shall be considered together.[38] Weight of each factor must be assessed on a case-by-case basis and none should occupy a position of preeminence *per se*.[39]

In the present case, the extraction of the Aquifer constitutes equitable and reasonable use considering: *first*, the population relying upon the Aquifer; *second*, the considerable volume of the Aquifer; *third*, the lack of alternatives due to Rahad's limited resources; *fourth*, the significantly urgent needs; *fifth*, the fact that Rahad contributes 65% of the Aquifer[40] and the Aquifer's nature of negligible flow; *sixth*, the long-lasting practice of utilizing the Aquifer across the Nomad Coast; and *seventh*, Rahad's intention to use the water as a short term solution.[41]

iii. In any event, the water extracted from the Aquifer has been used properly to serve Rahad's vital human needs.

In essence, the principle of equitable and reasonable use is a utilitarian concept,[42] where a cost-benefit analysis should be employed[43] to maximize the beneficial use[44]

36 ILC 'Draft Article on the Law of Transboundary Aquifers' (2008) UN Doc A/63/10 art 4.

37 'Report of the Secretary-General' (29 June 2011) UN Doc A/66/116 [72] (Libya Arab Jamahiriya) [99] (Saudi Arabia, Lebanon) [53]-[59] (China).

38 ILC Aquifers (n 36) art 5.

39 Helsinki Rules (n 31) art V.

40 ILC Aquifer Commentaries (n 4) art 5 [4].

41 *Compromis* [3]-[4] [14]-[15] [18]-[19] [22]; ILC Aquifers (n 36) art 5; Helsinki Rules (n 31) art VII; Berlin Rules on Water Resources (7 August 2004) 71 ILA 337 art 13.

42 Helsinki Rules (n 31) art V.

43 *Pulp Mills on the River Uruguay* (Argentina v Uruguay) (Judgment) [2010] ICJ Rep 14 [175]-[177]; Gabriel Eckstein and Yoram Eckstein, 'A Hydrogeological Approach to Transboundary Ground Water Resources and International Law' (2003)19 *American University International Law Review* 201, FN 145.

44 ILC Aquifers (n 36) art 4.

while minimize, instead of prohibiting, alleged detriment.[45]

Specifically, the beneficial use is of economic or social value.[46] The utilization of the Aquifer is not only economically and socially valuable, but indeed is 'life-giving' and sustains the immeasurable vital human needs,[47] which takes top priority.[48] In any circumstances, present and vital human needs must not be subordinated to prospective future requirements.[49] In contrast, the alleged damage to Atania, if any, was monetary loss which took only 3% of Atania's GDP and would not endanger human needs of Atania given its capability of exporting grains.[50]

Moreover, even though the extraction of the Aquifer restricted Atania's rights, Rahad has been pursuing the legitimate purpose of protecting its vital human needs[51] since the drought has constituted an emergency situation.[52]

D. MOREOVER, RAHAD HAS FULFILLED ITS PROCEDURAL OBLIGATIONS CONCERNING PROPER USE OF THE AQUIFER.

i. Rahad has fulfilled its obligation to cooperate with Atania.

a. Rahad has duly cooperated with Atania in good faith.

It is established that States initiating the project[53] are obliged to cooperate regarding

45 Helsinki Rules (n 31) art IV.

46 Helsinki Rules (n 31) art IV.

47 *Compromis* [22]; Stephen McCaffrey, *The Law of International Watercourse* (OUP 2007) 369-371.

48 ILC Aquifers (n 36) art 5(2); Helsinki Rules (n 31) art IV; Berlin Rules (n 41) art 14.

49 Helsinki Rules (n 31) art VII; Berlin Rules (n 41) art 40; Gabriel Eckstein, 'A Hydrogeological Perspective of the Status of Ground Water Resources under the UN Watercourse Convention' (2005) *Columbia Journal of Environmental Law* 30, 55.

50 *Compromis* [2] [27]-[29].

51 *Dispute Regarding Navigational and Related Rights* (Costa Rica v Nicaragua) (Judgment) [2009] ICJ Rep 213, 253.

52 ILC Aquifers (n 36) art 17.

53 *Lake Lanoux case* (Spain v France) [1957] 12 UNRIAA 281, 314; Rio Declaration on Environment and Development (adopted 14 June 1992) 31 ILM 874 (Rio Declaration) Principle 27; Declaration of the United Nations Conference on the Human Environment (adopted 16 June 1972) 11 ILM 1416 (Stockholm Declaration) Principle 24; 'Cooperation in the Field of Environment Concerning Natural Resources Shared by Two or More States' (18 December 1979) UN Doc A/RES/34/186.

shared resources,[54] including shared groundwater,[55] to the extent that they consider the rights of other States[56] in good faith.[57]

Rahad has fulfilled its obligation of good faith cooperation by (1) establishment of the hydrologists group;[58] (2) readiness to undertake further studies;[59] (3) willingness to accept assistance and expertise of independent third parties including the ILSA and the World Heritage Committee[60] and (4) timely response to Atania's request.[61]

b. Rahad has cooperated with Atania by notification.

Through televised address,[62] which Atania could access and respond to,[63] Rahad has duly cooperated with Atania by notifying its planned activities to Atania[64] accompanied by readily available information.[65] In doing so, Rahad was not obliged

---

54 *Gabčíkovo-Nagymaros Project* (Hungary/Slovakia) (Judgment) [1997] ICJ Rep 7 [32]; Agreement on Cooperation in Environmental Protection and Nature Conservation between Israel and Jordan (adopted 7 September 1995) art 1, cited in M Civic 'A Comparative Analysis of the Israeli and Arab Water Law Tradition and Insights for Modern Water Sharing Agreements' (1997) 26 *Denv J Int'l L &Pol'y* 437, 450-451; Seoul art III (3).

55 N Trac, 'Nubian Sandstone Aquifer Modelling and Groundwater Resources Planning for New Valley' (1984) UNESCO Technical Report PP/1981-1983/2/73/03 [58].

56 *Lake Lanoux* (n 53) 123-140; Philippe Sands, *Principles of International Environmental Law* (CUP 2003) 307.

57 ILC Aquifers (n 36) art 7(1); *Border and Transborder Armed Actions* (Nicaragua v Honduras) (Jurisdiction and Admissibility) [1988] ICJ Rep 69, 105.

58 *Compromis* [15] [18]; *Case concerning Land Reclamation by Singapore in and around the Straits of Johor* (Malaysia v Singapore) (Provisional Measures) [2005] 27 UNRIAA 133 [92]-[106].

59 *Compromis* [15] [33]; *Gabčíkovo-Nagymaros* (n 54) [107].

60 *Compromis* [21] [25]; *Clarifications* [3]; *Gabčíkovo-Nagymaros* (n 54) [143].

61 *Compromis* [25] [33]; *Clarifications* [3]; *Interpretation of the Agreement of 25 March 1951 between the WHO and Egypt* (Advisory Opinion) [1980] ICJ Rep 73, 96; *MOX Plant* (Ireland v UK) (Application) [2003] 42 ILM 1187 [33].

62 *Compromis* [22].

63 *Compromis* [23].

64 *Land Reclamation* (n 58) [47]; *Lake Lanoux* (n 53) [292].

65 ILC Aquifers (n 36) art 8; *Dispute over the Status and Use of the Waters of the Silala* (Chile/Bolivia) (Application of Chile) (Pending) [2016] ICJ [48].

to obtain consent,[66] pursue further negotiation,[67] or reach an agreement.[68]

ii. Rahad has fulfilled its obligations to prevent significant harm.

a. Rahad's legal obligations are procedural in nature.

Rahad is fully aware of its obligation to take preventive measures against significant transboundary damage[69] and that such obligation is fulfilled via due diligence, which is not intended to impose strict liability upon Rahad.[70]

b. Rahad has fully fulfilled its obligations to exercise due diligence.

Rahad has duly exercise due diligence by (1) properly conducting an *ex ante* EIA,[71] (2) employing best efforts to collect information,[72] and (3) monitoring on a continuous basis,[73] in preventing significant harm[74] up to its resources.[75]

In the present case, the EIA was properly conducted following domestic legislative standards[76] and was made public by communicating to the World Heritage Committee,

66 *Gut Dam Case* (US v Canada) [1969] 8 ILM 118 [128]; *Railway Traffic between Lithuania and Poland* (Advisory Opinion) [1931] PCIJ Rep Series A/B No 42, 116.

67 'Cooperation between States in the Field of Environment' (16 December 1972) UN Doc A/RES/2995(XXVII)[1, 2.]

68 *Pulp Mills* (n 43) [150].

69 *Corfu Channel case* (UK v Albania) (Merits) [1949] ICJ Rep 4, 22; *Trail Smelter case* (US v Canada) [1938/1941] 3 UNRIAA 1906, 1950; Rio Declaration Principle 2; Stockholm Declaration Principle 21; *Legality of the Threat or the Use of Nuclear Weapons* (Advisory Opinion) [1996] ICJ Rep 226, 241-242.

70 ILC 'Draft Articles on Prevention of Transboundary Harm from Hazardous Activities' (2001) UN Doc A/RES/56/10 art 3; Xue Hanqin, *Transboundary Damage in International Law* (CUP 2003) 133-134; Malcom Shaw, *International Law* (6th edn, CUP 2008) 853-855.

71 *Clarifications* [3]; ILC Aquifers (n 36) art 15; Rio Declaration Principle 17; *Pulp Mills* (n 43) [204].

72 *Compromis* [15] [20]; ILC Aquifers (n 36) art 8; Rio Declaration Principle 15.

73 *Gabčíkovo-Nagymaros* (n 54) [65].

74 ILC Aquifers (n 36) art 6.

75 Helsinki Rules (n 31) art IV; *Compromis* [20].

76 *Pulp Mills* (n 43) [205]; *MOX Plant* (n 61) 74-76; *Construction of a Road in Costa Rica Along the San Juan River* (Nicaragua v Costa Rica) (Judgment) [2015] ICJ Rep 665 [157].

a competent international organization,[77] making it sufficient for the purpose of due diligence.

II. RAHAD'S SAVALI PIPELINE OPERATIONS DO NOT VIOLATE ANY LEGAL OBLIGATIONS RELATING TO THE KIN CANYON COMPLEX.

Pursuant to the principle of state sovereignty[78] and non-intervention,[79] Rahad is entitled to perform all activities deemed necessary and beneficial to its people[80] and has fulfilled its legal obligations by not deliberately damaging [A], endeavoring to protect [B], and cooperating [C].

A. THE SAVALI PIPELINE OPERATIONS DID NOT VIOLATE THE LEGAL OBLIGATION NOT TO DELIBERATELY CAUSE DAMAGE.

i. The Complex was not damaged under WHC since its Outstanding Universal Value was not impaired.

The obligation 'not to take any deliberate measures which might damage' under WHC[81] entails no action shall be taken to threaten the integrity or value of the heritage concerned.[82] In assessing the Outstanding Universal Value, significant features are of ultimate importance.[83]

---

77 *Clarifications* [3]; United Nations Convention on the Law of the Sea (adopted 10 December 1982, entered into force16 November 1994) 1833 UNTS 3 art 205.

78 Convention for the Protection of the World Cultural and Natural Heritage (adopted 16 November 1972) 1037 UNTS 151 (WHC) art 6(1); 'Declaration on the Right to Development' (4 December 1986) UN Doc A/RES/41/128; Lucas Lixinski, 'Selecting Heritage-The Interplay of Art, Politics and Identity' (2011) 22(1) *European Journal of International Law* 81, 84.

79 Charter of the United Nations (adopted 26 June 1945, entered into force 24 October 1945) 1 UNTS XVI art 2; 'Declaration on the Inadmissibility of Intervention and Interference in the Internal Affairs of States' UN Doc A/RES/36/103 (9 December 1981) Preamble Second Recital.

80 Antonio Cassese, *International Law* (OUP 2005) 51.

81 WHC art 6(3).

82 'World Heritage Properties of the Democratic Republic of the Congo' UNESCO Doc 29 COM 7A (2005) 4, 11; 'Acts Constituting "Crimes against the Common Heritage of Humanity"' (11-16 December 2001) UN Doc WHC-01/CONF208/23, 12.

83 'UNESCO Operational Guidelines for the Implementation of the World Heritage Convention' (May 2015) UN Doc WHC15/01, 88-95; 'UNESCO Background Document on the Notion of Integrity, International World Heritage Expert Meeting on Integrity for Cultural Heritage' (7 March 2012) 7.

The features of the Complex lie in its aesthetic beauty[84] and it being 'a rich source of archaeological treasures',[85] including the Stronghold, the Sunrise Mesa and archaeological discoveries.[86] None of these features were found damaged in the present case.[87]

ii. Even though the Complex was damaged, such damage was not caused by any deliberate measures undertaken by Rahad.

Article 6(3) of WHC shall be interpreted in a narrow sense as only deliberately conducted damage is covered.[88] The Complex was not deliberately damaged because a discriminatory intent was absent [a], and the severity threshold was not met [b].

a. Rahad did not have a discriminatory intent.

To constitute a deliberate act, a discriminatory intent is required, which aims at a specific target[89] and precludes mere attitude[90] and collateral damage.[91] Demonstration of a discriminatory intent includes, *inter alia*, *first*, ordering[92] damage to specific statutes via an edict;[93] *second*, extensive physical interference such as looting,[94] arson,[95] poaching,[96] and military patrolling,[97] and *third*, repeated targeting[98] on certain

84 *Compromis* [5]; UNESCO Operational Guidelines (n 83) [77] (vii).

85 *Compromis* [6]; UNESCO Operational Guidelines (n 83) [77] (iii).

86 *Compromis* [5]-[6].

87 *Compromis* [30].

88 Francesco Francioni, *The 1972 World Heritage Convention A commentary* (OUP 2008) 126.

89 *Case Concerning Oil Platforms* (Islamic Republic of Iran v United States of America) (Judgment) [2003] ICJ Rep 161, 191-192.

90 *Corfu Channel* (n 69) 31.

91 *Prosecutor v Dario Kordic and Mario Cerkez* (Judgment) [2001] ICTY-95-14/2-T, 207.

92 *Partial Award: Central Front - Eritrea's Claims 2, 4, 6, 7, 8 & 22* [2004] 26 UNRIAA 115 [108].

93 'The Destruction of Relics and Monuments in Afghanistan' (1 May 2001) UN Doc A/RES/55/243 [2]; Francesco Francioni and Federico Lenzerini, 'The Destruction of the Buddhas of Bamiyan and International law' (2003) 14(4) *EJIL* 619, 620.

94 UN Doc A/RES/53/203A (18 Dec 1998) [21]; UN Doc A/RES/54/189A (17 Dec 1999) [30]; UN Doc A/RES/55/174A (19 Dec 2000) [30].

95 UNESCO, 'List of Factors Affecting the Properties' <http://whc.unesco.org/en/factors/> accessed 3 January 2017.

96 'World Heritage Properties of the Democratic Republic of the Congo' UNESCO Doc 29 COM 7A4 (2005) 11.

97 *Request for Interpretation of the Judgment of 15 June 1962 in the Case concerning the Temple of Preah Vihear* (Cambodia v Thailand) (Judgment) [2013] ICJ Rep 281, 317-318.

98 Council of Europe 'Information Report: The Destruction by War of the Cultural Heritage in Croatia and Bosnia-Herzegovina' (2 February 1993) Parliamentary Assembly Doc 6756 [155].

objects.

In the present case, none of the demonstration was found nor proved in the Savali Pipeline operations[99] and Rahad was certainly unable to foresee the outcome of any damage.[100]

b. The threshold of deliberate damage was not satisfied.

The Savali Pipeline is a pure civil project[101] and considerably below the high threshold of deliberate damage which is deemed as 'crimes against the common heritage of humanity'[102] or 'crimes of culture'.[103]

iii. Moreover, the Savali Pipeline operations caused no transboundary damage.

Pursuant to *sic utere tuo* principle,[104] the Savali Pipeline caused no transboundary damage since physical and human causation [a][105] and clear and convincing evidence were absent [b].[106]

a. The causation between the Savali Pipeline operations and the alleged damage could not be established.

The required causal relationship cannot be established due to the geological distance, the temporal separation and uncertain causes.[107]

First, the 'possible subsidence' noted in the 2005 World Heritage Committee decision was assumed on 'lands superjacent to the Aquifer'[108] while the Aquifer is

99 *Compromis* [30].

100 *Compromis* [25]-[26]; *Clarifications* [1].

101 *Compromis* [22].

102 'Acts Constituting "Crimes against the Common Heritage of Humanity"' (11-16 December 2001) UN Doc WHC-01/CONF208/23.

103 Francioni (n 93) 621.

104 *Trail Smelter* (n 69) [684]; *Corfu Channel* (n 69) [22]; Rio Principle 2; Stockholm Declaration Principle 7.

105 Xue (n 70) 3.

106 *Trail Smelter* (n 69) [1965].

107 See Generally *Construction of a Road in Costa Rica Along the San Juan River* (n 76).

108 *Compromis* [25].

not subjacent to the Complex,[109] and the alleged lowering of the water table occurred only south of the Complex.[110] *Second*, the Savali Pipeline operations began in 2006, while the alleged environmental degradation occurred not earlier than late 2010.[111] *Finally*, other factors may be relevant including Atania's consistent extraction of hydrocarbons.[112]

b. Atania has failed to provide clear and convincing evidence.

Atania, as the party asserting damage, should bear the burden of proof.[113] While the primary, and indeed the only evidence submitted was the geologists' investigation,[114] which was insufficient concerning its source,[115] method of production, and character.[116]

The geologists concerned followed the order of President Vhen and lacked the hydrological knowledge required to their conclusion, which undermined their independence and competence.[117] Also, the production of the results was unsatisfactory since that it only took weeks to reach unanimous conclusions,[118] failed to provide any clarified data[119] and lacked scientific certainty.[120]

Moreover, only the geologists' description of the images rather than their conclusion

109 *Clarifications* [1].

110 *Compromis* [28].

111 *Compormis* [26] [30]; Julio Barboza, *The Environment, Risk and Liability in International Law* (Martinus Nijhoff Publishers 2011) 11.

112 *Compromis* [2]; *Construction of a Road in Costa Rica Along the San Juan River* (n 76) [119].

113 *Preah Vihear* (n 18) 16; *Sovereignty over Pedra Branca/Pulau Batu Puteh, Middle Rocks and South Ledge* (Malaysia/Singapore) (Judgment) [2008] ICJ Rep 12, 31.

114 *Compromis* [30].

115 *Armed Activities* (DRC v Rwanda) (n 9) [61]; *Trail Smelter* (n 69) 1921.

116 *Application of the Convention on the Prevention and Punishment of the Crime of Genocide* (Bosnia and Herzegovina v Serbia and Montenegro) (Judgment) [2007] ICJ Rep 43 [204] [227].

117 *Compromis* [30]; *Pulp Mills* (n 43) [166]-[167].

118 *Compromis* [30].

119 *Pulp Mills* (n 43) [166]-[167].

120 *Pulp Mills on the River Uruguay* (Argentina v Uruguay) (Joint Dissenting Opinion of Judges Al-Khasawneh and Simma) [2010] ICJ Rep 14 [2]; *Pulp Mills on the River Uruguay* (Argentina v Uruguay) (Dissenting Opinion of Judge *Ad Hoc* Vinuesa) [2010] ICJ Rep 14 [95].

is of evidentiary value since '[t]he real value in expert opinion ... lies in their statements of appearance ... , rather than in their ultimate expressed opinions'.[121]

B. THE SAVALI PIPELINE OPERATIONS DID NOT VIOLATE THE LEGAL OBLIGATION TO PROTECT AND CONSERVE THE COMPLEX.

i. Articles 4 and 5 of WHC are not legal obligations.

In contrast to the word 'undertake' in Article 6 which is commonly used to impose legal obligations,[122] languages of Articles 4 and 5 of WHC, including 'will do all it can' and 'endeavor in so far as possible and as appropriate',[123] are hortatory, non-specific,[124] and unenforceable,[125] which leaves contents of the obligation to the discretion of State Parties. Such stipulations of Articles 4 and 5 can serve at most mere declarations of political intent[126] rather than impose legal obligations.[127]

ii. Peacetime protection of world heritage sites is not a customary legal obligation.

Languages employed in non-binding UNESCO instruments, including 'should',[128] 'recommend'[129] and 'responsibility',[130] are hortatory and avoiding formal terms 'legal obligation',[131] demonstrating no norm-creating character.[132] In the case of the

---

121 *Anderson v. American Smelting & Refining Co* 265 (1919) Federal Reporter 928, cited in Trail Smelter (n 69) 1922.

122 *Commonwealth of Australia v State of Tasmania* (1983) *HCA* 21.

123 WHC arts 4, 5, 6.

124 *Tasmania* (n 122).

125 O'Connel, *International Law* (Vol. 1, Stevens & Sons Ltd 1970) 246.

126 J Fawcett, 'The Legal Character of International Agreements' (1953) 30 *Brit YB Int'L* 381, 390-391.

127 'Declaration on the Responsibilities of the Present Generations towards Future Generations' (12 November 1997) UNESCO Doc 29C/Res 44 Preamble First Recital.

128 'Recommendation Concerning the Protection, at National Level, of the Cultural and Natural Heritage' (16 November 1972) UNESCO Doc 17C/Res 30 art 4.

129 'Recommendation on Participation by the People at Large in Cultural Life and their Contribution to It' (26 Nov 1976) UNESCO Doc 19C/Resolutions Annex I, 29, art 4.

130 'Situation of Human Rights in Afghanistan' (25 February 1999) UN Doc A/RES/53/165, 2.

131 O'Keefe, 'World Cultural Heritage: Obligations to the International Community as a Whole?' (2004) 53 *Int'L& Comp LQ* 189, 203.

132 'Acts Constituting "Crimes against the Common Heritage of Humanity"' UNESCO Doc 31C/46 [6] (c); *North Sea Continental Shelf* (n 11) [72]; 'Declaration Concerning the Intentional Destruction of Cultural Heritage'(17 October 2003) UNESCO 32C/Res 38 art IV.

destruction of Bamiyan Buddhas, only Ukraine characterized it as a violation of a legal obligation,[133] while the unanimous condemnation was indeed diplomatic. The *opinio juris* required for a customary legal obligation of peacetime protection of cultural heritage is insufficient.[134]

iii. Nevertheless, Rahad has endeavored to the utmost of its resources to protect and conserve the Complex.

Under WHC, Rahad's obligation of protection is set in the context of its own resources,[135] which are limited given it being a developing state.[136] By setting a 2-km buffer zone,[137] directing comprehensive studies,[138] limiting drilling areas[139] and conducting EIA,[140] Rahad has dedicated to the utmost of its resources to the protection of the Complex.

C. RAHAD HAS DULY COOPERATED WITH THE INTERNATIONAL COMMUNITY.

Rahad has fulfilled its obligations to cooperate with Atania [i] and the World Heritage Committee [ii].[141]

i. Rahad has duly cooperated with Atania.

As submitted *supra*, Rahad has fulfilled its obligation to cooperate with Atania by prior notification and regulatory studies accompanied with proper information.[142]

---

133 'Official Records of 94th Plenary Meeting' (9 March 2001) UN Doc A/55/PV94, 12.

134 O'Keefer (n 131) 205.

135 WHC Preamble arts 4, 5; Kanchana Wangkeo, 'Monumental Challenge: The Lawfulness of Destroying Cultural Heritage during Peacetime' (2003) 28 *Yale J Int'L* 183, 194.

136 WHC Commentary (n 88) 116.

137 *Compromis* [13]; UNESCO Operational Guidelines (n 83) [103].

138 *Compromis* [21] [26].

139 *Compromis* [30].

140 *Clarifications* [3].

141 WHC art 6; *Temple Interpretation* (n 97) 317; Janet Blake, *International Cultural Heritage Law* (OUP 2015) 94.

142 *Compromis* [22] [33].

ii. Rahad has duly cooperated with the World Heritage Committee.

The duty of cooperation in WHC[143] entails close cooperation with the Committee since it serves as a vehicle of international cooperation.[144]

a. Adding the Complex to the List of World Heritage in Danger violated due process.

The decision of the Committee to add the Complex on the List of World Heritage in Danger (the inscription) was based on Atanian geologists' investigation,[145] which was of no evidentiary value. Moreover, before inscription, consultation with States concerned is required[146] yet absent in the present case.[147] Rahad is therefore not obliged to implement any corrective measures arising from the inscription without its knowledge.[148]

b. Nevertheless, Rahad has actively cooperated with the World Heritage Committee.

By submitting the Savali Pipeline plan an *ex ante* EIA to the Committee,[149] limiting drilling areas,[150] and holding discussions,[151] Rahad has fully cooperated with the Committee in good faith.

III. RAHAD IS ENTITLED TO RETAIN POSSESSION OF THE RUBY SIPAR.

A. RAHAD IS ENTITLED TO POSSESS THE RUBY SIPAR TO PROTECT IT AS A CULTURAL HERITAGE UNDER INTERNATIONAL LAW.

i. The Ruby Sipar is a cultural heritage under international law.

The applicable scope of cultural heritage under WHC is extended[152] to 'movable' property.[153] In order to define a property as cultural heritage, the critical element to be

143 WHC art 6.

144 WHC art 7; Olena Melnychuk, 'Contemporary Interpretation of the Conception of World Heritage in International Law and Practice' (2011) 51(1) *Acta Juridica Hungarica* 54, 56.

145 *Compromis* [31].

146 WHC art 11 (6); UNESCO Operational Guidelines (n 83) [183].

147 *Compromis* [32].

148 *Clarifications* [6]; Brownlie (n 11) 447.

149 *Compromis* [24]; UNESCO Operational Guidelines (n 83) [172]; *Pulp Mills* (n 43) [204].

150 *Compromis* [26].

151 *Clarifications* [6].

152 WHC Commentary (n 88) 29.

153 UNESCO Operational Guidelines (n 83) [48].

concerned is 'Outstanding Universal Value'.[154] The criteria of assessing 'Outstanding Universal Value'[155] are that properties that 'bear a unique or at least exceptional testimony to a cultural tradition or to a civilization which is living or which has disappeared'.[156]

These criteria are met in the present case. Primarily, the Ruby Sipar is a unique and exceptional testimony to the Kin's tradition. It witnessed the legend of the Kin[157] and was further developed into miniature replicas as the symbol of protecting the traditions of the Kin.[158] Additionally, it reminds Clan Kin of their traditional culture while much of their history has already been lost through the ages.[159] Therefore, the Ruby Sipar shall be defined as 'culture heritage'.

In any event, the Ruby Sipar shall be defined as 'culture property', which forms part of the 'cultural heritage', according to the 1970 Convention.[160]

ii. Atania failed to fulfill its international obligations towards the Ruby Sipar.

a. Atania failed to fulfill its obligation of protecting the Ruby Sipar.

States have the obligation[161] to protect the cultural heritage.[162] However, Atania's removal of the Ruby Sipar from public display,[163] confiscation and destruction of the replicas by agents of law enforcement,[164] constitute the change of juridical status of the Ruby Sipar, which diminish the degree of its protection.[165] In addition, the

154 WHC Commentary (n 88) 29.

155 UNESCO Operational Guidelines (n 83) 48.

156 UNESCO Operational Guidelines (n 83) [77] (iii).

157 *Compromis* [8].

158 *Compromis* [9].

159 *Compromis* [9].

160 Convention on the Means of Prohibiting and Preventing the Illicit Import, Export and Transfer of Ownership of Cultural Property (adopted 14 November 1970) 823 UNTS 231 (1970 Convention) art 4.

161 WHC art 5(c); 1970 Convention art 5(c).

162 *City of Gotha and Federal Republic of Germany v Sotheby's and Cobert Finance SA*, High Court of Justice Queen's Bench Division [1993] C 3428 & [1997] G 185; *Government of the Islamic Republic of Iran v The Barakat Gallery Ltd* [2007] EWCA Civ 1374.

163 *Compromis* [44].

164 *Compromis* [43].

165 UNESCO Operational Guidelines (n 83) [179](b)(i).

success of removal of the Ruby Sipar from the Cultural Center also demonstrates the carelessness of Atania on its protection.[166]

b. Atania failed to make appropriate publicity when the Ruby Sipar disappeared.

To ensure the protection of the cultural heritage, States shall undertake to set up national services to make appropriate publicity given the disappearance of any items.[167] Clearly, Atania did not fulfill its obligation to make appropriate publicity when the Ruby Sipar disappeared, as it only knew of the loss after Rahad's notification.[168]

iii. Rahad is performing its international obligation towards the Ruby Sipar.

WHC obliges State Parties to take appropriate measures necessary for the protection and presentation of the cultural heritage.[169] Meanwhile, international instruments[170] and numerous examples[171] all emphasize that cultural heritage are of great importance of every people and should receive international protection.

In the present case, Rahad is providing protection to the Ruby Sipar and making it available to all those wish to see it.[172] The possession is a necessary step for Rahad to fulfill its obligation on protection and presentation of the Ruby Sipar for all human kind.[173] Otherwise the Ruby Sipar cannot receive better protection or be presented to

---

166 *Compromis* [50].

167 1970 Convention art 5(g).

168 *Compromis* [51].

169 WHC art 5(d).

170 1970 Convention Preamble [3]; 1954 Convention for the Protection of Cultural Property in the Event of Armed Conflict (adopted 14 May 1954) 249 UNTS 240 Preamble art 1; UN Doc WHC-14/38COM/INF5F (6 June 2014) [9].

171 Lyndel V Prott, *Witnesses to History: A Compendium of Documents and Writings on the Return of Cultural Objects* (UNESCO 2009) 43 [3].

172 *Compromis* [52].

173 John Merryman, 'Thinking about the Elgin Marble' (1985) 83(8) *Michigan Law Review* 1180, 1181; Rochelle Strahl, 'The Retention and Retrieval of Art and Antiquities through International and National Means: The Tug of War over Cultural Property' (1979) 5 *Brooklyn Journal of International Law* 103.

people due to its negative symbolic meaning regarded by Atania.[174]

B. RAHAD IS ENTITLED TO POSSESS THE RUBY SIPAR TO PROTECT INDIGENOUS CULTURAL RIGHTS OF CLAN KIN.

i. Clan Kin are indigenous people.

'Indigenous peoples' is a contested term without a universal and unambiguous definition.[175] Therefore, the criteria with main elements should be used to determine indigenous peoples.[176]Ancestral territories, continuity, self-identification, and distinctiveness are such elements to describe indigenous peoples.[177]

First, as Clan Kin venerated the Kin Canyons as the birthplace of their ancestors,[178] they are a group of people having a strong link with the ancestral territory, who enjoy a historical continuity of thousands of years. *Second*, Clan Kin established 'the Sisters of the Sun' to protect and preserve their culture and traditions[179] and constituted a local group with self-identification. *Third*, after the formation of Atania, Clan Kin migrated to Atania but remained politically and culturally isolated from the rest of Atania society, living off the land through farming, hunting and gathering,[180] which reflects their distinctiveness within Atania. Consequently, Clan Kin are indigenous

---

174 *Compromis* [43].

175 'United Nations Declaration on the Rights of Indigenous Peoples' GA Res 61/295 (13 September 2007) UN Doc A/RES/61/295 Preamble; Convention on Stolen or Illegally Exported Cultural Objects (adopted 24 June 1995) 2421 UNTS 457 Preamble.

176 'Report of the African Commission's Working Group of Experts on Indigenous Populations/ Communities' (2005) ACHPR/IWGIA 88.

177 José Martínez Cobo, 'Study of the Problem of Discrimination against Indigenous Populations' (July 1986) UN Doc E/CN4/Sub2/1986/7 and Add 1-4, 362-382; Working Group on Indigenous Populations (WGIP) 'Working Paper by the Chairperson-Rapporteur, Mrs. Erica-Irene A Daes, on the Concept of "Indigenous People"' (10 June 1996) UN Doc E/CN4/Sub2/AC4/1996/2 [69]; Committee of the Rights of Indigenous Peoples, 'Rights of Indigenous Peoples in International Law Association Report of the Seventy-Fifth Conference' (Sofia 2012) 2-3; Convention Concerning Indigenous and Tribal Peoples in Independent Countries (entered into force 27 June 1989) 72 ILO Official Bull 59 (ILO No 169) art 1.

178 *Compromis* [7].

179 *Compromis* [9].

180 *Compromis* [11].

people with the elements above satisfied.

ii. The Ruby Sipar is a cultural heritage of Clan Kin.

The cultural heritage of indigenous peoples is comprised of all objects, the nature or use of which is regarded as pertaining to a particular people,[181] including tangible and intangible manifestations of their ways of life and achievements.[182] Such manifestations and the objects associated therewith are therefore recognized by the indigenous peoples as part of their cultural heritage.[183]

The Ruby Sipar represented the heroic deed by Teppa, a warrior of Clan Kin, of saving the sacred Kin Canyons.[184] In memory of Teppa, Clan Kin established 'the Sisters of the Sun' whose members wear miniature replicas of the Ruby Sipar around their necks as a symbol of their loyalty.[185] In other words, the Ruby Sipar, whose nature is deeply pertaining to Clan Kin, is an object associated with the manifestation of the life and achievement of Clan Kin. It therefore belongs to the cultural heritage of Clan Kin. And Clan Kin has the right to control its cultural heritage[186] and turn it over to Rahad for its better protection.[187]

iii. The return of Ruby Sipar would violate cultural rights of Clan Kin.

According to Article 27 of the International Covenant on Civil and Political Rights

181 WGIP 'Report of the Seminar on the Draft Principles and Guidelines for the Protection of the Heritage of Indigenous People' (19 June 2000) UN Doc E/CN4/Sub2/2000/26 Annex I [12].

182 HRC 'Role of Languages and Culture in the Promotion and Protection of the Rights and Identity of Indigenous Peoples' UN Doc A/HRC/21/53 [52]; HRC 'Promotion and Protection of the Rights of Indigenous Peoples with Respect to their Cultural Heritage' UN Doc A/HRC/30/53 [6].

183 WGIP 'Review of the Draft Principles and Guidelines on the Heritage of Indigenous Peoples' (21 June 2005) UN Doc E/CN4/Sub2/AC4/2005/3 21 Annex Part III [1].

184 *Compromis* [8].

185 *Compromis* [9].

186 Declaration on the Rights of Indigenous Peoples (n 175) art 31; CESCR 'General Comment No 21: Right of Everyone to Take Part in Cultural Life [art 15 [1](a) of ICESCR]' (21 December 2009) UN Doc E/C12/GC/21 [37].

187 *Compromis* [50].

(ICCPR), persons who share in common a culture[188] in a State shall not be denied the right, in community with the other members of their group, to enjoy their own culture, including members of indigenous communities.[189] Accordingly, it is necessary for States to take positive measures to protect the rights of its members to enjoy and develop their culture.[190] Similarly, under Article 15 of the International Covenant on Economic, Social and Cultural Rights (ICESCR), everyone has the right to take part in cultural life,[191] also pertinent to the culture rights of individuals and communities, including indigenous peoples.[192] It follows that States have an obligation to respect the rights of indigenous peoples to have access to their culture heritage.[193]

In this sense, Atania violated the cultural rights of Clan Kin with respect to the Ruby Sipar. Atania removed the Ruby Sipar from public display and placed it in storage,[194] without meaningful participation and prior consent of Clan Kin,[195] which made it impossible for Clan Kin to enjoy culture without accessing their cultural heritage.[196] The right to cultural heritage[197] of Clan Kin was significantly violated by Atania in this way.

As Atania violated the cultural rights of Clan Kin with respect to the Ruby Sipar, it is inappropriate to return the Ruby Sipar to Atania. Rahad is entitled to possess the Ruby Sipar to protect the cultural rights of Clan Kin as 'indigenous peoples'.

---

188 CCPR 'General Comment No 23: Article 27 (Rights of Minorities)' (8 April 1994) UN Doc CCPR/C/21/Rev1/Add5, para 5.1.

189 General Comment 23 (n 188) para 3.2.

190 General Comment 23 (n 188) para 6.2.

191 International Covenant on Economic, Social and Cultural Rights (adopted 16 December 1966) 993 UNTS 3 (ICESCR) art 15(1).

192 General Comment 21 (n 186) [16](2).

193 General Comment 21 (n 186) [49](d).

194 *Compromis* [44].

195 Declaration on the Rights of Indigenous Peoples (n 175) art 19; *Angela Poma Poma v Peru,* HRC Communication No 1457/2006 (27 March 2009) UN Doc CCPR/C/95/D/1457/2006 para 7.6.

196 HRC 'Report of the Independent Expert in the Field of Cultural Rights, Farida Shaheed' (21 March 2011) UN Doc A/HR/C/17/38 [37].

197 UN Doc A/HR/C/17/38 (n 196) [21]; UN Doc A/HRC/21/53 [60].

C. IN ANY EVENT, RAHAD HAS NO OBLIGATION TO RETURN THE RUBY SIPAR TO ATANIA.

i. Rahad has no obligation to return the Ruby Sipar to Atania under the 1970 Convention.

Articles 7 and 13 of the 1970 Convention provide the obligation of State Parties to return the cultural property to other States. However, the conditions of both Articles cannot be established to facilitate the return of the Ruby Sipar to Atania.

According to Article 7(b)(ii), a State Party should take appropriate steps to recover and return stolen cultural property that has been imported illegally into that State. It is worth noting that the cultural property should be imported after the entry into force of the 1970 Convention in both States concerned.[198] In the present case, Rahad deposited its instrument of ratification with UNESCO on 30 September 2014[199] and the 1970 Convention therefore entered into force with respect to Rahad on 30 December 2014.[200] Even if the Ruby Sipar was regarded as 'stolen' from the Kin Canyon Complex Cultural Center in Atania, an institution similar to museums,[201] this illegal import took place before the 1970 Convention entered into force for Rahad.[202] In other words, the request by Atania of returning the Ruby Sipar cannot be supported under Article 7.[203]

As for Article 13 of the 1970 Convention, it requires State Parties to undertake to ensure that their competent services cooperate in facilitating the earliest possible restitution of illicitly exported cultural property to its rightful owner.[204] The ambiguous notion of 'rightful owner'[205] indicates that the demonstration of ownership

198 1970 Convention art 7(b)(ii).

199 *Corrections* [3].

200 1970 Convention art 21.

201 1970 Convention art 7(b)(i).

202 *Compromis* [50].

203 *R v Heller* (1983) 27 Alta LR (2d) 346; Appeal Decision (1984) 51 AR 73.

204 1970 Convention art 13(b).

205 Patrick O'Keefe, *Commentary on the 1970 UNESCO Convention on the Means of Prohibiting and Preventing the Illicit Import, Export and Transfer of Ownership of Cultural Property* (Institute of Art and Law 2007) 83.

by State Parties is necessary in order to allow for the return of the cultural property.[206] In Atania, there exists only export restriction legislation, without any State ownership laws.[207] As the export restriction is insufficiently clear to amount to an exertion of ownership,[208] Atania unsuccessfully claims to be the rightful owner of the Ruby Sipar. In this sense, Rahad has no obligation to return the Ruby Sipar to Atania.

ii. Rahad has no obligation to return the Ruby Sipar to Atania under customary international law.

In any event, there is no customary international law that offers protection for Atania concerning the return of the Ruby Sipar. The substance of customary international law must 'look for primarily in the actual practice and *opinio juris* of States',[209] but none of the two elements can be met in respect of returning of cultural property to the State of origin.

In the *Asylum* case, the Court laid down the basic rule that state practice of a customary rule must constitute 'constant and uniform usage'.[210] Similarly, in the *North Sea Continental Shelf* cases, the Court remarked that state practice had to be 'both extensive and virtually uniform'.[211] Unsuccessful cases of returning cultural property to States of origin[212] show that there exists no uniform state practice in this regard, which fails to form the basis of customary international law.

In the *Nicaragua* case, the *opinio juris* is expressed when the State has a belief that 'this practice is rendered obligatory'.[213] Additionally, a number of cases in the Court

206 UNESCO Operational Guidelines (n 83) [26].

207 *Compromis* [60].

208 *Government of Peru v Johnson*, 720 F Supp 810 (CD Cal 1989).

209 *Continental Shelf* (Libyan Arab Jamahiriya/Malta) (Judgment) [1985] ICJ Rep 13, 29.

210 *Columbian-Peruvian Asylum Case* (Columbia/Peru) (Judgment) [1950] ICJ 266, 276-277.

211 *North Sea Continental Shelf* (n 11) 43.

212 *Attorney-General of New Zealand v Ortiz and Others* [1982] QB 349 [1984] AC 1; *Islamic Republic of Iran v Wolfcarius,* Courd'Appel de Bruxelles 4eme Chambre-RG No 2002/AR/1993 (20 April 2011); *Greek Autocephalous Orthodox Church in Cyprus v Lans* Rotterdam Civil Court 44053HAZ95/2403 (4 February 1999).

213 *Nicaragua* (n 17) 108-109.

utilized General Assembly resolutions as confirming this subjective element, but what also matter are the content of the resolutions and the conditions of their adoption.[214] Even if there are General Assembly resolutions calling for the return of cultural property to the States of origin, in them no evidence of States' attitude towards a binding norm can be found.[215] Therefore, these resolutions fall short of establishing the existence of an *opinio juris* of returning the cultural property to States of origin.

With the above two elements unsatisfied, no customary international law exists to support the return of the Ruby Sipar to Atania, so Rahad does not have such an obligation.

IV. ATANIA MUST COMPENSATE RAHAD FOR ALL DIRECT AND INDIRECT EXPENSES INCURRED AND ACCRUING AS A RESULT OF ACCEPTING MEMBERS OF CLAN KIN FLEEING FROM ATANIA.

Article 42 of Draft Articles on Responsibility of States for Internationally Wrongful Acts provides that, 'the State is entitled as an injured State to invoke the responsibility of another State if the obligation breached is owed to a group of States including that State, and the breach of obligation specially affects that State.'[216] And as is stated in Article 31, 'the responsible State is under an obligation to make full reparation for the injury caused by the internationally wrongful act'.[217] This notion is emphasized in a number of leading cases.[218]

---

214 *Legality of the Threat or the Use of Nuclear Weapons* (n 69) 254-255; *Western Sahara* (Advisory Opinion) [1975] ICJ Rep 12, 31-33; *East Timor* (Portugal v Australia) (Judgment) [1995] ICJ Rep 90, 102; *Legal Consequences of the Construction of a Wall in the Occupied Palestinian Territory* (Advisory Opinion) [2004] ICJ Rep 136, 171-172.

215 See Generally GA Res 3026A (XXVII) (18 December 1972) UN Doc A/RES/3026A; GA Res 52/24 (25 November 1991) UN Doc A/RES/52/24; GA Res 70/76 (9 December 2015) UN Doc A/RES/70/76.

216 ILC 'Draft Articles on Responsibility of States for Internationally Wrongful Acts, with Commentaries' (2001) UN Doc A/56/10 art 42 (b)(i); *Questions relating to the Obligation to Prosecute or Extradite* (Belgium v. Senegal) [2012] (Judgment) ICJ Rep 422 [69].

217 ARSIWA (n 216) art 31.

218 *Case Concerning the Factory at Chorzów* (Germany v Poland) (Judgment) PCIJ Rep Series A No 9, 21; *Rainbow Warrior Case* (New Zealand v France) [1986] 19 UNRIAA 199, 218.

Atania must compensate Rahad for all expenses because Atania violates its international obligations by its conduct towards Clan Kin migrants [A], and this violation specially affects and causes damage to Rahad [B]. Rahad thereof requests Atania to compensate all expenses incurred and accruing as a result of Atania's wrongful act [C].

A. ATANIA VIOLATES ITS INTERNATIONAL OBLIGATIONS BY ITS CONDUCT TOWARDS CLAN KIN MIGRANTS.

i. Atania violates its international obligation to respect the right to 'water, food and life' of Clan Kin under international law.

ICESCR Article 11 obliges 'the State Parties to recognize the right of everyone'[219] to 'adequate food'[220] and 'water'.[221] It requires States to perform its national obligations to respect, protect and fulfil the right to food of its own citizens.[222] Meanwhile, ICCPR Article 6 emphasizeds 'every human being has the inherent right to life'.[223]

Atania knowingly and forcefully implements the WRAP Act to Clan Kin,[224] who are subsistence farmers,[225] and are neither qualified for an exemption,[226] nor able or allowed to pay for water licenses.[227] It makes more than 80% of Clan Kin in risk of lacking adequate water supply[228] for their subsistence farming,[229] which violates basic rights of Clan Kin to food and water.[230] And since no one can survive without adequate food and water, Atania's conducts constitute violation to the inherent right to

219 ICESCR art 11; Ben Saul *et al*, *International Covenant on Economic, Social and Cultural Rights Commentary, Cases and Material* (OUP 2014) 862 [1].

220 ICESCR art 11.

221 Saul *et al* (n 219) 867.

222 Saul *et al* (n 219) 867 [26].

223 ICCPR art 6.

224 *Compromis* [34] [37]-[38].

225 *Compromis* [11].

226 *Compromis* [37].

227 *Compromis* [37].

228 *Compromis* [36].

229 *Compromis* [11].

230 ICESCR art 11; Saul *et al* (n 219) 867.

life of Clan Kin.[231]

ii. Atania violates its international obligation to respect the right of 'peaceful assembly' and 'lawful arrest' under international law.

ICCPR states 'the right of peaceful assembly shall be recognized'[232] and 'no one shall be subjected to arbitrary arrest or detention'.[233] Though exceptions, under the circumstances of 'public order'[234] or 'procedure' 'established by law',[235] are considered, Atania's conducts cannot be justified, because the assembly by the Sisters of the Sun and Clan Kin members is peaceful [a], and Atania's arrests towards the Kin protesters are arbitrary [b].

a. The assembly by the Sisters of the Sun and Clan Kin members is peaceful.

In order to consider an assembly as a peaceful assembly, two requirements must be fulfilled: *first*, its organizers have professed peaceful intentions, and *second*, the conduct of the assembly is non-violent.[236]

Both elements are met in the present case: the intention of assembly of the Kin is to protest against 'the theft of their water, their food, and their way of life'[237] and to have the government 'listen to their cries'.[238] On one hand, the only purpose is to live back to their peaceful and subsistence farming tradition.[239] On the other hand, the worst impact of the Kin's assembly are blocking traffic and preventing employees from entering municipal offices,[240] which is not violent. As a result, the Kin's assembly is peaceful assembly.

231 ICCPR art 6.

232 ICCPR art 21.

233 ICCPR art 9(1).

234 ICCPR art 21.

235 ICCPR art 9(1).

236 OSCE Office for Democratic Institutions and Human Rights (ODIHR), *Guidelines on Freedom of Peaceful Assembly* (2nd edn, OSCE/ODIHR 2010) 15 [4].

237 *Compromis* [41].

238 *Compromis* [42].

239 *Compromis* [11] [40].

240 *Compromis* [42].

b. Atania's arrests towards the Kin protesters are arbitrary.

Arrest or detention as punishment for the legitimate exercise of the rights as guaranteed by ICCPR is arbitrary, including freedom of assembly.[241] Therefore, Atania's arrests of Clan Kin demonstrators during their peaceful assembly constitute arbitrary arrests.[242]

Meanwhile, arrest on discriminatory grounds is also in principle arbitrary.[243] In the current case, the arrest shall be defined as arbitrary because the WRAP Act,[244] which causes the Kin's Protest,[245] is itself discriminatory. The WRAP Act favored profit-generating farms, since they are qualified for exemptions or able to pay for licenses.[246] But Clan Kin are subsistence farmers[247] and unable to fulfill the WRAP Act obligations due to cultural and political isolation.[248] The exemptions covers nearly 86% farms in Atania,[249] but more than 80% of Clan Kin are still in excessive water usage.[250]

iii. Atania's conducts violate its obligation to take 'effective remedy' under international law.

ICCPR Article 2 requires State Parties to take 'effective remedy' to any person whose rights or freedoms as recognized in covenant are violated, notwithstanding that the violation has been committed by persons acting in an official capacity.[251]

Instead of taking measure to remedy obligations[252] violated by its previous conducts,

---

241 CCPR 'General Comment No 35 - Article 9: Liberty and Security of Person' (15 December 2014) UN Doc CCPR/C/GC/35 [17].

242 *Compromis* [45] [46].

243 CCPR *General Comment* (n 241) [17].

244 *Compromis* [34].

245 *Compromis* [41].

246 *Compromis* [41].

247 *Compromis* [11].

248 *Compromis* [41].

249 *Compromis* [35].

250 *Compromis* [37].

251 ICCPR art 3(a).

252 ICCPR art 6; ICCPR art 9(1) 21; ICESCR art 11.

Atania's amendments to the WRAP Act to punish Clan Kin,[253] and the pending trial towards arrested protesters[254] constitute violation of ICCPR Article 2.

iv. The obligations violated by Atania are obligations *erga omnes*.

Since human rights treaties create particular legal orders involving objective obligations to protect human rights,[255] human rights established under such treaties may constitute obligations *erga omnes* for the States Parties.[256] Atania's conducts which violate obligations obliged in ICCPR ICESCR, constitute violation of obligations *erga omnes*, which are owed to all states.[257]

B. ATANIA'S VIOLATION SPECIALLY AFFECTS AND CAUSES DAMAGE TO RAHAD.

i. Rahad is a specially affected State of Atania's wrongful acts.

Draft Articles entitles the injured State who is 'specially affected' by another State's international wrongful acts the right to invoke responsibility.[258] 'Specially affected' is frequently mentioned in cases.[259] And the State must be affected by the breach in a way which distinguishes it from the generality of other States to which the obligation is owed.[260] Considering Atania and Rahad are neighboring countries, also the only countries on the Nomad Coast,[261] and Clan Kin cannot flee to the desert or Ocean but Rahad,[262] Rahad is a specially affected State by the fleeing of Clan Kin,[263] which was caused by Atania's wrongful acts.[264]

---

253 *Compromis* [38].

254 *Clarifications* [7].

255 *Case Concerning Human rights in Northern Ireland* (Ireland v UK) (1978) 2 EHRR 25.

256 Shaw (n 70) 201; *Barcelona Traction, Light and Power Company, Limited* (Belgium v Spain) (Judgment) [1970] ICJ Rep 3, 4.

257 *Barcelona Traction* (n 256) 4, 32.

258 ARSIWA (n 216) art 42 (b)(i).

259 *North Sea Continental Shelf* (n 11) [74]; ARSIWA (n 216) 119 [12].

260 ARSIWA (n 216) 119 [12].

261 *Compromis* [1]

262 ARSIWA (n 216) art 42 (b)(i).

263 *Compromis* [47].

264 *Compromis* [38] [46]-[47].

ii. The fleeing of Clan Kin resulted from Atania's wrongful acts cause severe social and economic damage to Rahad.

As a result, the fleeing of Clan Kin caused severe economic damage, for example, spotted sporadic power outages in 85% of the country last for more than four hours at a time, more than 150,000 Rahadi families and countless Kin migrants in the camps are reduced clean water accesses,[265] etc. Meanwhile, the Rahad also suffers from social instability resulted from the migration, for instance, resettled refugees have problems of integration into the new society,[266] cannot acclimate to the culture of Rahad[267] and some even sleep in the streets.[268] And the damage is continuing accruing.[269]

C. THEREFORE, ATANIA SHOULD COMPENSATE ALL EXPENSES INCURRED AND ACCRUING AS A RESULT OF ITS INTERNATIONALLY WRONGFUL ACTS.

As is stated by Article 31 of ARSIWA, 'the responsible State is under an obligation to make full reparation for the injury caused by the internationally wrongful act'[270] and reaffirmed in a number of cases,[271] 'that reparation must, as far as possible, wipe out all the consequences of the illegal act and reestablish the situation which could, in all probability, have existed if that act had not been committed'.[272]

Therefore, Rahad requests Atania to compensate all direct and indirect expenses incurred, which amount to US$ 945,000,000,[273] as well as expenses continuing to accrue, from accepting Clan Kin refugees incurred as a result of Atania's wrongful act.[274]

---

265 *Compromis* [53].

266 *Compromis* [53].

267 *Compromis* [53].

268 *Compromis* [53].

269 *Compromis* [57].

270 ARSIWA (n 216) art 31.

271 *Chorzow Factory* (n 218) 21; *Armed Activities* (DRC v Uganda) (n 1) 168, 257; *Construction of a Wall* (n 214) 136, 198; ARSIWA (n 216) 119 [12].

272 *United States Diplomatic and Consular Staff in Tehran* (United States of America v Iran) (Judgment) [1980] ICJ Rep 3, 45.

273 *Compromis* [57].

274 *Compromis* [57].

CONCLUSION AND PRAYER FOR RELIEF

In view of the facts set forth in this Memorial and the arguments applying the law to the facts as stated;

May it please the Court, on behalf of the Kingdom of Rahad, Respondent herein, respectfully requests this Honorable Court to adjudge and declare that:

1. Rahad's extraction of water from the Aquifer does not violate Rahad's international legal obligations governing the proper use of shared resources;
2. Rahad's Savali Pipeline operations do not violate any legal obligations relating to the Kin Canyon Complex;
3. Rahad is entitled to retain possession of the Ruby Sipar; and
4. Atania must compensate Rahad for all direct and indirect expenses incurred and accruing as a result of accepting members of Clan Kin fleeing from Atania.

Respectfully submitted,
AGENTS FOR RAHAD

“Egart 与 Ibra 案”

Case Concerning the Egart and the Ibra (The People's Democratic Republic of Anduchenca v The Federal Republic of Rukaruku)

李子钰　李泽坤　廉雅雯　罗诗静　周睿哲　曹超

请求国书状

Memorials for the People's Democratic Republic of Anduchenca

TABLE OF CONTENTS

ii. Rukaruku's wrongfulness cannot be justified under international law.

B. ANDUCHENCA DID NOT VIOLATE ARTICLE 7 OF THE FCN TREATY WHEN IT CAPTURED THE EGART.

i. The freedom of commerce and navigation under Article 7 could not be applied to the Egart.

ii. The capture of the Egart is consistent with international law.

III. ANDUCHENCA DID NOT VIOLATE ARTICLE 16 OF THE FCN TREATY BY COMMISSIONING AND OPERATING THE IBRA.

A. ANDUCHENCA DID NOT VIOLATE ARTICLE VI OF NPT BY COMMISSIONING AND OPERATING THE IBRA.

i. Article VI of NPT is not binding on Anduchenca.

ii. Even if Article VI of NPT is binding on Anduchenca, it did not violate such obligation.

B. RESOLUTION 3790 DID NOT IMPOSE ANY DISARMAMENT OBLIGATIONS ON ANDUCHENCA.

IV. RUKARUKU VIOLATED ARTICLE 17 OF THE FCN TREATY WHEN IT ATTACKED THE COVFEFE AND WHEN IT CAPTURED THE IBRA.

A. RUKARUKU USED FORCE AGAINST THE TERRITORIAL INTEGRITY AND POLITICAL INDEPENDENCE OF ANDUCHENCA.

B. NOT PERMITTED UNDER INTERNATIONAL LAW, ATTACKING THE COVFEFE AND CAPTURING THE IBRA DID NOT CONSTITUTE THE EXCEPTION UNDER ARTICLE 17 OF THE FCN TREATY.

i. Resolution 3790 did not authorize Rukaruku to attack the Covfefe or to capture the Ibra.

ii. Rukaruku's use of force against the Covfefe and the Ibra did not constitute self-defense.

C. DUE TO THE VIOLATION OF PRINCIPLES OF PROPORTIONALITY AND NECESSITY, RUKARUKU'S MEANS AND METHODS ARE NOT PERMITTED UNDER INTERNATIONAL LAW.

i. Both principles of proportionality and necessity are binding on Rukaruku when it used force against Anduchenca.

ii. When attacking the Covfefe, Rukaruku violated the principle of proportionality

iii. When capturing the Ibra, Rukaruku violated the principle of necessity.

CONCLUSION AND PRAYER FOR RELIEF

STATEMENT OF JURISDICTION

On 3 July 2017, the People's Democratic Republic of Anduchenca (Anduchenca) filed in the Registry of the International Court of Justice (the Court) an Application against the Federal Republic of Rukaruku (Rukaruku) pursuant to Article 40(1) of the Court's Statute, in accordance with the Treaty of Friendship, Commerce and Navigation (the FCN Treaty) for submission to the Court of the dispute concerning the Egart and the Ibra, signed between the two parties on 12 March 1947. The Application was communicated to Rukaruku on 3 July 2017 pursuant to Article 40(2) of the Court's Statute. Rukaruku attended the proceedings.

QUESTIONS PRESENTED

People's Democratic Republic of Anduchenca respectfully requests the Court to adjudge:

I.

1. *Whether* the arbitral tribunal acts in excess of its power;

2. *Whether* there exists serious departure from fundamental rules of procedure.

II.

1. *Whether* the Egart's presence and data collection are prejudicial to Anduchenca's sovereignty;

2. *Whether* the Egart enjoys the right of freedom of navigation between both Parties' territory including the territorial sea;

3. *Whether* Anduchenca has the right to require foreign government vessel to obtain the prior authorization into its territorial sea.

III.

1. *Whether* Anduchenca is obliged to fulfill the obligation to implement disarmament programs;

2. *Whether* Anduchenca is obliged to pursue negotiation in good faith in accordance with Article VI of NPT;

3. *Whether* Anduchenca violated nuclear disarmament obligations under the United Nations Security Council Resolution 3790 (Resolution 3790).

IV.

1. *Whether* Rukaruku used force against Anduchenca's territorial integrity and political independence by attacking the Covfefe and capturing the Ibra;

2. *Whether* Rukaruku's use of force against Anduchenca was authorized by the United Nations Security Council Resolution 3790;

3. *Whether* Rukaruku's use of force could be justified by the right of self-defense;

4. *Whether* Rukaruku's use of force violated the principles of proportionality and necessity.

STATEMENT OF FACTS

The People's Democratic Republic of Anduchenca (Anduchenca) and the Federal Republic of Rukaruku (Rukaruku) are two coastal states on the Kumatqesh Ocean in the Odasarra Region, where interdependent trade prevails. Anduchenca is a developing country which contributes most of its military budget to its Navy. Rukaruku possesses aircraft carriers, surface ships and submarines.

World War II caused a proliferation of small arms and light weapons among the civilians in all the Odasarran States, except Rukaruku. After the War, Anduchenca participated in a program in which Rukaruku provided economic aid to help Anduchenca disarm and expanded its Navy deployment along the Kumatqesh coast.

On 12 March 1947, Anduchenca and Rukaruku signed the FCN Treaty. Hereafter Rukaruku offered a large amount of money to develop the cooperative disarmament program in Anduchenca. In 1967, Anduchenca underwent a *coup d'état*, under the leadership of General Rafiq Tovarish. In early 1969, Rukaruku terminated its economic assistance and the disarmament program, while it still deployed its navy along the Kumatqesh coast.

Anduchenca did not join the Treaty on the Non-Proliferation of Nuclear Weapons (NPT) and has declared its objection constantly over the past 50 years. Anduchenca also did not join the United Nations Convention on the Law of the Sea (UNCLOS) in 1982.

In August 2010, Anduchenca adopted a maritime security law providing any government vessel planning to enter its 12-nautical-mile territorial sea shall acquire authorization in advance. Correspondingly, Rukaruku ordered its vessel to keep 12 nautical miles away from the Anduchencan coast.

In August 2015, the Rukarukan Navy employed autonomous underwater vehicles

(AUVs) 'the Egart', equipped with advanced optical, acoustic, sonar, sense-and-avoid systems and can lift 5-kilogram objects from the ocean floor. It is designed to surface regularly to receive GPS signals.

On 25 September 2015, before the United Nations General Assembly, Mr. Tovarish condemned that Rukaruku operated the AUVs as spy drones and constituted a threat to international peace and security.

On 29 October 2015, Anduchenca stated that it captured the Egart navigating 11 nautical miles from the Anduchencan coast, which was gathering optical and acoustic data and they found it contained data important to Anduchencan national security.

After failure of negotiations, on 20 December 2015, Rukaruku instituted arbitration under Article 10(a) of the FCN Treaty in which Rukaruku claimed Anduchenca's violation of Article 7 the FCN Treaty by capturing the Egart and requested return.

Rukaruku selected Bhrasht Moyet as its arbitrator, who is of Rukarukan nationality and had been previously appointed by Rukaruku.

On 28 February 2016, Judge Alice Bacal appointed Mou Tong for Anduchenca. Two days later, Anduchenca sent a *Note Verbale* to Rukaruku and the tribunal asserting that the dispute was not arbitrable and the tribunal had no jurisdiction.

The arbitral proceedings proceeded without Anduchenca. On 2 March 2017, the tribunal rendered an award saying it had jurisdiction and decided in favor of Rukaruku. Anduchenca denounced it as null and void.

The Institute for Legal Studies of Arbitration (ILSA) is an international non-governmental organization, with significance online influence, reporting the inappropriate conduct of arbitrators with the aim of advocating transparency.

On 21 March 2017, the ILSA published a report revealing three pieces of undisclosed information accepted by both Parties, holding the tribunal's award as questionable.

First, Judge Moyet had three private telephone calls with Rukaruku's counsel Mr. Bouc Chivo, a lawyer in the Ministry of External Relations, before and during the tribunal's deliberations. In the conversations, Judge Moyet agreed to stress to the tribunal certain Rukarukan arguments as Mr. Chivo requested, which was criticized as a detriment to independence of Judge Moyet.

Second, the tribunal hired Mr. Mikkel Orvindari as assistant without notifying the parties in advance. Accounting showed that Mr. Orvindari spent 522 hours on the case but each arbitrator only billed between 57 and 62 hours. Mr. Orvindari's work contained 'summarizing arguments and evidence', 'attending tribunal deliberations', and 'drafting memoranda and award'.

Third, a note on a draft of the arbitral award same as the final version from Judge Tong was found, which read he would use Mr. Orvindari's original draft with no revision.

The report was widely spread on the media and Mr. Chivo resigned from Rukarukan Ministry of External Relations afterwards. On 27 March 2017, Rukaruku admitted the disclosed information but nevertheless stated the award as valid.

On 2 April 2017, *The Sydney Morning Herald* published an article reporting that Anduchenca had commissioned a nuclear submarine Ibra. Mr. Tovarish addressed that the Ibra would serve as a deterrent against who would persist in infringing its sovereignty. He further stated that Anduchenca attended the first session of the United Nations Conference to Negotiate a Legally Binding Instrument to Prohibit Nuclear Weapons (UN Conference) in March 2017, but would not attend the second substantive session or sign any treaty emerging therein.

On 8 May 2017, the United Nations Security Council (UNSC) adopted Resolution 3790 by a vote of nine to six on taking necessary action when confronting the Ibra.

Rukaruku said that it would commit to the enforcement.

On 6 June 2017, at 4:00 a.m. local time, two Rukarukan warships fired 12 cruise missiles at the unarmed supply ship Covfefe conveying provisions and personnel to the Ibra, which was 250 nautical miles away from the Anduchencan coast. Four of the 12 missiles hit their target, killing seven civilians onboard.

On 14 June 2017, the Rukarukan Navy discovered the Ibra. The six warships fired a series of torpedoes at the Ibra and eventually controlled it. The crew surrendered at once and was detained for questioning.

On 19 June 2017, the United Nations Security Council adopted a Resolution approving Rukaruku, the International Atomic Energy Agency (IAEA), and two NPT Nuclear Weapon States for dismantlement of the Ibra and removal of nuclear materials on board. The agreement had been carried out.

On 3 July 2017, Anduchenca filed in the Registry of the Court an Application instituting proceedings against Rukaruku. Rukaruku participated in the proceedings as Respondent.

SUMMARY OF PLEADINGS

FIRST PLEADING

The tribunal has no jurisdiction over the case since there exists no dispute concerning the interpretation and application of Article 7 of the FCN Treaty. Even if the dispute exists, the tribunal acts in excess of its power.

Additionally, the *ex parte* communications with Judge Moyet affected his ability to adjudicate the case independently and impartially, which also deprived Anduchenca's procedural right and constituted serious departure from fundamental rules of procedure. Moreover, Mr. Orvindari was improperly entrusted with substantive work. Judge Tong's decision-making function also delegated to Mr. Orvindari since he just signed off on the draft award made by Mr. Orvindari. Therefore, there existed serious departure of fundamental rules of procedure.

SECOND PLEADING

The Egart is a warship and it unlawfully entered into Anduchenca's territorial sea because the Egart did not obtain prior authorization from Anduchenca. Meanwhile, under customary international law, the warship does not enjoy the right of innocent passage in the territorial sea. Even if the prior authorization was not needed, the Egart's operation in Anduchenca's territorial sea was prejudicial to Anduchenca's sovereignty. Such wrongfulness could not be justified because Anduchenca made no consent.

Under Article 7 of the FCN Treaty, the Egart only enjoys freedom of navigation between the territories of both parties on High Seas. However, the Egart was operated in Anduchenca's territorial sea. Although the Egart enjoys immunity, Anduchenca was entitled to capture the Egart based on countermeasure, therefore Anduchenca did not violate Article 7 of the FCN Treaty.

THIRD PLEADING

Pursuant to Article 16 of the FCN Treaty, the disarmament obligation binding on Anduchenca under international law may involve nuclear disarmament obligation under Article VI of NPT and arguably under the United Nations Security Council Resolution 3790.

As for nuclear disarmament obligation under Article VI of NPT, since it is not a customary rule and Anduchenca is not a contracting party, but a persistent objector to NPT, such obligation is not binding on Anduchenca. Even if it is, Anduchenca has already fulfilled it by participating in the first session of the UN Conference to Negotiate a Legally Binding Instrument to Prohibit Nuclear Weapons (UN Conference).

Besides, Resolution 3790 did not impose any disarmament obligations on Anduchenca. To this end, Anduchenca did not violate Article 16 of the FCN Treaty by commissioning and operating the Ibra.

FOURTH PLEADING

By attacking the Covfefe and capturing the Ibra, Rukaruku used force against the territorial integrity and political independence of Anduchenca. Besides, attacking the Covfefe and capturing the Ibra were beyond the authorization of Resolution 3790 and could not be justified by the right of self-defense whether in accordance with Article 51 of the UN Charter or the doctrine of anticipatory self-defense.

Moreover, the means and methods used by Rukaruku were not permitted under international law. When attacking the Covfefe, Rukaruku violated the principle of proportionality, while when capturing the Ibra, it violated the principle of necessity. Therefore, Rukaruku's use of force against Anduchenca is not permitted under international law. To this end, by attacking the Covfefe and capturing the Ibra, Rukaruku violated Article 17 of the FCN Treaty.

PLEADINGS

I. THE ARBITRAL AWARD OF 2 MARCH 2017 IS NOT VALID.

The validity of an arbitral award may be challenged in cases of a manifest excess of powers or lack of jurisdiction, a serious departure from a fundamental rule of procedure or failure to state reasons for the award.[1] These grounds ensure control over the fundamental integrity of the arbitral process and the award rendered therein.[2] The award of 2 March 2017 is not valid since the tribunal has exceeded its power [A] and several procedural biases seriously infringed the fundamental rules of procedure [B].

A. THE TRIBUNAL HAS EXCEEDED ITS POWER.

The tribunal should exercise its power as entrusted by the parties' agreement. Here, the tribunal has exceeded its power since there was no dispute concerning Article 7 of the FCN Treaty before the initiation of the proceedings [i], and it violated the rules of interpretation in deciding its jurisdiction [ii].

i. The tribunal has no jurisdiction since no dispute concerning Article 7 of the FCN Treaty existed between Anduchenca and Rukaruku prior to the institution of the arbitration.

The existence of a dispute before the instituted proceeding[3] is a precondition for the tribunal's jurisdiction.[4] According to the *Marshall Island* case,[5] the date for

---

1 ILC 'Model Rules on Arbitral Procedure with a General Commentary' (1958) UN DOC A/13/9 art 35.

2 *Soufraki v The United Arab Emirates* (Decision on Annulment) [2007] ICSID Case No ARB/02/7 [123].

3 *Case Concerning Certain Property* (Liechtenstein v Germany) (Preliminary Objections) [2005] ICJ Rep 6 [25].

4 ICSID Convention, Regulations and Rules (entered into force 14 October 1966) art 25(1); 'Updated Background Paper on Annulment for the Administrative Council of ICSID' (2016) <http://documents.worldbank.org/curated/en/705861489478820495/Updated-background-paper-on-annulment-for-the-administrative-council-of-ICSID> accessed 11 January 2018 [85].

5 *Obligations Concerning Negotiations Relating to Cessation of the Nuclear Arms Race and to Nuclear Disarmament* (Marshall Islands v United Kingdom) (Preliminary Objections) [2016] ICJ Rep 833 [37].

determining the existence of the dispute should be the date on which the application to initiate the proceedings is submitted.[6] Under the 'awareness' standard[7] established in that case, a dispute exists when the subject-matter of the dispute is sufficiently clear in Applicant's statement to Respondent before instituting the proceeding so that Respondent is aware or cannot be unaware that Applicant's view is positively against its view,[8] which gives Respondent an opportunity to recognize or deny an international obligation.[9]

In the present case, there is no evidence showing that the alleged violation of Article 7 of the FCN Treaty was ever conveyed to Anduchenca. The subject of the communication between Anduchenca and Rukaruku prior to the initiation of the arbitration was only limited to the return of the Egart.[10] Anduchenca did not specifically allege any violation under the FCN Treaty, which is required according to the recent jurisprudence of ICJ.[11]

Therefore, the tribunal has no jurisdiction over the case since under the 'awareness' test, no legal dispute concerning Article 7 existed between the parties prior to the arbitration.

ii. Even if the dispute exists, there is manifest breach in the tribunal's interpretation of Article 7 of the FCN Treaty.

Although a tribunal has the power to decide its own jurisdiction[12] and to interpret the

6 *Alleged Violations of Sovereign Rights and Maritime Spaces in the Caribbean Sea* (Nicaragua v Colombia) (Preliminary Objections) [2016] ICJ Rep 3 [52]; *Case concerning Application of the International Convention on the Elimination of All Forms of Racial Discrimination* (Georgia v Russian Federation) (Preliminary Objections) [2011] ICJ Rep 70 [30].

7 *Marshall Islands* (n 5) 41, 49.

8 *Obligations concerning Negotiations Relating to Cessation of the Nuclear Arms Race and to Nuclear Disarmament* (Marshall Islands v United Kingdom) (Declaration of Judge Donoghue) [2016] ICJ Rep 1034 [8].

9 *Di Curzio Case* (Italy, United States) [1959] 391 RIAA 391-393.

10 *Case Concerning the Egart and the Ibra* (The People's Democratic Republic of Anduchenca v The Federal Republic of Rukaruku) (Statement of Agreed Facts) [2017] (*Facts*) [15]-[17] [19].

11 *Questions Relating to the Obligation to Prosecute or Extradite* (Belgium v Senegal) (Judgment) [2012] ICJ Rep 422 [54].

12 ILC Model Rules (n 1) art 9; Gary Born, *International Commercial Arbitration* (2nd edn, Wolters Kluwer Law & Business 2014) 1051.

instrument governing the jurisdiction,[13] the scope of the tribunal's jurisdiction and its limits are entrusted by the Parties' agreement.[14] The manifest breach[15] of the rules of interpretation will lead to the tribunal's excess of power.[16]

The manifest breach of a tribunal's competence can result from improperly interpreting the provisions governing its competence.[17] In the present case, the tribunal mechanically interpreted that the dispute was only concerned with the legality of the Egart's navigation[18] without addressing the scope of Article 7. The tribunal wrongfully determined that the ordinary meaning of Article 7 also covered government vessels, which is incompatible with the spirit, purpose and context of the FCN Treaty[19] since the scope of Article 7 only covers commercial vessels outside the territorial sea as submitted in section II(B)(i). Therefore, the tribunal's manifestly wrongful interpretation exceeded its competence conferred by the FCN Treaty.

B. THERE EXISTS SERIOUS DEPARTURE FROM FUNDAMENTAL RULES OF PROCEDURE.

The serious departure[20] from fundamental rules of procedure is recognized as a reason to vacate an arbitral award.[21] A departure enough to deprive a Party of the benefit or protection intended in the arbitral rules is serious.[22] Rules of natural justice concerning

---

13 *Nottebohm case* (Liechtenstein v Guatemala) (Preliminary Objection) [1953] ICJ Rep 111, 119; *Case Concerning the Arbitral Award of 31 July 1989* (Guinea-Bissau v Senegal) (Judgment) [1991] ICJ Rep 53 [68].

14 *Arbitral Award of 31 July 1989* (n 13) [49].

15 *Arbitral Award of 31 July 1989* (n 13) [47].

16 Background Paper (n 4) [87];

17 *Arbitral Award of 31 July 1989* (n 13) [48].

18 *Facts* [26].

19 *Facts* [Annex I].

20 Christoph Schreuer *et al*, *The ICSID Convention: A Commentary* (2nd edn, CUP 2009) 280, 282; *Maritime International Nominees Establishment (MINE) v Government of Guinea (Guinea)* (Decision on Annulment) [1989] ICSID Case No ARB/84/4 para 4.06.

21 ILC Model Rules (n 1) art 35(c); 'The Rules of Procedure of Arbitration Proceedings of ICSID' (adopted 2003) Doc ICSID/15/Rec 1 Rule 50(1)(c)(iii).

22 *MINE v Guinea* (n 20) para 5.05.

the essential fairness,[23] reflecting minimal international law procedural standards to be respected,[24] are regarded as fundamental. In the present case, the *ex parte* communications [i], the appointment of Mr. Orvindari and the work done by him [ii], and Judge Tong's signing off on the award drafted by Mr. Orvindari [iii] all constitute serious departure from fundamental rules of procedure.

i. The *ex parte* communications constitutes a serious departure from fundamental rules of procedure.

a. The ex parte communications infringed Judge Moyet's independence and impartiality.

The tribunal is obliged to protect the Parties' procedural rights which include the right to an impartial and independent arbitrator.[25] The independence and impartiality of an arbitrator[26] are a set of minimal standards of procedure to be respected under international law.[27] The standard of inquiry only requires an apparent lack of independence or impartiality, instead of actual bias or dependence, from the view of a reasonable and informed third party.[28] It is well established that the appointing-party shall not contact the arbitrator on either substantive or procedural[29] issues in private. Thus, by accepting the instructions from Rukaruku, there is no doubt that Judge Moyet lacks the appearance of independence and impartiality.

---

23 Schreuer (n 20) [286]; *CDC Group plc (CDC) v Republic of Seychelles (Seychelles)* (Award) [2003] ICSID Case No ARB/02/14 [49].

24 Schreuer (n 20) [284]; *Wena Hotels Ltd (Wena) v Arab Republic of Egypt (Egypt)* [2002] 41 ILM 896 [57].

25 *The Republic of Croatia v The Republic of Slovenia* (Partial Award) [2016] PCA Case No 2012-04 [227].

26 *CDC v Seychelles* (n 23) [49]; *Klöckner Industrie-Anlagen GmbH and others v United Republic of Cameroon and Société Camerounaise des Engrais* (Decision on Annulment) [1985] ICSID Case No ARB/81/2 [95].

27 *Wena v Egypt* (n 24) [57].

28 *Caratube International Oil Co LLP v Republic of Kazakhstan* (Decision on the Proposal for Disqualification of Bruno Boesc) [2014] ICSID Case No ARB/13/13, 1-2.

29 *Remmey v Paine Webber Inc* (1994) 4th Cir 32 F 3d 143; *Robert Schwartz v Merril Lynch & Co Inc* (2010) 2nd Cir Docket No 10-0826.

b. The ex parte communications deprived Anduchenca's right of equal treatment and hearing.

Ex parte communication between an arbitrator and the appointing-party is usually prohibited,[30] because it will unbalance and jeopardize the fundamental right of the other Party to be equally treated by the tribunal.[31] Such prohibition is considered as a fundamental rule.[32] *Ex parte* communication will also deprive the other Party of the right of hearing,[33] since it denies that Party's opportunity to respond to what has been submitted by the counter-party.[34]

In the private telephone conversations, Judge Moyet agreed to emphasize certain arguments to the tribunal at the request of Rukaruku's counsel,[35] which deprived Anduchenca of the chance to effectively respond to those arguments, and seriously departed from the principle of equal treatment.

The prohibition of *ex parte* communication is to ensure the procedural fairness.[36] *Ex parte* communication divests the Parties' benefit of equality in the proceedings.[37] With Anduchenca losing the right to respond to those emphasized arguments,[38] the inequality between the Parties contravened fairness. Therefore, the private telephone conversations constituted a serious departure from procedural fairness.

---

30 'UNCITRAL Model Law on International Commercial Arbitration' (United Nations Publications 2006) 24 ILM 1302 art 24(3); International Bar Association (IBA) 'Rules of Ethics for International Arbitrators' (1987) art 5.

31 Patricia Shaughnessy, Sherlin Tung, *The Powers and Duties of an Arbitrator: Liber Amicorum Pierre A Karrer* (Wolters Kluwer 2017) 73.

32 *MINE v Guinea* (n 20) para 5.06; Background Paper (n 4) [99]; Matti Kurkela, Santtu Turunen, *Due Process in International Commercial Arbitration* (2nd edn, OUP 2010) 206.

33 *Schwartz v Lynch* (n 29).

34 Born (n 12) 2228.

35 *Facts* [31].

36 *CDC v Seychelles* (n 23) [49].

37 Kurkela, Turunen (n 32) 206.

38 *Facts* [31].

ii. The appointment of and the work done by Mr. Orvindari without prior awareness and consent of Anduchenca and Rukaruku constitute a serious departure from the fundamental rules of procedure.

a. Mr. Orvindari was appointed without the Parties' awareness and consent.

Transparency constitutes a fundamental rule since it seeks to promote the procedural legitimacy.[39] Given that the potential substantive involvement[40] and impartiality and independence[41] of a secretary will affect the tribunal's decision,[42] the appointment of the secretary needs the Parties' awareness and consent[43] at earliest convenience,[44] which will give the Parties opportunities to promptly raise objections.[45]

Mr. Orvindari was appointed by the tribunal without the Parties' awareness and consent,[46] which violated the rule of transparency,[47] and also deprived Anduchenca of its procedural right. Therefore, it constituted a serious departure from fundamental rules of procedure.

b. The work was improperly entrusted to Mr. Orvindari by the tribunal.

There is no uniform standard concerning the restrictions to the role of a secretary[48]

---

39 Catherine Rogers, 'Transparency in International Commercial Arbitration' (2005) 54 *U Kan L Rev* 1301, 1309.

40 International Council for Commercial Arbitration '*Young ICCA Guide on Arbitral Secretaries*' (Young ICCA) (International Council for Commercial Arbitration 2014) art 3(1), (2)(e)(f)(i)(j).

41 Young ICCA (n 40) art 2(3) Commentary.

42 Rogers (n 39) 1306-1309.

43 Alan Redfern, Martin Hunter, *Law and Practice of International Commercial Arbitration* (4th edn, Sweet & Maxwell 2004) paras 4.195, 4.199; *Yukos case* (Hulley Enterprises Ltd, Yukos Universal Ltd, and Veteran Petroleum Ltd v the Russian Federation) (Expert Opinion of Professor Gorge Bermann) DDC Case No 1:14-cv-01996-ABJ [82].

44 Young ICCA (n 40) art 1(3).

45 Young ICCA (n 40) arts 1(2), 2(3), 2(4) Commentary; 'IBA Guidelines on Conflict of Interest in International Arbitration' (International Bar Association 2014) General Standard 5(b); International Commercial Disputes Committee 'Joint-Report of the International Commercial Disputes Committee and the Committee on Arbitration of the New York City Bar Association' (2006) 17 *American Review of International Arbitration* 575, 589-592.

46 *Facts* [32].

47 Young ICCA (n 40) art 1(2) Commentary.

48 Polkinghorne Michael, Charles B Rosenberg, 'The Role of the Tribunal Secretary in

under international law. Although it is generally accepted that a secretary can function beyond purely administrative aspects,[49] the tribunal should not entrust arbitrator's personal mandate,[50] such as decision-making function, to a secretary.

In this case, Mr. Orvindari has done a great deal of work far more than what the tribunal has done altogether. He billed 522 hours for the case, nearly ten times the average number of hours spent by the three arbitrators.[51] His summary of the Parties' arguments and evidence would indirectly influence the tribunal's evaluation of the case.[52] Moreover, his participation in the tribunal's deliberation and award drafting[53] would supersede the tribunal's decision-making function. Thus, the work accomplished by Mr. Orvindari deviated from the fundamental rules of procedure.

c. Rukaruku failed to prove Mr. Orvindari was under direction and supervision of the tribunal.

Mr. Orvindari should be under the tribunal's direction and supervision when he was entrusted with substantive work,[54] and the burden of proof should be borne by Rukaruku.[55] However, Rukaruku failed to substantiate this in its submission.

International Arbitration: A Call for a Uniform Standard' (2014) 8 *Dispute Resolution International* 107, 110.

49 Young ICCA (n 40) art 3(1) Commentary.

50 *Approved Judgment Made by Mr Justice Popplewell* [2017] EWHC 194 [65]; 'UNCITRAL Notes on Organizing Arbitral Proceedings' (2012) A/CN9/423 [27]; Redfern, Hunter (n 43) para 4.195; Hong Kong International Arbitration Center 'HKIAC Administered Arbitration Rules' (2013) art 3.4; International Chamber of Commerce 'ICC Note to Parties and Arbitral Tribunal on the Conduct of the Arbitration under the ICC Rules of Arbitration' (30 October 2017) art 2.

51 *Facts* [32].

52 *Facts* [32]; Young ICCA (n 40) art 3(2)(h).

53 *Facts* [32].

54 Young ICCA (n 40) art 3(1).

55 *Case Concerning the Arbitral Award Made by the King of Spain on 23 December 1906* (Honduras v Nicaragua) (Judgment) [1960] ICJ Rep 192, 206.

iii. Judge Tong entrusted his decision-making function to Mr. Orvindari and made no reasoning in the arbitral award.

a. The decision-making function was entrusted to Mr. Orvindari.

An arbitrator should not entrust the decision-making function to a secretary.[56] The Parties highly value the arbitrators' pivotal decision-making function,[57] thus this personal[58] and professional[59] mandate cannot be transferred to others,[60] which is recognized as a fundamental rule of procedure.[61] In fact, in the *Yukos* case,[62] the award was set aside after expert evidence showed that 79% of the award was written by the tribunal secretary.

Mr. Orvindari drafted the whole award which was identical to the final version,[63] and Judge Tong signed off on Mr. Orvindari's draft without making his own decision.[64] Those facts substantiate that the decision-making process was assumed by the secretary. Therefore, Judge Tong's personal and professional duty of decision-making was entrusted to the secretary, which rendered a serious departure from fundamental rules of procedure.

b. The tribunal made no reasoning in the arbitral award.

Failure to make reasoning is recognized as a ground to nullify an arbitral award.[65] It

56 *Approved Judgment* (n 50) [65]; UNCITRAL Notes (n 50) [27]; Redfern, Hunter (n 43) para 4.195; HKIAC Rules (n 50) art 3.4; ICC Note (n 50) art 2.

57 *Yukos Expert Opinion* (n 43) [81].

58 Constantine Partasides, 'The Fourth Arbitrator? The Role of Secretaries to the Tribunal in International Arbitration' (2002) 18 *Arbitration International* 147, 147; Eric Schwartz, 'The Rights and Duties of ICC Arbitrators' (1992) *Status of the Arbitrator* 67, 86.

59 *Yukos Expert Opinion* (n 43) [81].

60 *Yukos Expert Opinion* (n 43) [81]; American Arbitration Association and American Bar Association 'The Code of Ethics for Arbitrators in Commercial Disputes' (9 February 2004) Canon V (C).

61 Background Paper (n 4) [98].

62 *Yukos Universal Ltd (Isle of Man) v The Russian Federation* (Final Award) [2014] PCA Case No 2005-04/AA227.

63 *Facts* [33].

64 *Facts* [33].

65 ILC Model Rules (n 1) art 35 (c); ICSID Arbitration Rules (n 21) art 52; *Case Concerning*

is the tribunal that has to address its mind to the matters on which the contentions are based,[66] and draw its own conclusion therefrom.[67] However, the arbitral award was made by Mr. Orvindari, which signified the tribunal's own reasoning was not stated. Therefore, the arbitral award is invalid.

II. RUKARUKU VIOLATED ARTICLE 6 OF THE FCN TREATY WHEN THE EGART OPERATED IN ANDUCHENCAN TERRITORIAL SEA, BUT ANDUCHENCA DID NOT VIOLATE ARTICLE 7 OF THE FCN TREATY WHEN IT CAPTURED THE EGART.

A. RUKARUKU VIOLATED ARTICLE 6 OF THE FCN TREATY WHEN THE EGART OPERATED IN ANDUCHENCAN TERRITORIAL SEA.

States are required to comply with their treaty obligations in good faith.[68] Rukaruku violated Article 6 of the FCN Treaty because the Egart's entrance into Anduchencan territorial sea was unauthorized and did not constitute innocent passage [i], and Rukaruku's wrongfulness cannot be justified under international law [ii].

i. The Egart navigated into Anduchencan territorial sea without prior authorization, and its traverse was not innocent passage.

a. The Egart is a warship.

The AUV is consistent with the definition of warship[69] if one considers that the commanding officer of the launching ship is under the command of the AUV's navigation system and the crew operating the launching ship are 'manning' the AUV.[70]

---

the Arbitral Award of 31 July 1989 (Guinea-Bissau v Senegal) (Dissenting Opinion of Judge Weeramantry) [1991] ICJ Rep 53, 165; Georges Scelle, 'Report on Arbitration Procedure' (1950) UN Doc A/CN4/18, 67.

66 *Application for Review of Judgment No 333 of the United Nations Administrative Tribunal* (Advisory Opinion) [1987] ICJ Rep 18, 44.

67 *Arbitral Award of 31 July 1989* (Dissenting Opinion of Judge Weeramantry) (n 65) 162.

68 Vienna Convention on the Law of Treaties (adopted 22 May 1969, entered into force 27 January 1980) 1155 UNTS 331 (VCLT) art 26.

69 United Nations Convention on the Law of the Sea (adopted 10 December 1982, entered into force 16 November 1994) 1833 UNTS 3 (UNCLOS) art 29.

70 Jane Dalton, 'Future Navies-Present Issues' (2006) 82 *International Law Studies* 17.

Alternatively, as the 'component' of its launching ship,[71] the AUV could also satisfy the above requirements.

The Egart was employed by Rukarukan Navy, programmed to navigate autonomously and then return to its deploying ship.[72] Thus, the Egart should be deemed as, or as the extension of, Rukarukan warship.

b. The Egart does not enjoy the right of innocent passage under customary international law.

The international custom recognizes that the right of innocent passage[73] would *a priori* restrict coastal State's sovereignty over its territorial sea.[74] Even if *opinio juris* of States is confirmed by practice concerning the right of innocent passage of commercial ships,[75] the right of innocent passage of warships[76] not only is challenged by jurists,[77] but also lacks uniform[78] State practice.[79]

Respondent may cite the *Corfu Channel* case[80] to support warship's right of innocent passage. However, its judgment on the merits expressly limited that right to the passage in international straits, and hence is not applicable in the present case.[81] Thus,

71 Dalton (n 70); 'Rules for Building and Classing Underwater Vehicles, Systems, and Hyperbaric Facilities' (2002) American Bureau of Shipping <http://www.eagle.org/absdownloads/index.cfm> 155.

72 *Facts* [13]-[14].

73 UNCLOS art 17.

74 *North Sea Continental Shelf cases* (Federal Republic of Germany/Denmark; Federal Republic of Germany/Netherlands) (Judgment) [1969] ICJ Rep 3 [96].

75 Zou Keyuan, 'Innocent Passage for Warships: The Chinese Doctrine and Practice' (1998) 29 *Ocean Development & International Law* 195, 209.

76 Zou (n 75) 211.

77 L Oppenheim, Hersch Lauterpacht, *International Law: A Treatise* (7th edn, Longmans 1948-1952) 448.

78 *North Sea Continental Shelf cases* (n 74) [74].

79 Robert Smith, *Limits in the Seas: No 36 National Claims to Maritime Jurisdiction* (6th rev, United States Department of State: Bureau of Oceans and International Environmental and Scientific Affairs 1990).

80 *Corfu Channel case* (United Kingdom v Albania) (Judgment) [1949] ICJ Rep 4, 65.

81 *Corfu Channel case* (n 80) 30.

the Egart does not enjoy the right of innocent passage in Anduchencan territorial sea under customary international law.

c. The Egart should comply with Anduchenca's national law.

States are legitimate to have a 12-nautical-mile territorial sea,[82] where the coastal States extend their sovereignty,[83] so that they are entitled to enact national laws requiring government vessels to acquire prior authorization, and other States should comply with such regulations.[84] In the present case, Anduchenca requires all foreign government vessels to attain prior authorization.[85] However, the Egart did not acquire such authorization[86] and as such violated Anduchenca's national law.

d. Even if prior authorization is not required, the Egart's passage is prejudicial.

According to customary international law,[87] passage not prejudicial to the peace, good order and security of the coastal state will be innocent.[88] However, two requirements should be satisfied: the manner[89] of the passage is innocent and the passage is not prejudicial.[90]

(i) The Egart's passage is not innocent.

It is recognized that submarines and underwater vehicles should navigate on the surface and show their flags.[91] These requirements are to distinguish innocent passage from passage.[92] However, when the Egart entered into Anduchencan territorial sea, it

---

82 *Fisheries Jurisdiction case* (United Kingdom v Iceland) (Merits) [1974] ICJ Rep 3 [23].

83 Convention on the Territorial Sea and the Contiguous Zone (adopted 29 April 1958, entered into force 22 November 1964) 516 UNTS 205 (GCTS) art 2; UNCLOS art 3.

84 *United Nations Third Conference on the Law of the Sea* (Vol. 2, UN Publications 1975) 120.

85 *Facts* [12].

86 *Facts* [16].

87 Sarah Wolf, 'Territorial Sea' (2013) *Max Planck Encyclopedia of Public International Law* (MPEPIL) (2011); GCTS art 14; UNCLOS art 17.

88 UNCLOS art 19.

89 *Corfu Channel case* (n 80) 30.

90 UNCLOS art 19.

91 UNCLOS art 20; GCTS art 14(6); D O'Connell, I Shearer, *The International Law of the Sea* (Vol. I, Clarendon Press 1982) 294-295.

92 Myron Nordquist, *United Nations Convention on the Law of the Sea, 1982: A Commentary* (Vol. II, MNP 1993) 180.

neither navigated on the surface nor showed its flag.[93] Therefore, the Egart's passage is not innocent.

(ii) The Egart's non-innocent passage is prejudicial.

UNCLOS enumerates several activities which will be assumed prejudicial to coastal State,[94] including any act of collecting information in coastal State's territorial sea.[95] Even though it remains silent on the legality of foreign vessel's data collection in territorial sea against a third State, regard should be in view of the fact that intelligence gathering is most likely for the national defense of the third State rather than responding to collective maritime security threats.[96]

The Egart was collecting the optical and acoustic data when it was found in Anduchencan territorial sea.[97] Although Rukaruku might contend the data collection was intended to fight against the illicit international arms trafficking,[98] such a wide variety of intelligence gathering activities would constitute an abuse of right and were against the good faith.[99] Therefore, the Egart's passage is prejudicial to Anduchenca.

ii. Rukaruku's wrongfulness cannot be justified under international law.

a. The Egart's presence and data collection constituted internationally wrongful acts.

Internationally wrongful acts result from a breach of an international obligation,[100] and are attributable to the State[101] if done by its organ.[102] In the present case, the

93 *Facts* [16].

94 UNCLOS art 19.

95 UNCLOS art 19(2)(c).

96 Natalie Klein, *Maritime Security and the Law of the Sea* (OUP 2011) 217.

97 *Facts* [16].

98 *Facts* [5] [11].

99 UNCLOS art 300.

100 ILC 'Draft Articles on Responsibility of States for Internationally Wrongful Acts, with Commentaries' (ARSIWA) (2001) UN Doc A/56/10 art 2(b).

101 ARSIWA (n 100) art 2(a).

102 ARSIWA (n 100) art 4; *Difference Relating to Immunity from Legal Process of a Special Rapporteur of the Commission on Human Rights* (Advisory Opinion) [1999] ICJ Rep 62 [62].

Egart is employed by Rukarukan Navy.[103] Besides, its unauthorized presence and data collection activity constituted a violation of Article 6 of the FCN Treaty. Therefore, Rukaruku committed internationally wrongful acts.

b. Rukaruku's wrongful acts cannot be justified by consent.

(i) Anduchenca never consented to the Egart's presence and data collection in its territorial sea.

Although consent can preclude State's wrongfulness,[104] such consent should be made expressly rather than merely presumed.[105] Anduchenca has never expressly consented to the Egart's presence and data collection in Anduchencan territorial sea. Rukaruku may argue that the object and purpose of the FCN Treaty[106] constituted consent to Rukarukan Navy's presence in Anduchencan territorial sea.[107] However, it could not constitute an invitation or acceptance of such presence since the FCN Treaty serves the commercial purpose, and the Egart's presence is not intended for that purpose.

(ii) Even if there was consent, the Egart's presence and data collection did not fall within the scope of the consent.

Even if Anduchenca consented to Rukarukan Navy's presence, the consent was not open-ended.[108] Since Rukarukan Navy merely consisted of aircraft carriers, surface ships and submarines[109] during and after the conclusion of the FCN Treaty, Anduchenca never gave consent regarding the Egart. Furthermore, Anduchenca immediately posed objection once the Egart was operated.[110] Therefore, Anduchenca did not give consent to the Egart's operation in Anduchencan territorial sea.

---

103 *Facts* [13].

104 ARSIWA (n 100) 73; H Thirlway, 'The Law and Procedure of the International Court of Justice 1960-1989' (1995) 65 BYIL 1, 73.

105 ARSIWA (n 100) 73.

106 *Facts* [Annex I] Preamble.

107 *Facts* [5].

108 *Case Concerning Armed Activities on the Territory of the Congo* (Democratic Republic of the Congo v Uganda) (Judgment) [2005] ICJ Rep 168 [52].

109 *Facts* [3].

110 *Facts* [15].

(iii) Even if there was consent, it had been withdrawn by Anduchenca.

As the Court stated in the *Congo v. Uganda* case, consent antedated an agreement can be withdrawn regardless of formality.[111] Before the conclusion of the FCN Treaty, Rukarukan Navy's presence had already existed along the Kumatqesh coast.[112] Therefore, Anduchenca was free to withdraw its consent. Moreover, Anduchenca did withdraw its consent through its national law[113] and Mr. Rafiq Tovarish's declaration.[114]

c. Rukaruku's wrongful acts cannot be justified by force majeure.

A situation of *force majeure* shall be caused by irresistible force or an unforeseen event which is beyond control of the State concerned and make it materially impossible[115] to perform its obligation.[116] However, the Egart was equipped with a navigation system which enabled it to periodically surface to receive GPS signals.[117] Rukaruku was capable of ordering the Egart to navigate outside Anduchencan territorial sea. Considering that the navigation of Egart was under the control of Rukaruku, the requirements of *force majeure* were not satisfied.

B. ANDUCHENCA DID NOT VIOLATE ARTICLE 7 OF THE FCN TREATY WHEN IT CAPTURED THE EGART.

Anduchenca submits that it did not violate Article 7 of the FCN Treaty because Article 7 could not be applied to the Egart [i] and Anduchenca's capture of the Egart is consistent with international law [ii].

i. The freedom of commerce and navigation under Article 7 could not be applied to the Egart.

Considering the ordinary meaning of the terms and the object and purpose,[118]

---

111 *Armed Activities* (n 108) [47].

112 *Facts* [5].

113 *Facts* [12].

114 *Facts* [15].

115 *Gill* (Great Britain v United Mexican States) [1931] 5 RIAA 159.

116 ARSIWA (n 100) 76.

117 *Clarifications* [2].

118 VCLT art 31(1).

together with the circumstances of conclusion of the FCN Treaty,[119] Article 7 could not be applied to the Egart since it is not a commercial ship [a] and it navigated in Anduchencan territorial sea [b].

a. Article 7 could not be applied to a warship.

The FCN Treaty, concluded after World War II as part of the rehabilitation of the region,[120] aims at 'encouraging mutually beneficial trade and investment' and emphasizes its concern on 'commerce and navigation'.[121] Therefore, Article 7 can only be applied to commercial ships, which does not include the warship.

Even if Rukarukan warships were deployed along Anduchencan coast for the purpose of protecting commercial ships,[122] the Egart was not engaged in commerce and navigation since the act not bearing the traverse would not be assumed as engaged in 'navigation'[123] and ancillary activities are unrelated to commerce.[124] Thus, the Egart does not fall within the scope of Article 7.

b. Article 7 could only be applied outside Anduchencan territorial sea.

The ordinary meaning of the term 'territory' shall include land territory and territorial sea.[125] Thus, the term 'between the territories' in Article 7 clearly does not include the territorial seas of both parties. Besides, the term 'freedom of navigation' is usually recognized as a general rule[126] which applies to Exclusive Economic Zone and High Seas rather than territorial sea. Therefore, activities in the territorial sea do not fall within the scope of Article 7.

---

119 VCLT art 31(2).

120 *Facts* [5].

121 *Facts* [Annex I] Preamble, art 7.

122 *Facts* [5].

123 *Case Concerning Oil Platforms* (Islamic Republic of Iran v United States of America) (Judgment) [2003] ICJ Rep 161 [120].

124 *Oil Platforms* (n 123) [80].

125 Ian Brownlie, James Crawford, *Brownlie's Principles of Public International Law* (7th edn, OUP 2008) 203.

126 Convention on the High Seas (adopted 29 April 1958, entered into force 30 September 1962) 450 UNTS 11 art 2.

ii. The capture of the Egart is consistent with international law.

a. Anduchenca's capture of the Egart is a countermeasure.

As this Court recognized in *Gabčíkovo-Nagymaros* case, an injured State can take countermeasures against another State when that State violates its treaty obligations.[127] Anduchenca's capture of the Egart was a direct response to Rukaruku's prior breach of Article 6 of the FCN Treaty.[128] Therefore, any assertion of wrongfulness in respect of Anduchenca's capture of the Egart should be precluded since it was a valid and non-forcible countermeasure.

b. The countermeasure is proportionate.

The countermeasures must be proportionate, as the tribunal commented in the *Air Services* Arbitration. Judging the 'proportionality' of countermeasures is not an easy task and can at best be accomplished by approximation.[129] When the Egart was collecting data in Anduchencan territorial sea, only such urgent countermeasure could prevent Anduchencan information from being leaked to Rukaruku.

c. The countermeasure does not violate peremptory norm under international law.

As a government vessel, the Egart enjoys immunity.[130] However, the immunity can be waived by a State[131] or derogated under international law,[132] so that the immunity of warships does not constitute peremptory norm. Therefore, the countermeasure taken by Anduchenca does not violate peremptory norm under international law.

III. ANDUCHENCA DID NOT VIOLATE ARTICLE 16 OF THE FCN TREATY BY COMMISSIONING AND OPERATING THE IBRA.

Article 16 of the FCN Treaty requires Anduchenca to fulfill disarmament obligations

---

127 *Case Concerning the Gabčíkovo-Nagymaros Project* (Hungary/Slovakia) (Judgment) [1997] ICJ Rep 7 [106].

128 *Facts* [16].

129 *Air Services Agreement of 27 March 1946* (United States of America v France) [1979] 18 RIAA 416, 91, 94-96.

130 UNCLOS art 32.

131 United Nations General Assembly 'United Nations Convention on Jurisdictional Immunities of States and Their Property' (2 December 2004) UN Doc A/RES/59/38 art 16.

132 UNCLOS arts 32, 30.

binding on it under international law, which herein may involve nuclear disarmament obligation under Article VI of NPT [A] and the arguable disarmament obligation imposed by Resolution 3790 [B]. Anduchenca's commission and operation of the Ibra did not violate either of them.

A. ANDUCHENCA DID NOT VIOLATE ARTICLE VI OF NPT BY COMMISSIONING AND OPERATING THE IBRA.

i. Article VI of NPT is not binding on Anduchenca.

a. Article VI of NPT does not reflect customary international law.

The substance of customary international law must be looked for primarily in the actual practice and *opinio juris* of States,[133] and especially requires the positive acceptance of both (or all) Parties to the rule,[134] including that of States whose interests are specially affected.[135] Activities, including inaction,[136] on the international stage are an obvious form of State practice.[137]

As for Article VI of NPT, so far, States, especially nuclear-weapon States, for instance, China,[138] France,[139] India,[140] Pakistan,[141] Russia Federation,[142] the United States,[143] the

133 Malcom Shaw, *International Law* (6th edn, CUP 2008) 74; *Continental Shelf* (Libyan Arab Jamahiriya/Malta) (Judgment) [1985] ICJ Rep 13 [29].

134 *Case Concerning Right of Passage over Indian Territory* (Portugal v India) (Merits) [1960] ICJ Rep 6, 44.

135 *North Sea Continental Shelf* (n 74) [73].

136 ILC 'Report on the Work of the Sixty-Eighth Session' (1 May-2 June and 3 July-4 August 2017) UN Doc A/71/10 Conclusion 6.

137 *Arrest Warrant of 11 April 2000* (Democratic Republic of the Congo v Belgium) (Judgment) [2002] ICJ Rep 3, 23-24.

138 Chinese State Council 'China's National Defense in 2010' (Information Office of the Chinese State Council 2011) 39.

139 Olav Njølstad (ed.), *Nuclear Proliferation and International Order. Challenges to the Non-Proliferation Treaty* (Routledge 2011) 68.

140 Michael Quinlan, *Thinking About Nuclear Weapons: Principles, Problems, Prospects* (OUP 2009) 137.

141 Quinlan (n 140).

142 Dmitry Rogozin 'Russia Plans New Defense Strategy' (24 April 2012) United Press International <http://www.upi.com/Top_News/World-News/2012/04/24/Russia-plans-new-defense-strategy/UPI-81581335293440/> accessed 10 January 2018.

143 Committee on Nuclear Weapons, 'Non-Proliferation, and Contemporary International Law "Legal Aspects of Nuclear Disarmament—Second Report"' *International Law Association Report of*

United Kingdom,[144] etc., are still far from implementing it.[145] Even if some of those States are contracting Parties of NPT, their contradiction in practice still prevent the emergence of Article VI of NPT as customary international law.[146] Despite that the Treaty on the Prohibition of Nuclear Weapons (TPNW) was newly adopted, more than seventy states, including the above listed, did not attend the negotiation or vote.[147] The adoption itself cannot create a rule of customary international law.[148]

The Party which relies on a custom must prove that this custom is established in such a manner that it has become binding on the other Party.[149] Since State practice of Article VI of NPT is insufficient, it does not constitute a rule of customary international law, and therefore is not binding on Anduchenca, a non-contracting Party.[150]

b. Anduchenca is a persistent objector to NPT.

Declining to sign,[151] ratify[152] or accede to NPT, and expressly[153] stating its objection against NPT initially,[154] consistently[155] and persistently[156] on numerous occasions over

the Seventy-Sixth Conference (Washington 2014) 9.

144 John Simpson, 'Deterrence, Disarmament, Non-Proliferation and UK Trident' (British American Security Information Council 2013) 28.

145 Legal Aspects of Nuclear Disarmament (n 143) 9.

146 *Fisheries Jurisdiction* (United Kingdom v Iceland) (Joint Separate Opinion by Judges Forster, Bengzon, Jiménez de Aréchaga, Nagendra Singh and Ruda) [1974] ICJ Rep 3 [16].

147 UNGA 'Voting Result of Draft Treaty on the Prohibition of Nuclear Weapons' (7 July 2017) UN Doc A/CONF229/2017/L3/Rev1.

148 Report on the Work of the Sixty-Eighth Session (n 136) Conclusion 12 [1].

149 *Columbian-Peruvian Asylum case* (Columbia/Peru) (Judgment) [1950] ICJ Rep 266, 276.

150 VCLT art 34.

151 *Fisheries case* (United Kingdom v Norway) (Merits) [1951] ICJ Rep 116, 139.

152 *Asylum case* (n 149) 207.

153 Committee on Formation of Customary (General) International Law 'Statement of Principles Applicable to the Formation of General Customary International Law' in International Law Association Report of the Sixty-Ninth Conference (London 2000) 28.

154 *Asylum case* (n 149) 277-278; *Fisheries case* (n 151) 136.

155 *Fisheries* case (United Kingdom v Norway) (Counter-Memorial Submitted by the Government of the Kingdom of Norway) [1950] ICJ Pleading (Vol. I) 381-384.

156 *Siderman de Blake v Republic of Argentina* [1992] United States Court of Appeals for the Ninth Circuit 965 F2d, 54.

the past fifty years since NPT was concluded in 1968,[157] Anduchenca is a persistent objector to NPT, inasmuch as NPT could not be invoked against it.[158]

Besides, Anduchenca never signed any agreements[159] or treaties[160] which involved the obligation under Article VI of NPT. Even if it participated in the first session of the UN Conference to Negotiate a Legally Binding Instrument to Prohibit Nuclear Weapons (the UN Conference),[161] such a single contradiction[162] does not affect Anduchenca's willingness to remain exempt as a persistent objector[163] and is not inconsistent[164] with its former objection to Article VI of NPT, thus does not adversely affect its position as a persistent objector.

ii. Even if Article VI of NPT is binding on Anduchenca, it did not violate such obligation.

a. Anduchenca fulfilled the obligation of negotiation in good faith.

Negotiations require a genuine attempt by one Party to engage in discussions with other Parties[165] and the discussions must comprise more than merely going through a formal process.[166] To fulfill such obligation, *first*, Anduchenca entered into[167] the UN Conference.[168] *Second*, Anduchenca paid reasonable regard on the interests of the

157 *Facts* [9].

158 *Asylum case* (n 149) 207.

159 UN Department for Disarmament Affairs 'The United Nations Disarmament Yearbook' (1999) 24, 105.

160 *Commonwealth of Pennsylvania v Hector Huertas* Motion to Preclude the Commonwealth from Seeking the Death Penalty against a Juvenile and Consolidated Memorandum of Law (2002) CP 0009-0941 CTD 25.

161 *Facts* [39].

162 *Fisheries case* (n 151) 138.

163 James Green, *The Persistent Objector Rule in International Law* (OUP 2016) 121.

164 M Akehurst, 'Custom as a Source of International Law' (1974-1975) 47 *British Yearbook of International Law* 1, 24

165 *Elimination of All Forms of Racial Discrimination* (n 6) [157].

166 *North Sea Continental Shelf* (n 74) [85].

167 *South West Africa cases* (Ethiopia v South Africa; Liberia v South Africa) (Preliminary Objections) [1962] ICJ Rep 319 [188].

168 *Facts* [39].

other States[169] through general exchange of views on the UN Conference.[170] *Third,* Anduchenca, including its commission and operation of the Ibra, did not obstruct or break off the negotiations,[171] for instance interrupting communications or causing delays.[172] The UN Conference was, in fact, in a constructive atmosphere and in a collaborative spirit.[173]

b. Anduchenca's withdrawal from the UN Conference did not violate the obligation.

Anduchenca did not participate in further negotiation of the TPNW and its adoption, both of which took place in the second session of the UN Conference.[174] However, an obligation to negotiate does not imply an obligation to reach an agreement.[175] According to the ordinary meaning[176] and drafting history[177] of Article VI of NPT,[178] achieving a result is not obligatory. Therefore, Anduchenca's withdrawal from the UN Conference did not constitute a violation of Article VI of NPT.

Even if a precise result is required to be achieved, TPNW could not meet such requirement, since more than seventy States, including each nuclear weapon States,

---

169 *Application of the Interim Accord of 13 September 1995* (Macedonia v Greece) (Judgment) [2011] ICJ Rep 644 [132].

170 UN 'United Nations Conference to Negotiate Legally Binding Treaty Prohibiting Nuclear Weapons Will Hold Second Substantive Session, 15 June-7 July' (14 June 2017) Press Release DC/3709.

171 *Lake Lanoux Arbitration* (France v Spain) [1957] 12 RIAA 281, 128.

172 *Application of the Interim Accord of 13 September 1995* (n 169) [132]; *Fisheries Jurisdiction* (n 82) [78].

173 UN 'United Nations Conference to Negotiate Legally Binding Treaty Prohibiting Nuclear Weapons Will Hold Second Substantive Session, 15 June-7 July'.

174 *Facts* [39].

175 *Railway Traffic between Lithuania and Poland* (Advisory Opinion) PCIJ Rep Series A/B No 42 [29]; *Pulp Mills on the River Uruguay* (Argentina v Uruguay) (Judgment) [2010] ICJ Rep 14 [150]; *Elimination of All Forms of Racial Discrimination* (n 6) [158].

176 VCLT art 31(1).

177 VCLT art 32; ILC 'Documents of the Sixteenth Session Including the Report of the Commission to the General Assemble' (1964) UN Doc A/CN4/SERA/1964/ADD1, 20-21.

178 Mohamed Shaker, *The Nuclear Non-proliferation Treaty: Origin and Implementation, 1959-1979* (Vol. 3, Oceana Publications 1980) 567.

did not participate in the UN Conference or sign TPNW.[179] Anduchenca participated in the first session of the conference with a view to conclude an agreement,[180] however, the future treaty did not appear to be 'effective measures under strict and effective international control' and as such could not be regarded as a precise result.[181] Thus, by participating in the first session of the UN Conference, Anduchenca has already fulfilled the obligation to pursue a negotiation in good faith as far as possible.[182]

c. Anduchenca's commission and operation of the Ibra did not violate the obligation.

VCLT, in spite of contrary recommendation of the International Law Commission in the final draft codification,[183] finally does not impose any substantive obligations on negotiating States during the phase of negotiation.[184] Besides, it is further affirmed that statements made or actions taken during the negotiation which has not led to a complete agreement could not be taken into consideration.[185] Herein, Anduchenca commissioned the Ibra in the negotiation process of TPNW, during which it did not bear any substantive obligations and therefore did not as such violate the obligation of negotiation in good faith.

B. RESOLUTION 3790 DID NOT IMPOSE ANY DISARMAMENT OBLIGATIONS ON ANDUCHENCA.

Concerning the Ibra, the UNSC adopted Resolution 3790 on May 8, 2017,[186] which called upon all Member States to take such actions as may be appropriate to support the implementation of NPT and to restrict the proliferation of nuclear weapons and

179 UNGA 'Voting Result' (n 147).

180 *Railway Traffic* (n 175) [29].

181 *Legality of the Threat or Use of Nuclear Weapons* (Advisory Opinion) [1996] ICJ Rep 226 [100].

182 *Railway Traffic* (n 175) [116].

183 ILC 'Documents of the Second Part of the Seventeenth Session and of the Eighteenth Session including the Reports of the Commission to the General Assembly' (1966) UN Doc A/6309/Revl.

184 Paul Reuter, 'De l'obligation de négocier' (1975) *Mélanges Morelli* 711, 715.

185 *Case Concerning the Factory at Chorzów* (Germany v Poland) (Judgment) PCIJ Rep Series A No 17, 51; *Nuclear Tests* (Australia v France) (Judgment) [1974] ICJ Rep 253 [54].

186 *Facts* [41].

nuclear-armed vessels.[187]

The analyses of ordinary meaning of terms[188] and other resolutions of the UNSC on the same issue are required for the interpretation of the UNSC resolutions.[189] 'Call upon' is not generally intended to indicate a legally binding decision and has more the sense of strongly urging.[190] Compared with Resolution 3790, as for the resolutions adopted upon the nuclear weapon issues in DPRK, for instance Resolutions 1718, 1874, 2094, 2321 and 2397, the UNSC explicitly presented that DPRK should immediately abandon all nuclear weapons.[191] Therefore, Resolution 3790 did not purport to impose any disarmament obligations on Anduchenca.

IV. RUKARUKU VIOLATED ARTICLE 17 OF THE FCN TREATY WHEN IT ATTACKED THE COVFEFE AND WHEN IT CAPTURED THE IBRA.

By attacking the Covfefe and capturing the Ibra, Rukaruku used force against the territorial integrity and political independence of Anduchenca [A]. Such use of force did not possess authorization or justification permitted under international law [B] and violated the principle of proportionality and necessity [C]. To this end, Rukaruku violated Article 17 of the FCN Treaty.

A. RUKARUKU USED FORCE AGAINST THE TERRITORIAL INTEGRITY AND POLITICAL INDEPENDENCE OF ANDUCHENCA.

It is undisputed that armed force is within the scope of the fundamental notion of force,[192] and the terms 'territorial integrity' and 'political independence' are not intended to restrict the scope of the prohibition of the use of force.[193] Thus, attacking

187 *Facts* [Annex] II.

188 VCLT art 31.

189 *Accordance with International Law of the Unilateral Declaration of Independence in Respect of Kosovo* (Advisory Opinion) [2010] ICJ Rep 403 [94].

190 Quinlan n140 137.

191 United Nations Security Council (UNSC) UN Doc S/RES/1718 (14 October 2006); UNSC UN Doc S/RES/1874 (12 June 2009); UNSC UN Doc S/RES/2094 (7 March 2013); UNSC UN Doc S/RES/2321 (30 November 2016); UNSC UN Doc S/RES/2397 (22 December 2017).

192 H Kelsen, R Tucker, *Principles of International Law* (Holt 1996) 86.

193 Lassa Oppenheim, *International Law: Disputes, War and Neutrality* (Vol. 2, H lauterpacht ed.,

the Covfefe and capturing the Ibra, which are placed in the same as national territory,[194] fall into the scope of the prohibition under Article 17 of the FCN Treaty.

B. NOT PERMITTED UNDER INTERNATIONAL LAW, ATTACKING THE COVFEFE AND CAPTURING THE IBRA DID NOT CONSTITUTE THE EXCEPTION UNDER ARTICLE 17 OF THE FCN TREATY.

Two exceptions of use of force exist in relation to collective measures taken by the UNSC [i] and with regard to the right of self-defense [ii],[195] neither of which is in the case.

i. Resolution 3790 did not authorize Rukaruku to attack the Covfefe or to capture the Ibra.

Interpretation of Resolution 3790 is within the scope of competence of the Court.[196] If Resolution 3790 is to be interpreted as mandating the use of force, clear indications thereof are required.[197] However, taking the UNSC Resolution 1973, 2146 and 2182 as references,[198] the term 'all measures commensurate' used in Resolution 3790 does not indicate authorization of use of force.

a. Resolution 3790 did not authorize Rukaruku to attack the Covfefe.

When interpreting a UNSC Resolution, the rules on treaty interpretation embodied in VCLT may provide guidance.[199] According to Resolution 3790, the UNSC only authorized actions to be taken in confronting the Ibra.[200] On the basis of ordinary

---

7th edn, Longmans, Green and Co 1952) 154

194 *SS 'Lotus'* (France v Turkey) (Judgment) PCIJ Rep Series A No 10, 25.

195 Charter of the United Nations (entered into force 24 October 1945) 1 UNTS XV (UN Charter) art 2(4), 42, 51; Malcom Shaw (n 142) 1123.

196 *Kosovo* (n 189) [46].

197 Ugo Villani, 'The Security Council's Authorization of Enforcement Action by Regional Organizations' (2002) 6 *Max Planck Yearbook of United Nations Law* 535, 543.

198 UNSC UN Doc S/RES/1973 (17 March 2011); UNSC UN Doc S/RES/2146 (19 March 2014); UNSC UN Doc S/RES/2182 (24 October 2014).

199 ILC 'Report of the International Law Commission: 68th Session' (2 May-10 June and 4 July-12 August 2016) UN Doc A/71/10 [76]; Richard K Gardiner, *Treaty Interpretation* (OUP 2015) 12-17.

200 *Facts* [Annex] II.

meaning[201] of 'confronting the Ibra', the attack against the Covfefe, a supply ship,[202] is not included in the scope of authorization.

b. Resolution 3790 did not authorize Rukaruku to capture the Ibra.

When interpreting a UNSC Resolution, the intention of the Council as expressed by words used in resolutions and the circumstances of the adoption of the resolution[203] should also be taken into consideration.[204]

Resolution 3790 was adopted in the context[205] that Anduchenca's possession of a nuclear-armed submarine was merely based on news resources and its own oral statements,[206] and was lacking of material evidence. Besides, considering the whole resolution,[207] the UNSC also expressed its uncertainty on whether Anduchenca actually developed the Ibra and explicitly focused its concern on the Ibra's undisclosed location.[208] Thus, under a logical and systematic interpretation,[209] the authorization of actions against the Ibra should be limited to the confirmation of the development of the Ibra and its location. To this end, capturing the Ibra is not included in the scope of authorization.

ii. Rukaruku's use of force against the Covfefe and the Ibra did not constitute self-defense.

a. Rukaruku was not entitled to use force in self-defense in accordance with Article 51 of the UN Charter.

Since Article 51 represents an exception to the ban instated by Article 2(4), it should

---

201 VCLT art 31(1).

202 *Facts* [43].

203 *Legal Consequences for States of the Continued Presence of South Africa in Namibia (South West Africa) notwithstanding Security Council Resolution 276* (1970) (Advisory Opinion) [1971] ICJ Rep 16 [53].

204 *Kosovo* (n 189) [94].

205 *Al-Jedda v the United Kingdom* (Judgment) (7 July 2011) ECtHR App No 27021/08 [76].

206 *Facts* [37]-[38].

207 *United Nations Juridical Yearbook 2003* (United Nations Publications 2003) 538-539.

208 *Facts* [Annex] II.

209 *Prosecutor v Tadic* (Decision on the Defense Motion for Interlocutory Appeal on Jurisdiction) (2 October 1995) ICTY-94-1-AR72, 71-78.

be interpreted in a restrictive manner.[210] The right to self-defense does not exist if an armed attack has not yet occurred,[211] thus a state may not use force in self-defense unless and only[212] until there exists an armed attack.[213] In the present case, Anduchenca had no action of armed force[214] or specific intention of harming[215] against Rukaruku,[216] therefore, Rukaruku was not entitled to use force in self-defense.

b. Rukaruku was not entitled to use force in anticipatory self-defense or pre-emptive self-defense.

Even if the right of anticipatory self-defense prevails, it requires that other non-forcible means are exhausted[217] and the threatened attack is imminent,[218] i.e. instant, overwhelming, no moment for deliberation.[219] However, neither the Covfefe nor the Ibra appeared to launch any attack. The occurrence of an attack from Anduchenca in the very near future was still doubted.[220] Thus, Rukaruku was not entitled to use force in anticipatory self-defense. As for pre-emptive self-defense, it is going beyond as

210 Tom Ruys, *'Armed Attack' and Article 51 of the UN Charter: Evolutions in Customary Law and Practice* (CUP 2010) 259.

211 UN Charter art 51; Sean Murphy, 'The Doctrine of Preemptive Self-Defense' (2005) 50 *Villanova Law Review* 699, 706.

212 Emanuel Gross, 'Thwarting Terrorist Acts by Attacking the Perpetrators or Their Commanders as an Act of Self-Defense: Human Rights Versus the State's Duty to Protect its Citizens' (2001) 15 *Temple International and Comparative Law Journal* 195, 213.

213 Ian Brownile, *International Law and the Use of Force by States* (Clarendon Press 1963) 278; Louis Henkin, *International Law: Politics, Values and Functions* (Martinus Nijhoff 1990) 156; Phillip Jessup, *A Modern Law of Nations* (Hamden, CT: Archon Books 1968) 166.

214 *Oil Platforms* (n 123) [51].

215 *Oil Platforms* (n 123) [64].

216 *Facts* [43]-[46].

217 Matthew Waxman, 'The Use of Force against States That Might Have Weapons of Mass Destruction' (2009) 31 *Michigan Journal of International Law* 1, 8.

218 UN High-Level Panel on Threats, Change, and United Nations, *A More Secure World: Our Shared Responsibility: Report of the High-Level Panel on Threats, Challenges, and Change* (2004) [188].

219 'Letter from Daniel Webster, US Secretary of State, to Lord Ashburton, British Plenipotentiary (6 August 1842)' in John Bassett Moore, *A Digest of International Law* (Vol. 2, Princeton University Press 1906) 412.

220 V Andreias, 'Anticipatory Self-Defense in International Law: Legal or Just a Construct for Using Force?' <http://arno.uvt.nl/show.cgi?fid=122935> assessed 12 January 2018.

what is currently acceptable in international law,[221] so that cannot justify Rukaruku's use of force either.

C. DUE TO THE VIOLATION OF PRINCIPLES OF PROPORTIONALITY AND NECESSITY, RUKARUKU'S MEANS AND METHODS ARE NOT PERMITTED UNDER INTERNATIONAL LAW.

i. Both principles of proportionality and necessity are binding on Rukaruku when it used force against Anduchenca.

It is prohibited to cause unnecessary losses and excessive suffering,[222] so that States do not have unlimited freedom of choice of means and methods they use.[223] Such fundamental rules, as principles of customary international law, bound all States[224] either in their actions taken for self-defense[225] or in accordance with the UNSC Resolutions.[226]

ii. When attacking the Covfefe, Rukaruku violated the principle of proportionality.

The principle of proportionality determines the amount of force that can legitimately be used to achieve the goal pursued.[227] Even if Resolution 3790 authorized Rukaruku to use force against the Covfefe, which is not the case, from the perspective of the whole operation,[228] using 12 cruise missiles[229] to attack the Covfefe, a supply ship,[230]

221 UN High-Level (n 218) [189]; Elizabeth Wilmhurs, 'The Chatham House Principles of International Law on the Use of Force in Self-Defense' (2006) 55 *International & Comparative Law Quarterly* 963, 968.

222 Jean-Marie Henckaerts, Louise Doswald-Beck, *Customary International Humanitarian Law* (Vol. 1, CUP 2009) 237 Rule 70.

223 *Legality of Nuclear Weapon* (n 181) [257].

224 *Oil Platforms* (n 123) [74].

225 *Legality of Nuclear Weapons* (n 181) [30]; *Armed Activities on the Territory of the Congo* (n 108) [147].

226 *Legality of Nuclear Weapon* (n 181) [41]; UN Charter art 42.

227 Judith Gardam, 'Proportionality and Force in International Law' (1993) 87 *American Journal of International Law* 391, 403; Christopher Greenwood, 'The Relationship between *Jus ad Bellum* and *Jus in Bello*' (1985) 9 *Review of International Studies* 224.

228 *Oil Platforms* (n 123) [72].

229 *Facts* [43].

230 Judith Gardam, *Necessity, Proportionality and the Use of Force by States* (CUP 2004) 158.

to sink[231] merely for the purpose of depriving the Ibra of supplies[232] was over the size and scope[233] of the threat or danger the Covfefe caused,[234] therefore violated the principle of proportionality.

iii. When capturing the Ibra, Rukaruku violated the principle of necessity.

The principle of necessity centered upon the availability of other means[235] to halt the attack so that the state attacked ...must not have had any means of halting the attack[236] other than resort to armed force.[237] When capturing the Ibra, Rukaruku fired a series of torpedoes to the Ibra to force it to surface.[238] However, as stated by the Prime Minister of Rukaruku, their object to attack the Covfefe was also to indirectly force the Ibra to surface,[239] which hindered the necessity of firing torpedoes.

Besides, it is prohibited to employ methods or means of warfare which ... may be expected, to cause widespread, long-term and severe damage to the natural environment.[240] To this end, when confronting the Ibra, a nuclear-armed submarine, Rukaruku was obliged to seriously consider[241] environmental protection, which further affirmed the unnecessity of using torpedoes against the Ibra.

---

231 *Clarifications* [9].

232 *Facts* [44].

233 *Legality of Nuclear Weapon* (n 181) 41-43.

234 Robert Zayac, 'United States' Authority to Legally Implement the Self-Defense and Anticipatory Doctrines to Eradicate the Threat Posed by Countries Harboring Terrorists and Producing Weapons of Mass Destruction' (2005) 29 *Southern Illinois University Law Journal* 433, 452.

235 *Oil Platforms* (n 123) [73].

236 Bin Cheng, *General Principles of Law as Applied by International Courts and Tribunals* (CUP 1994) 71.

237 UNHCR 'Eighth Report on State Responsibility by Mr Roberto Ago' (1980) UN Doc A/CN4/318/Add5-7, 69.

238 *Facts* [46].

239 *Facts* [44].

240 Henckaerts, Doswald-Beck (n 222) 151 Rule 45; Protocol Additional to the Geneva Conventions of 12 August 1949, and Relating to the Protection of Victims of International Armed Conflicts (Protocol I) (adopted 8 June 1977, entered into force 7 December 1978) 1125 UNTS 3 art 35(3).

241 *Legality of Nuclear Weapons* (n 181) 30, 33.

CONCLUSION AND PRAYER FOR RELIEF

In view of the facts set forth in this Memorial and the arguments applying the law to the facts as stated;

May it please the Court, on behalf of The People's Democratic Republic of Anduchenca, Applicant herein, respectfully requests this Honorable Court to adjudge and declare that:

1. The arbitral award of 2 March 2017 is not valid;
2. Rukaruku violated Article 6 of the FCN Treaty when the Egart operated in Anduchenca's territorial sea, while Anduchenca did not violate Article 7 of the FCN Treaty when it captured the Egart;
3. Anduchenca did not violate Article 16 of the FCN Treaty by commissioning and operating the Ibra; and
4. Rukaruku violated Article 17 of the FCN Treaty when it attacked the Covfefe and when it captured the Ibra.

Respectfully submitted,

AGENTS FOR ANDUCHENCA

被告国书状

Memorials for the Federal Republic of Rukaruku

TABLE OF CONTENTS

B. ANDUCHENCA VIOLATED ARTICLE 7 BY CAPTURING THE EGART BECAUSE OF THE VIOLATION OF FREEDOM OF NAVIGATION BETWEEN BOTH PARTIES' TERRITORIES.

i. Anduchenca deprived Rukaruku of freedom of navigation under the FCN Treaty.

ii. Anduchenca's wrongful acts could not be justified under international law.

iii. Anduchenca committed internationally wrongful acts by capturing and detaining the Egart and hence should return it to Rukaruku.

III. ANDUCHENCA VIOLATED ARTICLE 16 OF THE FCN TREATY BY COMMISSIONING AND OPERATING THE IBRA.

A. ANDUCHENCA VIOLATED THE OBLIGATION TO PURSUE NEGOTIATIONS IN GOOD FAITH FOR NUCLEAR DISARMAMENT.

i. Anduchenca bears the obligation to pursue negotiations in good faith for nuclear disarmament under customary international law.

ii. The policy of deterrence could not justify the violation of the nuclear disarmament obligation.

iii. Anduchenca, by commissioning and operating the Ibra, breached the nuclear disarmament obligation.

B. ANDUCHENCA VIOLATED THE DISARMAMENT OBLIGATION TO NEUTRALIZE THE THREAT POSED BY THE IBRA UNDER RESOLUTION 3790.

i. Operative paragraph one of Resolution 3790 constitutes a binding decision.

ii. Operative paragraph one of Resolution 3790 imposes a disarmament obligation on Anduchenca.

iii. Anduchenca violated such disarmament obligation by continuing operating the Ibra.

IV. RUKARUKU DID NOT VIOLATE ARTICLE 17 OF THE FCN TREATY BY ATTACKING THE COVFEFE OR BY CAPTURING THE IBRA.

A. RUKARUKU WAS ENTITLED TO USE FORCE AGAINST THE IBRA UNDER RESOLUTION 3790.

i. Resolution 3790 is adopted within the legal limits under the UN Charter.

ii. Resolution 3790 authorizes Rukaruku to use force against both the Ibra and the Covfefe.

B. RUKARUKU WAS ENTILED TO USE FORCE AGAINST THE COVFEFE

AND THE IBRA WITH THE RIGHT OF ANTICIPATORY SELF-DEFENSE.

i. Rukaruku enjoys the inherent right of anticipatory self-defense.

ii. Anduchenca's commission and operation of the Ibra endowed Rukaruku with the condition to exercise the right of anticipatory self-defense.

C. RUKARUKU'S ATTACK AT THE COVFEFE AND CAPTURE OF THE IBRA WERE PERMITTED UNDER INTERNATIONAL LAW.

i. Both the Covfefe and the Ibra are military objectives.

ii. Rukaruku's actions were necessary and proportionate.

CONCLUSION AND PRAYER FOR RELIEF

STATEMENT OF JURISDICTION

On 3 July 2017, the People's Democratic Republic of Anduchenca (Anduchenca) filed in the Registry of the International Court of Justice (the Court) an Application against the Federal Republic of Rukaruku (Rukaruku) pursuant to Article 40 (1) of the Court's Statute, in accordance with the Treaty of Friendship, Commerce and Navigation (the FCN Treaty) for submission to the Court of the dispute concerning the Egart and the Ibra, signed between the two Parties on 12 March 1947. The Application was communicated to Rukaruku on 3 July 2017 pursuant to Article 40 (2) of the Court's Statute. Rukaruku attended the proceedings.

QUESTIONS PRESENTED

The Federal Republic of Rukaruku respectfully requests the Court to adjudge:

I.

1. Whether the arbitral tribunal acts in excess of its power;

2. Whether the arbitral tribunal is properly constituted;

3. Whether there exists serious departure from fundamental rules of procedure during the arbitral proceedings.

II.

1. Whether the Egart could navigate in Anduchencan territorial sea;

2. Whether the Egart's presence and data collection are prejudicial to Anduchenca;

3. Whether Article 7 can be applied to government vessels navigating in the territorial sea.

III.

1. Whether Anduchenca bears the obligation of implementing disarmament programs and negotiation under Article VI of NPT;

2. Whether Anduchenca's commission and operation of the Ibra violated the obligation to pursue negotiations in good faith for nuclear disarmament under customary international law;

3. Whether Anduchenca's commission and operation of the Ibra violated the obligation to disarm the nuclear weapons under the United Nations Security Council Resolution 3790 (Resolution 3790).

IV.

1. Whether Resolution 3790 is valid and binding on Rukaruku;

2. Whether Rukaruku was entitled to use force against both the Ibra and the Covfefe under the authorization of Resolution 3790;

3. *Whether* Rukaruku was entitled to act under the right of anticipatory self-defense;

4. *Whether* Rukaruku's capture of the Ibra and attack at the Covfefe were permitted under international law.

STATEMENT OF FACTS

Anduchenca and Rukaruku are two coastal States on the Kumatqesh Ocean in the Odasarra Region. Rukaruku is a developed country with a gross domestic product which is 25 times larger than that of Anduchenca, a developing country.

After World War II, Rukaruku provided financial aid to help initiate disarmament programs respectively in the four other Odasarran countries to advance stability in the region. On 12 March 1947, Rukaruku concluded the FCN Treaty with Anduchenca as it did with the three other countries, which included plans to boost the disarmament programs.

In the next two decades, Rukaruku offered Anduchenca economic aid, part of which helped implementation of the disarmament program, and this span of time was highlighted by the sound bilateral political relations.

On 26 October 1967, General Rafiq Tovarish ruled Anduchenca through a *coup d'état*, highly condemned by the other Odasarran States. Soon in 1969, Rukaruku terminated the program in Anduchenca and the finical aid. In the 1970s, the two countries were constantly involved in nonviolent conflicts.

Anduchenca has not signed, ratified or acceded to Treaty on the Non-Proliferation of Nuclear Weapons in 1968 and the United Nations Convention on the Law of the Sea (UNCLOS) in 1982 as it asserted that the former included an intrinsic inequality and the compulsory dispute settlement stipulated in Part XV of the latter was excessive.

In 2010, Anduchenca, in its maritime security law, stipulated prior authorization as a prerequisite for any foreign government vessel entering its 12-nautical-mile territorial sea. Rukaruku objected to it as lawless under international law.

In August 2015, the Rukarukan Navy deployed autonomous underwater vehicles

(AUVs) 'the Egart' to guarantee the safety in the region, which was set to keep no less than 12 nautical miles from the Anduchencan coast.

On 29 October 2015, the Anduchencan Navy drew in and captured the Egart 11 nautical miles away from its coastline by interfering its communication and transmitting false GPS signals and refused to return it.

On 20 December 2015, Rukaruku initiated arbitration against Anduchenca under Article 10(a) of the FCN Treaty, arguing Anduchenca's breach of Article 7 of the FCN Treaty by capturing the Egart and claimed restitution. Rukaruku chose its citizen Bhrasht Moyet as its arbitrator and the presiding arbitrator Judge Alice Bacal appointed Mou Tong for Anduchenca as Anduchenca did not respond within the 60-day limit.

On 1 March 2016, Anduchenca sent a *Note Verbale* denying the jurisdiction of the tribunal and refused to join the arbitration. The proceedings then continued without Anduchenca's presence. All communications and materials were sent to Anduchenca and equal time was given for submission of responses and arguments, but Anduchenca made no avail of them. On 2 March 2017, the tribunal decided that it had jurisdiction and supported Rukaruku's argument.

The Institute for Legal Studies of Arbitration (ILSA) is an international non-governmental organization which reports the incorrect behavior of arbitrators to promote transparency.

On 21 March 2017, the ILSA published a report featuring the arbitration between Rukaruku and Anduchenca by disclosing three pieces of information: *First*, Judge Moyet had three *ex parte* telephone conversations with Rukaruku's arbitration counsel Mr. Bouc Chivo about the earlier presented arguments which Judge Moyet stressed to the other arbitrators after the conversations. *Second,* Mr. Mikkel Orvindari was hired by the tribunal without disclosure to the parties as assistant of the tribunal who spent 522 hours on the case, doing summarizing and drafting work. *Third*, a note from

Judge Tong indicated that he had checked Mr. Orvindari's draft and would use it.

On 27 March 2017, a spokesman of Rukaruku stated that these three pieces of information did not notably affect the award and thus the award was nevertheless valid.

On 2 April 2017, *The Sydney Morning Herald* published an article reporting that Anduchenca had commissioned a nuclear submarine Ibra. Mr. Tovarish later addressed that the Ibra equipped with top nuclear weapons and ballistic missiles, available to hit targets precisely anywhere in the region, would be deployed and serve as a deterrent.

Anduchenca attended the first session of the United Nations Conference to Negotiate a Legally Binding Instrument to Prohibit Nuclear Weapons (UN Conference) in March 2017, but Mr. Tovarish added in the April speech of the Ibra that Anduchenca would not attend the second substantive session in June and July, thus denying any treaty from it.

On 8 May 2017, the Security Council adopted Resolution 3790 despite Anduchenca's opposition, authorizing Member States to take all measures necessary to defend against the Ibra which constitutes a threat to international peace and security. Rukaruku expressed its willingness to act under the Resolution.

On 6 June 2017, two Rukarukan warships fired cruise missiles on the high seas at the supply ship Covfefe delivering communication equipment and personnel to the Ibra. Besides the Anduchancan sailors, the people died abroad were from the High Seas Supplies (HSS) employed by the Anduchencan Navy. Before the attack, the Rukaruku Navy had communicated six times with the Cofveve but all in vain as none received response. Rukaruku claimed the attack was essential to facilitate the surface of the Ibra.

Eight days after the attack, Rukaruku eventually found the Ibra only 20 nautical miles from the Anduchencan coast. Rukarukan warships fired torpedoes pushing the Ibra to surface and successfully captured it. After questioning, all the crew was taken to the Anduchencan Embassy in Rukaruku. Rukaruku at once reported its attack and capture to the Security Council, referring to Article 51 of the UN Charter and Resolution 3790.

On 19 June 2017, the Security Council adopted a Resolution confirming the consent among Rukaruku, the International Atomic Energy Agency (IAEA), and two NPT nuclear weapon States for utter dismantlement of the Ibra and removal of nuclear materials on it. The IAEA later confirmed the implementation of the agreement and preliminarily learned that all the weapons found on the Ibra were produced by Anduchenca.

On 3 July 2017, Anduchenca filed in the Registry of the Court an Application against Rukaruku. Rukaruku participated in the proceedings as Respondent.

SUMMARY OF PLEADINGS

FIRST PLEADING

The arbitral tribunal has the jurisdiction over the case since there exists the dispute concerning the interpretation and application of Article 7 of the FCN Treaty between both Parties. Though Judge Moyet is of Rukarukan nationality and had been appointed by Rukaruku, the tribunal is properly constituted. The arbitral tribunal has not exceeded its power during the proceedings.

Though Rukaruku's counsel privately made phone conversations with Judge Moyet, the *ex parte* communication does not seriously depart from the fundamental rules of procedure. The appointment of and work done by Mr. Orvindari do not seriously depart from the fundamental procedure rules either. Meanwhile, Judge Tong did not delegate the decision-making function to Mr. Orvindari.

SECOND PLEADING

The Egart is employed by Rukarukan Navy and its mission is to collect the information and share with all of the States of the Region. The Egart's navigation in Anduchenca's territorial sea is not prejudicial to its sovereignty. Even if the Egart's operation violated Article 6 of the FCN Treaty, such wrongfulness was precluded due to the consent made by Anduchenca.

Under Article 7 of the FCN Treaty, the Egart enjoys the freedom of navigation between the territories of both Parties including the territorial sea. The Egart does not need prior authorization from Anduchenca to navigate in its territorial sea because Anduchencan domestic law is inconsistent with international law. Therefore, Anduchenca violated Article 7 of the FCN Treaty.

THIRD PLEADING

By commissioning and operating the Ibra, Anduchenca violated the disarmament obligations under Article 16 of the FCN Treaty, *i.e.* the negotiation obligation under Article VI of NPT and the disarmament obligation to neutralize the threat posed by the Ibra under Resolution 3790.

As Article VI of NPT constitutes customary international law and Anduchenca is not a persistent objector towards such a rule, Anduchenca bears the obligation to negotiation in good faith for nuclear disarmament. However, by commissioning and operating the Ibra, Anduchenca did not satisfy the requirement of meaningful negotiation and of continuation under the obligation. The policy of deterrence, which does not have any legal force, could not justify the actions.

Article 16 of FCN Treaty further requires Anduchenca to carry out the disarmament obligation to neutralize the threat posed by the Ibra under Resolution 3790. Operative paragraph one of Resolution 3790 indicates its binding force on Anduchenca and imposes disarmament regulation. Specifically, Anduchenca's continuation of commissioning and operating the Ibra was deliberate violation of its obligation.

FOURTH PLEADING

Rukaruku was entitled to use force against the Ibra under Resolution 3790 and the right of anticipatory self-defense. Resolution 3790 was adopted within the legal limits under the UN Charter and authorized Rukaruku to use force against both the Ibra and the Covfefe. Further, Rukaruku also enjoyed the right of anticipatory self-defense as the threat posed by the Ibra was imminent and Rukaruku acted before effective measures were taken by the UNSC.

As both the Covfefe and the Ibra were military objectives and Rukaruku's capture of the Ibra and attack at the Covfefe were necessary and proportionate, Rukaruku's actions were permitted under international law, proved by the report from Rukaruku to the UNSC.

PLEADINGS

I. THE ARBITRAL AWARD OF 2 MARCH 2017 IS VALID.

The tribunal has jurisdiction over the case [A], and is properly constituted [B]. Besides, neither the *ex parte* communications with Judge Moyet nor the appointment of and work done by Mr. Orvindari seriously depart from the fundamental rules [C]. Moreover, the tribunal did not delegate decision-making function to the secretary [D].

A. THE TRIBUNAL HAS JURISDICTION OVER THE DISPUTE CONCERNING THE CAPTURE OF THE EGART AND THE ISSUE INVOLVED IS ARBITRABLE.

The tribunal has jurisdiction over this case because there is a valid arbitration clause in the FCN Treaty [i]. Also, the Parties have disputes [ii] regarding the interpretation and application of Article 7 of the FCN Treaty [iii] before Rukaruku initiated the proceedings.

i. The arbitration clause of the FCN Treaty is valid.

Whereas the nullity of the undertaking to arbitrate or the facts would be a reason to challenge the validity of an award,[1] such a rule would be considered belated if challenge is advanced after rendering the award,[2] which is the case here as Anduchenca never claimed to the tribunal that the FCN Treaty is null before Rukaruku instituted arbitration proceedings.[3] Therefore, the arbitration clause in the FCN Treaty is valid.

ii. There exists a dispute between Rukaruku and Anduchenca.

A dispute is 'a disagreement on a point of law or fact, a conflict of legal views or

1 International Law Commission (ILC) 'Model Rules on Arbitral Procedure with a General Commentary' (1958) UN DOC A/13/9 arts 9, 35(d); United Nations General Assembly (UNGA) Res 1262 (XIII) (14 November 1958) UN Doc A/RES/1262.

2 Karin Oellers-Frahm, 'Judicial and Arbitral Decisions, Validity and Nullity' (2013) *Max Planck Encyclopedia of Public International Law* (MPEPIL).

3 *Facts* [20] [25].

of interests'[4] between the Parties, and one Party's claim is positively opposed by another.[5] The existence of a dispute shall be determined objectively,[6] taking into account the statements of the Parties.[7] The position of a Party can be established by inference and not necessarily by *expressis verbis*.[8]

In this case, the subject-matter[9] of the dispute falls within the scope of Article 10 of the FCN Treaty. After Anduchenca captured the Egart, both Parties mentioned the territorial sea and the passage of the Egart,[10] which reflected the existence of a dispute concerning the interpretation of Article 7 of the FCN Treaty, *i.e.* the legality of the Egart navigation.[11] Thus, there are disputes between the Parties before Rukaruku initiated the proceedings.

iii. The dispute falls within the scope of interpretation and application of Article 7 of the FCN Treaty.

It is recognized the tribunal has the power to decide its own jurisdiction[12] and interpret the instrument which governs that jurisdiction.[13] If the relevant words of the

4 *The Mavrommatis Palestine Concessions* (Judgment) [1924] PCIJ Rep Series A No 2, 11.

5 *South West Africa cases* (Ethiopia v South Africa; Liberia v South Africa) (Preliminary Objections) [1962] ICJ Rep 319, 328.

6 *Alleged Violations of Sovereign Rights and Maritime Spaces in the Caribbean Sea* (Nicaragua v Colombia) (Preliminary Objections) [2016] ICJ Rep 3 [50].

7 *Questions relating to the Obligation to Prosecute or Extradite* (Belgium v Senegal) (Judgment) [2012] ICJ Rep 422 [50]-[55].

8 *Case Concerning the Land and Maritime Boundary between Cameroon and Nigeria* (Cameroon v Nigeria) (Preliminary Objections) [1998] ICJ Rep 275 [89].

9 *Case Concerning Application of the International Convention on the Elimination of All Forms of Racial Discrimination* (Georgia v Russian Federation) (Preliminary Objections) [2011] ICJ Rep 70 [30].

10 *Facts* [17] [19].

11 *Facts* [Annex I] art 7.

12 ILC Model Rules (n 1) art 9; Res 1262 (n 1); Gary Born, *International Commercial Arbitration* (2nd edn, Wolters Kluwer Law & Business 2014) 1051.

13 *Nottebohm case* (Liechtenstein v Guatemala) (Preliminary Objection) [1953] ICJ Rep 111, 119; *Case concerning the Arbitral Award of 31 July 1989* (Guinea-Bissau v Senegal) (Judgment) [1991] ICJ Rep 53 [46].

instrument in their natural and ordinary meaning make sense in their context,[14] then other means of interpretation are unnecessary. Besides, Parties' subsequent statements are also relevant to clarify the scope of the dispute.[15]

The tribunal's opinion, in essence, was concerned with the legality of the Egart's navigation in the territorial sea.[16] Anduchenca contended that the object of freedom of navigation should only include the commercial vessels, and the geographic scope of that was limited to between the two States on the high seaes,[17] which constitutes another interpretation of Article 7 of the FCN Treaty regarding the words 'between the territories' and 'freedom of navigation'. Therefore, the Parties' dispute regarding the interpretation of those words falls within the jurisdiction of the tribunal.

Whereas ICJ is not the appellate body,[18] it is not allowed to reconsider how the tribunal interpreted the FCN Treaty when deciding upon its jurisdiction, and it should not decide which interpretation is preferable. Therefore, the tribunal has jurisdiction to interpret such article.

B. THE TRIBUNAL IS PROPERLY CONSTITUTED.

The arbitral award in this case was made by an *ad hoc* tribunal[19] concerning the maritime issue[20] between two States.[21] While the applicable tests in international commercial[22] and investment[23] arbitrations are different, only the rules applicable to

---

14 *Competence of the General Assembly for the Admission of a State to the United Nations* (Advisory Opinion) [1950] ICJ Rep 4, 8.

15 *Cameroon v Nigeria* (n 8) [93].

16 *Facts* [26].

17 *Facts* [23].

18 *Guinea-Bissau v Senegal* (n 13) [47].

19 *Facts* [Annex I] art 10.

20 *Facts* [Annex I] art 7.

21 *Facts* [27].

22 *AWG Group Limited v Argentine Republic* (Decision on a Second Proposal for the Disqualification of a Member of the Arbitral Tribunal) [2008] UNCITRAL Arbitration [22].

23 *Suez, Sociedad General de Aguas de Barcelona SA, and InterAguas Servicios Integrales de Agua SA v Argentine Republic* [2003] ICSID Case No ARB/03/17; *Suez, Sociedad General de Aguas de Barcelona SA and Vivendi Universal SA v Argentine Republic* [2003] ICSID Case No ARB/03/19.

and practice of inter-State cases[24] should be applied in the present case, unless there exists a lacuna in the law allowing private rules to be applied by analogy.[25]

First, numerous inter-State arbitrations[26] have established that the standard of challenging the independence and impartiality of the arbitrator should be based on justifiable grounds,[27] while the nationality of the arbitrator[28] should not be deemed as such.[29] In the present case, the mere fact that Judge Moyet is of Rukarukan nationality cannot constitute a bias or a ground to nullify an award.

Second, even if private rules could be applied here by analogy,[30] the rules shall be assessed on a case-by-case basis.[31] The fact that the arbitrator is of one party's nationality and the arbitrator's previous appointment by one Party only requires that arbitrator's disclosure[32] rather than sufficing for a ground to nullify an arbitral award. And Anduchenca's failure to raise such issues before can be deemed to have waived its right to raise this as a ground for annulment.[33]

Thus, in the present case Judge Moyet's nationality and previous appointment cannot

---

24 *Chagos Marine Protected Area Arbitration* (Mauritius v United Kingdom) (Reasoned Decisions on Challenge) [2011] PCA Case No 2011-03 [168].

25 Silja Vöneky, 'Analogy in International Law' (2008) *MPEPIL* [4].

26 Eritrea-Ethiopia Boundary Commission Rules of Procedure (adopted 11 April 2002) art 8; Rules of Procedure for The Arbitral Tribunal Constituted Under the OSPAR Convention Pursuant to the Request of Ireland (2001) art 6; Rules of Procedure for the MOX Plant case (Ireland v United Kingdom) (2001) art 6.

27 *Chagos Arbitration* (n 24) [166].

28 Alan Redfern, Martin Hunter, *Droit et pratique de l'arbitrage commercial international* (2nd edn, LGDJ 1994) 182.

29 Redfern, Hunter (n 28).

30 Vöneky (n 25) [4].

31 'IBA Guidelines on Conflict of Interest in International Arbitration' (IBA Conflicts Guidelines) (23 October 2014) 19.

32 IBA Conflicts Guidelines (n 31) 19.

33 *Azurix Corp v Argentine Republic* [2009] ICSID Case No ARB/01/12 [291]; *Compagnie d'Exploitation du Chemin de Fer Transgabonais v Gabonese Republic* [2010] ICSID Case No ARB/04/5, 129-130.

constitute the ground to nullify the arbitral award.

C. THERE EXISTS NO SERIOUS DEPARTURE FROM FUNDAMENTAL RULES OF PROCEDURE DURING THE PROCEEDINGS.

Neither the *ex parte* communications between Judge Moyet and Rukaruku's counsel [i], nor the appointment of and work done by Mr. Orvindari [ii] constitute serious departure from fundamental rules of procedure.

i. The *ex parte* communications with Judge Moyet do not seriously infringe the fundamental rules of procedure.

a. The ex parte communications do not deprive Anduchenca's right of fair hearing.

Contacts not included in the record[34] will not be a departure from fundamental rules if it does not infringe the procedural balance between the Parties.[35] The content of the *ex parte* contacts in this case only concerned the already presented arguments and Judge Moyet just emphasized these to the other arbitrators.[36] Hence, Anduchenca's procedural right of fair hearing will not be infringed as it was given due opportunities to respond to those arguments when they were presented before.[37]

b. The ex parte communications do not affect the independence and impartiality of Judge Moyet.

Ex parte communications will not infringe the fundamental rules of procedure if they do not unbalance and jeopardize the fundamental right of the other party to be equally treated by the tribunal.[38] The already presented arguments would not affect Judge Moyet's ability to adjudicate the case independently and impartially.

---

34 Born (n 12) 2228.

35 *The Republic of Croatia v The Republic of Slovenia* (Partial Award) [2016] PCA Case No 2012-04 [195].

36 *Facts* [31].

37 *Facts* [25].

38 Patricia Shaughnessy, Sherlin Tung, *The Powers and Duties of an Arbitrator: Liber Amicorum Pierre A Karrer* (Wolters Kluwer 2017) 70.

c. Anduchenca failed to prove that the subject-matters of the ex parte conversations were related to the essence of the dispute's merits and influenced the outcome of the award.

Ex parte contacts that do not concern disputed substantive or procedural[39] issues will not constitute grounds for annulment[40] of an arbitral award.[41] Additionally, the burden of proof is on Anduchenca to prove[42] that the contacts would affect the deliberation.[43] However, Anduchenca failed to substantiate this.

ii. The appointment of and work done by Mr. Orvindari do not infringe fundamental rules of procedure.

a. The tribunal has the right to appoint a secretary without disclosing the hiring to the parties.

A secretary can be appointed to assist the tribunal in large and complex international arbitrations.[44] It is also recognized that the tribunal is competent to formulate the rules of procedure[45] when the Parties do not stipulate or the procedure in the agreement is insufficient.[46] Also, it remains a widespread practice to hire a tribunal secretary without formal appointment.[47] Such undisclosed appointment[48] of the secretary does

39 *Roberta Schwartz v Merrill Lynch & Co* (2011) US 2nd Circuit No 10-0826; *Remmey v Paine Webber, Inc* (1994) US 4th Circuit No 93-2059 [25].

40 *The Consignment of Russian Styrene Monomer* (Judgment) [2008] Swiss International Arbitration Law Reports DFT 4A_294/2008 para 3.2.2; *Webber* (n 39).

41 *Glass, Molders, Pottery, Plastics & Allied Workers Int'l Union, AFL-CIO, CLC, Local 182B v Excelsior Foundry Company* (1995) US 7th Circuit No 94-3734, 846.

42 *Case Concerning the Arbitral Award Made by the King of Spain on 23 December 1906* (Honduras v Nicaragua) (Judgment) [1960] ICJ Rep 192, 205.

43 *National Bulk Carriers, Inc v Princess Management Company* 597 F2d 819 (2nd Cir 1979); *David SPECTOR and Specurity Industrial Ltd v Dov TORENBERG, Ximena Florez, Nicolas Fucci, TRS Computers, Ltd, and Microguard, Inc* (1994) SDNY No 93 Civ 5865 (PKL) 209.

44 Alan Redfern, Martin Hunter, *Law and Practice of International Commercial Arbitration* (4th edn, Sweet & Maxwell 2004) 224; International Council for Commercial Arbitration, 'Young ICCA Guide on Arbitral Secretaries' (International Council for Commercial Arbitration 2014) art 2(1) Commentary.

45 ILC Model Rules (n 1) art 12(1).

46 *Facts* [ANNEX art 10]; Born (n 12) 2045.

47 Young ICCA (n 44) 5; Benjamin Hughes, 'The Problem of Undisclosed Assistance to Arbitral Tribunals', in Patricia Shaughnessy, Sherlin Tung (eds.), *The Powers and Duties of an Arbitrator* (Wolter Kluwer, 2017) 163.

48 *Facts* [32].

not constitute a serious[49] departure from a fundamental rule of procedure.[50]

b. The work done by the secretary is consistent with international law.

There is no uniform standard as to the restrictions to the role of secretary[51] under international law, yet the secretary can legitimately handle substantive tasks[52] so long as the arbitrator does not rely on their work exclusively and the secretary does not take the role of the arbitrator to review underlying authorities.[53]

First, a secretary can assist the arbitrator in acquiring greater familiarity with a case by producing memoranda summarizing the Parties' respective submissions and evidence,[54] further supported by the practice when the legal assistant of fora similarly assists judges without illegitimate derogation of decision-making function.[55] Therefore, the secretary can also assist arbitrators by producing summaries from his or her review of the file.

Second, most institutional rules admit that the arbitral secretary can be present during the deliberations,[56] as long as he or she avoids participating in the private deliberations leading to the award.[57] Therefore, the fact that the secretary attended the tribunal deliberations does not deviate from the fundamental procedure rules.

---

49 *Maritime International Nominees Establishment (MINE) v Government of Guinea (Guinea)* [1989] ICSID Case No ARB/84/4 para 5.05.

50 ILC Model Rules (n 1) art 35(c).

51 Michael Polkinghorne, Charles B Rosenberg, 'The Role of the Tribunal Secretary in International Arbitration: A Call for a Uniform Standard' (2014) 8(2) *Dispute Resolution International* 107, 110.

52 *Sonatrach v Statoil* [2014] EWHC 875 (Comm) 46-50.

53 *Iran-United States Claims Tribunal Reports* (Vol. 27, Grotius Publications 1992) 328-336.

54 Constantine Partasides, 'The Fourth Arbitrator? The Role of Secretaries to the Tribunal in International Arbitration' (2002) 18 *Arbitration International* 147, 157.

55 Young ICCA (n 44) art 3(2)(h) Commentary.

56 Young ICCA (n 44) art 3(i); Hong Kong International Arbitration Center (HKIAC), 'HKIAC Administered Arbitration Rules' (adopted 2013) art 3.4(e); International Chamber of Commerce, 'ICC Note to Parties and Arbitral Tribunal on the Conduct of the Arbitration under the ICC Rules of Arbitration' (30 October 2017) art 2.

57 Redfern, Hunter (n 44) para 4.194.

Third, drafting the memoranda such as the procedural orders and similar documents can be entrusted to the secretary[58] so long as it does not release the tribunal from its own duty to review the files.[59]

Fourth, the secretary may legitimately prepare the first draft of certain parts of the award,[60] as long as the arbitrator can retain control of the decision-making process by restricting a secretary's participation to 'highly structured' tasks, and by subjecting the arbitrator's output to critical review.[61] Accordingly, the secretary is capable of drafting the award[62] so long as the tribunal's decision-making power is not sacrificed.

Thus, the fact that Mr. Orvindari summarized the Parties' arguments and evidence, attended tribunal deliberations, drafted memoranda to the President of the tribunal, and drafted the award[63] will not render the award invalid.

D. JUDGE TONG DID NOT DELEGATE THE DECISION-MAKING FUNCTION TO THE SECRETARY.

The secretary's substantial involvement is accepted by legal scholars[64] and is evidenced by case law.[65] Assisting arbitrators to draft award does not mean that the secretary is involved in the decision-making process.

---

58 Young ICCA (n 44) art 3(g); 'Instructions for the Registry of International Court of Justice' (20 March 2012) art 45(c).

59 ICC Note (n 56) art 2.

60 Young ICCA (n 44) art 3(j) Commentary; Partasides (n 54) 158; *Iran-United States Claim* (n 53) 333; Instructions (n 58) art 45.

61 Partasides (n 54) 157.

62 *Facts* [32]; Partasides (n 54) 158.

63 *Facts* [32].

64 Young ICCA (n 44); HKIAC, 'Guidelines on the Use of a Secretary to the Arbitral Tribunal' (2014) arts 3.4-3.6:

65 *Hulley Enterprises Limited (Cyprus) v The Russian Federation* (Interim Award on Jurisdiction and Admissibility) [2009] PCA Case No 2005-03/AA226 [78]; *Methanex Corporation v United States* (Final Award) (2005) UNCITRAL 44 ILM 1345.

The decision does not necessarily need to be expressed[66] since the essence of it is to address one's mind to the matters on which the contention is and to draw its conclusions therefrom.[67] Even though the draft was made by Mr. Orvindari,[68] Judge Tong made his decision by the implication that the part of the draft prepared by Mr. Orvindari *de facto* reflected Judge Tong's own mind.

Moreover, the tribunal's control over the decision-making process would not be sacrificed if the fact of a dispute or even its outcome is in the tribunal's view sufficiently clear and uncontroversial.[69] In the present case, Judge Tong, by reviewing the draft, made sure that the draft was consistent with his own decision.

II. EVEN IF THE ARBITRAL AWARD IS NOT VALID, RUKARUKU DID NOT VIOLATE ARTICLE 6 OF THE FCN TREATY, BUT ANDUCHENCA VIOLATED ARTICLE 7 OF THE FCN TREATY BY CAPTURING THE EGART.

The Egart is entitled to navigate into Anduchencan territorial sea, which is consistent with Article 6 of the FCN Treaty [A]. Thus, Anduchenca violated Article 7 by capturing the Egart [B].

A. RUKARUKU DID NOT VIOLATE ARTICLE 6 SINCE IT DID NOT INFRINGE ANDUCHENCA'S SOVEREIGNTY UNDER INTERNATIONAL LAW.

The Egart's data collection activity is against the illicit arms traffickers instead of Anduchenca, so it is not prejudicial to Anduchenca's sovereignty [i]. Even if the Egart's activity was not in conformity with the FCN Treaty, such wrongfulness can be justified by Anduchenca's consent and *force majeure* [ii].

i. The Egart's data collection is not prejudicial to Anduchenca's sovereignty.

The rules in the UNCLOS which have constituted customary norms[70] should prevail

66 *Application for Review of Judgment No 333 of the United Nations Administrative Tribunal* (Advisory Opinion) [1987] ICJ Rep 18, 45.

67 *Application for Review* (n 66) 44.

68 *Facts* [33].

69 Partasides (n 54) 158.

70 *Continental Shelf* (Tunisia/Libyan Arab Jamahiriya) (Judgment) [1982] ICJ Rep 18 [24].

in this case. One of the rules regulates that any act aimed at collecting information[71] to the prejudice of the defense or security of the coastal State during the passage would be considered as prejudicial to coastal State. However, data collection in the territorial sea of one coastal State by a foreign vessel against a third Party was lawful under such rules.

The Egart was employed by Rukarukan Navy to collect information along Odasarra Region's coast and to share with all the States of the Region,[72] with an aim to reduce the illicit arms trafficking.[73] Therefore, such data collection against a third Party, *i.e.,* the illicit arms traffickers, does not violate the obligation owed to the coastal State.[74]

ii. Even if Rukaruku breached the FCN Treaty, the wrongfulness could be precluded.

Were the Court to find Rukaruku *prima facie* breached Article 6 of the FCN Treaty, the wrongfulness could be justified[75] under international law by consent[76] and *force majeure.*[77]

a. Anduchenca made its consent as to the presence of and data collection conducted by Rukarukan Navy in its territorial sea.

Anduchenca's acquiescence of Rukarukan Navy deployment is equivalent to tacit recognition[78] which could be construed as consent. The legal basis of such consent also lies in the FCN Treaty, which should be interpreted based on its wording and

---

71 United Nations Convention on the Law of the Sea (adopted 10 December 1982, entered into force 16 November 1994) 1833 UNTS 3 (UNCLOS) art 19(2)(c).

72 *Facts* [5].

73 *Facts* [11].

74 James Kraska, 'Putting Your Head in the Tiger's Mouth: Submarine Espionage in Territorial Waters' (2015) *Columbia Journal of Transnational Law* 164, 219.

75 *Case Concerning Oil Platforms* (Islamic Republic of Iran v United States of America) (Judgment) [2003] ICJ Rep 161 [280]; ILC 'Draft Articles on Responsibility of States for Internationally Wrongful Acts, with Commentaries' (2001) UN Doc A/56/10, 71.

76 ARSIWA (n 75) art 20.

77 *Denkavit Belgi ë NV v Belgian State* (1987) EHRR Case 145/85, 565.

78 *Delimitation of the Maritime Boundary in the Gulf of Maine Area* (Canada/United States of America) (Judgment) [1984] ICJ Rep 246 [130].

purpose,[79] taking into account subsequent practice[80] and the circumstances of its conclusion.

First, the word 'ensuring perpetual peace and stability'[81] in the preamble of the FCN Treaty constitutes an 'invitation or acceptance'[82] from Anduchenca for Rukaruku to send Rukarukan Navy to Anduchencan territorial sea.

Second, the subsequent practice of the absence of Anduchenca's objection[83] to the presence of Rukarukan Navy along its coast, and the sharing of the data collected by Rukarukan Navy, together with the signing of the FCN Treaty support that the continued presence and data collection were permitted by virtue of the FCN Treaty.

Thus, the Egart's presence in Anduchencan territorial sea and its data collection activity[84] all fell within the scope of the consent.

b. Anduchenca did not withdraw its consent.

First, as the *Temple* case suggests, one is precluded by its conduct to assert the opposite position if it enjoys the benefit and other Parties rely on its prior conduct.[85] Anduchenca enjoyed the benefit of a stable coast conferred by Rukarukan Navy deployment,[86] while Rukaruku has been fighting against illicit arms trafficking in the region for decades with reliance on Anduchenca's consent under the FCN Treaty.[87] Therefore, Anduchenca should be precluded from withdrawing its consent.

---

79 Vienna Convention on the Law of Treaties (adopted 22 May 1969, entered into force 27 January 1980) 1155 UNTS 331 (VCLT) art 31(1).

80 VCLT art 31(3)(b); *Case concerning the Temple of Preah Vihear* (Cambodia v Thailand) (Judgment) [1962] ICJ Rep 6, 32.

81 *Facts* [Annex I] Preamble.

82 *Armed Activities on the Territory of the Congo* (Democratic Republic of the Congo v Rwanda) (Jurisdiction and Admissibility) [2006] ICJ Rep 6, 33.

83 *Facts* [5] [8].

84 *Facts* [16].

85 *Temple case* (n 80) 32.

86 *Facts* [4] [5].

87 *Facts* [5] [11].

Second, the content of the declaration made by Mr. Tovarish before the UNGA[88] is too ambiguous[89] to withdraw the consent. The wording 'drone' in his declaration usually means 'a pilotless aircraft or missile directed by remote control',[90] which does not specifically refer to the Egart. The wording 'espionage' usually refers to 'a consciously deceitful collection of information, ordered by a government... accomplished by humans unauthorized by the target to do the collection',[91] which is totally contrary to the Egart's data collection activity. Therefore, the declaration did not point at Rukarukan Navy's data collection activity and its presence, nor could it be construed as a withdrawal of consent.

c. Even if there is no consent, the Egart's entry can be justified by force majeure.

A situation of *force majeure* exists when irresistible force or an unforeseen event which is beyond control of the state concerned makes it materially impossible[92] for the State to perform its obligation.[93]

The Egart is equipped with an advanced sense-and-avoid system[94] which would avoid navigating beyond its programmed field, making its navigation into Anduchenca's 12-nautical-mile territorial sea unforeseeable by Rukaruku.[95] Moreover, it is programmed to navigate for one week and then return autonomously,[96] and it would fall beyond Rukaruku's control if malfunction or any other situations happens during its operation. Therefore, the Egart's entering into Anduchencan territorial sea can be justified by *force majeure*.

---

88 *Facts* [15].

89 *Congo case* (n 82) [51].

90 Brendan Gogarty, Isabel Robinson, 'Unmanned Vehicles: A (Rebooted) History, Background and Current State of the Art' (2011) 21 *Journal of Law, Information and Science* 1, 2.

91 Gogarty, Robinson (n 90).

92 *Gill (Great Britain) v United Mexican States* [1931] 5 RIAA 159.

93 ARSIWA (n 75) 76.

94 *Facts* [14].

95 *Facts* [17].

96 *Facts* [14].

B. ANDUCHENCA VIOLATED ARTICLE 7 BY CAPTURING THE EGART BECAUSE OF THE VIOLATION OF FREEDOM OF NAVIGATION BETWEEN BOTH PARTIES' TERRITORIES.

Anduchenca's capture of the Egart violated Article 7 of the FCN Treaty because Rukaruku enjoys freedom of navigation under that article [i]. Also, there is no justification for Anduchenca's wrongful act under international law [ii]. Since Anduchenca's act is internationally wrongful, it should return the Egart to Rukaruku [iii].

i. Anduchenca deprived Rukaruku of freedom of navigation under the FCN Treaty.

a. The Egart is a non-commercial government vessel under international law.

Vessel is a 'human-made device, capable of traversing the sea'[97] including submersibles,[98] which is not necessarily a means of transportation.[99] Since the Egart is employed by Rukarukan Navy[100] without engaging in commerce,[101] the Egart should be deemed as a non-commercial government vessel.

b. The scope of freedom of navigation shall include government vessel operating between the territories which include the territorial sea of the parties.

The scope of Article 7 should be interpreted by its wording and in light of its purpose and object,[102] taking into account subsequent practice[103] and the circumstances of its conclusion.[104]

First, the freedom of navigation regulated under Article 7 of the FCN Treaty is a

---

97 George Walker, 'Defining Terms in the 1982 Law of the Sea Convention III: The International Hydrographic Organization ECDIS Glossary' (2004) 34 *California Western International Law Journal* 211, 238.

98 International Convention for the Prevention of Pollution of Ships (adopted 2 November 1973, entered into force 2 October 1983) 1340 UNTS 184 art 2.

99 *The Estate of Kenneth Wenzel by its Special Administrator Winston Mirikitani, Edward Wenzel and Anna M Steinberg v Seaward Marine Services Inc* (1983) US 9th Circuit No 82-4619.

100 *Facts* [13].

101 *Facts* [17].

102 VCLT art 31(1).

103 VCLT art 31(3)(b).

104 VCLT art 32.

general term which is not territorially restricted to exclusive economic zone and high seas. Though coastal State's sovereignty extends to its territorial sea, foreign vessels enjoy certain rights of freedom.[105]

Second, before and after the conclusion of the FCN Treaty, Rukaruku has deployed its Navy along the Anduchenca's coast for decades[106] with Anduchenca's acquiescence,[107] and the deployment is to ensure the perpetual peace and stability of the region.[108] Therefore, the wording of Article 7 should include government vessel and extend to territorial sea.

c. Anduchenca's Maritime security law, which requires prior authorization for foreign government vessels into its territorial sea, is not consistent with international law.

The right of innocent passage,[109] which restricts State's sovereignty in its territorial sea, could not be hindered,[110] since all ships[111] could enjoy innocent passage if the requirements are satisfied. However, Anduchenca's domestic law would hamper innocent passage if foreign ship is not authorized to traverse its territorial sea and is thus inconsistent with international law.

ii. Anduchenca's wrongful acts could not be justified under international law.

a. Anduchenca's domestic law could not justify its wrongful acts.

It is a general principle that wrongful acts cannot be evaded by domestic law.[112] Anduchenca's wrongfulness concerning the infringement on the Egart's

105 *Military and Paramilitary Activities in and against Nicaragua* (Nicaragua v United States of America) (Merits) [1986] ICJ Rep 14 [214].

106 *Facts* [5] [8] [11].

107 *Facts* [5] [8] [11].

108 *Facts* [Annex I] Preamble.

109 UNCLOS art 17.

110 UNCLOS art 24; Convention on the Territorial Sea and the Contiguous Zone (adopted 29 April 1958, entered into force 22 November 1964) 516 UNTS 205 art 15.

111 'Joint Statement with Attached Uniform Interpretation of Rules of International Law Governing Innocent Passage' (1989) 28 ILM 1444.

112 ARSIWA (n 75) art 3; VCLT art 27; *Fisheries case* (United Kingdom v Norway) (Judgment) [1951] ICJ Rep 116, 132; *Applicability of the Obligation to Arbitrate under Section 21 of the United Nations Headquarters Agreement of 26 June 1947* (Advisory Opinion) [1988] ICJ Rep 12 [57].

navigation under Article 7 of the FCN Treaty could not be precluded by its domestic law.[113]

b. Anduchenca cannot justify its acts by countermeasures either.

First, an injured State may only take countermeasures against a State which is responsible for an internationally wrongful act in order to induce the latter to comply with its international obligations.[114] However, as Rukaruku did not commit a prior breach of its obligation, Anduchenca could not take such countermeasures.

Second, even if Rukaruku indeed breached its obligation, a legitimate countermeasure should be 'necessary and reasonable'[115] and should be sufficient to induce the responsible State to comply with its obligations, without having a punitive effect.[116] Anduchenca did not respect the necessity requirement as it jammed the communication links of the Egart and transmitted false GPS coordinates to capture the Egart,[117] rather than propelling it to leave Anduchencan territorial sea. Further, Anduchenca's act was not proportionate, as the Egart employs a navigation system to periodically surface to receive GPS[118] and an advanced sense-and-avoid system, so that the Egart can correct its navigation by itself.

iii. Anduchenca committed internationally wrongful acts by capturing and detaining the Egart and hence shall return it to Rukaruku.

Government vessels enjoy sovereign immunity.[119] Even if the Egart's passage was not

113 *Facts* [12].

114 *Air Services Agreement of 27 March 1946* (the United States of America v France) [1979] 18 RIAA 416; James Crawford, *The International Law Commission's Articles on State Responsibility: Introduction, Text and Commentaries* (CUP 2002) 168.

115 *Archer Daniels Midland Company and Tate & Lyle Ingredients Americas, Inc v the United Mexican States* [2007] ICSID Case No ARB(AF)/04/05 [153]; ARSIWA (n 75) art 49;

116 *United States-Subsidies on Upland Cotton, Recourse to Arbitration by the United States under Article 22.6 of the DSU and Article 4.11 of the SCM Agreement* [2009] WTO Case No WT/DS267/ARB/1 para 4.113.

117 *Facts* [16].

118 *Facts* [14].

119 UNCLOS art 32.

consistent with the coastal State's laws and regulations, acts taken by coastal State would only be limited to require such vessel to leave.[120] It is internationally wrongful to capture and detain the Egart, and therefore, Anduchenca is under an obligation to make restitution[121] via returning it to Rukaruku.

III. ANDUCHENCA VIOLATED ARTICLE 16 OF THE FCN TREATY BY COMMISSIONING AND OPERATING THE IBRA.

Article 16 of the FCN Treaty stipulates that 'Each Contracting Party shall ... comply with all disarmament obligations binding on it under international law'. 'Under International law' is a generic term, whose content the Parties expected would change through time,[122] therefore the obligation of implementing negotiation under Article VI of NPT [A] and of neutralizing the threat by disarming the Ibra under Resolution 3790 [B] are involved in Article 16 of the FCN Treaty.

A. ANDUCHENCA VIOLATED THE OBLIGATION TO PURSUE NEGOTIATIONS IN GOOD FAITH FOR NUCLEAR DISARMAMENT.

i. Anduchenca bears the obligation to pursue negotiations in good faith for nuclear disarmament under customary international law.

a. The obligation of negotiation is a primary disarmament obligation stressed in Article VI of NPT, which constitutes customary international law.

The obligation to pursue negotiations in good faith for nuclear disarmament under Article VI of NPT,[123] as a twofold obligation to pursue and to conclude negotiations,[124] should be regarded as customary international law, qualifying the elements of state practice and *opinio juris*.[125] The fact that 191 States, a vast majority of international

---

120 UNCLOS art 30.

121 ARSIWA (n 75) art 35.

122 *Kasikili/Sedudu Island case* (Botswana/Namibia) (Declaration of Judge Higgins) [1999] ICJ Rep 1045 [2].

123 Treaty on the Non-Proliferation of Nuclear Weapons (adopted 1 July 1968, entered into force 5 March 1970) 729 UNTS 161 (NPT) art VI.

124 *Legality of the Threat or Use of Nuclear Weapons* (Advisory Opinion) [1996] ICJ Rep 226 [100].

125 Statute of the International Court of Justice (adopted 26 June 1945, entered into force 24 October 1945) 33 UNTS 993 art 38(2); *Continental Shelf* (Libyan Arab Jamahiriya/Malta) (Judgment) [1985] ICJ Rep 13 [27].

community,[126] have joined NPT, especially the five nuclear weapon States,[127] proves a uniform State practice,[128] while the consistent endorsement[129] in the UNGA resolutions[130] calling upon the fulfillment of this obligation from all States[131] has clearly demonstrated the *opinio juris*.[132] Additionally, UNSC Resolutions 984/1995 and 1887/2009 also call upon all States to fulfill this obligation.[133] Particularly, all five nuclear weapon States adopt these resolutions and show their *opinio juris*.

b. Anduchenca is not a persistent objector.

Persistent objectors[134] require initial objection,[135] sustained objection[136] with persistency[137] and consistency,[138] and other States' toleration,[139] which Anduchenca did

126 *Legality of Nuclear Weapons* (n 124) [100]; '191 States according to Status of the Treaty on the Non-Proliferation of Nuclear Weapons' <http://disarmament.un.org/treaties/t/npt> accessed 8 January 2018.

127 *Legality of Nuclear Weapons* (n 124) [100].

128 *North Sea Continental Shelf* (Federal Republic of Germany/Denmark; Federal Republic of Germany/Netherlands) (Judgment) [1969] ICJ Rep 3 [73].

129 UNGA Res 70/33 (7 December 2015) UN Doc A/RES/70/33 (adopted by 138 Votes to 12, with 34 Abstentions); UNGA Res 70/52 (7 December 2015) UN Doc A/RES/70/52 (adopted by 127 to 43, with 15 Abstentions).

130 UNGA Res 51/45 (10 December 1996) UN Doc A/RES/51/45; UNGA Res 56/24 (29 November 2001) UN Doc A/RES/56/24; UNGA Res 61/83 (6 December 2006) UN Doc A/RES/61/83; UNGA Res 66/46 (2 December 2011) UN Doc A/RES/66/46; UNGA Res 70/56 (7 December 2015) UN Doc A/RES/70/56.

131 *Obligations concerning Negotiations relating to Cessation of the Nuclear Arms Race and to Nuclear Disarmament* (Marshall Islands v United Kingdom) (Dissenting Opinion of Judge Cançado Trindade) [2016] ICJ Rep 907 [56].

132 *Military and Paramilitary Activities* (n 105) [99]-[100] [188].

133 United Nations Security Council (UNSC) UN Doc S/RES/984 (11 April 1995); UNSC UN Doc S/RES/1887 (24 September 2009).

134 ILC 'Third Report on Identification of Customary International Law' (2015) UN Doc A/CN4/682 [85].

135 *Columbian-Peruvian Asylum case* (Columbia/Peru) (Judgment) [1950] ICJ Rep 266, 277-278; *Fisheries case* (n 112) 136.

136 *Fisheries case* (n 112) 131.

137 *Fisheries case* (n 112) 137-138.

138 *Fisheries case* (n 112) 137-138.

139 *Fisheries case* (n 112) 138-139.

not fulfill.[140]

First, what Anduchenca opposed to is the inequality in NPT between Nuclear Weapon States and Non-Nuclear Weapon States.[141] However, Article VI of NPT does not aggravate the inequality as it involved all States with the same aim to completely eliminate nuclear weapons, which was to balance such inequality. Thus, Anduchenca did not raise initial objection to Article VI.[142] *Second*, the consistency should be absolute,[143] denying any inconsistent practice,[144] as confirmed by State practice.[145] However, Anduchenca's participation in the 2017 UN Conference to negotiate for nuclear disarmament[146] undermined its consistency, which resulted in inconsistent objection.

ii. The policy of deterrence could not justify the violation of the nuclear disarmament obligation.

The policy of deterrence is a political concept[147] with no legal force.[148] Judge Bravo in *Legality of Nuclear Weapons* case also noted that deterrence could not justify the threat or use of nuclear weapons.[149] Thus, deterrence grants Anduchenca no right to commission or operate the Ibra.

---

140 Ruwanthika Gunaratne, 'Anglo Norwegian Fisheries Case (Summary on Customary International Law)' <https://ruwanthikagunaratne.wordpress.com/2014/04/11/anglo-norwegian-fisheries-summary/> accessed 8 January 2018.

141 *Facts* [9].

142 Mark Newcomb, 'Non-Proliferation, Self-Defense, and the Korean Crisis' (1994) 27 *Vand J Transnat'l L* 603, 607.

143 James Green, *The Persistent Objector Rule in International Law* (1st edn, OUP 2016) 117.

144 Green (n 143) 117.

145 *Negotiation to Nuclear Disarmament* (n 131) [145].

146 *Facts* [39].

147 *Legality of Nuclear Weapons* (Declaration of Judge Shi) (n 124) 277.

148 *Legality of Nuclear Weapons* (Declaration of Judge Bravo) (n 124) 226, 283; *Negotiation to Nuclear Disarmament* (n 131) [145].

149 *Legality of Nuclear Weapons* (Declaration of Judge Bravo) (n 124) 284.

iii. Anduchenca, by commissioning and operating the Ibra, breached the nuclear disarmament obligation.

a. Anduchenca did not satisfy the requirement of meaningful negotiation.

Good faith negotiation must be meaningful,[150] which requires negotiation with a view to arrive at an agreement[151] and to prohibit 'acts defeating the object and purpose of the future treaty'.[152]

Thus, to be a good faith negotiator, Anduchenca should have born a genuine view to reach an agreement toward the goal of the 2017 UN Conference. However, proved by Mr. Tovarish's speech, Anduchenca was commissioning and preparing to operate the Ibra during the negotiation in the 2017 UN Conference.[153] Anduchenca's actions reflected its complete ignorance of the object and purpose of the negotiation, which should be 'total elimination',[154] and its reluctance to reach an agreement. Therefore, it violated the obligation thereof.

b. Anduchenca did not satisfy the requirement of continuation under good faith negotiation.

First, the obligation itself requires continuing the negotiation to reach a precise result, *i.e.*, nuclear disarmament in all aspects.[155] *Second*, good faith, which regulates obligation performance,[156] demands continuation of negotiations unless a failure or futility exists.[157]

---

150 *Railway Traffic between Lithuania and Poland* (Advisory Opinion) [1931] PCIJ Rep Series A/B No 42, 116; *North Sea Continental Shelf* (n 128) [85].

151 *Railway Traffic* (n 150) 116; *North Sea Continental Shelf* (n 128) [85]; *Application of the Interim Accord of 13 September 1995* (Macedonia v Greece) (Judgment) [2011] ICJ Rep 644 [132].

152 Antonio Cassese, 'The Israel-PLO Agreement and Self-Determination' (1993) 4 *EJIL* 564, 567.

153 *Facts* [37]-[38].

154 UNGA Res 71/258 (23 December 2016) UN Doc A/RES/71/258.

155 *Legality of Nuclear Weapons* (n 124) [99].

156 *Nuclear Tests* (Australia v France) (Judgment) [1974] ICJ Rep 253 [46]; *Pulp Mills on the River Uruguay* (Argentina v Uruguay) (Judgment) [2010] ICJ Rep 14 [145]; *Legality of Nuclear Weapons* (n 124) [102].

157 *South West Africa* (n 5) 345-346; *Headquarters Agreement* (n 112) [55]; *Elimination of All Forms of Racial Discrimination* (n 9) [159].

Anduchenca's withdrawal from the second session of the 2017 UN Conference[158] facilitated Ibra's operation, since this session would conclude a treaty restricting such operation.[159] As the first session indicated no failure or futility regarding the precise result to nuclear disarmament,[160] Anduchenca's operation of the Ibra, which induced the opting-out, failed to satisfy the continuation requirement of negotiation in good faith.

B. ANDUCHENCA VIOLATED THE DISARMAMENT OBLIGATION TO NEUTRALIZE THE THREAT POSED BY THE IBRA UNDER RESOLUTION 3790.

i. Operative paragraph one of Resolution 3790 constitutes a binding decision.

According to the Advisory Opinion of *Legal Consequences for States of the Continued Presence of South Africa in Namibia* case, all circumstances, including the terms of the resolution should be considered to determine the binding effect of a Resolution.[161] Here, considering that the UNSC has already determined that 'the current situation along the Kumatqesh coast in the Odasarra Region constitutes a threat to international peace and security',[162] operative paragraph one of Resolution 3790 should be deemed as a binding decision and therefore imposes obligations to Anduchenca.

Although operative paragraph one uses 'calls upon',[163] the word can also impose obligations, as in the Advisory Opinion of *Legal Consequences for States of the Continued Presence of South Africa in Namibia*, a provision (operative paragraph five) which began with the words 'calls upon all States' was found to be legally binding.[164] Another example is UNSC Resolution 2177, which only used 'encourages', 'calls

158 *Facts* [39].

159 UN 'United Nations Conference to Negotiate Legally Binding Treaty Prohibiting Nuclear Weapons Will Hold Second Substantive Session' (14 June 2017) Press Release DC/3709.

160 Press Release DC/3706 (n 159).

161 *Legal Consequences for States of the Continued Presence of South Africa in Namibia (South West Africa) notwithstanding Security Council Resolution 276* (Advisory Opinion) [1971] ICJ Rep 16 [114].

162 *Facts* [Annex II] Preamble.

163 *Facts* [Annex II] 1.

164 *Namibia case* (n 161) [115].

on', 'urges' and 'commends' in its operative paragraphs when dealing with countries' actions against the outbreak of the Ebola virus.[165] However, the Repertoire of the Practice of the Security Council 19th Supplement (2014-2015) deems it as indeed a decision with binding effect.[166]

Further, operative paragraph four of Resolution 3790 authorizes actions to neutralize such threat,[167] which further confirms that operative paragraph one is binding.

ii. Operative paragraph one of Resolution 3790 imposes a disarmament obligation on Anduchenca.

A binding determination made by a competent organ of the United Nations to the effect that a situation is illegal cannot remain without consequence.[168] Provided the UNSC has decided that the Ibra was a threat to peace, Anduchenca's actions were against the purpose of the UN Charter and should be deemed as illegal. Anduchenca thus, as a State responsible for the illegal actions, was under the disarmament obligation to put an end to it, *i.e.,* to disarm the nuclear weapons on the Ibra.

iii. Anduchenca violated such disarmament obligation by continuing operating the Ibra.

After the adoption of Resolution 3790, instead of disarming the Ibra, Anduchenca continuously deployed and operated it on the high seas.[169] Thus, Anduchenca violated the disarmament obligation under operative paragraph one of Resolution 3790.

IV. RUKARUKU DID NOT VIOLATE ARTICLE 17 OF THE FCN TREATY BY ATTACKING THE COVFEFE OR BY CAPTURING THE IBRA.

Two exceptions of threat or use of force exist in relation to collective measures taken by the UNSC resolutions [A] and with regard to the right of self-defense [B].[170]

165 UNSC UN Doc S/RES/2177 (18 September 2014).

166 Repertoire of the Practice of the Security Council 19th Supplement (2014-2015) 9.

167 *Facts* [Annex II] 4.

168 *Namibia case* (n 161) [117].

169 *Facts* [46].

170 Charter of the United Nations (entered into force 24 October 1945) 1 UNTS XV (UN Charter)

Acting within the requirements of both, Rukaruku's actions were permitted under international law [C].

A. RUKARUKU WAS ENTITLED TO USE FORCE AGAINST THE IBRA UNDER RESOLUTION 3790.

i. Resolution 3790 is adopted within the legal limits under the UN Charter.

The UNSC resolutions are subject to both procedural and substantive limits under the UN Charter.[171] For procedural limits, Resolution 3790 is adopted in correct formal procedures, with Anduchenca's attendance,[172] and necessary majority,[173] *i.e.,* nine to six.[174]

For substantive limits, *first*, the aspiration of Resolution 3790 to neutralize the threat to 'international peace and security'[175] is in accordance with Articles 1(1) and 24(2) of the UN Charter.[176] *Second*, the UNSC does not compel Anduchenca to comply with NPT,[177] as NPT was only mentioned in the preamble rather than the operative paragraphs of Resolution 3790,[178] which generally only presents the considerations on what actions to take.[179]

ii. Resolution 3790 authorizes Rukaruku to use force against both the Ibra and the Covfefe.

a. The Security Council fulfills the preconditions for the authorization of the use of force.

First, Resolution 3790 is adopted under Chapter VII of the UN Charter when there

arts 2(4), 42, 51.

171 UN Charter arts 2(5), 25; Anne Peters, 'Article 25' in Bruno Simma (eds.), *The Charter of the United Nations: A Commentary* (Vol. 1, 3rd edn, OUP 2012) [74].

172 UN Charter art 31; *Clarifications* [6].

173 UN Charter art 27(2).

174 *Facts* [41].

175 *Facts* [ANNEX II Preamble].

176 UN Charter arts 1(1), 24(2).

177 *Facts* [42].

178 *Facts* [ANNEX II Preamble].

179 'Security Council Resolutions' <http://www.un.org/en/sc/documents/resolutions/ > accessed 9 January 2018.

exists a threat to international peace and security.[180] The concept of such threat has been expanding to include the proliferation of nuclear weapons,[181] which was first exemplified by the 1992 statement of President of the UNSC[182] and was later reaffirmed by the UNSC resolutions[183] with little opposition.[184] Provided the UNSC had determined Anduchenca's commission and operation of the Ibra[185] caused such threat, the UNSC could authorize the use of force under Chapter VII.[186]

Second, Resolution 3790, using 'with their specific circumstances in confronting the Ibra',[187] specifies the means and extent of the action to remove this threat,[188] which only requires separation of the determination of a threat and the decision on action,[189] as indicated by Resolution 678[190] and 1973.[191]

b. The language of Resolution 3790 indicates the authorization to use force.

The language of Resolution 3790, after careful analysis,[192] indicated such authorization. The rules on treaty interpretation in VCLT may guide the interpretation of the UNSC resolutions,[193] together with 'other resolutions on the same issue'.[194]

---

180 UN Charter arts 39, 42; *Facts* [Annex] II Preamble.

181 UNSC 'Note by the President of the Security Council' (31 January 1992) UN Doc S/23500.

182 UN Doc S/23500 (n 181).

183 UNSC UN Doc S/RES/1172 (6 June 1998); UNSC UN Doc S/RES/1540 (28 April 2004); UNSC UN Doc S/RES/1718 (14 October 2006).

184 Nico Krisch, 'Article 39' in Bruno Simma (eds.) *The Charter of the United Nations: A Commentary* (Vol. 2, 3rd edn, OUP 2012) [16].

185 *Facts* [38].

186 UN Charter art 39.

187 *Facts* [Annex II] 4.

188 UN Charter art 42; Nico Krisch, 'Article 42' in Simma (n 184) [20].

189 Nico Krisch, 'Article 42' in Simma (n 184) [20].

190 UNSC UN Doc S/RES/678 (29 November 1990).

191 UNSC UN Doc S/RES/1973 (17 March 2011).

192 *Namibia case* (n 161) [114].

193 *Accordance with International Law of the Unilateral Declaration of Independence in Respect of Kosovo* (Advisory Opinion) [2010] ICJ Rep 403 [94].

194 *Kosovo* (n 193).

First, considering the Ibra's ability to accurately strike targets[195] and potential to destroy all civilizations and the entire ecosystem,[196] 'all measures commensurate with the specific circumstances'[197] should be interpreted to authorize use of force.

Second, in light of the past UNSC resolutions, the UNSC uses similar language to authorize use of force. The UNSC Resolution 2240 contains the similar wording 'all measures commensurate' and authorizes States to use force when inspecting or capturing the vessels engaging in human trafficking in Libya.[198]

The destructive capability of the Ibra was even more severe than the vessels engaging in human trafficking, and it could be inferred that Rukaruku was authorized to use force under Resolution 3790.

c. Rukaruku could use force against both the Covfefe and the Ibra to neutralize the threat posed by the Ibra.

Primary importance should be attached to the ordinary meaning of the text in the light of its object and purpose,[199] as applied in Advisory Opinion of *Kosovo*.[200] The object and purpose of Resolution 3790 is to 'neutralize the threat' posed by the Ibra,[201] and the subsequent resolution further proves that the final aim was to dismantle the Ibra.

With the object and purpose of 'neutralizing the threat',[202] which was posed by both the existence and the undisclosed locations of the Ibra,[203] attack at targets which were essential for dismantling the Ibra should be within the authorization, further proved

195 *Clarifications* [5].

196 *Legality of Nuclear Weapons* (n 124) [35].

197 *Facts* [Annex II] 4.

198 UNSC UN Doc S/RES/2240 (9 October 2015).

199 Alexander Orakhelashvili, 'Unilateral Interpretation of Security Council Resolutions: UK Practice' (2010) 2 *Goettingen Journal of International Law* 823, 826.

200 *Kosovo* (n 193) [96]-[100].

201 *Facts* [Annex II] 4.

202 *Facts* [Annex II] 4.

203 *Facts* [Annex II] 4.

by the subsequent resolution affirming the dismantlement.[204] As the deprivation of communication equipment on the Covfefe would force the Ibra to surface,[205] which was essential for capturing the Ibra,[206] both the Covfefe and the Ibra were appropriate targets under Resolution 3790.

B. RUKARUKU WAS ENTILED TO USE FORCE AGAINST THE COVFEFE AND THE IBRA WITH THE RIGHT OF ANTICIPATORY SELF-DEFENSE.

i. Rukaruku enjoys the inherent right of anticipatory self-defense.

First, the right of anticipatory self-defense is enshrined in Article 51 of the UN Charter, which preserves the 'inherent' right of self-defense existing pre-Charter.[207] As reflected in the famous 1837 Caroline incident[208] and the judgments of the Nuremberg[209] and Tokyo[210] international military tribunals, the phrase 'if an armed attack occurs' in Article 51 of the UN Charter cannot eliminate such right of anticipatory self-defense.

Second, State practice also supports the right, with the recognition from the UN Secretary General's High-Level Panel on Threats, Challenges and Change,[211] and

---

204 *Facts* [47].

205 *Facts* [44].

206 Berenice Baker, 'Deep Secret-Secure Submarine Communication on a Quantum Level' (2013) Naval Technology <http://www.naval-technology.com/features/featuredeep-secret-secure-submarine-communication-on-a-quantum-level/> accessed 9 January 2018.

207 Sean Murphy, 'The Doctrine of Preemptive Self-Defense' (2005) 50 *Villanova Law Review* 699; Ashley Deeks, 'Taming the Doctrine of Pre-Emption' in Marc Weller (ed.), *The Oxford Handbook of the Use of Force in International Law* (OUP 2015) 665.

208 Deeks (n 207) 665; 'Letter from Daniel Webster, US Secretary of State, to Lord Ashburton, British Plenipotentiary (6 Aug 1842)' in John Bassett Moore, *A Digest of International Law* (1906) 2 *American Journal of International* 412.

209 'Judgment of the Nuremberg International Military Tribunal 1946' (1947) 41 AJIL172, 205.

210 'International Military Tribunal at Tokyo (1948)' in Leon Friedman (ed.), *The Law of War: A Documentary History* (Vol. 2, Random House 1972) 1029, 1157-1159.

211 UN High-level Panel on Threats, Change, and United Nations, *A More Secure World: Our Shared Responsibility: Report of the High-level Panel on Threats, Challenges, and Change* (2004) [188].

the little criticism for Israel in the UNSC or UNGA[212] for Israel's use of force under anticipatory self-defense.[213]

ii. Anduchenca's commission and operation of the Ibra endowed Rukaruku with the condition to exercise the right of anticipatory self-defense.

a. The threat posed by Anduchenca's commission and operation of the Ibra was imminent to Rukaruku.

In response to efforts by some States to acquire Weapons of Mass Destruction, 'it is imperative to update the concept of imminence'[214] in the *Caroline* principle,[215] which is the precondition for exercising anticipatory self-defense,[216] confirmed by the United States National Security Strategy (2002)[217] and proved by the near total lack of international criticism on Israel's preemptive actions in the al-Kibar bombings[218] when the Syrian reactor hardly met the *Caroline* principle.[219]

The new imminence threshold could be determined through three factors:[220] the nature and quantum of the threat,[221] the potential harm,[222] and the urgency and specificity

212 Rosalyn Higgins, 'The Attitude of Western States Towards Legal Aspects of the Use of Force' in Antonio Cassese, *The Current Legal Regulation of the Use of Force* (MNP 1986) 443; Deeks (n 207) 665.

213 Yoram Dinstein, *War, Aggression and Self-defence* (CUP 2017) 173.

214 Matthew Waxman, 'The Use of Force against States That Might Have Weapons of Mass Destruction' (2009) 31 *Michigan Journal of International Law* 1, 12; Deeks (n 207) 670.

215 Letter from Daniel Webster (n 208).

216 Letter from Daniel Webster (n 208).

217 The White House Washington 'The National Security Strategy of the United States of America' (September 2002) <http://www.au.af.mil/au/awc/awcgate/nss/nss_sep2002.pdf> accessed 9 January 2018 .

218 Leonard Spector, Avner Cohen, 'Israel's Airstrike on Syria's Reactor: Implications for the Non-Proliferation Regime' (2008) *Arms Control Today* 15.

219 Spector (n 218); Andrew Garwood-Gowers, 'Israel's Airstrike on Syria's Al-Kibar Facility: A Test Case for the Doctrine of Pre-emptive Self-Defence?' 16 *Journal of Conflict and Security Law* 263, 268.

220 Deeks (n 207) 675.

221 Abraham Sofaer, 'On the Necessity of Pre-Emption' (2003)14 *European Journal of International Law* 209, 220; Christopher Greenwood, 'International Law and the Pre-emptive Use of Force: Afghanistan, Al-Qaida, and Iraq' (2003) 4 *San Diego International Law Journal* 7, 16.

222 Sofaer (n 221); Greenwood (n 221).

of the threat.[223] Here, nuclear weapons on the Ibra with the deadly precision of the ballistic missiles aboard[224] were able to release immeasurable heat and radiation, and destroy all civilizations and the entire ecosystem,[225] and would cause extreme threat towards Rukaruku, especially during the time of a deteriorated bilateral relationship.[226] Moreover, Anduchenca had already deployed the Ibra to an undisclosed location and threatened to use the Ibra against any country persisting in infringing its sovereignty.[227] As Anduchenca accused Rukaruku of invading its territorial water,[228] its operation of the Ibra under deterrence,[229] 'which must include a threat of possible use',[230] further materialized the threat to be imminent.

b. There existed no effective UNSC measures to maintain international peace and security.

The reference to 'measures' under Article 51 of the UN Charter suggests that the mere passage of a resolution cannot remove the right of self-defense,[231] supported by the fact that UNSC resolutions did not hinder Kuwait's right of self-defense in 1990.[232] Here, Rukaruku's immediate report to the UNSC after the capture of the Ibra and the attack at the Covfefe[233] not only indicated that Rukaruku acted under self-defense,[234] but also affirmed the lack of effective measures from the UNSC.

C. RUKARUKU'S ATTACK AT THE COVFEFE AND CAPTURE OF THE IBRA WERE PERMITTED UNDER INTERNATIONAL LAW.

i. Both the Covfefe and the Ibra were military objectives.

Rukaruku's actions complied with international humanitarian law and were directed at

---

223 Sofaer (n 221); Greenwood (n 221).

224 *Clarifications* [5].

225 *Legality of Nuclear Weapons* (n 124) [35].

226 *Facts* [8].

227 *Facts* [38].

228 *Facts* [16] [19].

229 *Facts* [38].

230 *Legality of Nuclear Weapons* (Dissenting Opinion of Vice-President Schwebel) (n 124) 314.

231 Greenwood (n 221) [33].

232 Greenwood (n 221) [33].

233 *Clarifications* [7].

234 *Military and Paramilitary Activities* (n 105) [200].

only military objectives, as required by both UNSC resolutions[235] and the right of self-defense.[236]

Military objectives are objectives 'which by their nature, location, purpose or use make an effective contribution to military action and whose total or partial destruction, capture or neutralization, in the circumstances ruling at the time, offers a definite military advantage'.[237]

The Ibra was undeniably military objective being part of Anduchencan Navy.[238] The Covfefe also qualified as a military objective. The Covfefe supplied communication equipment to the Ibra,[239] and destruction of it would give Rukaruku a definite military advantage as the Ibra would face increasing risks of detection without the communication equipment.[240]

ii. Rukaruku's actions were necessary and proportionate.

Rukaruku's actions met the requirements of necessity [a] and proportionality [b][241] as required by both Chapter VII of the UN Charter[242] and self-defense.[243]

a. Rukaruku's actions were necessary.

Necessity exists when there is no 'measure of discretion',[244] while the ICJ also

---

235 UN Charter art 1(3); Peters (n 171) [130].

236 *Oil Platforms* (n 75) [51].

237 Protocol Additional to the Geneva Conventions of 12 August 1949, and relating to the Protection of Victims of International Armed Conflicts (Protocol I) (adopted 8 June 1977, entered into force 7 December 1978) 1125 UNTS 3 (API) art 52(2).

238 *Facts* [38].

239 *Clarifications* [8]; *Facts* [44].

240 H Singh, Rajendra Pal, 'Submarine Communications' (1993) 43 *Defense Science Journal* 43.

241 UN Charter art 42; *Military and Paramilitary Activities* (n 105) [176]; *Legality of Nuclear Weapons* (n 124) [41].

242 UN Charter art 42.

243 *Legality of Nuclear Weapons* (n 124) [30].

244 *Oil Platforms* (n 75) [73].

develops more specific geographical[245] criterion.

First, the capture of the Ibra was necessary, as there were no peaceful means to restore security. Anduchenca admitted that many States expressed their concerns on the Ibra.[246] However, Anduchenca refused to moderate the behavior, but withdrew from the negotiation of the 2017 UN Conference. Considering that Anduchenca's deteriorated relationship with all the countries around the Odasarra Region, the possibility of any peaceful diplomatic solution was ruled out.

Second, the actions of capturing the Ibra were necessary considering the geographical factor, as the Ibra was only 20 nautical miles from the Anduchencan Coast when being enclosed,[247] which necessitated immediate firing of torpedoes in case the Ibra would escape the capture when it moved into Anduchencan territorial sea.

Third, the actions of attacking the Covfefe were necessary as the last resort. If Rukaruku relinquished attacking the Covfefe, locating the Ibra would be practically impossible as the submarine deeply submerged could not be detected by sonars.[248]

Further, the Covfefe did not respond to Rukarukan warships' six communication attempts or change its course.[249] Considering the Covfefe was *en route* to give supply to the Ibra, Rukaruku needed to stop the possibility and immediately disable the Covfefe.

b. Rukaruku's actions were proportionate.

Proportionality demands consideration of the size and scope[250] of the threat and the scale of the whole operation.[251] Attacks affecting civilians are not inevitably unlawful

245 *Armed Activities on the Territory of the Congo* (Democratic Republic of the Congo v Uganda) (Judgment) [2005] ICJ Rep 168 [147].

246 *Facts* [40].

247 *Facts* [46].

248 Baker (n 206).

249 *Facts* [43]; *Clarifications* [9].

250 *Legality of Nuclear Weapons* (n 124) [41]-[43].

251 *Oil Platforms* (n 75) [77].

provided the damage to civilians is incidental and not excessive,[252] prescribing that civilians are not needlessly injured by carelessness.[253]

First, considering the scale of the whole operation,[254] actions in capturing the Ibra,[255] as normal State practice,[256] were proportionate. *Second*, considering the size and scope[257] of the threat posed by the Ibra, which constituted an imminent threat to international peace and security,[258] actions in attacking the Covfefe[259] were proportionate.

Additionally, the death of the seven civilians on the military objective Covfefe was neither excessive given the military advantage gained, *i.e.*, checking the Ibra, nor needless as the Covfefe's failure to respond rendered Rukaruku's knowledge of the civilians on board impossible, where Rukaruku had fulfilled the precautionary obligation of carefulness.[260]

---

252 *Prosecutor v Kupreskic et al* (Judgment) [2000] ICTY-95-16-T-14 [524]; Jean-Marie Henckaerts, Louise Doswald-Beck, *Customary International Humanitarian Law* (Vol. 1, CUP 2005) 29.

253 *Prosecutor v Kupreskic et al* (n 252) [524].

254 *Oil Platforms* (n 75) [77].

255 *Facts* [46].

256 Gudmundur Helgason, 'Captured U-boats' (1997) <https://uboat.net/fates/captured.htm> accessed 11 January 2018.

257 *Legality of Nuclear Weapons* (n 124) [41]-[43].

258 *Facts* [Annex II] Preamble.

259 *Facts* [43].

260 API art 57(2)(c).

CONCLUSION AND PRAYER FOR RELIEF

In view of the facts set forth in this Memorial and the arguments applying the law to the facts as stated;

May it please the Court, on behalf of the Federal Republic of Rukaruku, Respondent herein, respectfully requests this Honorable Court to adjudge and declare that:

1. The arbitral award of 2 March 2017 is valid;
2. Even if the arbitral award is not valid, Rukaruku did not violate Article 6 of the FCN Treaty when the Egart operated in Anduchencan territorial sea, but Anduchenca violated Article 7 of the FCN Treaty by capturing the Egart, which it therefore must return to Rukaruku;
3. Anduchenca violated Article 16 of the FCN Treaty by commissioning and operating the Ibra; and
4. Rukaruku did not violate Article 17 of the FCN Treaty by attacking the Covfefe or by capturing the Ibra.

Respectfully submitted,

AGENTS FOR RUKARUKU

“Kayleff 牦牛案”

Case Concerning the Kayleff Yak
(The State of Aurok v The Republic of Rakkab)

杨一梁　李冰清　钟青萌　叶欧仪　陈然

请求国书状

Memorials for the State of Aurok

TABLE OF CONTENTS

III. THE HARVESTING OF THE YAK IN RAKKAB VIOLATES THE CULTURAL AND RELIGIOUS RIGHTS OF THE PEOPLE OF AUROK, AND RAKKAB MUST PROHIBIT SUCH HUNTING FORTHWITH.

A. AUROK HAS STANDING TO BRING THE CLAIM.

B. THE YAK HARVESTING IN RAKKAB VIOLATES AUROKANS' CULTURAL RIGHTS UNDER ICESCR.

i. ICESCR is extraterritorially applicable.

ii. The Yak harvesting in Rakkab violates Aurokans' right to participate in cultural life under Article 15 of ICESCR.

iii. The Yak harvesting in Rakkab is not validly justified.

C. RAKKAB VIOLATES AUROKANS' RELIGIOUS RIGHTS UNDER ARTICLE 18 OF ICCPR.

i. ICCPR is extraterritorially applicable.

ii. The Yak harvesting in Rakkab violates Aurokans' rights to manifest their religion under Article 18 of ICCPR.

iii. The Yak harvesting in Rakkab is not validly justified.

D. THE YAK HARVESTING IN RAKKAB VIOLATED AUROKANS' PARTICIPATORY RIGHTS AS INDIGENOUS PEOPLE.

i. Rakkab has extraterritorial obligations to respect Aurokans' indigenous rights under ILO No 169.

ii. Rakkab violates Aurokans' participatory rights.

E. RAKKAB MUST PROHIBIT THE YAK HARVESTING IN RAKKAB.

IV. RAKKAB MUST PAY AUROK A PORTION OF THE PROFITS REALIZED FROM SALES OF THE DRUG GALLVECTRA.

A. RAKKAB UTILIZED AUROKANS' KNOWLEDGE CONCERNING THE HEALTH BENEFITS OF CONSUMING THE YAK'S GALLBLADDER.

i. Aurokans' knowledge concerning the health benefits of consuming the Yak's gallbladder is traditional knowledge.

ii. Dr. Bello utilized Aurokans' traditional knowledge.

B. THE DEVELOPMENT OF GALLVECTRA WITHOUT COMPENSATION IS INCONSISTENT WITH INTERNATIONAL LAW.

i. Rakkab's utilization without benefit-sharing violates CBD and the Nagoya Protocol.

ii.Rakkab's utilization without benefit-sharing violates the Paris Convention.

C. RAKKAB SHOULD PAY THE PROFITS TO AUROK.

CONCLUSION AND PRAYER FOR RELIEF

STATEMENT OF JURISDICTION

The State of Aurok (Aurok), and the Republic of Rakkab (Rakkab) hereby submit the present dispute to the International Court of Justice (the Court) pursuant to Article 40(1) of the Court's Statute, in accordance with the *Compromis* for submission to the Court of the differences concerning the Kayleff Yak, signed in the Hague, The Netherlands, on the fourteenth day of September in the year two thousand eighteen. Both States have accepted the jurisdiction of this Court pursuant to Article 36(1) of its Statute.

QUESTIONS PRESENTED

The State of Aurok respectfully requests the Court to adjudge:

I.

1. Whether Rakkab is responsible for DORTA's actions attributable to it;

2. Whether Rakkab is responsible for its own failure to prevent DORTA from committing the wrongful acts.

II.

1. Whether the harvesting of the Yak constitutes a kind of taking under CMS;

2. Whether the harvesting of the Yak is justified by the exceptions of CMS;

3. Whether Rakkab bears the obligation to cease the harvesting of the Yak.

III.

1. Whether Aurok has standing to bring the claim;

2. Whether Rakkab has the obligations to respect and protect Aurokans' cultural and religious rights under ICCPR, ICESCR and ILO No 169;

3. Whether the harvesting of the Yak in Rakkab violates Aurokans' cultural and religious rights;

4. Whether the violation can be justified.

IV.

1. Whether Rakkab must share the profits realized from the selling of Gallvectra with Aurokans under the Nagoya Protocol;

2. Whether Rakkab must make the restitution by compensating Aurokans a portion of profits realized from the selling of Gallvectra under the Paris Convention;

3. Whether the profits should be paid to Aurok.

STATEMENT OF FACTS

The State of Aurok (Aurok), and the Republic of Rakkab (Rakkab), are neighboring countries on the Gaur Highlands (Gaur), the exclusive habitat of the Kayleff Yak (Yak) for more than 250,000 years. The Yak is a migratory species, born and staying in Aurok in (northern hemisphere) spring and summer, and in Rakkab in autumn and winter.

The Pivzao civilization (Pivzao) is a civilization arising in the Gaur relied upon subsistence hunting of the Yak, from which almost entirely Aurokan people descend. Traditional Yak hunting is a complex community event. People who participate in the kill are rewarded with a traditional dish called Tirhinga Nos Lustuk (soup of the nasty bits of the Yak), which not only symbolizes gratitude to the Yak but also is considered as conferring of health benefits and longevity according to the Pivzao traditions. To the present day, many Aurokans continue to observe those traditions, and the Yak remains of prime religious and cultural significance.

DORTA M/S (DORTA), whose predecessor is the Department of Research, Technology & Application of Rakkab, is a corporation registered under the laws of Rakkab, which is subsidized by Rakkab and possesses a legislatively-granted and government-enforced monopoly on the sale of prescription medication within Rakkab. A month after its privatization, DORTA began to publicly trade its shares on the New York Stock Exchange. As of the present date, Rakkab holds approximately 12% of DORTA's voting stock. And DORTA's 15-member Board of Directors includes four former Rakkabi Cabinet Ministers and three former leaders of Rakkab's major political parties. Besides, representatives of the government of Rakkab regularly meet with the CEO and senior executives of DORTA to discuss Rakkab's national priorities.

The Gallvectra is a medication derived from the Lustuk Enzyme, a key ingredient in Tirhinga Nos Lustuk, whose inventor is Dr. Bello, the employee of a DORTA-operated private hospital. On 11 November 2004, DORTA filed a patent application with the Rakkabi Intellectual Property Ministry for the Gallvectra, the Ministry granted it on 21 May 2006. As of 2018, DORTA has sold the Gallvectra in more than 85 countries and profited much from it.

In January 2005, an anthropologist Cressida Cauty, published an article in the international peer-reviewed sociology journal *Human Organization* and noted that through their consumption of Tirhinga Nos Lustuk, observant Aurokans ingested hundreds of grams of the Lustuk Enzyme each year.

In March 2005, the Aurokan Minister of Intellectual Property, Tom Wynet, wrote to his Rakkabi counterpart, emphasizing that the Aurokan people, rather than Dr. Bello, first discovered the health benefits of the Yak's gallbladders.

In April 2005, patent attorneys for DORTA replied to Minister Wynet's letter, stating that it was Dr. Bello who directly isolated the Lustuk Enzyme and the Aurokan people never produced a reliable, consistent prescription drug for human use.

In February 2016, the Brisbane-based *Courier Mail* published a lengthy investigative report, noting that in 2011, after DORTA's harvesting the number of Yak hunting license applications increased to more than 300, nearly all of which were granted; the number of licenses has increased every year since then in Rakkab. And according to this report, from October 2015 to February 2016, hunters killed nearly 30,000 Yak within the territory of Rakkab and delivered their gallbladders to DORTA.

In late February 2016, the Aurokan Parliament enacted a bill to fund Yak research, emphasizing developing successful breeding methods for Yak in captivity. Besides, the Parliament also legislated a five-year moratorium on the hunting of female Yak of breeding age.

In March 2016, DORTA announced that it was initiating a captive breeding program of its own. However, it has not met with any success.

In June 2016, the Yak Life Sciences Academy (YLSA), an international NGO, concluded in its 2016 report that the total Kayleff Yak population had decreased by more than five percent since June 2015 and the only possible reason was DORTA's sponsored harvesting of the herd within Rakkab. Following the release of YLSA report, the Aurokan Prime Minister Sumun issued a statement depicting DORTA Yak harvest as 'a danger to Aurokan culture'.

In the spring of 2016, Aurokan villagers throughout the country also described a significant decline in the size of Yak herds. And in a nationwide survey, YLSA reported that townspeople in Aurok were seeing herd sizes notably smaller than that in 2010.

On 2 October 2016, the Aurokan Prime Minister Sumun visited Rakkab to discuss the issue of the Yak with Rakkabi Prime Minister Derlap Frangie and with DORTA CEO Ms. Alexander. Rakkabi Prime Minister Frangie expressed his confidence that 'DORTA will act responsibly to conserve this vital cultural and health resource' .

On 16 November 2016, the Rakkabi Ministry of Agriculture released on all major digital platforms an application called 'YakTrakker'. Although according to the YLSA, it was also used by Yak hunters to hunt the herds more efficiently, Rakkab made no reply, and the YakTrakker app remains in operation and available for download to the present day.

In March 2017, Gallvectra was added to the WHO Model List of Essential Medicines. Rakkab welcomed the decision. However, the Aurokan Minister of Health criticized the decision, stating that the Aurokan people were the ones who discovered Gallvectra and that they were harmed by the irresponsible harvesting.

On 29 September 2017, the Yak was included in Appendix III of the Convention on International Trade in Endangered Species of Wild Fauna and Flora (CITES).

On 19 September 2017, the Aurokan Prime Minister Sumun addressed to the United Nations General Assembly. She concluded that the extinction of the Yak would lead to the end of Aurokan life.

On 5 October 2017, Prime Ministers Sumun and Frangie met in Transcentral. Prime Minister Sumun presented her counterpart a demarche demanding that the DORTA-sponsored Yak harvest cease, and that the Rakkabi government 'pay Aurok and the Aurokan people their rightful share of the profits that DORTA has made from the Aurokan people's traditions, and from their ancestors' knowledge of which they are the current custodians.'

In October 2017, the Yak was included in Appendix I of the Convention on Migratory Species (CMS).

On 15 November 2017, the Rakkabi Ministry of Agriculture promulgated Regulation AG/2017-0300 to regulate the Yak harvesting. After the promulgation, DORTA promptly announced that it was suspending its payments for Yak gallbladders until it received a license.

On 20 December 2017, DORTA was granted a Yak hunting license by the Ministry of Agriculture, only 28 days after its application. And the numerical limitation on the Yak hunting is the same as before, 30,000. Later, the Aurokan Ambassador in Rakkab sent a formal diplomatic note to the Foreign Ministry, protesting the issuance of the license as 'plainly a violation of CMS'.

On 2 January 2018, DORTA publicly announced that it was again offering payment for Yak gallbladders, but only to registered agents of the company. YLSA's annual survey indicated that DORTA agents killed approximately 28,500 Yak during January and February 2018.

SUMMARY OF PLEADINGS

FIRST PLEADING

Rakkab is responsible for the internationally wrongful acts *infra*. The acts of DORTA should be attributed to Rakkab since DORTA is empowered by Rakkab to exercise governmental authority. Alternatively, DORTA is acting under the effective control of Rakkab in carrying out the conducts. In any event, Rakkab is responsible for its own failure to prevent DORTA from committing the wrongful acts. Rakkab fails to undertake its obligation to prevent damage to the environment of Aurok and fails to observe due diligence to prevent the transboundary damage.

SECOND PLEADING

The harvesting of the Yak in Rakkab violates Rakkab's international obligations to protect endangered species and the environment under CMS. Rakkab is obliged to prohibit the taking of the Yak since the Yak was included in Appendix I of CMS, to which Rakkab is a Party. The Yak harvesting in Rakkab constitutes a taking. Such taking is not under the exceptions of Article III(5) of CMS since it is not for scientific purposes, does not satisfy extraordinary circumstances and does not satisfy the restrictions of exception. Therefore, Rakkab must end the Yak harvesting on its territory under its obligation to cease continuing internationally wrongful acts.

THIRD PLEADING

The harvesting of the Yak in Rakkab violates the cultural and religious rights of the people of Aurok. Rakkab has extraterritorial obligations to respect Aurokans' right to participate in cultural life, right to manifest religion and participatory rights under Article 15(1)(a) of the International Covenant on Economic Social and Cultural Rights (ICESCR), Article 18(1) of the International Covenant on Civil and Political Rights (ICCPR) and Articles 6 and 7 of the International Labor Organization's Convention concerning Indigenous and Tribal Peoples in Independent Countries (ILO No 169). The Yak harvesting in Rakkab violates Aurokans' cultural, religious and participatory rights given the interference with Aurokans' access to the Yak, the potential extinction of the Yak and Rakkab's failure to consult Aurokans effectively in advance. The violations cannot be justified under Article 4 of ICESCR or Article 18(3) of ICCPR. Therefore, Rakkab is under the obligation to prohibit such harvesting.

FOURTH PLEADING

Rakkab must pay Aurok a portion of the profits realized from sales of the drug Gallvectra. Rakkab has the benefit sharing obligation under the Convention of Biological Diversity (CBD) and the Nagoya Protocol on Access to Genetic Resources and the Fair and Equitable Sharing of Benefits Arising from Their Utilization to the Convention on Biological Diversity (the Nagoya Protocol). Aurokans' knowledge concerning the health benefits of consuming Yak's gallbladder is traditional knowledge. Dr. Bello appropriated and exploited the traditional knowledge since it made substantial contribution to the research and development of Gallvectra. Alternatively, Rakkab must return the profits to Aurokans under the principle of unjust enrichment since Rakkab benefited from Aurokans' traditional knowledge at Aurokans' expense without just factors.

PLEADINGS

I. THE ACTS OF DORTA SHOULD BE ATTRIBUTED TO RAKKAB AND RAKKAB HAS THE RESPONSIBILITY TO PREVENT THE ALLEGED ACTS.

A. DORTA'S ACTIONS ARE ATTRIBUTABLE TO RAKKAB.

DORTA's actions are attributable to Rakkab since DORTA is empowered by Rakkab to exercise governmental authority [i] or DORTA is acting under the effective control of Rakkab [ii].

i. DORTA is empowered by Rakkab to exercise governmental authority.

The conduct of an entity empowered by the law of a State to exercise governmental authority shall be attributable to that State.[1] Such empowerment requires the entity to exercise specified functions which are akin to those normally exercised by organs of the State[2] and the functions can refer to a public function usually reserved to the State.[3] Besides, the scope of a public function relies on 'the particular society, and its history and traditions'.[4]

In Rakkab, until 1996, pharmaceutical research, production and distribution were State functions exercised by the State's Department of Research, Technology and Application.[5] DORTA was privatized from the State's Department[6] and it preserves a 'legislatively-granted and government-enforced monopoly'[7] on the sales of prescription medicine, maintaining the same function as its predecessor's. Therefore,

1 International Law Commission (ILC) 'Draft Articles on Responsibility of States for Internationally Wrongful Acts, with Commentaries' (2001) UN Doc A/56/10 (ARSIWA) art 5.

2 ARSIWA (n 1) art 5 Commentary [2].

3 *Maffezini v Spain* (Award) [2000] ICSID Case No ARB/97/07 [48][57]; *Salini v Morocco* (Decision on Jurisdiction) [2001] ICSID Case No ARB/00/4 [33].

4 ARSIWA (n 1) art 5 Commentary [6].

5 *Compromis* [9].

6 *Compromis* [10].

7 *Compromis* [11].

in the Rakkabi context, DORTA is exercising an element of governmental authority when it hunts the Yak because this activity is an integral part of DORTA's healthcare/pharmaceutical activities. Accordingly, the hunting of Yak can be attributed to Rakkab in these circumstances.

ii. DORTA is acting under the effective control of Rakkab in carrying out the alleged acts.

A State should be responsible for the conduct carried out by an entity which is on the instructions of, or under the direction or the control of that State.[8] These three tests are not cumulative but rather disjunctive.[9] Therefore, actions will be attributed to a State when the entity is under the control of that State.

In *Nicaragua* case, the Court adopted the standard of 'effective control', which requires the State to direct or enforce the perpetration of the acts.[10] The State must have exercised control on specific operation and the conduct complained of should have been an integral part of that operation.[11] In determining whether the control over cooperation is specific and integral or not, factors like government ownership, government presence on the board of directors[12] and specific government control[13] are considered in judicial practices.[14]

---

8 ARSIWA (n 1) art 8.

9 ARSIWA (n 1) art 8 Commentary [7]; Antonio Cassese, 'The Nicaragua and Tadić Tests Revisited in Light of the ICJ Judgment on Genocide in Bosnia' (2007) 18 *European Journal of International Law* 649, 650.

10 *Military and Paramilitary Activities in and against Nicaragua* (Nicaragua v United States of America) (Merits) [1986] ICJ Rep 14 [115].

11 ARSIWA (n 1) art 8 Commentary (3); *Application of the Convention on the Prevention and Punishment of the Crime of Genocide* (Bosnia and Herzegovina v Serbia and Montenegro) (Judgment) [2007] ICJ Rep 43 [401].

12 United States-Definitive Anti-Dumping and Countervailing Duties on Certain Products from China [2011] WTO WT/DS379/AB/R [343].

13 *Leo Hertzberg et al v Finland* [1985] Communication No R14/61 para 9.1.

14 *Foremost Tehran, Inc v The Government of the Islamic Republic of Iran* [1986] Iran-US Claims Tribunal (Vol. 10) 228; *American Bell International Inc v The Islamic Republic of Iran* [1986] Iran-US Claims Tribunal (Vol. 10) 170.

First, as a company privatized by legislation, the Rakkabi government still owns 12% of the voting shares in accordance with DORTA's private Charter.[15] Considering that DORTA is a quoted company on the New York Stock Exchange, 12% of the shares occupy the position of controlling shares.[16] Besides, the harvesting licenses have been kept issuing to DORTA,[17] without which, DORTA couldn't continue marketing and selling Gallvectra to the present day.[18] Therefore, Rakkab's control over DORTA is indispensable.

Second, in the present case of DORTA, 7 out of the 15 board members are former senior government officials,[19] remaining regular discussion on Rakkab's national priorities with government representatives,[20] making DORTA's actions impossible to get rid of Rakkab's specific instructions. Apart from providing subsidies for DORTA's research and development activities,[21] Rakkab keeps granting licenses to each hunter employed by DORTA.[22] 'YakTrakker' released by Rakkabi Ministry of Agriculture is another evidence in proving its specific operation on DORTA's harvesting[23] because it would effectively provide operational support to Yak hunters.[24]

Thus, Rakkab's control over DORTA satisfied the degree of 'effective control' and hence Rakkab is responsible for DORTA's actions.

B. RAKKAB IS RESPONSIBLE FOR ITS OWN FAILURE TO PREVENT DORTA FROM COMMITTING THE WRONGFUL ACTS.

Rakkab is responsible for its own failure to prevent DORTA from committing the wrongful acts because Rakkab fails to undertake its obligation to prevent damage

15 *Compromis* [10].

16 *Compromis* [10].

17 *Compromis* [23] [44].

18 *Clarifications* [5].

19 *Compromis* [11].

20 *Clarifications* [4].

21 *Compromis* [11].

22 *Compromis* [23].

23 *Compromis* [34].

24 *Compromis* [35].

to the environment of other States [i] and Rakkab fails to fulfill its due diligence [ii]. Further, Rakkab's obligation under the other international conventions will be demonstrated in Pleadings II-IV.

i. Rakkab fails to undertake its obligation to prevent damage to the environment of other States.

The Principle[25] that has been recognized as a customary international law[26] requires the State not to knowingly allow its territory[27] and jurisdiction[28] to be used for activities which would cause damage[29] to other States.[30]

a. The damage to Yaks is significant.

Transboundary damage suffered by States should be serious[31] or significant,[32] and it should lead to a real detrimental effect on the property or the environment in other States.[33] The damage can be measured by size, location, and effect of the activity in order to determine whether it is significant.[34]

Scientists from the non-governmental organization YLSA concluded in 2016 that the

---

25 *Certain Activities Carried out by Nicaragua in the Border Area* (Costa Rica v Nicaragua) and *Construction of a Road in Costa Rica Along the San Juan River* (Nicaragua v Costa Rica) (Judgment) [2015] ICJ Rep 665 [104].

26 *Pulp Mills on the River Uruguay* (Argentina v Uruguay) (Judgment) [2010] ICJ Rep 14 [101].

27 *Corfu Channel case* (United Kingdom v Albania) (Merits) [1949] ICJ Rep 4, 22.

28 Rio Declaration on Environment and Development (adopted 14 June 1992) ILM 874 (Rio Declaration) art 2.

29 *Environment and Human Rights* (Advisory Opinion) [2017] IACHR No Oc-23/17 art III(a).

30 Convention on Biological Diversity (adopted 5 June 1992, entered into force 29 December 1993) 30619 UNTS 1760 (CBD) art 3.

31 *Trail Smelter case* (US v Canada) [1938/1941] 3 RIAA 1906, 1965.

32 Hanqin Xue, *Transboundary Damage in International Law* (CUP 2003) 8; *Trail Smelter* (n 31) 1965.

33 ILC 'Draft Articles on Prevention of Transboundary Harm from Hazardous Activities, Commentaries' (2001) UN Doc A/56/10 152-153.

34 UN Economic Commission for Europe 'Convention on Environmental Impact Assessment in a Transboundary Context' (2001) UN Doc A/56/10 (Espoo Convention) Appendix III.

Yak population was down nearly 10 percent from two years ago,[35] and Yak's herd size was notably smaller than that in 2010.[36] Besides, the damage to Yak is significant as it was included in Appendix I of CMS on the recommendation of CMS Scientific Council.[37] Based on subsequent annual surveys of YLSA,[38] it is estimated that the Yak will be extinct by 2040. In addition, since Yaks migrate to Rakkab during the mating season,[39] DORTA's hunting behavior would bring a negative impact on the young and female groups, which is also in line with YLSA's report.[40]

b. The damage can be proved by clear and convincing evidence.

The serious injury should be established by clear and convincing evidence.[41] In order to prove the significance of damages, a series of evidence is corroborated together and leads to a logical conclusion.[42]

First, YLSA is an independent organization, and its reports have weighty value since they were not prepared for litigation.[43] Reports covering different times[44] and scales[45] lead to the same conclusion that the damage to the Yak is significant.[46] Besides, consistent press releases would contribute to the existence of such damage.[47] As the article released by *Courier Mail* was widely distributed on the Internet and on social media,[48] it has formed public knowledge worldwide and contributed to the facts of the

35 *Compromis* [36].
36 *Compromis* [29].
37 *Compromis* [43].
38 *Compromis* [28].
39 *Compromis* [1].
40 *Compromis* [27].
41 *Trail Smelter* (n 31) 1965; *Ethiopia's Damages Claims* (Eritrea v Ethiopia) [2009] 26 RIAA 631 [35].
42 *Corfu Channel* (n 27) 18.
43 *Ethiopia's Damages Claims* (n 41) [36].
44 *Compromis* [28].
45 *Compromis* [29].
46 *Compromis* [27].
47 *United States Diplomatic and Consular Staff in Tehran* (United States v Iran) (Judgment) [1980] ICJ Rep 3 [13].
48 *Compromis* [24].

damage on the Yak,[49] which should be weighed heavily.[50]

In addition, CMS would incorporate a species when it is threatened with danger under the recommendation of Scientific Council.[51] Yak's inclusion further proves the damage is serious.[52] Therefore, the damage to the Yak is significant and it can be proved by clear and convincing evidence.

c. The damage is caused by DORTA's harvesting.

Causation is understood as the process of connecting an act with an outcome as cause and effect.[53] In the *San Juan River* case, sufficiency, proximity and interference factors are considered by the Court when building up the causal link,[54] which is also echoed with the standard of ILC.[55]

With the introduction of modern weapons to DORTA's harvesting,[56] roughly 5 percent of Yak was killed within a limited time, especially among females of breeding age.[57] This kind of hunting mode is detrimental to the Yak population since it doesn't fit the Yak's reproduction rate comparing with what Aurokan cultural practices have evolved after a millennia coexistence with the Yak.[58] According to YLSA's reports in 2016, the decrease of Yak is not attributable to natural causes but instead, it is a consequence of DORTA-sponsored harvesting.[59] Therefore it can be sufficiently concluded that the damage is caused by DORTA's harvesting.

---

49 *Tehran* (n 47) [12].

50 *Nicaragua case* (n 10) [63]; *Tehran* (n 47) [12].

51 Convention on the Conservation of Migratory Species of Wild Animals (adopted 23 June 1979, entered into force 1 November 1983) 1651 UNTS 333 (CMS) art III(1).

52 *Compromis* [28].

53 Ilias Plakokefalos, 'Causation in the Law of State Responsibility and the Problem of Overdetermination' (2015) 26 *European Journal of International Law* 471, 472.

54 See Generally *Border Area* (n 25).

55 ARSIWA (n 1) art 31 Commentary [10].

56 *Compromis* [24].

57 *Compromis* [36].

58 *Compromis* [27].

59 *Compromis* [27].

ii. Rakkab fails to observe due diligence to prevent the damage.

The principle of prevention, as a customary rule, has its origins in the due diligence required of a State in its territory.[60] Due diligence requests States not only to take rules and measures, but also adopt certain vigilance in their enforcement and exercise.[61] The standard of due diligence should be appropriate and proportional to the degree of risk of transboundary harm.[62]

a. Rakkab fails to carry out a preliminary assessment of the risk.

Preliminary assessment should be carried out in determining the existence of risk.[63] The risk can be measured by the nature and magnitude of the project and the context in which the conduct was to be carried out.[64] In *San Juan River* case, a State should adduce evidence to prove that it has carried out such preliminary assessment.[65]

In the present case, DORTA's pharmaceutical project would lethally exploit a large amount of Yak,[66] and due to its effectiveness in the treatment of diabetes and related disorders,[67] the potential market would be immense.[68] However, Rakkab only submitted the experts' assertion,[69] instead of study or report on the risk of harvesting,[70] which is insufficient to prove that a preliminary assessment has been carried out.

b. Rakkab fails to carry out an EIA in advance.

As the Court noted in *Pulp Mills* case, it may now be considered a general international law to undertake an environmental impact assessment (EIA)[71] where

---

60 *Pulp Mills* (n 26) [101]; *Gabčikovo-Nagymaros Project* (Hungary/Slovakia) (Judgment) [1997] ICJ Rep 7 [140]; Xue (n 32) 163.

61 *Pulp Mills* (n 26) [97]; *Enviroment and Human Rights* (n 29) art III(b).

62 ILC Hazardous Activities (n 33) art 3(11) 152-153.

63 *San Juan River* (n 25) [154].

64 *San Juan River* (n 25) [155].

65 *San Juan River* (n 25) [154].

66 *Compromis* [24].

67 *Compromis* [14].

68 *Compromis* [20].

69 *Compromis* [33].

70 *Border Area* (n 25) [105].

71 *Pulp Mills* (n 26) [204].

certain activities have risks of significant adverse impact[72] in a transboundary context,[73] and it should be conducted prior to the decision.[74]

The harvesting required an EIA because it has the risk of significant transboundary damage.[75] However, Rakkab didn't conduct an EIA until October 2017 as part of the administrative rule-making process.[76] Its overdue action in carrying out an EIA in October 2017 violated its procedural obligation under customary international law.[77]

c. Rakkab failed to continuously monitor the effects of its conduct.

The obligation to carry out EIA is a continuous one.[78] The Court states in *Pulp Mill* case that continuous monitoring of its effects on the environment shall be undertaken throughout the project.[79]

Rakkab mentioned the impact of continued hunting of Yak in its first EIA only and didn't make further monitoring.[80] Although Rakkabi Prime Minister Frangie promised to monitor the issue,[81] it didn't communicate any action consistent with its assessment to keep monitoring the adverse effects of the harvesting.

d. Rakkab failed to negotiate with Aurok in good faith.

Consultations and negotiations[82] should be conducted in good faith[83] when States

---

72 CBD art 14(1) (a).

73 *Border Area* (n 25) [104].

74 *Pulp Mills* (n 26) [205].

75 See Section I B i a.

76 *Clarifications* [7].

77 *Pulp Mills* (n 26) [204].

78 *San Juan River* (n 25) [161].

79 *Pulp Mills* (n 26) [205].

80 *Clarifications* [7].

81 *Compromis* [31].

82 CBD art 14(1)(c).

83 Convention on the Law of the Non-navigational Uses of International Watercourses (adopted 21 May 1997) 36 ILM 700 art 17.

failed to reachan agreement[84] towards the project. It must be genuine and must not be merely going through a formal process,[85] neither of the Parties should insist upon their own position without contemplating any modification of it.[86] Bad faith includes abnormal delay or systematic refusals to take into consideration adverse proposals or interests.[87]

In the present case, Aurok tried to communicate with Rakkab by sending an official letter early in 2005,[88] but Rakkab didn't make any response to the letter, the only response was made by DORTA's patent attorneys,[89] who are not the counterpart of the Aurokan Minister of Intellectual Property.[90] Besides, Aurok conducted two meetings with Rakkab respectively in 2016 and 2017, but Aurok's concerns were ignored and denied by Rakkabi Prime Minister Frangie and DORTA's CEO.[91] In addition, Aurok had made a concession by legislating a five-year moratorium on the hunting of female Yak of breeding age in 2016,[92] but in contrary, the Regulation promulgated by Rakkab didn't make any substantial change to show good faith.[93]

e. Rakkab fails to adopt or enforce appropriate rules.

DORTA was granted the patent in 2006[94] and began its pharmaceutical business early in 2011.[95] Being well aware that the harvesting has given rise to and has caused certain damages to other States,[96] especially to the Yak population[97] and Aurokan

84 ILC 'International Liability for Injurious Consequences Arising out of Acts Not Prohibited by International Law' (2002) UN Doc A/CN4/SERA/2002/Add1 art 9(3).

85 *Lake Lanoux case* (Spain v France) [1957] 12 RIAA 281, 15-16.

86 *North Sea Continental Shelf* (Federal Republic of Germany v Denmark) (Judgment) [1969] ICJ Rep 3 [85].

87 *Lake Lanoux case* (n 85) 23; *Tacna-Arica Question* (Chile, Peru) [1925] 2 RIAA 921, 933.

88 *Compromis* [17].

89 *Compromis* [18].

90 *Compromis* [17].

91 *Compromis* [31] [42].

92 *Compromis* [25].

93 *Compromis* [45].

94 *Correction* [1]; *Compromis* [19].

95 *Compromis* [20].

96 *Compromis* [31].

97 *Compromis* [36].

traditions,[98] Rakkab did nothing to prevent it but rather supported the harvesting through subsidies.[99] Considering the significant damage, Rakkab's failure to perform duties of prevention entails State responsibility.[100]

II. THE HARVESTING OF THE YAK IN RAKKAB VIOLATES ITS INTERNATIONAL OBLIGATIONS TO PROTECT ENDANGERED SPECIES AND THE ENVIRONMENT, AND RAKKAB IS OBLIGATED TO END YAK HARVESTING.

Rakkab has violated the substantive obligation to protect endangered species and the environment endowed by CMS, especially the obligation under Article III [A], and its violation cannot be justified [B].

A. THE HARVESTING OF THE YAK VIOLATES ITS OBLIGATION UNDER CMS.

Article III strengthens that Parties shall prohibit the taking of animals belonging to species included in Appendix I.[101] 'Taking' means taking, hunting, fishing, capturing, harassing, deliberate killing, or attempting to engage in any such conduct.[102] The harvesting of the Yak constitutes a kind of taking because it would lethally hunt the Yak. Since the Yak was included in Appendix I of CMS in October 2017 without reservation of Rakkab,[103] Rakkab is obliged to prohibit the harvesting of the Yak.

B. THE HARVESTING IS NOT JUSTIFIED BY THE EXCEPTIONS OF ARTICLE III (5) OF CMS.

Species listed in Appendix I shall be prohibited to take unless taking falls in the exceptions listed in Article III (5).[104]

98 *Compromis* [41].

99 *Compromis* [11].

100 ILC International Liability (n 84) 443.

101 CMS art III (5).

102 CMS art I (1) (i).

103 *Compromis* [43].

104 CMS art III (5).

i. The harvesting is not for scientific purposes.

Two elements are determinative in deciding whether an act is in accordance with the purpose of scientific research—the exploitation should foster scientific knowledge and should be sustainable.[105]

Although research on a synthetic alternative to the Lustuk Enzyme is a kind of scientific practice,[106] hardly any output was seen through the whole project of harvesting.[107] Besides, for most parameters of scientific research, the sample sizes calculated are in the range of 800-1,000 animals, as the Court noted in the *Whaling* case.[108] In contrary, the hunting consisting of 30,000 of Yak annually largely exceeds that number,[109] since DORTA didn't come up with sustainable alternatives other than lethal method as well,[110] the harvesting of the Yak conducted by DORTA is unsustainable.

Therefore, since the selling of Gallvectra would yield lucrative profits, the harvesting of the Yak is for the development and manufacture of Gallvectra, instead of for the purpose of scientific research because it doesn't foster scientific knowledge or use the Yak sustainably.

ii. The harvesting doesn't satisfy extraordinary circumstances.

Only when extraordinary circumstances so require would taking be excepted from prohibition.[111] Extraordinary circumstances require cases of accidental taking when all means to reduce incidental taking have been demonstrably employed.[112] 'So require' indicates a complete absence of reasonable alternatives.[113]

---

105 *Whaling in the Antarctic* (Australia v Japan: New Zealand intervening) (Judgment) [2014] ICJ Rep 226 [58].

106 *Compromis* [33].

107 *Whaling* (n 105) [219].

108 *Whaling* (n 105) [182].

109 *Compromis* [24].

110 *Whaling* (n 105) [83].

111 CMS art III (5) (d).

112 'Interpretation of Certain Terms Used in the Convention' (1997) UNEP/CMS/CONF 5.16.

113 Arie Trouwborst, 'Aussie Jaws and International Laws: The Australian Shark Cull and the Convention on Migratory Species' (2014) 2 *Cornell International Law Journal Online* 41, 44.

In the present case, the harvesting is on purpose and it is beyond the scope of 'accidental' since DORTA consciously pursued patent and license for its activities.[114] Neither DORTA nor Rakkab observes due diligence in reducing incidental taking since alternative approaches other than lethal method are ignored in the harvesting.[115] Moreover, 'Gallvectra' is not the only option since other alternative essential medicines, including Gliclazide or Glucagon, are also effective in treating diabetes and other lifestyle-related diseases as well.[116] Therefore, the harvesting of the Yak doesn't satisfy extraordinary circumstances.

iii. The harvesting doesn't satisfy the restrictions of the exception.

Exceptions may be made provided that such exceptions are precise as to content and limited in space and time, and such taking should not operate to the disadvantage of the species.[117] Based on the textual interpretation, 'disadvantage' means a condition or situation that causes problems.[118]

However, the harvesting does operate to the disadvantage of the species since it causes significant decrease on Yak population.[119] Therefore, the harvesting doesn't satisfy the restrictions of exceptions as well and Rakkab fails to prevent the harvesting of the Yak.

C. RAKKAB HAS AN OBLIGATION TO CEASE THE HARVESTING.

The internationally wrongful act is under obligation to cease if the wrongful act has a continuing character[120] and that the violated rule is still in force.[121] Rakkab's obligations are continuing since those conventions and customary international laws are still in force till today. Besides, DORTA continues marketing and selling

114 *Compromis* [20][45].

115 *Compromis* [46].

116 WHO 'Model List of Essential Medicines 20th List' (March 2017) 41, section 18.5.

117 CMS art III (5) (d).

118 Trouwborst (n 113) 43.

119 See Section I B b i a.

120 ARSIWA (n 1) art 14 Commentary [5].

121 *Rainbow Warrior case* (New Zealand v France) [1986] 19 RIAA 199 [114].

Gallvectra to the present day,[122] indicating that Rakkab constantly breaches its obligations. Therefore, the harvesting should cease.

III. THE HARVESTING OF THE YAK IN RAKKAB VIOLATES THE CULTURAL AND RELIGIOUS RIGHTS OF THE PEOPLE OF AUROK, AND RAKKAB MUST PROHIBIT SUCH HUNTING FORTHWITH.

A. AUROK HAS STANDING TO BRING THE CLAIM.

The State of nationality is entitled to exercise diplomatic protection of its national injured by another State if the injured national has exhausted all local remedies.[123] The Aurokan village leaders had filed a civil suit in Rakkab against such harvesting, alleging the violation of their cultural and religious rights in 2017.[124] Local remedies have been exhausted since Aurokans' claim was dismissed and no further review was available.[125] Therefore, Aurok has standing to bring the claim before the Court.

B. THE YAK HARVESTING IN RAKKAB VIOLATES AUROKANS' CULTURAL RIGHTS UNDER ICESCR.

i. ICESCR is extraterritorially applicable.

A treaty can apply extraterritorially if it does not contain territorial or jurisdictional restriction.[126] In *Georgia v Russia Federation* case, the Court held that the provisions of International Convention on the Elimination of All Forms of Racial Discrimination (CERD), which do not contain 'a specific territorial restriction', applied to the Russian forces in Georgia.[127] Regarding ICESCR, only Article 14, regulating the education right, has reference to 'territory' and 'jurisdiction'.[128] This indicates that

---

122 *Clarifications* [5].

123 ILC 'Draft Articles on Diplomatic Protection' (2006) UN Doc A/61/10 arts 3, 14; *Nottebohm case* (Liechtenstein v Guatemala)(Judgment) [1955] ICJ Rep 4, 24; *Thompson v Panama* [1994] UNHRC UN Doc CCPR/C/52/D/438/1990 para 5.2.

124 *Clarifications* [3].

125 *Clarifications* [3].

126 *Application of the International Convention on the Elimination of All Forms of Racial Discrimination* (Georgia v Russian Federation) (Order) [2008] ICJ Rep 353 [109].

127 *Georgia v Russian Federation* (n 126) [109].

128 International Covenant on Economic Social and Cultural Rights (adopted 16 December 1966, entry into force 3 January 1976) 993 UNTS 3 (ICESCR) art 14.

other provisions of ICESCR, including Article 15, shall apply extraterritorially.[129]

The extraterritorial obligations require State Parties to refrain from interfering with the enjoyment of human rights of persons outside their territory,[130] and prevent corporations, over which they can exercise control, from committing such infringements.[131] States may seek to regulate corporations which are incorporated under their laws or have principal place of business on their national territories.[132] DORTA is under Rakkab's control since DORTA is registered in Rakkab and carries out its main business activities there.[133] Therefore, Rakkab has the obligations to respect Aurokans' rights under ICESCR and prevent DORTA's human rights violations.

ii. The Yak harvesting in Rakkab violates Aurokans' right to participate in cultural life under Article 15 of ICESCR.

a. Aurokans' Yak harvesting and associated activities fall within the scope of 'cultural life'.

Article 15 (1)(a) of ICESCR protects individuals' rights to take part in cultural life.[134] Culture in this sense means 'the sum total of the material and spiritual activities and products of a given social group'[135] that distinguish the group from others.[136]

---

129 *Georgia v Russian Federation* (n 126) [109].

130 Committee on Economic, Social and Cultural Rights (CESCR) 'General Comment No 24 on State Obligations under the International Covenant on Economic, Social and Cultural Rights in the Context of Business Activities' (10 August 2017) UN Doc E/C12/GC/24 [29].

131 General Comment 24 (n 130) [30]; UN Committee on the Elimination of Racial Discrimination (CERD) 'Concluding Observations of the Committee: Canada' (2012) UN Doc CERD/C/CAN/CO/19-20 [14].

132 General Comment 24 (n 130) [31]; Committee on the Rights of the Child (CRC) 'General Comment No 16 on State Obligations Regarding the Impact of the Business Sector on Children's Rights' (2013) UN Doc CRC/C/GC/16 [46]; Observations of Canada (n 131) [14].

133 *Compromis* [10].

134 ICESCR art 15(1)(a).

135 CESCR 'General Comment No 21: Right of Everyone to Take Part in Cultural Life' (2009) UN Doc E/C12/GC/21 [10].

136 *Centre for Minority Rights Development (Kenya) and Minority Rights Group (on behalf of Endoro is Welfare Council) v Kenya* [2003] ACHPR 276/03 (Endorois) [241].

Specifically, culture encompasses ways of life,[137] ceremonies and traditions.[138]

The Yak harvesting constitutes Aurokans' unique way of life, as Aurokans rely upon it for virtually every aspect of their life.[139] The Yak hunting and associated activities are cultural ceremonies reflecting Aurokans' worldview.[140] Therefore, these activities are under the protection of ICESCR and Aurokans have the rights to practice them freely.

b. The Yak harvesting in Rakkab causes substantial adverse impact to Aurokans' cultural rights.

Violation occurs when the alleged violating activities, including the approved future activities, cause a substantial adverse impact to the cultural rights.[141] To take part in cultural life requires accessibility to follow a way of life associated with the use of natural resources.[142] Assessment of violation is made regarding the tie between the culture and the natural resources[143] as well as the magnitude (size[144] and time[145]) of the activity.

First, there is a close tie between Aurokans' cultural life and the Yak harvesting. Aurokans' cultural practices have evolved to fit the migration and number of the Yaks,[146] which is manifested by Aurokans' special calendar based upon the animals' regular migration and the central festivals coordinated with Yaks' movement.[147]

---

137 *Yanner v Eaton* (1999) High Court of Australia (HCA) 53, 258; *Moiwana Village v Suriname* (Judgment) [2005] IACHR Series C No 124 [98] [103]; Human Rights Committee (HRC) 'General Comment No 23: Article 27 (Rights of Minorities)' (1994) UN Doc CCPR/C/21/Rev1/Add5 [7].

138 General Comment 21 (n 135) [13].

139 *Compromis* [2].

140 *Compromis* [2].

141 *Länsman v Finland* (Länsman No 671/95) [1996] UN Doc CCPR/C/58/D/671/1995 para 10.1; *Länsman et al v Finland* (Länsman No 511/92) [1994] UN Doc CCPR/C/52/D/511/1992 para 9.1.

142 Comment 21 (n 135) [15 (c)].

143 *African Commission on Human and People's Rights v Republic of Kenya* (*Ogiek case*) (Judgment) [2017] ACHPR Application No 006/2012[164]; General Comment 21 (n 135) [36].

144 *Länsman* No 511/92 (n 141) paras 9.7, 9.8; *Länsman* No 671/95 (n 141) para 10.6.

145 *Länsman* No 511/92 (n 141) para 9.5.

146 *Compromis* [27].

147 *Compromis* [2].

This indicates that any interference with access to the Yak would cause considerable repercussion on the enjoyment of Aurokans' culture.[148]

Second, the magnitude of the Yak harvesting in Rakkab is substantial. Nearly 30,000 Yaks were killed annually since 2015[149] in their mating season in Rakkab,[150] which made it hard for their number to recover. The harvesting has caused a visible decline of the Yak herds' size in Aurok.[151]

The Yak harvesting in Rakkab to the present date has deprived young Aurokans in the North of the opportunities to participate in the Yak hunting, which greatly disrupted their lives.[152] Regarding future activities, Rakkab's approval for DORTA to hunt 30,000 Yaks annually will generate Yak's extinction according to YLSA's report.[153] Yak's extinction would completely deprive Aurokans of access to the Yak, making their culture baseless and generating serious repercussion on their enjoyment of their culture.

In conclusion, the adverse impact on Aurokans' cultural rights brought by the Yak harvesting in Rakkab amounts to the level of violation.

c. Rakkab did not prevent DORTA's Yak harvesting.

Rakkab's extraterritorial obligations also require it to adopt legislative, administrative, as well as other appropriate measures to prevent DORTA's interfering activities.[154] There is no evidence indicating that Rakkab has taken measures to require DORTA to respect Aurokans' culture. On the contrary, Rakkab granted DORTA to harvest the 30,000 Yaks annually, which would cause Yak's extinction.[155]

---

148 *Ogie kcase* (n 143) [164].

149 *Compromis* [27] [36] [46].

150 *Compromis* [1].

151 *Compromis* [36].

152 *Compromis* [41].

153 *Compromis* [27].

154 General Comment 24 (n 130) [14].

155 *Compromis* [41] [45].

iii. The Yak harvesting in Rakkab is not validly justified.

Pursuant to Article 4 of ICESCR, the limitation to rights must be determined by law, be compatible with the nature of the rights and solely for the purpose of promoting the general welfare in a democratic society.[156]

First, there is no law regulating such limitation. The law shall be implemented by competent authorities.[157] Regulation AG/2017-0300 was promulgated by the Ministry of Agriculture, which is not a competent authority to limit people's cultural rights.[158] Further, the Regulation only regulates the license to harvest Yak but not the number of Yak that can be harvested.[159]

Second, the Yak harvesting in Rakkab is not solely for promoting general welfare. DORTA harvested the Yaks for selling Gallvectra, which yields lucrative profits.[160] This is a commercial activity, thus not solely for promoting general welfare.

Third, the harvesting is incompatible with the nature of cultural rights. Compatible limitation shall not be 'applied so as to jeopardize the essence of the right concerned'.[161] Aurokans' cultural rights are centered on the Yak harvesting. However, the continuance of Yak harvesting in Rakkab will cause the Yak's extinction, rendering the essence of Aurokans' cultural rights baseless.

C. RAKKAB VIOLATES AUROKANS' RELIGIOUS RIGHTS UNDER ARTICLE 18 OF ICCPR.

i. ICCPR is extraterritorially applicable.

ICCPR requires that a State Party must 'respect and ensure the rights laid down in

156 ICESCR art 4; General Comment 21 (n 135) [1].

157 *Singh v France* (2012) UNHRC Communication 1876/2008 para 8.4.

158 *Compromis* [44].

159 *Compromis* [44]-[45].

160 *Compromis* [21].

161 ECOSOC 'Limburg Principles on the Implementation of the International Covenant on Economic, Social and Cultural Rights' (1987) E/CN4/1987/17 [56].

ICCPR to anyone within its jurisdiction',[162] even if the individuals are not situated in its territory.[163] In terms of transboundary damage, the victims are under the jurisdiction of the State of origin as long as the State exercises effective control over the 'conduct' which has a causal link with the damage and the consequent violation of human rights.[164]

Aurokans' human rights should be respected and protected under ICCPR as Rakkab exercises effective control over the conduct of DORTA's Yak harvesting,[165] generating its extraterritorial obligations under ICCPR.

ii. The Yak harvesting in Rakkab violates Aurokans' rights to manifest their religion under Article 18 of ICCPR.

Article 18 of ICCPR guarantees individuals' right to manifest their religion or belief in worship, observance and practice.[166] Worship extends to ceremonies or rituals giving direct expression to the belief.[167] Aurokans believed that the Yak is the avatar of the Great God Kayleff.[168] The Yak harvesting and consumption of the Tirhinga Nos Lustuk, of which Yak's gallbladder is the key ingredient, are rituals, reflecting Aurokans, belief in Kayleff Yak.[169] Therefore, Aurokans' religious ritual depends on the free access to the Yak and the Yak herd's sustainability.

Due to the great reliance of Aurokans' religion on accessing Yak, any interference with the access to the Yak would cause considerable repercussion on Aurokans'

162 International Covenant on Civil and Political Rights (adopted 16 December 1966, entered into force 23 March 1976) 999 UNTS 171 (ICCPR) art 2.

163 CCPR 'General Comment No 31[80]: The Nature of the General Legal Obligation Imposed on States Parties to the Covenant' (26 May 2004) UN Doc CCPR/C/21/Rev1/Add13 [10].

164 *Environment and Human Rights* (n 29) art II (h).

165 See Section I A i.

166 ICCPR art 18.

167 HRC 'General Comment No 22: Article 18 (Freedom of Thought, Conscience or Religion)' (30 July 1993) UN Doc CCPR/C/21/Rev1/Add4 [4].

168 *Compromis* [2].

169 *Compromis* [4] [7].

ritual acts.[170] The Yak harvesting in Rakkab is unsustainable and its continuance will generate the Yak's extinction.[171] Young Aurokans in the North have been prevented from participating in the religious rite of passage into adulthood.[172] With Yak's extinction, Aurokans will have no way to practice their religious rituals. Therefore, the Yak harvesting in Rakkab violates Aurokans' rights to manifest their religion.

iii. The Yak harvesting in Rakkab is not validly justified.

With respect to the freedom to manifest religion, the limitation must be prescribed by law and be necessary to protect public health or other fundamental rights and freedoms of others.[173]

First, as established before, Regulation AG/2017-0300 is not a qualified legislation regulating the limitation.[174] *Second*, the limitation does not serve the purpose to protect public health. The purpose is served with the premise that the limited religion creates concrete risk to the public health.[175] However, Aurokans' religious practices do not present a threat to the public health as Aurokans have coexisted with Yak harmoniously for millennia,[176] and have even developed beneficial traditional knowledge associated with the Yak.[177] *Third*, even if the aim is legitimate, the limitation is by no means necessary. A necessary limitation shall be proportionate.[178] Additionally, there shall be no other less onerous alternatives to meet the legitimate aim.[179] On the one hand, the Yak harvesting in Rakkab is unsustainable, imposing great threat to both the biodiversity[180] and Aurokans' religious rights.[181] On the other

170 *Ogiek case* (n 143) [164].

171 *Compromis* [27].

172 *Compromis* [7].

173 ICCPR art 18(3).

174 See Section III B iii.

175 *Singh v France* (n 157) para 8.7.

176 *Compromis* [27].

177 *Compromis* [16].

178 *Ogiek case* (n 143) [129]; *Singh v France* (n 157) para 8.5.

179 *Ogiek case* (n 143) [167].

180 *Compromis* [27].

181 *Compromis* [27]; See Section III C.

hand, there is no pressing social need for Gallvectra since diabetes and obesity are chronic diseases. Further, alternatives without such adverse impacts are available to defeat diabetes and obesity.[182] For example, there are other available medicines listed by the WHO.[183] People can also mind their lifestyles since these diseases are lifestyle-oriented.[184]

D. THE YAK HARVESTING IN RAKKAB VIOLATED AUROKANS' PARTICIPATORY RIGHTS AS INDIGENOUS PEOPLE.

ILO No 169 guarantees indigenous people's participatory rights.[185] Rakkab has extraterritorial obligations to respect Aurokans' indigenous rights under ILO No 169 [i], which it violates [ii].

i. Rakkab has extraterritorial obligations to respect Aurokans' indigenous rights under ILO No 169.

a. ILO No 169 applies extraterritorially.

ILO No 169 lacks a jurisdictional clause and can apply extraterritorially pursuant to *Georgia v Russian Federation.*[186] Besides, given the distinctive relationship between indigenous people and the environment,[187] the harm faced by indigenous people does not only come from the domestic government but also from the outer world through transboundary environmental damage.[188] It is unreasonable to limit the obligation to domestic government.

---

182 *Ogiek case* (n 143) [167]; *Endorois* (n 136) [249]; General Comment 21 (n 135) [19].

183 Model List (n 116) section 18.5.

184 *Compromis* [12].

185 The International Labor Organization's Convention (No 169) Concerning Indigenous and Tribal Peoples in Independent Countries (adopted 27 June 1989, entered into force 5 September 1991) 1650 UNTS 383 (ILO No 169) arts 6, 7.

186 *Georgia v Russian Federation* (n 126) [109].

187 *Mayagna v Nicaragua* (Judgment) [2001] IACHR [149]; *Maya Indigenous Community of the Toledo District v Belize* (Judgment) [2000] IACHR Case 12.053 Report No 78/00 [114].

188 Special Procedures of the United Nations Human Rights Council 'Mapping Human Rights Obligations Relating to the Enjoyment of a Safe, Clean, Healthy and Sustainable Environment, Individual Report on the Rights of Indigenous Peoples' (2013) Report No 8 [118].

b. Aurokans are indigenous people.

Pursuant to ILO No 169, there are three constituent factors for indigenous people: prior inhabitation in the region; a voluntary perpetuation of cultural distinctiveness; and self-identification as a distinct collectivity.[189] Self-identification as indigenous people is the fundamental factor under ILO No 169.[190]

First, Aurokans' ancestors have been living in the Gaur Highlands since 1000 BCE,[191] long before the colonization by the Kingdom of Jeramia.[192] *Second*, they have developed their own distinct culture and religion of which the Yak is the central element,[193] and Aurokans voluntarily observe them in the modern time.[194] Most importantly, nearly all Aurokans self-identify themselves as indigenous people.[195] Therefore, Aurokans should be deemed as indigenous people under ILO No 169.

ii. Rakkab violates Aurokans' participatory rights.

States have the obligations to consult the indigenous people as to any decision affecting them,[196] and get their 'free, prior and informed consent'.[197] Alternatively, the consultation shall be conducted with the aim to achieve consent.[198]

---

189 *Ogiek case* (n 143) [107] [108]; UN Economic and Social Council 'Sub-commission on Prevention of Discrimination and Protection of Minorities, Working Group on Indigenous Populations, Standard-setting Activities: Evolution of Standards Concerning the Rights of Indigenous People' (1996) E/CN4/Sub2/AC4/1996/2 [69].

190 ILO No 169 art 2; *Ogiek case* (n 143) [107] [108].

191 *Compromis* [2].

192 *Compromis* [6] [7].

193 *Compromis* [2].

194 *Compromis* [7].

195 *Clarifications* [1].

196 ILO No 169 arts 6, 7; United Nations General Assembly (UNGA) 'United Nations Declaration on the Rights of Indigenous Peoples' (13 September 2007) UN Doc A/RES/61/295 art 18; *Kichwa Indigenous People of Sarayaku v Ecuador* (Judgment) [2012] IACHR Case No 245 [157]; *Poma Poma v Peru* [2006] UNHRC Communication 1475/06 para 7.6.

197 *Kichwa case* (n 196) [178]; *Poma Poma v Peru* (n 196) para 7.6; General Comment 21 (n 135) [36] [37].

198 ILO No 169 art 7.

Facing a substantial adverse impact on Aurokans' culture and religion,[199] Rakkab did not get Aurokans' 'free, prior and informed consent' as Aurokans have been protesting against the DORTA-sponsored harvesting openly[200] and have filed a civil suit in Rakkab against such harvesting.[201]

Neither was Rakkab's consultation with the aim of achieving Aurokans' consent. States should conduct social and cultural impact assessment if the decision would influence culture and religion.[202] However, the EIA conducted by Rakkab only assessed the impact of Regulation AG/2017-0300 on Yak's number.[203] It did not take into account the cultural and religious impact that the Yak harvesting granted by the Regulation might have. Therefore, the Yak harvesting in Rakkab violated Aurokans' participatory rights.

E. RAKKAB MUST PROHIBIT THE YAK HARVESTING IN RAKKAB.

The State responsible for the international wrongful act is under the obligation to cease if the wrongful act has a continuing character[204] and that the violated rule is still in force.[205] Rakkab's obligations are continuing since those Conventions are still in force till today. Besides, DORTA continues the Yak harvesting to the present day,[206] indicating that Rakkab constantly breaches its obligations. Therefore, Rakkab must prohibit the Yak harvesting within its territory.

IV. RAKKAB MUST PAY AUROK A PORTION OF THE PROFITS REALIZED FROM SALES OF THE DRUG GALLVECTRA.

Rakkab appropriated and exploited Aurokans' traditional knowledge [A], which is inconsistent with international law [B]. Thus, Rakkab must pay Aurok a portion of the

---

199 See Section III C b.

200 *Compromis* [30].

201 *Clarifications* [3].

202 *Kichwa case* (n 196) [205].

203 *Clarifications* [7].

204 ARSIWA (n 1) art 14 Commentary [5].

205 *Rainbow Warrior* (n 121) [114].

206 *Clarifications* [5].

profits realized from sales of the drug Gallvectra [C].

A. RAKKAB UTILIZED AUROKANS' KNOWLEDGE CONCERNING THE HEALTH BENEFITS OF CONSUMING THE YAK'S GALLBLADDER.

i. Aurokans' knowledge concerning the health benefits of consuming the Yak's gallbladder is traditional knowledge.

a. The knowledge concerning the health benefits of the Yak's gallbladder is traditional knowledge.

Traditional knowledge is defined as knowledge, know-how, skills and practices[207] that are developed, sustained and passed on from generation to generation within a community, often forming part of the community's cultural or spiritual identity.[208] This definition does not require that the traditional knowledge should be specific as to the curative effect.

The Pivzao attributed great health benefits to the Yak's gallbladder[209] and the knowledge is passed on to Aurokans in the modern time within the Pivzao community.[210] The knowledge is associated with a solemn, ritualized event of the consumption of the Tirhinga Nos Lustuk, of which the Yak's gallbladder is the key ingredient, and symbolizes Aurokans' gratitude to Kayleff for nature's bounty.[211] Therefore, the knowledge concerning the health benefits of the Yak's gallbladder is traditional knowledge integral to Aurokans' cultural identity.

b. The traditional knowledge is held by Aurokans.

The holders of traditional knowledge are indigenous people and local communities.[212]

---

207 CBD art 8 (j); International Council for Science 'ICSU Series on Series for Sustainable Development No 4: Science, Traditional Knowledge and Sustainable Development' (2002) 24, 9.

208 World Intellectual Property Organization (WIPO) 'The Protection of Traditional Knowledge: Draft Articles-REV 2' (2018) WIPO/GRTKF/IC/37/FACILITATORS TEXT art 1.

209 *Compromis* [4] [16].

210 *Compromis* [16].

211 *Compromis* [4].

212 CBD art 8(j); Nagoya Protocol on Access to Genetic Resources and the Fair and Equitable Sharing of Benefits Arising from Their Utilization to the Convention on Biological Diversity (adopted 29 October 2010, entered into force 12 October 2014) (Nagoya Protocol) art 5(1).

As established before, Aurokans are indigenous people.[213] Alternatively, Aurokans belong to a local community.

ii. Dr. Bello utilized Aurokans' traditional knowledge.

a. Dr. Bello intended to use the traditional knowledge for 'research and development'.

Under systematic interpretation,[214] utilization of traditional knowledge can be understood as hinging on the same intent of that of genetic resources, which is 'research and development'.[215] Based on the words' ordinary meaning,[216] 'research and development' in conjunction refer to two closely related processes intended to create new products through technological innovation.[217]

Dr. Bello was aspired to find a way in Aurok to cure diabetes since the rate of diabetes among his Aurokan patients was consistently and markedly low.[218] Hence, he observed Aurokans' dietary and cultural practices, of which Aurokans' traditional knowledge is embodied in.[219] The knowledge was used in the process of researching the beneficial enzyme and developing the new drug Gallvectra.[220] Thus, the intention element is met.

b. The traditional knowledge made substantial contribution to the research and development of Gallvectra.

Utilization is triggered when the traditional knowledge contributes to the discovery or investigation phase of the research and development process.[221] According to the

---

213 See Section III D i a.

214 VCLT art 31(2).

215 Nagoya Protocol art 2.

216 *Sovereignty over Pulau Ligitan and Pulau Sipadan* (Indonesial/Malaysia) (Judgment) [2002] ICJ Rep 625 [37] [43]; VCLT art 31(1).

217 Elisa Morgera *et al*, *Unraveling the Nagoya Protocol: A Commentary on the Nagoya Protocol on Access and Benefit-sharing to the Convention on Biological Diversity* (Brill 2014) 63; 'Research and Development' in *Encyclopedia Britannica Online* <www.britannica.com/EBchecked/topic/499010/research-and-development> accessed 6 January 2019.

218 *Compromis* [13].

219 *Compromis* [4] [13].

220 *Compromis* [4] [13].

221 United Nations Conference on Trade and Development 'BioTrade and Access and Benefit Sharing: From Concept to Practice: A Handbook for Policymakers and Regulators' UNCTAD/DITC/TED/2017/6, 52.

preparatory work of CBD and the Nagoya Protocol,[222] the reason to protect traditional knowledge is that it provides clue to identify the beneficial properties of a genetic resource,[223] which increases the efficiency of screening natural resources.[224] For example, the traditional use of *Hoodia* guided the scientist to investigate the plant.[225] Consequently, whether the traditional knowledge is utilized does not depend on the similarity between the traditional use of the resources and the modern use in the end-product made through the research and development process.[226]

The significance of Aurokans' traditional knowledge for the development of Gallvectra is similar to that of the traditional use of *Quassiaamara* in French Guiana for the patented Simalikalactone E (SkE). Inspired by the traditional use of *Quassiaamare* in tea, the French Institute for Development and Research (IRD) successfully isolated a new antimalarial molecule from the plant using alcohol-based extraction.[227] Despite that the molecule was discovered by the scientist, the IRD carried out its benefit sharing obligation because it was the traditional knowledge which led the scientist to examine *Quassiaamare* and not thousands of other plants. [228]

The value of Gallvectra lies in the beneficial enzyme contained in the Yak's gallbladder.[229]

---

222 VCLT art 31(2).

223 'Report of the Sixth Meeting of the Ad Hoc Open-ended Inter-Sessional Working Group on Article 8(j) and Related Provisions of the Convention on Biological Diversity' UNEP/CBD/COP/10/2 Annex II, iii - v.

224 Gurdial Nijar, 'Incorporating Traditional Knowledge in an International Regime on Access to Genetic Resources and Benefit Sharing: Problems and Prospects' (2010) 21(2) *European Journal of International Law* 457, 458.

225 Roger Chennells, 'Traditional Knowledge and Benefit Sharing after the Nagoya Protocol: Three Cases from South Africa' (2013) 9(2) *Law Environment and Development Journal* 165, 169.

226 'Report of the Meeting of the Group of Technical and Legal Experts on Traditional Knowledge Associated with Genetic Resources in the Context of the International Regime on Access and Benefit-sharing' (Report on ABS) UNEP/CBD/WG-ABS/8/2 Annex [14].

227 Genevieve Bourdy *et al*, 'Quassia "Biopiracy" Case and the Nagoya Protocol: A Researcher's Perspective' (2017) 206 *Journal of Ethnopharmacology* 290, 291.

228 'French Institute Agrees to Share Patent Benefits after Biopiracy Accusations' <https://www.sciencemag.org/news/2016/02/french-institute-agrees-share-patent-benefits-after-biopiracy-accusations> accessed 6 January 2019.

229 *Compromis* [13].

Like the traditional use of *Quassiaamare*, Aurokans' traditional knowledge over the health benefits of the Yak's gallbladder, which is reflected in their dietary practices observed by Dr. Bello, led Dr. Bello to examine the Yak's Gallbladder and identify the beneficial enzyme.[230] This limited the scope of screening among a variety of resources and saved Dr. Bello great efforts and time. Therefore, Aurokans' traditional knowledge is 'utilized' as it contributed to the investigation phase of Gallvectra's development by leading Dr. Bello to investigate the Yak's gallbladder. It does not matter that the enzyme was first discovered and isolated by Dr. Bello.

B. THE DEVELOPMENT OF GALLVECTRA WITHOUT COMPENSATION IS INCONSISTENT WITH INTERNATIONAL LAW.

Rakkab's utilization of Aurokans' traditional knowledge generates its benefit-sharing obligation under CBD and the Nagoya Protocol [i] and the general principle of unjust enrichment [ii].

i. Rakkab's utilization without benefit-sharing violates CBD and the Nagoya Protocol.

a. The Nagoya Protocol applies to the continuing utilization of Aurokans' traditional knowledge.

Pursuant to Article 28 of VCLT, a treaty binds a party in relation to any act, fact or situation which took place before the date of the treaty's entry into force but does not cease to exist after that date.[231] Therefore, the Nagoya Protocol applies to the continuing use of traditional knowledge, even if the knowledge was accessed before its entry into force. Article 5(1) of the Nagoya Protocol provides that the benefits arising from the utilization of genetic resources as well as subsequent commercialization shall be shared.[232] Under systematic interpretation, this article also applies to the benefit-sharing concerning traditional knowledge.[233]

Even though Dr. Bello accessed the traditional knowledge before the Nagoya Protocol's

230 *Compromis* [13].

231 VCLT art 28.

232 Nagoya Protocol art 5(1).

233 VCLT art 31(2).

entry into force, which is in 2014, the utilization as well as commercialization of the traditional knowledge do not cease to exist in terms of Article 28 of VCLT.[234] In 2017, the Rakkabi government granted Yak harvesting licenses to DORTA for the development and manufacture of the Gallvectra.[235] Since DORTA has not succeeded in developing a synthetic alternative yet,[236] the development of the Gallvectra is still based on the traditional knowledge that the Yak's gallbladder possesses properties which can promote health.[237] Further, DORTA is manufacturing and marketing Gallvectra to the present day, generating lucrative profits.[238] Therefore, the generation of profits arising from the continuing utilization and commercialization of Aurokans' traditional knowledge is subject to the Nagoya Protocol.

b. Aurokans' traditional knowledge is protected under CBD and the Nagoya Protocol.

The traditional knowledge protected under CBD and the Nagoya Protocol should be relevant to the sustainable use of biological diversity[239] and associated with genetic resources.[240]

First, Aurokans' traditional knowledge is consistent with the sustainable use of biological diversity. 'Sustainable use' means that the use of traditional knowledge should not lead to a long-term decline of biological diversity for the needs and aspirations of present and future generations.[241] The Aurokans' harvesting is in accordance with Yak's migration pattern and its reproduction rate,[242] which can keep the sustainability of the Yak's populations. This is further confirmed by the fact that Aurokans have coexisted with the Yaks for millennia[243] and there is no sign of the decrease in the Yak's number before the introduction of DORTA-sponsored Yak

234 VCLT art 28.
235 *Compromis* [45].
236 *Compromis* [27].
237 *Compromis* [13].
238 *Compromis* [38].
239 CBD art 8(j).
240 Nagoya Protocol art 5(5).
241 CBD art 2; Nagoya Protocol art 1.
242 *Compromis* [27].
243 *Compromis* [27].

harvesting.[244] Therefore, the traditional knowledge over the health benefits of Yak's gallbladder is relevant for the sustainable use of the Yaks.

Second, Aurokans' traditional knowledge is associated with genetic resources. In the context of the Nagoya Protocol, 'genetic resources' not only refer to materials containing functional units of heredity, but more broadly to the derivatives.[245] Further, 'associated' only requires the knowledge to be in 'general relationship' with the genetic resources, and not necessarily to be specific.[246] Aurokans know that the Yak's gallbladder is beneficial to health. This function is actually attributed to the enzyme contained in the gallbladder.[247] Since the enzyme is a kind of derivative,[248] Aurokans' traditional knowledge is associated with genetic resources.

In conclusion, Rakkab should share a portion of profits realized from the sales of Gallvectra, as a monetary form,[249] with Aurokans for the utilization of their traditional knowledge.

c. Rakkab's utilization without benefit-sharing violated CBD and the Nagoya Protocol.

Article 8(j) of CBD requires the State to encourage equitable benefit sharing of utilization of traditional knowledge.[250] Article 5(5) of the Nagoya Protocol further stipulates that State Parties shall take legislative, administrative or policy measures to ensure the benefit sharing arising from the utilization of traditional knowledge associated with genetic resources.[251] However, Rakkab, as a State Party, utilized Aurokans' traditional knowledge but did not share any profits generated through the sales of Gallvectra.[252] It is inconsistent with Rakkab's benefit-sharing obligation under

244 *Compromis* [27].

245 Morgera (n 217) 65, 71.

246 Report on ABS (n 226) [12].

247 *Compromis* [3] [14] [16].

248 Morgera (n 217) 71.

249 Nagoya Protocol Annex.

250 CBD art 8(j).

251 Nagoya Protocol art 5(5).

252 *Compromis* [37].

CBD and the Nagoya Protocol.

ii. Rakkab's utilization without benefit-sharing violates the Paris Convention.

The Paris Convention for the Protection of Industrial Property (the Paris Convention) prohibits unfair competition,[253] including dishonest practice like unjust enrichment.[254] Unjust enrichment, as an independent cause of action,[255] is regarded as a general principle of law.[256] It requires one to return profits if he is enriched at the expense of another without just factors.[257]

a. Rakkab is enriched by utilizing Aurokans' traditional knowledge.

'Enrichment' means anything of value, whether tangible or intangible.[258] Dr. Bello utilized Aurokans' traditional knowledge over the health benefits of consuming the Yak's gallbladder to identify the beneficial enzyme.[259] This saved Dr. Bello efforts and time to search for resources in the Guar Highlands and brought large profits to DORTA through the royalties from the patent granted.[260] Therefore, DORTA is enriched by Aurokans' traditional knowledge.

b. The enrichment is at Aurokans' expense.

'Enrichment at the expense of another' indicates the link between the parties as transfer or and transferee of value.[261] The patenting of the Gallvectra directly led to

253 Paris Convention for the Protection of Industrial Property (adopted 14 July 1967, entered into force 26 April 1970) 828 UNTS 305 art 10 *bis*.

254 WIPO 'The Protection of Traditional Knowledge: Updated Draft Gap Analysis' (2018) WIPO/GRTKF/IC/37/6 [48].

255 C Schreuer, 'Unjustified Enrichment in International Law' (1974) 22 *American Journal of Comparative Law* 281, 281.

256 *Sea-Land Service Inc v The Government of the Islamic Republic of Iran* [1986] Iran-US Claims Tribunal (Vol. 4) 149, 169; *Inceysa Vallisoletana SL v Republic of El Salvador* [Award] [2006] ICSID Case No ARB/03/26 [253]-[254]; Schreuer (n 255) 301.

257 *Benjamin Isaiah v Bank Mellat* [1983] Iran-US Claims Tribunal (Vol. 2) 236-237.

258 *Sea-Land case* (n 256) 149, 169.

259 *Compromis* [13].

260 *Compromis* [2] [38].

261 E Weinrib 'Unjust Enrichment' <https://www.law.upenn.edu/live/files/335-weinribunjustenrichmentpdf> accessed 6 January 2019, 8.

the diminishment of Aurokans' right over their traditional knowledge, as they were deprived of the opportunity to use such knowledge to develop similar products in the future.[262]

c. The enrichment is without just factors.

International law recognizes indigenous people's intangible property rights over their traditional knowledge, that they have the right to maintain, control, protect and develop their traditional knowledge.[263] However, Rakkab obtained the traditional knowledge without reciprocation.[264] Aurokans also did not express any consent to DORTA about the appropriation of their traditional knowledge for commercial use.[265] Therefore, the use of the traditional knowledge is not justified.

In conclusion, the utilization of Aurokans's traditional knowledge constitutes unjust enrichment, and Rakkab must make restitution by compensating Aurokans a portion of profits realized from the sales of Gallvectra.

C. RAKKAB SHOULD PAY THE PROFITS TO AUROK.

Aurokans, as the right holder of the traditional knowledge, have exhausted local remedies by alleging the appropriation of their traditional knowledge in Rakkab.[266] Therefore, Aurok, as the nationality State,[267] can exercise diplomatic protection to claim the benefit-sharing or compensation for Aurokans. Rakkab should pay the profits arising from the appropriation of Aurokans' traditional knowledge to Aurok.

---

262 *Compromis* [15]; Babatunde Oni *et al* 'Combating the Scourge of Insider Biopiracy in Nigeria: Can the Law of Unjust Enrichment Offer a Solution to the Misappropriation of Traditional Knowledge on the Medicinal Uses of Plants?' (2016) 5 *International Journal of Law and Policy Review* 159, 179.

263 UNDRIP (n 196) art 3 (1).

264 *Compromis* [37] [42].

265 *Clarifications* [3].

266 *Clarifications* [3].

267 *Nottebohm case* (n 123) 24.

CONCLUSION AND PRAYER FOR RELIEF

In view of the facts set forth in this Memorial and the arguments applying the law to the facts as stated;

May it please the Court, on behalf of the State of Aurok, Applicant herein, respectfully requests this Honorable Court to adjudge and declare that:

1. Rakkab is responsible for the internationally wrongful acts because DORTA's actions are attributable to Rakkab, or in the alternative, Rakkab is responsible for its own failure to prevent DORTA from committing those wrongful acts;

2. The harvesting of the Yak in Rakkab violates Rakkab's international obligations relating to the protection of endangered species and the environment, including those under relevant conventions, and Rakkab is obligated to end the Yak harvesting on its territory;

3. The harvesting of the Yak in Rakkab violates the cultural and religious rights of the people of Aurok, and Rakkab must prohibit such hunting forthwith;

4. Rakkab must pay Aurok, a portion (to be determined in subsequent proceedings) of the profits realized from sales of the drug Gallvectra, because the appropriation and exploitation of traditional knowledge belonging to the Aurokan people without compensation is inconsistent with international law.

Respectfully submitted,
AGENTS FOR AUROK

被告国书状

Memorials for the Republic of Rakkab

TABLE OF CONTENTS

ii. Rakkab has fulfilled the obligation to minimize the risk.

C. RAKKAB IS NOT OBLIGED TO CEASE THE HARVESTING.

III. THE HARVESTING OF YAK IN RAKKAB DOES NOT VIOLATE THE CULTURAL AND RELIGIOUS RIGHTS OF AUROKANS AND RAKKAB IS NOT OBLIGATED TO PROHIBIT SUCH HUNTING.

A. RAKKAB HAS NO OBLIGATION OVER AUROKANS' CULTURAL AND RELIGIOUS RIGHTS UNDER INTERNATIONAL LAW.

i. Rakkab has no obligation under ILO No 169 and UNDRIP.

ii. Rakkab has no obligation under ICCPR and ICESCR.

B. ALTERNATIVELY, RAKKAB DOES NOT VIOLATE THE CULTURAL AND RELIGIOUS RIGHTS OF AUROKANS.

i. Rakkab does not violate Aurokans' cultural rights.

ii. Rakkab does not violate Aurokans' religious rights.

C. ALTERNATIVELY, YAK HARVESTING IN RAKKAB CAN BE JUSTIFIED BY THE NECESSARY LIMITATIONS TO CULTURAL AND RELIGIOUS RIGHTS.

IV. RAKKAB DOES NOT NEED TO PAY AUROK A PORTION OF THE PROFITS REALIZED FROM SALES OF THE DRUG GALLVECTRA.

A. THE CONSUMPTION OF TIRHINGA NOS LUSTUK IS NOT TRADITIONAL KNOWLEDGE PROTECTED WITHIN THE SCOPE OF CBD AND THE NAGOYA PROTOCOL.

i. The consumption of TNL is not traditional knowledge as it is not relevant for the conservation and sustainable use of biodiversity.

ii. Besides, the consumption of TNL is not traditional knowledge associated with genetic resources.

B. ALTERNATIVELY, THE PRODUCTION OF GALLVECTRA DOES NOT APPROPRIATE AND EXPLOIT THE TRADITIONAL KNOWLEDGE BELONGING TO AUROKANS.

i. The traditional knowledge does not exclusively belong to Aurokans.

ii. The traditional knowledge has made no contribution to the production of Gallvectra due to its vagueness.

iii. The production of Gallvectra is based on Dr. Bello's independent discovery and there is no misappropriation of the traditional knowledge.

iv. The traditional knowledge falls in public domain knowledge and is freely available.

C. ALTERNATIVELY, RAKKAB IS NOT OBLIGED TO OBSERVE THE BENEFIT-SHARING PRINCIPLE UNDER CBD AND THE NAGOYA PROTOCOL.

i. Rakkab is not obligated to benefit-sharing under CBD.

ii. Rakkab is not obligated to benefit-sharing under the Nagoya Protocol as the Nagoya Protocol is not retroactively applicable.

D. RAKKAB DOES NOT NEED TO PAY THE STATE OF AUROK A PORTION OF PROFIT AS AUROK DOES NOT HAVE THE RIGHT TO CLAIM BENEFIT-SHARING.

CONCLUSION AND PRAYER FOR RELIEF

STATEMENT OF JURISDICTION

The State of Aurok (Aurok), and the Republic of Rakkab (Rakkab) hereby submit the present dispute to the International Court of Justice (the Court) pursuant to Article 40(1) of the Court's Statute, in accordance with the *Compromis* for submission to the Court of the differences concerning the Kayleff Yak, signed in the Hague, The Netherlands, on the fourteenth day of September in the year two thousand eighteen. Both States have accepted the jurisdiction of this Court pursuant to Article 36(1) of its Statute.

QUESTIONS PRESENTED

The Republic of Rakkab respectfully requests the Court to adjudge:

I.

1. *Whether* Rakkab is responsible for DORTA's acts;

2. *Whether* Rakkab is responsible for its own failure to prevent DORTA from committing the wrongful acts.

II.

1. *Whether* the harvesting of Yak violates the substantive obligations under the CMS and CITES;

2. *Whether* the harvesting of the Yak violates the procedural obligations;

3. *Whether* Rakkab is obliged to cease the harvesting.

III.

1. *Whether* Rakkab has the obligation to respect Aurokan peoples' cultural and religious rights under ILO No 169 and UNDRIP;

2. *Whether* Rakkab has the obligation to respect Aurokan peoples' cultural and religious rights under ICCPR, ICESCR and UDHR;

3. *Whether* Rakkab violates the cultural and religious rights of Aurokans;

4. *Whether* Yak harvesting in Rakkab can be justified by the necessary limitations to cultural and religious rights.

IV.

1. *Whether* the consumption of Tirhinga Nos Lustuk forms the traditional knowledge protected under CBD and the Nagoya Protocol;

2. *Whether* Rakkab has appropriated or exploited the traditional knowledge belonging to Aurokans;

3. *Whether* Rakkab is obliged to share the profits realized from the selling of Gallvectra under CBD and the Nagoya Protocol;

4. *Whether* Aurok as a State has the right to claim benefit-sharing.

STATEMENT OF FACTS

The State of Aurok (Aurok), and the Republic of Rakkab (Rakkab), are neighboring countries on the Gaur Highlands (Gaur), the exclusive habitat of the majestic Kayleff Yak (Yak) for more than 250,000 years. The Yak is a migratory species, born and staying in Aurok in (northern hemisphere) spring and summer, and in Rakkab in autumn and winter.

The Pivzao civilization (Pivzao) is a civilization arising in the Gaur relied upon subsistence hunting of the Yak. Traditional Yak hunting is a complex community event. People who participate in the killing are rewarded with a traditional dish called Tirhinga Nos Lustuk (soup of the nasty bits of the Yak), which not only symbolizes gratitude to the Yak, but also is considered as conferring of health benefits and longevity according to the Pivzao traditions. To the present day, many Aurokans continue to observe those traditions, and the Yak remains of prime religious and cultural significance.

DORTA M/S (DORTA) is a corporation registered under the laws of Rakkab, privatized from the Department of Research, Technology & Application of Rakkab. Public trading of its shares began on the New York Stock Exchange in May 1996. As of the present date, Rakkab holds approximately 12% of DORTA's stock, which complies with the legislative act privatizing the Department and DORTA's private charter. And DORTA's 15-member Board of Directors includes four former Rakkabi Cabinet Ministers and three former leaders of Rakkab's major political parties.

The Gallvectra is a medication derived from the Lustuk Enzyme, a key ingredient in Tirhinga Nos Lustuk, whose inventor is Dr. Bello, the employee of a DORTA-operated private hospital. On 11 November 2004, DORTA filed a patent application with the Rakkabi Intellectual Property Ministry for Gallvectra, the Ministry granted it on 21 May 2006. As of 2018, DORTA has sold Gallvectra in more than 85 countries and profited much from it.

In January 2005, an anthropologist Cressida Cauty, published an article in the international peer-reviewed sociology journal *Human Organization* and noted that through their consumption of Tirhinga Nos Lustuk, observant Aurokans ingested hundreds of grams of the Lustuk Enzyme each year.

In March 2005, the Aurokan Minister of Intellectual Property, Tom Wynet, wrote to his Rakkabi counterpart, emphasizing that the Aurokan people, rather than Dr. Bello, first discovered the health benefits of the Yak's gallbladders.

In April 2005, patent attorneys for DORTA replied to Minister Wynet's letter, stating that it was Dr. Bello who directly isolated the Lustuk Enzyme and the Aurokan people never produced a reliable, consistent prescription drug for human use.

In October 2015, Carla Alexander, the Chief Executive Officer of DORTA stated on the meeting of shareholders of DORTA that the Gallvectra was without question the most successful pharmaceutical product in the history of this company.

In February 2016, the Brisbane-based *Courier Mail* published a lengthy investigative report, noting that in order to hunt Yak—or, indeed, any other wild animal in Rakkab—an individual must be awarded a license, specific to the animal to be hunted. And in this report, the author quoted a spokesperson for DORTA as stating that only about 4 percent of the Yak per year had been taken to produce Gallvectra, while Aurokans had for decades culled hundreds of thousands of Yak for their traditional purposes.

In March 2016, DORTA's researchers met with the Aurokans to discuss the sustainability of the Yak population and announced that it was initiating a captive breeding program of its own.

In June 2016, the Yak Life Sciences Academy (YLSA), an international NGO, concluded in its 2016 report that the number of Yak harvested by Aurokans was much larger than the 30,000 or so killed by DORTA hunters last winter.

On 2 October 2016, the Rakkabi Prime Minister Derlap Frangie discussed the issue of the Yak with the Aurokan Prime Minister Sumun and DORTA CEO Ms. Alexander. Rakkabi Prime Minister Frangie expressed his confidence that 'DORTA will act responsibly to conserve this vital cultural and health resource' and promised to monitor the issue and to cooperate with Aurok.

On 1 November 2016, at DORTA's annual shareholder meeting, DORTA CEO Ms. Alexander contended that Gallvectra continued to help countless people worldwide and that the number of the Yak killed by DORTA was only a quarter of the number killed each year by the Aurokans for more than 10 years.

On 16 November 2016, the Rakkabi Ministry of Agriculture released on all major digital platforms an application called 'YakTrakker'. And the purpose of the application was 'to allow scientists and conservationists to make accurate estimates of the health and vitality of the Yak population'.

In March 2017, Gallvectra was added to the WHO Model List of Essential Medicines, which manifests the global recognition of Gallvectra's fundamental importance and its enormous value.

On 29 September 2017, the Yak was included in Appendix III of the Convention on International Trade in Endangered Species of Wild Fauna and Flora (CITES). And the Ministry of Agriculture of Rakkab is a designated Management Authority under Article IX of CITES. Since 29 September 2017, the Ministry has issued certificates of origin for the Lustuk Enzyme in all batches of Gallvectra exported from Rakkab. The Ministry keeps appropriate records with respect to all such certificates issued.

On 5 October 2017, Prime Ministers Frangie and Sumun met in Transcentral. Prime Minister Sumun presented her counterpart a demarche demanding that the DORTA-sponsored Yak harvest cease, and that the Rakkabi government 'pay Aurok and the Aurokan people their rightful share of the profits that DORTA has made from the Aurokan people's traditions, and from their ancestors' knowledge of which they are the current custodians'. However, the Rakkabi Prime Minister denied that his government was legally or practically responsible for the actions of DORTA in manufacturing or selling Gallvectra.

In October 2017, the Yak was included in Appendix I of the Convention on Migratory Species (CMS). On 15 November 2017, the Rakkabi Ministry of Agriculture promulgated Regulation AG/2017-0300 to regulate the Yak harvesting, which provided for criminal and civil sanctions. Additionally, all licenses issued under Section 3 of Regulation AG/2017-0300 are notified to CMS Secretariat in a manner consistent with Article III (7) of CMS.

Beginning in October 2017, as part of the administrative rule-making process that resulted in the issuance of Regulation AG/2017-0300, Rakkab conducted a comprehensive environmental impact assessment, which concluded that Regulation AG/2017-0300 would be adequate to protect the sustainability of the Yak population.

On 20 December 2017, DORTA was granted a Yak hunting license by the Ministry of Agriculture. And there was a number limitation on the Yak hunting, 30,000. Besides, upon the expiration of the DORTA license, the authorities 'will review the continuing scientific and medical benefits of then-current hunting levels, and the impact upon the Yak population'.

On 2 January 2018, DORTA publicly announced that it was again offering payment for Yak gallbladders, but only to registered agents of the company. YLSA's annual survey indicated that DORTA agents killed approximately 28,500 Yak during January and February 2018.

SUMMARY OF PLEADINGS

FIRST PLEADING

Rakkab is not responsible for the acts conducted by DORTA because DORTA's acts are not attributable to Rakkab. *First,* DORTA is not an organ of Rakkab and does not exercise elements of governmental authority. *Second*, Rakkab has never instructed, directed nor controlled DORTA. *Third*, Rakkab has never adopted DORTA's actions. Moreover, Rakkab is not responsible for its own failure to prevent DORTA from committing those wrongful acts.

SECOND PLEADING

The harvesting of Yak in Rakkab does not violate Rakkab's international obligations to the protection of endangered species and the environment and Rakkab is not obliged to cease the harvesting. *First*, Rakkab fulfills its substantive obligations under CMS due to the scientific purpose or extraordinary circumstance so required. *Second*, Rakkab fulfills its substantive obligations under CITES since an export permit is not required. *Third*, Rakkab fulfills its procedure obligation.

THIRD PLEADING

The harvesting of Yak in Rakkab does not violate the cultural and religious rights of Aurokans, and Rakkab is not obligated to prohibit such hunting. *First,* Rakkab has no obligation to respect Aurokans' cultural and religious rights under international law. *Second,* Rakkab does not violate Aurokans' cultural and religious rights. Alternatively, the Yak harvesting in Rakkab can be justified by the necessary limitations to the rights.

FORTH PLEADING

Rakkab does not need to pay Aurok a portion of the profits realized from sales of the drug Gallvectra. *First*, the consumption of Tirhinga Nos Lustuk is not traditional knowledge protected within the scope of CBD and the Nagoya Protocol. *Second,* the production of Gallvectra does not appropriate and exploit traditional knowledge belonging to Aurokans. *Third*, Rakkab is not obliged to observe the benefit-sharing principle under CBD and the Nagoya Protocol. *Fourth,* Rakkab does not need to pay the State of Aurok a portion of profit as Aurok does not have the right to claim benefit-sharing.

PLEADINGS

I. THE ACTS OF DORTA CANNOT BE ATTRIBUTED TO RAKKAB AND RAKKAB HAS NO RESPONSIBILITY TO PREVENT THE ALLEGED ACTS.

A. THE ACTS OF DORTA CANNOT BE ATTRIBUTED TO RAKKAB.

i. DORTA is not an organ of Rakkab.

A State shall be responsible for the conduct of its organs,[1] whether they belong to the legislative, executive, or judicial department of the government.[2] DORTA is a private company,[3] a legal entity separating from Rakkab.[4] Therefore, the acts of DORTA cannot be attributed to Rakkab.

ii. DORTA does not exercise elements of governmental authority.

The conduct of a person or entity which is not an organ of the State can be attributed to the State only when it is empowered by the law of that State [a] to exercise elements of the governmental authority and acting in that capacity [b] in the particular complained situations.[5]

a. DORTA is not empowered by the law of Rakkab to exercise elements of the governmental authority.

The empowerment from the internal law must be context-specific and fact intensive,[6] the general regulation of the affairs of the community cannot be regarded as

---

1 International Law Commission (ILC) 'Draft Articles on Responsibility of States for Internationally Wrongful Acts, with Commentaries' (2001) UN Doc A/56/10 art 4.

2 *Salvador Commercial Company Case* (El Salvador v United States) [1902] 15 RIAA 455, 477; *Chattin case* (United States v United Mexican States) [1927] 4 RIAA 282, 285-286; *Dispute Concerning the Interpretation of Article 79 of the Treaty of Peace* (Italy v Tunisia) [1955] 13 RIAA 389, 438.

3 *Compromis* [10].

4 *Noble Ventures, Inc v Romania* [2005] ICSID Case No ARB/01/11[69].

5 ARSIWA (n 1) art 5; *Bosh International Inc and B&P Ltd Foreign Investment Enterprise v Ukraine* [2012] ICSID Case No ARB/08/11 [164].

6 *EDF (Services) Limited v Romania* [2019] ICSID Case No ARB/05/13 [192]; ARSIWA (n 1) art 5 Commentary [3].

such empowerment.[7] However, no internal law specifically delegated any power to DORTA. Although the Regulation AG/2017-0300 provided for criminal and civil sanctions,[8] it functions to limit the Yak hunting[9] with neither specifying the object of the empowerment[10] nor specifying that the power to choose hunter is the governmental authority to DORTA.

b. DORTA is not exercising governmental authority in any event.

The internal law has to define the relevant competence and powers of governmental authority,[11] which are not normally opened to private business.[12] The purpose for which the power is to be exercised, the content of the power, and the extent to which the entity is publicly accountable for their exercise are relevant to assessing whether the authority is 'governmental' or not.[13]

In the present case, the Regulation AG/2017-0300[14] doesn't provide any requirement within the scope of governmental role to sell the medicine at affordable costs or at accessible geographical locations,[15] but instead, Yak hunting and the sale of prescription medication are private conducts[16] irrelevant to any sovereign act.[17] Monopoly on the sales of DORTA is only accountable to the Government as a shareholder for its commercial performance, not for public health.[18]

In conclusion, DORTA does not exercise elements of the governmental authority

---

7 ARSIWA (n 1) art 5 Commentary [7].

8 *Clarifications* [8].

9 *Compromis* [45].

10 *Compromis* [23] [44].

11 *Noble* (n 4) [72].

12 *Emilio Augustin Maffezini v The Kingdom of Spain* [2000] ICSID Case NO ARB/97/7 [26]; *Flemingo Duty Free Shop Private Limited v Poland* (Award) [2016] UNCITRAL [428].

13 ARSIWA (n 1) art 5 Commentary [6].

14 *Compromis* [44].

15 WHO 'Public-Private Roles in the Pharmaceutical Sector: Implications for Equitable Access and Rational Drug Use' (1997) WHO/DAP/97.12 [3]-[4].

16 *Compromis* [21]

17 *Bosh* (n 5) [162].

18 *Compromis* [11].

when harvesting Yak and producing Gallvectra.

iii. DORTA is neither acting on the instructions of, nor under the direction or control of Rakkab.

A State will be responsible for the conduct carried out by an entity which is acting on the instructions of, or under the direction [a] or the control of that State [b]. [19] Neither of these conditions is satisfied in the present case.

a. DORTA is not acting on the instructions of Rakkab.

The instructions of the State commonly refer to the supplement of a State organ by recruiting or instigating private persons or group while the official structure of the State is remained.[20] The instructions are often conveyed through an official of the State.[21]

DORTA operates independently since it is a private company[22] and has its own shareholders' meeting.[23] Besides, Rakkab only grants DORTA patents[24] and licenses,[25] but never recruits or instigates it. Furthermore, there is no evidence showing that Rakkabi officials have given orders to DORTA.[26] Rakkabi Prime Minister only promised to monitor DORTA's actions,[27] which is different from command.[28] Therefore, DORTA is not acting on the instructions of Rakkab.

b. Rakkab does not have effective control over DORTA.

The degree of control may vary according to the factual circumstances of each case.[29]

19 ARSIWA (n 1) art 8.

20 ARSIWA (n 1) art 8 Commentary [2].

21 *Zafiro case* (Great Britain v United States) (1925) 6 RIAA 160, 163; *Stephens case* (USA v United Mexican States) (1927) 4 RIAA 265 [6].

22 *Compromis* [10].

23 *Compromis* [21].

24 *Compromis* [21].

25 *Compromis* [45].

26 *Stephens case* (n 21) [267].

27 *Compromis* [31].

28 *Zafiro case* (n 21) 161.

29 *Prosecutor v Duško Tadic* (Judgment) [1999] ICTYIT-94-1-A [117].

The standard of 'overall control' is applied by the International Criminal Tribunal for the former Yugoslavia (ICTY)[30] flexibly in determining whether or not the acts of an individual criminal is attributable to State,[31] which is irrelevant to the current State responsibility case. Indeed, Judge Shahabuddeen noted that a higher degree of control is required to attribute violations of international law to States.[32] Therefore, the standard of 'overall control' is inapplicable.

In *Nicaragua* case, the Court adopted the standard of 'effective control', which requires the State to direct or enforce the perpetration of the acts.[33] The State must have exercised control on specific operation and the conduct complained of should have been an integral part of that operation.[34]

First, as a listed company in New York Stock Exchange,[35] shareholder's approval is a prerequisite in significant situations,[36] and such approval should be expressed through majority of votes.[37] DORTA's harvesting is a regular operation which does not need the approval of shareholders and 12% of voting shares.[38] Besides, Rakkab would hold no more than 19.9% of shares[39] and current government officials are prohibited in DORTA's board,[40] indicating that Rakkab consciously avoids any excessive influence in private companies.

---

30 Generally *Tadic case* (n 29).

31 *Application of the Convention on the Prevention and Punishment of the Crime of Genocide* (Bosnia and Herzegovina v Serbia and Montenegro) (Judgment) [2007] ICJ Rep 43 [403]-[407]; *Prosecutor v Duško Tadic* (Separate Opinion of Judge Shahabuddeen) [1999] ICTY [14] [18]; ARSIWA (n 1) art 8 Commentary [5].

32 *Tadic case* (Separate Opinion of Judge Shahabuddeen) (n 31) [18].

33 *Military and Paramilitary Activities in and against Nicaragua* (Nicaragua v United States of America) (Merits) [1986] ICJ Rep 14 [115].

34 ARSIWA (n 1) art 8 Commentary [3]; *Genocide* (n 31) [401].

35 *Compromis* [10].

36 New York Stock Exchange Listed Company Manual 312.03.

37 New York Stock Exchange Listed Company Manual 312.07.

38 *Compromis* [10].

39 *Compromis* [10].

40 *Compromis* [11].

Second, the control over specific operation,[41] namely the taking of Yak, cannot be deduced by the regular meeting between representatives of the government of Rakkab and DORTA's officials.[42] In fact, Rakkab regulates DORTA by granting patents[43] and licenses[44] to limit its hunting activities, which is part of the general regulatory function of Rakkabi government.

Third, there's no evidence indicating that Rakkab's subsidies upon DORTA[45] constitute the main financial source of it as DORTA, the eighth-largest pharmaceutical manufacturer worldwide,[46] is able to operate apart from that subsidy.

Therefore, DORTA was not under Rakkab's effective control when harvesting the Yak and producing Gallvectra.

iv. Rakkab has never acknowledged nor adopted DORTA's acts.

Conduct shall be considered as an act of the State if and to the extent that the State acknowledges and adopts the conduct as its own.[47] The standard of attribution should not be a general acknowledgment of a factual situation, but rather that the State identifies the conduct as its own.[48] However, Rakkabi Prime Minister merely expressed his confidence towards DORTA's conservation of the Yak.[49] He publicly denied that Rakkab was legally or practically responsible for the acts of DORTA,[50] indicating that Rakkab has never adopted DORTA's actions as its own. Therefore, they cannot be attributed to Rakkab.

---

41 *Tadic case* (n 29) [118]-[119] [141].

42 *Clarifications* [4].

43 *Compromis* [23].

44 *Compromis* [44].

45 *Compromis* [32].

46 *Compromis* [11].

47 ARSIWA (n 1) art 11.

48 ARSIWA (n 1) art 11 Commentary [6]; *United States Diplomatic and Consular Staff in Tehran* (United States of America v Iran) (Judgment) [1980] ICJ Rep 3 [74].

49 *Compromis* [31].

50 *Compromis* [42].

B. ALTERNATIVELY, RAKKAB IS NOT RESPONSIBLE FOR ITS OWN FAILURE TO PREVENT DORTA FROM COMMITTING THE WRONGFUL ACTS.

The Principle[51] that States should ensure[52] activities within their territory[53] and jurisdiction[54] do not cause damage[55] to the environment of other States[56] is now a part of the *corpus*[57] of international law. Further, States should protect the human rights from being infringed by transboundary environmental damage.[58] Accordingly, a State will not be under such obligation when the activity has no risk of significant transboundary harm [i] and the activity does not cause significant transboundary harm [ii].

i. The harvesting in Rakkab has no risk of significant transboundary harm.

The term 'risk' refers to the possibility of harm caused by activity,[59] which should be assessed on the basis of an objective evaluation of all the relevant circumstances including the nature and magnitude of the project and the context in which the conduct was to be carried out,[60] instead of being deduced from the result[61] of certain activities.

Aurokans have been harvesting more than 140,000 Yaks annually for a long time,[62]

---

51 *Certain Activities Carried out by Nicaragua in the Border Area* (Costa Rica v Nicaragua) and *Construction of a Road in Costa Rica Along the San Juan River* (Nicaragua v Costa Rica) (Judgment) [2015] ICJ Rep 665 [104].

52 'Declaration of the United Nations Conference on the Human Environment' (adopted 16 June 1972) 11 ILM 1416 Principle 21.

53 *Corfu Channel case* (United Kingdom v Albania) (Merits) [1949] ICJ Rep 4, 22.

54 Rio Declaration on Environment and Development (adopted 14 June 1992) ILM 874 Principle 2.

55 *Environment and Human Rights* (Advisory Opinion) [2017] IACHR No Oc-23/17 art III(a).

56 Convention on Biological Diversity (adopted 5 June 1992, entered into force 29 December 1993) 30619 UNTS 1760 (CBD) art 3.

57 *Legality of the Threat or the Use of Nuclear Weapons* (Advisory Opinion) [1996] ICJ Rep 226 [29].

58 *Environment and Human Rights* (n 55) art II(h).

59 ILC 'Draft Articles on Prevention of Transboundary Harm from Hazardous Activities with Commentaries' (2001) UN Doc A/RES/56/10 art 1 Commentary (7).

60 *Certain Activities* and *Construction of a Road* (n 51) [155].

61 *Certain Activities* and *Construction of a Road* (n 51) [155].

62 *Compromis* [24].

while DORTA's harvesting constitutes only a quarter of Aurok's hunting[63] and 5% of whole population of Yak.[64] Besides, experts in Rakkab[65] have conducted a preliminary assessment[66] to ascertain the sustainability of Yak harvesting level. Based upon an objective assessment of these facts, there is no reason to believe that such limited and cautious harvesting has risk of significant transboundary harm.

ii. The harvesting of the Yak in Rakkab does not cause significant transboundary harm.

a. The alleged harm cannot be proved by clear and convincing evidence.

The alleged harm should be supported by clear, convincing[67] and conclusive[68] evidence. Since there is no direct evidence[69] in the present case, the standard for indirect evidence submitted by Aurok should leave no room for reasonable doubt.[70] Therefore, the indirect evidence has to base on a series of facts linked together and leading logically to a single conclusion.[71] Evidence in the present case fails to satisfy that standard.

First, the media reports should not be treated as evidence[72] to establish the existence of harm. The acceptable media reports have to constitute public knowledge worldwide.[73] However, both *Courier Mail* and *Aurok Truth* are national newspapers[74] and fail to reach the standard of public knowledge which requires extensive coverage

63 *Compromis* [24].

64 *Compromis* [36].

65 *Compromis* [33].

66 *Certain Activities* and *Construction of a Road* (n 51) [154].

67 *Pulp Mills on the River Uruguay* (Argentina v Uruguay)(Judgment) [2010] ICJ Rep 14 [225] [228] [230]; *Trail Smelter* (United States of America v Canada) [1938/1941] 3 RIAA 1905, 1950, 1965.

68 *Corfu Channel* (n 53) 16-17.

69 *Corfu Channel* (n 53) 16-17.

70 *Corfu Channel* (n 53) 18.

71 *Corfu Channel* (n 53) 18.

72 *Military and Paramilitary Activities* (n 33) [63].

73 *Staff in Tehran* (n 48) [12].

74 *Compromis* [22].

in the world.[75] Besides, these media reports only mentioned the facts that the Yak was killed by DORTA without linking the damage to the harvesting. Therefore, the reports lack consistency and concordance[76] to the main facts and circumstances of the case.[77]

Second, NGO report used for proving has to be gathered in a certain way[78] and be specific to the claim.[79] YLSA's reports provide no details on how the information was gathered and it only speculates the causes of reduction of Yak without offering convincible reasons.[80] Furthermore, the evidence will become less reliable if it is driven from one source.[81] Therefore, YLSA's report lacks reliability because there is no other independent research supporting it.[82]

Third, the statements of witness from the north part of Aurok cannot prove itself [83] because the statements are personal and subjective.[84] The witness' statement can be used to assist in determining the fact when it is in conjunction with other provable evidence.[85] But in the present case, Aurok fails to provide any other provable evidence.

In conclusion, no significant transboundary harm can be proved due to the insufficiency of clear and convincing evidence.

iii. The causal link cannot be established between the harvesting in Rakkab and the reduction of Yak population.

The causal link has to be established between the alleged activity and the result.[86] In

---

75 *Staff in Tehran* (n 48) [12].

76 *Staff in Tehran* (n 48) [12].

77 *Staff in Tehran* (n 48) [12].

78 *Armed Activities on the Territory of the Congo* (Democratic Republic of Congo v Uganda) (Judgment) [2005] ICJ Rep 168 [61].

79 *Armed Activities* (n 78) [298].

80 *Compromis* [27].

81 *Military and Paramilitary Activities* (n 33) [63].

82 *Compromis* [28].

83 *Military and Paramilitary Activities* (n 33) [68].

84 *Military and Paramilitary Activities* (n 33) [68].

85 *Military and Paramilitary Activities* (n 33) [68].

86 *Certain Activities* and *Construction of a Road* (n 51) [119].

Certain Activities and *Construction of a Road* case, factors of sufficiency, proximity and interference are considered by the Court when building up a causal link,[87] which is also confirmed by the standard of International Law Commission (ILC).[88] However, neither of those is satisfied in the present case.

First, the total number of Yak harvested in Rakkab is 30,000 annually,[89] roughly 5% of the entire Yak population, and about only one-third of the number of Yak harvested by Aurokans.[90] Giving by the proportion, the decline of Yak should be attributed to Aurok instead of Rakkab.

Second, YLSA's reports provide no details on how the information was cross-examined,[91] it only speculates the causes of reduction of Yak without offering convincible evidences and no other independent research can support it.[92] While no decrease of Yak population was reported before 2016[93] since the increase of Yak harvesting started in 2011,[94] the temporal gap between the harvesting in Rakkab and the decline of Yak population leaves room for reasonable doubt that there may exist other factors[95] influencing the Yak population. In conclusion, the causation cannot be established.

To sum up, the harvesting of Yak is carried out without risk of significant harm and there is no evidence leading to such harm. Moreover, causal link can't be established between the Yak harvesting in Rakkab and the decline of the Yak population. Thus, Rakkab is not obliged to prevent the harvesting.

---

87 *Certain Activities* and *Construction of a Road* (n 51) [181]-[216].

88 ARISIWA (n 1) art 31 Commentary [10].

89 *Compromis* [36].

90 *Compromis* [36].

91 *Armed Activities* (n 78) [61].

92 *Armed Activities* (n 78) [61].

93 *Compromis* [27].

94 *Compromis* [23].

95 *Certain Activities* and *Construction of a Road* (n 51) [119].

II. THE HARVESTING OF YAK IN RAKKAB DOES NOT VIOLATE INTERNATIONAL OBLIGATION TO THE PROTECTION OF ENDANGERED SPECIES AND THE ENVIRONMENT.

DORTA's harvesting of the Yak in Rakkab did not violate Rakkab's international obligations under substantive obligations [A] or procedure obligations [B].

A. RAKKAB DOES NOT VIOLATE ITS SUBSTANTIVE OBLIGATIONS.

i. The harvesting does not violate Rakkab's obligation under CMS.

According to CMS Article III(5), animals in Appendix I are prohibited from any kinds of taking unless the exceptions[96] are made. The exceptions include takings for scientific purposes [a] and extraordinary circumstance so required [b].[97]

a. The harvesting of Yak is for scientific purpose.

While CMS does not define 'scientific purpose', referential guidance can be found in this Court's *Whaling in the Antarctic* judgment,[98] where the Court concentrated on whether the specific elements of the scientific program's design and implementation were reasonable in relation to achieving its stated scientific objectives.[99] Peer-reviewed[100] scientific outcomes[101] that beneficial to the community,[102] the use of lethal method[103] and the environmental sustainability[104] are taken as criteria in assessing the conformity of scientific purpose by the application of other Conventions.[105]

---

96 Convention on the Conservation of Migratory Species of Wild Animals (adopted 23 June 1979, entered into force 1 November 1983) 1651 UNTS 333 (CMS) art III 5.

97 CMS art III 5 (a)(d).

98 *Whaling in the Antarctic* (Australia v Japan: New Zealand intervening) (Judgment) [2014] ICJ Rep 226 [227].

99 *Whaling* (n 98) [67] [88].

100 *Whaling* (n 98) [74] [84].

101 *Whaling* (n 98) [219].

102 Mauritius Fisheries and Marine Resources Act (2007) Section 16(2).

103 *Whaling* (n 98) [67][128]-[146].

104 'Chile National Report' (2019) COP13 UNEP/CMS/COP13/NR023; 'Peru National Report' (2019) COP13 UNEP/CMS/COP13/NR095.

105 'Transfer of Technology and Technology Cooperation' UNEP/CBD/COP/DEC/7/29, 6; CBD Secretariat, *Handbook of the Convention on Biological Diversity Including Its Cartagena Protocol on Biosafety* (3rd edn Montreal 2005) 158.

The initial aim behind DORTA's harvesting was to pursue and disseminate the scientific discoveries, including new medicines and treatments.[106] As no alternative method other than lethal one is available,[107] the harvesting of Yak is needed and the Gallvectra manifests itself with great scientific output of the harvesting,[108] as it is highly effective in treating the diabetes and related disorders.[109]

In addition, State owes a degree of latitude in implementing its own domestic policies in good faith.[110] As Regulation AG/2017-0300[111] and other sufficient mechanisms have been introduced to ensure that the harvesting adheres to this purpose on a continuing basis, the harvesting is in conformity with its stated object and satisfies the exception of scientific purpose.

b. Alternatively, the harvesting of Yak satisfied the extraordinary circumstance so required.

The extraordinary circumstance does not manifest itself in CMS context, but explanation can be interpreted in the context of Article III as a whole[112] and various environmental law treaties,[113] covering a range of subject matter and circumstances, instead of limiting within the scope of preventing extraordinary harm.[114] Besides, 'so required' indicates an absence of reasonable alternatives other than the necessity of taking.[115]

106 *Compromis* [9].

107 *Compromis* [26] [33].

108 *Compromis* [13] [15]

109 *Compromis* [14].

110 *LaGrand* (Germany v United States) (Judgment) [2001] ICJ Rep 466 [124].

111 *Compromis* [44]; *Clarifications* [7].

112 Vienna Convention on the Law of Treaties (adopted 22 May 1969, entered into force 27 January 1980) 1155 UNTS 331(VCLT) art 31(1).

113 Convention on Wetlands of International Importance Especially as Waterfowl Habitat (adopted 2 February 1971, entered into force 21 December 1975) 996 UNTS 245 (Ramsar Convention) art 4; Berne Convention on the Conversation of European Wildlife and Natural Habitats arts 4, 9; Convention for the Protection of Migratory Bird between the United States and Great Britain art VII.

114 Arie Trouwborst, 'Aussie Jaws and International Laws: The Australian Shark Cull and the Convention on Migratory Species' (2014) 2 *Cornell InL Jour Online* 41, 43.

115 Trouwborst (n 114) 44.

The Yak harvesting provides extraordinary medical benefits, and potentially could be a cure for diseases such as diabetes, which will almost certainly prolong the lives on an almost unprecedented scale, as it has been added to the WHO Model List of Essential Medicines,[116] indicating that it is the medicine that satisfies the priority health care needs of the population and should be available within the health system adequately.[117] This permanent solution to a life-threatening illness is required since other method including non-lethal alternatives is absent.[118] Therefore, the harvesting can be justified by the extraordinary circumstance since it is for the interest of public health[119] and other reasonable alternatives are absent in the present situation.

c. The harvesting of Yak satisfied the general restrictions to the exceptions.

The exceptional taking should be precise to content, limited in space and time and not operate to the disadvantage of the species, and Parties shall inform the Secretariat when it made exceptions.[120] The Yak harvesting is under the Regulation which imposes the restriction on the total number of the Yak harvested in Rakkab.[121] All licenses issued under Regulation are notified to CMS Secretariat.[122] Besides, as the EIA had confirmed, the sustainability of Yak population would not be influenced.[123] Therefore, no disadvantage had been made.

ii. The harvesting does not violate Rakkab's obligation under CITES.

a. An export permit is not required.

Although Yak has been included in Appendix III of CITES[124] and Gallvectra is a kind

116 *Compromis* [37].

117 'Essential Medicines; Definition' <http://www.who.int/medicines/services/essmedicines_def/en/> accessed 10 January 2019.

118 *Whaling* (n 98) [82].

119 Treaty on the Prohibition of Nuclear Weapons (adopted 7 July 2017, opened for signature 20 September 2017) UN Doc A/CONF229/2017/8 (TPNW) art 17.

120 CMS art III 7.

121 *Compromis* [45].

122 *Clarifications* [8].

123 *Clarifications* [7].

124 *Compromis* [40]; Convention on International Trade in Endangered Species of Wild Fauna

of derivatives of the Yak,[125] an export permit is only required when the Appendix III specimen is being exported from the country that requested the addition of the species to Appendix III.[126] The Kayleff Yak was added to Appendix III at the request of Aurok, not Rakkab.[127] Therefore, an export permit was not required for the export of Gallvectra, but only a certificate of origin was required.[128]

b. Alternatively, the breach does not require DORTA to cease the harvesting.

The purpose of CITES is to regulate international trade, particularly the activities of poachers and illegal traders, it does not prohibit the taking of the Yak.[129] The harvesting of the Yak was under the Regulation and the Lustuk Enzyme was obtained in a legal way,[130] and Rakkab has already issued export permit.[131] Therefore, the taking alone does not justify discontinuation of DORTA's harvesting of the Yak.

B. RAKKAB DOES NOT VIOLATE ITS PROCEDURAL OBLIGATIONS.

i. Rakkab has fulfilled its preventive obligation.

States are required to act with due diligence in preventing significant transboundary harm resulting from activities in its territory.[132] However, as this Court noted in the *Genocide* case, due diligence obligation is one of conduct and not one of result.[133] Rakkab has fulfilled its preventive obligation to conduct an EIA consistent with its customary obligation [a] and notify, negotiate and consult with Aurok in good faith [b].

---

and Flora (adopted 3 March 1973, entered into force 1 July 1975) 993 UNTS 243 (CITES).

125 Derivatives: Any Processed Part of an Animal or Plant (e.g. Medicine). See CITES, 'CITES Glossary' <https://www.cites.org/eng/resources/terms/glossary.php#d> accessed 10 January 2019.

126 CITES art V(2); Cyrille de Klemm, 'Guidelines for Legislation to Implement CITES' (1993) 26 *IUCN Environmental Policy and Law Paper* 1, 29.

127 *Compromis* [40].

128 *Clarifications* [6].

129 CITES Preamble; Michael Bowman *et al*, *Lyster's International Wildlife Law* (2nd edn, CUP 2010) 486.

130 *Compromis* [44]-[45].

131 *Clarifications* [6].

132 *Trail Smelter* (n 67) 1965; *Nuclear Weapons* (n 57) [29]; *Genocide Convention* (n 31) [430]; *Pulp Mills* (n 67) [187].

133 *Genocide Convention* (n 31) [430].

a. Rakkab has fulfilled its obligation to conduct an EIA.

As the Court noted in *Pulp Mills* case, it may now be considered a general international law to undertake an EIA[134] where certain activities have risks of significant adverse impact[135] in a transboundary context,[136] and it should be conducted prior to the decision.[137] Even when the harvesting of Yak in Rakkab has no risk of significant transboundary harm and the obligation of conducting an EIA has been exempted, Rakkab still carries out the assessment consistent to the customary international law.[138]

First, as is required by the customary international law,[139] EIA had been taken prior to the implementation of certain activities.[140] In the present case, Rakkabi experts had ascertained the sustainability of Yak harvesting in Rakkab.[141] EIA involving consultation with DORTA scientists, YLSA representatives, Rakkabi Pivzao adherents, government officials from Aurok was conducted in October 2017,[142] before the issuance of Regulation[143] and the result of the assessment confirmed that the harvesting of DORTA would not lead to the negative influence of the sustainability of Yak population.[144]

Second, Rakkab has continuously monitored the effects on the environment throughout the project.[145] As Rakkabi Ministry of Agriculture promised,[146] an

134 *Pulp Mills* (n 67) [204].

135 CBD art 14(1) (a).

136 *Certain Activities* and *Construction of a Road* (n 51) [104].

137 *Pulp Mills* (n 67) [205].

138 *Pulp Mills* (n 67) [204]; Rio Principle 17.

139 *Pulp Mills* (n 67) [204]

140 *Pulp Mills* (n 67) [205].

141 *Compromis* [33].

142 *Clarifications* [7].

143 *Clarifications* [7].

144 *Clarifications* [7].

145 *Pulp Mills* (n 67) [205].

146 *Compromis* [31].

application called 'YakTrakker' was released in Rakkab.[147] Scientists[148] could monitor the project's effects,[149] including the health and vitality of the Yak population with that application.[150]

b. Rakkab has notified, negotiated and consulted with Aurok in good faith.

A State is obliged to notify and consult in good faith[151] with the potentially affected State when EIA confirms that there is a risk of significant transboundary harm[152] and that certain activity to be carried is liable to cause such harm.[153] A State should also negotiate with the potentially affected State[154] and seek cooperation between the Parties.[155] Although EIA had confirmed the inexistence of risk,[156] the obligations had been fulfilled.

First, the notification contained technical data enables the notified Party to assess the probable impact of the certain activity.[157] The spokesperson of DORTA had notified the amount and purpose of harvesting in Rakkab.[158]

Second, the consultation and negotiation are arranged in good faith[159] and are not limited in formal process.[160] The purpose of the consultation and negotiation is to achieve acceptable solutions[161] which take an equitable balance of interests of

---

147 *Compromis* [34].

148 *Compromis* [34].

149 *Certain Activities* and *Construction of a Road* (n 51) [161].

150 *Compromis* [34].

151 *Certain Activities* and *Construction of a Road* (n 51) [104].

152 *Certain Activities* and *Construction of a Road* (n 51) [104].

153 *Pulp Mills* (n 67) [119].

154 *Pulp Mills* (n 67) [59].

155 *Pulp Mills* (n 67) [58].

156 *Clarifications* [7].

157 *Pulp Mills* (n 67) [112].

158 *Compromis* [24].

159 ILC Draft Articles on Prevention (n 59) art 9 Commentary [2].

160 *North Sea Continental Shelf* (Federal Republic of Germany v Denmark; Federal Republic of Germany v The Netherlands) (Judgment) [1969] ICJ Rep 3 [85].

161 Draft Articles on Prevention (n 59) art 9.

both Parties[162] into consideration. Rakkabi Prime Minister and DORTA's CEO had discussed the issue of Yak with Aurokan authority.[163] Both Parties agreed on the importance of the sustainability of Yak Population.[164] Rakkab also promised to monitor the harvesting and cooperate with Aurok[165] for mutual interest.

ii. Rakkab has fulfilled the obligation to minimize the risk.

The due diligence,[166] according to which a State is obliged to take actions to avoid significant transboundary harm, also requires reasonable effort[167] to minimize the risk.[168] The efforts have to be proportioned to the magnitude of the subject[169] and embodied as factual and legal implementation.[170] However, the total prevention of the significant harm is not necessarily required.[171]

The legislation and administrative regulations had been designed and enforced[172] in Rakkab. Rakkab came up with the Regulation of providing licenses with a limited number and period of the Yak harvesting[173] to avoid unconstrained overkill. The strengthened regulation was in conformity with the effort to minimize the risk of harvesting.

C. RAKKAB IS NOT OBLIGED TO CEASE THE HARVESTING.

The internationally wrongful act is under obligation to cease if it has a continuing character[174] and the violated rule is still in force.[175] However, as proved above, Rakkab

162 Draft Articles on Prevention (n 59) art 9.

163 *Compromis* [31].

164 *Compromis* [31].

165 *Compromis* [31].

166 *Pulp Mills* (n 67) [101].

167 Draft Articles on Prevention (n 59) art 3 Commentary [10].

168 Draft Articles on Prevention (n 59) art 3 Commentary [7].

169 Draft Articles on Prevention (n 59) art 3 Commentary [11].

170 Draft Articles on Prevention (n 59) art 3 Commentary [10].

171 Draft Articles on Prevention (n 59) art 3 Commentary [7].

172 Draft Articles on Prevention (n 59) art 3 Commentary [10].

173 *Compromis* [44].

174 ARSIWA (n 1) art 14 Commentary [5].

175 *Rainbow Warrior case* (New Zealand v France) [1986] 19 RIAA 199 [114].

does not violate any international obligations to protect endangered species and the environment. Therefore, Rakkab is not obliged to cease the harvesting.

III. THE HARVESTING OF YAK IN RAKKAB DOES NOT VIOLATE THE CULTURAL AND RELIGIOUS RIGHTS OF AUROKANS AND RAKKAB IS NOT OBLIGATED TO PROHIBIT SUCH HUNTING.

A. RAKKAB HAS NO OBLIGATION OVER AUROKANS' CULTURAL AND RELIGIOUS RIGHTS UNDER INTERNATIONAL LAW.

i. Rakkab has no obligation under ILO No 169 and UNDRIP.

a. Aurokans are not indigenous people.

Only indigenous people are under the protection of ILO No 169 and United Nations Declaration on the Rights of Indigenous Peoples (UNDRIP). Indigenous people should form the non-dominant sectors of societies and should be distinct from other sectors prevailing in those territories.[176] The rationale for protection is based on their vulnerability of being disadvantaged and suffering from historic injustices[177] for their differences from the national dominant society.[178]

In the present case, Aurok is composed almost entirely of adherents of the Pivzao civilization since its independence.[179] The Pivzao civilization adherents form the dominant and prevailing sector of the Aurokan society and have not experienced

---

176 'United Nations Declaration on the Rights of Indigenous Peoples, Historical Overview' <https://www.un.org/development/desa/indigenouspeoples/declaration-on-the-rights-of-indigenous-peoples.html> accessed 1 January 2019; Benedict Kingsbury 'Indigenous Peoples in International Law:A Constructivist Approach to the Asian Controversy'(1998) 92 (3) *American Journal of International Law* 414, 453.

177 United Nations General Assembly (UNGA) 'United Nations Declaration on the Rights of Indigenous Peoples' (13 September 2007) UN Doc A/RES/61/295 Preamble.

178 UNDRIP (n 177) Preamble; Convention (No 169) Concerning Indigenous and Tribal Peoples in Independent Countries (adopted 27 June 1989, entered into force 5 September 1991) 1650 UNTS383 (ILO No 169) art 2; *African Commission on Human and Peoples' Rights v Republic of Kenya* [2017] ACHPR Application No 006/2012 [107]; *Centre for Minority Rights Development (Kenya) and Minority Rights Group International on Behalf of Endorois Welfare Council v Kenya* [2003] ACHPR Communication No 276-2003 [148]; Irene Daes 'On the Concept of "Indigenous People"' UN Doc E/CNA/Sub2/ACA/1996/2 [69].

179 *Compromis* [7].

any disadvantage. Therefore, the Aurokan population should not be recognized as indigenous people and should not be protected under ILO No. 169 and UNDRIP.

b. ILO No 169 is not applicable extraterritorially.

ILO No 169 aims at protecting the aspirations of indigenous people recognized by ILO within the framework of the States in which they live.[180] Besides, it takes the approach that the cultures and institutions of indigenous peoples must be respected within their national societies.[181] Therefore, the indigenous people only own rights against their own government in the context of ILO No 169.

In the present case, even if the Aurokan group is recognized as indigenous people, their rights are only recognized within the framework and national society of Aurok, not in Rakkab.

c. UNDRIP is not applicable.

First, UNDRIP, as a General Assembly's resolution, is not a legally binding instrument. Under the UN Charter, the authority of the General Assembly is only to make 'recommendations'.[182] It is rarely resorted to in practice.[183]

Second, UNDRIP does not reflect customary international law.[184] A resolution adopted by the UN cannot create a rule of customary international law unless the provision corresponds to a general practice that is accepted as law (*opinio juris*).[185] UNDRIP was not adopted by a unanimous vote. Four countries voted against it and eleven

180 ILO No 169 Preamble.

181 'Leaflet No 8: The ILO and Indigenous and Tribal Peoples OHCHR', <https://www.ohchr.org/Documents/Publications/GuideIPleaflet8en.pdf> accessed 1 January 2019.

182 *Obligation to Negotiate Access to the Pacific Ocean* (Bolivia v Chile) (Judgment) [2018] ICJ Rep 507 [171].

183 Economic and Social Council 'Report of the Commission on Human Rights' (1962) E/3616/Rev [105].

184 'Rights of Indigenous Peoples' 75th Conference of the International Law Association Held in Sofia, Bulgaria (26 to 30 August 2012) Resolution No 5/2012 [3].

185 *Nuclear Weapons* (n 57) [73]; *Military and Paramilitary Activities* (n 33) [183].

countries chose abstentions[186] while these countries are home to large indigenous populations whose rights are especially affected.[187] Besides, some of the States who voted in favor expressed that they had no intention to lay down rules of international law.[188] Therefore, UNDRIP cannot be established as customary international law.[189] Rakkab has no obligation under UNDRIP.

ii. Rakkab has no obligation under ICCPR and ICESCR.

International Covenant on Civil and Political Rights (ICCPR) explicitly limits States obligations to individuals in their territory and subject to their jurisdiction.[190] International Covenant on Economic, Social and Cultural Rights (ICESCR) guarantees rights which are essentially territorial[191] and shall apply with respect to situations within the State's national territory, and outside the national territory over which States Parties may exercise effective control.[192]

Therefore, 'jurisdiction' is a critical issue in determining Rakkab's obligation under these instruments. 'Jurisdiction' occurs when the State exercises effective control[193]

---

186 UNDRIP (n 177) adopted by a Vote of 143 in Favor to 4 against (Australia, Canada, New Zealand and United States) with 11 Abstentions (Azerbaijan, Bangladesh, Bhutan, Burundi, Colombia, Georgia, Kenya, Nigeria, Russian Federation, Samoa and Ukraine) <https://www.un.org/development/desa/indigenouspeoples/declaration-on-the-rights-of-indigenous-peoples.html> assessed 1 January 2019.

187 *North Sea Continental Shelf* (n 160) [73].

188 'Draft Resolution A/61/L67' UNGA 61st Session 107th Plenary Meeting (13 September 2007) UN Doc A/61/PV107, 22, 26.

189 'Rights of Indigenous Peoples' (n 184) [3].

190 International Covenant on Civil and Political Rights (adopted 16 December 1966, entered into force 23 March 1976) 999 UNTS 171 (ICCPR) art 2; Human Rights Committee (HRC) 'General Comment No 31: The Nature of the General Legal Obligation Imposed on States Parties to the Covenant' (26 May 2004) UN Doc CCPR/C/21/Rev1/Add13 [10].

191 *Legal Consequences of the Construction of a Wall in the Occupied Palestinian Territory* (Advisory Opinion) [2004] ICJ Rep 136 [106]-[112].

192 *Sergio Euben Lopez Burgos v Uruguay* [1981] UN Doc CCPR/C/13/D/52/1979 para 12.2; *Wall Palestine* (n 191) [112]; *Armed Activities* (n 78) [216]-[217]; *Loizidou v Turkey* [1995] ECHR 10 [68] [71].

193 *Burgos* (n 192) para 12.2.

over either the territory[194] or individuals.[195] 'Effective control' is established through the State's own armed forces or through a subordinate local administration.[196] In the present case, Rakkab's effective control over Aurokan territory or populations cannot be established. Aurokans are neither within Rakkab's territory nor under its jurisdiction.[197] Hence, Rakkab has no obligation over Aurokans under ICCPR and ICESCR.

B. ALTERNATIVELY, RAKKAB DOES NOT VIOLATE THE CULTURAL AND RELIGIOUS RIGHTS OF AUROKANS.

i. Rakkab does not violate Aurokans' cultural rights.

Cultural rights are rights related to 'culture',[198] which means the sum total of the material and spiritual activities and products of a given social group[199] that distinguish it from others.[200] Violation of cultural rights occurs when States prevent access to cultural life,[201] especially in terms of evictions from land,[202] effective denial of the right to enjoy cultural life,[203] and banning the use of languages.[204] These confirm a considerably high threshold of violation of cultural rights that it happens upon prevention or restriction of access to cultural life. Besides, according to the UN Human

194 *Loizidou* (n 192) [68] [71]; *Wall Palestine* (n 191) [107]-[113]; *Armed Activities* (n 78) [216] [217].

195 *Burgos* (n 192) para 12.2.

196 *Loizidou* (n 192) [52]; *Cyprus v Turkey* (Merits) ECHR 2001-IV [76]; *Banković and Others v Belgium and Others* (Admissibility) ECHR 2001-XII [70].

197 *Compromis* [7] [8].

198 United Nations Educational, Scientific and Cultural Organization (UNESCO) 'Universal Declaration on Cultural Diversity' (2 November 2001) Preamble [5]; UNESCO 'Recommendation on Participation by the People at Large in Cultural Life and Their Contribution to It' (26 November 1976) 19 C/Resolutions + CORR Preamble [5 (a) (c)].

199 Committee on Economic, Social and Cultural Rights (CESCR) 'General Comment No 21: Right of Everyone to Take Part in Cultural Life' (2009) UN Doc E/C12/GC/21 [11].

200 *Endorois Welfare Council* (n 178) [241].

201 General Comment No 21(n 199) [62].

202 *African Commission on Human and Peoples' Rights* (n 178) [183]; *Khurshid Mustafa and Tarzibachi v Sweden* [2008] ECHR Application No 23883/06 [44].

203 *Länsman and Others v Finland* [1994] CCPR UN Doc CCPR/C/52/D/511/1992 para 9.5.

204 Office of the United Nations High Commissioner for Human Rights 'Frequently Asked Questions on Economic, Social and Cultural Rights' Fact Sheet No 33, 18.

Rights Committee, 'limited impact' does not amount to violation of cultural rights.[205]

In the present case, Aurokans have access to and are able to practice their rights with the existing amount of the Yak and their continuous harvesting.[206] There has been no significant increase in the rate of malnutrition in Aurok since 2000,[207] indicating that Aurokans' consumption of the Yak has remained on a stable level. Aurokans' religious and cultural rights exercised through the Yak harvesting are therefore not violated.

Rakkab had taken Aurokans' interests into consideration.[208] It had consulted Aurokans before initiating the Regulation, and restricted the Yak harvesting number to the minimum level, which can guarantee the sustainability of the Yak's population.[209] It is also dedicated that Rakkab is determined to find out alternative ways like captive breeding and synthetic alternatives.[210] Therefore, the threshold of violation is not met.

ii. Rakkab does not violate Aurokans' religious rights.

Religious rights include the right to freedom of thought, conscience and religion and freedom to manifest religion or belief.[211] Rakkab violates neither of the rights.

a. Rakkab has not violated Aurokans' right to freedom of religion.

Freedom of religion includes the freedom to have or to adopt a religion or belief of his choice.[212] In this case, Aurokans enjoy the freedom to practice their religious rights through the Yak hunting and the traditional use of the Yak is not precluded.[213]

---

205 *Länsman* (n 203) para 10.5.

206 *Compromis* [18] [20] [27].

207 *Clarifications* [2].

208 Läns*man* (n 203) para 10.5.

209 *Compromis* [45]; *Clarifications* [7].

210 *Compromis* [26] [33].

211 ICCPR art 18(1); CCPR 'General Comment No 22: Article 18 (Freedom of Thought, Conscience or Religion)' (30 July 1993) UN Doc CCPR/C/21/Rev1/Add4 art 18[4]; *Free Legal Assistance Group v Zaire* [1995] ACHPR Comm No 25/89, 47/90, 56/91,100/93 [45].

212 General Comment No 22 (n 211) [1].

213 *Compromis* [20].

b. Rakkab has not violated Aurokans' right to freedom to manifest religion and belief.

Violation of the right to manifest religion has a considerably high threshold. It occurs under situations when it is impossible to undertake religious practice, including the eviction of populations from land,[214] deprivation of natural resources central to religion,[215] banning religious activities,[216] prohibiting the opening of places of worship.[217]

In the present case, Aurokans are still able to conduct ritual and ceremonial acts and customs with the existing amount of the Yak.[218] Through continuous harvesting, Aurokans have the possibility of performing the right to manifest religion. The Yak harvesting in Rakkab does not preclude Aurokans from worship, observance, practice and teaching of their religion or belief.[219] Hence, Aurokan people's right to freedom to manifest religion and belief is not violated.

C. ALTERNATIVELY, YAK HARVESTING IN RAKKAB CAN BE JUSTIFIED BY THE NECESSARY LIMITATIONS TO CULTURAL AND RELIGIOUS RIGHTS.

Limitations to cultural and religious rights are allowed and necessary if it is determined by law[220] and proportionate[221] to a legitimate aim.[222] The legitimate aim for limitations to religious rights is to protect public health and the fundamental rights and freedoms

---

214 *African Commission on Human and Peoples' Rights* (n 178) [166].

215 *Cha'are Shalom Ve Tsedek v France* (Merits) [2000] ECHR 2000-VII [80].

216 *Jehovah's Witnesses of Moscow and Others v Russia* (Merits and Just Satisfaction) [2010] ECHR Application No 302/02 [103].

217 *Jehovah's Witnesses of Moscow and Others* (n 216) [102].

218 *Compromis* [18] [20] [27].

219 General Comment 21 (n 199) [4].

220 *Singh v France* (Merits) UN Doc CCPR/C/106/D/1852/2008 para 8.4; ICCPR art 18(3); International Covenant on Economic, Social and Cultural Rights (adopted 16 December 1966) 993 UNTS 3 (ICESCR) art 4.

221 *African Commission on Human and Peoples' Rights* (n 178) [167]; General Comment 21 (n 199) [19]; General Comment 22 (n 211) [8].

222 *African Commission on Human and Peoples' Rights* (n 178) [184]; ICCPR art 18(3); ICESCR art 4.

of others, especially the right to health[223] for the promotion of general welfare in a democratic society.[224] States are obligated to allocate 'maximum available resources'[225] to realize the right to health,[226] which includes the right of access to essential medicines and the right to treatment of diseases.[227]

First, the limitation is prescribed by Rakkabi law and has a legitimate aim. The limitation to Aurokans' rights is to guarantee the fundamental rights to health worldwide by developing Gallvectra, which can treat obesity and diabetes effectively.[228] The implementation of the Regulation AG/2017-0300 provides that the Yak harvesting is mainly for developing Gallvectra.[229]

Second, the limitation is proportionate. Gallvectra is included in the WHO Model list of Essential Medicines and has been widely used to treat diseases in over 85 countries.[230] Besides, the Yak harvesting is the least restrictive measure till now since alternative methods are still under development.[231] Moreover, the number of harvesting is restricted to the lowest level,[232] which guarantees the sustainability of the Yak population.[233] Therefore, the impact brought by the Yak harvesting in Rakkab forms a necessary limitation.

In conclusion, the harvesting of the Yak in Rakkab is not wrongful acts since it does

---

223 ICCPR art 18 (3); *Karnel Singh Bhinder v Canada* [1989] UN Doc CCPR/C/37/D/208/1986 para 6.2; *Sergei Malakhovsky and Alexander Pikul v Belarus* [2005] UN Doc CCPR/C/84/D/1207/2003 para 7.5; *Gareth Anver Prince v South Africa* [2007] UN Doc CCPR/C/91/D/1474/2006 para 7.3.

224 ICESCR art 4; General Comment 21 (n 199).

225 ICESCR art 2(1).

226 WHO 'The Right to Health Factsheet No 31' (2008) 24.

227 The Right to Health Factsheet No 31 (n 226).

228 *Compromis* [14] [20] [37].

229 *Compromis* [45]; *Clarifications* [9].

230 *Compromis* [20].

231 *Compromis* [26] [33].

232 *Compromis* [45].

233 *Clarifications* [7].

not violate Aurokans' cultural and religious rights. Therefore, Rakkab is not obligated to prohibit such hunting forthwith.[234]

IV. RAKKAB DOES NOT NEED TO PAY AUROK A PORTION OF THE PROFITS REALIZED FROM SALES OF THE DRUG GALLVECTRA.

A. THE CONSUMPTION OF TIRHINGA NOS LUSTUK IS NOT TRADITIONAL KNOWLEDGE PROTECTED WITHIN THE SCOPE OF CBD AND THE NAGOYA PROTOCOL.

Traditional knowledge under the Convention on Biological Diversity (CBD) refers to the traditional knowledge, innovations and practices of indigenous and local communities embodying traditional lifestyles relevant for the conservation and sustainable use of biological diversity.[235] The consumption of Tirhinga Nos Lustuk (TNL) is not protected under CBD and the Nagoya Protocol on Access to Genetic Resources and the Fair and Equitable Sharing of Benefits Arising from Their Utilization to the Convention on Biological Diversity (the Nagoya Protocol) as it is not relevant for the conservation and sustainable use of biodiversity [i]; it is not traditional knowledge associated with genetic resources [ii].

i. The consumption of TNL is not traditional knowledge as it is not relevant for the conservation and sustainable use of biodiversity.

Conservation and sustainable use of biodiversity is a key factor in determining traditional knowledge under CBD.[236] It means that the use of traditional knowledge should not lead to a long-term decline of biological diversity for the needs and

234 ARSIWA (n 1) art 14.

235 CBD Preamble, art 8(j); CBD 'Akwé: Kon Guidelines' (2004) CBD-COP 7 Decisions VII/16 F, 7; 'The Tkarihwaié: ri Code of Ethical Conduct'(2010) CBD-COP 10 Decision X/42, 3; International Treaty on Plant Genetic Resources for Food and Agriculture (adopted 3 November 2001, entered into force 29 June 2004) 2400 UNTS 303 art 9.2; World Intellectual Property Organization (WIPO) 'List and Brief Technical Explanation of Various Forms in which Traditional Knowledge May Be Found' (2010) WIPO/GRTKF/IC/17/INF/9, 9.

236 Elisa Morgera *et al*, *Unraveling the Nagoya Protocol: A Commentary on the Nagoya Protocol on Access and Benefit-sharing to the Convention on Biological Diversity* (Brill 2014) 27.

aspirations of present and future generations.[237]

The consumption of TNL is incompatible with the conservation and sustainable use of biodiversity. *First,* an Aurokan town of 100 people might kill as many as 15 or 16 Yak during seasonal migrations.[238] Considering the 1.2 million population of Aurok[239] and their monthly communal eating habits,[240] the consumption of TNL generates a massive amount of killing of the Yak,[241] approximately one-fifth of the entire population annually.[242] *Second*, the long-term consumption contributes to the decline of the Yak population and its possible extinction,[243] posing a threat upon the future generations of the community.[244] *Third*, as the Yak cannot be bred in captivity, [245] Aurokans make no contributions but only adverse impact on the conservation and sustainable use of biodiversity. Hence, the consumption of TNL does not form traditional knowledge within the scope of CBD.

ii. Besides, the consumption of TNL is not traditional knowledge associated with genetic resources.

The Nagoya Protocol applies to traditional knowledge associated with genetic resources,[246] which refer to genetic material of actual or potential value[247] or genetic

---

237 CBD art 2; Nagoya Protocol on Access to Genetic Resources and the Fair and Equitable Sharing of Benefits Arising from Their Utilization to the Convention on Biological Diversity (adopted 29 October 2010, entered into force 12 October 2014) (Nagoya Protocol) art 1; 'Bonn Guidelines on Access to Genetic Resources and Fair and Equitable Sharing of the Benefits Arising out of Their Utilization' (2002) CBD-COP 6 Decision VI/24.

238 *Compromis* [3].

239 *Compromis* [7].

240 *Compromis* [4].

241 *Compromis* [27].

242 *Compromis* [24].

243 *Compromis* [36].

244 *Compromis* [22].

245 *Compromis* [1].

246 Nagoya Protocol art 3; WIPO 'The Protection of Traditional Knowledge: Updated Draft Gap Analysis' (2018) WIPO/GRTKF/IC/38/6 Annex I, 280.

247 CBD art 2; Morgera (n 236) 55.

or biochemical composition.[248] Genetic material refers to any material of plant, animal or other origin containing functional units of heredity (ie DNA).[249] Genetic or biochemical composition refers to that of the gene or of organism.[250]

In the present case, TNL is a soup of nasty bits of the Yak containing numerous other ingredients like roots and wild grains.[251] The soup, as a simple mixture of various ingredients, is not associated with any genetic material or genetic or biochemical composition. Besides, Aurokans lack of knowledge of the biochemical composition of TNL as they have failed to identify the enzyme[252] and produce a reliable, consistent drug from the soup.[253] Moreover, an enzyme does not possess any DNA. Therefore, the Nagoya Protocol is not applicable to the consumption of TNL as it is not traditional knowledge associated with genetic resources.

B. ALTERNATIVELY, THE PRODUCTION OF GALLVECTRA DOES NOT APPROPRIATE AND EXPLOITTHE TRADITIONAL KNOWLEDGE BELONGING TO AUROKANS.

i. The traditional knowledge does not exclusively belong to Aurokans.

Holders of traditional knowledge are indigenous peoples or local communities.[254] In the present case, Rakkabi adherents to the Pivzao traditions are also the holders of the alleged traditional knowledge.[255]

ii. The traditional knowledge has made no contribution to the production of Gallvectra due to its vagueness.

Appropriation refers to ‘a taking of possession’.[256] In practice, appropriation and

---

248 WIPO ‘Matters Concerning the Intergovernmental Committee on Intellectual Property and Genetic Resources, Traditional Knowledge and Folklore (IGC)’ (2013) WO/GA/43/14 Annex A [2]; WIPO General Assembly ‘Matters concerning the IGC’ WO/GA/43/14 Annex A [2].

249 CBD, art 2; Morgera (n 236) 60.

250 Morgera (n 236) 60 Footnote 8.

251 *Compromis* [16].

252 *Compromis* [13].

253 *Compromis* [18].

254 The Protection of Traditional Knowledge (n 246) 5.

255 *Compromis* [8].

256 *Black's Law Dictionary* (8th edn, CUP 2005) 117.

exploitation of traditional knowledge in pharmaceutical field happens when indigenous people or local communities have knowledge about the exact function of a specific kind of organism, for instance curing insect stings, toothache, malaria and diabetes,[257] holding back thirst and hunger[258] and wound healing.[259]

In the present case, Aurokans has not identified gallbladder as the key ingredients of TNL before Dr. Bello's published his findings[260] and they were not aware of the specific functions of the soup or the gallbladder of treating obesity or diabetes.[261] Therefore, Aurokans' knowledge about TNL is too vague and general. It has made no contributions to the identification of the critical enzyme or the production of Gallvectra. Hence, there is no appropriation or exploitation of the traditional knowledge.[262]

iii. The production of Gallvectra is based on Dr. Bello's independent discovery and there is no misappropriation of the traditional knowledge.

Misappropriation occurs when one party has made investments to extract information which the other party takes with no similar investment, causing the first party's suffering from a competitive injury.[263] Misappropriation is excluded when the traditional knowledge is acquired by lawful means such as independent discovery or creation.[264]

In the present case, acquisition of traditional knowledge was conducted through

---

257 Tobias Kiene, *The Legal Protection of Traditional Knowledge in the Pharmaceutical Field: An Intercultural on the International Agenda* (Waxmann, 2011) 16.

258 Kiene (n 257) 19.

259 Kiene (n 257) 19.

260 *Compromis* [13] [16].

261 *Compromis* [4].

262 CBD Secretariat 'Access and Benefit-sharing in Practice: Trends in Partnerships Across Sectors' (2008) CBD Technical Series No 38, 20.

263 WIPO 'Glossary of Key Terms Related to Intellectual Property and Genetic Resources, Traditional Knowledge and Traditional Cultural Expressions' (2018) WIPO/GRTKF/IC/38/INF/7 Annex 26.

264 The Protection of Traditional Knowledge (n 246) 4.

the independent discovery of Dr. Bello. Hence, there is no misappropriation of the knowledge. Dr. Bello observed the low rate of obesity of Aurokans by himself, paid great efforts in locating the key ingredient of gallbladder and identifying the new enzyme through fieldwork and subsequent laboratory studies.[265] The hereafter isolation of the enzyme and the invention of Gallvectra took almost 4 years of dedication of Dr. Bello's team.[266] This work was accomplished independently by Dr. Bello's team and cannot be attributed to the use of Aurokans' traditional knowledge. Therefore, Rakkab is not obliged to pay a remedy for misappropriation.[267]

iv. The traditional knowledge falls in public domain knowledge and is freely available.

Traditional knowledge has often been deemed to be in the public domain and hence freely available once it has been accessed and removed from its particular cultural context and disseminated,[268] except when constituting secret traditional knowledge. If traditional knowledge falls in public domain, it constitutes legitimate use and no liability can be derived from it.[269]

In the present case, Aurok has not taken any measures to maintain secrecy of the knowledge.[270] Dr. Bello learnt about the consumption of TNL simply through fieldwork, indicating that this knowledge is not regarded as secret by Aurokans.[271] Knowledge about TNL is accessible to anyone interested out of the cultural context

265 *Compromis* [13].

266 *Compromis* [14]-[15].

267 WIPO 'The Protection of Traditional Knowledge: Revised Objectives and Principles' (22 March 2010) WIPO/GRTKF/IC/16/5.

268 'Report of the Meeting of the Group of Technical and Legal Experts on Traditional Knowledge Associated with Genetic Resources in the Context of the International Regime on Access and Benefit-sharing' UNEP/CBD/WG-ABS/8/2 [122].

269 WIPO 'Report on the International Patent System' (2009) SCP/13/REF-SCP/12 [237]; List and Brief Technical Explanation of Various Forms (n 235) 9.

270 *Compromis* [3] [5].

271 Agreement on Trade-related Aspects of Intellectual Property Rights, Marrakesh Agreement Establishing the World Trade Organization, Annex 1C (15 April 1994) 1869 UNTS 299 (TRIPS Agreement) art 39; The Protection of Traditional Knowledge (n 246) Annex I, 14.

and is therefore disseminated.[272] Hence, the traditional knowledge falls in public domain and is freely available.

C. ALTERNATIVELY, RAKKAB IS NOT OBLIGED TO OBSERVE THE BENEFIT-SHARING PRINCIPLE UNDER CBD AND THE NAGOYA PROTOCOL.

i. Rakkab is not obligated to benefit-sharing under CBD.

Article 8(j) of CBD encourages benefit-sharing.[273] The terms used by Parties in international law would indicate their legal commitments.[274] Therefore, Article 8(j) is weak in imposing of obligation in this respect on the Parties[275] by leaving them considerable discretion as to the circumstances in which, the extent to which, and how, they will share benefits.[276] Therefore, Rakkab is not bound by CBD to conduct benefit-sharing.

ii. Rakkab is not obligated to benefit-sharing under the Nagoya Protocol as the Nagoya Protocol is not retroactively applicable.

In line with international law,[277] a treaty is not to be regarded as intended to have retroactive effects unless such an intention is expressed in the treaty.[278] The Nagoya Protocol does not apply retroactively to activities that took place before its entry into force[279] without any special clause or any special object necessitating retroactive interpretation.[280] Access and utilization of genetic resources and traditional knowledge

272 *Compromis* [8].

273 CBD art 8(j).

274 *Pacific Ocean* (n 182) [91].

275 Malgosia Fitzmaurice, 'The Dilemma of Traditional Knowledge: Indigenous Peoples and Traditional Knowledge' (2008) 10 *International Community Law Review* 255, 278.

276 CBD 'Traditional Forest-related Knowledge and the Convention on Biological Diversity' (1996) UNEP/CBD/COP/3/Inf53, 3.

277 VCLT art 28.

278 ILC 'Draft Articles on the Law of Treaties with Commentaries' (1966) UN Doc A/6309/Rev1 art 24 Commentary.

279 Mark Villiger, *Commentary on the 1969 Vienna Convention on the Law of Treaties* (Brill 2009) 383.

280 Villiger (n 279) 381; *Mavrommatis Palestine Concessions* [1924] PCIJ Series A No 2, 34.

associated with genetic resources taken place previously would not be covered by the Protocol.

The Nagoya Protocol entered into force October 2014. In the present case, Dr. Bello started his research in 2001[281] and Gallvectra was invented in 2004.[282] The production and marketing of Gallvectra are irrelevant to 'research and development', therefore do not constitute utilization of traditional knowledge. Hence, all the potential situations of access and utilization of traditional knowledge happened before 2014 and are not covered by the Nagoya Protocol.

D. RAKKAB DOES NOT NEED TO PAY THE STATE OF AUROK A PORTION OF PROFIT AS AUROK DOES NOT HAVE THE RIGHT TO CLAIM BENEFIT-SHARING.

Beneficiaries of the protection of traditional knowledge should be the traditional holders of traditional knowledge which are indigenous peoples or local communities.[283] A State would not be the beneficiary unless the traditional knowledge is not specifically attributable to or confined to indigenous peoples or local community, or it is not possible to identify the community that has generated it.[284] Besides, a State can only represent its people and conduct diplomatic protection when local remedies are exhausted.

In the present case, the consumption of TNL is observed by Aurokan and Rakkabi adherents to the Pivzao civilization.[285] The traditional knowledge does not exclusively belong to Aurokans. Religious leaders from both countries have represented their communities respectively in the previous law suit. This indicates that the holders of

281 *Compromis* [13].

282 *Compromis* [15].

283 WIPO 'Glossary of Key Terms Related to Intellectual Property and Genetic Resources, Traditional Knowledge and Traditional Cultural Expressions' (2012) WIPO/GRTKF/IC/22/INF/8 Annex 2; The Protection of Traditional Knowledge (n 267) 36.

284 Report of the Meeting of the Group of Technical and Legal Experts (n 268); Glossary of Key Terms (n 283) Annex 3.

285 *Compromis* [7]-[8].

the alleged traditional knowledge are identifiable and should be the Rakkabi Pivzao community and the Aurokan Pivzao community.[286] Besides, the Aurokan community has not exhausted local remedies regarding their claim of benefit-sharing. Therefore, the State of Aurok is not the holder of the traditional knowledge and does not have the right to claim benefit-sharing.

286 *Clarifications* [3].

CONCLUSION AND PRAYER FOR RELIEF

In view of the facts set forth in this Memorial and the arguments applying the law to the facts as stated;

May it please the Court, on behalf of the Republic of Rakkab, Respondent herein, respectfully requests this Honorable Court to adjudge and declare that:

1. Rakkab is not responsible for the alleged acts because DORTA's actions are not attributable to Rakkab and Rakkab is not responsible to prevent DORTA from committing those wrongful acts;

2. The harvesting of the Yak in Rakkab does not violate Rakkab's international obligations relating to the protection of endangered species and the environment and Rakkab is not obligated to end the Yak harvesting on its territory;

3. The harvesting of the Yak in Rakkab does not violate the cultural and religious rights of the people of Aurok, and Rakkab does not need to prohibit such hunting forthwith;

4. Rakkab does not need to pay Aurok for the Aurokan people, a portion of the profits realized from sales of the drug Gallvectra.

Respectfully submitted,
AGENTS FOR RAKKAB

“Helian 风信子案”

Case Concerning the Helian Hyacinth
(The State of Adawa v The Republic of Rasasa)

叶欧仪　林泽宇　李奕慧　王姿月　余施语　严帅东

请求国书状

Memorials for the State of Adawa

TABLE OF CONTENTS

of protection for the right to life.

C. RASASA'S DEVELOPMENT AND DEPLOYMENT OF THE WALL VIOLATES THE INTERNATIONAL HUMANITARIAN LAW (IHL).

i. The IHL is applicable as the conflicts between Rasasa and the criminal gangs constitute armed conflicts.

ii. Rasasa's development and deployment of the WALL constitutes a violation of the Martens Clause under the IHL.

iii. Rasasa's development and deployment of the WALL is inconsistent with the principle of distinction and proportionality.

D. RASASA SHOULD DISMANTLE AND REMOVE THE WALL.

III. THE COURT MAY ADJUDICATE ADAWA'S CLAIM THAT RASASA'S IMPOSITION OF TARIFFS AT ISSUE VIOLATES THE CHC TREATY, AND ADAWA IS ENTITLED TO COMPENSATORY DAMAGES.

A. DISPUTES IN THE CHC TREATY FALL WITHIN THE COURT'S JURISDICTION AND ARE ADMISSIBLE.

i. The Court has jurisdiction over the disputes at issue.

ii. There are no reasons for the Court to decline its jurisdiction.

B. RASASA'S IMPOSITION OF TARIFFS ON HELIAN PRODUCTS FROM ADAWA VIOLATES THE CHC TREATY, AND ADAWA IS ENTITLED TO COMPENSATORY DAMAGES.

i. The imposition of tariffs at issue violates Article 3 of the CHC Treaty.

ii. The imposition of tariffs at issue cannot be justified under Article 22(b) of the CHC Treaty.

iii. Adawa is entitled to compensatory damages reflecting the financial harm it has suffered to date.

IV. THE ARREST AND DETENTION OF MS. GREY ARE CONSISTENT WITH ADAWA'S OBLIGATIONS UNDER INTERNATIONAL LAW, AND ADAWA MAY PROCESS TO RENDER HER TO ICC.

A. ADAWA IS OBLIGED TO COOPERATE FULLY WITH ICC UNDER ARTICLE 86 OF THE ROME STATUTE.

i. The ICC has jurisdiction over this case and Ms. Grey is in the process of the international criminal proceedings.

ii. Adawa bears no obligation to examine the appropriateness of the warrant.

iii. Adawa should comply with the request to arrest and detain Ms. Grey and may process to render her to the ICC under Article 59 of the Rome Statute.

B. ADAWA'S COOPERATION WITH THE ICC DOES NOT VIOLATE ADAWA'S OBLIGATIONS WITH RESPECT TO THE IMMUNITY UNDER INTERNATIONAL LAW.

i. Adawa does not violate customary international law.

ii. Adawa does not violate the CHC Treaty.

C. ADAWA DOES NOT VIOLATE ITS OBLIGATIONS WITH RESPECT TO THE IMMUNITY UNDER ARTICLE 98(1) OF THE ROME STATUTE.

i. The conflict of Adawa's cooperation obligation and international obligation to respect immunity does not exist.

ii. Even if the conflict of obligations exists, Adawa should still cooperate with the ICC.

CONCLUSION AND PRAYER FOR RELIEF

STATEMENT OF JURISDICTION

The State of Adawa (Adawa) and the Republic of Rasasa (Rasasa) accept the compulsory jurisdiction of the Permanent Court of International Justice (PCIJ) in the Botega Treaty. Adawa hereby submits the present dispute to the International Court of Justice (the Court) pursuant to Article 37 of the Statute of the Court, by virtue of the Statement of Agreed Facts jointly signed by both Parties on 20 September 2019. Both States should accept the Court's decision as final and binding and execute it in good faith.

QUESTIONS PRESENTED

The State of Adawa respectfully requests the Court to adjudge:

I.

1. Whether Adawa is a Party to the Treaty of Botega;

2. Whether the Court has jurisdiction over the present case.

II.

1. Whether Rasasa's development of the WALL is consistent with international law;

2. Whether Rasasa's deployment of the WALL is consistent with international law.

III.

1. Whether Adawa's claim concerning the CHC Treaty falls out of the Court's jurisdiction;

2. Whether Adawa's claim concerning the CHC Treaty is inadmissible;

3. Whether the imposition of tariffs is consistent with the CHC Treaty.

IV.

1. Whether the apprehension and detention of Ms. Grey violates customary international law;

2. Whether the apprehension and detention of Ms. Grey violates the CHC Treaty;

3. Whether the apprehension and detention of Ms. Grey violates the Rome Statute.

STATEMENT OF FACTS

THE BACKGROUND

Adawa and Rasasa are neighboring countries in the Crosinia Region, the only place on Earth where the Helian hyacinth is cultivated. Exports of Helian spice contribute significantly to all six Crosinian States, which were all provinces of the Kingdom of Crosinia. The last king of the Kingdom Narang III died in 1924 without a competent descendant. Scattered violence and skirmishing over the next three years became a full-fledged civil war in 1927.

On 29 October 1929, the remaining belligerents Adawa, Zeitounia and Rasasa concluded negotiations to end the bloodshed. Rasasa declared itself an independent republic. Adawa and Zeitounia united to form the independent monarchy Adawa-Zeitounia Union (AZU). The newly installed President of Rasasa and Queen Goleta of AZU signed the Treaty of Botega on Armistice and Pacification (the Botega Treaty).

On 1 January 1939, the two provinces of AZU amicably agreed to dissolve their Union. Adawa and Rasasa joined the United Nations in 1947 and acceded to the Statute of the International Court of Justice (ICJ Statute). Neither State has filed a declaration accepting the Court's compulsory jurisdiction under Article 36(2) of the Statute.

All of the Crosinian States engaged in the highly profitable Helian industry. To facilitate the Helian industry, the six Crosinian States formed an unofficial round table in 1964. Five years later, that arrangement was formalized in a treaty, signed on 20 June 1969 and ratified by all six Member States, declaring the formation of the Crosinian Helian Community (CHC). The Parties to the CHC agreed to impose no customs duties within the CHC on Helian spice or the equipment and materials used to harvest or process the Helian hyacinth.

In 1998, Adawa became an original Party to the Rome Statute establishing the

International Criminal Court (ICC). Rasasa is not a Party to the Rome Statute.

THE BORDER ISSUE AND THE WALL

On 14 July 2012, a catastrophic tropical cyclone struck the entire Region, following which crime rates skyrocketed throughout the Region. In October 2012, in a meeting convened by the President of Rasasa, the 'Weaponized Autonomous Limitation Line' (WALL) was advocated.

On 6 July 2015, the project of the WALL was completed. Neither of the governments elected to purchase it. Both Adawa and Rasasa stated that it was neither economically feasible nor politically desirable to go further with the project. Rasasan Robotics Corporation (RRC) reportedly marketed the WALL in the ensuing years, but there has been no public confirmation of its deployment by other governments.

Since July 2012, some criminal gangs have been constantly committing cross border crimes. In 2016, they turned well-armed and organized, regularly entered Rasasa illegally, assaulting and killing villagers. In September 2016, Adawa cooperated with Rasasa and jointly decided to establish a high-level task force to tackle the border problem.

In February 2017, the Rasasan Border Police reported that the militia had become organized. Proved by the United Nations Office on Drugs and Crime and eyewitnesses, the militias were heavily armed with military-grade weapons and equipment. They established a permanent and well-defended encampment which they used as the base for international drug trafficking. Both Adawa and Rasasa declared that their domestic police efforts had been ineffective in counteracting the militias.

On 25 June 2017, President Pindro of Rasasa authorized the deployment of the Rasasan Army against the militia camps within Rasasa, as well as the purchase of the WALL from the RRC and its installation along the border. The 10-meter-tall towers are deployed every 200 meters along the 201-kilometer-long border. The WALL closely monitors all ground and aerial activity within a 130,000 square meter area and carries fully automatic .50 caliber machine guns. In addition, the system is fully autonomous, taking actions independently without human control. Decisions are made so rapidly that second-guessing by human is practically impossible.

The President of Adawa strongly objected the deployment of the WALL. He stated that so long as the possibility existed that this autonomous system might be unleashed against Adawan people or on Adawan soil, its deployment would be incompatible with the Botega Treaty and other rules under international law.

Rasasa made no response to Adawa's objections. In May 2018, in response to recommendations from the task force, Adawa stationed unarmed human monitors on its side of the border and reiterated its opposition to the program *de jure*.

THE IMPOSITION OF TARIFFS ON HELIAN PRODUCTS

The storm caused severe death and drastic damages to the town to each of the six States. More than 60% of the Helian hyacinths in Rasasa, 20% of those in Adawa, and between 15% and 20% of those in the other four States were destroyed. Additionally, unemployment rate began to increase across the Region.

The newly elected President Pindro submitted the bill concerning Helian products for legislative approval. He invoked 'essential security interests' and provided for the introduction of tariffs of 25% *ad valorem* on Helian bulbs, live plants, and pollen imported into Rasasa, in an effort to encourage Rasasa's domestic processors to return to local farms for their feedstock. The proposal was adopted by the Rasasan Parliament in January 2018.

In October 2018, Adawa formally requested consultations with Rasasa pursuant to Article 1 and Article 4 of the Understanding on Rules and Procedures Governing the Settlement of Disputes (DSU) of the WTO. Government officials from both Adawa and Rasasa met with each other, but no amicable resolutions were made. In February 2019, Adawa requested the establishment of a panel pursuant to Article 6(2) of the DSU, alleging that Rasasa's tariffs on Helian products were an unjustifiable breach of its commitment to maintaining the bound rate of zero on such items.

THE ARREST AND DETENTION OF MS. DARIAN GREY

From 1979 to 2016, Ms. Darian Grey served as the founder and chief executive officer of the RRC. The RRC was involved in the 2007-2009 civil war in Garantia by selling weapon systems and providing training to government militias, which was referred to the Prosecutor of ICC. Ms. Grey was appointed as the Minister of Foreign Affairs of Rasasa by President Pindro in January 2017.

In accordance with the ICC procedures, the Office of the Prosecutor opened an investigation against Ms. Grey in August 2009. On 13 April 2019, the Prosecutor requested the issuance of a warrant for the arrest of Ms. Grey pursuant to Article 58 of the Rome Statute, assigning to her criminal responsibility for certain alleged activities of the RRC in Garantia between 2007 and 2009.

Ms. Grey, representing Rasasa, arrived in the capital city of Adawa on 18 June 2019 for the four-day regular annual session of the CHC. On 20 June 2019, a Pre-Trial Chamber of the ICC granted the Prosecutor's 13 April 2019 request and issued a warrant of arrest for Ms. Grey. Two days later, officers of the Novazora police approached and arrested Ms. Grey. The Rasasan Ambassador to Adawa was promptly notified of her arrest, and Rasasan consular agents were provided access to her. During the arrest, Ms. Grey's judicial appeal was denied by a magistrate and she would remain under house arrest at a monitored diplomatic guesthouse in Adawa, pending this Court's disposition of the case.

SUMMARY OF PLEADINGS

FIRST PLEADING

The Court has jurisdiction over Adawa's claims because Adawa is a Party to the 1929 Botega Treaty. *First*, it was a customary international law in 1939 to succeed treaties universally when the dissolution occurred. *Second,* Adawa has succeeded to the Botega Treaty as it is a territorial treaty concerning the common interests of Crosinia. *Third,* the Court has jurisdiction over Adawa's claims based on Article 37 of ICJ Statute.

SECOND PLEADING

Rasasa's development and deployment of the WALL along the border between Adawa and Rasasa is in violation of international law, and the WALL should be dismantled and removed forthwith. *First*, Rasasa's deployment of the WALL violates the principle of prohibition of the threat or use of force. *Second*, Rasasa's development and deployment of the WALL violates Adawan's right to life under the international human rights law. *Third*, Rasasa's development and deployment of the WALL violates the international humanitarian law. *Fourth*, Rasasa is obligated to dismantle and remove the WALL.

THIRD PLEADING

Adawa's claim falls into the scope of the Court's jurisdiction and is admissible, and it is entitled to compensatory damages. *First*, the Court has jurisdiction over the dispute at issue. *Second*, there are no reasons for the Court to decline its jurisdiction. *Third,* the dispute before the Court is different from the one before the WTO. Alternatively, even if the two disputes submitted are substantially identical, the Court may still preserve its jurisdiction. *Fourth,* Rasasa's imposition of tariffs on Helian products from Adawa violates the Treaty Establishing the Crosinian Helian Community (CHC Treaty), and thus it is entitled to compensatory damages.

FOURTH PLEADING

The arrest and detention of Ms. Grey are consistent with Adawa's obligations under international law. *First,* Adawa is obliged to cooperate fully with the ICC under the Rome Statute. *Second*, Adawa's cooperation with the ICC does not violate Adawa's obligations with respect to the immunity under international law. *Third,* Adawa does not violate its obligations with respect to the immunity under Article 98(1) of the Rome Statute. Hence, Adawa may process to render her to the ICC.

PLEADINGS

I. THE COURT HAS JURISDICTION OVER ADAWA'S CLAIMS BECAUSE ADAWA IS A PARTY TO THE BOTEGA TREATY.

A. ADAWA IS A PARTY TO THE BOTEGA TREATY.

i. Universal succession of treaties when dissolution occurred was a customary international law before 1939.

A juridical fact must be appreciated in light of the law contemporary with it, but not of the law in force at the time when a dispute arises.[1] Before the dissolution of Adawa-Zeitounia Union (AZU) in 1939,[2] it had formed a customary international law that the successor State should succeed universally the treaties of the predecessor State when dissolution occurred. To identify the existence of a customary international law, two aspects must be examined: the general practice [a] and *opinio juris* [b].[3]

a. The universal succession after dissolution qualified the element of State practice.

The relevant practice must be general, indicating that it must be sufficiently widespread, representative and consistent.[4] It is not necessary to show that all the States have participated in the practice in question,[5] but State practice, including that of States whose interests are particularly affected, should have been both extensive and virtually uniform.[6]

Before 1939, State practices were fairly uniform that newly-emerging States remained

1 *The Island of Palmas case* (Netherlands/USA) [1928] 2 RIAA 829, 845.

2 *Case Concerning the Helian Hyacinth* (Adawa v Rasasa) (Statement of Agreed Facts) [2019] (*Facts*) [7].

3 International Law Commission (ILC) 'Draft Conclusions on Identification of Customary International Law, with Commentaries' UN Doc A/73/10 (2018) Conclusion 2; *North Sea Continental Shelf cases* (Federal Republic of Germany/Denmark; Federal Republic of Germany/Netherlands) (Judgment) [1969] ICJ Rep 3 [77].

4 ILC Draft Conclusions (n 3) 120.

5 ILC Draft Conclusions (n 3) 136.

6 *North Sea Continental* (n 3) [74].

bound by the former treaties when dismemberments occurred.[7] Abundant precedents support this conclusion, *inter alia* the dissolution of Great Colombia in 1829-1831, Union of Norway and Sweden in 1905, Austro-Hungarian Empire in 1918.[8] On the contrary, the negation of the validity of particular treaties was determined by special agreements between particular States.[9] In other practices, the new States refused to succeed the treaties of the predecessor States. However, these practices were performed under the circumstance of secession rather than dissolution.[10]

b. The universal succession after dissolution qualified the element of opinio juris.

The States concerned must feel that they are obliged to conform to a settled practice.[11] *Opinio juris* manifests in government legal opinions, diplomatic correspondence, treaties' provisions or tribunal's decisions.[12] After the dissolution of Great Colombia, the King's legal advisor confirmed that the treaties are 'still acknowledged to be in force' between Great Britain and the successor States.[13] In the *Mechanic* arbitration, the Mixed Commission adjudged that the 1795 Treaty still bound the successor State Ecuador after the dissolution of Great Colombia.[14] After the dissolution of Sweden-Norway Union, Swedish government noticed British government that treaties concluded by the Union would be valid.[15] After the dissolution of Austro-Hungarian Empire, the Treaties of St-Germain and Trianon stipulated that the bilateral treaties 'should be in force' and the number of contracting

7 D Muralt, *The Problem of State Succession with Regard to Treaties* (W P Van Stockum & Zoon 1954) 91.

8 ILC 'Report of the International Law Commission on the Work of Its Twenty-sixth Session' (6 May-26 July 1974) UN Doc A/9610/Rev 1, 260-265; Arnold McNair, *The Law of Treaties* (Clarendon Press 1961) 606-616.

9 McNair (n 8) 606-670.

10 Reviewed by C Emanuelli, 'State Succession, Then and Now, with Special Reference to the Louisiana Purchase (1803)' (2003) 63 *Louisiana Law Review* 1278, 1283.

11 *Jurisdictional Immunities of the State* (Germany v Italy: Greece intervening) (Judgment) [2012] ICJ Rep 99 [55].

12 ILC Draft Conclusions (n 3) 120-121.

13 Public Record Office 'Law Officers' Reports' FOR 83 2254.

14 *Case of the Schooner Mechanic* (Atlantic and Hope Insurance Companies v Ecuador) [1862] 29 RIAA 108, 109.

15 'Baron de Bildt to the Marquess of Lansdowne' 98 British and Foreign State Papers 833-834.

Parties was up to 23.[16]

Therefore, in the present case, under the customary international law of the time AZU dissolved, Adawa should succeed the Botega Treaty on Armistice and Pacification (the Botega Treaty).

ii. Adawa should succeed the Botega Treaty as it is a territorial treaty concerning the common interests of Crosinia.

a. It has been a customary international law to succeed the territorial treaties.

Article 12 of Vienna Convention on the Succession of States in Respect of Treaties (VCSST) prescribes that succession of States does not affect obligations or rights relating to territory for the benefits of other States and considered as attached to that territory.[17]

The succession of territorial treaties had been established by a number of convincing precedents before the dissolution of AZU.[18] Aaland islands of Finland remained demilitarization after Finland declared independence from Russia and the Committee of Jurist adjudged that Finland could not escape the obligations imposed by the 1856 Treaty of Paris as the Treaty regulated European interest.[19] Similarly, the Permanent Court of International Justice (PCIJ) in the *Free Zone* case confirmed that France must succeed the obligations imposed on Sardinia to neutralize Savoy by the 1815 Treaty of Versailles as it related to the interest of Powers.[20] Therefore, the treaty operating in the common interests of a particular region shall not be affected by the succession of

16 Treaty of Saint-Germain-en-Laye art 241; Treaty of Trianon art 224.

17 Vienna Convention on the Succession of States in Respect of Treaties (1978) 1946 UNTS 3 (VCSST) art 12.

18 ILC 'Draft Articles on Succession of States in Respect of Treaties with Commentaries' *Yearbook of the International Law Commission* (1974) UN Doc A/CN4/SERA/1974/Addl (Part One) 204 [30].

19 'Report of the International Committee of Jurists Entrusted by the Council of the League of Nations with the Task of Giving an Advisory Opinion upon the Legal Aspects of the Aaland Islands Question' (1920) *League of Nations Official Journal*, Special Supplement No 3, 18.

20 *Free Zones of Upper Savoy and the District of Gex* (Switzerland/France) Judgment [1932] PCIJ Rep Series A/B No 46, 145.

State and is independent of the will of the Parties.[21]

Based on these precedents, the International Court of Justice (the Court) affirmed that Article 12 of VCSST reflects a customary international law.[22]

b. The Botega Treaty is of territorial character.

Treaties concerning demilitarization of a particular territory have been regarded as a category of territorial treaties.[23] A typical form of demilitarization is the establishment of a zone of peace.[24]

In the present case, along with the armistice, the Botega Treaty established a zone of peace to which the citizens of both Parties can access.[25] It regulates the settlement relating to the territory, rendering the Botega Treaty territorial.

c. The Botega Treaty is concerned with the interests of other States.

The interests of other States include the utilization of part of territory[26] or the maintenance of peace.[27] *First*, the Contracting Parties signed the treaty with aspiration of saving Crosinians from the scourge of war generation by generation.[28] The Botega Treaty is treaty of armistice[29] which indicates a suspension of hostilities rather the permanent peace.[30] Abandoning the Botega Treaty renders the reoccurrence of

---

21 *Free City of Danzig and International Labour Organization* (Advisory Opinion) [1930] PCIJ Rep Series B No 18, 29.

22 *Case Concerning the Gabčíkovo-Nagymaros Project* (Hungary/Slovakia) (Judgment) [1997] ICJ Rep 7 [123].

23 Draft Articles on Succession of States in Respect of Treaties (n 18) [30].

24 Peter Macalister-Smith, 'Zone of Peace' Max Planck Encyclopedias of International Law <https://opil.ouplaw.com/view/10.1093/law:epil/9780199231690/law-9780199231690-e451?rskey=sO5tvu&result=1&prd=MPIL> accessed 1 January 2020.

25 *Facts* [Annex A] art II.

26 *Arbitration Regarding the Iron Rhine Railway* (Belgium v Netherland) [2005] 27 RIAA 35 [241].

27 Aaland Islands Report (n 19) 17.

28 *Facts* [Annex A] Preamble.

29 *Facts* [Annex A].

30 Convention Concerning the Laws and Customs of War on Land [1907] 205 CTS 277 art 36; *Dalmia Cement Limited v National Bank of Pakistan* (Award) [1984] 67 ILR 611, 642.

war possible. Hence, the Treaty preserves the peace, protects the Helian fields and safeguards all Crosinian.[31] *Second*, the freely accessible zone of peace endows rights to the Adawans, Zeitounians and Rasasans and consequently relates to the utilization of tripartite territory. Therefore, the Botega Treaty is concerned with the interests of the three States and the common interest of Crosinia.

In conclusion, the Botega Treaty with territorial character established the zone of peace, concerning the benefits of other States and guaranteeing the regional interest of the entire Crosinia. It should be succeeded by Adawa based on the established customary international law.

B. THE COURT HAS JURISDICTION OVER ADAWA'S CLAIMS BASED ON ARTICLE 37 OF ICJ STATUTE

Article 37 of ICJ Statute stipulates that the Court can exercise jurisdiction pursuant to treaty in force providing for reference of a matter to the PCIJ.

i. The Botega Treaty is in force.

A treaty is by principle indivisible. Any grounds for the termination of a treaty can only be invoked to the treaty as a whole.[32] According to the *ICAO* case, a dispute settlement clause is an integral part of a treaty, and its judicial force cannot be considered in isolation.[33]

Based on the argument aforementioned, Adawa has succeeded the Botega Treaty. One of the objectives of the Botega Treaty is to 'ensure the pacific settlement of future disputes'[34] and the Parties reiterated this objective in the provisions.[35] Hence, as a dispute settlement clause, Article VI is inseparable from the other provisions of the

31 *Facts* [Annex A] Preamble.

32 Vienna Convention on the Law of Treaties (adopted 22 May 1969, entered into force 27 January 1980) 1155 UNTS 331(VCLT) art 44(2).

33 *Appeal Relating to the Jurisdiction of the ICAO Council* (India v Pakistan) (Judgment) [1972] ICJ Rep 46 [25].

34 *Facts* [Annex A] Preamble.

35 *Facts* [Annex A] art II.

Botega Treaty.

ii. The jurisdiction of the PCIJ has been transferred to the Court.

Article 37 transfers the jurisdiction of the PCIJ to the Court. This transference is voluntarily assumed by the Member States of the United Nations[36] whenever they join in the ICJ Statute.[37] Precedents of the Court have supported the application of Article 37 of the ICJ Statute. In *South West Africa* case, the Union of South Africa is under an obligation to accept the compulsory jurisdiction of the Court according to 1927 Mandate which specifies the jurisdiction of the PCIJ.[38] In certain cases, although the Court denies its jurisdiction when the Parties invoke Article 37, the denials are on the account of other reasons, including the lack of retroactivity,[39] reservation made by States[40] and unqualified to access to the Court.[41] However, these reasons do not exist in the present case. Furthermore, Article 37 and Article 36 provide independent sources of jurisdiction.[42] If Article 37 is applicable, there is no need to consider other jurisdictional bases provided for in Article 36.[43]

In the present case, the Botega Treaty prescribes the compulsory jurisdiction of the PCIJ. Pursuant to Article 37 of the ICJ Statute, the Court has jurisdiction over the dispute.

---

36 *South West Africa cases* (Ethiopia v South Africa; Liberia v South Africa) (Preliminary Objections) [1962] ICJ Rep 319, 334-335.

37 *The Barcelona Traction case* (Belgium v Spain) (Preliminary Objections) [1964] ICJ Rep 6, 34-37.

38 *International Status of South West Africa* (Advisory Opinion) [1950] ICJ Rep 128, 138; *South West Africa* (n 36) 334-335.

39 *Ambatielos case* (Greece v United Kingdom) (Preliminary Objection) [1952] ICJ Rep 28, 41.

40 *Case of Certain Norwegian Loans* (France/Norway) (Judgment) [1957] ICJ Rep 9, 27; *Aegean Sea Continental Shelf case* (Greece/Turkey) (Questions of Jurisdiction and Admissibility) [1978] ICJ Rep 3 [90].

41 *Case Concerning Legality of Use of Force* (Serbia and Montenegro v United Kingdom) (Preliminary Objections) [2004] ICJ Rep 1307 [113].

42 A. Zimmermann *et al* (eds.), *The Statute of the International Court of Justice: A Commentary* (OUP 2006) 670 [25].

43 *ICAO* (n 33) [25].

II. RASASA'S DEVELOPMENT AND DEPLOYMENT OF THE WALL ALONG THE BORDER BETWEEN ADAWA AND RASASA IS IN VIOLATION OF INTERNATIONAL LAW, AND THE WALL SHOULD BE DISMANTLED AND REMOVED FORTHWITH.

A. RASASA'S DEPLOYMENT OF THE WALL VIOLATES THE PRINCIPLE OF PROHIBITION OF THE THREAT OR USE OF FORCE.

i. The deployment of the WALL constitutes threat of force.

Charter of the United Nations requires States to refrain from the threat or use of force.[44] In international relations, respect for territorial sovereignty is essential.[45] Attacks from outside a State's territory are prohibited.[46] Besides, the Court affirms that if the envisaged use of force is unlawful, the threat to use such force would also be unlawful.[47]

In the present case, a tower of the WALL is deployed every 200 meters all along its 201-kilometer-long border.[48] It includes Adawan territory into its killing range. The WALL can unleash force to deter illegal behaviors when people are still in Adawa.[49] The use of weapons against Adawan territory violates the Adawan sovereignty and constitutes unlawful use of force. Therefore, with the possibility to use this unlawful force, the deployment of the WALL constitutes a threat of force.

ii. The two exceptions of the principle are not applicable.

There are two exceptions of the principle, including actions taken by the UN Security Council (UNSC)[50] and Member States' practice of the right of self-defense.[51]

---

44 Charter of the United Nations (adopted 26 June 1945, entered into force 24 October 1945) (UN Charter) art 2(4); *Armed Activities on the Territory of the Congo* (Democratic Republic of the Congo v Uganda) (Merits) [2005] ICJ Rep 168 [148].

45 *Corfu Channel case* (United Kingdom v Albania) (Merits) [1949] ICJ Rep 4, 35.

46 *Legal Consequences of the Construction of a Wall in the Occupied Palestinian Territory* (Advisory Opinion) [2004] ICJ Rep 136 [139].

47 *Legality of the Threat or Use of Nuclear Weapons* (Advisory Opinion) [1996] ICJ Rep 226 [47].

48 *Clarifications* [1]; *Facts* [2] [24].

49 *Facts* [37].

50 UN Charter art 51(1).

51 UN Charter arts 42, 51(1).

The situation of the present case constitutes neither of the exceptions. *First*, Rasasa's acts are neither taken nor authorized by the UNSC. *Second*, the right of self-defense can only be exercised when armed attacks occur[52] between States.[53] In the present case, Adawa has actively cooperated with Rasasa to resolve the problems[54] and the criminal gangs' behaviors are not attributable to Adawa.[55] Therefore, neither of the exceptions is applicable.

B. RASASA'S DEVELOPMENT AND DEPLOYMENT OF THE WALL VIOLATES ADAWAN'S RIGHT TO LIFE UNDER THE INTERNATIONAL HUMAN RIGHTS LAW (IHRL).

Article 6 of the International Covenant on Civil and Political Rights (ICCPR) protects the right to life of all human beings and prohibits arbitrary deprivations of life.[56] The right of life is a supreme right which cannot be derogated under any circumstances, including for public emergency or national security.[57]

i. The development and deployment of the WALL *per se* violates the right to life.

The Human Rights Committee contends that non-human decision-making weapon system regarding deprivations of life is inherently arbitrary[58] and the development and use of such weapon systems should be prohibited.[59] The WALL independently makes decisions and takes actions to deter those attempting to cross illegally the

---

52 UN Charter art 51(1).

53 *Construction of a Wall* (n 46) [139]; *Armed Activities* (n 44) [146]-[147]; *Case Concerning Oil Platforms* (Islamic Republic of Iran v United States of America) (Judgment) [2003] ICJ Rep 161 [51].

54 *Facts* [29] [42].

55 *Facts* [34] [35].

56 International Covenant on Civil and Political Rights (adopted 16 December 1966, entered into force 23 March 1976) 999 UNTS 171 (ICCPR) art 6(1).

57 ICCPR art 4(2); *Nuclear Weapons* (n 47) [25].

58 Human Rights Council (HRC) 'Report of the Special Rapporteur on Extrajudicial, Summary or Arbitrary Executions, Christof Heyns' (2013) A/HRC/23/47 [90]; United Nations Office for Disarmament Office, 'Perspectives on Lethal Autonomous Weapon System' UNODA Occasional Papers No 30, 5.

59 HRC 'General Comment No 36' UN Doc CCPR/C/GC/36 [65]; United Nations Office at Geneva (UNOG) 'Report of the 2018 Session of the Group of Governmental Experts on Emerging Technologies in the Area of Lethal Autonomous Weapons Systems' (2018) CCW/GGE1/2018/3 [21].

border. During its operation, no human control or intervention is involved.[60] Besides, it has been proved that it is possible for the WALL to make mistakes[61] and when it misjudges, a second-guessing by human is impossible.[62] Equipped with more than a thousand . 50 caliber machine guns,[63] hence, the machine totally controls the decision of life-or-death. The development of such weapons is against the requirement of ICCPR and constitutes a violation of the IHRL.

ii. Rasasa's development and deployment of the WALL does not meet the requirement of protection for the right to life.

An arbitrary deprivation of life is established if the relevant acts are inappropriate, disproportionate[64] and violate due process of law.[65] Violation of the right to life does not require an actual result of life deprivation[66] and will be established when foreseeable threats to life generating from the governmental measures exist.[67]

First, the WALL breaches the principle of proportionality.[68] It is even disproportionate to use lethal force when the targets pose no threat to the law enforcement official's life.[69] In the present case, no human lives but only machines are involved. Moreover, proportionality requires that States must adopt less harmful means before resorting to weapons.[70] The application of lethal force must be the last resort after the exhaustion of other alternatives.[71] In the present case, Rasasa could have employed less harmful

60 *Facts* [24].

61 *Facts* [25].

62 *Facts* [24].

63 *Facts* [24].

64 HRC 'Concluding Observations on Liechtenstein' UN Doc CCPR/CO/81/LIE [10].

65 *Gorji-Dinka v Cameron*, UNHRC Communication No 1134/2002 para 5.1.

66 General Comment No 36 (n 59) [6].

67 *Marcellana and Gumanoy* v *Philippines,* UNHRC Communication No 1560/2007 para 7.7.

68 HRC 'Consideration of Reports Submitted by States Parties under Article 40 of the Covenant Concluding Observations of the Human Rights Committee' UN Doc CCPR/C/ISR/CO/3 [9]-[10].

69 *Finogenov et al v Russia*, ECHR App No 18299/03 and 27311/03 [220]; United Nations General Assembly (UNGA) 'Basic Principles on the Use of Force and Firearms by Law Enforcement Officials' (1990) UN Doc A/CONF144/28/Rev1, 114 [9].

70 HRC 'Concluding Observations of the Human Rights Committee' UN Doc CCPR/CO/74/SWE [10].

71 *Suarez de Guerrero v Colombia*, UNHRC Communication No R 11/45 para 13.2.

means such as stronger patrol, regular border fence or even stationing army. However, Rasasa directly chose to deploy the WALL with a lethal method.[72] Therefore, the deployment of the WALL is disproportionate.

Second, to protect the right to life, States should organize their State organs and establish adequate institutions and procedures by law.[73] Effective institutional safeguards must be provided to prevent arbitrary deprivations of life[74] and ensure accountability.[75] The WALL was deployed with the absence of such institution and valid Rasasan law. Rasasa has not fulfilled this obligation as required by the IHRL.

Third, considering due process, any deprivation of life under exceptional circumstances, for instance, death penalty, must be explicitly prescribed by law and defined with sufficient precision to avoid overly broad or arbitrary interpretation or application.[76] Without its internal legislative approval, Rasasa's act does not have any legal basis.[77] Therefore, Rasasa's acts cannot be justified.

In conclusion, the development and deployment of the WALL is inconsistent with the requirement of the IHRL to respect the right to life.

C. RASASA'S DEVELOPMENT AND DEPLOYMENT OF THE WALL VIOLATES THE INTERNATIONAL HUMANITARIAN LAW (IHL).

i. The IHL is applicable as the conflicts between Rasasa and the criminal gangs constitute armed conflicts.

The IHL applies to armed conflicts.[78] Non-International Armed Conflict (NIAC) exists when there is protracted armed violence between the State and an organized armed group.[79] Intensity of the conflict and organizations of the Parties shall be considered

---

72 *Facts* [37].

73 *Case of González et al v Mexico* [2009] IACHR Series C No 205 [236].

74 General Comment 36 (n 59) [10].

75 *Sathasivam et al v Sri Lanka,* UNHRC Communication No1436/2005 para 3.11.

76 HRC 'General Comment No 35' UN Doc CCPR/C/GC/35 [22].

77 *Facts* [33].

78 *Construction of a Wall* (n 46) [95].

79 *Prosecutor v Tadić* (Judgment) [1997] ICTY No IT-94-1-A [561].

when determining an armed conflict.[80] The International Criminal Tribunal for the former Yugoslavia (ICTY) identifies certain factors when determining organization, including military units,[81] existence of headquarters[82] and sustained and concerted military operations.[83] Regarding the intensity level, the ICTY considers the type of weapons used[84] and the intervention of military force.[85]

In the present case, the parties to the conflict are Rasasa and the Adawan criminal gangs which is a non-State actor.[86] The criminal gangs are well-armed and organized with well-defended encampments and have conducted several well-armed and organized attacks to Rasasa.[87] Rasasa has deployed the WALL with lethal weapons and its army to exterminate the gangs.[88] Therefore, an NIAC can be established and the IHL is applicable.

ii. Rasasa's development and deployment of the WALL constitutes a violation of the Martens Clause under the IHL.

The development of the WALL must follow the Martens Clause.[89] It prevents the assumption that anything which is not explicitly prohibited is permitted,[90] and ensures that civilians and combatants remain under the protection of custom, principles of

80 *Tadić* (n 79) [562].

81 *Prosecutor v Tadić* (Appeals Judgment) [1999] ICTY No IT-94-1-A [120].

82 *Prosecutor v Haradinaj* (Judgment) [2008] ICTY No IT-04-84-T [60].

83 Protocol Additional to the Geneva Convention of 12 August 1949, and Relating to the Protection of Victims of Non-International Armed Conflict (adopted 6 August 1977, entered into force 7 December 1978)1125 UNTS 609 (Protocol II) art 1(2).

84 *Tadić* (n 79) [565]; *Prosecutor v Limaj* (Judgment) [2005] ICTY No IT-03-66-T [158].

85 *Prosecutor v Boškoski and Tarčulovski* (Judgment) [2008] ICTY No IT-04-82-T [178].

86 *Facts* [37].

87 *Facts* [34] [35] [36].

88 *Facts* [37].

89 UNOG 'Report of the 2019 Session of the Group of Governmental Experts on Emerging Technologies in the Area of Lethal Autonomous Weapons Systems' (2019) UN Doc CCW/GGE1/2019/3 [17].

90 International Committee of the Red Cross (ICRC), *Commentaries on the Additional Protocols* (Geneva 1987) 39.

humanity and public conscience.[91] To verify the conformity with the Martens Clause, a criterion is whether the WALL will be condemned as inhumane by society.[92]

Weapons similar to the WALL cannot be tolerated by custom, principles of humanity, public conscience.[93] According to the International Committee of the Red Cross (ICRC), it denigrates the value of life by allowing machines to have the power of life and death over human beings.[94] The UN Secretary-General, along with other 28 countries,[95] has been explicitly calling for a ban on this kind of weaponry for its moral repugnancy.[96] More than 200 organizations and 3,000 artificial intelligence scientists have pledged out of morality to neither participate in nor support its development.[97] Causing such great amount of objections, the development and deployment of the WALL, greatly exacerbating Adawan's fear,[98] violates the Martens Clause.

iii. Rasasa's development and deployment of the WALL is inconsistent with the principle of distinction and proportionality.

The principles of distinction[99] and proportionality[100] are basic rules of the IHL and

---

91 Protocol Additional to the Geneva Convention of 12 August 1949, and Relating to the Protection of Victims of International Armed Conflict (adopted 6 August 1977, entered into force 7 December 1978) 1125 UNTS 3 (Protocol I) art 1(2).

92 *Legality of the Threat or Use of Nuclear Weapons* (Verbatim Record) [1995] [10].

93 'Making the Case: The Dangers of Killer Robots and the Need for a Pre-emptive Ban' (9 December 2016) Human Rights Watch <https://www.hrw.org/report/2016/12/09/making-case/dangers-killer-robots-and-need-preemptive-ban> accessed 10 January 2020.

94 Christof Heyns Report (n 58) [109].

95 'Country Views on Killer Robots' (22 November 2018) Campaign to Stop Killer Robots <https://www.stopkillerrobots.org/wp-content/uploads/2018/11/KRC_CountryViews22Nov2018.pdf> accessed 10 January 2020.

96 United Nations 'UN Secretary-General António Guterres' Address to the Paris Peace Forum' SG/SM/19338.

97 'Lethal Autonomous Weapons Pledge' (19 July 2018) Future of Life Institute <https://futureoflife.org/lethal-autonomous-weapons-pledge/?cn-reloaded=1> accessed 10 January 2020.

98 *Facts* [40].

99 Protocol I arts 48, 51, 52; St. Petersburg Declaration; Convention on Prohibitions or Restrictions on the Use of Certain Conventional Weapons Which May be Deemed to be Excessively Injurious or to Have Indiscriminate Effects (adopted 10 October 1980, entered into force 2 December 1983) 1342 UNTS 137 art 3; Laws and Customs of War on Land (29 July 1899) Treaty Series 403 Annex.

100 *Nuclear Weapons* (n 47) [41]; *Military and Paramilitary Activities in and against Nicaragua* (Nicaragua v USA) (Judgment) [1986] ICJ Rep 14 [176].

have been recognized as customary international law.[101] The WALL as a weapon used in the armed conflict must respect these principles.

a. Rasasa's development and deployment of the WALL violates the principle of distinction.
During armed conflicts, Parties must distinguish between civilians and combatants.[102] Bandits of the criminal gangs must be distinguished from civilians. However, this distinction cannot be comprehensively described[103] and must be made based on a reasonable evaluation of the prevailing circumstances.[104]

In the present case, the algorithm of the WALL presets the same levels of force against them and is at risk of using lethal weapons against civilians.[105] All tests of the WALL are implemented in the laboratory and supervised by human.[106] Its reliability of distinction has not been examined by actual combats. The WALL is equipped with lethal force and totally controls the 201-kilometer-long border.[107] One mistake may create humanitarian disasters. Deployment of such questionable weapons is inconsistent with the principle of distinction.

b. Rasasa's development and deployment of the WALL violates the principle of proportionality.
An attack shall not cause incidental harm to civilians, or exceed military advantages anticipated.[108] The kind and degree of force cannot be predetermined but must be decided according to the relevant circumstances.[109] When determining proportionality, it is necessary to examine whether a reasonably well-informed person will conduct

101 *Nuclear Weapons* (n 47) [61]; *Prosecutor v Martic* (Review of the Indictment) [1996] ICTY No IT-95-11-R61 [139]; *Prosecutor v Kupreškić et al* (Judgment) ICTY No IT-95-16-T [524].

102 Protocol I art 48.

103 *Prosecutor v Galic* (Judgment) [2003] ICTY No IT-98-29-T [50].

104 Nils Melzer, *Interpretive Guidance on the Notion of Direct Participation in Hostilities under International Humanitarian Law* (ICRC 2009) 69.

105 *Facts* [37].

106 *Facts* [20].

107 *Facts* [2] [24].

108 Protocol I art 51 (5) (b).

109 European Parliament 'Human Rights Implications of the Usage of Drones and Unmanned Robots in Warfare' EXPO/B/DROI/2012/12, 29.

the same behavior.[110]

In the present case, the operation of the WALL is totally preset by algorithm which is based on the former datum.[111] The means and levels of attack are also limited and preset.[112] Without human involvement, the standard of well-informed person cannot be executed during the operation. Hence, it cannot meet the requirement of proportionality. Without specific loss, the cumulative effect of questionable attack in proportionality is also contrary to this principle.[113]

D. RASASA SHOULD DISMANTLE AND REMOVE THE WALL.

States are burdened with international responsibility when its acts are incompatible with a recognized rule[114] and the acts can be imputed to the States.[115] States are obligated to cease the wrongful act when it is continuous and the violated rule is still in force.[116]

The deployment of the WALL breaches the principle of prohibition of threat of force, violates the IHRL and the IHL and therefore constitutes a wrongful act. The deployment of the WALL is attributable to Rasasa[117] and continues to threaten the security and sovereignty of Adawa. Therefore, Rasasa is obligated to dismantle and remove the WALL.

---

110 *Prosecutor v Galić* (n 103) [58].

111 *Facts* [37].

112 *Facts* [37].

113 *Prosecutor v Kupreškić et al* (n 101) [526].

114 ILC 'Draft Articles on Responsibility of States for Internationally Wrongful Acts, with Commentaries' UN Doc A/56/10 art 30(a); *Military and Paramilitary Activities* (n 100) [186].

115 *Military and Paramilitary Activities* (n 100) [86].

116 *Case Concerning the Rainbow Warrior Affair* (New Zealand/France) [1990] 20 RIAA 215 [114].

117 *Facts* [37].

III. THE COURT MAY ADJUDICATE ADAWA'S CLAIM THAT RASASA'S IMPOSITION OF TARIFFS AT ISSUE VIOLATES THE CHC TREATY, AND ADAWA IS ENTITLED TO COMPENSATORY DAMAGES.

A. DISPUTES IN THE CHC TREATY FALL WITHIN THE COURT'S JURISDICTION AND ARE ADMISSIBLE.

i. The Court has jurisdiction over the disputes at issue.

As demonstrated in the first pleading, the Court has jurisdiction over Adawa's claims because Adawa is a Party to the Botega Treaty.

ii. There are no reasons for the Court to decline its jurisdiction.

a. The WTO rules cannot preclude the Court's jurisdiction.

Under Article 1 of the Understanding on Rules and Procedures Governing the Settlement of Disputes (DSU), its rules and procedures apply to disputes in 'covered agreements'.[118] Under Article 23, the WTO has exclusive jurisdiction only over the covered agreements,[119] which are interpreted as including the WTO Agreement, the Agreements in Annexes 1 and 2 and Plurilateral Trade Agreements in Annex 4 of the DSU.[120] Particularly, it is well settled in WTO case law that its dispute settlement mechanism does not apply to violations of rules in a Free Trade Agreement which is not among covered agreements.[121] In the present case, since the CHC Treaty is not within the covered agreements, the Dispute Settlement Body (DSB) lacks jurisdiction over this dispute.

b. The CHC Treaty does not preclude the Court's jurisdiction.

Choice of forum clauses or exclusive forum clauses are stipulated in some Regional Trade Agreements, specifying the forum to refer to when disputes arise or further confirming the selected forum's exclusive jurisdiction once dispute settlement

---

118 Understanding on Rules and Procedures Governing the Settlement of Disputes (1994) 1896 UNTS 401 (DSU) art 1(1).

119 DSU art 23(1).

120 *Brazil-Measures Affecting Desiccated Coconut* (Appellate Body Report) [1997] WTO No WT/DS22/ABR 13.

121 *Mexico-Tax Measures on Soft Drinks and Other Beverages* (Panel Report) [2005] WTO No WT/DS308/R para 7.15.

procedures have been initiated.[122] Although the Treaty was notified as a Regional Trade Agreement,[123] it does not contain the clauses aforementioned. Nothing in this treaty precludes the Court's jurisdiction.

c. The dispute before the Court is different from the one before the DSB.

There are three elements to identify a dispute, *i.e.* the identity of Parties,[124] cause of action,[125] and subject matter.[126] To identify the cause of action of disputes, legal basis was deemed a decisive factor.[127] Characterization of the true subject matter of disputes requires consideration upon object of claims.[128] As long as one of these three factors in the two disputes is different, it will be safe to conclude that these two disputes are not substantially identical. In the present case, the legal basis [i] and object of claims [ii] are not the same.

(i) The legal basis is different.

Different treaties are universally recognized as different legal basis. *First*, different treaties may provide different protection.[129] *Second*, the rights they create are not in all aspects the same.[130] *Third*, even though articles in different treaties are similar or identical, the interpretation of them may not be the same with different contexts, objects, subsequent practice and *travaux préparatoires*.[131]

---

122 North American Free Trade Agreement (17 December1992) 32 ILM 289 (1993) Chapter 20; EC-Chile Free Trade Agreement (2002) art 189(4)(c).

123 *Clarification* [5].

124 *Case Concerning Certain German Interests in Polish Upper Silesia* (German/Poland) [1926] PCIJ Rep Series A No 6, 20; Filip De Ly, Audley Sheppard, 'ILA Final Report on *Lis Pendens* and Arbitration' (2009) 25(1) *Arbitration International* 3 para 5.6.

125 *Mobil Investments v Canada (II)* (Decision on Jurisdiction and Admissibility) [2013] ICSID Case No ARB/15/6 [207].

126 *CME Czech Republic BV* (The Netherlands v Czech Republic) (Final Award) [2003] UNCITRAL [435].

127 Case C-406/92, *The Owners of the Cargo Lately Laden on Board the Ship 'Tatry' v The Owners of the Ship 'Mcciej Rataj'* [1994] ECR I-5475 [39].

128 *Nuclear Tests case (*Australia v France*)* (Judgment) [1974] ICJ Rep 253 [29].

129 *CME* (n 126) [432].

130 *CME* (n 126) [433].

131 *MOX Plant case* (Ireland/United Kingdom) (Provisional Measures) ITLOS Reports 2001 [51].

In the present case, the two claims are based on violations of different obligations under different treaties, regardless of whether the measure in question is the same. The dispute referred to the DSB is based on the violation of concession schedule in Article II of the General Agreement on Tariffs and Trade (GATT 1994), while the dispute before the Court is based on the violation of Article 3 of the CHC Treaty. The GATT 1994 is the fundamental treaty of an influential international organization, while the CHC Treaty is a regional treaty within six countries.

(ii) The object is different.

The UNCITRAL's tribunal in cases like the *Lauder v Czech Republic*[132] considers the remedies sought by Parties when identify particular proceedings. Additionally, in the *Chorzów Factory* case, the Court distinguishes 'declaratory judgment' from judgment seeking an 'indemnity'.[133]

In the present case, the two submissions seek different redress. The submission before the WTO only asked for declaration of violation. However, the submission before the Court has dual purposes. For one thing, Adawa requests the Court to confirm the violation under the CHC Treaty. For another, it also seeks monetary reparation, a remedy 'not typically awarded by WTO Panels'.[134] Under the WTO, retaliation is the commonly authorized remedy.[135] Though 'voluntary compensation' is an alternative,[136] it has only been utilized once.[137] However, conditions to receive compensation are always examined by the Court,[138] and the awarding of compensation exists in

132 *Lauder v Czech Republic* (Final Award) [2001] UNCITRAL [174].

133 *Case Concerning the Factory at Chorzów* (Germany v Poland) (Dissenting Opinion of Judge Anzilotti) [1927] PCIJ Rep Series A No 13 [27].

134 *Facts* [57].

135 General Agreement on Tariffs and Trade (1994) 1896 UNTS 401 (GATT) art XXIII.

136 DSU art 22; *EEC-Restrictions on Imports of Apples from Chile* (Panel Report) [1980] GATT L/5074-27S/98 para 4.6.

137 *Japan-Taxes on Alcoholic Beverages* (Appellate Body Report) WTO WT/DS8/AB/R, WT/DS11/AB/R 33.

138 *Land and Maritime Boundary between Cameroon and Nigeria* (Cameroon/Nigeria) (Judgment) [2002] ICJ Rep 303 [311]-[315]; *Military and Paramilitary Activities* (n 100) [148].

practice.[139]

Moreover, right to seek different legal protection granted in two different treaties cannot be deprived.[140] Precluding the Court's jurisdiction denies the possibility to have the compensation claim tried,[141] thus diminishes the Party's right to seek redress of a violation of obligations,[142] and impairs its interests.

d. Even if the two disputes submitted are substantially identical, the Court may still preserve its jurisdiction.

First, the incidence of parallel proceedings cannot affect the forum's jurisdiction,[143] or undermine the Parties' rights.[144] In other words, in the 'same' dispute, the fact that one tribunal is competent to adjudicate the dispute does not necessarily affect the authority of another court.[145] Additionally, whether the doctrine of *lis pendens* applies in international relations remains highly disputed.[146]

Second, declining to exercise its jurisdiction, a forum will fail to fulfil its obliged tasks.[147] The Court has a primary and fundamental role in international law, as being established as the principle judicial organ of the United Nations.[148] Though it is admitted that the Court has inherent power to remove disputes from the List cited by the Court,[149] using that power to decline the Court's jurisdiction 'must be considered

139 *Corfu Channel case* (n 45) 244; *Ahmadou Sadio Diallo* (Republic of Guinea/DRC) (Judgment) [2012] ICJ Rep 324 [56].

140 *CME Czech Republic BV v The Czech Republic* (Partial Award) [2001] UNCITRAL [419].

141 *CME Czech Republic BV v The Czech Republic* (Judgment) [2003] SVEA Court of Appeal Case No T 8753-01, 70.

142 *Mexico-Soft Drinks* (n 121) [53].

143 *CME* (n 140) [410].

144 *Lauder* (n 132) [174].

145 *German Interests* (n 124) 20; *American Bottle Company (USA) v United Mexican States* [1929] 4 RIAA 435, 437.

146 *German Interests* (n 124) 20.

147 *Mexico-Soft Drinks* (n 121) [53].

148 Statute of the International Court of Justice art 1.

149 *Legality of the Use of Force* (Serbia and Montenegro v Belgium) (Preliminary Objection) (Separate Opinion of Judge Higgins) [2004] ICJ Rep 279, 338 [9].

as highly exceptional'.[150] When defining its jurisdiction in relation to that of another tribunal, PCIJ has ruled that it cannot give away without a sufficiently clear clause to do so.[151]

In the present case, with no express clause precluding the Court's jurisdiction, the fact that the DSB has seized the dispute concerning the tariffs at issue is by no means a compelling reason for the Court to decline its own jurisdiction.

B. RASASA'S IMPOSITION OF TARIFFS ON HELIAN PRODUCTS FROM ADAWA VIOLATES THE CHC TREATY, AND ADAWA IS ENTITLED TO COMPENSATORY DAMAGES.

i. The imposition of tariffs at issue violates Article 3 of the CHC Treaty.

Under Article 3 of the Treaty, there shall be no customs duties on Helian products and related goods. The imposition of 25% *ad valorem* on Helian bulbs, live plants, and pollen imported into Rasasa[152] obviously constitutes an infringement of this article.

ii. The imposition of tariffs at issue cannot be justified under Article 22(b) of the CHC Treaty.

According to Article 22(b) of the Treaty, measures necessary to protect a Member State's essential security interest are allowed as an exemption from obligations under this treaty.[153] However, the tariffs imposed at issue do not accord with this article.

a. The tariffs at issue were not imposed for Rasasa's 'essential security interest'.

First, 'essential security interest' is typically linked with military action and war. For instance, the US-Ukraine Bilateral Investment Treaty stipulates that measures permitted for the protection of a Party's essential security interests include security-related actions taken in a time of war or national emergency or have clear and direct

150 *Nuclear Test* (Joint Dissenting Opinion) (n 128) 322 [22].

151 *Chorzów* (n 133) 30.

152 *Facts* [33].

153 Treaty Establishing the Crosinian Helian Community (20 June 1969) *Facts* [Annex B] (CHC Treaty) art 22(b).

relationship with the essential security interest of the Party involved.[154] In both *Military* case and *Oil Platform* case, the essential security clause is examined in the context of alleged armed attacks.[155] In the present case, the tariffs at issue is aimed to bring Rasasa's domestic processors back to local farms for the interests of Helian industry,[156] having no link with military action or war, and thus not for the essential security interests of Rasasa.

Secondly, when considering economic and social factors for essential security, the International Centre for Settlement of Investment Disputes (ICSID) takes total economic and social collapse requisite in several cases like *CMS v Argentine Republic*.[157] In the *Russia-Traffic in Transit* case, the Panel finds this term referred to 'those interests relating to the quintessential functions of the state'.[158] Here, Helian industrial is not the pillar industry in Rasasa, since it has developed a robust robotics industry.[159] The damage of this industry will not lead to the collapse of Rasasa's domestic economy or society. Additionally, the challenge faced by Rasasa's Helian industry is not urgent. According to the report of the Rasasan Helian Growers Association, the alleged catastrophic effects are not existing but just possible, which will only occur if the current trends continue.[160]

b. The tariffs at issue are not necessary.

Referring to the application of necessity test in international law,[161] four elements will

154 Treaty Concerning the Encouragement and Reciprocal Protection of Investment, Argentina-United States (1994) art IX.

155 *Military and Paramilitary Activities* (n 100) [128]; *Oil Platform* (n 53) [78].

156 *Facts* [33].

157 *CMS Gas Transmission Company v the Republic of Argentine (Award)* [2005] ICSID Case No ARB/01/08 [305].

158 *Russia-Measures Concerning Traffic in Transit* (Panel Report) [2019] WTO WT/DS512/R para 7.130.

159 *Facts* [9].

160 *Facts* [30].

161 *Korea-Measures Affecting Imports of Fresh, Chilled and Frozen Beef* (Appellate Body Report) [2000] WTO WT/DS161/AB/R [164]; *United States-Section 337 of the Tariff Act of 1930 and Amendments Thereto* (Panel Report) [2000] WTO WT/DS186/2 para 5.26.

be examined in the present necessity test, including: the relative importance of the measure; the contribution of the measure to its objective; the restrictive effect of the measure, and whether a less restrictive measure is available as an alternative.

First, as indicated above, the objective of increasing domestic demand of raw materials falls out of the ambit of 'essential security interest' and is of a relatively low importance.

Second, the imposition of these tariffs is not efficient or effective to achieve its objective. Though a price advantage is foreseeable, the insufficient quantity of Rasasa's raw materials still cannot meet the need. Additionally, due to the long cultivation period of Helian spice and the profit-seeking nature of commercial environment, Rasasan processors' purchase from Adawa is less likely to decrease.

Third, the measure at issue does not only cause considerable losses to Adawa, but also hinders the goal and future implementation of the CHC Treaty. On one hand, Adawa relies highly on the Helian industry, and as a direct result of the tariffs, Adawan farmers have suffered a heavy loss, which would increase in coming years.[162] On the other hand, by creating an exception of that obligation, the disputed measure also hinders the stability, predictability and the authority of the Treaty, exerting adverse effects on the future implementation of it.

Fourth, the imposition of these tariffs is by no means the last resort. As alternative, the government could have played an important role for the recovery of this industry by offering financial support. What's more, Rasasa could have taken advantage of its advanced robotic industry to cover the shortage of related equipment and the possible shortage of labour force. In addition, Rasasa could have resorted to the regional cooperation mechanism provided by the CHC first, instead of taking unilateral measures directly.[163]

---

162 *Facts* [46].

163 CHC Treaty art 2(a).

iii. Adawa is entitled to compensatory damages reflecting the financial harm it has suffered to date.

It is a well-established rule that to the extent restitution is materially impossible,[164] or insufficient to ensure full reparation,[165] the suffering Party is entitled to compensation. The Court has ruled that an injured State is entitled to obtain compensation from the State which has committed an internationally wrongful act for the damage caused by it.[166] In the present case, since Rasasa's violation of obligation under the CHC Treaty has caused considerable damages to Adawa, and restitution of the pecuniary loss is impossible, Adawa is entitled to compensatory damages, such amount to be determined in subsequent proceedings.

IV. THE ARREST AND DETENTION OF MS. GREY ARE CONSISTENT WITH ADAWA'S OBLIGATIONS UNDER INTERNATIONAL LAW, AND ADAWA MAY PROCESS TO RENDER HER TO ICC.

A. ADAWA IS OBLIGED TO COOPERATE FULLY WITH ICC UNDER ARTICLE 86 OF THE ROME STATUTE.

Pursuant to Article 86 of the Rome Statute, States Parties shall cooperate fully with the ICC in its investigation and prosecution of crimes within its jurisdiction.[167] States Parties undertake this cooperation obligation in the whole process of arrest, detention, and surrender.[168]

i. The ICC has jurisdiction over this case and Ms. Grey is in the process of the international criminal proceedings.

The ICC can exercise its jurisdiction if the conduct in question occurred on the territory of the State Parties.[169] According to the principle of territorial jurisdiction,

164 *Chorzów* (n 133) [76].

165 *Différend Dame Mélanie Lachenal* [1954] 13 RIAA 117 [130]-[131].

166 *Project* (n 22) [152]; *Fisheries Jurisdiction* (Federal Republic of Germany v Iceland) (Merits) [1974] ICJ Rep 3 [71]-[76].

167 Rome Statute of the International Criminal Court (adopted 17 July 1998, entered into force 1 July 2002) 2187 UNTS 3 (Rome Statute) art 86.

168 Rome Statute arts 59, 89.

169 Rome Statute art 12(2)(a).

the ICC may have jurisdiction over alien perpetrators of a non-State Party,[170] when at least one material or constituent element of an offense occurs within the state.[171] In the present case, the transportation of prohibited weapons systems, the training and supervision of paramilitary forces occurred in Garantia, a State Party of the Rome Statute.[172] As the chief executive officer of the RRC,[173] Ms. Grey should be held responsible for the crimes committed by the corporation.

ii. Adawa bears no obligation to examine the appropriateness of the warrant.

Under Article 59(4), custodial State is not allowed to consider whether the warrant of arrest is properly issued,[174] prohibiting instead of entitling Adawa to question the warrant's authority. Therefore, no obligation is imposed on Adawa to consider whether the warrant is appropriate.

iii. Adawa should comply with the request to arrest and detain Ms. Grey and may process to render her to the ICC under Article 59 of the Rome Statute.

a. Adawa is obliged to arrest and detain Ms. Grey under Article 59(1).

Under Article 59(1), a State Party which has received a request shall immediately take steps in accordance with related provisions of the Statute.[175] Considering the short term of the meeting as well as Rasasa's refusal to declare Ms. Grey guilty or initiate domestic criminal proceedings against her, arresting her was urgent. If Adawa did not take prompt actions in two days after receiving the request,[176] it would have failed to discharge the cooperation request.[177]

---

170 Mark Klamberg *et al* (eds.), *Commentary on the Law of the International Criminal Court* (Torkel Opsahl Academic EPublisher 2017) 171.

171 M Cherif Bassiouni (ed.), *International Criminal Law, Volume 2: Multilateral and Bilateral Enforcement Mechanism* (Brill 2008) 101.

172 *Clarifications* [4].

173 *Facts* [14].

174 Rome Statute art 59(4).

175 Rome Statute art 59(1).

176 *Clarifications* [8].

177 *Facts* [49].

b. Adawa may process to render her to the ICC under Article 59(7).

Once ordered to be surrendered by the custodial State, the person shall be delivered to the ICC as soon as possible.[178] After this Court's disposition,[179] Adawa may arrange for her transfer to The Hague.

B. ADAWA'S COOPERATION WITH THE ICC DOES NOT VIOLATE ADAWA'S OBLIGATIONS WITH RESPECT TO THE IMMUNITY UNDER INTERNATIONAL LAW.

i. Adawa does not violate customary international law.

The immunity *ratione personae* does not apply in criminal proceedings before international courts.[180] Non-recognition of immunity in the international proceedings has been historically endorsed.[181] In the *Bashir* case, the Pre-Trail Chamber declares that customary international law creates an exception to immunity *ratione personae* when international courts seek a Head of State's arrest for the commission of international crimes.[182] To determine the existence and content of a rule of customary international law, it is necessary to ascertain whether there is a general practice that is accepted as law (*opinio juris*).[183]

a. The exemption of immunity ratione personae qualifies the element of state practice.

State practice could be embodied in treaties[184] and decisions of courts and tribunals.[185]

In treaties, it had long been upheld that there is no immunity in international circumstances since the end of the First World War,[186] and the following Second World

---

178 Rome Statute art 59(7).

179 *Facts* [52].

180 Klamberg (n 170) 666.

181 *Prosecutor v Omar Hassan Ahmad Al Bashir* (Decision on the Failure by Malawi to Comply with the Cooperation Requests) [2011] ICC No ICC-02/05-01/09-139 [38].

182 *Malawi* (n 181) [43]; *Bashir* (Decision on the Refusal of the Chad to Comply with the Cooperation Requests) [2011] ICC No ICC-02/05-01/09-140 [13].

183 ILC Draft Conclusions (n 3) conclusion 2.

184 ILC Draft Conclusions (n 3) conclusion 11.

185 ILC Draft Conclusions (n 3) conclusion 13.

186 Treaty of Versailles (1919) art 227.

War.[187] This tenet is also enshrined in the ICTY Statute,[188] the ICTR (International Criminal Tribunal for Rwanda)Statute[189] and the Rome Statute.[190]

Many judicial decisions have advocated that customary international law creates such an exception.[191] Among, the Special Court for Sierra Leone (SCSL) holds that the principle established that the sovereign equality of states does not prevent a Head of State from being prosecuted before an international criminal tribunal or court.[192] In the *Bashir* case, it is ruled that immunity cannot be invoked to oppose a prosecution by an international court, which applies to sitting Heads of non-party States to the Statute.[193]

b. The exemption of immunity ratione personae qualifies the element of opinion juris.

Opinio juris manifests itself in legislative acts[194] and treaties,[195] especially when adopted by a representative of majority.[196] There is a relatively broad consensus on ending the impunity of international crimes.[197] The universally supported the Rome

---

187 Charter of the International Military Tribunal (8 August 1945) 82 UNTS 280 art 7.

188 United Nations Security Council (UNSC) 'International Criminal Tribunal for the Former Yugoslavia' (25 May 1993) UN Doc S/RES/827 art 7(2).

189 UNSC 'Establishment of an International Tribunal and adoption of the Statute of the Tribunal' (1994) UN Doc S/RES/955 art 6(2).

190 Rome Statute art 27(2).

191 *Prosecutor v Slobodan Milosevic* (Decision on Preliminary Motions) [2001] ICTY IT-99-37-PT [28]; *Arrest Warrant of 11 April 2000* (Democratic Republic of the Congo v Belgium) (Judgment) [2002] ICJ Rep 3 [61]; *Prosecutor v Charles Ghankay Taylor* (Decision on Immunity from Jurisdiction) [2004] SCSL No SCSL-2003-01-I [52].

192 *Charles* (n 191) [52].

193 *Malawi* (n 181) [36].

194 ILC Draft Conclusions (n 3) conclusion 10.

195 ILC Draft Conclusions (n 3) conclusion 11.

196 Anthea Roberts, 'Traditional and Modern Approaches to Customary International Law: A Reconciliation' (2001) 95 *American Journal of International Law* 757, 757.

197 'Summary Record of the 2nd Plenary Meeting, United Nations Diplomatic Conference of Plenipotentiaries on the Establishment of an International Criminal Court' UN Doc A/CONF183/SR2 [12] (Australia), [15] (South Africa), [33] (UK), [63] (Canada), [82] (Korea); 'Summary Record of the 3rd Plenary Meeting' UN Doc A/CONF183/SR3 [46] (Brazil), [86] (Armenia); 'Summary Record of the 4th Plenary Meeting' UN Doc A/CONF183/SR4 [8] (Philippines), [16] (Senegal), [18] (Syria), [23] (Colombia), [27] (Portugal), [36] (Ukraine), [40] (Austria), [45] (Macedonia); 'Summary Record of the 6th Plenary Meeting' UN Doc A/CONF183/SR6 [61] (New Zealand), [99] (Argentina).

Statute, adopted by a vote of 120 to 7, firmly indicates States' determination to end impunity for the perpetrators of egregious crimes and to enhance international justice.[198] The relevant legislations of Canada, New Zealand and German provide that no person may rely on immunities in international proceedings instituted pursuant to an ICC request.[199]

ii. Adawa does not violate the CHC Treaty.

a. The immunity provided in the CHC Treaty is interstate.

A treaty provision should be interpreted in light with the ordinary meaning of the terms, the object and purpose,[200] together with the circumstances of conclusion of the Treaty.[201]

First, the interpretation of 'immunity' in Article 32 of the Treaty should accord with the object of it. Referring to Article 1,[202] the overall objective is to enhance the Community's interests in Helian industry. The immunity clause is to achieve the goal in Helian related diplomatic affairs within the Community. Involvement in States' arm conflicts is by no means related to the interstate object and thus cannot be justified by this article.

Second, during the conclusion process of the Treaty, the drafters confined it to the territory of the six countries and set rights and obligations among them.[203] Consequently, the Treaty provides Contracting States immunity in other five States' national criminal proceedings. Additionally, the ICC has not yet been established then, suggesting that the Crosinian States had no intention to provide immunity in

198 Rome Statute Preamble.

199 Canada Crimes against Humanity and War Crimes Act (2000) Chapter 24 arts 48, 70; New Zealand International Crimes and International Criminal Court Act (2000) art 31(1); Gerichtsverfassungsgesetz (GVG) (German) (1950) Section 21.

200 VCLT art 31(1); *Territorial Dispute* (Libyan Arab Jamahiriya/Chad) (Judgment) [1994] ICJ Rep 6 [41]; *Maritime Delimitation and Territorial Questions between Qatar and Bahrain* (Qatar v Bahrain) (Jurisdiction and Admissibility) [1995] ICJ Rep 6 [33].

201 VCLT art 32; *Oil Platform* (n 53) [23].

202 CHC Treaty art 1.

203 *Facts* [10].

international criminal proceedings.

b. The arrest taken by Adawa is an extension of ICC's jurisdiction.

State Parties are entitled to exercise the *ius puniendi* on behalf of the ICC as its extension.[204] The 'indirect enforcement model' makes it possible for non-party State to cooperate with the ICC without breaking its international obligations.[205] State arrest in a national setting shall be distinguished from that in international criminal law *strictosensu*.[206] Therefore, Adawa exerted the jurisdiction of the ICC without violation of its international obligations.

C. ADAWA DOES NOT VIOLATE ITS OBLIGATIONS WITH RESPECT TO THE IMMUNITY UNDER ARTICLE 98(1) OF THE ROME STATUTE.

i. The conflict of Adawa's cooperation obligation and international obligation to respect immunity does not exist.

a. Immunity ratione personae is not covered by immunities enshrined in Article 98(1).

The State is no longer requested to cooperate if this obligation conflicts with obligations concerning State or diplomatic immunity.[207] Considering the ordinary meaning of the terms,[208] State and diplomatic immunity differ from immunity *ratione personae*.

State immunity differs from immunity *ratione personae*.[209] An official who enjoys immunity *ratione personae* may do so even in respect of acts which are performed in a private capacity and thus crimes are not attributable to the State and do not engage

204 *Malawi* (n 181) [46]; Claus Kreß, Kimberly Prost, *Commentary on the Rome Statute of the International Criminal Court: Observers' Notes, Article by Article* (2nd edn, Hart Publishing 2008) 786.

205 Klamberg (n 170) 666.

206 Kreß, Prost (n 204) 1607.

207 Rome Statute art 98.

208 VCLT art 31(1).

209 *Jurisdictional Immunities* (n 11) [100]; UNGA 'United Nations Convention on Jurisdictional Immunities of States and Their Property' (2 December 2004) UN Doc A/RES/59/38 art 3(2).

its responsibility.[210] Diplomatic immunity is also different from this principle.[211] It refers solely to members of diplomatic missions, i.e. Embassy and Consulate staff.[212] In the present case, Ms. Grey does not act in the State capacity and she is the Minister of Foreign Affairs, rather than an ambassador or a consul. Thus, she does not possess State immunity and diplomatic immunity covered by Article 98(1).

b. Even if immunity ratione personae is covered by Article 98(1), Ms. Grey doesnot possess it before the ICC.

Ms. Grey does not enjoy immunity in the international proceedings considering the exception of immunity *ratione personae.* In addition, Adawa exerted the ICC's jurisdiction instead of its domestic jurisdiction. Thus, there is no conflict between contracting States' obligations towards the ICC and their obligations under customary international law and Article 98(1) does not apply in the present circumstance.

ii. Even if the conflict of obligations exists, Adawa should still cooperate with the ICC.

a. Adawa's cooperation obligation prevails over its international obligation.

In international criminal responsibility of an individual,[213] a *jus cogens* norm enjoys a higher rank than treaty law and ordinary customary rules.[214] With a hierarchy in obligations under customary international law, less important obligations concerning personal immunities shall give way to obligations of preventing impunity from violations of *jus cogens*[215] norms regarding accountability. Those norms include prohibitions on war crimes, crimes against humanity, and genocide.[216] In the present

210 ILC 'Fourth Report on the Immunity of State Officials from Foreign Criminal Jurisdiction by Concepción Escobar Hernández, Special Rapporteur' (2015) UN Doc A/CN4/686 [48] [109].

211 *Arrest Warrant* (n 191) [52]; *Certain Questions of Mutual Assistance in Criminal Matters* (Djibouti/France) (Judgment) [2008] ICJ Rep 177 [193].

212 ILC 'Draft Articles on Diplomatic Intercourse and Immunities with Commentaries' *Yearbook of the International Law Commission* (1958) 89.

213 *Al-Adsani v United Kingdom* [2001] ECHR 2001-XI [61].

214 *Prosecutor v Furundzija* (Judgment) [1998] ICTY No IT-95-17/I-T [153]; *Regina v Bow Street Metropolitan Stipendiary Magistrate and Others, ex parte Pinochet Ugarte* (No 3 Judgment) [1999] 2 All ER 97; *Arrest Warrant* (Dissenting Opinion of Judge Van den Wyngaert) (n 191) [28].

215 VCLT art 53.

216 *East Timor* (Portugal v Australia) (Judgment) [1995] ICJ Rep 90 [29]; *Nuclear Weapons* (n 47) [83].

case, Ms. Grey was charged with war crimes and other serious violations concerning armed conflicts. Thus, Adawa's obligation to cooperate with the ICC to prevent her escape from her criminal responsibility prevails over its customary obligation to other States regarding personal immunities.

b. Adawa should respect the sole authority of the ICC to decide whether the immunity is applicable.

The ICC is the arbiter of the application of Article 98[217] and this article does not allow States Parties to refuse to cooperate.[218] Pursuant to the *Malawi* Decision,[219] *Chad* Decision[220] and *Congo* Decision,[221] the ICC has sole authority to determine whether immunities applied in any particular case, deriving from Article 119(1) of the Rome Statute.

Whether a conflict between the ICC's request for cooperation and the requested State's international obligation exists are ultimately determined by the ICC, instead of the concerned State itself, on a case-to-case basis.[222] In addition, to interpret Article 98(1) as allowing the refusal to cooperate would disable the ICC and the justice.[223] Accordingly, Adawa is not allowed to decide unilaterally whether the ICC has acted *ultra vires*. Any determination based on this would not be accepted. Therefore, Adawa has had no choice but to comply with the ICC's cooperation request.

---

217 William Schabas, *The International Criminal Court: A Commentary on the Rome Statute* (2nd edn, OUP 2016) 1039.

218 *Bashir* (Decision on the Non-compliance by Jordan Regarding Bashir) [2017] ICC No ICC-02/05-01/09 [43].

219 *Malawi* (n 181) [11].

220 *Chad* (n 182) [10].

221 *Bashir* (Decision on the Cooperation of Congo Regarding Bashir) [2014] ICC No ICC-02/05-01/09-195 [16].

222 Kreß, Prost (n 204) 1603.

223 *Malawi* (n 181) [41].

CONCLUSION AND PRAYER FOR RELIEF

In view of the facts set forth in this Memorial and the arguments applying the law to the facts as stated;

May it please the Court, on behalf of the State of Adawa, Applicant herein, respectfully requests this Honorable Court to adjudge and declare that:

1. The Court has jurisdiction over Adawa's claims because Adawa is a party to the Botega Treaty;

2. The development and deployment of the WALL along the border between Adawa and Rasasa is inconsistent with international law, and the WALL should be dismantled and removed forthwith;

3. Adawa's claim falls within the Court's jurisdiction and is admissible, Rasasa's imposition of tariffs on Helian products from Adawa violates the CHC Treaty, and Adawa is entitled to compensatory damages reflecting the financial harm it has suffered to date; and

4. The arrest and detention of Ms. Grey were consistent with Adawa's obligations under international law, and that Adawa may proceed to render her to the International Criminal Court.

Respectfully submitted,

AGENTS FOR ADAWA

被告国书状

Memorials for the Republic of Rasasa

TABLE OF CONTENTS

ii. Rasasa's deployment of the WALL does not violate Adawans' human rights.

iii. Rasasa's deployment of the WALL does not violate the International Humanitarian Law (IHL).

III. ADAWA'S CLAIM DOES NOT FALL INTO THE SCOPE OF THE COURT'S JURISDICTION OR IS INADMISSIBLE; IN THE ALTERNATIVE, THE IMPOSITION OF TARIFFS DOES NOT VIOLATE THE CHC TREATY.

A. ADAWA'S CLAIM DOES NOT FALL INTO THE SCOPE OF THE COURT'S JURISDICTION OR IS INADMISSIBLE.

i. The Court does not have jurisdiction over the dispute.

ii. Alternatively, Adawa's claim is inadmissible.

B. THE IMPOSITION OF TARIFFS DOES NOT VIOLATE THE CHC TREATY.

i. Rasasa's essential security interest is under threat.

ii. The measure is necessary to protect Rasasan essential security interest.

IV. ADAWA'S ARREST AND DETENTION OF MS. GREY CONSTITUTE INTERNATIONAL WRONGFUL ACTS, AND SHE MUST BE IMMEDIATELY REPATRIATED TO RASASA.

A. ADAWA'S ARREST AND DETENTION OF MS. GREY VIOLATE HER IMMUNITY RATIONE PERSONAE IN THE FOREIGN CRIMINAL PROCEEDINGS.

i. Adawa's arrest and detention violate Ms. Grey's immunity ratione personae under customary international law.

ii. Adawa's arrest and detention violate Ms. Grey's immunity ratione personae under the CHC Treaty.

B. ALTERNATIVELY, ADAWA'S ARREST AND DETENTION VIOLATE MS. GREY'S IMMUNITY RATIONE PERSONAE IN THE ICC'S CRIMINAL PROCEEDINGS.

i. Rasasa is not a contracting Party to the ICC.

ii. The exception of the immunity ratione personae in the international proceedings is not customary international law.

C. ADAWA'S COOPERATION OBLIGATION IS IN CONFLICT WITH ITS OBLIGATION TO RESPECT FOR MS. GREY'S IMMUNITY UNDER ARTICLE 98(1) OF THE ROME STATUTE AND ADAWA FAILED TO ASSIST THE ICC.

i. Adawa's cooperation obligation is in conflict with its international obligation to respect for Ms. Grey's immunity under Article 98(1) of the Rome Statute.

ii. Adawa failed to assist the ICC to cope with the conflict.

D. MS. GREY MUST BE IMMEDIATELY REPATRIATED TO RASASA.

CONCLUSION AND PRAYER FOR RELIEF

STATEMENT OF JURISDICTION

The Republic of Rasasa (Rasasa) hereby objects the jurisdiction of the International Court of Justice (the Court) for the reason that the State of Adawa (Adawa) is not a Party to the Botega Treaty. Furthermore, neither Rasasa nor Adawa has given consent to accept the jurisdiction of the Court, and the compulsory jurisdiction of the Permanent Court of International Justice (PCIJ) cannot be transferred to the Court. Both Parties have agreed that the Statement of Agreed Facts jointly signed on 20 September 2019 was without prejudice to Rasasa's objection.

QUESTIONS PRESENTED

The Republic of Rasasa respectfully requests the Court to adjudge:

I.

1. Whether Adawa is a Party to the Botega Treaty;

2. Whether the Court has jurisdiction over the present case.

II.

1. Whether Rasasa's development of the WALL is consistent with international law;

2. Whether Rasasa's deployment of the WALL is consistent with international law.

III.

1. Whether Adawa's claim concerning the CHC Treaty falls out of the Court's jurisdiction;

2. Whether Adawa's claim concerning the CHC Treaty is inadmissible;

3. Whether the imposition of tariffs is consistent with the CHC Treaty.

IV.

1. Whether the apprehension and detention of Ms. Grey violates customary international law;

2. Whether the apprehension and detention of Ms. Grey violates the CHC Treaty.

STATEMENT OF FACTS

THE JURISDICTION ISSUE

Adawa and Rasasa are neighboring countries with a 201-kilometer-long shared border in the Crosinia Region. The Region is the only place on Earth where the Helian hyacinth is cultivated. Exports of Helian spice contribute significantly to all six Crosinian States.

On 29 October 1929, Rasasa declared independence from its former Kingdom Crosinia, and the provinces of Adawa and Zeitounia united to form the Adawa-Zeitounia Union (AZU). The President of Rasasa and Queen Goleta of the AZU signed the Treaty of Botega on Armistice and Pacification (the Botega Treaty). These States promptly became Parties to the Statute of the Permanent Court of International Justice.

On 1 January 1939, the two provinces of AZU amicably agreed to dissolve their Union, and each declared its independence as of that date. Both Adawa and Rasasa joined the United Nations in 1947 and acceded to the Statute of the International Court of Justice. Neither State has filed a declaration accepting the Court's compulsory jurisdiction under Article 36(2) of the Statute.

THE DEVELOPMENT OF THE 'WEAPONIZED AUTONOMOUS LIMITATION LINE' (WALL)

The WALL employed machine learning algorithms and featured an advanced form of 'supervised learning', in which the training data acquired from 11 States had been meticulously 'tagged' by Rasasan Robotics Corporation (RRC). All six CHC Member States provided leading exports to the development phase of the project.

During the development process of the WALL, for its compliance with international law, Rasasa has conducted a review by advisers. The system was subjected to the close supervision of Rasasa and Adawa. Every element of the system has been extensively peer-reviewed and tested by government and private experts in more than 30 countries. The head of the Adawan team recognized the accuracy and reliability of the WALL, as it demonstrated a 'false positive' rate of less than 0.0001% and would mistakenly use excessive force no more than once in two hundred million encounters.

Since July 2012, the Adawan criminal gangs have been constantly committing cross border crimes. In 2016, they turned well-armed and organized. The Adawan gangs regularly entered Rasasa illegally, assaulting and even killing villagers. In September 2016, the Rasasan and Adawan governments decided to establish a high-level task force to tackle this problem. This, afterwards, failed to formulate a comprehensive plan. In February 2017, the Rasasan Border Police reported that the Adawan disorganized gangs had become organized militias. Proved by the United Nations Office on Drugs and Crime and eyewitnesses, the Adawan militias were heavily armed with military-grade weapons and equipment, and had established permanent and well-defended encampments within Rasasan territory, which they used as bases for international trafficking of illegal drugs. Both Adawa and Rasasa declared that their domestic police efforts had been ineffective in counteracting the Adawan militia.

THE DEPLOYMENT OF THE WALL

On 1 June 2017, the militia simultaneously attacked nine Rasasan Border Police stations, killing 21 officers. On 25 June 2017, President Pindro authorized the purchase of the WALL from the RRC and also its installation along the Rasasa-Adawa border. The WALL was deployed entirely within Rasasan territory, between 6 and 35 meters from the Rasasa-Adawa border. There are no permanent human settlements within 200 meters of the border. The WALL will deploy, on the basis of graduated sequencing, demonstrative measures to preset levels of force, based upon its training data, against anyone attempting to cross the border illegally, in either direction.

The task force reviewed reports from both States' national police forces indicated that in the four months following the deployment of the WALL, reports of trans-border incidents decreased more than 80 percent. To this date, the WALL has on approximately 100 occasions issued verbal warnings and in five instances non-lethal 'warning shots'. No injuries are known to have occurred as a result of these measures. Meanwhile, there have been no reports of any incidents of lethal force deployed by the WALL.

THE IMPOSITION OF TARIFFS ON HELIAN PRODUCTS

On 14 July 2012, an unprecedented and catastrophic tropical cyclone struck the entire Region, causing severe death and drastic damages to the town to each of the six States. More than 60% of the Helian hyacinths in Rasasa, 20% of those in Adawa, and between 15% and 20% of those in the other four States were destroyed. Additionally, unemployment rate began to increase across the Region.

Considering that the Helian industry has a significant impact on the wellbeing of Rasasan citizens, the newly elected President Pindro invoked 'essential security interests' and submitted the bill concerning Helian products for legislative approval. It provided for the introduction of tariffs of 25% *ad valorem* on Helian bulbs, live plants, and pollen imported into Rasasa, in an effort to encourage Rasasan domestic processors to return to local farms for their feedstock. The proposal was adopted by the Rasasa's Parliament in January 2018.

In October 2018, Adawa formally requested consultations with Rasasa pursuant to Article 1 and Article 4 of the Understanding on Rules and Procedures Governing the Settlement of Disputes (DSU) of the WTO. Government officials from both Adawa and Rasasa met, but no amicable resolutions were made. In February 2019, Adawa requested the establishment of a panel pursuant to Article 6(2) of the DSU, alleging that Rasasa's tariffs on Helian products constituted an unjustifiable breach of its commitment to maintaining the bound rate of zero on such items.

THE ARREST AND DETENTION OF MS. DARIAN GREY

From 1979 to 2016, Ms. Darian Grey served as the founder and chief executive officer of the RRC. The RRC was involved in the 2007–2009 civil war in Garantia by selling weapons systems and providing training to government militias, which was referred to the Prosecutor of the International Criminal Court (ICC) by Garantia. Ms. Grey was appointed as the Minister of Foreign Affairs of Rasasa by President Pindro in January 2017.

In accordance with the ICC procedures, the Office of the Prosecutor opened an investigation against Ms. Grey in August 2009. On 13 April 2019, the Prosecutor requested the issuance of a warrant for the arrest of Ms. Grey pursuant to Article 58 of the Rome Statute, assigning to her criminal responsibility for certain alleged activities of the RRC in Garantia between 2007 and 2009.

Ms. Grey, representing Rasasa, arrived in the capital city of Adawa on 18 June 2019 for the four-day regular annual session of the CHC. On 20 June 2019, a Pre-Trial Chamber of the ICC granted the Prosecutor's 13 April 2019 request and issued a warrant of arrest of Ms. Grey. Two days later, officers of the Novazora police approached and arrested Ms. Grey. The Rasasan Ambassador to Adawa was promptly notified of her arrest, and Rasasan consular agents were provided access to her. During the arrest, Ms. Grey's judicial appeal was denied by a magistrate and she would remain under house arrest at a monitored diplomatic guesthouse in Adawa, pending this Court's disposition of the case.

In 1998, Adawa became an original Party to the Rome Statute establishing the International Criminal Court (Rome Statute). Adawa remains a party to that treaty. Rasasa is not a party to the Rome Statute.

SUMMARY OF PLEADINGS

FIRST PLEADING

Adawa is not a Party to the 1929 Botega Treaty and the Court does not have jurisdiction over Adawa's claims. *First*, Adawa is neither a contracting Party nor a successor to the Botega Treaty under applicable international law. *Second*, Rasasa and Adawa have not given consent to accept the jurisdiction of the Court, and the compulsory jurisdiction of the Permanent Court of International Justice cannot be transferred to the Court.

SECOND PLEADING

Rasasa's development and deployment of the WALL along the Adawa-Rasasa border is consistent with international law. *First*, the deployment of the WALL is not restricted by conventions or customary international law. *Second*, the deployment of the WALL is in compliance with international law. For one thing, Rasasa is entitled to use force on its border during law enforcement activities. For another, the deployment of the WALL does not violate Adawan's human rights and the International Humanitarian Law.

THIRD PLEADING

Adawa's claim concerning the CHC Treaty does not fall into the scope of the Court's jurisdiction or is inadmissible. *First*, the Court has no jurisdiction since Adawa is not a Party to the Botega Treaty. *Second*, adjudicating on Adawa's claim will constitute parallel proceedings, which are barred from by *lis pendens* principle. Alternatively, the Court should decline its jurisdiction pursuant to principle of comity. *Third*, the imposition of tariff can be justified under Article 22 of the CHC Treaty.

FOURTH PLEADING

Adawa's arrest and detention of Ms. Grey constitute international unlawful act for violating its obligation to respect for Ms. Grey's immunity *ratione personae. First,* the arrest and detention of Ms. Grey violate her immunity in the foreign criminal proceedings. *Second*, the arrest and detention violate her immunity *ratione personae* in the ICC's criminal proceedings. Thus, Adawa's obligation to cooperate with the ICC conflicts with its obligation to respect Ms. Grey's immunity and it fails to assist the ICC. Hence, Adawa's act is unlawful and Adawa should immediately repatriate Ms. Grey.

PLEADINGS

I. ADAWA IS NOT A PARTY TO THE BOTEGA TREATY AND THE COURT DOES NOT HAVE JURISDICTION OVER ADAWA'S CLAIMS.

A. ADAWA IS NOT A PARTY TO THE BOTEGA TREATY UNDER APPLICABLE INTERNATIONAL LAW.

i. Adawa is not a contracting Party to the Botega Treaty and has not given consent to be bound by it.

According to the Vienna Convention on the Law of Treaties (VCLT), a Party is a State which has consented to be bound by the treaty in force,[1] whether in forms of signature, ratification, acceptance, or by any other means if so agreed.[2] The Treaty of Botega on Armistice and Pacification (the Botega Treaty) is signed between the Adawa-Zeitounia Union (AZU) and Rasasa long before the establishment of Adawa.[3] Adawa has neither signed the treaty nor consented to be bound by it. Therefore, Adawa is not a contracting Party to the Botega Treaty. Besides, Parties of the Botega Treaty have not agreed that participation in negotiation constitutes a form of consent. Therefore, Adawan representatives' participation in the negotiation process of the treaty should neither be regarded as giving consent to be bound by it nor indicate that Adawa is a contracting Party to it.

ii. Adawa is not a successor State to the Botega Treaty under VCLT.

VCLT is the only international legal instrument concerning treaty application of which Adawa is a contracting Party.[4] According to Article 73 of VCLT, the convention

---

1 Vienna Convention on the Law of Treaties (adopted 22 May 1969, entered into force 27 January 1980) 1155 UNTS 331 (VCLT) art 2(1)(g); International Law Commission (ILC) 'Draft Articles on the Law of Treaties with Commentaries' *Yearbook of the International Law Commission* (Vol. II, 1966) UN Doc A/CN4/SER A/1966/Add1,190.

2 VCLT art 11.

3 Treaty of Botega on Armistice and Pacification (1 November 1929) Case Concerning the Helian Hyacinth (Adawa v Rasasa) (Statement of Agreed Facts) [2019] (*Facts*) [Annex A] (Botega Treaty) Preamble.

4 *Facts* [60].

shall not prejudge any question that may arise in regard to a treaty from a succession of State.[5] Therefore, Adawa could not succeed to the Botega Treaty by referring to VCLT.

iii. Adawa is not a successor State to the Botega Treaty under VCSST.

a. Adawa and Rasasa are not contracting Parties to VCSST.

Neither Adawa nor Rasasa is a contracting Party to the Vienna Convention on Succession of States in respect of Treaties (VCSST). Besides, according to VCLT,[6] a treaty is not to be regarded as intended to have retroactive effects unless such an intention is expressed in the treaty.[7] Without any special clause or any special object necessitating retroactive interpretation.[8] VCSST is not applicable retroactively to the conclusion of the Botega Treaty[9] which was concluded before its entry into force[10] in 1978.

b. Article 34 of VCSST does not constitute customary international law.

Article 34 VCSST regulates States succession in cases of separation of parts of a State.[11] It has been widely recognized that for an international convention to create a rule of customary international law, the provision must correspond to a general practice that is accepted as law (*opinio juris*).[12] State practice in connection with treaties and decisions of the International Court of Justice (the Court) should be considered for the identification.[13] Where the relevant acts are divergent to the

5 ILC 'Summary Records of the Eighteenth Session' (1966) UN Doc A/CN4/SERA/1966, 302.

6 VCLT art 28.

7 Draft Articles on the Law of Treaties with Commentaries (n 1) 211.

8 *Mavrommatis Palestine Concessions* (Greece v United Kingdom) (Objection to the Jurisdiction of the Court) [1924] PCIJ Rep Series A No 2, 34.

9 *Facts* [5].

10 *Ambatielos case* (Greece/United Kingdom) (Preliminary Objection) [1952] ICJ Rep 28, 40.

11 Vienna Convention on Succession of States in Respect of Treaties (adopted 23 August 1978, entered into force 6 November 1996) 1946 UNTS 3 (VCSST) art 34.

12 *North Sea Continental Shelf cases* (Federal Republic of Germany/Denmark; Federal Republic of Germany/Netherlands) (Judgment) [1969] ICJ Rep 3 [77].

13 ILC 'Draft Conclusions on Identification of Customary International Law, with Commentaries' (2018) UN Doc A/73/10 Conclusions 6 and 13, 120-121.

extent that no pattern of behavior can be discerned, no general practice can be said to exist.[14]

In the *Gabčíkovo-Nagymaros* case, the Court does not affirm Article 34 of VCSST as customary international law.[15] Only 23 States have ratified VCSST.[16] The USA considered all its treaties with the Central American Federation abrogated when the federation was dissolved.[17] Austria persisted that it was a new State not *ipso jure* bound by those treaties after the termination of the Austro-Hungarian Empire.[18] The state practice of Article 34 of VCSST is neither widespread nor consistent. Accordingly, it does not constitute customary international law. Adawa could not succeed to the Botega Treaty on this ground.

c. Adawa is not a successor State to the Botega Treaty under Article 12 of VCSST.

(i) Article 12 of VCSST is not applicable as the Botega Treaty does not concern the interests of any other States.

Article 12 of VCSST is designed to secure the benefits of foreign States, a group of States or all State from the potential effects of State successions.[19] In the present case, the Botega Treaty is for the pacific settlement of future disputes which may arise between AZU and Rasasa.[20] The Armistice Demarcation Line and the International Zone of Peace[21] are both exclusively for the interests of AZU and Rasasa. Besides, as the component provinces of AZU, Adawa and Zeitounian should by no means be

---

14 *Asylum case* (Colombia v Peru) (Judgment) [1950] ICJ Rep 266, 277.

15 *Case Concerning the Gabčíkovo-Nagymaros Project* (Hungary/Slovakia) (Judgment) [1997] ICJ Rep 7 [123].

16 United Nations Treaty Collection (UNTC) 'Status of VCSST' <https://treaties.un.org/Pages/ViewDetails.aspx?src=TREATY&mtdsg_no=XXIII-2&chapter=23&clang=_en> accessed 1 January 2020.

17 Arthur Keith, *Theory of State Succession* (Palala Press 2016) 19.

18 United Nations Secretariat 'Succession of States in Respect of Bilateral Treaties' UN Doc A/CN4/229 [116].

19 VCSST art 12(1)(2); *Gabčíkovo-Nagymaros* (n 15) [123]; International Law Association (ILA) 'Final Report, Committee on Aspects of the Law of State Succession' (2008) 27-31 [9].

20 Botega Treaty Preamble.

21 Botega Treaty art 1.

regarded as foreign States.[22] Therefore, the Botega Treaty is a bilateral regime, which does not influence the interests of other States. Thus, Article 12 of VCSST is not applicable.

(ii) Only the obligations and rights relating to territory, rather than the whole Botega Treaty, can be succeeded.

Article 12 of VCSST requires that a succession of States shall not affect the obligations and rights established by a treaty relating to the use of any territory, or to restrictions upon its use.[23]

First, the Botega Treaty as a whole cannot be succeeded as it is not a territorial treaty. As is widely accepted, treaties of a territorial character constitute a special category and are not affected by the succession of States.[24] According to the *Gabčíkovo-Nagymaros* case, if the major elements of a treaty relate to the respective territories, the treaty itself then fall within the territorial category.[25] In the present case, territory does not constitute the major elements of the Botega Treaty. Only two articles of it are to a limited extent related to territorial issues. As clarified in its preamble, the Botega Treaty should be regarded as a step toward the restoration of peace and security to people,[26] rather than a permanent settlement on demarcation or territorial disputes.[27] Therefore, the major elements of the treaty are irrelevant to territories.

Second, only Article I and III, rather than Article VI of the Botega Treaty may be succeeded. Article 12 of VCSST provides that the obligations and rights concerned shall not be affected by State succession. The International Law Commission considers this rule only relates to the objective effects of the treaty on deciding

22 *Facts* [5].

23 VCSST art 12 (1)(2).

24 ILC 'Draft Articles on Succession of States in Respect of Treaties with Commentaries' *Yearbook of the International Law Commission* (Part I, 1974) UN Doc A/CN4/SERA/1974/Addl, 197.

25 VCLT art 12; *Gabčíkovo-Nagymaros* (n 15) [123].

26 Botega Treaty Preamble.

27 Botega Treaty Preamble.

territorial issues. It is irrelevant to the succession of the treaty.[28] Therefore, Article VI as a dispute resolution clause cannot be succeeded.

B. MEANWHILE, THE COURT DOES NOT HAVE JURISDICTION IN THE PRESENT CASE.

In the auspice of the principle of the sovereign equality,[29] the jurisdiction of the Court cannot be established without a State's consent.[30] Jurisdiction of the Court can either be established through a specific consent given to it, or transferred from the Permanent Court of International Justice (PCIJ).

i. Neither Rasasa nor Adawa has given a specific consent to accept the jurisdiction of the present Court.

A declaration is the only formal and indispensable requirement acknowledged by both the Statute of the International Court of Justice (ICJ Statute) and the Court.[31] When States accept the compulsory jurisdiction of the Court through declarations,[32] such declarations shall be deposited with the United Nations Secretary-General (UNSG) under Article 36(4) of the ICJ Statute.[33]

In the present case, neither Adawa nor Rasasa has filed a declaration accepting the Court's compulsory jurisdiction.[34] Moreover, no deposition to the UNSG has been made.[35] Therefore, the Court does not have compulsory jurisdiction over the present

28 Draft Articles on Succession of States in Respect of Treaties (n 24) 206 [36].

29 Charter of the United Nations (adopted 26 June 1945, entered into force 24 October 1945) (UN Charter) art 2(1); *Western Sahara* (Advisory Opinion) [1975] ICJ Rep 12 [33].

30 Statute of the International Court of Justice (ICJ Statute) art 36(1); *Continental Shelf* (Libyan Arab Jamahiriya/Malta) (Judgment) [1985] ICJ Rep 13[10].

31 *Case Concerning the Temple of Preah Vihear* (Cambodia v Thailand) (Preliminary Objections) [1961] ICJ Rep 17, 31.

32 ICJ Statute art 36(4).

33 *Temple* (n 31) 32.

34 *Facts* [7].

35 *Facts* [8]; Declarations Recognizing the Jurisdiction of the Court as Compulsory <https://www.icj-cij.org/en/declarations> accessed 1 January 2020.

case on this ground.[36]

ii. The jurisdiction of PCIJ cannot be transferred to the present Court.

a. The compulsory jurisdiction of PCIJ cannot be transferred to the Court through Article 36 (5) of the ICJ Statute.

The AZU and Rasasa recognized the compulsory jurisdiction of PCIJ by referring to Article 36 of PCIJ Statute.[37] Two requirements should be fulfilled to transfer the compulsory jurisdiction to the present Court. *First*, declarations made for the jurisdiction of PCIJ should be in force when the State becomes a Party to the ICJ Statute.[38] According to *Ariel Incident* case and *Temple* case, such declarations are no longer in force if the State joined the United Nations later than 16 April 1946 when PCIJ was dissolved.[39] *Second*, the acceptance of compulsory jurisdiction shall be deposited to the UNSG according to Article 36(4) of the ICJ Statute, as the only formal and inalienable requirement of the ICJ Statute.[40]

Both Rasasa and Adawa joint the United Nations and acceded to the ICJ Statute in 1947 after the dissolution of PCIJ.[41] Therefore, the acceptance set out in that declaration was devoid of object since PCIJ was no longer in existence. Moreover, neither of the Parties has deposited any of their declarations to the UNSG.[42] Failing to fulfill these requirements, the jurisdiction over the present case of PCIJ cannot be transferred to the Court.

b. The compulsory jurisdiction of PCIJ cannot be transferred to the Court through Article 37 of the ICJ Statute.

Article 37 of the ICJ Statute states that whenever a treaty in force provides for

36 *Barcelona Traction, Light and Power Company, Limited* (Belgium v Spain) (Preliminary Objections) [1964] ICJ Rep 6, 32.

37 Botega Treaty art VI.

38 ICJ Statute art 36(5); *Case Concerning the Aerial Incident of 27 July 1955* (Israel v Bulgaria) (Preliminary Objections) [1959] ICJ Rep 127, 144.

39 *Aerial Incident* (n 38) 143-144; *Temple* (n 31) 25-26.

40 *Temple* (n 31) 31.

41 *Facts* [6].

42 *Facts* [8]; Declarations Recognizing the Jurisdiction of the Court as Compulsory (n 35).

reference of a matter to PCIJ, the matter shall, as between the Parties to the present Statute, be referred to the Court.[43] Concerning the present case, there are two essential prerequisites for applying this article. *First,* a genuine consent must be given.[44] *Second,* the treaty itself must be 'in force',[45] as Article 37 formally related not to the clause as such but to the instrument containing it.[46]

Neither of the requirements was fulfilled in the present case. *First,* Rasasa firmly determined that the Botega Treaty was only binding upon AZU and Rasasa, and Adawa did not become a Party to the treaty.[47] Within Rasasa's understanding, there was no legal instrument in force between Adawa and itself. It was neither possible for nor intended by Rasasa to give a genuine consent to accept the jurisdiction of the Court through Article 37. *Second,* as illustrated above, no treaty exists between Adawa and Rasasa. Therefore, the jurisdiction of PCIJ cannot be transferred to the Court upon Article 37 of the ICJ Statute.

II. RASASA'S DEVELOPMENT AND DEPLOYMENT OF THE WALL ALONG THE BORDER BETWEEN ADAWA AND RASASA IS CONSISTENT WITH INTERNATIONAL LAW.

A. RASASA'S DEVELOPMENT OF THE WALL IS CONSISTENT WITH INTERNATIONAL LAW.

i. The development of the WALL is not restricted by any conventions.

According to the *Lotus* case, the rules of law binding upon States emanate from their own free will as expressed in conventions or by usages generally accepted as expressing principles of law. Restrictions upon the independence of States cannot be presumed.[48] In absence of contrary legal instruments, development of

43 ICJ Statute art 37.

44 *Barcelona Traction* (n 36) 35.

45 *Barcelona Traction* (n 36) 32; *Legality of Use of Force* (Serbia and Montenegro v Netherlands) (Preliminary Objections) [2004] ICJ Rep 1011 [124]; Shabtai Rosenne, *The Law and Practice of the International Court (1920-2005)* (4th edn, Vol. II, Martinus Nijhoff Publishers 2006) 665.

46 *Barcelona Traction* (n 36) 29-30.

47 *Facts* [58] [61].

48 *S.S. Lotus* (France v Turkey) (Judgment) [1927] PCIJ Rep Series A No 10 [44].

certain technology shall be decided by States themselves.[49] In the present case, no international legal instruments have been established concerning prohibition of the development of autonomous weaponry system.

ii. The development of the WALL is not restricted under customary international law.

Customary international law concerning the restriction of autonomous weaponry cannot be established in lack of a general practice and *opinio juris*.[50] It cannot be established when the rule is accepted by some States but rejected by others.[51] Regarding the development of autonomous weaponry system, major powers including the US, China and India have expressed their support.[52] The Netherlands considered this system equally fair.[53] Besides, officials and experts from 15 States have participated in the development of the WALL and Adawa have supported its entire development process.[54] The customary international law cannot be established. Therefore, Rasasa's development of the WALL is legitimate.

B. RASASA'S DEPLOYMENT OF THE WALL DOES NOT VIOLATE APPLICABLE INTERNATIONAL LAW.

Although applied by Rasasa, the WALL is against anyone attempting to cross the border illegally in either direction.[55] In its essence, the system is a border control measure designed to detect threats, and to prevent them from becoming reality.[56]

---

49 *Accordance with International Law of the Unilateral Declaration of Independence in Respect of Kosovo* (Advisory Opinion) [2010] ICJ Rep 403 [121].

50 *North Sea Continental Shelf* (n 12) [77].

51 *Fisheries case* (United Kingdom v Norway) [1951] ICJ Rep 116, 131.

52 IPSO 'Global Advisor Data on Autonomous Weapons Systems (AWS)' <https://www.ipsos.com/en-us/news-polls> accessed 1 January 2020.

53 Ilse Verdiesen, 'An Empirical Study Using the Value Sensitive Design Approach' (2017) 38 *IEEE Technology and Society Magazine*, 34-44.

54 *Facts* [19] [20] [21] [22] [25].

55 *Facts* [37].

56 *Facts* [37].

i. Rasasa has the legitimate right to use force and firearms for law enforcement on its border.

States have supreme authority within their territory, the plenitude of internal jurisdiction and their freedom from other States' intervention on their territory.[57] According to *Guyana v Suriname* case, force may be used in law enforcement activities in international law.[58]

In the present case, the Adawan militia has been constantly interfering and violating Rasasa's sovereignty in almost five years in an escalating trend.[59] The militia has been using its permanent camps within Rasasan territory as a headquarters for its global trafficking of illegal drugs.[60] On 1 June 2017, the Adawan militia attacked nine Rasasan Police Stations and killed 21 officers.[61] A threat to the life and safety of law enforcement officials means a threat to the stability of Rasasa society as a whole.[62] Rasasa has the right to exercise enforcement jurisdiction over breaches of its rules by using force in border law enforcement activities.[63]

ii. Rasasa's deployment of the WALL does not violate Adawans' human rights.

a. The deployment of the WALL does not violate Adawan's human rights, especially the right to life.

The deployment of the WALL does not constitute arbitrary deprivation of life

---

57 UN Charter art 2(4)(7).

58 *Arbitral Tribunal Constituted Pursuant to Article 287, and in Accordance with Annex VII of the United Nations Convention on the Law of the Sea in the Matter of an Arbitration between Guyana and Suriname* [2007] 30 RIAA 1 [445]; *SS 'I'm Alone'* (Canada/United States) [1935] 3 RIAA 1609, 1615; *The M/V 'SAIGA' case* (Saint Vincent and the Grenadines v Guinea) (Judgment) ITLOS Reports 1999, 7.

59 *Facts* [17] [27] [36].

60 *Facts* [35].

61 *Facts* [35] [36].

62 UNCHR 'Principles on the Use of Force and Firearms by Law Enforcement Officials' <https://www.ohchr.org/en/professionalinterest/pages/useofforceandfirearms.aspx> accessed 1 January 2020.

63 Bernard Oxman, 'Jurisdiction of States' Max Planck Encyclopedias of International Law <https://opil.ouplaw.com/view/10.1093/law:epil/9780199231690/law-9780199231690-e1436?rskey=S1UYd8&result=2&prd=MPIL> accessed 1 January 2020.

prohibited by Article 6(1) of the International Covenant on Civil and Political Rights (ICCPR).[64] The Human Rights Committee,[65] the Inter-American Commission and Court[66] and the African Commission,[67] established the standards for the determination of 'arbitrary' through the rule of law, necessity and proportionality.[68]

In the present case, the WALL has not and will not arbitrarily deprive anyone's life. *First,* as mentioned above, Rasasa is faced with the necessity to exercise enforcement jurisdiction and take actions according to its internal law. *Second,* the WALL is a proportionate measure. The WALL is carefully deployed in a manner preventing potential harm. The system is embedded with rules instructing the software to favor non-lethal deterrence[69] and equipped with numerous precautionary methods[70] with a negligible mistake rate.[71] Every tower making up the WALL is situated within Rasasan territory, keeping adequate distance from the border.[72] Most importantly, Rasasa's deployment of the WALL is based on the prerequisite that no permanent human settlements exist within 200 meters of the border.[73] Therefore, the deployment of the WALL does not violate anyone's right to life.

b. Conversely, the WALL has a positive impact in safeguarding the human rights of both Adawan and Rasasan.

According to the task force reviewed reports from both States, in the four months

64 International Covenant on Civil and Political Rights (adopted 16 December 1966, entered into force 23 March 1976) 999 UNTS 171 (ICCPR) art 6(1).

65 Human Rights Committee 'General Comment No 36 (2018) on Article 6 of the International Covenant on Civil and Political Rights, on the Right to Life' (30 October 2018) UN Doc CCPR/C/GC/36 [12]; *Suarez de Guerrero v Colombia*, HRC Communication No R 11/45 para 13.2.

66 *Constantine and Benjamin et al v Trinidad and Tobago* [2002] IACHR Series C No 94 [106].

67 African Commission on Human and Peoples' Rights 'General Comment No 3 on the African Charter on Human and Peoples' Rights: The Right to Life (Article 4)' (2015) [12].

68 United Nations Office on Drugs and Crime '*Arbitrary Deprivation of Life*' <https://www.unodc.org/e4j/en/terrorism/module-8/key-issues/arbitrary-deprivation-of-life.html> accessed 1 January 2020.

69 *Facts* [25].

70 *Facts* [37].

71 *Facts* [37].

72 *Clarifications* [3].

73 *Clarifications* [3].

following the deployment of the WALL, reports of transborder incidents decreased more than 80 percent.[74] The WALL has effectively deterred more than 100 illegal occasions without causing any injuries.[75] It has never deployed lethal force and no injuries have ever occurred.[76] Recognized by the joint task force, the WALL has without question had a positive impact in reducing and deterring cross-border crime.[77] Therefore, the deployment of the WALL does not violate Adawan's human rights.

iii. Rasasa's deployment of the WALL does not violate the International Humanitarian Law (IHL).

a. The WALL is in compliance with the basic principles of the IHL.

(i) The WALL complies with the principle of military necessity.

The principle of military necessity is an essential component of International Humanitarian Law.[78] It means the necessity for measures which are essential to attain the goals of war, and which are lawful in accordance with the laws and customs of war.[79] It permits a belligerent, subject to the laws of war, to apply any amount and kind of force to compel the complete submission of the enemy with the least possible expenditure of time, life, and money.[80]

The Adawan militia has committed serious criminal acts, including but not limited to attacking and assaulting Rasasa civilian,[81] killing Rasasan officials,[82] and running international illegal drug trafficking business in Rasasa.[83] Domestic police efforts

---

74 *Facts* [41].

75 *Clarifications* [4].

76 *Facts* [42]; *Clarifications* [4].

77 *Facts* [42].

78 The International Committee of the Red Cross (ICRC) 'Military Necessity' <https://casebook.icrc.org> accessed 1 January 2020; Declaration Renouncing the Use, in Time of War, of Explosive Projectiles under 400 Grammes Weight, Saint Petersburg (1868) (St Petersburg Declaration).

79 Instructions for the Government of Armies of the United States in the Field (Lieber Code) (1863) art 14; D Schindler and J Toman, *The Laws of Armed Conflicts* (Martinus Nijhoff Publishers 1988) 3-23.

80 *The United States of America v Wilhelm List et al* (Judgment) US Military Tribunal at Nuremberg [1253].

81 *Facts* [17].

82 *Facts* [36].

83 *Facts* [35].

and joint task force have been ineffective in tackling the problem.[84] Both countries admitted that the free movement of criminal operatives across the border had contributed to the current situation.[85] Rasasa had the concrete and direct military advantage anticipated to reestablish the stability of the border and provide the Rasasan victims a normal and safe life. As declared by both States, this should be realized through tightening border controls and eliminating armed incursions.[86]

(ii) The WALL complies with the principle of proportionality.

The principle of proportionality regarding the use of force is a basic principle of the IHL.[87] According to the Protocol Additional to the Geneva Conventions of 12 August 1949, and relating to the Protection of Victims of International Armed Conflicts (API), attacks which would be excessive in relation to the concrete and direct military advantage anticipated shall be prohibited.[88] Proportionality is an element that must be taken into account by Parties when undertaking targeting decisions, and making decisions on choice of weaponry.[89]

In the present case, the deployment of the WALL is proportionate to Rasasa's military necessity. The WALL is embedded with rules instructing the software to favor non-lethal deterrence[90] and takes measures in proportionate to the illegal

---

84 *Facts* [29] [34] [35].

85 *Facts* [35].

86 *Facts* [32] [35].

87 *Legality of the Threat or Use of Nuclear Weapons* (Advisory Opinion) [1996] ICJ Rep 226 [41]; *Military and Paramilitary Activities in and against Nicaragua* (Nicaragua v USA) (Judgment) [1986] ICJ Rep 14 [176].

88 Protocol Additional to the Geneva Convention of 12 August 1949, and relating to the Protection of Victims of International Armed Conflict (adopted 6 August 1977, entered into force 7 December 1978) 1125 UNTS 3 (Protocol I) arts 51(5)(b), 57(2)(a)(i), 57(2)(b); Protocol Additional to the Geneva Convention of 12 August 1949, and relating to the Protection of Victims of Non-International Armed Conflict (adopted 6 August 1977, entered into force 7 December 1978) 1125 UNTS 609 (Protocol II) art 3(3)(c).

89 Emily Crawford, 'Proportionality' at Max Planck Encyclopedia of International (MPIL) <https://opil.ouplaw.com/view/10.1093/law:epil/9780199231690/law-9780199231690-e1459?rskey=VgMt1b&result=1&prd=MPIL> accessed 1 January 2020.

90 *Facts* [25].

behaviors. Normally, dispersal of disabling chemicals and non-lethal warning shots would resolve the problem without causing any injuries.[91] In conclusion, the WALL is designed to generate the least amount of loss or damage to the population while improving border stability with a negligible mistake rate.[92]

The principle of proportionality also requires that Parties shall take all feasible precautions in the choice of means and methods of attack to avoid or minimize damage.[93] The WALL deploys all demonstrative measures before resorting to preset levels of force.[94]

Therefore, the deployment of the WALL complies with the principle of proportionality.

(iii) The WALL complies with the principle of distinction.

The principle of distinction is another basic principle of the IHL.[95] According to the API, the Parties to the conflict shall at all times distinguish between the civilian population and combatants, civilian objects and military objectives.[96] Indiscriminate attacks are prohibited.[97]

In the present case, the WALL is enabled by its tagging system to recognize indicators of retreat, surrender, incapacity and other factors that would render an individual effectively *hors de combat*.[98] Data from 11 countries were collected and tagged

---

91 *Facts* [37]; *Clarifications* [4].

92 *Facts* [25].

93 Protocol I art 57(2)(a)(ii); *McCann and Others v United Kingdom*, ECHR Application No 18984/91 [194]; *Nadege Dorzema et al v Dominican Republic* [2012] IACHR Series C No 251 [87]; UNCHR 'Report of the Special Rapporteur on Extrajudicial, Summary or Arbitrary Executions, Christof Heyns' UN Doc A/HRC/26/36 [63].

94 *Facts* [37].

95 Protocol I arts 48, 51, 52; St Petersburg Declaration; Convention on Prohibitions or Restrictions on the Use of Certain Conventional Weapons Which May be Deemed to be Excessively Injurious or to Have Indiscriminate Effects (adopted 10 October 1980, entered into force 2 December 1983) 1342 UNTS 137 (CCW) art 3; Laws and Customs of War on Land (29 July 1899) Treaty Series 403 Annex.

96 Protocol I arts 48, 49, 51, 52, 57; Protocol II art 3 (3)(c).

97 Protocol I arts 49(1), 51(4).

98 *Facts* [21].

meticulously.[99] Proved by a report signed by 12 States' police and military technology experts,[100] the WALL is capable of distinguishing between civilian, combatants, the *hors de combat* and react accurately to the transition between different identities.[101] Besides, the WALL is proportionate as a preventive measure for future escalated border conflicts since the seriousness of Adawa militia's criminal behaviors has been increasingly growing in the past five years.[102]

b. The WALL is in compliance with the rules of Methods and Means of Warfare under the IHL.

Parties shall follow the rules concerning methods and means of warfare under the IHL.[103] Weapons, projectiles and material and methods of warfare of a nature to cause superfluous injury or unnecessary suffering are prohibited.[104] Several weapons are explicitly prohibited, including spike batons[105] and bacteriological weapons,[106] etc.

In the present case, the WALL's force equipment includes disabling chemicals, non-targeted explosions and fully automatic .50 caliber machine guns. None of these measures will cause superfluous injury or unnecessary suffering. With its application strictly limited, the WALL is a legitimate method and means of warfare.

c. The WALL is in compliance with the Martens Clause.

The Martens Clause is a principle preventing the assumption that anything not

99 *Facts* [20].

100 *Facts* [20].

101 *Facts* [20].

102 *Facts* [17] [27] [35] [36].

103 Convention Concerning the Laws and Customs of War on Land and Its Annex: Regulations Respecting the Laws and Customs of War on Land (adopted 18 October 1907, entered into force 26 January 1910) 205 CTS 277 (Hague IV) arts 22, 23(a)(b)(e).

104 Protocol I art 35(3); St Petersburg Declaration; CCW Preamble.

105 European Commission Council 'European Commission Council Regulation Concerning Trade in Certain Goods Which Could be Used for Capital Punishment, Torture, or Other Cruel, Inhumane, or Degrading Treatment or Punishment' No 1236/2005.

106 Claude Pilloud *et al*, *Additional Protocols: of 8 June 1977 to the Geneva Conventions of 12 August 1949* (Martinus Nijhoff Publishers 1987) 1412.

explicitly prohibited by the relevant treaties is permitted.[107] It states that cases not covered by current legal instruments remain under the protection and authority of the principles of international law derived from established custom, principles of humanity and the dictates of public conscience.[108]

As mentioned above, the WALL is in compliance with the principles of international law. It is also in accordance with public conscience. After its deployment, trans-border incidents decreased more than 80 percent.[109] The WALL has been recognized by Adawan force as having a positive impact in reducing and deterring cross-border crime.[110] Rasasa efficiently and effectively solved this problem which had troubled both countries for more than 5 years[111] without generating any injuries.[112] Since the urgent need for peace of both Rasasan and Adawan, the deployment of the WALL accords with the dictates of public conscience and the Martens Clause.

III. ADAWA'S CLAIM DOES NOT FALL INTO THE SCOPE OF THE COURT'S JURISDICTION OR IS INADMISSIBLE; IN THE ALTERNATIVE, THE IMPOSITION OF TARIFFS DOES NOT VIOLATE THE CHC TREATY.

A. ADAWA'S CLAIM DOES NOT FALL INTO THE SCOPE OF THE COURT'S JURISDICTION OR IS INADMISSIBLE.

i. The Court does not have jurisdiction over the dispute.

As demonstrated in the first pleading, the Court does not have jurisdiction over Adawa's claims for Adawa is not a Party to the Botega Treaty.

ii. Alternatively, Adawa's claim is inadmissible.

The adjudication of Adawa's claim will constitute parallel proceedings [*a*]. *Lis*

107 *Nuclear Weapons* (n 87) [78]; S Miyazaki 'The Martens Clause and International Humanitarian Law' in Christophe Swinarski (ed.), *Studies and Essays on International Humanitarian Law and Red Cross Principles in Honour of Jean Pictet* (Springer 1984) 433.

108 Hague IV Preamble; Protocol I art 1(2); Protocol II Preamble.

109 *Facts* [41].

110 *Facts* [42].

111 *Facts* [14], [41].

112 *Clarifications* [4].

pendens principle bars the Court from initiating parallel proceedings as a general principle of law [*b*]. Alternatively, the Court should decline its jurisdiction according to the principle of comity [*c*].

a. Adawa's claims constitute parallel proceedings.

A parallel proceeding is a situation where different courts hear 'the same or substantially the same' dispute concurrently.[113] The term 'same dispute' comprises of three elements: same Parties,[114] same cause of action,[115] and same objective.[116] In the present case, the concerning Parties are the same to the pending case before the Dispute Settlement Body of WTO (DSB).[117]

(i) The causes of action of two claims are substantially the same.

A 'cause of action' comprises facts which give rise to the relief.[118] According to the *Tatry* case, legal ground is also a factor of cause of action.[119] According to the *Southern Bluefin Tuna* case, albeit based on different treaties, different grounds may be 'artificial'[120] when they refer to the same legal obligation and will lead to the rejection of jurisdiction.[121]

---

113 ILA 'Final Report on *Lis Pendens* and Arbitration' (2009) 25 *Arbitration International* 3, 32 para 5.6.

114 *Case Concerning Certain German Interests in Polish Upper Silesia* (German/Poland) [1926] PCIJ Rep Series A No 6, 20.

115 *CME Czech Republic* BV (The Netherlands v Czech Republic) (Final Award)[2003] UNCITRAL [435]; Judgment of *the Administrative Tribunal of the ILO upon Complaints Made against the UNESCO* (Advisory Opinion) [1956] ICJ Rep 77, 89.

116 *Nuclear Tests case* (Australia v France) (Judgment) [1974] ICJ Rep 253 [29];Bin Cheng, *General Principles of Law as Applied by International Courts and Tribunals* (CUP 1953) 340.

117 *Facts* [47] [57].

118 ILA 'Interim Report of the Committee on International Commercial Arbitration on *Res Judicata* and Arbitration' Berlin Conference (2004) [4].

119 Case C-406/92, *The Owners of the Cargo Lately Laden on Board the Ship 'Tatry' v The Owners of the Ship 'Mcciej Rataj'* [1994] ECR I-5475 [39].

120 *Southern Bluefin Tuna* (New Zealand/Japan; Australia/Japan) (Award on Jurisdiction and Admissibility) [2000] 23 RIAA 1 [54].

121 *Southern Bluefin Tuna* (n 120) [38(c)] [52] [59].

In the present case, *first*, both claims arise from the imposition of tariff [122] and thus rely on the same fact. *Second*, both claims are based on the alleged breach of substantially identical legal obligations. Under Article 3 of the Treaty Establishing the Crosinian Helian Community (the CHC Treaty), which came into effect in 1969, two Parties shall impose zero tariffs on Helian products.[123] Thus, when the Parties joined the World Trade Organization (WTO) in 1982 and 1985 respectively,[124] the tariff of Helian in their 'then-applicable' tariff schedules is zero. Both schedules result in the same commitment of zero bound rate under the General Agreement on Tariffs and Trade 1994 (GATT).[125] Hence, the commitment under the GATT is an implementation of obligation under Article 3 of the CHC Treaty. Two obligations are thus closely linked and substantially identical.

(ii) The objectives of two claims are substantially the same.

In the pending dispute before the DSU, Adawa seeks for the declaration that Rasasan imposition of tariff violates its obligation. In the present case, Adawa claims for compensation in addition to the former relief.[126] Nonetheless, the decision in declaration has a decisive effect on the claim of compensation[127] for no compensation will be awarded if the declaration is objected. The monetary relief added to the present claim cannot make the two claims distinctive. Thus, the 'essence'[128] of both claims is whether the imposition of the tariff can be justified and therefore the objectives of two claims are substantially the same.

In conclusion, Adawa's claims are based on the same facts and legal grounds, concerning the same Parties, and pursuing the same objective, which will lead to parallel proceedings.

122 *Facts* [47] [57].

123 Treaty Establishing the Crosinian Helian Community (20 June 1969) *Facts* [Annex B] (CHC Treaty) art 3.

124 *Facts* [12].

125 *Facts* [12].

126 *Facts* [57].

127 James George, 'International Parallel Litigation–A Survey of Current Conventions and Model Laws' (2002) 37 *Texas International Law Journal* 499, 500.

128 *Royal Indem Co v Apex Oil Co* (2008) 511 F 3d 788 [10]; *Gubisch Maschinenfabrik KG v Giulio Palumbo* (Judgment) [1987] ECJ C-144/86 [9].

b. The Court should decline its jurisdiction by applying lis pendens as a general principle of law.

Lis pendens operates to bar parallel proceeding by mandating the subsequent court to decline jurisdiction.[129] As a procedural mechanism to prevent conflicting judgments, it is manifested in domestic law,[130] decisions of national courts,[131] European Union law[132] as well as international jurisprudence.[133]

Based on the need of ensuring stability in the international trading system,[134] *Lis pendens* is also widely manifested as a solution to jurisdictional conflicts between the WTO and Regional Trade Agreement (RTA).[135] In the present case, the CHC Treaty is notified as an RTA.[136] According to the forum selection clause of many RTAs,[137] if the

---

129 *Certain German Interests* (n 114) 20; *Final Report* (n 113) 32 para 5.12; Ishaya Paul Amaza, 'Multiplicity of International Dispute Settlement Forums: Avoiding the Risk of Parallel Proceedings' (2012) 2 *Dispute Resolution International* 149, 156.

130 Code of Civil Procedure (1980) art 261 (Germany); New Code of Civil Procedure (2007) art 100 (France); Reformed Statute on Private International Law (1995) art 7 (Italy); Federal Act on Private International Law (1987) art 9 (Switzerland); Code of Judicial Procedure (1948) Chapter 13 Section 6 (Sweden); see also Gary Born, *International Civil Litigation in United States Courts* (3rd edn, Aspen 1996) 461.

131 *The Abidin Daver* [1984] AC 398 [483]; *Colorado River Water Conservation District v United States*, 424 US 800 (1976) [818]-[819]; *O'Connor v Sherry Fitzgerald Limited & Ors* [2018] IECA 67 [5]-[6].

132 Convention on Jurisdiction and the Enforcement of Judgments in Civil and Commercial Matters (27 September 1968) 29 ILM 1413; Convention on Jurisdiction and the Enforcement of Judgments in Civil and Commercial Matters (16 September 1988) 28 ILM 620.

133 Europe Convention for the Protection of Human Rights and Fundamental Freedoms (4 November 1950) ETS 5 art 35(2); *Certain German Interests* (n 114) 20.

134 Caroline Henckels, 'Overcoming Jurisdictional Isolationism at the WTO-FTA Nexus: A Potential Approach for the WTO' (2008) 19 *the European Journal of International Law* 571, 597.

135 Kyung Kwak, Gabrielle Marceau, 'Overlaps and Conflicts of Jurisdiction between the World Trade Organization and Regional Trade Agreements' (2003) *Canadian Yearbook of International Law* 83, 98; Pauwelyn, 'Going Global, Regional or Both? Dispute Settlement in the Southern African Development Community and Overlaps with the WTO and Other Jurisdictions' (2004) 13 *Minnesota J Global Trade* 231, 285.

136 *Clarifications* [5].

137 United States-Mexico-Canada Agreement(adopted 30 November 2018) art 31.3; Olivos Protocol for the Settlement of Disputes in Mercosur (entered into force 10 February 2004); EC-Chile Free Trade Agreement(entered into force 20 December 2002) art189(4)(c); United States-Singapore Free Trade Agreement (entered into force 1 January 2004) art 20.4(3); Free Trade Agreement between the Government of Canada and the Government of the Republic of Costa Rica (entered into force 1 November 2002) art XIII.6.

obligations under a RTA and WTO agreement are 'equivalent in substance',[138] a Party may not seek redress for the breach of such obligations in both forums.

Therefore, the principle of *lis pendens* is recognized and applicable as a general principle of law in the sense of Article 38 of the Court's Statute.[139] As demonstrated above, the same dispute is *de facto* pending before the DSB and the concurring jurisdictions create the risk of conflicting decisions,[140] rendering *lis pendens* principle applicable. Thus, the Court should accordingly decline its jurisdiction.

c. Alternatively, the Court should decline its jurisdiction according to the principle of comity.

Comity operates to permit a court to limit its jurisdiction where exercise of that jurisdiction would be inappropriate in the particular circumstances.[141] In the *MOX Plant* case, the Tribunal did not hear the case due to the considerations of mutual respect and comity[142] since conflicting judgments on the same issue would not be helpful for the resolution of the dispute. According to the *Chan Chin Cheung* case, risk of conflicting judgments is a factor supporting the stay of proceeding.[143]

In the present case, *first*, even if falling short of parallel proceedings, due to the considerable overlap in both disputes, there is a risk of 'irreparable'[144] conflicting

138 Comprehensive Economic and Trade Agreement between Canada and the European Union (entered into force 21 September 2018) art 29.3(1)-(2); Free Trade Agreement between the European Union and the Socialist Republic of Vietnam (30 June 2019) art 24(2).

139 A Reinisch, 'The Use and Limits of Res Judicata and *Lis Pendens* as Procedural Tools to Avoid Conflicting Dispute Settlement Outcomes' (2004) 2 *Law and Practice of International Courts and Tribunals* 37, 48.

140 *Facts* [58].

141 *Northern Cameroons* (Cameroon v United Kingdom) (Preliminary Objections) [1963] ICJ Rep 15 [37]; *Free Zones of Upper Savoy and the District of Gex* (France v Switzerland) (Judgment) [1932] PCIJ Rep Series A/B No 46, 161.

142 *MOX Plant case* (Ireland v United Kingdom) (Order No 3, Suspension of Proceedings on Jurisdiction and Merits and Request for Further Provisional Measures) [2003] PCA Case No 2002-01 [28].

143 *Chan Chin Cheung v Chan Fatt Cheung and Others* [2009] SGCA 62 [45].

144 *Alleged Violations of the 1955 Treaty of Amity, Economic Relations, and Consular Rights* (Islamic Republic of Iran v United States) (Order) [2018] ICJ Rep [77].

judgments if two forums proceed with the cases concurrently. *Second*, it would be more appropriate for the WTO tribunal to adjudicate the case. The WTO has exclusive jurisdiction over dispute arising from its covered agreement.[145] Since present dispute falls within the specific field of trade and is substantially identical to the dispute pending before the DSB, the Court's staying its proceeding can promote justice[146] and respect for the authority of the DSB and minimize the risk of conflicting judgment.[147] Thus, the Court should apply its inherent authority[148] and decline its jurisdiction.

B. THE IMPOSITION OF TARIFFS DOES NOT VIOLATE THE CHC TREATY.

i. Rasasa's essential security interest is under threat.

'Essential' means 'indispensable',[149] which needs to be assessed on a case-by-case basis.[150] Interest relating to the protection of the State against any danger seriously compromising its internal or external situations can be recognized as 'essential'.[151] In the *Oil Platforms* case, the flow of commerce could be recognized as security interests.[152] Additionally, economic security of State and population can wreak havoc on the lives of an entire population.[153]

145 DSU art 23(1).

146 *Southern Pacific Properties v Egypt* (Preliminary Jurisdiction) [1985] ICSID Case No ARB/84/3 [16].

147 *Chan Chin Cheung* (n 143) [46]; Giorgio Gaja, *The Statute of the International Court of Justice: A Commentary* (3rd edn, OUP 2012) 655.

148 *Nuclear Tests* (n 116) 23; *SGS Socute Generate de Surveillance SA v Philippines* (Jurisdiction) [2004] ICSID Case No ARB/02/06 [171].

149 *China-Measures Related to the Exportation of Various Raw Materials* (Panel Report) [2011] WTO WT/DS394/R para 7.275.

150 *Gabčíkovo-Nagymaros* (n 15) [53]; ILC 'Report on the Work on Its Fifty-Third Session' (2001) UN Doc A/56/10, 83 [15].

151 *LG&E International Inc v The Argentine Republic* (Decision on Liability) [2006] ICSID Case No ARB/02/1 [251].

152 *Case Concerning Oil Platforms case (Islamic Republic of Iran v United States of America)* (Judgment) [2003] ICJ Rep 161 [73].

153 *Continental Casualty Co v Argentine Republic*(Award) [2008] ICSID Case No ARB/03/9 [175]; *LG&E* (n 151) [238].

In the present case, *first*, Helian hyacinth is a particular product in Crosinia region, contributing significantly to Rasasa's GDP and employment,[154] and the survival of Helian hyacinth has a fundamental impact on Rasasan economy and national security.[155] *Second*, due to the unprecedented hurricane and attacks by Adawan criminal gangs, Rasasan farmers' lives and properties were impaired. The massive increase in unemployment has also been alarming.[156] If the current trend continues, the collapse of Helian industry is foreseeable since the domestic material stocks, local market and the global share of it all suffered drastically, which will impair Rasasan economy and society in general.[157] Hence, it is reasonable to deduce that Rasasa's essential security interest is under threat.

ii. The measure is necessary to protect Rasasan essential security interest.

Under Article 22 of the CHC Treaty, the application of measures necessary to protect a Member State's essential security interests can be justified.[158] Under international law,[159] factors which need to be considered include: *first*, the relative importance of the objective pursued by the measure; *second*, the contribution of the measure to the objective; *third*, the restrictive effect of the measure on international commerce; and *fourth*, whether there exist reasonably available alternative measures that are less restrictive.

First, as demonstrated above, the objective of imposing the tariff falls within the ambit of 'essential security interest'. The maintenance of Helian industry is essential for the well-being of Rasasa.[160] Thus, the objective is of vital importance.

Second, the measure can effectively contribute to its objective. The measure will

154 *Facts* [1] [2] [11].

155 *Facts* [31].

156 *Facts* [16] [28].

157 *Facts* [30].

158 CHC Treaty art 22.

159 *Korea-Measures Affecting Imports of Fresh, Chilled and Frozen Beef* (Appellate Body Report) [2000] WTO WT/DS161/AB/R [164]; *United States-Section 337 of the Tariff Act of 1930 and Amendments thereto* (Panel Report) [2000] WTO WT/DS186/2 para 5.26.

160 *Facts* [19] [44].

draw Rasasan buyers back to domestic suppliers, making the recovery of the industry possible, hereby preventing the collapse of it. In addition, the employment can also be improved.

Third, the measure exerts the least restrictive effect on international Helian commerce. Despite the great loss of Helian plants and related equipment of Helian industry, Rasasa only imposed tariffs on unprocessed materials.[161] The measure does not indiscriminately lead to hindrances to all imported Helian-related products. Hence, the impact of the measure was minimized and would only result in a reasonable restrictive effect.

Fourth, there are no other alternative measures. Given the twenty-year cultivation period of Helian hyacinth, as well as the alarming trend that may result in the collapse of the industry,[162] immediate measures are urgent. Based on the severe and emergent situation, the measure is irreplaceable for the desired level of the objective. There exists no other resort that is less trade-restrictive, while making an equivalent contribution to the objective.[163]

IV. ADAWA'S ARREST AND DETENTION OF MS. GREY CONSTITUTE INTERNATIONAL WRONGFUL ACTS, AND SHE MUST BE IMMEDIATELY REPATRIATED TO RASASA.

A. ADAWA'S ARREST AND DETENTION OF MS. GREY VIOLATE HER IMMUNITY RATIONE PERSONAE IN THE FOREIGN CRIMINAL PROCEEDINGS.

i. Adawa's arrest and detention violate Ms. Grey's immunity *ratione personae* under customary international law.

To ensure the effective performance of functions on behalf of a State,[164] certain

161 *Facts* [43].

162 *Facts* [1].

163 *Brazil-Measures Affecting Imports of Retreaded Tyres* (Panel Report) [2007] WTO WT/DS332/R para 7.149.

164 *Arrest Warrant of 11 April 2000* (Democratic Republic of the Congo v Belgium) (Judgment) [2002] ICJ Rep 3 [53].

holders of high-ranking office in a State such as Minister for Foreign Affairs, enjoy immunities from criminal jurisdiction in other States.[165] The immunity *ratione personae* accorded to incumbent senior officials from foreign domestic criminal jurisdiction and arrest is absolute and applies even when the official is accused of committing an international crime.[166] In the *Arrest Warrant* case, the Court declared that there exists no exception to the customary international law which accords foreign ministers immunity in foreign criminal jurisdiction, even when they are accused of international crimes.[167]

In the present case, Ms. Grey explicitly stated that she enjoyed diplomatic immunity,[168] which protects her against any act of authority of other States that would hinder her in the performance of duties. However, Adawa exercised its domestic jurisdiction by taking Ms. Grey into custody regardless of her immunity. Thus, Adawa's arrest and detention violate Ms. Grey's immunity *ratione personae* under customary international law.

ii. Adawa's arrest and detention violate Ms. Grey's immunity *ratione personae* under the CHC Treaty.

Pursuant to Article 32 of the CHC Treaty, representatives of Member States at meetings convened by the Community shall enjoy immunity from personal arrest or detention and immunity from legal process of every kind.[169] As a contracting party of the CHC Treaty,[170] Adawa must have known Ms. Grey enjoys immunity as the representative of Rasasa, but still took her into custody. Therefore, Adawa's arrest and detention violate the obligation to respect for Ms. Grey's immunity *ratione personae* under the CHC Treaty.

165 *Arrest Warrant case* (n 164) [58].

166 *Arrest Warrant case* (n 164) [58].

167 *Arrest Warrant case* (n 164) [58].

168 *Facts* [51].

169 CHC Treaty art 32.

170 *Facts* [10].

B. ALTERNATIVELY, ADAWA'S ARREST AND DETENTION VIOLATE MS. GREY'S IMMUNITY RATIONE PERSONAE IN THE ICC'S CRIMINAL PROCEEDINGS.

i. Rasasa is not a contracting Party to the ICC.

The ICC is a treaty-based court[171] and its existence and establishment rests upon the direct consent of contracting States,[172] and thus the obligations to cooperate with the ICC remain 'only' treaty obligations.[173] The ICC stated that the removing of immunity under Article 27(2) of the Rome Statute should be confined to States Parties.[174] In the present case, Rasasa is not a contracting Party to the ICC and expressly refused to waive Ms. Grey's immunity. Therefore, Ms. Grey is entitled to immunity *ratione personae* before the ICC.

ii. The exception of the immunity *ratione personae* in the international proceedings is not customary international law.

The exception of immunity has not yet established as a customary international law.[175] In general, the substance of customary international law must be looked for in the State practice and *opinio juris*.[176]

a. The exception of the immunity ratione personae does not qualify the element of State practice.

State practice could be embodied in verbal acts.[177] However, the relevant exception

171 Robert Cryer *et al*, *Introduction to International Criminal Law and Procedure* (2nd edn, CUP 2010) 9.

172 VCLT art 34.

173 Morten Bergsmo, LING Yan (eds.), *State Sovereignty and International Criminal Law* (Torkel Opsahl Academic E Publisher 2012) 72.

174 *Prosecutor v Omar Hassan Ahmad Al Bashir* (Decision on the Cooperation of Congo Regarding Bashir) [2014] ICC No ICC-02/05-01/09-195 [26].

175 Dapo Akande, 'International Law Immunities and the International Criminal Court' (2004) 98 *American Journal of International Law* 407, 417.

176 Identification of Customary International Law(n 13) conclusion 12; *North Sea Continental Shelf* (n 12) [77]; *Continental Shelf* (n 30) [27]; *Nuclear Weapons* (n 87) [73]

177 Identification of Customary International Law (n 13) conclusion 6.

is not general in practice.[178] Contrarily, some States have made reservations on this issue, while other States have expressed clear opposition. The United States argued that conferral of jurisdiction over nationals of non-party States would breach Article 34 of VCLT, which declares that international treaties cannot be binding on the third States.[179] France,[180] India,[181] China[182] and other countries[183] clearly stated their opposition to the exercise of jurisdiction over non-parties at the international level.[184] The sparsity of State practice indicates that immunity *ratione personae* in the international criminal proceedings still exists.[185]

b. The exception of the immunity ratione personae does not qualify the element of opinio juris.

Opinion juris manifests in legislative acts[186] and treaties.[187] Concerning the legislative acts, Chad, Malawi, Democratic Republic of the Congo, South Africa and Jordan have refused to cooperate with the ICC by stating that such cooperation would be in breach of its international obligations.[188] Various African Union resolutions have also required

178 Identification of Customary International Law (n 13) conclusion 8.

179 William Schabas, *The International Criminal Court: A Commentary on the Rome Statute* (OUP 2010) 279.

180 A/CONF183/SR6 [76].

181 A/CONF183/SR4 [47] [49].

182 A/CONF183/SR3 [37].

183 A/CONF183/SR5 [11] [36]; A/CONF183/SR7 [12]; A/CONF183/SR3 [91].

184 Mark Klamberg, *Commentary on the Law of the International Criminal Court* (Torkel Opsahl Academic EPublisher 2017) 169-170.

185 Claus Kreß, Kimberly Prost, *Commentary on the Rome Statute of the International Criminal Court: Observers' Notes, Article by Article* (2nd edn, Hart Publishing 2008) 1611.

186 Identification of Customary International Law (n 13) conclusion 10.

187 Identification of Customary International Law (n 13) conclusion 11.

188 *Bashir* (Decision on the Failure by Malawi to Comply with the Cooperation Requests) [2011] ICC No ICC-02/05-01/09-139 [21]; *Bashir* (Decision on the Refusal of Chad to Comply with the Cooperation Requests)[2011] ICC No ICC-02/05-01/09-140 [12]; *Bashir Congo*(n 174) [7]; *Bashir* [Decision under Article 87(7) of the Rome Statute on the Non-compliance by South Africa with the Request by the Court for the Arrest and Surrender of Omar Al-Bashir] [2017] ICC No ICC-02/05-01/09 [16]; *Bashir* (Decision on the Non-compliance by Jordan Regarding Bashir) [2017] ICC No ICC-02/05-01/09 [8].

its members not to cooperate with the ICC regarding the warrant of arrest issued against Omar Al Bashir.[189] Chinese government believed that the international court should not exercise jurisdiction without the consent of the countries concerned.[190] The United States declared that ‘it is not a party to the ICC’s Rome Statute and has consistently voiced its unequivocal objections to any attempts to assert the ICC’s jurisdiction over American personnel’.[191]

In general, exceptions of the immunity *ratione personae* could be triggered by the United Nations Security Council (UNSC),[192] and it is the obligation that is created by the UN Charter rather than Rome Statute. In the present case, there is no such a resolution to create the exception.

In light of the current situation on State practice and *opinio juris*, the exception of the immunity *ratione personae* does not constitute a customary international law, rendering the arrest and detention of Ms. Grey unlawful.

---

189 African Union Assembly (AUA) ‘Decision on the Meeting of African States Parties to the Rome Statute of the International Criminal Tribunal’ (2009) Assembly/AU/13(XIII) [10]; AUA ‘Decision on the Progress Report of the Commission on the Implementation of Decision Assembly/AU/Dec270(XIV) on the Second Ministerial Meeting on the Rome Statute of the International Criminal Court’ (2010) Assembly/AU/10(XV) [5]-[6].

190 ‘Summary Record of the 3rd Plenary Meeting’ (1998) United Nations Diplomatic Conference of Plenipotentiaries on the Establishment of an International Criminal Court UN Doc A/CONF183/SR3 [35]-[38].

191 Michael Pompeo, ‘U.S. Policy on the International Criminal Court Remains Unchanged’ (9 October 2019) <https://www.state.gov/u-s-policy-on-the-international-criminal-court-remains-unchanged/> assessed 1 January 2020.

192 Security Council Resolution 827(1993) UN Doc S/RES/827 art 7(2); Security Council Resolution 955(1994) UN Doc S/RES/955 art 6(2).

C. ADAWA'S COOPERATION OBLIGATION IS IN CONFLICT WITH ITS OBLIGATION TO RESPECT FOR MS. GREY'S IMMUNITY UNDER ARTICLE 98(1) OF THE ROME STATUTE AND ADAWA FAILED TO ASSIST THE ICC.

i. Adawa's cooperation obligation is in conflict with its international obligation to respect for Ms. Grey's immunity under Article 98(1) of the Rome Statute.

a. Ms. Grey possesses immunity ratione personae and Rasasa does not voluntarily waive her immunity in accordance with Article 98(1).

In the *Bashir* case, the ICC declared that a tension may exist between the duty to cooperate and the obligation to respect for immunities according to Article 98(1).[193] The ICC should thus first obtain the waiver of the third State to ensure State Parties to carry out their obligations to cooperate.[194] In the present case, Rasasa does not waive Ms. Grey's immunity to cooperate with the ICC.[195]

b. Adawa's obligation to cooperate should not prevail over its obligation to respect for Ms. Grey's immunity.

The object and purpose of Article 98(1) is to prevent the State from acting inconsistently with its obligation towards the third Party's *ratione personae.*[196] Thereby, insisting on cooperating with the ICC will violate the objective of Article 98(1). According to existing practice, cooperation obligation shall prevail over other existing obligations of the State[197] only in the presence of the UNSC Resolutions pursuant to Article 103 of the UN Charter.[198] Therefore, Adawa's obligation to cooperate does not surpass the obligation to respect for Ms. Grey's immunity without the UNSC Resolution, and thus the conflict of obligations exists.

ii. Adawa failed to assist the ICC to cope with the conflict.

a. Adawa did not challenge the validity of warrant of arrest.

Rule 117(3) of *Rules of Procedure and Evidence* provides the custodial State with

193 *Bashir Jordan* (n 188) [41].

194 Rome Statute art 98(1).

195 *Facts* [53].

196 *Bashir Congo* (n 174) [27].

197 *Bashir Jordan* (n 188) [78].

198 UN Charter art 103.

access to challenging the validity of the arrest warrant to the Pre-Trial Chamber.[199] The warrant was inappropriately issued by the Pre-Trail Chamber for neglecting the existence of Ms. Grey's immunity.[200] However, instead of challenging the warrant, Adawa took Ms. Grey into custody directly and immediately.[201]

b. Adawa failed to assist the ICC in the application of Article 98(1).

Article 98(1) requires a State to contest any request if it deems that a conflict has arisen.[202] Rule 195(1) requires the State Party concerned to provide the ICC with any information relevant to assist the ICC in the application of Article 98(1).[203] The requested State shall provide the information on possible violation of obligations to a third country before the execution, so that the ICC can negotiate in fully to grasp the attitude of the third Party, in order to obtain the waiver of immunity.[204] Pending a response by the ICC, the requested State may postpone execution of the request for cooperation.[205]

Even though Adawa was fully aware of the immunity under customary international law and the CHC Treaty, it didn't provide any material to the ICC concerning the conflict of obligations, notify the ICC to seek the waiver or wait until the ICC has obtained the cooperation of Rasasa for the waiver, but arrested and detained her without hesitation.

D. MS. GREY MUST BE IMMEDIATELY REPATRIATED TO RASASA.

International wrongful acts result from a breach of an international obligation[206]

---

199 'Rules of Procedure and Evidence' in 'The Official Records of the Assembly of States Parties to the Rome Statute of the International Criminal Court' (3-10 September 2002) ICC-ASP/1/3 and Corr1 Part II.A art 117(3).

200 *Facts* [50].

201 *Facts* [52].

202 Kreß, Prost (n 185) 1039.

203 Rules of Procedure and Evidence (n 199) art 195.

204 Kreß, Prost (n 185) 1063.

205 Proposal Submitted by France Concerning Part 9 of the Rome Statute of the International 'Criminal Court, on International Cooperation and Judicial Assistance '(Part 9 of the Rome Statute) (1999) PCNICC/1999/WGRPE(9)/DP2, 6.

206 ILC'Draft Articles on Responsibility of States for Internationally Wrongful Acts, with commentaries' (ARSIWA) (2001) A/56/10 art 2(b), 34.

attributable to the State.[207] If the act is continuing, the State is under an obligation to cease it.[208] Adawa's arrest and detention violate Ms. Grey's immunity *ratione personae* under customary international law and the CHC Treaty, and thus constitute an international wrongful act. The detention is continuous and Adawa should immediately cease the detention and repatriate Ms. Grey to Rasasa.

207 ARSIWA art 2(a).

208 ARSIWA art 30; *Case Concerning The Rainbow Warrior Affair* (New Zealand/France) [1990] 20 RIAA 215 [114].

CONCLUSION AND PRAYER FOR RELIEF

In view of the facts set forth in this Memorial and the arguments applying the law to the facts as stated;

May it please the Court, on behalf of the Republic of Rasasa, Respondent herein, respectfully requests this Honorable Court to adjudge and declare that:

1. Adawa is not a Party to the Botega Treaty and the Court does not have jurisdiction over Adawa's claims;

2. Rasasa's development and deployment of the WALL is consistent with international law;

3. Adawa's claim concerning the CHC Treaty falls outside the Court's jurisdiction or is inadmissible. Alternatively, the imposition of the tariffs does not violate the CHC Treaty; and

4. The apprehension and detention of Ms. Grey constitute internationally wrongful acts and she must be immediately released.

Respectfully submitted,
AGENTS FOR RASASA

第二部分

问题研究

跨界环境影响评价的习惯国际法规则研究

——以国际法院案例为例

刘燕彬

摘要：国际法院在 2010 年“关于乌拉圭河沿岸的纸浆厂案”中确认了环境影响评价是“一般国际法”的要求，这里的“一般国际法”应理解为习惯国际法。环境影响评价是为了预防风险，这意味着评价的对象为可能存在的风险，而相关活动最终是否实际造成损害与此无关。国际法院在 2015 年“关于尼加拉瓜在边界地区开展某些活动案”以及“哥斯达黎加沿圣胡安河修建道路案”两起诉讼案件判决中，进一步澄清了启动环境影响评价义务的门槛标准，即需要通过预评估判断拟进行的活动是否有可能造成重大跨界环境损害的风险。但法院在两案中对是否达到门槛标准的问题采取了不同的论证逻辑，其中在哥斯达黎加诉尼加拉瓜“关于尼加拉瓜在边界地区开展某些活动案”中的论证思路存在一定问题。此外，法院进一步明晰了环境影响评价作为习惯国际法义务的具体内容。

关键词：环境影响评价；一般国际法；习惯国际法；风险预防原则；重大跨界损害

借助科学技术手段，人类提高了判断自身活动是否会对自然环境造成破坏的能力。科技的发展也成为国际环境法发展的主要驱动力之一。[1] 环境影响评价（Environmental Impact Assessment，EIA）本质上是一种技术手段。通过该程序可以确认国家拟采取的活动对环境造成的潜在影响，国内法和国际法都注意到了环境影响评价制度的必要性。在国际法层面，国际法院（以下简称法院）关于环境影响评价义务的最新实践是 2015 年尼加拉瓜诉哥斯达黎加“哥斯达黎加沿圣胡安河修建道路案”（后简称“修建道路案”）以及哥斯达黎加诉尼加拉

1 *Gabčíkovo-Nagymaros Project (Hungary/Slovakia), ICJ Reports 1997, Separate Opinion of Vice-President Weeramantry*, p. 110.

瓜“关于尼加拉瓜在边界地区开展某些活动案”（后简称“边界地区活动案”）。2010 年 11 月 18 日，哥斯达黎加向法院提起诉讼程序，主张尼加拉瓜在哥斯达黎加领土上部署军队，侵犯了其领土主权，并且尼加拉瓜在圣胡安河进行的疏浚活动违反了包括跨界环境影响评价在内的多项义务。[2] 2011 年 12 月 22 日，尼加拉瓜向法院提起诉讼，主张哥斯达黎加在两国边界进行的大规模道路建设工作造成了重大环境损害。2013 年 4 月 17 日，法院将上述两案合并审理（以下简称“尼加拉瓜与哥斯达黎加两案”）。[3]

虽然早在 2010 年阿根廷诉乌拉圭“关于乌拉圭河沿岸的纸浆厂案”（以下简称“纸浆厂案”）中，法院就已确认，对于可能造成的严重跨界环境损害进行环境影响评价不仅仅是条约义务，而且是一般国际法（general international law）的要求。但问题在于，法院使用了“一般国际法”而非“习惯国际法”来说明环境影响评价义务的法律地位，并且该义务的具体内容仍然较为模糊。本文将结合尼加拉瓜与哥斯达黎加两案的判决对上述问题进行研究，并评析相关案例。

一、环境影响评价的习惯国际法地位

国际海洋法法庭在 2011 年“国家对国际海底区域内活动的责任与义务的咨询意见案”中，更加直接地指明，环境影响评价本身就是“习惯国际法规定的一般义务”，并援引了“纸浆厂案”中法院的说理，认为该案所使用的“一般国际法”等于习惯国际法，即环境影响评价是习惯国际法义务。[4] 而法院在四年后的“修建道路案”中并没有援引国际海洋法法庭的观点，也没有确认环境影响评价已成为习惯国际法，而是继续沿用了“纸浆厂案”中“一般国际法”的表述。[5] 那么，是什么构成了一般国际法？作为法院裁判依据的《国际法院规约》第 38 条并没有对“一般国际法”进行说明。此外，2015 年“修建道路案”中，

2 “Certain Activities Carried Out by Nicaragua in the Border Area (Costa Rica v. Nicaragua): Overview of the Case,” ICJ, https://www.icj-cij.org/en/case/150 (Last visited on 6 July 2020).

3 “Construction of a Road in Costa Rica along the San Juan River (Nicaragua v. Costa Rica): Overview of the Case,” ICJ, https://www.icj-cij.org/en/case/152 (Last visited on 6 July 2020).

4 *Responsibilities and obligations of States with respect to Activities in the Area, Advisory Opinion, 1 February 2011, ITLOS Reports 2011*, p. 50, para. 145.

5 *Certain Activities Carried Out by Nicaragua in the Border Area (Costa Rica v. Nicaragua) and Construction of a Road in Costa Rica along the San Juan River (Nicaragua v. Costa Rica), Separate Opinion of Judge Owada*, pp. 4-5, para. 14.

部分法官在其单独意见中就环境影响评价的法律地位表达了不同立场。鉴于此，有必要对环境影响评价的法律地位进行探究。

国内有学者认为，“一般国际法”与“习惯国际法”的内涵并不相同。[6] 国际法委员会亦承认，“一般国际法”这一用语有多种不同含义。国际法委员会在《关于“习惯国际法的形成与证据”秘书处备忘录》(以下简称《秘书处备忘录》)中指出，委员会有时使用“一般国际法”来“泛指除条约规则之外的国际法规则”，有时交替使用了“一般国际法”和“习惯国际法”这两种表述，还可能将“一般国际法”作为“同时包括习惯国际法和一般国际法原则的总称使用”。[7] 虽然法院认为环境影响评价是一般国际法的要求，但由于存在多种可能性，所以应当结合具体语境来分析其内涵。

部分法官在 2015 年“修建道路案”的单独意见中讨论了“一般国际法”这一用语。其中，多诺霍法官（Judge Donohue）和杜加尔德专案法官（*ad hoc* Judge Dugard）对“一般国际法”的内涵作出了直接的论述，认为进行环境影响评价构成了习惯国际法；其他部分法官虽然没有直接回应“一般国际法”的内涵，但亦在其各自的单独意见中分析了环境影响评价义务的法律地位，如特林达德法官（Judge Trindade）和班达里法官（Judge Bhandari）认为，进行环境影响评价是国际法一般原则。[8] 虽然法官们对“一般国际法”的内涵及环境影响评价义务的法律地位的看法有一定分歧，但进行跨界环境影响评价应当已构成习惯国际法。

首先，回顾环境影响评价的司法实践，法院对环境影响评价义务的判断是对应着环境影响评价国家实践的发展逐渐形成的。其次，法院在“纸浆厂案”中确认进行环境影响评价是一般国际法的要求时，其上下文对“习惯国际法”和“一般国际法”两个用语的使用并无明显差别，这也是杜加尔德法官支持该语境下“习惯国际法”与“一般国际法”具有相同内涵的原因。[9] 值得注意的

6　禾木:《当代国际法学中的“一般国际法”概念——兼论一般国际法与习惯国际法的区别》,《中山大学学报》2014 年第 5 期，第 168—170 页。

7　国际法委员会秘书处:《习惯国际法的形成与证据：国际法委员会以前工作中与本专题特别相关的要素》,《国际法委员会第 65 届会议秘书处备忘录》，UN Doc A/CN.4/659，2013，第 37 页。

8　Rumiana Yotova, “Case and Comment: The Principles of Due Diligence and Prevention in International Environmental Law,” *Cambridge Law Journal,* Vol. 75, No. 3, 2016, p. 447.

9　*Certain Activities Carried Out by Nicaragua in the Border Area (Costa Rica v. Nicaragua) and Construction of a Road in Costa Rica along the San Juan River (Nicaragua v. Costa Rica), Separate Opinion of Judge Donohue*, p. 1, para. 2.

是，哥斯达黎加或尼加拉瓜都没有否认该义务对它们有约束力，尽管各自的诉状仍然遵循了“纸浆厂案”中“一般国际法”的表述。当事方对该用语的含义并没有争论，表明其均认可它是习惯国际法的同义词。[10]最后，国际法委员会在《秘书处备忘录》中指出：“在法院自1947年7月31日至2015年12月31日发布的所有667项命令、判决和咨询意见中，其中64项明确讨论或适用了习惯国际法。”[11]其中，脚注36列举的实践包括“边界地区活动案（哥斯达黎加诉尼加拉瓜）– 修建道路案（尼加拉瓜诉哥斯达黎加）”，[12]表明国际法委员会也认为该案中关于“一般国际法”的表述指向的就是习惯国际法。因此，法院在环境影响评价问题上所使用的“一般国际法”用语具有习惯国际法的内涵。

法院在“纸浆厂案”中，主要通过演绎推理（deductive reasoning），即审查某一习惯国际法规则“源自表述更为宽泛的规则”的方法，并没有使用传统的两要素的“归纳推理法”，即考虑国家实践和法律确信，这是比较少见的实践。[13]虽然国际法委员会也认为“‘两要素法’事实上并未排除演绎法”，但仍应当避免单独使用演绎法认定习惯国际法，因为虽然演绎法可以在很大程度上确定法律确信要素，但对于确定国家实践的作用较小。

就“两要素法”而言，目前环境影响评价义务已被大量国际条约规定，超过170个国家或地区制定了相关立法；[14]并且在联合国大会的相关决议中，投票记录也反映出多数国家支持该义务。[15]因此，环境影响评价义务具有习惯国际

---

10 *Certain Activities Carried Out by Nicaragua in the Border Area (Costa Rica v. Nicaragua) and Construction of a Road in Costa Rica along the San Juan River (Nicaragua v. Costa Rica), Separate Opinion of Judge ad hoc Dugard*, p. 5, para. 17.

11 国际法委员会秘书处:《习惯国际法的识别：就确定习惯国际法而言国家法院的判决在普遍性国际法院和法庭的案例法方面发挥的作用》,《国际法委员会第68届会议秘书处备忘录》, A/CN.4/691，2016，第8页，第18段。

12 国际法委员会秘书处:《习惯国际法的识别：就确定习惯国际法而言国家法院的判决在普遍性国际法院和法庭的案例法方面发挥的作用》,《国际法委员会第68届会议秘书处备忘录》, A/CN.4/691，2016，第10页，脚注36。

13 国际法委员会:《国际法委员会第68届大会报告》, A/71/10，2016年，第81页，第5—6段。

14 *Legislation*, ECOLEX, https://www.ecolex.org/result/?q=EIA&type=legislation&xdate_min=&xdate_max= (Last visited on July 7, 2020).

15 对1972年涉及环境影响评价的联合国大会第2995号（XXVII）决议，115个国家表示支持，无反对意见，see *Voting Record of A/RES/2995(XXVII)*, UNGA, http://research.un.org/en/docs/ga/quick/regular/27 (Last visited on July 14, 2020)；联合国大会第42届会议通过了以“环境领域的国际合作”为题的决议，并在决议中表明支持《环境规划署关于环境影响评价的目标和原则》，149个国家投票支持，仅有1个国家反对，see *Voting Records of A/Res/42/184*, UNGA, http://research.un.org/en/docs/ga/quick/regular/42 (Last visited on 14 July 2020)。

法的地位应当是明确的。

二、环境影响评价的义务来源：谨慎注意义务和风险预防原则

追根溯源，法院最早处理涉及环境影响评价义务的问题是在 1995 年新西兰诉法国“核试验案”中出现的。威拉曼特里法官（Judge Weeramantry）在其异议意见中认为，环境影响评价是风险预防原则（precautionary principle）的附属原则，因而国家在条约义务之外仍应进行环境影响评价，该义务正在“获得广泛的国际接受，并达到了法院应该注意的普遍认可程度”。[16] 而法院在 1997 年匈牙利诉斯洛伐克“加布奇科沃 – 大毛罗斯工程案”中，首次确认国家应当进行环境影响评价，[17] 但是该案并没有对环境影响评价义务的来源做进一步阐述。

在威拉曼特里法官发表异议意见 15 年后，法院在“纸浆厂案”中认定，在出现可能造成严重跨界环境损害的风险时，进行环境影响评价不仅仅是条约义务，而且是一般国际法的要求。法院从分析国家有避免跨界损害的义务出发，总结出作为习惯国际法的损害预防原则来源于国家在其领土内承担的谨慎注意义务（due diligence），[18] 并援引了 1949 年英国诉阿尔巴尼亚“科孚海峡案”，确认“每个国家有义务不能有意将其领土用于违反其他国家的权利”。[19] 基于此，“国家有义务采取其所能调动的一切手段，避免在其领土或其管辖的区域内发生的活动对其他国家的环境造成重大（significant）损害”。[20] 而环境影响评价正是履行谨慎注意义务的“一切手段”的重要一环。

尽管杜加尔德法官认为环境影响评价的义务来源是损害预防原则，[21] 但其来

---

16 *Request for an Examination of the Situation in Accordance with Paragraph 63 of the Court's Judgment of 20 December 1974 in the Nuclear Tests Case (New Zealand v. France), Order, Dissenting Opinion of Judge Weeramantry*, p. 345.

17 *Gabcikovo-Nagymaros Project (Hungary/Slovakia), Judgment, ICJ Reports 1997*, p. 73, para. 125.

18 *Pulp Mills on the River Uruguay (Argentina v. Uruguay), Judgment, ICJ Reports 2010 (I)*, pp. 55-56, para. 101.

19 *Corfu Channel (United Kingdom v. Albania), Merits, Judgment, ICJ Reports 1949*, p. 22

20 *Pulp Mills on the River Uruguay (Argentina v. Uruguay), Judgment, ICJ Reports 2010 (I)*, pp. 55-56, para. 101.

21 *Certain Activities Carried Out by Nicaragua in the Border Area (Costa Rica v. Nicaragua) and Construction of a Road in Costa Rica along the San Juan River (Nicaragua v. Costa Rica), Separate Opinion of Judge ad hoc Dugard*, p. 2, para. 7.

源应当为谨慎注意义务和风险预防原则。杜加尔德法官认为，将谨慎注意义务作为环境影响评价的义务来源将允许当事国以“最终没有造成损害”为由进行追溯式的抗辩。然而，恰恰相反，仅将损害预防原则作为环境影响评价的义务来源才会产生此类问题。

传统的损害预防原则要求，只有在因果关系及损害结果有明确可信的证据证明时，才能要求国家采取防止措施；而风险预防原则的逻辑核心在于——如果存在严重或不可逆转的环境损害的风险，即使因果关系存疑或科学证据不足也不能以缺乏完全的科学确定性为理由延迟采取防止措施。[22] 虽然上述两项原则均可能要求事前进行环境影响评价作为防止措施；[23] 对比而言，风险预防原则的主要关注点在于是否“有重大损害的风险”。特林达德法官在其单独意见中也再次重申，“损害预防原则提供了可以客观地评估风险以避免损害的假设，而风险预防原则涉及评估面临不确定性的风险，并将人类和环境的脆弱性、造成不可逆转损害的可能性考虑在内”。[24] 因此，实际是否造成了损害并不重要，事后未发生损害结果不能作为前期存在重大损害风险却未及时采取防止措施的抗辩理由。通过对环境影响评价义务来源的分析可以发现，该义务的门槛标准并不适用造成实际重大跨界损害的高标准。据此，即使争议发生时，当事国证明其行为没有造成重大跨界损害，也不能免除其进行环境影响评价的义务。

虽然目前风险预防原则的法律地位仍有争议，但是法院在“修建道路案”中的论述暗含了该原则的逻辑核心。如果法院只考虑损害预防原则，该原则仅要求避免损害结果的发生；此时，事前的环境影响评价义务仅是预防损害的辅助手段，只要无损害发生则没有违反环境影响评价义务。然而，虽然法院最后确认哥斯达黎加修建道路的行为没有造成损害，但这不妨碍判定其违反了环境影响评价义务。因此，虽然法院在 2010 年“纸浆厂案”中讨论了损害预防原则，但是，不应据此认为环境影响评价的义务来源仅是损害预防原则。

---

22 Principle 15, *Rio Declaration on Environment and Development*, A/CONF.151/26, 14 June, 1992.

23 刘泽：《国际环境法中的风险预防原则——一种功能性的认识》，《中国国际法年刊》（2014 年卷），法律出版社，2015，第 287 页。

24 *Certain Activities Carried Out by Nicaragua in the Border Area (Costa Rica v. Nicaragua) and Construction of a Road in Costa Rica along the San Juan River (Nicaragua v. Costa Rica), Separate opinion of Judge Cançado Trindade*, p. 14, para. 55.

三、环境影响评价的习惯国际法内涵

在厘清环境影响评价义务来源的基础上，可以借助基础原则（underlying principle）的内涵与要求来理解法院在“修建道路案”中对环境影响评价义务内容的进一步阐释。第一，法院扩大了适用环境影响评价义务的项目或活动范围。与“纸浆厂案”中环境影响评价仅涉及工业活动不同，法院在“修建道路案”中明确指出，因为基础原则适用于所有可能产生重大跨界环境损害的活动，因此，环境影响评价的适用条件更加普遍化。第二，法院进一步澄清了环境影响评价义务的门槛及时间要求。以项目的时间发展为线索进行说明：[25]在某个项目或活动开始前，进行相关活动的国家应当通过预评估、筛查等方式预先判断潜在影响，客观确定是否有可能造成重大跨界环境损害风险，一旦发现存在此种风险可能性，即满足门槛标准，则应当启动正式的环境影响评价程序。[26]一旦国家通过环境影响评价确认相关活动存在重大跨界环境损害风险，该国应当通过通知及协商等途径寻找减少损害的方式。此外，项目开始后的整个阶段，环境影响评价应持续进行，并且“确认有重大跨界损害风险—通知与协商—采取减少损害措施”等环节可能重复进行。

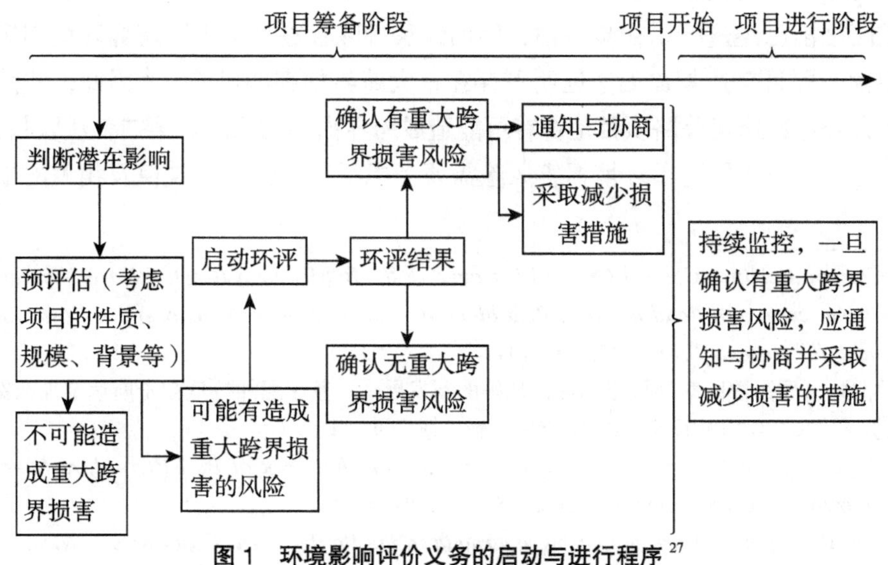

图 1　环境影响评价义务的启动与进行程序[27]

25　详见图 1“环境影响评价义务的启动与进行程序”。

26　边永民：《跨界环境影响评价的国际习惯法的建立和发展》，《中国政法大学学报》2019 年第 2 期，第 41 页。

27　作者依据对“修建道路案”和“边界地区活动案”的总结绘制本图。

（一）门槛标准：存在重大跨界损害的风险

在“修建道路案”中，哥斯达黎加主张环境影响评价的门槛标准未满足，因而无须承担环境影响评价义务。哥斯达黎加没有在事前进行环境影响评价，而是通过嗣后的环境影响评价报告来证明修建道路的活动没有造成严重的跨界损害，从而以此为由主张不存在环境影响评价义务。然而，这一主张并没有被法院接受，法院判决指出，“一旦此种重大风险（即重大跨界损害风险）存在，就会触发环境影响评价的要求”。[28]

对于“风险程度”的证明，风险预防原则只要求有充分的科学证据可以表明风险程度，但不要求具有百分之一百的科学确定性。[29]国际法委员会在《防止危险活动跨境损害的条款草案》中对风险的定义，包括“造成灾难性损害的较低可能性”及“造成重大损害的较高可能性”等。[30]这意味着，随着损害影响程度加深，对于风险发生可能性的要求也会降低。因此，法院在“修建道路案”中分析环境影响评价的门槛标准是否满足时，考虑更多的是项目的性质、规模和背景等因素，评估潜在的损害影响程度是否重大及环境的易破坏程度。

法院在“修建道路案”中认为，哥斯达黎加违反了在开始修建道路之前进行环境影响评价的义务。[31]原因包括：第一，哥斯达黎加没有证明它在开始修建道路之前已经进行了初步评估，因而无法排除存在“重大”跨界环境损害的可能性，即哥斯达黎加无法证明不存在重大跨界损害的风险。[32]因此，法院不得不另外考察修建公路项目是否有可能造成跨界损害的风险。第二，法院指出，是否存在“重大”跨界环境损害风险需要考虑活动的性质、规模及相关的地理

---

28 *Certain Activities Carried Out by Nicaragua in the Border Area (Costa Rica v. Nicaragua) and Construction of a Road in Costa Rica along the San Juan River (Nicaragua v. Costa Rica), Judgment, ICJ Reports 2015*, p. 45, para. 104.

29 邓华：《国际法院对环境影响评价规则的新发展——基于尼加拉瓜和哥斯达黎加两案的判决》,《中山大学法律评论》第 16 卷第 1 辑，第 9 页。

30 *Report of the International Law Commission on the Work of Its Fifty - third Session*, International Law Commission, UN Doc. A/56/10, 2001, p. 146.

31 *Certain Activities Carried Out by Nicaragua in the Border Area (Costa Rica v. Nicaragua) and Construction of a Road in Costa Rica along the San Juan River (Nicaragua v. Costa Rica), Judgment, ICJ Reports 2015*, pp. 59-63, paras. 153, 159, 161, 168.

32 *Certain Activities Carried Out by Nicaragua in the Border Area (Costa Rica v. Nicaragua) and Construction of a Road in Costa Rica along the San Juan River (Nicaragua v. Costa Rica), Judgment, ICJ Reports 2015*, p. 59, para. 154.

条件。哥斯达黎加规划的道路较长（160 公里），境内修建的道路离圣胡安河非常近，该道路还与具有国际重要性的湿地邻近，并且会穿越一块哥斯达黎加湿地的事实，均表明了环境的敏感性和易破坏性，增加了“重大”跨界环境损害的风险。[33]

与之相对的是，在“边界地区活动案”中，法院认为没有满足启动环境影响评价的门槛标准，因而尼加拉瓜无须承担环境影响评价义务。该案中，法院判决的主要证据为 2006 年尼加拉瓜对其疏浚计划可能产生的环境影响所进行的环境影响研究（EIS）。该研究表明，该计划不会对河流的流量产生重大影响，并且这一结论后来得到了双方专家的证实。[34]

通过对比可以发现，法院在尼加拉瓜和哥斯达黎加两案中关于义务门槛是否满足的论证方法是不同的。事前进行环境影响评价的义务应当按照“三步走”的判断逻辑：第一，应当初步判断是否需要进行环境影响评价，即其门槛标准是否满足；第二，应当判断环境影响评价义务履行的最低要求是否满足；第三，应当对重大跨界风险的存在与否进行确认，这将影响当事国是否将承担通知、协商等义务。而在“边界地区活动案”中，法院多数意见的论证逻辑似乎通过第三步的结论来溯及解决第一步的问题。法院将尼加拉瓜 2006 年进行的研究作为“预评估”看待，认为该预评估已经表明不存在重大跨界损害的风险，因而没有正式进行启动环境影响评价程序的必要。

值得注意的是，回顾尼加拉瓜在该案中提交的书状可以发现，尼加拉瓜所主张的是其已经进行了完善的环境影响评价，并且主张 2006 年的环境影响研究符合其国内法关于环境影响评价的要求。[35] 由此可见，2006 年的研究应当被视为一个正式的环境影响评价。因此，即使该研究确认不存在重大的跨界损害风险，其所解决的是第三步，尼加拉瓜无须承担通知与协商义务的问题，而非第一步尼加拉瓜是否需要进行环境影响评价的问题。正如杜加尔德法官在尼加拉瓜与哥斯达黎加两案的单独意见，法院多数意见没有在两案中采用相同的论证

---

33 *Certain Activities Carried Out by Nicaragua in the Border Area (Costa Rica v. Nicaragua) and Construction of a Road in Costa Rica along the San Juan River (Nicaragua v. Costa Rica), Judgment, ICJ Reports 2015*, pp. 56-60, paras. 146-162.

34 *Certain Activities Carried Out by Nicaragua in the Border Area (Costa Rica v. Nicaragua) and Construction of a Road in Costa Rica along the San Juan River (Nicaragua v. Costa Rica), Judgment, ICJ Reports 2015*, p. 46, para. 105.

35 *Certain Activities Carried Out by Nicaragua in the Border Area (Costa Rica v. Nicaragua), Counter Memorial of the Republic of Nicaragua*, pp. 134-149.

方式。[36]笔者认为，法院采取此种方式论证尼加拉瓜的疏浚活动没有达到启动环境影响评价的门槛要件很大程度上是因为第二步正式的环境影响评价确认了没有重大跨界损害的风险，因此进行了倒推，无须额外再进行预评价；此外，双方专家均确认没有重大跨界损害风险的事实也是论证的重要原因。

（二）时间要求：事先进行与持续进行环境影响评价

如前文所述，环境影响评价的义务来源是风险预防原则。相对于损害预防原则，该原则大大提前了采取防止措施的时间。[37]在该基础原则要求下的环境影响评价义务应当衡量的是，项目或活动开始前是否存在重大跨界环境损害的风险。因此，环境影响评价必须在项目或活动开始前进行。在"修建道路案"中，哥斯达黎加所有的相关研究均发生在修建道路项目开始后，因此不满足"事先"的要求。[38]

哥斯达黎加主张尼加拉瓜占领争议地区伊斯拉－波蒂略斯（Isla Portillos）实施疏浚活动及派遣军队的行为造成了哥斯达黎加的紧急状态；而其国内法规定紧急状态可以免除环境影响评价义务。[39]但是，环境影响评价的内容由国内法规定，并不代表一国国内法可以免除其在国际法中的环境影响评价义务。法院已经确认，事先评价是习惯国际法的要求之一。国内法的紧急状态无法免除事先进行环境影响评价的义务，[40]而哥斯达黎加最早进行的环境影响评价为2012年的一份环境管理计划，远晚于开始修建道路的时间。因此，结合上述两方面的因素，哥斯达黎加违反了环境影响评价义务。

---

36 *Certain Activities Carried Out by Nicaragua in the Border Area (Costa Rica v. Nicaragua) and Construction of a Road in Costa Rica along the San Juan River (Nicaragua v. Costa Rica), Separate Opinion of Judge ad hoc Dugard*, p. 2, para. 5.

37 刘泽：《国际环境法中的风险预防原则——一种功能性的认识》，载《中国国际法年刊》（2014年卷），法律出版社，2015，第286页。

38 *Certain Activities Carried Out by Nicaragua in the Border Area (Costa Rica v. Nicaragua) and Construction of a Road in Costa Rica along the San Juan River (Nicaragua v. Costa Rica), Judgment, ICJ Reports 2015*, pp. 61-62, para. 161.

39 *Certain Activities Carried Out by Nicaragua in the Border Area (Costa Rica v. Nicaragua) and Construction of a Road in Costa Rica along the San Juan River (Nicaragua v. Costa Rica), Judgment, ICJ Reports 2015*, p. 56, para. 148.

40 *Certain Activities Carried Out by Nicaragua in the Border Area (Costa Rica v. Nicaragua) and Construction of a Road in Costa Rica along the San Juan River (Nicaragua v. Costa Rica), Judgment, ICJ Reports 2015*, p. 59, para. 157.

此外，环境影响评价义务的履行应当贯穿项目始终。这有两方面原因：一方面，环境影响评价是为了避免损害，但预防损害和风险不是一劳永逸的，损害随时可能发生；另一方面，环境影响评价义务的履行需要达到谨慎注意义务的标准。[41] 谨慎注意义务贯穿整个行为过程，“这意味着在授权和开展活动后，谨慎注意义务不会终止；只要活动继续进行，就继续监测活动的执行情况”。[42]

四、违反环境影响评价义务的国家责任

在“边界地区活动案”之后，法院于 2018 年 2 月 2 日对该案涉及的国家责任问题作出判决。法院在多数意见中首先回顾了国家责任的相关原则，重申了违反义务就要引起赔偿（reparation），并且赔偿应当是充分的，旨在“消除不法行为的所有后果，重建如果不法行为不发生则完全可能存在的状态”，同时应当避免造成惩罚性的后果。[43]《国家对国际不法行为的责任条款草案》（以下简称《国家责任条款草案》）第 34 条规定，对国际不法行为造成的损害充分赔偿，应单独或合并采取恢复原状（restitution）、补偿（compensation）和抵偿（satisfaction）的方式。[44]

值得注意的是，法院在“纸浆厂案”和“边界地区活动案”等案件中均对环境影响评价、通知与协商等程序性义务和不造成跨界损害等实体义务进行了区分。在“纸浆厂案”中，相关条约没有规定违反程序性义务的后果，根据国际法，难以认定仅因为违反程序性义务，法院就可以判决拆除纸浆厂或对阿根廷进行补偿。[45]

类似的，在“修建道路案”的判决中，法院指出，虽然哥斯达黎加违反了环境影响评价的程序性义务，但其并未违反不对尼加拉瓜造成显著跨界损害、尊重主权和领土完整等实体义务。由于哥斯达黎加没有违反国际法规定的实体义务，恢复原状和补偿均不适用。对于违反程序性义务，法院仅强调当事国应

41 *Pulp Mills on the River Uruguay (Argentina v. Uruguay), Judgment, ICJ Reports 2010 (I)*, p. 83, para. 204.

42 International Law Commission, *Yearbook of the International Law Commission*, 2001, Vol. II, Part Two, p. 165, para. 2.

43 *Factory at Chorzów, Merits, Judgment No. 13, 1928, P.C.I.J., Series A, No. 17*, p. 47.

44 Art. 34, *Draft articles on Responsibility of States for Internationally Wrongful Acts, with commentaries*, International Law Commission, UN Doc A/56/10, 2001.

45 *Pulp Mills on the River Uruguay (Argentina v. Uruguay), Judgment, ICJ Reports 2010 (I)*, paras. 267-281.

当继续合作并履行对环境的谨慎注意义务；而且，对于实体义务的违反，也应进一步区分其是否造成物质损害。如 2018 年哥斯达黎加诉尼加拉瓜“边界地区活动案”中，法院确认尼加拉瓜违反了尊重哥斯达黎加领土主权的实体义务，但宣告相关行为违反国际法已经为哥斯达黎加受到的非物质损害提供了足够的抵偿。[46] 只有造成物质损害，如违反“预防跨界损害的义务”（obligation to prevent transboundary harm），才可能引起恢复原状或补偿的责任承担形式。考虑到环境的脆弱性和环境损害的难以逆转，要求通过恢复原状的形式承担国家责任几乎不可能。因此，将环境损害量化并给予相应金额补偿的方式是恰当的，这种做法符合《国家责任条款草案》第 35 条的要求，也被法院的实践所支持。[47]

结论

随着国际社会逐渐意识到环境损害的不可逆转及赔偿机制的局限性，环境影响评价成为公认的避免重大环境损害的必要环节。从 1995 年法院多数意见“保持沉默”到 2015 年法院进一步阐释了环境影响评价作为习惯国际法的适用条件和内涵，其实践推动了环境影响评价制度的发展。虽然法院在 2010 年“纸浆厂案”中没有使用“习惯国际法”而是使用了“一般国际法”这一用语来表述环境影响评价义务的法律地位，但基于对具体语境的分析及法院使用的法律推理方法的逻辑，此语境下“一般国际法”与“习惯国际法”并无区别。环境影响评价的义务来源于谨慎注意和风险预防的要求，这意味着环境影响评价的对象是较低标准的风险而不问最终有无实际损害结果。法院在尼加拉瓜与哥斯达黎加两案中对环境影响评价义务的门槛标准、时间要求进行了澄清，为各国进行跨界环境影响评价提供了参考。

也需注意到，虽然跨界环境影响评价能够促进共享资源的合理利用，也符合可持续发展原则的要求，但如果一国行为没有造成实质损害，仅违反环境影响评价义务将不会引起恢复原状和补偿等国家责任。法院在 2015 年尼加拉瓜与哥斯达黎加两案中对于程序性义务和实体义务的不同结论也体现了这一点。因

---

46 *Pulp Mills on the River Uruguay (Argentina v. Uruguay), Judgment, ICJ Reports 2010 (I)*, pp. 103-104, para. 273; *Certain Activities Carried Out by Nicaragua in the Border Area (Costa Rica v. Nicaragua), Compensation, Judgment, ICJ Reports 2018*, p. 15, para. 31.

47 *Pulp Mills on the River Uruguay (Argentina v. Uruguay), Judgment, ICJ Reports 2010 (I)*, pp. 103-104, para. 273; *Certain Activities Carried Out by Nicaragua in the Border Area (Costa Rica v. Nicaragua), Compensation, Judgment, ICJ Reports 2018*, p. 15, para. 31.

此，法院仅能在确认违法和督促义务履行的层面上要求国家承担责任。现实中，仍然需要各国认识到国际社会在环境问题上是人类命运共同体，只有秉持合作共赢、安危与共的理念，[48] 才能更好地解决跨界环境损害的事前预防问题。

48　车丕照：《“人类命运共同体”理念的国际法学思考》，《吉林大学社会科学学报》2018 年第 6 期，第 15—20 页。

论国际法上的核裁军义务

李子钰　罗诗静

摘要：核裁军是国际法上的热点问题。尽管核武器具有巨大的破坏性，但核裁军却进展缓慢。本文认为，核裁军义务包括核裁军实体义务和核裁军谈判义务。首先，核裁军实体义务被规定在《禁止核武器条约》第4条，但《禁止核武器条约》缺少有核武器国家参与，实践意义有限，难以成为习惯国际法。联合国大会通过的核裁军相关决议也不能证明核裁军实体义务的存在。其次，核裁军谈判义务被规定在《不扩散核武器条约》第6条中，该义务已经成为习惯国际法，其内涵包括行为义务和结果义务，并且各国均不能援引一贯反对者规则排除该义务。但就核裁军谈判义务的实践而言，以《禁止核武器条约》的谈判为例，由于该条约的保障监督标准并非严格、有效，即使一国没有参与该条约的谈判，也没有违反谈判义务，仍可以通过积极参与裁军谈判会议和《不扩散核武器条约》缔约国审议大会等方式履行核裁军谈判义务。

关键词：核裁军；实体义务；谈判义务；习惯国际法；一贯反对者

引言

核武器及核裁军问题是当今世界最为重要的问题之一。在1996年“以核武器进行威胁或使用核武器的合法性的咨询意见案”中，国际法院（以下简称法院）指出了核武器的破坏性和灾难性，并指出核武器会给人类带来巨大痛苦，甚至灭绝人类，具有“摧毁地球上所有文明和整个生态系统的潜力”。[1]尽管如此，国际社会在核裁军问题上仍进展缓慢，难以达成有效共识。在国际法方面，与核裁军问题最紧密相关的两个条约是2017年的《禁止核武器条约》（Treaty on the Prohibition of Nuclear Weapons）与1968年的《不扩散核武器条约》（Treaty on the Non-Proliferation of Nuclear Weapons）。此外，联合国大会也通过了多个与之相关的决议。但这些国际法规则是否建立了有效的核裁军义务？目前的国

1　*Legality of the Threat or Use of Nuclear Weapons, Advisory Opinion, ICJ Reports 1996*, p. 243, para. 35.

际法规则存在哪些问题？本文将从以下几个方面展开研究：首先，分析目前国际核裁军存在的现实问题；其次，探讨 2017 年《禁止核武器条约》中规定的核裁军实体义务，分析该义务的要求及实践适用问题；最后，讨论 1968 年《不扩散核武器条约》第 6 条规定的核裁军谈判义务，分析该义务的要求以及法律地位，并对核裁军谈判义务的实践进行评析。

一、国际核裁军存在的现实问题

首先，有核武器国家并不会主动进行全面的核裁军。《不扩散核武器条约》第 9 条中仅承认了五个有核武器国家（Nuclear Weapon State），分别为中国、法国、俄罗斯、英国和美国，但在 2018 年 10 月 24 日，这五个国家发表了联合声明，表示不会在现阶段进行核裁军。其次，有部分无核武器国家（Non-Nuclear Weapon State）发展并取得了核武器，[2] 并且表示不会进行核裁军。例如，朝鲜曾作为无核武器国家加入《不扩散核武器条约》，但在 2003 年 1 月退出了该条约，[3] 并于 2006 年开始核试验。截至 2020 年 12 月，联合国安全理事会通过了多项关于朝核问题的决议，并逐步加强了制裁。[4]2018 年 9 月 6 日，在开始与美国的谈判后，朝鲜首次承诺将进行核裁军，实现"朝鲜半岛完全无核化"，[5]但由于双方的反复，谈判进展较为缓慢。最后，法院在核武器和核裁军问题上亦采取保守态度。在 2016 年马绍尔群岛诉英国"停止核军备竞赛和核裁军谈判义务案"（以下简称"谈判义务案"）中，法院认为两国不存在争端，因而对案件没有管辖权，不会审理该案的实体问题。特林达德法官（Judge Trindade）在其反对意见中批评了法院的回避态度，认为"法院在审理案件的可受理性、管辖权

2　参见《禁止核试验国际日——终止核试验》，联合国，https://www.un.org/zh/observances/end-nuclear-tests-day/history；"巴基斯坦已发展和部署用于战场的战术核武器"，参见《巴基斯坦首次承认有战术核武》，新华网，2015 年 10 月 23 日，http://www.xinhuanet.com/world/2015-10/23/c_128348939.htm（最后访问日期：2021 年 2 月 28 日）。

3　《朝鲜宣布退出〈不扩散核武器条约〉（声明、背景）》，中国新闻网，2003 年 1 月 1 日，https://www.chinanews.com/n/2003-01-10/26/262255.html（最后访问日期：2021 年 2 月 28 日）。

4　包括联合国安理会第 1718 号决议、第 1874 号决议、第 1928 号决议、第 1985 号决议、第 2050 号决议、第 2087 号决议、第 2094 号决议、第 2141 号决议、第 2207 号决议、第 2270 号决议、第 2276 号决议、第 2321 号决议、第 2345 号决议、第 2356 号决议、第 2371 号决议、第 2375 号决议、第 2397 号决议、第 2407 号决议、第 2464 号决议、第 2515 号决议。

5　《韩媒：金正恩承诺实现半岛无核化》，澎湃网，2018 年 9 月 6 日，https://www.thepaper.cn/newsDetail_forward_2413273（最后访问日期：2020 年 7 月 6 日）。

和实体问题时必须牢记人道主义”。[6]实践中，多国以发展或禁止核武器为谈判手段，但没有真正考虑进行有效核裁军。

二、《禁止核武器条约》中的核裁军实体义务

2016 年 12 月 23 日，联合国大会通过第 71/258 号决议，决定在 2017 年召开一次国际会议，“尽快缔结一项具有法律约束力的禁止核武器并彻底消除核武器的文书”。[7]最终，联合国在 2017 年 7 月 7 日通过了《禁止核武器条约》，122 国表示赞成。[8]

（一）核裁军实体义务的内容

《禁止核武器条约》对于核裁军问题而言是一个突破，建立了一套全面禁止参加任何核武器活动的规定，全方位地禁止缔约国参与任何与核武器相关的活动，[9]包括承诺不发展、试验、生产、获取、拥有、储存、使用或威胁使用核武器。该条约第 1 条规定，“不发展、试验、生产、制造或以其他方式获得、拥有或储存核武器或其他核爆炸装置；不直接或间接向任何接受者转让核武器或其他核爆炸装置或对此种武器或爆炸装置的控制权；不直接或间接接受核武器或其他核爆炸装置的转让或对此种武器或爆炸装置的控制权；不使用或威胁使用核武器或其他核爆炸装置；不以任何方式协助、鼓励或诱导任何人从事本条约禁止缔约国从事的活动；不以任何方式寻求或接受任何人为从事本条约禁止缔约国从事的活动而提供的援助；不允许在其领土或其管辖或控制的任何地方安置、安装或部署核武器或其他核爆炸装置。”第 4 条进一步规定，在不发展新的核武器的同时，各缔约国也必须采取措施“逐步实现彻底消除核武器”，即拥有

---

6 *Obligations concerning Negotiations relating to Cessation of the Nuclear Arms Race and to Nuclear Disarmament (Marshall Islands v. United Kingdom), Dissenting Opinion of Judge Cancado Trindade, ICJ Reports 2016*, para. 310.

7 *Taking forward Multilateral Nuclear Disarmament Negotiations*, United Nations General Assembly, A/RES/71/258, 2017, p. 4, para. 12.

8 “Conference to Negotiate Legally Binding Instrument Banning Nuclear Weapons Adopts Treaty by 122 Votes in Favour, 1 against, 1 Abstention” (7 July 2017), https://www.un.org/press/en/2017/dc3723.doc.htm (Last visited on 6 July 2020).

9 《禁止核武器条约》，A/CONF.229/2017/8，2017 年 7 月 7 日通过，39 个国家批准或加入，https://www.un.org/zh/documents/treaty/files/A-CONF.229-2017-8.shtml（最后访问日期：2020 年 7 月 6 日）。

核武器或者核爆炸装置的缔约国必须立即停止运行并销毁它们。此外，该条约第 6 条还要求缔约国向对其管辖地区内受核武器使用或试验影响的个人充分提供相应的帮助，并对其管辖地区内受核武器使用或试验影响而受污染的地区，采取必要和适当的措施进行补救。并且，该条约不接受任何保留。[10]

《禁止核武器条约》第 4 条具体规定了核裁军义务：首先，核裁军义务的主体为拥有、掌握或控制核武器或其他核爆炸装置的国家，即目的是针对拥有或主张拥有核武器的国家。其次，核裁军义务的履行方式为缔约国向各缔约国或缔约国向指定的国际主管当局提交核裁军计划，并根据核准后的计划进行核裁军。最后，需要为核裁军义务设置期限并经过核准，在《禁止核武器条约》对其生效之日起 60 天内，拥有、掌握或控制核武器或其他核爆炸装置的各缔约国应向国际主管当局提交核裁军计划进行核准，并按照核裁军计划，立即解除核武器的临战状态，尽快并最迟于核准确定的最后期限销毁核武器。第 4 条从不同方面详细设定了核裁军义务的内涵与范围。从措辞上看，第 4 条隐含着各缔约国应当尽快进行核裁军的期望，这也是国际条约中第一次规定核裁军实体义务。

联合国裁军事务副秘书长兼裁军事务厅高级代表中满泉（Izumi Nakamitsu）认为，该条约体现了国际社会对于推进核裁军进程的认同，其中的各项规定更使各缔约国无法再逃避履行《不扩散核武器条约》；但中满泉也表示，有核武器国家可“以自己的方式”逐步禁止与消除核武器。参加会议的新加坡和瑞士代表强调了《不扩散核武器条约》的重要性，认为《禁止核武器条约》不能影响《不扩散核武器条约》项下缔约国的权利和义务。[11]

（二）《禁止核武器条约》及其核裁军义务的实际困境

尽管《禁止核武器条约》创设了核裁军实体义务，但由于有核武器国家均对其表示了反对，《禁止核武器条约》面临着缺少有核武器国家参与、难以形成习惯国际法等困境。

1. 缺少有核武器国家参与

根据《禁止核武器条约》第 15 条的规定，只有在第 50 份批准书、接受书、核准书或签署书交存 90 天后条约才能生效。目前该条约已有 86 个国家加入，

---

10 《禁止核武器条约》第 16 条规定“本条约各项条款不接受保留”。

11 “Conference to Negotiate Legally Binding Instrument Banning Nuclear Weapons Adopts Treaty by 122 Votes in Favour, 1 against, 1 Abstention,” (7 July 2017), https://www.un.org/press/en/2017/dc3723.doc.htm (Last visited on 6 July 2020).

于 2021 年 1 月 22 日正式生效，[12] 对缔约国具有约束力。

需要注意的是，所有实际拥有核武器的国家都没有参与该条约的谈判和缔结过程，也没有签署该条约。2018 年 10 月 24 日，联合国五个常任理事国（以下简称五常，均为有核国家）甚至发表联合声明，反对《禁止核武器条约》，认为只有逐步的核裁军过程才能实现无核武器世界，而该条约忽视了国际安全环境和区域挑战，没有增加各国之间的信任和透明度，该条约并不能达到消除核武器的效果，也不能满足不扩散的最高标准。[13] 五常重申其不会支持、签署或批准该条约。鉴于《禁止核武器条约》第 4 条规定的核裁军义务主体为有核武器国家，但目前这些国家都没有加入该条约，所以其规定的核裁军义务只具有宣示意义，缺乏实际效果。五常的上述声明表明，《禁止核武器条约》中的核裁军义务只具有宣示效果，缺乏实际意义。

2. 难以成为习惯国际法

只有当《禁止核武器条约》中的核裁军义务具有习惯国际法属性时，才能约束非缔约国。根据联合国国际法委员会 2018 年《关于习惯国际法的识别的结论草案》[14] 第 2、5、9 条，习惯国际法的识别要考虑两个要件：国家实践（state practice）和法律确信（*opinio juris*）。[15]

在衡量国家实践时，特别受影响国家（specially affected states）的实践需要特别考虑，[16] 五常在核裁军问题上显然属于"特别受影响国家"。但并不是只有这五个国家是"特别受影响的国家"，在 2016 年"谈判义务案"中，法院指出，长期以来，马绍尔群岛被广泛用于核试验，其人民遭受了巨大痛苦，所以，马绍尔群岛对核裁军也有着特殊的关切。[17] 因此，法院间接承认了即使不是《不

---

12 "Status of the Treaty on the Prohibition of Nuclear Weapons," United Nations Office for Disarmament Affairs (UNODA), http://disarmament.un.org/treaties/t/tpnw(Last visited on 24 February 2022).

13 UK Mission to UN in New York & UK Mission to the WTO, UN and other International Organizations (Geneva), "P5 Joint Statement on the Treaty on the Non-Proliferation of Nuclear Weapons," Government of UK, 24 October 2018, https://www.gov.uk/government/news/p5-joint-statement-on-the-treaty-on-the-non-proliferation-of-nuclear-weapons (Last visited on 6 July 2020).

14 *Report of the International Law Commission Seventieth Session*, International Law Commission (ILC), A/73/10, 2018, p. 120.

15 *Continental Shelf (Libyan Arab Jamahiriya/Malta), Judgment, ICJ Reports 1985*, para. 27.

16 *North Sea Continental Shelf cases (Federal Republic of Germany/Denmark; Federal Republic of Germany/Netherlands), Judgment, ICJ Reports 1969*, para. 74.

17 *Obligations concerning Negotiations relating to Cessation of the Nuclear Arms Race and to Nuclear Disarmament (Marshall Islands v. United Kingdom), Preliminary Objection, Judgment, ICJ Reports 2016*, para. 44.

扩散核武器条约》承认的有核武器国家，也可能成为“特别受影响国家”。考虑到核武器的破坏性，这一论断有其合理性。

无论如何，2018 年 10 月 24 日的联合声明都清楚表明了五常反对《禁止核武器条约》下的核裁军实体义务，并且“不接受任何关于该条约有助于形成习惯国际法的主张”。[18]即使《禁止核武器条约》的61个缔约国（State Party）[19]确有法律确信，但也数量甚微。虽然也存在这样一种可能性，即参与实践的国家数量较少，但其他国家对该实践没有反应，也可以认为这种默认的情形满足了法律确信的要件，[20]然而五常明确表示反对显然不属于这种情形。习惯国际法的形成与建立需要大国的参与和支持，[21]由于五常正是当今世界上的重要大国，它们的反对使《禁止核武器条约》中的核裁军实体义务很难成为习惯国际法规则。

此外，自 1994 年起，联合国大会每年均通过与核裁军问题相关的决议，呼吁各国进行核裁军谈判并进行实体核裁军。[22]虽然这些决议反映了国际社会对核裁军问题的关注，但也不能证明核裁军实体义务成为习惯国际法。尽管各国对某些联合国大会决议的态度可以反映法律确信，[23]但联合国大会决议本身并不能为各国设置法律义务。[24]此外，这些决议的用语也表明其没有为国家创设国际法义务的意图。因为决议使用了“呼吁”（calls upon）而不是“决定”（decides）的用语，一般而言，“呼吁”一词并不能创设国际法义务。[25]因此，联合国大会

18 UK Mission to UN in New York & UK Mission to the WTO, UN and other International Organizations (Geneva), “P5 Joint Statement on the Treaty on the Non-Proliferation of Nuclear Weapons,” Government of UK, 24 October 2018, https://www.gov.uk/government/news/p5-joint-statement-on-the-treaty-on-the-non-proliferation-of-nuclear-weapons (Last visited on 6 July 2020).

19 “Status of the Treaty on the Prohibition of Nuclear Weapons,” United Nations Office for Disarmament Affairs (UNODA), http://disarmament.un.org/treaties/t/tpnw (Last visited on 5 June 2022).

20 *Report of the International Law Commission Sixty-Eighth Session*, International Law Commission, A/71/10, 2016, p. 94.

21 Malcom N. Shaw, *International Law* (Cambridge University Press, 2014), 7th edn, p. 57.

22 参见附表“联合国大会有关核裁军义务的决议”。

23 *Military and Paramilitary Activities in and against Nicaragua (Nicaragua v. United States of America), Merits, Judgment, ICJ Reports 1986*, paras. 99-100.

24 *Legality of the Threat or Use of Nuclear Weapons, Advisory Opinion, ICJ Reports 1996*, para. 70.

25 Ivan Shalev, “EIP Explainer: How to Read UN Security Council resolutions,” European Institute of Peace, http://eip.org/en/news-events/eip-explainer-how-read-un-security-council-resolutions (Last visited on 6 July 2020).

的系列决议虽然具有建议性，却并不能证明核裁军实体义务已成为有约束力的习惯国际法。

三、《不扩散核武器条约》中的核裁军谈判义务

《不扩散核武器条约》是一项具有里程碑意义的国际条约，其目标是防止核武器和技术的扩散，促进和平利用核能方面的合作，并推进实现核裁军和全面彻底裁军。[26]《不扩散核武器条约》是目前唯一的有核武器国家作出承诺的具有约束力的条约。该条约于 1968 年 7 月 1 日开放供签署，1970 年 3 月 5 日生效。[27]1995 年 5 月 11 日，联合国《不扩散核武器条约》的审议和延长大会决定无限期延长该条约。[28] 截至 2022 年 6 月，共有 191 个国家加入了该条约，其中包括五常。[29] 由于联合国只有 193 个会员国，批准《不扩散核武器条约》的国家数量比任何其他军备控制和裁军条约的都多，证明了该条约的广泛适用性和重要性。但《不扩散核武器条约》中的核裁军义务只是一种谈判义务，而非实体义务，它没有要求有核国家减少核储备、实体上进行核裁军，而只要求缔约国就核裁军问题进行谈判。

（一）核裁军谈判义务的内容

《不扩散核武器条约》第 6 条规定的核裁军谈判义务的内容是：每个缔约国承诺就及早停止核军备竞赛和核裁军方面的有效措施，以及就一项在严格和有效国际监督下的全面彻底裁军条约，真诚地进行谈判。根据该条款，核裁军谈判义务可以分为两个方面：行为义务和结果义务。

1. 行为义务

根据谈判义务的一般要求，结合第 6 条的具体规定，核裁军方面真诚谈判的行为义务主要包括以下四个方面的要求。

---

26 参见《不扩散核武器条约》引言部分。

27 “Status of the Treaty on the Prohibition of Nuclear Weapons,” UNODA, http://disarmament.un.org/treaties/t/tpnw (Last visited on 5 June 2022).

28 “1995 Review and Extension Conference of the Parties to the Treaty on the Non-Proliferation of Nuclear Weapons, Decision 3: Extension of the Treaty on the Non-Proliferation of Nuclear Weapons,” UNODA, 17 April-12 May 1995, https://www.un.org/disarmament/wmd/nuclear/npt1995/ (Last visited on 6 July 2020).

29 “Status of the Treaty on the Prohibition of Nuclear Weapons,” UNODA, http://disarmament.un.org/treaties/t/tpnw (Last visited on 5 June 2022).

第一，国家有义务真诚地开始并持续进行谈判。真诚地进行谈判的义务首先要求缔约国参与谈判，[30] 这是履行谈判义务的前提。各国必须要首先参与谈判，才有可能就议题交换意见、进行磋商，最终达成协议。在开始谈判后，缔约国有必要持续参与谈判，不能在中途随意退出谈判，否则缔约国的谈判义务可能沦为形式。法院在 2011 年格鲁吉亚诉俄罗斯联邦"《消除一切形式种族歧视国际公约》的适用问题案"中指出，只有当谈判最终失败、最终达成协议或者陷入僵局时，才可以认为国家完成了谈判义务。[31] 根据国际海洋法法庭在 2003 年马来西亚诉新加坡"在柔佛海峡及附近填海案"中的论述，当谈判失去达成结果的可能性时，可以被认为陷入僵局，缔约国才可以退出谈判。[32]

第二，谈判的主题应当与核裁军相关。根据 2011 年"《消除一切形式种族歧视国际公约》的适用问题案"，谈判的主题必须涉及相关条约及其所载的实质性义务。[33] 根据《不扩散核武器条约》第 6 条的规定，谈判的主题应当涉及核裁军的有效措施或者在严格有效国际监督下的全面彻底裁军。

第三，国家有义务进行有意义的谈判。缔约国在谈判时，不能仅仅只是为了履行义务而进行一种流程，必须要有达成协议的真诚愿望。[34] 这种愿望需要通过外在的真诚谈判行为表现。例如，各国应当合理考虑另一方的利益，[35] 并作出适当让步。[36] 并且，参与谈判的国家不能不正当地阻碍谈判的进程，中断交

---

30 *Application of the International Convention on the Elimination of All Forms of Racial Discrimination (Georgia v. Russian Federation), Preliminary Objections, Judgment, ICJ Reports 2011*, p. 132, para. 157.

31 *Application of the International Convention on the Elimination of All Forms of Racial Discrimination (Georgia v. Russian Federation), Preliminary Objections, Judgment, ICJ Reports 2011*, p. 133, para. 159.

32 *Land Reclamation by Singapore in and around the Straits of Johor (Malaysia v. Singapore), Provisional Measures, Order of 8 October 2003, ITLOS Reports 2003*, p. 19, para. 47.

33 *Application of the International Convention on the Elimination of All Forms of Racial Discrimination (Georgia v. Russian Federation), Preliminary Objections, Judgment, ICJ Reports 2011*, p. 133, para. 161.

34 *North Sea Continental Shelf cases (Federal Republic of Germany/Denmark; Federal Republic of Germany/Netherlands), Judgment, ICJ Reports 1969*, pp. 46-47, para. 85.

35 *Application of the Interim Accord of 13 September 1995 (the former Yugoslav Republic of Macedonia v. Greece), Judgment of 5 December 2011, ICJ Reports 2011*, p. 685, para. 132.

36 *South West Africa (Ethiopia v. South Africa; Liberia v. South Africa), Preliminary Objection, Judgment, ICJ Reports 1962*, pp. 345-346.

流、造成谈判程序延误等行为都是违反真诚谈判义务的行为。[37]

第四，缔约国在谈判过程中不能从事违反谈判目的和宗旨的行为。该要件来源于国际法上履行义务的善意原则（principle of good faith）。法院在1974年澳大利亚诉法国“核试验案”中指出，善意原则是国际法上履行义务的基本原则。[38]善意原则要求，在履行义务时，各方应当以合理的方式并以实现其目的的方式进行。[39]因此，缔约国在进入谈判后，不能作出违反谈判主题的行为，这既是缔约国真诚缔约的体现，也是善意原则的要求。在核裁军谈判义务中，这意味着国家在进行谈判时，应当停止发展、试验、生产、获取、拥有、储存、使用或威胁使用核武器。

2. 结果义务

关于谈判义务的内容在学界早有争论，有两种不同内涵的谈判义务——缔约承诺（pactum de contrahendo）义务和谈判承诺（pactum de negotiando）义务。缔约承诺为谈判各方施加了未来加入所缔结协议的义务；谈判承诺则只要求谈判各方有真诚谈判的行为，而不要求最终达成结果。[40]在1996年“以核武器进行威胁或使用核武器的合法性的咨询意见案”中，法院认为，核裁军谈判义务不只是一种真诚进行谈判的行为义务，还是一种必须实现确切结果的结果义务。[41]但时任法院副院长的施韦贝尔法官（Judge Schwebel）发表了不同看法，他认为，由于联合国大会只请求法院确定使用或威胁使用核武器的合法性问题，咨询意见中涉及的核裁军谈判义务只是附带意见，因而不具有法律约束力。[42]尽管如此，施韦贝尔法官主要质疑法院对核裁军谈判义务发表咨询意见的管辖权，[43]并没有否定核裁军谈判义务的双重义务属性。

37 *Fisheries Jurisdiction (United Kingdom v. Iceland), Merits, Judgment, ICJ Reports 1974*, p. 33, para. 78.

38 *Nuclear Tests (Australia v. France), Judgment, ICJ Reports 1974*, p. 268, para. 46.

39 *Gabcikovo-Nagymaros Project (Hungary v. Slovakia), Judgment, ICJ Reports1997*, pp. 78-79, para. 142.

40 Antonio Cassese, “The Israel-PLO Agreement and Self-Determination,” *European Journal of International Law,* Vol. 4, 1993, pp. 566-567.

41 *Legality of the Threat or Use of Nuclear Weapons, Advisory Opinion, ICJ Reports1996*, pp. 263-264, para. 99.

42 *Legality of the Threat or Use of Nuclear Weapons, Dissenting Opinion of Vice-President Schwebel, ICJ Reports 1996*, p. 329.

43 *Second Report: Legal Aspects of Nuclear Disarmament*, International Law Association Washington Conference, 2014, p. 3, para. 4.

判断一个谈判义务是缔约承诺还是谈判承诺主要取决于对条约内容的解释。[44] 例如，1993 年《关于在被占领土上巴勒斯坦临时自治政府安排的原则宣言》第 5 条规定，“以色列政府和巴勒斯坦人民的代表之间的永久地位谈判应尽快开始……谈判的主题应包括耶路撒冷、难民、移民点、安全安排、边界、同其他邻国的关系和合作以及共同关心的其他问题”，该条款被认为是规定了谈判承诺；第 7 条规定，“以色列代表团和巴勒斯坦代表团将就过渡时期谈判一项协定……临时协定……应规定理事会的结构、成员人数、权力和责任、成立安排等”，该条款被认为是规定了缔约承诺。[45] 由此可见，如果条款明确规定了缔结协议的义务且概述了未来协议的基本内容，那么可以认为该条款创设了缔约承诺义务；如果条款仅概括规定了未来协议的主题，那么该条款仅创设了谈判承诺义务。

尽管《不扩散核武器条约》第 6 条没有详细规定核裁军谈判应达成的协议，但考虑到其明确界定了核裁军谈判的主题，即达成核裁军的有效措施或在严格有效国际监督下的全面彻底裁军条约，因此，其中的核裁军义务应当被认为是缔约承诺义务，不仅包括行为义务，也包括结果义务。结果义务不仅要求各缔约国谈判后确定全面彻底核裁军条约的文本，同时还暗含了各缔约国有义务签署该条约并受其约束。前者是真诚谈判行为义务的应有之意，后者则为缔约国创设了更高的要求，也符合缔约承诺的内涵。

（二）核裁军谈判义务的习惯国际法属性

截至 2022 年 1 月，共有 191 个国家加入了《不扩散核武器条约》，其中包括 5 个有核武器国家，[46] 印度和巴基斯坦未加入，朝鲜于 2003 年退出了该条约。若要使所有国家均受该条约第 6 条中核裁军谈判义务的约束，则必须证明该义务的习惯国际法属性，需要考察相关国家实践和法律确信。

1. 国家实践

国家实践必须具有普遍性，也就是国家实践应当足够广泛、有代表性以及

---

44 Owada Hisashi, “Pactum de Contrahendo, Pactum de Negotiando,” Max Planck Encyclopedia of Public International Law, 2008, para. 9, http://opil.ouplaw.com/view/10.1093/law:epil/9780199231690/law-9780199231690-e1451?print=pdf (Last visited on 6 July 2020).

45 Antonio Cassese, “The Israel-PLO Agreement and Self-Determination,” *European Journal of International Law,* Vol. 4, 1993, p. 565.

46 “Status of Treaty on the Non-Proliferation of Nuclear Weapons,” UNODA, http://disarmament.un.org/treaties/t/npt (Last visited on 15 January 2022).

一致。[47] 就足够广泛和有代表性而言，国家实践有多种形式，包括与国际组织或政府间会议通过决议有关的行为，或者与条约有关的行为。[48] 因此，191 个国家加入《不扩散核武器条约》并同意受核裁军谈判义务约束，该事实可以反映广泛和有代表性的国家实践。另外，有核武器国家作为“特别受影响国家”，其实践确认了国家实践的足够广泛和有代表性。例如，五常均参加了裁军谈判会议（Conference on Disarmament），确定了永久性的法定裁军谈判任务，在 2016 年 6 月 14 日也讨论了停止核军备竞赛和核裁军问题。[49] 就重要国家的实践而言，2010 年，美国和俄罗斯也就限制和裁减核武器达成了《新削减战略武器条约》，该条约于 2011 年 2 月 5 日生效。根据该条约，美国和俄罗斯必须在 2018 年 2 月 5 日之前达到裁减相当数量的战略性核武器的目标。[50]

关于国家实践的一致性，需要指出，如果一个国家进行了相反的实践，但通过诉诸规则本身所包含的例外或理由来维护其行为的合法性，那么该相反的实践实质上将确认了规则的有效性。[51] 也就是说，并不是所有的相反实践都会有损国家实践的一致性，重点须关注各国对于相反实践的解释、态度和理由。例如，在 2016 年“谈判义务案”中，法院曾经讨论过英国对联合国大会通过的核裁军谈判决议均投票表示反对，似乎构成了一种相反实践。但在 2016 年 3 月 23 日的书面答复中，英国援引各种政治和法律因素说明了它对这些决议的立场，而非拒绝该义务。[52] 因此，国家实践实际上也基本符合一致性的要求。

2. 法律确信

法律确信要求国家必须因为相信义务的要求而采取某种实践。证明法律确

---

47 *Report of the International Law Commission Seventieth Session*, ILC, A/73/10, 2018, p. 120, Conclusion 8.

48 *Report of the International Law Commission Seventieth Session*, ILC, A/73/10, 2018, p. 120, Conclusion 6.

49 *Report of the Conference on Disarmament (2016 Session)*, United Nations General Assembly, A/71/27, 2016, p.14, para. 44.

50 “New START Treaty,” U.S. Department of State, https://www.state.gov/t/avc/newstart/ (Last visited on 6 July 2020).

51 *Military & Paramilitary Activities in and against Nicaragua (Nicaragua v. United States of America), Merits, Judgment, ICJ Reports1986*, p. 98, para. 186.

52 *Obligations concerning Negotiations relating to Cessation of the Nuclear Arms Race and to Nuclear Disarmament (Marshall Islands v. United Kingdom), Written Reply of the United Kingdom of Great Britain and Northern Ireland to Questions from Judges Cançado Trindade and Greenwood, ICJ Reports 2016*, p. 1, para. 2.

信有多种形式。例如，可以从各国对某些国际组织决议的态度进行推断，[53]如果联大决议是在国家一致同意或绝大多数同意的情况下通过的，则可能证明法律确信的存在。在 1996 年“以核武器进行威胁或使用核武器的合法性的咨询意见案”公布后，联合国大会每年均通过决议呼吁就全面禁止核裁军问题展开多边谈判，大部分国家投票表示赞成。[54] 例如，联合国大会 2015 年 12 月 7 日“关于推进多边核裁军谈判的决议”，投票结果为 138 票赞成、12 票反对、34 票弃权；12 月 7 日“关于核裁军的决议”，投票结果为 127 票赞成、43 票反对、15 票弃权。[55] 这些压倒性的投票结果也从侧面证明了《不扩散核武器条约》第 6 条已经被国际社会所广泛认同，[56]可能满足习惯国际法构成要件中的法律确信。[57] 此外，五常的联合声明重申将遵守《不扩散核武器条约》，也体现了法律确信。

（三）核裁军谈判义务的一贯反对者

尽管核裁军谈判义务构成习惯国际法，因而对国家具有普遍拘束力，但其并不能拘束该规则的一贯反对者（persistent objector）。[58] 习惯国际法规则的一贯反对者需要满足四个条件：第一，一国从习惯国际法规则形成之始就对此表示反对；[59] 第二，该国持续（persistent）表示反对；第三，该国始终如一地（consistent）表示反对；[60] 第四，其他国家对该反对表示承认或容忍。[61]

需要强调的是，国家单纯拒绝加入《不扩散核武器条约》并不能构成对第 6 条中的核武器谈判义务的反对。国家不批准条约的决定可能是因为条约中的任意条款，并且部分国家虽然不加入某一条约，但并不影响其遵守条约

53 *Military & Paramilitary Activities in and against Nicaragua (Nicaragua v. United States of America), Merits, Judgment, ICJ Reports 1986*, pp. 99-100, para. 188.

54 参见附表“联合国大会有关核裁军义务的决议”。

55 *Taking forward Multilateral Nuclear Disarmament*, UNGA, A/RES/70/33, 2015; UNGA, *Nuclear disarmament*, A/RES/70/52, 2015.

56 参见附表“联合国大会有关核裁军义务的决议”。

57 *Military & Paramilitary Activities in and against Nicaragua (Nicaragua v United States of America), Merits, Judgment, ICJ Reports 1986*, pp. 58-59, paras. 99-100.

58 *Report of the International Law Commission Seventieth Session*, ILC, A/73/10, 2018, p. 152, Conclusion 15.

59 *Columbian-Peruvian Asylum Case (Columbia/Peru), Judgment, ICJ Reports 1950*, pp. 277-278; *Fisheries Case (United Kingdom v Norway), Judgment, ICJ Reports 1951*, p. 136.

60 *Fisheries Case (United Kingdom v Norway), Judgment, ICJ Reports 1951*, pp. 137-138.

61 *Fisheries Case (United Kingdom v Norway), Judgment, ICJ Reports 1951*, pp. 138-139.

中的特定规则。因此，在判断国家拒绝加入条约是否能构成对其中特定义务的反对时，应当重点关注国家拒绝或者加入条约的原因。[62] 例如，巴基斯坦和印度之所以拒绝加入《不扩散核武器条约》，是因为它们认为该条约存在歧视（discriminatory）。[63] 这种歧视性表现为：第一，无核武器国家有义务签署《全面保障监督协定》（Comprehensive Safeguards Agreements），将其所有核活动开放给国际原子能机构核查，而有核武器国家却不受此类要求的限制，只需要签署《自愿承诺协定》（Voluntary Offer Agreements）；[64] 第二，无核武器国家根据《不扩散核武器条约》无法获得核武器，而有核武器国家却可以保留其核武器。但《不扩散核武器条约》第 6 条中的核裁军谈判义务本身不具有歧视性，它要求所有缔约国都参与谈判，并且最终的目标是全面核裁军。因此，并不能认为这些国家拒绝加入《不扩散核武器条约》构成了对核裁军谈判义务的反对。

作为一贯反对的国家，其反对必须是始终如一的。对于始终如一的标准，在国际法上有绝对一致和基本一致两种标准。前者要求国家在某一习惯国际法规则形成期间的任何时候都不得肯定或接受该规则，任何不一致的做法都会使该国丧失成为一贯反对者的可能性；后者则只要求国家在大多数情况下保持其反对者的立场，偶尔接受该规则并不一定会使其丧失一贯反对者地位。[65] 实践表明，大部分国家认为只有绝对一致的反对才能使国家成为一贯反对者。[66] 习惯国际法规则对国际社会所有成员具有同等效力，国家不可以随意单方面排除习惯国际法规则。[67] 由于一贯反对者是唯一的例外，所以，其适用标准必须足够高，否则可能造成对一贯反对者规则的滥用，使习惯国际法规则形同虚设。而事实上，伊朗、朝鲜、印度、巴基斯坦都参加了裁军谈判会议，并在 2016 年

---

62 James A. Green, *The Persistent Objector Rule in International Law* (Oxford: Oxford University Press, 2016), p. 86.

63 "India says no to NPT again, terms it discriminatory," Hindustan Times, https://www.hindustantimes.com/delhi/india-says-no-to-npt-again-terms-it-discriminatory/story-CywfgdfgKsQcMjVKvKeceK.html (Last visited on 6 March 2021).

64 Tadashi Tanaka, "Some Legal Aspects of Disarmament," *Japanese Annual of International Law*, Vol. 30, 1987, p. 26.

65 James A. Green, *The Persistent Objector Rule in International Law* (Oxford University Press, 2016), p. 117.

66 James A. Green, *The Persistent Objector Rule in International Law* (Oxford University Press, 2016), p. 117.

67 *North Sea Continental Shelf Cases (Federal Republic of Germany/Denmark; Federal Republic of Germany/Netherlands), Judgment, ICJ Reports 1969*, pp. 38-39, para. 63.

6 月 14 日的裁军谈判会议上，都表示将参加以裁军谈判会议为平台的全面禁止核武器条约的谈判。

综上所述，核裁军谈判义务已经构成习惯国际法，且各国都难以主张自己属于该义务的一贯反对者。因此，各国应当遵守该义务，参与完全禁止核武器条约的谈判。

（四）《禁止核武器条约》与核裁军谈判义务

《不扩散核武器条约》第 6 条规定的核裁军谈判义务明确界定了核裁军谈判的目标和宗旨，即采取核裁军的有效措施，或者缔结一个存在严格有效国际监督的全面彻底的核裁军条约。因此，如果一个正在进行的谈判没有或不可能实现该目标和宗旨，即使国家不参与该谈判，也并不意味着其违反了核裁军谈判义务。本文将以《禁止核武器条约》为例说明，由于该条约缺乏严格和有效的国际监督保障机制，不参与该条约的谈判并不一定构成对核裁军谈判义务的违反。

1.《禁止核武器条约》的保障监督标准过低

首先，《禁止核武器条约》中的保障监督标准比《不扩散核武器条约》中的保障监督标准更低，可能会对《不扩散核武器条约》的履行造成一定的障碍。

国际原子能机构（International Atomic Energy Agency）通过保障监督机制，核查无核武器国家是否履行不将核计划用于核武器目的的义务。国际原子能机构有三种不同“保障监督协定”模板：《全面保障监督协定》（针对无核武器国家）、《自愿承诺协定》（针对有核武器国家）、《特定项目保障监督协定》（Item-specific Safeguards Agreements，针对非《不扩散核武器条约》缔约国）。[68] 同时，在“保障监督协定”的基础上，各国还可以签订《国际原子能机构示范附加议定书》（IAEA Model Additional Protocol，以下简称《示范附加议定书》）。《示范附加议定书》是为了解决国际原子能机构在伊拉克秘密核武器的发现中暴露出来的问题，[69] 因此，其在监督检查方面要严格于“保障监督协定”。

根据《禁止核武器条约》第 3 条和第 4 条，该条约的最低标准为《全面保障监督协定》，而非附加有《示范附加议定书》的“保障监督协定”。有学者认为，《禁止核武器条约》规定缔约国至少有义务维持其现有的保障监督标准（即《全面保障监督协定》），并且要求有核国家有谈判、缔结和维持适当的“保障监

68 “More on Safeguards agreements,” IAEA, https://www.iaea.org/topics/safeguards-legal-framework/more-on-safeguards-agreements (Last visited on 2 March 2020).

69 “Nuclear Weapon Prohibition Treaty: A Safeguards Debacle,” Trust & Verify, p. 3, http://www.vertic.org/media/assets/TV/TV158.pdf (Last visited on 6 July 2020).

督协定”的直接义务，超越了《不扩散核武器条约》中的规定。[70]然而，《不扩散核武器条约》并没有认定《全面保障监督协定》为最低标准，而只是笼统地规定“每个无核武器的缔约国承诺接受按照国际原子能机构规约及该机构的保障制度与该机构谈判缔结的协定中所规定的各项保障措施”。

实践中，已有多数国家采取了较高标准，即在《全面保障监督协定》的基础上附加签订《示范附加议定书》。截至 2020 年 12 月 31 日，《示范附加议定书》已经在 136 个国家生效，另外还有 14 个国家签署了该协议。[71]另外，白俄罗斯、伊朗、马来西亚、塞尔维亚和泰国也签署了《示范附加议定书》，只是还没有批准。目前在拥有重大核活动的无核武器国家中，已有 90% 的国家缔结或至少签署了《示范附加议定书》。[72]也就是说，《禁止核武器条约》严格适用了一项可能已经过时的保障监督协定标准，这显然是不合时宜的。

2.《禁止核武器条约》取得保障监督协定的期限过长

《禁止核武器条约》延长了《不扩散核武器条约》中规定的取得“保障监督协定”的期限，不能起到严格有效的保障监督作用。[73]《禁止核武器条约》第 3 条规定，缔约国须在《禁止核武器条约》对该国生效后 18 个月内取得有效的“保障监督协定”。而《不扩散核武器条约》第 3 条第 4 款规定的期限为：（1）无核武器国家需要在《不扩散核武器条约》最初生效后（1970 年 3 月 5 日）的 180 天内与国际原子能机构开始就“保障监督协定”进行谈判，“保障监督协定”不迟于谈判开始之日起 18 个月内生效；（2）在 180 天期限届满后（1970 年 9 月 1 日）加入《不扩散核武器条约》的各国，需要自加入《不扩散核武器条约》之日起开始谈判，“保障监督协定”应不迟于谈判开始之日起 18 个月内生效。由此可见，《禁止核武器条约》延长了《不扩散核武器条约》规定的期限，其保障监督机制更不能被认为是严格有效的。

---

70 Eirini Giorgou, “Safeguards Provisions in the Treaty on the Prohibition of Nuclear Weapons,” *Arms Control Law*, 11 April 2018, https://armscontrollaw.com/2018/04/11/safeguards-provisions-in-the-treaty-on-the-prohibition-of-nuclear-weapons/ (Last visited on 6 July 2020).

71 “Additional Protocol,” IAEA, https://www.iaea.org/topics/additional-protocol (Last visited on 2 March 2020).

72 See “Nuclear Weapon Prohibition Treaty: A Safeguards Debacle,” Trust & Verify, p. 3, http://www.vertic.org/media/assets/TV/TV158.pdf (Last visited on 6 July 2020).

73 “Nuclear Weapon Prohibition Treaty: A Safeguards Debacle,” Trust & Verify, p. 3, http://www.vertic.org/media/assets/TV/TV158.pdf (Last visited on 6 July 2020).

结论

本文通过分析研究2017年的《禁止核武器条约》和1968年的《不扩散核武器条约》以及联合国大会通过的核裁军相关决议，确定了国际法上两类核裁军义务的法律地位和效力。首先，《禁止核武器条约》下的核裁军实体义务仍然只是条约义务，由于该条约缺少有核武器国家参与，实践意义有限，因此难以成为习惯国际法。其次，《不扩散核武器条约》下的核裁军谈判义务已经具有了习惯国际法效力，并且各国均不能援引一贯反对者规则以排除该义务。对核裁军谈判义务的实践而言，以《禁止核武器条约》的谈判为例，由于《禁止核武器条约》的保障监督标准并非严格、有效，因此，即使一国没有参加《禁止核武器条约》谈判，也不能认为其违反《不扩散核武器条约》中的核裁军谈判义务。

附表：联合国大会有关核裁军义务的决议

<table>
<tr><th>联合国决议编号</th><th>年份</th><th>题目</th><th>相关表述</th><th>投票结果</th><th>内容</th></tr>
<tr><td>A/RES/49/75H</td><td>1994 年</td><td rowspan="6">为最终消除核武器进行核裁军</td><td>呼吁有核武器国家致力于核裁军，以期按全面彻底裁军的架构实现消除核武器的最终目标。</td><td>163 票赞成，0 票反对，8 票弃权</td><td rowspan="6">实体裁军义务</td></tr>
<tr><td>A/RES/50/70C</td><td>1995 年</td><td rowspan="3">呼吁有核武器国家继续作出坚决、系统而逐步的努力，争取全球裁减核武器，而最终目标是消除这种武器，呼吁所有国家继续坚决争取在严格而有效的国际管制下全面彻底裁军，并请它们将取得的进展和所做的努力随时通知联合国会员国。</td><td>154 票赞成，0 票反对，10 票弃权</td></tr>
<tr><td>A/RES/51/45G</td><td>1996 年</td><td>159 票赞成，0 票反对，11 票弃权</td></tr>
<tr><td>A/RES/52/38K</td><td>1997 年</td><td>156 票赞成，0 票反对，10 票弃权</td></tr>
<tr><td>A/RES/53/77U</td><td>1998 年</td><td rowspan="2">呼吁有核武器国家坚决地为裁减全球的核武器作出系统和逐步的努力，以消除这些武器为最终目标，并呼吁所有国家在严格而有效的国际管制下坚决地致力于全面彻底裁军。</td><td>160 票赞成，0 票反对，11 票弃权</td></tr>
<tr><td>A/RES/54/54D</td><td>1999 年</td><td>153 票赞成，0 票反对，12 票弃权</td></tr>
<tr><td>A/RES/50/70P</td><td>1995 年</td><td rowspan="5">核裁军</td><td rowspan="4">1. 呼吁有核武器国家逐步减少核威胁，实施逐步而均衡地大幅度削减核武器的分期方案，并执行有效的核裁军措施，以便在一个时限框架内彻底消除此种武器；
2. 呼吁裁军谈判会议优先设立一个核裁军特设委员会，在下一年年初（笔者注）就核裁军的分期方案以及通过一项核武器公约在明确时限框架内最终消除核武器展开谈判。</td><td>106 票赞成，39 票反对，17 票弃权</td><td rowspan="5">实体裁军义务+谈判义务</td></tr>
<tr><td>A/RES/51/45O</td><td>1996 年</td><td>110 票赞成，39 票反对，20 票弃权</td></tr>
<tr><td>A/RES/52/38L</td><td>1997 年</td><td>109 票赞成，39 票反对，18 票弃权</td></tr>
<tr><td>A/RES/53/77X</td><td>1998 年</td><td>110 票赞成，41 票反对，18 票弃权</td></tr>
<tr><td>A/RES/54/54P</td><td>1999 年</td><td>1. 重申吁请有核武器国家逐步减少核威胁，吁请并执行有效的核裁军措施，以便全面消除此种武器；</td><td>104 票赞成，41 票反对，17 票弃权</td></tr>
</table>

续表

联合国决议编号	年份	题目	相关表述	投票结果	内容
A/RES/55/33T	2000 年	核裁军	2. 敦促有核武器国家在适当阶段把进一步大幅裁减核武器作为一项核裁军的有效措施，相互展开复边/诸边谈判； 3. 再次呼吁裁军谈判会议，在下一年年初（笔者注）优先设立处理核裁军问题的特设委员会，并就最终消除核武器的核裁军分阶段方案展开谈判； 4. 呼吁早日召开讨论核裁军所有方面问题的国际会议，以确定并讨论具体的核裁军措施。	109 票赞成，39 票反对，20 票弃权	实体裁军义务 + 谈判义务
A/RES/56/24R	2001 年			103 票赞成，41 票反对，17 票弃权	
A/RES/57/79	2002 年			107 票赞成，41 票反对，21 票弃权	
A/RES/58/56	2003 年			112 票赞成，45 票反对，20 票弃权	
A/RES/59/77	2004 年			117 票赞成，43 票反对，21 票弃权	
A/RES/60/70	2005 年			113 票赞成，45 票反对，20 票弃权	
A/RES/61/78	2006 年			115 票赞成，48 票反对，18 票弃权	
A/RES/62/42	2007 年			117 票赞成，47 票反对，17 票弃权	
A/RES/63/46	2008 年			117 票赞成，45 票反对，19 票弃权	
A/RES/64/53	2009 年			111 票赞成，45 票反对，19 票弃权	
A/RES/65/56	2010 年			120 票赞成，45 票反对，18 票弃权	
A/RES/66/51	2011 年			117 票赞成，45 票反对，18 票弃权	
A/RES/67/60	2012 年			124 票赞成，44 票反对，18 票弃权	
A/RES/68/47	2013 年			122 票赞成，44 票反对，17 票弃权	
A/RES/69/48	2014 年			121 票赞成，44 票反对，17 票弃权	
A/RES/70/52	2015 年		1. 再次促请有核武器国家执行有效的核裁军措施，以期在规定的时限内彻底消除核武器； 2. 敦促有核武器国家就以不可逆、可核查和透明的方式进一步大幅裁减核武器作为一项核裁军的有效措施，在适当阶段进行诸边谈判；	127 票赞成，43 票反对，15 票弃权	

续表

<table>
<tr><th>联合国决议编号</th><th>年份</th><th>题目</th><th>相关表述</th><th>投票结果</th><th>内容</th></tr>
<tr><td>A/RES/71/63</td><td>2016 年</td><td rowspan="3">核裁军</td><td rowspan="2">3. 再次呼吁召开裁军谈判会议，在下一年年初（笔者注）优先设立处理核裁军问题的特设委员会，并就导致最终消除核武器的核裁军分阶段方案展开谈判；
4. 呼吁最迟于 2018 年举行一次核裁军问题的联合国高级别国际会议，以审查在这方面取得的进展情况。</td><td>122 票赞成，44 票反对，17 票弃权</td><td rowspan="3">实体裁军义务＋谈判义务</td></tr>
<tr><td>A/RES/72/38</td><td>2017 年</td><td>119 票赞成，41 票反对，20 票弃权</td></tr>
<tr><td>A/RES/73/50</td><td>2018 年</td><td>1. 再次促请有核武器国家执行有效的核裁军措施，以期在规定的时限内彻底消除核武器；
2. 敦促有核武器国家就以不可逆、可核查和透明的方式进一步大幅裁减核武器作为一项核裁军的有效措施，在适当阶段展开诸边谈判；
3. 再次呼吁召开裁军谈判会议，在 2019 年初优先设立处理核裁军问题的特设委员会，并就最终消除核武器的核裁军分阶段方案展开谈判；
4. 呼吁尽快举行一次核裁军问题的联合国高级别国际会议，以审查在这方面取得的进展情况。</td><td>125 票赞成，40 票反对，18 票弃权</td></tr>
<tr><td>A/RES/51/45M</td><td>1996 年</td><td>国际法院关于以核武器进行威胁或使用核武器的合法性的咨询意见</td><td>……
3. 强调国际法院的一致结论，认为各国有义务真诚地开展和完成将导致在严格有效的国际监督之下实现所有方面的核裁军的谈判；
4. 吁请所有国家立即履行其义务，于 1997 年开展多边谈判，以求早日缔结一项禁止发展、生产、试验、部署、储存、转让核武器以及以核武器进行威胁或使用核武器，并规定消除此种武器的公约。</td><td>115 票赞成，22 票反对，32 票弃权

实体部分第 3 句：139 票赞成，7 票反对，20 票弃权
第 4 句：110 票赞成，27 票反对，29 票弃权</td><td>谈判义务</td></tr>
</table>

续表

联合国决议编号	年份	题目	相关表述	投票结果	内容
A/RES/52/38O	1997 年	国际法院关于以核武器进行威胁或使用核武器的合法性的咨询意见	1. 再次强调国际法院的一致结论，认为各国有义务真诚地开展和完成将导致在严格有效的国际监督下实现所有方面的核裁军的谈判； 2. 再次吁请所有国家立即履行上述义务，在下一年（笔者注）开展多边谈判，以求早日缔结一项禁止发展、生产、试验、部署、储存、转让核武器以及以核武器进行威胁或使用核武器，并规定消除此种武器的公约。	116 票赞成，26 票反对，24 票弃权 实体部分第 1 句：152 票赞成，6 票反对，6 票弃权 第 2 句：106 票赞成，34 票反对，24 票弃权	谈判义务
A/RES/53/77W	1998 年	国际法院关于“以核武器进行威胁或使用核武器的合法性”的咨询意见的后续行动		123 票赞成，25 票反对，25 票弃权 实体部分第 1 句：159 票赞成，4 票反对，8 票弃权	
A/RES/54/54Q	1999 年			114 票赞成，28 票反对，22 票弃权 实体部分第 1 句：156 票赞成，3 票反对，3 票弃权 第 2 句：107 票赞成，29 票反对，26 票弃权	
A/RES/55/33X	2000 年			119 票赞成，28 票反对，22 票弃权 实体部分第 1 句：162 票赞成，4 票反对，1 票弃权	
A/RES/56/24S	2001 年			111 票赞成，29 票反对，21 票弃权 实体部分第 1 句：153 票赞成，4 票反对，2 票弃权	

续表

联合国决议编号	年份	题目	相关表述	投票结果	内容
A/RES/57/85	2002 年	国际法院关于“以核武器进行威胁或使用核武器的合法性”的咨询意见的后续行动	1. 再次强调国际法院的一致结论，认为各国有义务真诚地开展和完成将导致在严格有效的国际监督下实现所有方面的核裁军的谈判； 2. 再次吁请所有国家立即履行上述义务，开展多边谈判，以求早日（无相关时间限制，笔者注）缔结一项禁止发展、生产、试验、部署、储存、转让核武器以及以核武器进行威胁或使用核武器，并规定消除此种武器的公约。	117 票赞成，30 票反对，24 票弃权 实体部分第 1 句：161 票赞成，4 票反对，1 票弃权	谈判义务
A/RES/58/46	2003 年			124 票赞成，29 票反对，22 票弃权 实体部分第 1 句：165 票赞成，4 票反对，3 票弃权	
A/RES/59/83	2004 年			132 票赞成，29 票反对，24 票弃权 实体部分第 1 句：170 票赞成，5 票反对，4 票弃权	
A/RES/60/76	2005 年			126 票赞成，29 票反对，24 票弃权 实体部分第 1 句：165 票赞成，3 票反对，4 票弃权	
A/RES/61/83	2006 年			125 票赞成，27 票反对，29 票弃权 实体部分第 1 句：168 票赞成，3 票反对，5 票弃权	
A/RES/62/39	2007 年			127 票赞成，27 票反对，27 票弃权	
A/RES/63/49	2008 年			127 票赞成，30 票反对，23 票弃权	
A/RES/64/55	2009 年			124 票赞成，31 票反对，21 票弃权	

续表

联合国决议编号	年份	题目	相关表述	投票结果	内容
A/RES/65/76	2010 年	国际法院关于“以核武器进行威胁或使用核武器的合法性”的咨询意见的后续行动		133 票赞成，28 票反对，23 票弃权	谈判义务
A/RES/66/46	2011 年			130 票赞成，26 票反对，23 票弃权	
A/RES/67/33	2012 年			135 票赞成，22 票反对，26 票弃权	
A/RES/68/42	2013 年			133 票赞成，24 票反对，25 票弃权	
A/RES/69/43	2014 年			134 票赞成，23 票反对，23 票弃权	
A/RES/70/56	2015 年			137 票赞成，24 票反对，25 票弃权	
A/RES/71/58	2016 年			136 票赞成，25 票反对，22 票弃权	
A/RES/72/58	2017 年		（引言部分）： 深信核武器的继续存在对人类和地球上的所有生命构成威胁，确认防止核灾难的唯一办法就是彻底消除核武器并确保永远不再生产核武器。 （正文部分）： 1. 再次强调国际法院的一致结论，即各国有义务真诚地开展和完成在严格有效的国际监督下实现所有方面核裁军的谈判； 2. 再次促请所有国家立即开展导致在严格有效的国际监督下，包括根据《禁止核武器条约》，实现所有方面的核裁军的多边谈判。	131 票赞成，31 票反对，18 票弃权 引言部分相关段落：125 票赞成，35 票反对，13 票弃权 实体部分第 2 句：123 票赞成，35 票反对，15 票弃权	实体裁军义务+谈判义务
A/RES/73/64	2018 年			138 票赞成，32 票反对，17 票弃权 实体部分第 2 句：121 票赞成，35 票反对，18 票弃权	

资料来源：

投票结果参见：United Nations Digital Library Voting Data, https://digitallibrary.un.org/search?ln=en&cc=Voting+Data&p=&f=&action_search=Search&rm=&ln=en&sf=&so=d&rg=50&c=Voting+Data&c=&of=hb&fti=0&fti=0；

决议内容参见：https://www.un.org/zh/sections/documents/general-assembly-resolutions/index.html2。

国家同意原则在国际法院咨询管辖权中的作用

——“查戈斯分离咨询意见案”评述

高正霖

摘要：国际法院认定有权在“查戈斯分离咨询意见案”中可以行使咨询管辖权：法院认为国家同意原则可能促使其拒绝行使咨询管辖权，但当事国的政治动机不影响法院行使咨询管辖权，且属于联合国大会职能框架中的议题将限制国家同意原则的适用。同时，法院对于国家同意原则提出了一些新的论述：第一，只有对于受到联合国相关机构“长期且始终”关注的法律问题，法院才不会因缺乏国家同意而拒绝行使咨询管辖权；第二，法院如果判定可以行使咨询管辖权，则可能在缺乏相关国家同意的前提下，通过咨询意见限制其权利，或者为相关国家设立义务。

关键词：国际法院；咨询管辖权；国家同意；查戈斯群岛

国家同意原则反映了国家主权平等，是一项国际法基本原则，得到了联合国国际法院（以下简称法院）的认可。[1]未获得当事国同意，法院对争端不具有诉讼管辖权。[2]对于咨询管辖权而言，法院首先需要判定其是否具有咨询管辖权；在确立了具有管辖权的基础上，法院会进一步考虑是否应当行使咨询管辖权。[3]而国家同意原则是法院判定其是否应当行使咨询管辖权的考量因素之

1 *Case of the Monetary Gold Removed from Rome in 1943, Preliminary Question, Judgment, ICJ Reports 1954,* pp. 19, 32; *Western Sahara, Advisory Opinion, ICJ Reports 1975,* p. 25, para. 33; *Interpretation of Peace Treaties with Bulgaria, Hungary and Romania, First Phase, Advisory Opinion, ICJ Reports 1950,* p. 71.

2 Anders Henriksen, *International Law* (Oxford: Oxford University Press, 2019), p. 235; Malcolm D. Evans *et al.*, *International Law* (Oxford: Oxford University Press, 2014), 4th edn, p. 595.

3 *Legality of the Use by a State of Nuclear Weapons in Armed Conflict, Advisory Opinion, ICJ Reports 1996,* p. 73, para. 14; *Legal Consequences of the Separation of the Chagos Archipelago from Mauritius in 1965, Advisory Opinion,* p.17, para. 54.

一：[4]法院可以（might）基于迫不得已的理由（compelling reasons），拒绝发表咨询意见；[5]但是，如果请求问题涉及的双边冲突源自（arise from）联合国大会正在讨论的议题，法院不应当以缺乏国家同意为由拒绝作出咨询意见。[6]

不可否认，部分国家出于对自身国力或者社会经济因素的考量，企图回避国家同意原则，通过寻求国际或者区域法庭作出判决或者发表咨询意见的方式，强迫其他当事国解决争端。这种做法不仅侵害国家主权原则，同时也会损害相关法庭的公信力。实质上，这种做法也不利于从根本上解决争端，实现国际社会长期和平与稳定。

本文将基于“1965年查戈斯群岛从毛里求斯分裂的法律后果咨询意见案”（以下简称“查戈斯分离咨询意见案”）中法院对于国家同意原则的论述，厘清法院在该案中决定行使咨询管辖权的理由；同时，结合法院过往的咨询意见，分析利益相关国家的同意在何种程度上会影响法院咨询管辖权的行使；最后，探讨“查戈斯分离咨询意见案”中，法院所提出的关于国家同意原则影响其行使咨询管辖权的新论述及其影响。

一、“查戈斯分离咨询意见案”概述

（一）案件背景

2017年6月22日，联合国大会通过第71/292号决议，请求法院就查戈斯群岛1965年从毛里求斯分裂的法律后果发表咨询意见。[7]法院2019年2月5日作出了咨询意见，判定法院可以对该案行使咨询管辖权，并且毛里求斯的非殖民化进程在该国独立时尚未结束，英国需要尽快结束其在查戈斯群岛的管辖。[8]

法院在事实认定部分查明，在毛里求斯获得独立之前，查戈斯群岛是毛里

---

4 *Western Sahara,* p. 25, para. 33; *Legal Consequences of the Separation of the Chagos Archipelago,* p. 22, para. 85.

5 *Western Sahara,* p. 25, para. 33.

6 *Legal Consequences of the Construction of a Legal Consequences of the Construction of a Wall in the Occupied Palestinian Territory , Advisory Opinion, ICJ Reports 2004,* p. 158, para. 47.

7 *Request for an Advisory Opinion of the International Court of Justice on the Legal Consequences of the Separation of the Chagos Archipelago from Mauritius in 1965,* United Nation General Assembly (UNGA), A/RES/71/292, 2017.

8 *Legal Consequences of the Separation of the Chagos Archipelago,* pp. 43-44, para. 183.

求斯的附属群岛。[9]1964 年，美国向英国表示其希望在查戈斯群岛设立军事基地，[10] 英国为此建立了英属印度洋领地（British Indian Ocean Territory），其范围包括查戈斯群岛。[11] 这一行为引起了联合国大会以及联合国非殖民化专门委员会（以下简称第二十四委员会）的关注，并导致联合国作出了 1965 年第 2066（XX）号决议、1966 年第 2232（XXI）号决议，以及 1967 年第 2357（XXII）号决议，敦促英国停止分裂毛里求斯领土主权的行为。[12]1965 年 11 月，英国政府为正当化其行为，在毛里求斯独立前，与殖民统治下的毛里求斯政府签订了《兰开斯特宫承诺》（*Lancaster House Undertakings*），毛里求斯政府同意分离查戈斯群岛。[13] 随后，1966 年 12 月，英国与美国签署了《关于将英属印度洋领地用于军事用途的协定》（以下简称《1966 年协定》），同意授予美国对该地区 50 年的使用期限。[14]1968 年，毛里求斯独立。但直到 1980 年，毛里求斯未就查戈斯群岛问题提出过异议。[15]1980 年后，毛里求斯先后在多个国际场合明确反对英国分离查戈斯群岛的做法，并在 2010 年申请依照《联合国海洋法公约》附件七组建了仲裁庭，就英国在查戈斯群岛周围建立海洋保护区问题进行仲裁。2015 年仲裁庭作出裁决，认定两国之间的争端实质是关于查戈斯群岛的主权争端，而非关于《联合国海洋法公约》解释和适用的争端，遂以缺乏管辖权为由，拒绝审理部分诉求。[16]2016 年，《1966 年协定》中规定的 50 年使用期到期，英国与美国达成新协议，将该期限延长 20 年。[17]

---

9 *Legal Consequences of the Separation of the Chagos Archipelago,* p.13, para. 29.

10 *Legal Consequences of the Separation of the Chagos Archipelago,* p.13, para. 31.

11 *Legal Consequences of the Separation of the Chagos Archipelago,* p.14, para. 33.

12 UNGA,UN Doc A/RES/2066 (XX), 1965; UNGA, UN Doc A/RES/2232 (XXI), 1966; UNGA, UN Doc A/RES/2357 (XXII), 1967.

13 *Legal Consequences of the Separation of the Chagos Archipelago,* p. 28, paras. 110-112.

14 *Legal Consequences of the Separation of the Chagos Archipelago,* p.14, para. 36.

15 *Legal Consequences of the Separation of the Chagos Archipelago from Mauritius in 1965 (Requested by the United Nations General Assembly for an Advisory Opinion) Written Comments of the United Kingdom and Northern Ireland (15 February 2018),* p. 76, para. 5.6.

16 *In the Matter of the Chagos Maritime Protection Area Arbitration (Mauritius/United Kingdom),* Award of 18 March 2015, p. 90, para. 221; *Legal Consequences of the Separation of the Chagos Archipelago,* pp.15-16, paras. 45-50.

17 *Legal Consequences of the Separation of the Chagos Archipelago,* p.16, para. 51.

（二）“查戈斯分离咨询意见案”中对国家同意原则的考量

在分析实体问题之前，咨询意见着重论述了法院是否可以行使咨询管辖权。法院的裁判大致可以分为三部分。首先，法院认可，缺乏利益相关国同意可能构成迫不得已的理由，使法院拒绝行使咨询管辖权；但原则上，法院不会拒绝发表咨询意见。[18] 在本案中，联合国大会的请求旨在寻求法院的协助，解决毛里求斯非殖民化进程的问题，而非为了解决双边冲突；法院发表咨询意见仅是为了协助联合国大会完成其职能。[19] 其次，法院认为，非殖民化作为联合国大会长期且始终（long and consistent）致力于完成的职责之一，是联合国大会的关注焦点（particular concern），因此，意见所涉法律问题应当被置于非殖民化的广阔历史背景中考虑。[20] 最后，虽然争端当事方可能对于咨询意见所涉法律问题存在显著分歧，但存在分歧本身并不意味着，法院就该法律问题发表咨询意见相当于解决双边争端。[21] 基于上述理由，法院认为其不应当因国家同意原则而拒绝行使咨询管辖权。

二、国家同意原则在法院咨询意见中的适用

（一）法院对国家同意原则的谨慎态度

《国际法院规约》（以下简称《规约》）第 65 条第 1 款和《联合国宪章》（以下简称《宪章》）第 96 条是关于咨询管辖权的主要法律规定。[22] 虽然这两条没有明确要求获得相关国家同意是法院建立咨询管辖权的前提，但是基于法院以往发表的咨询意见，各国倾向于以缺乏国家同意为由，要求法院拒绝行使管辖权，而非否定法院具有管辖权。[23]

---

18 *Legal Consequences of the Separation of the Chagos Archipelago,* p. 22, para. 85.

19 *Legal Consequences of the Separation of the Chagos Archipelago,* pp. 22-23, para. 86.

20 *Legal Consequences of the Separation of the Chagos Archipelago,* p. 23, paras. 87-88.

21 *Legal Consequences of the Separation of the Chagos Archipelago,* p. 23, para. 89.

22 《规约》第 65 条第 1 款规定：“1. 法院对于任何法律问题如经任何团体由《联合国宪章》授权而请求或依照《联合国宪章》而请求时，得发表咨询意见。”《宪章》第 96 条规定：“1. 大会或安全理事会对于任何法律问题得请国际法院发表咨询意见。2. 联合国其他机关及各种专门机关，对于其工作范围内之任何法律问题，得随时以大会之授权，请求国际法院发表咨询意见。”

23 Andreas Zimmermann *et al.*, *The Statute of the International Court of Justice: A Commentary* (Oxford University Press, 2012), 2nd edn, p. 1617, para. 33.

综观法院及其前身常设国际法院迄今审理的全部咨询意见案，仅有一起案件法院以缺乏国家同意为由，拒绝发表咨询意见。[24] 在 1923 年“东卡雷利亚地位咨询意见案”中，常设国际法院拒绝发表咨询意见，理由是：苏联既不是《常设国际法院规约》成员国，也不是国际联盟会员国；且苏联不同意依照《国际联盟盟约》第 17 条规定，接受国际联盟参与解决其与芬兰的冲突。因此，由于缺乏苏联的同意，常设国际法院无法作出一个对苏联既得权产生不利影响的咨询意见。[25]此外，因为该咨询意见涉及双边争端，苏联作为当事方之一拒绝参与程序，使常设国际法院无法就该双边争端发表合理的咨询意见。[26]在国际法院时期，1923 年“东卡雷利亚地位咨询意见案”被相关国家多次援引，作为否定法院行使咨询管辖权的先例。但是法院在多个咨询意见中明确指出了该案的特殊之处：拒绝行使管辖权是因为苏联既不是《常设国际法院规约》成员国，也不是国际联盟会员国。[27] 由于目前几乎所有国家均是《国际法院规约》成员国或者联合国会员国，1923 年“东卡雷利亚地位咨询意见案”的现实意义已降低。[28]

虽然 1923 年“东卡雷利亚地位咨询意见案”的参考价值已降低，但这并不否定国家同意原则依然是法院判定是否应当行使咨询管辖权时的重要考虑因素。正如法院在 1970 年“西撒哈拉咨询意见案”中一段被广为引用的判词所言：“在特殊情况下，缺乏国家同意可能使得法院在违背其司法性质（judicial character）的情况下发表咨询意见。”[29]如果法院认为，回复该咨询意见请求可能导致争端当事方以缺乏国家同意的方式解决双边冲突，法院有权基于迫不得已的理由，拒绝行使咨询管辖权。但自 1923 年“东卡雷利亚地位咨询意见案”至今，法院并未以缺乏国家同意为由，拒绝发表咨询意见。[30] 由此可见，法院对

---

24 国际法院处理的咨询意见案详见：“Advisory Proceedings,” https://www.icj-cij.org/en/advisory-proceedings (Last visited on 6 July 2020)。

25 *Status of Eastern Carelia, Advisory Opinion of 23 July 1923, P.C.I.J., Series B, No. 5,* pp. 27-28.

26 *Status of Eastern Carelia, Advisory Opinion of 23 July 1923, P.C.I.J., Series B, No. 5,* pp. 28-29.

27 *Western Sahara,* pp. 23-24, para. 30; *Legal Consequences for States of the continued Presence of South Africa in Namibia (South West Africa) notwithstanding Security Council Resolution 276 (1970), Advisory Opinion, ICJ Reports 1971,* pp. 23-24, para. 31; *Legality of the Threat or Use of Nuclear Weapons, Advisory Opinion, ICJ Reports 1996,* pp. 235-236, para. 14.

28 R. Kolb, *The Elgar Companion to the International Court of Justice* (Cheltenham: Edward Elgar Publishing, 2014), p. 273.

29 *Western Sahara,*p. 25, para. 33.

30 国际法院处理的咨询意见案详见：“Advisory Proceedings,” https://www.icj-cij.org/en/advisory-proceedings (Last visited on July 6, 2020)。

利用国家同意原则阻却其咨询管辖权的行使，采取了一种极为谨慎的态度。

法院采取这种谨慎态度的原因在于，咨询管辖与诉讼管辖之间存在较大区别。在 1950 年“与保加利亚、匈牙利和罗马尼亚的和平条约的解释咨询意见案”（以下简称 1950 年“和平条约咨询意见案”）中，法院认为咨询意见的作用是为联合国认为有必要的事项提供指引（enlightenment）；作出咨询意见体现的是法院作为联合国机关之一，参与联合国的活动；况且咨询意见是向请求意见的联合国机关作出，并非面向单独的国家作出。[31] 因此，除非有迫不得已的原因，法院认为其在原则上不应当拒绝发表咨询意见。[32] 作为联合国唯一的司法机关，法院需要发挥其在联合国中的关键作用：以提供法律咨询的方式辅助其他机关完成职能。[33] 如果法院轻易拒绝联合国大会或其他适格主体的咨询意见请求，那么将导致相关机关难以获得必要的司法协助，从而无法更好地解决其面临的问题，这将从整体上掣肘联合国发挥其维持国际和平与安全的职能。因此，法院原则上不会拒绝作出咨询意见。这也就增加了以缺乏国家同意为由，要求法院拒绝发表咨询意见的难度。

（二）当事国政治动机的无关性

在考量是否拒绝发表咨询意见的过程中，法院并不关注国家向联合国大会提交咨询管辖申请的动机，而更看重请求咨询意见的国际组织的职能。[34]

在“查戈斯分离咨询意见案”中，虽然毛里求斯将查戈斯群岛问题提交多个国际组织以及国际法庭寻求解决，并且其官员在多个场合坦言，查戈斯群岛问题实质上就是双边领土主权问题，[35] 但是法院在咨询意见中并未对此有任何论

31　*Interpretation of Peace Treaties,* p.71.

32　*Legal Consequences of the Construction of a Wall,* p. 156, para. 44; *Accordance with International Law of the Unilateral Declaration of Independence in respect of Kosovo, Advisory Opinion, ICJ Reports 2010,* p. 416, para. 30.

33　*Interpretation of Peace Treaties,* p. 71; *Difference Relating to Immunity from Legal Process of a Special Rapporteur of the Commission on Human Rights, Advisory Opinion, ICJ Reports 1999,* pp. 78-79, para. 29; *Legal Consequences of the Construction of a Wall,* p. 156, para. 44.

34　法院唯一一次拒绝作出咨询意见的理由正是，咨询管辖申请的内容不属于提出该申请的国际组织章程的范畴。See *Legality of the Use by a State of Nuclear Weapons in Armed Conflict,* p. 84, para. 31.

35　*Legal Consequences of the Separation of the Chagos Archipelago Written Comments of the United Kingdom and Northern Ireland (15 February 2018),* pp. 75-85, paras. 5.3-5.21; *Legal*

述，而是着重强调了联合国大会在非殖民化问题上的“长期且始终”（long and consistent）的努力。[36] 正如法院在 2010 年“科索沃单方宣布独立是否符合国际法咨询意见案”（以下简称 2010 年“科索沃咨询意见案”）中所强调的：提请或者支持联合国大会向法院提交咨询意见申请的国家的动机，不是法院是否行使咨询管辖的考虑内容。[37] 在 1996 年“威胁使用或使用核武器的合法性咨询意见案”中，法院表明：提出咨询意见申请的起因、政治历史背景，或者是该申请在联合国大会的表决情况，均不是法院决定是否行使咨询管辖权的考虑因素。[38]

政治问题和法律问题是紧密相连的，很多法律问题不可避免地会掺杂政治因素。在法院以往的咨询意见中，有许多法律问题都涉及了敏感的政治议题。例如，纳米比亚情势、[39] 以色列在巴勒斯坦被占领土上修建隔离墙的合法性问题，[40] 以及科索沃单方宣告独立的合法性问题，[41] 等等。由此可见，法院不会仅仅因为一个法律问题中存在政治因素就拒绝作出咨询意见。[42] 事实上，正是因为受到政治因素的羁绊，相关国际组织才向法院寻求咨询意见，期望从法律的角度理性看待并解决相关问题。[43]

（三）属于联合国职能框架中的议题将限制国家同意原则的适用

在法院以往的咨询意见中，咨询意见请求涉及的事项均已进入联合国大会或者安理会的讨论。在 1971 年“南非不顾安全理事会第 276（1970）号决议继续留驻纳米比亚（西南非洲）对各国的法律后果咨询意见案”（以下简称 1971 年“纳米比亚咨询意见案”）中，法院出具意见的背景是，联合国安理会第 276

Consequences of the Separation of the Chagos Archipelago Written Comments of the United States of America (1 March 2018), pp. 3-7, paras. 2.10-2.22.

36 *Legal Consequences of the Separation of the Chagos Archipelago,* p. 23, para. 87.

37 *Unilateral Declaration of Independence in respect of Kosovo,* pp. 416-417, para. 33.

38 *Legality of the Threat or Use of Nuclear Weapons,* p. 237, para. 16.

39 *Legal Consequences for States of the Continued Presence of South Africa in Namibia,* p. 16.

40 *Legal Consequences of the Construction of a Wall,* p.136.

41 *Unilateral Declaration of Independence in Respect of Kosovo,* p. 403.

42 *Application for Review of Judgment No. 158 of the United Nations Administrative Tribunal, Advisory Opinion, ICJ Reports 1973,* p. 172, para. 14; *Legality of the Threat or Use of Nuclear Weapons,* p. 234, para. 13; *Legal Consequences of the Construction of a Wall,* p. 155, para. 41; *Unilateral Declaration of Independence in respect of Kosovo,* p. 415, para. 27.

43 *Interpretation of the Agreement of 25 March 1951 between the WHO and Egypt, Advisory Opinion, ICJ Reports 1982,* p. 87, para. 33.

（1970）号决议表明南非在纳米比亚的持续存在不符合国际法，并且号召南非执行该决议的内容。[44] 在 1970 年“西撒哈拉咨询意见案”中，法院也认可了西撒哈拉问题是在联合国大会的讨论过程中产生的，[45]因此该问题不应当被认为是独立产生和发展的一个双边冲突，[46]法院的咨询意见将协助联合国大会发挥其在西撒哈拉执行非殖民化职能。[47] 同样的观点也得到 2004 年“巴勒斯坦被占领土上修建隔离墙法律后果咨询意见案”（以下简称 2004 年“隔离墙咨询意见案”）的支持：该案件涉及以色列与巴勒斯坦的双边争端，但是考虑到联合国维护世界和平与安全的职责，尤其是根据联合国大会第 57/107 号决议，按照国际法，联合国大会负有解决巴勒斯坦问题的永久责任。此外，还需要考虑到联合国通过了巴勒斯坦委任统治和分治决议，并且安理会和联合国大会在其组织框架中通过了多个决议，建立了若干专门辅助机构以帮助实现巴勒斯坦人民不可剥夺的权利。[48]因此，法院认为该双边冲突落入了（located in）联合国大会更广泛的职能框架中，法院不应当以缺乏国家同意为由拒绝作出咨询意见。[49]

在“查戈斯分离咨询意见案”中，法院延续其在 1970 年“西撒哈拉咨询意见案”与 2004 年“隔离墙咨询意见案”中的观点。[50] 作为联合国大会“长期且始终”关注的议题，法院可以对查戈斯群岛问题作出咨询意见。[51]

三、“查戈斯分离咨询意见案”对国家同意原则的发展

“查戈斯分离咨询意见案”中，法院延续了以往咨询意见所确立的原则，没有基于国家同意原则拒绝行使咨询管辖权。但是，法院对于咨询管辖也提出了新的看法。

（一）将“长期且始终”作为联合国大会职能框架议题的判断标准

针对“查戈斯分离咨询意见案”，英国主张该案属于双边争端，因此，如果

44 *Legal Consequences for States of the Continued Presence of South Africa in Namibia*, p. 45.

45 *Western Sahara,* p. 25, para. 34.

46 *Western Sahara,* p. 26, para. 38.

47 *Western Sahara,* pp.18-19, para. 39.

48 *Legal Consequences of the Construction of a Wall,* p. 159, para. 49.

49 *Legal Consequences of the Construction of a Wall*, p. 159, para. 50.

50 *Legal Consequences of the Separation of the Chagos Archipelago,* p. 23, paras. 88, 90.

51 *Legal Consequences of the Separation of the Chagos Archipelago,* p. 23, para. 87.

缺乏当事方英国的同意，法院不能行使咨询管辖权。[52] 英国认为，自毛里求斯1968年独立之后，查戈斯群岛非殖民化问题并未进入联合国大会或者安理会的讨论，因而该案事实上不涉及非殖民化问题。[53] 正如部分法官在2010年“科索沃咨询意见案”的反对意见中所言，如果联合国大会没有将请求法院发表咨询意见的事项纳入其讨论计划中，则可以认为联合国大会就该事项获得咨询意见不具有充分的利益基础（a sufficient interest）。[54]

对于上述观点，在“查戈斯分离咨询意见案”中，法院认为：只有相关法律问题受到联合国相关机构“长期且始终”的关注，才能够认定该法律问题“落入联合国大会的更广泛的职能框架”中，法院才不会因缺乏国家同意而拒绝行使咨询管辖权。[55]“长期且始终”这一判断标准，有效弥补了之前咨询意见中可能存在的漏洞。个别国家可能将法院的咨询意见作为规避国家同意的借口，扩大解读法院咨询意见：将凡是被认为危及国际社会和平与安全的双边冲突，都解释成违反《宪章》第39条的规定，从而主张其属于联合国的关注事项，进而要求法院在缺乏当事国同意的前提下，对这些双边冲突作出咨询意见。[56] 这将构成对国家同意原则的极大危害。[57] 因为仅仅是进入联合国的讨论范畴尚不足以认定为“落入了联合国大会的更广泛的职能框架”中，这种讨论必须是“长期且始终”的。以非殖民化为例：自从联合国成立以来，非殖民化进程始终是联合国大会关注的核心议题；[58]联合国在过去的数十年中，通过民族自决的方

---

52 *Legal Consequences of the Separation of the Chagos Archipelago Written Comments of the United Kingdom and Northern Ireland (15 February 2018),* p. 116, para. 7.21.

53 *Legal Consequences of the Separation of the Chagos Archipelago Written Comments of the United Kingdom and Northern Ireland (14 May 2018),* p. 48, para. 3.18 (a). 英国的观点也得到了美国的支持，See *Legal Consequences of the Separation of the Chagos Archipelago Written Comments of the United States of America (15 May 2018),* p. 12, paras. 2.24-2.25; pp. 13-14, paras. 3.22-3.23。

54 *Unilateral Declaration of Independence in respect of Kosovo, Declaration of Judge Tomka,* paras. 2, 5; *Unilateral Declaration of Independence in respect of Kosovo, Dissenting Opinion of Judge Bennouna,* paras. 19-20.

55 *Legal Consequences of the Separation of the Chagos Archipelago*, pp. 23-24, paras. 86-89.

56 *Legal Consequences of the Separation of the Chagos Archipelago Written Comments of the United Kingdom and Northern Ireland (2 February 2018),* pp. 103-104, para. 7.9.

57 Andreas Zimmermann *et al*, *The Statute of the International Court of Justice: A Commentary* (Oxford: Oxford University Press, 2012), 2nd edn, p.1618, para. 36.

58 Julia Wagner, “The Chagos Request and the Role of the Consent Principle in the ICJ’s Advisory Jurisdiction, or: What to Do When Opportunity Knocks,” *Questions of International Law*, Vol. 55, 2018, p.184.

式在多个国家实现了非殖民化，为促进世界和平与稳定作出了重要贡献。[59]《宪章》第 1 条规定了各国权利平等以及民族自决的权利；第 73 条要求各会员国将其所管理的非自治领土的“经济、社会及教育情形之统计及具有专门性质之情报，递送秘书长，以供参考”。1960 年，联合国大会通过第 1514（XV）号决议，这标志着非殖民化问题成为联合国大会关注的核心议题之一；同时，该决议重申了非殖民化进程中应当尊重相关国家的主权和领土完整。[60] 同一年，联合国大会又通过了第 1541（XV）号决议，进一步明确了会员国向联合国汇报其管理下非自治领土信息的流程以及原则。[61]联合国大会第四委员会以及其后的联合国非殖民化特别委员会负责关注世界去殖民化进程和相关民族自决问题。[62] 就查戈斯群岛的问题，联合国大会先后作出了 1965 年第 2066（XX）号决议、1966 年第 2232（XXI）号决议以及 1967 年第 2357（XXII）号决议，敦促英国停止分裂毛里求斯领土主权的行为，遵守并执行联合国大会第 1514（XV）号决议，并要求联合国非殖民化委员会持续关注该问题。[63] 因此，明显可见，非殖民化议题受到联合国大会“长期且始终”的关注，属于联合国大会更广泛的职能框架中，法院不应当以缺乏国家同意为由拒绝作出咨询意见。

但不可否认，法院对于“长期且始终”这一标准的定义依然较为模糊宽泛。如上文所述，“查戈斯分离咨询意见案”被放置在非殖民化这一特殊的历史背景下，而非殖民化问题毋庸置疑属于联合国长期关注的事项，[64] 且联合国大会针对查戈斯群岛分离问题专门作出了决议。因此法院在该咨询意见中，并没

59 Antonio Cassese, *Self-Determination of Peoples: A Legal Reappraisal* (Cambridge University Press, 1998), pp. 76-79; Ralph Wilde, *International Territorial Administration: How Trusteeship and the Civilizing Mission Never Went Away* (Oxford University Press, 2008), pp.161-188.

60 *Declaration on the Granting of Independence to Colonial Countries and People,* UNGA, A/RES/1514(XV), 1960, para. 6.

61 *Principles which Should Guide Members in Determining whether or not an Obligation Exists to Transmit the Information Called for Under Article 73 E of the Charter*, UNGA, A/RES/1541(XV), 1960.

62 *Legal Consequences of the Separation of the Chagos Archipelago,* p. 39, paras. 163-167.

63 UNGA, UN Doc A/RES/2066(XX), 1965, pp. 57-58; UNGA, UN Doc A/RES/2232 (XXI), 1966, pp.74-75; UNGA, UN Doc A/RES/2357(XXII), 1967; UNGA, UN Doc A/RES/ 1514(XV), 1960; *Legal Consequences of the Separation of the Chagos Archipelago,* pp. 39-40, paras.163-169.

64 Antonio Cassese, *Self-Determination of Peoples: A Legal Reappraisal* (Cambridge University Press, 1998), pp. 76-79; Ralph Wilde, *International Territorial Administration: How Trusteeship and the Civilizing Mission Never Went Away* (Oxford University Press, 2008), pp.161-188.

有详细论述何为“长期”？如何界定“始终”？譬如，对于“长期且始终”的判断可以按照一项争端曾经是否被列入联合国相关机构的讨论议程来判定吗？抑或一项争端是否只有经过联合国相关机构反复且实质的讨论，并最终形成了决议，才符合“长期且始终”的判定标准？此外，如果一项法律争端被认为违反了《宪章》所确立的基本原则，但尚未有联合国相关机构对其作出具体决议，则该争端是否属于联合国相关机构“长期且始终”的关注？例如，一国情报机构干涉他国总统选举，抑或一国军机未经事先许可进入他国领空执行反恐任务等。法院在上述情形下是否可以基于不干涉他国内政原则，或者国家主权原则，认定相关法律争端受到联合国相关机构“长期且始终”的关注，从而行使咨询管辖权？

国家同意原则实际上是国家主权原则的体现。如何在尊重国家主权与协助联合国政治机关解决争端之间取得平衡，需要法院在作出咨询意见时仔细权衡。一方面，如果法院不顾国家主权，一味接受联合国其他机构的申请，在缺乏国家同意的前提下作出咨询意见，那么这不仅将有损法院的司法正当性，还很可能导致相关国家拒绝认可法院咨询意见的有效性，使争端依然无法得到真正解决。另一方面，如果法院过分受制于国家主权原则，一旦意见所涉问题的当事国不同意就拒绝发表咨询意见，则无法充分有效发挥其作为联合国司法机关的作用。毕竟如法院所言，咨询管辖不同于诉讼管辖，作出咨询意见体现的是法院作为联合国机关之一参与联合国活动的职能，并且咨询意见是向请求机关作出，并非面向个体国家。[65]正是基于此，法院提出了“长期且始终”的标准：只有相关法律问题受到联合国相关机构“长期且始终”的关注，法院才不会因为缺乏国家同意而拒绝行使咨询管辖权。通过设立较高的标准，法院在力图防止国家通过滥用国际政治组织多数表决的方式，解决国家间争端的同时，也发挥了其通过司法方式协助联合国机关行使职能的作用。但是该标准的具体认定标准依然较为模糊，需要法院在今后的咨询意见中进行不断发展和完善。

（二）法院可能在缺乏国家同意的情况下影响国家的权利和义务

在 1950 年“和平条约咨询意见案”中，法院认为联合国大会并没有请求法院关注条约的实体性问题，因此该申请事项仅限于条约中关于争端解决的程序性问题，其咨询意见不会对各当事方的法律地位产生影响。[66]在 1970 年“西

65 *Interpretation of Peace Treaties*, p. 71.

66 *Unilateral Declaration of Independence in respect of Kosovo*, p. 72.

撒哈拉咨询意见案”中，法院明确表示西班牙作为西撒哈拉委任统治国的地位不会受到其咨询意见的影响，特别是联合国大会 1974 年第 3292（XXIX）号决议认可了西班牙当时作为（西撒哈拉）委任统治国的地位。[67] 在 1989 年“关于《联合国特权与豁免公约》第 6 条第 22 节适用问题的咨询意见案”中，法院区分了《联合国特权与豁免公约》的可适用性（applicability）以及如何适用（application）两个问题；法院为了避免违反国家同意原则，仅仅就该公约的可适用性问题发表了咨询意见，而不涉及如何适用该公约。[68]

“查戈斯分离咨询意见案”的情势则略有不同，法院的咨询意见不可避免地影响了英国的具体权利和义务。该咨询意见涉及两个问题，其中第二个问题关注：根据国际法义务，英国继续管理查戈斯群岛将产生何种后果，包括对毛里求斯无法执行在查戈斯群岛重新安置其国民尤其是原查戈斯群岛岛民的计划的后果。为了判断非殖民化进程是否结束，法院在咨询意见中必须认定英国与毛里求斯 1965 年签订的《兰开斯特宫承诺》的有效性问题。法院不认为《兰开斯特宫承诺》是国际协议：首先，该文件是殖民时期的毛里求斯政府与英国签订的；其次，该协议不能够反映毛里求斯人民的真实意愿。[69] 此外，由于《兰卡斯特宫承诺》的无效性，法院认为英国应当尽速完成毛里求斯的非殖民化进程，并有义务尽快终止其在查戈斯群岛的行政管理。[70] 这实质上承认了毛里求斯对查戈斯群岛居民行使一定的主权权利，进而直接影响英国在该群岛上的既得权。[71] 虽然法院援引了 2010 年“科索沃咨询意见案”的观点，主张应由联合国大会决定执行非殖民化进程的方式，[72] 但是联合国大会在 2017 年第 71/292 号决议中明确，请求法院基于国际法，认定英国继续管理查戈斯群岛将产生何种后果。换言之，联合国司法机关依照国际法发表了“查戈斯分离咨询意见”。[73] 事实上，

67　*Western Sahara,*p. 27, paras. 42-43.

68　*Applicability of Article VI, Section 22, of the Convention on the Privileges and Immunities of the United Nations, Advisory Opinion, ICJ Reports 1989,*p. 191, para. 38.

69　*Legal Consequences of the Separation of the Chagos Archipelago,* pp. 40-41, para.172.

70　*Legal Consequences of the Separation of the Chagos Archipelago,* p. 42, para.179; p. 43, para.182.

71　*Legal Consequences of the Separation of the Chagos Archipelago Written Comments of the United Kingdom and Northern Ireland (2 February 2018),* pp.110-111, para. 7.16.

72　*Unilateral Declaration of Independence in respect of Kosovo,* p. 421, para. 44.

73　*Legal Consequences of the Separation of the Chagos Archipelago Written Comments of the United Kingdom and Northern Ireland (14 May 2018),* p. 46, para. 3.14.

这是在规避英国同意的前提下，直接限制了英国在查戈斯群岛上的权力。当然，法院的这种做法并非无先例可循。在 2004 年“隔离墙咨询意见案”中，法院就以巴以双边冲突落入了联合国大会更广泛的职能框架中、属于其“长期且始终”关注的事项为由，拒绝了因缺乏国家同意而放弃行使咨询管辖权，并且法院在咨询意见中为以色列设定了诸多义务。[74] 但是 2004 年“隔离墙咨询意见案”并不涉及判定一项协议的有效性问题。然而，法院在“查戈斯分离咨询意见案”中直接认定《兰开斯特宫承诺》不是一项有效的国际协议，进而判定毛里求斯的非殖民化进程尚未结束，从而要求英国尽速结束其对查戈斯群岛的管理。

当然，我们必须注意到，法院强调，由于咨询意见不同于诉讼判决，不具有法律拘束力，[75] 因此，咨询意见是否被采纳以及在何种程度上被执行，完全取决于请求机关。理论上，法院的咨询意见不会影响当事方的权利与义务，但是在实践中，法院作出的咨询意见具有相当重要的效力。在法院作出 2004 年“隔离墙咨询意见案”后，联合国大会于 2004 年召开特别会议，通过 A/RES/ES-10/15 决议。决议中强调了“尊重国际法院及其职能是在国际事务中以法和以理服人所必不可少的”，并且“要求占领国以色列履行咨询意见中提及的法律义务”。[76] 同样，在法院作出 2004 年“科索沃咨询意见案”判决后，联合国大会在 2010 年通过了 A/RES/64/298 号决议，承认了法院的咨询意见，并欢迎欧盟做好促进建立科索沃对话机制的准备。[77] 不可否认的是，如果作为联合国司法机关的法院的咨询意见认定一国行为不符合国际法，会使得该国继续坚持其行为合法性的主张更加难以被世界各国所接受。[78] 由此可见，法院作出的咨询意

---

74 *Legal Consequences of the Construction of a Wall,* pp. 201-203, para. 163.

75 *Interpretation of Peace Treaties,* p. 71.

76 *Advisory opinion of the International Court of Justice on the Legal Consequences of the Construction of a Legal Consequences of the Construction of a Wall in the Occupied Palestinian Territory in the Occupied Palestinian Territory, including in and around East Jerusalem,* UNGA, A/RES/ES-10/15, 2004.

77 *Request for an Advisory Opinion of the International Court of Justice on Whether the Unilateral Declaration of Independence of Accordance with International Law of the Unilateral Declaration of Independence in respect of Kosovo is in accordance with International Law,* UNGA, A/RES/64/298, 2010.

78 Malcolm D. Evans *et al*, *International Law* (Oxford: Oxford University Press, 2014), p. 611.

见仍然具有重要的法律意义。[79]

结论

作为一项国际法基本原则，国家同意原则得到了法院的认可。但是，由于《规约》第 65 条没有明确限制法院在确立咨询管辖权阶段需要考虑国家同意，这为部分国家利用法院咨询意见规避国家同意原则提供了可能。基于对法院过往咨询意见的分析可以发现：首先，法院可以因为缺乏相关国家的同意而拒绝发表咨询意见；其次，对于因国家同意原则而拒绝行使咨询管辖权的问题，法院采取了一种谨慎的态度，因为作为联合国的司法机关，为了辅助联合国政治机关解决争端，法院原则上不会拒绝发表咨询意见；再次，在判断是否应当行使咨询管辖权时，法院主要关注提出咨询管辖请求的联合国机关的职责，而非向联合国机关提交争议的国家的政治动机；最后，如果一项请求属于联合国大会更广泛的职能框架中，法院不会以缺乏国家同意为由而拒绝发表咨询意见。

法院在“查戈斯分离咨询意见案”中延续了上述以往咨询意见中形成的结论，同时又有所突破。首先，法院进一步明确界定了“落入联合国大会更广泛的职能框架”的判断标准——只有相关法律问题受到联合国相关机构“长期且始终”的关注，法院才不会因缺乏国家同意而拒绝行使咨询管辖权。这体现出法院通过设立较高的标准力图防止国家滥用国际政治组织的多数表决解决国家间争端。其次，法院如果判定可以行使咨询管辖权，则可能在缺乏相关国家同意的前提下，通过咨询意见限制其权利，或者为相关国家设立义务。但此种影响的实际意义有多大，值得深思。正如“查戈斯分离咨询意见案”之后发生的情况，因为咨询意见没有法律拘束力，即使咨询意见本身为相关国家设定了义务，相关国家依然无国际法义务去履行。

79　Andreas Zimmermann *et al*, *The Statute of the International Court of Justice: A Commentary* (Oxford University Press, 2012), 2nd edn p.1621, para. 45; 宋岩：《国家同意原则对国际法院行使咨询管辖权的限制——兼论“查戈斯群岛咨询意见案”的管辖权问题》，《国际法研究》2018 年第 1 期，第 10 页。

国际野生动物保护条约中的“科学例外”研究

陈然

摘要：“科学例外”是国际野生动物保护条约中较为常见的一种例外许可。出于改善生物种群的生存状态、促进生物多样性发展的需求，“科学例外”有助于人们更好地了解生物种群的生活方式、遗传基因和种群状态。因此，许多野生动物保护条约允许国家通过制定“科学例外”，对受保护的野生动物进行捕杀或捉捕。但是，由于“科学例外”的表述及适用较为宽泛，缺乏官方解释，使“科学例外”可能成为某些国家实现自身利益、追求经济效益的法律漏洞，也直接限制了国际野生动物保护条约的拘束力与有效性。本文通过梳理各项国际野生动物保护条约中“科学例外”的表述及适用，归纳总结认定“科学例外”的原则与方法，并对“科学例外”的发展进行展望。

关键词：“科学例外”；科学研究；为了科研目的；野生动物

引言

随着人类活动与全球化的不断发展，环境问题的全球性逐渐凸显，越来越成为国际社会关注的焦点。其中，人类活动对野生动物的生存环境和生存状态产生了巨大的负面影响。因此，国际社会通过制定各项国际野生动物保护条约，对人类的活动加以限制，以减少人类对野生动物的干扰，改善生物种群的生存状态，促进生物多样性发展。

虽然各项国际野生动物保护条约严格限制人类对受保护野生动物的捕猎、捕杀或进出口贸易，并设立了专门的科学研究机构，建立了汇报等监督机制，但是许多条约仍通过“人工繁殖”“为了科学研究（for scientific research）”“为了科研目的（for the purpose of scientific research）”“文化传统”等例外条件，[1]允许部分人类对受保护动物的干扰行为。其中，“为了科学研究目的”构成的“科学例外（scientific exemption）”由于其判断标准不明，[2]相关国家实践和学术研究

1　详见本文第一部分及附表 1：“规定‘科学例外’的主要国际野生动物保护条约及其情况”。

2　Patricia Birnie, Alan Boyle, *International Law and the Environment* (Oxford University Press, 1994), p. 441.

存在一定的空白，许多国家以此为借口，[3]进行捕杀活动，在科学研究的掩饰下从事野生动物商业贸易，为国际野生动物多样性带来了较大威胁。[4]这种“科学例外”的实践逐渐成为某些国家规避国家责任的一种方式，不仅削弱了相关条约保护生物多样性、促进生物资源可持续发展的能力，还在实质上对受保护的野生动物造成了不可逆的伤害。因此，亟须明确“科学例外”的判断标准，以保障各项国际野生动物保护条约的宗旨及目的得到有效落实。这既需防止人类活动对野生动物资源的危害，明确国际不法行为的国家责任，又需在合理的范围内推动动物保护和人类社会的共同进步。

本文主要分为三个部分：首先，总结主要国际野生动物保护条约中关于“科学例外”的规定，介绍相关条约的基本情况；其次，分析“科学例外”的相关解释及适用，归纳认定“科学例外”的原则与标准；最后，分析“科学例外”适用中突出存在的监管问题，指出未来“科学例外”的发展趋势，并提出应对措施。

一、国际野生动物保护条约对“科学例外”[5]的规定

（一）《保护迁徙野生动物物种公约》中的“为了科学目的”

《保护迁徙野生动物物种公约》（Convention on the Conservation of Migratory Species of Wild Animals，后简称《CMS公约》），[6]又称《波恩公约》，是为保护迁徙野生动物而制定的一项国际条约。由于迁徙物种具有周期性的迁徙规律，其迁徙路线往往跨越多个国家边界，且较为依赖迁徙路线上的生态环境。[7]因此，在保护迁徙动物、维护其族群稳定时，需要区域内国家协调一致，共同为迁徙动物创造良好的迁徙条件。

《CMS 公约》在序言部分指出，现今野生动物的基因、科学价值越来越高，

3　Elizabeth Baldwin, “Twenty-five Years under the Convention on Migratory Species: Migration Conservation Lessons from Europe,” *Environmental Law,* Vol. 41, 2011, p. 535.

4　David Hunter *et al*, *International Environmental Law and Policy* (Foundation Press, 2007), p. 836.

5　各主要国际野生动物保护条约的具体情况和规定参见附表 1。

6　Convention on the Conservation of Migratory Species of Wild Animals, adopted 23 June 1979, entered into force 1 November 1983, 1651 UNTS 333.

7　Beyerlin Ulrich, Thilo Marauhn, *International Environmental Law* (Bloomsbury Publishing, 2011), p. 189.

为保证人类能够世世代代拥有地球资源，各国应有义务明智地使用生物资源。为保护野生迁徙动物的可持续发展，该公约第 2 条、第 3 条规定，区域国家不得对附录一、二中受保护的野生迁徙动物进行任何形式的“捕捉（taking）”，包括猎捕、开展渔业、抓获、侵扰、故意杀害或其他任何相似行为。考虑到相关需求，公约第 3 条第 5 款规定，涉及相关保护物种迁徙区域的成员国“为了科学目的”，可以对附录一所列的迁徙物种进行捕捉。[8] 同时规定，该种例外情况必须确切，时间和空间要有限制，并且这类捕捉不应给此类物种带来不良影响。除此之外，公约第 3 条第 7 款规定，国家在自行作出第 3 条第 5 款的例外许可后，要及时向公约秘书处进行报告。

目前，《CMS 公约》共有 129 个成员，但美国、加拿大、俄罗斯、中国等重要国家却不在其中。野生动物保护工作需要国家间的相互协调，没有这些国家的参与，《CMS 公约》在保护野生动物方面的能力会受到一定限制。

（二）《国际捕鲸管制公约》中的“为了科研目的”

《国际捕鲸管制公约》（International Convention for the Regulation of Whaling，后简称《ICRW 公约》）[9] 是在国际捕鲸委员会（International Whaling Commission）的指导下，于 1946 年制定的有关合理开发鲸鱼种群的公约。现代捕鲸业的发展起源于 19 世纪。人们出于对鲸油、鲸骨和鲸肉的需求，曾广泛开展捕鲸活动。人类曾经认为海洋资源取之不尽、用之不竭，但是自 1883 年开始，人们逐渐意识到这种无限制捕杀鲸鱼的方式，会对鲸鱼种群的可持续生存能力造成巨大的威胁。[10]1937 年，国际社会达成《国际捕鲸管制协议》，尝试对人类捕鲸活动进行管制，但是最终由于缺乏有效的管理机构，致使该协议并没有达到预期的目的。1946 年，国际社会制定了《ICRW 公约》，通过设立国际捕鲸委员会，对捕鲸活动加以限制，旨在协调鲸鱼种群和人类捕鲸活动。《ICRW 公约》共分为公

---

8 《保护迁徙野生动物物种公约》第 3 条第 5 款规定：“凡属于其分布区域国的成员国应禁止捕捉附录所列的迁徙物种，唯有下列情况不在禁止之列：1. 为了科研目的；2. 为了提高该物种的繁殖率和生存机会；3. 为了满足这类物种传统食用者生活的需要；4. 特殊情况下必须捕捉。”

9 International Convention for the Regulation of Whaling, adopted 2 December 1946, entered into force 10 November 1948, signed or ratified by 88 countries, 161 UNTS 72.

10 Malgosia Fitzmaurice, “International Convention for the Regulation of Whaling,” *United Nations Audiovisual Library of International Law,* 2007, https://legal.un.org/avl/ha/icrw/icrw.html (Last visited on June 27, 2020).

约文本和公约计划书（Schedule）两个部分。

公约文本在序言中表示，该公约并非限制捕鲸行为，而是旨在对鲸鱼进行合理保护的同时，给予鲸鱼一定的恢复时间，以对鲸鱼进行合理的捕杀。[11]虽然公约第 5 条对捕鲸行为进行了诸多限制，但公约第 8 条规定，缔约政府对本国国民为科学研究的目的而对鲸鱼进行的捕获、击杀和加工处理，可按该政府认为适当的限制数量，发给特别许可证。

为防止公约在适用中出现分歧，国际捕鲸委员会在公约计划书中，对“为了科研目的”作出了更加细致的规定。[12]计划书第 30 条指出，各国“为了科研目的”的捕鲸许可需提前报批国际捕鲸委员会的科学委员会进行审查，且许可内容应包含：研究目标，采样的数量、性别分布、年龄大小和种群名称，科学家和其他国家合作参与的机会，对鲸鱼种群潜在的影响。

无论是公约文本、公约计划书，还是 1986 年决议，国际捕鲸委员会尝试对“科学例外”进行限制，以防止某些国家滥用公约第 8 条的相关规定。《ICRW 公约》并非只为保护鲸类种群而设立，而是同时兼顾鲸鱼保护与人类捕鲸活动的良性发展。因此，公约在适用过程中仍出现了一定的争议。公约现有 88 个成员，加拿大、菲律宾、埃及、委内瑞拉在 20 世纪末相继退出本公约，且受到国际法院“南极捕鲸案”裁决影响，日本也于 2019 年退出了本公约。[13]

（三）《濒危野生动植物物种国际贸易公约》中的“为了科学交换”

《濒危野生动植物物种国际贸易公约》（Convention on International Trade in Endangered Species of Wild Fauna and Flora，后简称《CITES 公约》）又称《华盛顿公约》，[14]制定于 1963 年，旨在限制或禁止濒危野生动植物的跨国贸易，对贸易条件、手续进行规范。由于濒危物种的国际贸易会对其生存状态造成严重影响，因此公约第 2 条规定对附录一、附录二所列濒危物种及其衍生物不允许

11　Wichert Nussbaum, Martha Nussbaum, “Scientific Whaling? The Scientific Research Exception and the Future of the International Whaling Commission,” *Journal of Human Development and Capabilities*, Vol. 18, No. 3, 2017, p. 359.

12　International Whaling Commission (IWC), International Convention for the Regulation of Whaling 1946 Schedule, amended by the Commission at the 67th Meeting, Brazil, 2018.

13　IWC, “Membership and Contracting Governments,” https://iwc.int/members (Last visited on 27 June 2020).

14　Convention on International Trade in Endangered Species of Wild Fauna and Flora, adopted 3 March 1973, entered into force 1 July 1975, signed or ratified by 183 countries, 27 UNTS 1087.

进行贸易。但公约第 7 条第 6 款对其贸易限制规定了例外许可，允许国家之间以非商业租借、捐赠、科学家或科研机构之间的交换为目的对附录一、附录二中的濒危物种及其衍生物进行跨国运输。

在表述方面，《CITES 公约》中的“为了科学交换（to exchange between scientists or scientific institutions）”属于一种特殊的“科学例外”，即科学家或科研机构之间的濒危物种交换，并未要求该种交换要以“研究”为前提，但仍需满足“为了”和“科学”两个要件。《CITES 公约》第 15 届全体成员大会修订通过第 5.10 号文件《“以商业为主要目的（primarily commercial purposes）”的定义》对此进行了详细的规定，并对“以商业为主要目的”以外的“科学目的”进行了解释。[15] 解释认为，“科学目的”是指相关的跨国运输活动必须以科学为主要目的，进口者必须是进口国管理机构认可的科研机构或科学家，且由进口产生的商业利益，包括转卖或展览所得，不应成为该种交换的初始目的。

在科研机构的定义及科学交换方面，大会第 11.15 号文件《博物馆样品、植物标本、研究样本诊断及检验中的非商业租赁、捐赠或交换》指出，各国应建立“濒危物种清单”，及时更新所列物种，并每五年上报用于科研交换的具体科研机构的名称；与此同时，该文件还针对不同物种，对所交换的样本进行严格的限制，包括血液体积、器官或表皮组织样本大小、分泌物体积等，通过此种方法防止滥用第 7 条所规定的例外情况。[16]

《CITES 公约》对保护物种的规定较为详细，但其并不能从根本上限制对濒危物种的捕杀，因此保护野生动物的能力仍然较弱。在“科学例外”的规定方面，较难把握“科学交换”的具体内涵。《CITES 公约》现有 183 个成员，美国、中国、俄罗斯等联合国安理会常任理事国在内的世界绝大部分国家签署了该条约。

（四）其他国际野生动物保护条约对“科学例外”的规定

除上述条约外，“科学例外”还广泛存在于针对特定物种或特定地理范围的国际野生动物保护条约中。

《保护南极海豹公约》[17] 是根据 1959 年《南极公约》中有关南极动植物保护

---

15 *Definition of “Primarily Commercial Purposes,”* CITES, Conf. 5.10 (Rev. CoP15), 1985, p. 2, Annex b.

16 *Non-Commercial Loan, Donation or Exchange of Museum, Herbarium, Diagnostic and Forensic Research Specimens*, CITES, Conf. 11.15 (Rev. CoP18), 2000, pp. 1-2, Article. 3 (b) (g: ii, iv, vi), Annex.

17 Convention for the Conservation of Antarctic Seals, adopted 1 June 1972, entered into force 11 March 1978, signed or ratified by 18 countries, 1080 UNTS 175.

相关措施制定的保护南极海豹的公约，该公约于 1972 年制定，现有 18 个成员。该公约第 4 条规定，在符合公约的宗旨和原则的情况下，允许国家“为了科学研究”，对海豹在有限的范围内进行捕杀，且应在最短时间内通知其他公约成员及国际科学联盟理事会南极研究科学委员会。关于“为了科学研究”的具体内涵，公约附录第 7 条第 2 段指出，这类研究应包括从保护和合理利用南极海豹资源及人性化的角度出发，对捕杀海豹方法的有效性进行研究。

《益农鸟类保护公约》[18] 于 1902 年签订，旨在保护对农业生产有益的鸟类，该公约现有 10 个成员。公约第 7 条规定，有关部门可以“为了科学目的”或者以“鸟类繁育”为由，准许针对益农鸟类进行捕杀的个别例外情况，但有关机构应保证在作出例外许可前，采取任何可能滥用该许可的预防措施。

《西半球自然保护和野生动物保护公约》[19] 和《南太平洋自然保护公约》[20] 分别签订于 1940 年和 1976 年，旨在保护特定区域的野生动物或自然环境。两项公约的文本较为相似，都在“科学例外”方面赋予各国政府较大的自由裁量权。例如，《西半球自然保护和野生动物保护公约》在第 3 条、第 7 条和第 8 条规定，只要是符合公约保护野生动物的宗旨，各国机构均有权在自行认为合理且符合合理使用的情况下，作出“为了科学研究和调查（scientific study and investigation）”的许可，但此种许可只能在进一步进行科学研究的特殊情况下，或是在对发现该动植物的地区进行管理时必不可少（essential）的情况下，才可以作出。《南太平洋自然保护公约》第 3 条在《西半球自然保护和野生动物保护公约》的基础上，增加了对保护生态平衡必不可少的情况，规定也能作出“为了科学研究和调查”的许可。

综上所述，“科学例外”有多种表述方法，主要包括“为了科学研究（for scientific research）”“为了科学目的（for scientific purpose）”“为了科研目的（for the purpose of scientific research）”和“为了科学交换（to exchange between scientists or scientific institutions）”等，都是由“为了”和“科学”两个要件组成，仅在用语方面有细微的差别。无论采取何种表述，“科学例外”都允许国家

18 Convention for the Protection of Birds Useful to Agriculture, adopted 19 March 1901, entered into force 6 December 1905, signed or ratified by 10 countries, IUCN TRE-000067.

19 Convention on Nature Protection and Wild Life Preservation in the Western Hemisphere, adopted 12 October 1940, entered into force 1 May 1942, signed or ratified by 22 countries, 161 UNTS 193.

20 Convention on Conservation of Nature in the South Pacific, adopted 12 June 1976, entered into force 26 June 1990, signed or ratified by 6 countries, IUCN TRE-000540.

在保护野生动物的大背景下对受保护动物进行一定的捕杀活动。

二、关于“科学例外”的解释与适用

尽管“科学例外”的表述有所区别，但是其实质都是由“科学研究”和“为了科学研究目的”两方面组成的：前者为客观构成要件，强调一项例外的科学性；后者为主观构成要件，强调一项例外在主观上的目的性。在解释“科学例外”时，可以依照国际法院（后简称法院）2014年澳大利亚诉日本“南极捕鲸案”中所采取的“两分法”，从科学研究和为了科学研究目的两个方面分别进行分析。[21]法院认为，两个要素为累积（cumulative）关系，由此，即便一个捕鲸项目涉及科学研究，其对鲸鱼的捕杀、捕获和处理也不一定符合《ICRW公约》第8条的相关规定，除非这些项目是为了科学研究目的。[22]

（一）科学研究的认定

科学研究关注项目的科学性，即从文本解释的角度出发，认定科学研究的具体内涵及构成要素，从而判断一个项目是否符合科学研究的定义。《ICRW公约》框架下的“南极捕鲸案”对科学研究的定义进行了分析。该案中，国际法院从澳大利亚所提出的四点标准出发，分析日本JARPA II捕鲸项目是否符合科学研究的构成要素，即研究目标、致死手段与非致死手段、国际合作与同行评审（peer review）及消极影响评估，最终认为澳大利亚提出的四点标准是对科学研究的广义定义，并不能直接用于解释《ICRW公约》的相关内容。[23]尽管如此，由于“科学研究”在其他公约的适用中也出现了类似标准，所以这四点标准仍然具有一定的参考价值。

1. 研究目标

研究目标包括一个项目的研究问题和研究假设，[24]既需要有关国家制定可行的促进物种保护和管理的研究目标，又需要有关国家在许可中明确采样的数量、性别、年龄和采样种群名称。

在“南极捕鲸案”中，日本JARPA II的研究目标包括监测南极生态环境、

---

21 *Whaling in the Antarctic (Australia v Japan: New Zealand intervening) (Whaling case), Judgment, ICJ Reports 2014,* p. 254, para. 67.

22 *Whaling case,*p. 255, para. 71.

23 *Whaling case,*p. 258, para. 86.

24 *Whaling case,*p. 255, para. 74.

对比鲸鱼种群管理模型、阐明鲸鱼种群时间和空间上的变化，以及改善南极抹香鲸种群的管理方法。[25] 在将研究目标作为科学研究的认定标准上，日本并未提出异议，但日本对研究目标中研究假设的详细程度存在不同意见。[26] 就JARPA II 的研究目标是否达到科学研究的标准，亚伯拉罕法官（Judge Abraham）在其不同意见中指出，日本的研究项目本质上是科学的，提出了科学研究的目标和实施方法，并依照国际捕鲸委员会的相关规定与其科学委员会进行了及时的沟通。[27] 国际法院并未就此点深究日本 JARPA II 项目中研究目标的合理性。

除"南极捕鲸案"外，意大利的国内立法也采用了相似的要求，以规范科学研究例外的实施。《CMS 公约》第十二届全体成员大会通过第 12.9 号决议，决定通过加强各国国内立法程序，以达到对迁徙物种的保护与可持续管理的目的。[28] 在此背景下，意大利回顾了欧盟于 1992 年、2009 年分别通过的《保护自然栖息地及野生动植物群的指令》[29] 和《保护野生鸟类指令》[30]，对黄爪隼、白眼潜鸭、地中海鸥、长须鲸和抹香鲸等物种作出了科学研究的例外许可，例如"伊斯基亚水域幼年抹香鲸的声音和行为的研究"。这些研究都需要具有明确的研究目标和研究内容，在研究对象的数量、年龄方面具有详细的规定，且在研究时间、空间上作出了严格的限制。[31]

2. 致死手段与非致死手段

在各国际野生动物保护条约的"科学例外"的规定中，均允许对科研对象采用捕猎、捕杀的方法进行人为干扰，并且在科学研究中并未要求不得使用致死手段。尽管如此，澳大利亚通过引用《ICRW 公约》的相关决议，尤其是 1986 年有关"科学研究特殊许可"的决议，来证明各国在进行科学研究时，应

25　*Report of the Expert Workshop to Review the Japanese JARPA II Special Permit Research Programme*, IWC Scientific Committee (24-28 February 2014), https://www.icrwhale.org/pdf/SC-65b-Rep02.pdf (Last visited on 27 June 2020).

26　*Whaling case,* p. 255, para. 77.

27　*Whaling case, Dissenting Opinion of Judge Abraham,* p. 328, para. 28.

28　*Establishment of a Review Mechanism and a National Legislation Programme,* CMS, UNEP/CMS/Resolution 12.9, 2017, p. 2, Art. I.

29　*Council Directive on the Conservation of Natural Habitats and of Wild Fauna and Flora*, European Union (EU) Document 92/43/EEC, 1992.

30　*Directive of the European Parliament and of the Council on the Conservation of Wild Birds*, European Union (EU) Document 2009/147/EC, 2009.

31　*Italy National Report COP12*, Convention on the Conservation of Migratory Species of Wild Animals, CMS, UNEP/CMS/COP12/Inf.25.50, 2017.

采用合理的手段，即只有在其他手段不可行的情况下才可采用致死手段。日本方面对此提出了反对意见。首先，日本认为《ICRW 公约》第 8 条的规定本身为“捕杀”鲸鱼提供例外许可，在实质上允许对鲸鱼种群使用致死手段进行科学研究。其次，日本认为其所采用的致死手段并未超过所需的范围。[32]

法院认为，澳大利亚所引证的大会决议只是意见性建议，并非所有国家均认可并接受了这些决议的内容，尤其是日本并没有接受这些决议。同时，这些意见性决议并没有指出，只有在其他手段不可行的情况下才可采用致死手段。因此，不能仅因为一个项目使用了致死手段，就否定该项目在手段上的合法性，也不能否认这个项目的科学性。[33]

3. 国际合作与同行评审

澳大利亚认为，科学研究的内容应该接受同行评审，这一点也与《ICRW 公约》计划书第 30 条有关国际合作的要求相吻合。法院认为，同行评审是科学领域的普遍实践，但不能仅仅通过一个项目是否存在同行评审而判定其是否为科学研究项目。尽管如此，法院结合《ICRW 公约》计划书第 30 条的内容，认为项目需要提前由国际捕鲸委员会科学委员会进行审议，以符合相关程序义务。[34] 除此之外，优素福法官（Judge Yusuf）在其反对意见中指出，日本积极与科学委员会进行定期沟通，分享 JARPA II 项目的初始结果，科学委员会也对其作出了高度评价。既然国际捕鲸委员会下设的科学委员会认可 JARPA II 项目在未来捕鲸管理中起到的重要作用，JARPA II 项目应该被认为是一项科学研究项目。[35]

因此，如果条约建立了汇报机制，相关汇报的完成情况应被纳入认定科学研究的标准之中，由此可以通过科学委员会或者其他科学家的第三方认定，来判断一个项目是否符合科学研究的标准。

4. 消极影响评估

澳大利亚认为，对于鲸鱼种群的科学研究不应对鲸鱼种群造成负面影响，这一点符合《ICRW 公约》计划书第 30 条有关“对鲸鱼种群潜在的影响”的要求。日本对此也表示认同。[36] 除此之外，在《CMS 公约》的国家实践中，例如，比利时佛兰芒（Flemish）地区允许以科学目的为由对鸟类的“捉捕”作出

32 *Whaling case,* p. 256, para. 80.

33 *Whaling case,* p. 257, para. 83.

34 *Whaling case,* p. 257, para. 84.

35 *Whaling case, Dissenting Opinion of Judge Yusuf,* p. 396, paras. 37-38.

36 *Whaling case,* p. 258, para. 85.

例外许可，但这种许可只针对物种种群而非特定物种，且必须提供环境影响评价（environmental impact assessment），以综合判断该种例外对其他潜在种群的影响。[37] 因此，在认定科学研究时，应考虑项目对相关种群的负面影响。[38]

综上，认定某一项目是否构成科学研究时，主要考察的标准包含研究目标、致死手段与非致死手段、同行评审和消极影响评估等。但需要注意，科学研究并不能完全独立地分析，应结合具体项目对于科研目标、数据处理、研究成果等方面进行综合分析。正如国际法院在“南极捕鲸案”中的认定一样，日本的研究项目之所以在广义上可以被认定为科学研究，是因为其具有一定的研究目标，其研究项目都按时提交科学委员会进行审议，其致死手段的使用本身也没有违反相关法律规定，且澳大利亚方面无法证明日本的项目设计会对鲸鱼种群造成负面影响。[39] 因此，科学研究的认定虽然具有一定的客观标准可以遵循，但标准相对宽松和灵活。

（二）为了科学研究目的的认定

虽然为了科学研究目的是一种主观标准，但并不能完全取决于当事方的自由裁量，仍应根据客观情况推断主观目的。[40] 相关国际野生动物保护条约中对为了科学研究目的的认定较少，目前最直接相关的实践是国际法院审理的“南极捕鲸案”。法院在分析该用语时使用了“与实现所称目标合理相关（reasonable in relation to achieving its stated objectives）”的标准，即研究项目的设计与实施是否与其所声称的目标存在合理的相关性，并认为该种标准是一种客观标准。而实质上，该标准关注的是科学研究项目各项措施的必要性（necessary），特别是使用致死手段及其他措施对实现所称目标的必要性。

必要性的判断标准曾多次出现在国际法院的判决中，用以分析某项行为或措施能否构成合法例外。如 1986 年尼加拉瓜诉美国“军事活动和准军事活动案”中，美国认为其在尼加拉瓜港口埋设水雷，破坏尼加拉瓜港口和油气设施的行为能够保护美国的根本安全利益。但是国际法院从必要性的角度出发，认为这些行为并不是维护美国根本安全利益的必要行为。[41] 在 2009 年哥斯达黎加

37　*Belgium National Report COP13*, CMS, UNEP/CMS/COP13/NR.012, 2019.

38　*Whaling case,* p. 258, para. 85.

39　*Whaling case,* p. 257, para. 83.

40　*Whaling case,* p. 253, para. 61.

41　*Case Concerning Military and Paramilitary Activities in and against Nicaragua (Nicaragua v United States of America), Judgment, ICJ Reports 1986*, p. 117, para. 224.

诉尼加拉瓜"航行权利和相关权利争端案"中，哥斯达黎加认为，尼加拉瓜对圣胡安河（San Juan River）上哥斯达黎加的船舶截停并审查证件的行为是出于侵扰的目的。国际法院从必要性的角度出发，认为尼加拉瓜只是依照国家主权的原则进行合法审查，以保护尼加拉瓜的主权、环境和航行安全。[42] 国际法院的两项判决都采用了必要性标准，分析相关行为是否在主观上能够满足特定目的，将国家行为正当化。

必要性标准还出现在《关税与贸易总协定》(GATT）例外条款的适用中。[43] 作为一种例外，GATT 第 20 条的条款乙允许国家采取保护人类、动植物的生命或健康所必需的措施。在实践中，2000 年美国诉韩国"鲜牛肉和冷藏、冷冻牛肉进口措施案"[44] 和 2000 年欧洲共同体诉美国"1930 年关税法第 337 节及其修正案"[45] 在分析必要性时考虑了四个要点：第一，该种措施所要达成的目标的相对重要性；第二，该种措施对目标的贡献程度；第三，该种措施对国际贸易产生的限制性影响；第四，是否存在一个限制性影响更小的合理替代措施。由于 GATT 中对必要性的规定也出现在例外条款中，且"南极捕鲸案"中，国际法院在认定为了科学研究目的时所分析的研究方法必要性与 GATT 第 20 条的适用具有重合之处，因此相关解释标准也可以作为参考依据。

1. 目标的相对重要性

在科学研究项目所要达成目标的相对重要性方面，国际法院在"南极捕鲸案"中，并未对日本 JARPA II 项目设计目标的重要性提出异议，因为国际捕鲸委员会科学委员对该项目作出了高度评价，认为日本的捕鲸项目能够在未来捕鲸管理中起到重要作用。[46] 除此之外，其他国际野生动物保护类条约对项目目标的重要性进行了规定，如《益农鸟类保护公约》要求国家为了科学目的的例外许可应促进鸟类的繁育；《保护南极海豹公约》要求相关研究项目应注重合理利用南极海豹资源；秘鲁"第 004–2014 号判例"规定，为了科研目的的例外必

---

42 *Dispute Regarding Navigational and Related Rights (Costa Rica v Nicaragua), Judgment, ICJ Reports 2009,* pp. 253-258, paras. 100-118.

43 General Agreement on Tariffs and Trade, adopted 20 October 1947, entered into force 1 January 1948, 64 UNTS 187.

44 *Measures Affecting Imports of Fresh, Chilled and Frozen Beef (the United States v. Republic of Korea), Appellate Body Report, WTO, WT/DS161/AB/R, 2000,* p. 50, para. 164.

45 *Section 337 of the Tariff Act of 1930 and Amendments thereto (European Committee v. the United States), Panel Report, WTO, WT/DS186/2, 2000,* p. 45, para. 5.26.

46 *Whaling case, Dissenting Opinion of Judge Yusuf,* p. 396, paras. 37-38.

须对科学知识和物种保护作出贡献。[47]

2.研究方法对目标的贡献程度

关于该要素，实践中最主要的争议问题是致死手段的使用。若某一科学研究项目使用致死手段，则需分析致死手段对实现研究目标是否必要，以及致死手段必要的限度。如国际法院在“南极捕鲸案”中指出，由于 JARPA II 项目需要对鲸鱼内脏的相关数据进行研究，日本和澳大利亚方面都认同部分研究内容无法通过非致死手段达成，致死手段对部分研究内容确为必要。[48]但是，尽管日本采用了致死手段，但 JARPA II 项目 6 年间只产出了 2 篇论文。因此，致死手段的使用对 JARPA II 项目的贡献程度值得商榷。[49]

与此同时，尽管法院认可了 JARPA II 研究项目在部分研究目标上需要使用致死手段，但是法院更关注该种致死手段必要的限度。法院认为，为达成项目所称目标而使用的致死手段不应超过必要的限度。[50]法院通过分析日本捕杀鲸鱼的数量、计划捕杀和实际捕杀数量之间的关系，以及 JARPA II 和其前身 JARPA 两个项目之间样本大小的变化，最终认为日本在 JARPA II 项目中致死手段的使用超过了其研究目标所必要的范围，因而认定日本的 JARPA II 项目并非以科学研究为目的。[51]

除“南极捕鲸案”外，《CMS 公约》下设的国家立法项目中，部分国家实践也对致死手段的使用提出了限制要求。例如，秘鲁最高法“第 004–2014 号判例”规定，只有在自然历史博物馆或科研机构中确无相关样本的情况下，才可以在研究中采用致死手段。[52]《保护南极海豹公约》指出，只有在“特殊情况”下才可对海豹进行为了科学研究的捕杀。虽然该公约并未明晰特殊情况，但也从侧面反映出，致死手段的使用需要严格的限制。

3. 限制负面影响

如前文所述，“南极捕鲸案”和《CMS 公约》均强调“科学例外”不应对受保护动物产生负面影响，GATT 第 20 条例外规定的适用中也对必要措施的限制性影响进行考量，因此，对受保护动物种群的负面影响也应成为分析必要性

---

47 *Peru National Report COP13*, CMS, UNEP/CMS/COP13/NR.095, 2019.

48 *Whaling case,* p. 269, para. 133.

49 *Whaling case,* p. 291, para. 219.

50 *Whaling case,* p. 270, para. 137.

51 *Whaling case,* p. 293, para. 227.

52 *Peru National Report COP13*, CMS, UNEP/CMS/COP13/NR.095, 2019.

的因素之一。在认定和限制负面影响时，可从相关科学研究项目的设计与实施两方面入手，对项目的负面影响进行评估。

项目设计方面，《CMS 公约》第 3 条第 5 款规定，国家所作出的例外许可应具有详细的设计内容，并且在时间和空间上有所限制。“南极捕鲸案”中国际法院也指出，日本的 JARPA II 项目应设置具体的时间计划和阶段性目标。[53] 因此，项目在时间、空间以及阶段目标方面的规定能够在一定范围内限制项目的负面影响。

在项目的实施方面，除要求致死手段为必要外，项目中非致死手段的使用也应注意动物实验的道德及伦理规范。《CMS 公约》的国家立法实践中，阿尔及利亚“第 88–08 号法案”禁止对动物进行虐待，相关动物实验也只能在必需的情况下才可开展，且应注意动物实验的道德及伦理规范。[54] 因此，项目在实施方面的规定也能够限制项目的负面影响，使项目满足必要性标准。

4. 考虑负面影响最小的替代措施

相关研究项目应考虑对受保护动物伤害更小的替代性措施的可行性，分析是否存在负面影响更小的合理替代措施。在“南极捕鲸案”中，日本声称非致死手段费时费力，不切实际，但并未提供相关证据证明这种观点，且日本也未对非致死手段推广的可能性进行探究。除此之外，国际法院还对是否可以将非致死手段的适用范围扩大等问题对日本进行了询问，但日本均未作出合理回应。因此，在没有证据支撑的情况下，法院认为日本的研究设计，尤其是在非致死手段分析的应用和适用范围方面，存在一定的缺陷。[55]

值得注意的是，法院对于致死手段必要性的分析仍存在一定争议。例如有学者认为，法院在“南极捕鲸案”中认定日本致死手段的使用超过了其研究目标所必要的范围，拔高了以科学研究为目的的适用标准。这种严格的解释与公约所规定的“政府认为适当（thinks fit）”的要求相冲突，[56] 因为后者给予国家较

---

53 *Whaling case,* p. 290, para. 216.

54 *Algeria National Report COP13,* CMS, UNEP/CMS/COP13/NR.003, 2019.

55 *Whaling case,* p. 271, para. 144.

56 《国际捕鲸管制公约》第 8 条第 1 款：“尽管有本公约的规定，缔约政府对本国国民为科学研究的目的而对鲸进行捕获、击杀和加工处理，可按该政府认为适当的限制数量，得发给特别许可证。按本条款的规定对鲸的捕获、击杀和加工处理，均不受本公约的约束。各缔约政府应将所有发出的上述特别许可证迅速通知委员会。各缔约政府可在任何时期取消其发出的上述特别许可证。”

大的自由裁量权，未将致死手段规制于必要的范围内。[57] 除《ICRW 公约》外，《西半球自然保护和野生动物保护公约》第 7 条也采用了国家认为合理的表述，给予国家在此问题上较大的自由裁量权。因此，根据这种表述，部分学者认为只要国家认为其致死手段的使用存在合理性，就应当认定具有合理性，法院不能推定国家具有恶意。[58] 尽管如此，因为相关国际野生动物保护条约中对为了科学研究目的的认定较少，目前最直接相关的实践是“南极捕鲸案”，所以法院的解释为今后的国际法实践提供了一定的参考。[59]

三、适用“科学例外”的监管问题

由于“科学例外”在解释和适用方面存在一定的模糊性，因此需要有力的监管制度以防止该例外被滥用。然而，在“科学例外”的监管方面，同样存在诸多问题，主要体现在四个方面：通知时间、通知内容、事中监管和责任制度。

（一）通知时间

不同的条约对通知时间进行了不同的规定，而国家在作出“科学例外”后的通知时间早晚，可能直接影响国际条约适用的效果。

《ICRW 公约》第 8 条第 1 款规定，各缔约政府应将所有发出的上述特别许可证迅速通知委员会。与此同时，《ICRW 公约》计划书第 30 条规定，国家在作出“科学例外”许可前，应留足够的时间通知公约秘书处，使国际捕鲸委员会科学委员会能够对其进行审查。这种事前汇报机制可能防止国家滥用“科学例外”，防止对野生动物保护产生负面影响。

《CMS 公约》第 3 条第 7 款规定，国家在自行作出第 3 条第 5 款的例外许可后，要及时向公约秘书处报告。这种事后汇报机制允许国家在其国内先作出“科学例外”许可，对保护动植物进行捉捕，再向公约秘书处或管理机构报备，使得保护动植物的实现基本依赖于国家的自觉，且存在严重的滞后性。部分条

57　Leifan Wang, Fenghua Li, “Alternative interpretation to Article VIII of the International Convention for the Regulation of Whaling: Implications from Article XX of the GATT,” *Marine Policy,* Vol. 117, 2020, p. 6.

58　*Whaling case, Dissenting Opinion of Judge Abraham,* pp. 332-333, paras. 41-42.

59　Asier Garrido-Munoz, “Managing Uncertainty: The International Court of Justice, Objective Reasonableness and the Judicial Function,” *Leiden Journal of International Law,* Vol. 30, No. 2, 2017, pp. 468-469.

约不能有效限制对受保护动植物的损害。例如意大利基于欧盟通过的《保护自然栖息地及野生动植物群的指令》和《保护野生鸟类指令》进行的报备并未公布其研究成果，仅在事后向大会秘书处按时进行了报备。[60]

因此，国际野生动物保护类条约应尽量改变事后汇报的监管机制，化被动为主动，定期要求各成员国提交相关受保护动物的生态报告，以及人类对其潜在的影响报告等，建立科学委员会并事先对各国的“科学例外”措施的可行性进行专家评审，从而有助于更好落实各条约的“科学例外”规定。

（二）通知内容

在通知内容方面，《ICRW 公约》的规定较为详细，在公约计划书第 30 条中，国际捕鲸委员会详细规定了四点许可汇报的内容，包括：研究目标，采样的数量、性别分布、年龄大小和种群名称，科学家和其他国家合作参与的机会，以及项目对鲸鱼种群潜在的影响。[61] 这种规定使得“科学例外”许可的发布更加规范。

但是，《CMS 公约》《CITES 公约》以及其他国际野生动物保护公约在通知内容方面并未作明确的规定。国家通知各管理机构的内容存在空白，使管理机构可能无法掌握国家采取“科学例外”措施的详细内容，可能导致“科学例外”的滥用。

（三）事中监管

除通知时间和内容外，“科学例外”的监管还离不开实施过程中的持续监督。目前，仅有《ICRW 公约》详细规定了“科学例外”在实施过程中的监管制度，《CMS 公约》规定的方式较为模糊。

《ICRW 公约》第 8 条第 3 款规定，各缔约政府应尽可能将该政府收到的有关鲸类和捕鲸的科学资料，包括本条第 1 款和第 4 条进行的调查研究结果，寄送委员会指定的机构，各次寄送的间隔时间不应超过一年。除此之外，国际捕鲸委员会在 1986 年通过的《科学研究特殊许可》的决议中规定了审查各国作出的“科学例外”许可的方式，包括：研究目标是否无法通过非致死手段实现，研究项目是否能够对鲸鱼种群管理提供至关重要的信息，研究项目的完成是否

---

60 *Italy National Report COP12*, CMS, UNEP/CMS/COP12/Inf.25.50, 2017.

61 IWC, International Convention for the Regulation of Whaling 1946 Schedule, amended by the Commission at the 67th Meeting, Brazil, 2018.

必须采集相应数量、性别和年龄的样本，以及捕杀鲸鱼的方式是否符合公约第三部分的相关规定。[62] 通过定期更新和审查，《ICRW 公约》可以及时对各国“科学例外”的实施进行审查、提出建议并进行监管。

《CMS 公约》第十二届全体成员大会通过第 12.9 号决议，决定通过加强各国国内立法程序，以达到对迁徙物种的保护与可持续管理目的。[63] 从各国提交的国内立法文件来看，只有 7 个国家在国内立法中作出了与“为了科学目的”相关的例外许可。[64] 这些文件仅列举了各国国内立法中作出“科学例外”许可的相关法律依据以及特定物种，但是并未详细说明监管内容和审查标准。因此，这种方式在“科学例外”实施过程中的监管力度较弱。

（四）责任制度

各国际野生动物保护条约并未明确规定严格的责任制度，使得国家损害受保护动物的违法成本较低。例如，尽管国际法院认定日本违反了其在《ICRW 公约》框架下的国际义务，要求日本立即停止捕鲸行为，[65] 但事实上，日本之后并未遵守该判决，而是提出重新修订其捕鲸项目，继续开展捕鲸作业。[66]

各国际野生动物保护条约应试图建立责任制度，加强各国间的沟通协调，提高国家损害受保护动物的成本，在国家责任和赔偿方面进行细化。[67] 例如，在多边机制下建立“黑名单”制度，约束不负责任的国家。此外，还应针对濒危物种设立生态红线，杜绝大范围使用致死手段等不可逆的研究手段，推动人道主义、科学责任和道德标准成为“科学例外”的实施原则。[68]

---

62 *1986-Appendix 2 Resolution on Special Permits for Scientific Research*, IWC, 1986, p. 1.

63 *Establishment of a Review Mechanism and a National Legislation Programme,* CMS, UNEP/CMS/Resolution 12.9, 2017, p. 2, Art. I.

64 参见附表 2 “《CMS 公约》国家实践中的‘科学例外’”。

65 *Whaling case,* p. 299, para. 247.

66 McCurry Justin, Readfearn Graham, “Japan to resume commercial whaling after leaving IWC–report,” *the Guardian,* 20 December 2018, https://www.theguardian.com/environment/2018/dec/20/japan-to-resume-commercial-whaling-after-leaving-iwc-report (Last visited on June 27, 2020).

67 Elizabeth Baldwin, “Twenty-five Years under the Convention on Migratory Species: Migration Conservation Lessons from Europe,” *Environmental Law,* Vol. 41, 2011, p. 535.

68 Alexander Gillespie, *International Environmental Law, Policy, and Ethics* (Oxford University Press, 2014), p. 124.

结论

“科学例外”经常会成为某些国家实现自身利益、追求经济效益的法律漏洞，也直接限制了国际环境法的拘束力与有效性。“科学例外”在不同条约中有不同的规定，但都具有主观上的“为了”和客观上的“科学”两个构成要素。在认定过程中，可以遵循国际法院在“南极捕鲸案”中的两分法，从“科学研究”和“为了科学研究目的”两个角度进行分析。根据国家实践和条约解释，判断某一项目是否构成科学研究时，可以借鉴的标准包括研究目标、同行评审和消极影响评估等，相对宽松和灵活。科学例外适用的难点在于“为了科学研究目的”的认定。在判断某一项目是否是“为了科学研究目的”时，可以参考GATT第20条例外条款的相关解释和适用，结合“南极捕鲸案”中的解释方法，考虑项目目标的相对重要性、研究方法对目标的贡献程度、限制负面影响，以及考虑替代措施等。

在监管方面，各条约中有关“科学例外”的规定在通知时间、通知内容、事中监管和责任制度等方面均存在问题。滞后的通知时间、模糊的通知内容、含糊的审查方式，以及笼统的责任制度会对各条约的适用产生严重的负面影响。国际社会应尽量改变事后汇报的监管机制，细化通知内容，强化对“科学例外”的全过程监督，并建立有效的责任制度，使各国际野生动物保护条约落到实处。

需要明确的是，在实际适用中，本文所总结的“科学例外”的认定标准和考虑因素仍存在一定的局限性。部分国际条约的成员国数量较少，国际法庭的相关判例仍然非常有限，并且各条约的文本规定和目的宗旨存在差异，因此不能将个别案例泛化。所以，“科学例外”仍是国际环境法领域中需要进一步明确的概念。随着科学技术的不断发展，该问题的意义将日益凸显，因此应密切关注实践并进行研究。在利用“科学例外”推动人类社会不断进步的同时，保护地球生物多样性，为子孙后代及整个人类家园创造可持续的未来。

附表 1　规定“科学例外”的主要国际野生动物保护条约及其情况

条约名称	生效日期	“科学例外”条款	“科学例外”的表述	缔约国数量
《保护南极海豹公约》	1978 年 3 月 11 日	第 4 条	为了科学研究	18
《西半球自然保护和野生动物保护公约》	1942 年 5 月 1 日	第 3、7、8 条	为了科学研究和调查	22
《南太平洋自然保护公约》	1990 年 6 月 26 日	第 3 条	为了科学研究和调查	6
《保护迁徙野生动物物种公约》	1983 年 11 月 1 日	第 3 条第 5 款	为了科学目的	129
《益农鸟类保护公约》	1905 年 12 月 6 日	第 7 条	为了科学目的	10
《国际捕鲸管制公约》	1948 年 11 月 10 日	第 8 条	为了科研目的	88
《濒危野生动植物物种国际贸易公约》	1975 年 7 月 1 日	第 7 条第 6 款	为了科学交换	183

本表格根据《联合国条约集》整理，https://treaties.un.org/Pages/AdvanceSearch.aspx?tab=UNTS&clang=_en，最后访问日期：2020 年 6 月 27 日。

附表 2 《CMS 公约》国家实践中的“科学例外”

国家	立法名称	与“为了科学目的”相关的因素
阿尔及利亚	第 04–07 号捕猎法	严格限制时间、地点和对象
	第 06–05 号法令	允许以“为了科学研究与繁育”为由对部分鸟类作出例外许可
	第 88–08 号法案	禁止对动物进行虐待
比利时	Flemish 地区法律	允许以“为了科学研究”为由对部分鸟类进行“捉捕”
		（需提供环境影响评估）
智利	第 4601、19473 号法律	允许以“为了科学研究”为由对陆地哺乳动物和鸟类进行“捉捕”
毛里塔尼亚	第 045 号环境法规	允许以“为了科学目的”为由对鸟类作出例外许可
马里	第 95–031 号法案	允许以“科学目的”为由的特殊情况下作出例外许可
欧盟	《保护自然栖息地及野生动植物群的指令》	允许以“为了科学研究”为由作出例外许可
	《保护野生鸟类指令》	
秘鲁	第 004–2014 号判例	“为了科研目的”的例外必须要对科学知识和物种保护作出贡献

本表格根据“《CMS 公约》国家立法项目”整理，https://www.cms.int/en/activities/national-legislation-programme，最后访问日期：2020 年 6 月 27 日。

跨界环境损害中人权条约域外适用的困境与路径

钟青萌

摘要：环境损害与人权损害关系密切。环境损害经常跨越边界，但在传统理论下，国家仅对"受其管辖之人"承担人权义务，因此跨界环境损害中的条约域外适用面临困境。在既有理论与实践的框架下，对以《经济、社会及文化权利国际公约》为代表的不包含管辖条款的条约的域外适用，不应当施加"管辖"前提；对以《公民及政治权利国际公约》为代表的含有管辖条款的条约，可以扩张解释管辖条款的含义。此外，在认定国家的域外人权义务时应当区分尊重、保护和实现三个不同层次的国家义务。

关键词：跨界环境损害；《公民及政治权利国际公约》；《经济、社会及文化权利国际公约》；域外适用；管辖条款

引言

2018 年 2 月，美洲国家间人权法院（Inter-American Court of Human Rights）发布了一项关于环境与人权的咨询意见案，认为基于环境与人权的不可分性，《美洲人权公约》在跨界环境损害的情形下可以域外适用。[1] 这一地标性案件引发了对于跨界环境损害中人权条约域外适用的激烈争论。[2]

传统上，人权条约的目的是将国家与其国民之间的关系置于国际监督之下，

---

1 *Environment and Human Rights*, *Advisory Opinion OC-23/17 of 15 November 2017*, Requested by the Republic of Colombia, Inter-American Court of Human Rights (IACHR), Official Summary Issued by the Inter-American Court, p. 4, para. II.h.

2 Monica Feria-Tinta, Simon Milnes, "The Rise of Environmental Law in International Dispute Resolution: Inter-American Court of Human Rights issues Landmark Advisory Opinion on Environment and Human Rights," *Yearbook of International Environment Law*, Vol. 27, No. 1, 2016, p. 75; Lorraine Aboagye, Giovanny Vega-Barbosa, "A Commentary on the Advisory Opinion of the Inter-American Court of Human Rights on the Environment and Human Rights," *DPCE Online*, Vol. 34, No. 1, 2018, p. 296.

不涉及跨界人权保护的问题。[3] 现有理论与实践也将人权条约的域外适用限定于军事占领等情形。[4] 因而，单纯的跨界环境损害难以满足人权条约域外适用的条件。

在全球化的今天，世界各国联系日益密切，全球气候变暖、边境大型工程建设以及跨国公司的存在，都给人权保护带来了极大挑战。然而，根据传统观点，虽然损害是跨界的，但是法律责任却不能跨界。此类问题在司法实践中逐渐显现。2005 年，分布于四个国家的因纽特人向美洲人权委员会起诉，主张美国政府导致的全球气候变暖损害其根据《美洲人权公约》享有的生存权和文化权。[5]2008 年，厄瓜多尔以空中喷洒除草剂为由在国际法院对哥伦比亚提起诉讼，两国就人权条约的适用问题展开了激烈争论。[6] 遗憾的是，因为程序中断，两个案件中法院均没有对此问题作出解释。

这类问题也得到了全社会的广泛关注。联合国多次呼吁国家尊重域外人权。例如，2017 年 6 月，联合国经济、社会及文化权利委员会（Committee on Economic, Social and Cultural Rights，以下简称经社文委员会）建议澳大利亚重新审视本国在煤炭运输方面的政策，因为其将对全球气候造成极大影响，进而影响全世界人民的经济、社会和文化权利。[7] 此外，学术界还涌现出了 ETO 组织（extraterritorial obligations organizations），专门研究国家在经济、社会和文化权利领域的域外义务，呼吁各界重视国家的域外人权义务。[8]

---

3 Sigrun Skogly, Mark Gibney, "Transnational Human Rights Obligations," *Human Rights Quarterly*, Vol. 24, No. 3, 2002, p. 783. 转引自于亮：《国家在经济、社会和文化权利方面的域外义务》,《法制与社会发展》2016 年第 1 期，第 82 页。

4 *Legal Consequences of the Construction of a Wall in the Occupied Palestinian Territory, Advisory Opinion, ICJ Reports 2004*, pp. 179-181, para. 110; *Armed Activities on the Territory of the Congo (Democratic Republic of the Congo v. Uganda), Judgment, ICJ Reports 2005*, p. 243, para. 216.

5 *Petition to the Inter American Commission on Human Rights Seeking Relief from Violation Resulting from Global Warming Caused by Acts and Omissions of the United States*, 7 December 2005, p. 70.

6 *Aerial Herbicide Spraying (Ecuador v. Colombia)*, Overview of the Case, https://www.icj-cij.org/en/case/138 (Last visited on 6 July 2019).

7 *Concluding Observations on the Fifth Periodic Report of Australia*, Committee on Economic, Social and Cultural Rights (CESCR), UN Doc E/C.12/AUS/CO/5, 2017, paras. 11-12.

8 The ETO Consortium, https://www.etoconsortium.org/en/main-navigation/about-us/eto-consortium/ (Last visited on 6 July 2019).

本文旨在以《公民及政治权利国际公约》(后简称 ICCPR)和《经济、社会及文化权利国际公约》(后简称 ICESR)两大国际人权条约为代表，通过分析条约本身、国际法院和其他司法机构判例、学者学说，以及国际组织报告，结合国际法的最新发展，探究跨界环境损害中人权条约域外适用的可行性与条件。本文共三个部分：第一部分将探讨跨界环境损害与人权损害的联系；第二部分将通过国际司法机构关于人权条约域外适用的判例，指出在环境领域内人权条约域外适用存在的困境；第三部分旨在通过现存国际法规则，结合国际法最新发展趋势，探究解决跨界环境损害中人权条约域外适用困境的路径。

一、跨界环境损害与人权损害联系密切

一国可能直接(如在边境建设大型工程)或者间接(如资助、授权或者不规制私人行为)造成跨界环境损害。跨界环境损害形式多样，主要包括全球气候变化和大型工程建设导致的生态系统破坏。基于环境和人权的不可分性，跨界环境损害将威胁到域外人权。

(一)环境与人权的关系

威拉曼特里(Weeramatry)副院长在 1997 年匈牙利和斯洛伐克“加布奇科沃 - 大毛罗斯工程案”的个别意见中指出：“保护环境是人权领域的重要组成部分，因为它是诸多人权的重要因素。”[9]保护环境和实现人权之间有着不可否认的联系。[10]

首先，环境是人生存的基础，环境损害直接影响人的生存。在 2019 年“卡塞雷斯诉巴拉圭案”中，两个农民家庭中的成员因为附近工厂大量使用农药和杀虫剂而生病，因此控告巴拉圭国没有尽到保护环境的义务。[11]联合国人权事务委员会认定，巴拉圭政府没有尽到保护个人不受环境损害的义务，违反了 ICCPR 第 6 条(生存权)和第 17 条(保护家庭权)。[12]在 2012 年“萨拉亚库土

9　*Case concerning the Gabcikovo-Nagymaros Project (Hungary/Slovakia), ICJ Reports 1997, Separate Opinion of Judge Weeramantry*, pp. 91-92.

10　*Views adopted by the Committee under Article 5 (4) of the Optional Protocol, concerning Communication No. 2751/2016*, Human Rights Committee (CCPR), CCPR/C/126/D/2751/2016, 2016, p. 14, para. 7.4.

11　*Views adopted by the Committee under Article 5 (4) of the Optional Protocol, concerning Communication No. 2751/2016*, CCPR, CCPR/C/126/D/2751/2016, 2016, p. 2, para. 1.

12　*Views adopted by the Committee under Article 5 (4) of the Optional Protocol, concerning Communication No. 2751/2016*, CCPR, CCPR/C/126/D/2751/2016, 2016, p. 14, paras. 7.6-7.7.

著群体诉厄瓜多尔案”中，厄瓜多尔政府授权私人公司在土著人生活区域从事石油勘探和开采活动，破坏了森林、水源以及地下河流，导致动物外迁，从而扰乱该地区土著人的生活方式。[13]美洲国家间人权法院最终认为这一破坏环境的举措损害了萨拉亚库人的生存权。[14]

此外，环境还是经济文化活动的依托，这一点在少数族裔和土著居民身上尤为显著。在1990年“伯纳德·奥米纳亚克诉加拿大案”中，加拿大政府与私人公司签订合同，授权私人公司在卢比康湖边（Lack Lubicon）湖边开采石油和天然气，破坏了周边环境。而湖旁生活着一群从远古时期开始便在此狩猎和捕鱼的土著群体。联合国人权事务委员会判定环境损害破坏了土著人生存的经济基础和文化，损害了他们在ICCPR第27条项下的少数群体权利。[15]在1996年“拉斯曼等诉芬兰案”中，芬兰政府授权私人主体在萨米人生活的森林里进行采石业和建设相关基础设施。联合国人权事务委员会认为，在森林中进行的驯鹿养殖是萨米人文化的重要组成部分，如果采石业的规模在现有基础上扩大，便有可能侵犯萨米人的少数群体权利。[16]

（二）环境损害可能影响的两公约中的人权

联合国人权理事会于2012年3月任命了一名独立专家约翰·诺克斯（John Knox）作为特别报告员来研究与环境有关的人权。根据其报告，环境损害将影响两大人权公约下的权利。具体来说，ICCPR中与环境有关的权利主要包括：第6条规定的生存权；第17条规定的任何人的私生活及家庭不得被非法侵害的权利；第27条规定的保障少数群体享受其固有文化的权利。[17]ICESCR中与环境有关的权利主要包括：第11条规定的为自己及家庭获得相当生活水准的权利

---

13 *Kichwa Indigenous People of Sarayaku v. Ecuador*, Merits and Reparations, 2012, IACHR No. 78/00, pp. 66-67, para. 233.

14 *Kichwa Indigenous People of Sarayaku v. Ecuador*, Judgment, 2012 (Merits and Reparations), IACHR No. 78/00, p. 71, para. 249.

15 *Bernard Ominayak, Chief of the Lubicon Lake Band v. Canada*, 26 March 1990, Communication No. 167/1984, para. 33.

16 *Jouni Länsman, et al v. Finland*, (1996), UNHRC, UN Doc CCPR/C/58/D/671/1995, para. 9.8.

17 United Nations, Special Procedures of the United Nations Human Rights Council, *Mapping Human Rights Obligations Relating to the Enjoyment of a Safe, Clean, Healthy and Sustainable Environment*, Individual Report on the International Covenant on Civil and Political Rights, December, 2013.

（包括足够的衣着、食物和住房）；第 12 条规定的人人有权享有能达到最高身体与精神健康的权利；第 15 条规定的参与文化生活的权利。[18]

综上，适宜的环境是人权的基础，环境损害与人权损害有着不可分割的联系，国家需要对造成的环境损害行为承担相应的人权责任。

二、跨界环境损害中人权条约域外适用的困境

人权条约适用范围的规定方式分两种：一种是条约明文包含管辖或者领土条款（jurisdiction or territory provision），如 ICCPR 第 2 条规定，一国需尊重并确保“所有境内受其管辖之人”的权利，为条约的适用范围设定了地域和管辖条件。[19] 另一种则是没有明文规定条约适用的领土或管辖限制，如 ICESCR 第 2 条作为一般性规定条款没有提及领土或管辖。[20]

（一）ICCPR 的适用范围

国际法的发展已经承认了含有管辖条款的 ICCPR 可以在域外适用。国际法院在 2004 年“关于在被占领的巴勒斯坦地区修隔离墙的法律后果的咨询意见案”（以下简称 2004 年“隔离墙案”）中认为，ICCPR 第 2 条的“境内”和“受其管辖”两个要件是分离的（disjunctive），不需要同时满足。[21] 且公约第 2 条的立法准备文件显示，公约起草者在选择用语的时候，没有意图让国家在行使域外管辖的时候逃避国家责任。他们只是希望防止居住在国外的公民向其国籍国主张本应当由居住国处理的事项。[22] 人权事务委员会在《第 31 号一般性意

18　United Nations, Special Procedures of the United Nations Human Rights Council, *Mapping Human Rights Obligations Relating to the Enjoyment of a Safe, Clean, Healthy and Sustainable Environment*, Individual Report on the International Covenant on Economic, Social and Cultural Rights, December 2013.

19　ICCPR 第 2 条第 1 款规定：“本公约每一缔约国承担尊重和保证在其领土内和受其管辖的一切个人享有本公约所承认的权利，不分种族、肤色、性别、语言、宗教、政治或其他见解、国籍或社会出身、财产、出生或其他身份等任何区别。”

20　ICESCR 第 2 条第 1 款规定：“本盟约缔约国承允尽其资源能力所及，各自并借国际协助与合作，特别在经济与技术方面之协助与合作，采取种种步骤，务期以所有适当方法，尤其包括通过立法措施，逐渐使本盟约所确认之各种权利完全实现。”

21　*Legal Consequences of the Construction of a Wall in the Occupied Palestinian Territory, Advisory Opinion, ICJ Reports 2004*, p. 180, para. 112.

22　*Official Records of the General Assembly*, 10th Session, Annexes, A/2929, 1955, Part II, Chap. V, para. 4.

见》中也明确表示，该公约适用于所有在国家“权威和有效控制”之下的个人，不管该个人是否处于该国领土内。因此，公约适用范围讨论的焦点在于权利人是否处于义务国的“管辖范围”内。[23]

公约本身没有对“管辖”和“权威与控制”作出定义。传统上，人权条约下的“管辖”与一般国际法上的“管辖权”类似，强调主权性权利。人权条约下的“管辖权”包含两种模式：一种是“空间模式”（spatial model），即国家对于个人所在领土的有效控制；另一种是“个人模式”（personal model），即国家对于个人的权威与控制。[24]

1.“空间模式”下的管辖

“空间模式”最接近国际公法对于管辖权的定义。[25] 在国际公法中，管辖权涉及国家根据国际法规制或者以其他方式影响人民、财产和情况的权力。[26] 因此，它的特征之一就是体现国家主权原则。[27]“空间模式”下的管辖指国家对特定领土实施有效控制。欧洲人权法院在 2001 年“班科维奇诉比利时案”中对管辖权作出了如下解释：《欧洲人权公约》第 1 条的管辖权应当根据一般国际公法的管辖权概念解释。一国的管辖权首先应当是域内的。[28] 域外管辖仅存在于例外情形下，是通过对相关领土和领土上的居民实施有效控制实现的。法院列举了两种主要情形：一种是军事占领，另一种是一国同意、邀请或者承认另一国政府在该国领土上实施本应由本国政府实施的全部或者部分公共权力。[29] 国际法院的判例也采纳了这一方式。在 2004 年“隔离墙案”中，法院认为 ICCPR 可

---

23 *General Comment No. 31: The Nature of the General Legal Obligation Imposed on States Parties to the Covenant*, Human Rights Committee, CCPR/C/21/Rev.1/Add/ 13, p. 4, para. 10.

24 Nicola Wenzel, "*Human Rights, Treaties, Extraterritorial Application and Effects*," Max Planck Encyclopedia of Public, 2008, para. 21, https://opil.ouplaw.com/view/10.1093/law:epil/9780199231690/law-9780199231690-e819 (Last visited on 6 July 2020).

25 Marko Milanovic, *Extraterritorial Application of Human Rights Treaties: Law, Principles, and Policy* (Oxford: Oxford University Press, 2011), p. 123.

26 Malcolm N. Shaw, *International Law* (Cambridge University Press, 2008), p. 645.

27 Marko Milanovic, *Extraterritorial Application of Human Rights Treaties: Law, Principles, and Policy* (Oxford University Press, 2011), p. 123.

28 *Bankovic v. Belgium and 16 Other Contracting States*, Decision on Admissibility of 12 December 2001, ECHR 2001-XII [GC], para. 56.

29 *Bankovic v. Belgium and 16 Other Contracting States*, Decision on Admissibility of 12 December 2001, ECHR 2001-XII [GC], para. 71.

以适用的原因是以色列对巴勒斯坦地区实施了长达 37 年的军事占领。[30] 在 2005 年刚果诉乌干达“刚果境内军事行动案”中，法院重申了 2004 年“隔离墙案”中的观点，即国际人权条约可以适用于一国在其境外实施管辖时的行为，尤其是在被占领地区。[31]

2.“个人模式”下的管辖

“个人模式”指“权威和控制”可以直接建立在国家与个人之间。[32]“个人模式”最早是由人权理事会在 1981 年“洛佩兹·布尔乔亚诉乌拉圭案”中提出的。该案指出，ICCPR 也适用于一国代理人在境外对公民实施权威或者有效控制的情形，即使国家对于该被害人所在的领土没有实施任何的控制。[33]“个人模式”也包含两类情形：一类是关于一国的领事或者外交代表在外国领土上的行为，例如，一国在外国的领事官员拒绝为本国公民更新护照。[34] 另一类是关于一国在境外的抓捕或者拘留行为，这也将使个人处于国家的权威与控制之下。[35] 虽然“个人模式”相较“空间模式”更为宽松和灵活，但是控制的范围仍然限于国家代理人实施的行为。

（二）ICESCR 的适用范围

ICESCR 不包含领土和管辖条款，但是国际法院的判例仍将管辖视为其域外适用的前提。2004 年“隔离墙案”是国际法院唯一的关于 ICESCR 域外适用的案件。法院认为，ICESCR 之所以不包含管辖条款，是因为公约保护的权利本质上是“域内的”（essentially territorial），但是当国家对特定领土实施有效控制时，公约仍可以适用。[36] 由此看出，法院的方式是通过解释案件中的权利人

30　Nicola Wenzel, “Human Rights, Treaties, Extraterritorial Application and Effects,” Max Planck Encyclopedia of Public, 2008, para. 21.

31　*Armed Activities on the Territory of the Congo (Democratic Republic of the Congo v. Uganda), Judgment, ICJ Reports 2005*, p. 243, para. 216.

32　Nicola Wenzel, “Human Rights, Treaties, Extraterritorial Application and Effects,” Max Planck Encyclopedia of Public, 2008, para. 21.

33　*Sergio Euben Lopez Burgos v. Uruguay* (1981), UN Doc A/36/40, 6 June 1979, p.136, para. 12.3.

34　*Montero v Uruguay*, Merits, Communication No 106/1981, UN Doc CCPR/C/18/D/106/1981, 31 March 1983, para. 5.

35　*Sergio Euben Lopez Burgos v. Uruguay* (1981),UN Doc A/36/40, 6 June 1979, p.136, para. 12.3.

36　*Legal Consequences of the Construction of a Wall in the Occupied Palestinian Territory, Advisory Opinion, ICJ Reports 2004*, p. 180, para. 112.

符合“在国家的管辖下”来肯定公约的域外适用。这相当于为公约的域外适用设置了默认的管辖前提，其域外适用条件与含有管辖条款的 ICCPR 相同。

（三）缺乏跨界损害下有效保障人权的“斜行义务”

从上述两公约的适用前提可以总结出，虽然国际法已经承认一国承担的人权义务不止步于国境，但是无论条约是否包含管辖条款，其域外适用均以管辖为前提。跨界环境损害的特殊之处在于，虽然其与人权损害有直接的关联，但损害行为通常发生在一国境内，只是会造成域外后果。损害来源国通常没有对受害人所在国家进行军事占领或者在受害者所在国家行使公共权力，因而在单纯的跨界损害中，损害来源国没有对受害人所在领土实施有效控制，不符合管辖的“空间模式”。并且，损害来源国与受害人之间的唯一关联是环境损害导致人权损害，因而也没有对个人实施“个人模式”下的权威与控制。总之，跨界环境损害不满足传统意义上的管辖条款，难以引发国家的域外人权义务。

缺乏跨界环境损害中的域外人权义务将导致人权保护出现真空。跨界环境损害中的人权保护是一项环境法和人权法的交叉议题。国际环境法上的国家义务是典型的“平行义务”（horizontal obligation），即国家之间互负的义务。人权法上的国家义务在传统上是典型的“垂直义务”（vertical obligation），即国家对本国国民承担的义务。[37] 在国际环境法下，国家原则上对国家承担责任，不对境外的个人承担责任；在人权法下，国家原则上对本国公民承担责任，也不需要对境外的个人负责。[38] 受跨界环境损害影响的个人没有直接的救济途径。[39] 因此，只有当国家承担“斜行义务”（diagonal obligation），即对境外个人负担的义务时，才能有效保障境外受害人个人的权利。但是，管辖条款的存在使得损

37 John Knox, “Diagonal Environmental Rights,” in Mark Gibney, Sigrun Skogly, eds., *Universal Human Rights and Extraterritorial Obligations* (University of Pennsylvania Press, 2010), p. 148; Monica Feria-Tinta, Simon Milnes, “The Rise of Environmental Law in International Dispute Resolution: Inter-American Court of Human Rights issues Landmark Advisory Opinion on Environment and Human Rights,” *Yearbook of International Environment Law*, Vol. 27, No. 1, 2016, p. 75.

38 John Knox, “Diagonal Environmental Rights,” in Mark Gibney, Sigrun Skogly, eds., *Universal Human Rights and Extraterritorial Obligations* (University of Pennsylvania Press, 2010), p. 148.

39 Monica Feria-Tinta, Simon Milnes, “The Rise of Environmental Law in International Dispute Resolution: Inter-American Court of Human Rights issues Landmark Advisory Opinion on Environment and Human Rights,” *Yearbook of International Environment Law*, Vol. 27, No. 1, 2016, p. 75.

害来源国不需要对境外个人遭受的人权损害承担责任，导致受害人的人权不能得到应有的保障。

综上，跨界环境损害不满足传统意义上人权条约域外适用的管辖前提，将导致人权保护的真空。

三、解决跨界环境损害中人权条约域外适用的路径

到目前为止，关于跨界环境损害中人权条约域外适用的司法实践仅有美洲国家间人权法院的咨询意见案一例，且根据以往的实践，跨界环境损害本身并不能使受害人处于义务国管辖下。但是，通过条约解释，仍然可以在不突破两大人权条约规定的前提下，实现人权条约在跨界环境损害中的域外适用。

（一）否认默示管辖条款

2004 年“隔离墙案”中，法院认为 ICESCR 中的权利本质上是“域内的”，因此条约适用以管辖为前提。这种观点将“管辖”视为不需要明文规定的默示条件。但是在 2008 年格鲁吉亚与俄罗斯“关于《消除一切形式的种族歧视公约》的适用问题案”中，国际法院认为，因为该公约的第 2 条和第 5 条不包含领土或者管辖上的限制，所以俄罗斯在公约下的义务可以适用于格鲁吉亚境内一切可以归责于俄罗斯的行为。俄罗斯应当尽其所能确保政府部门和其控制下的公共机构不从事任何形式的种族歧视行为。[40] 在该案中，条约的域外适用是单纯的条约解释问题，即应当根据《维也纳条约法公约》第 31 条推断条约的适用是否以管辖为前提，而不应预设本不存在的管辖条款。2011 年，体现欧洲学者共识的《关于国家域外的经济、社会以及文化义务的马斯特里赫特原则》（以下简称《马斯特里赫特原则》）出台。该原则并没有创设国际法，而是对现存国际法规则的阐明。[41] 该原则认为国家对域内和域外的个人均负有人权义务。[42] 国家的域外经济、社会以及文化义务可以通过条约解释的方法推断出来。根据条

40　*Application of the International Convention on the Elimination of All Forms of Racial Discrimination (Georgia v.Russian Federation), Provisional Measures, Order of 15 October 2008, ICJ Reports 2008*, p. 353, para. 22.

41　Article I (3), Maastricht Principles on Extraterritorial Obligations of States in the area of Economic, Social and Cultural Rights (“Maastricht Principles”), https://archive.crin.org/en/library/legal-database/maastricht-principles-extraterritorial-obligations-states-area-economic.html (Last visited on 23 April 2019).

42　Maastricht Principles, Preamble.

约解释，ICESCR 的域外适用不以管辖权为前提。

1. 条约的通常含义和上下文

与 ICCPR 相比，ICESCR 没有明确的管辖条款，因此不应对两公约施加以相同的域外适用条件。2004 年“隔离墙案”在论证公约权利域内性时提及的是该公约第 14 条（教育权），[43]该条明确指向了领土与管辖限制，但是类似的表述没有出现在第 2 条的一般性规定条款和其他任何的具体权利条款中，更加佐证了“管辖”这一条件需要条约的明确规定。也就是说，人权条约的域外适用不是建立在积极规定的基础上，相反，只要没有消极的限制规定，条约即可域外适用。[44]此外，条约第 2 条明确指出了“国际协作”，既然有协作义务，至少可以推断出国家负有不损害域外人权的义务。[45]

2. 人权条约监督机构的解释

联合国经济、社会及文化权利委员会的解释亦佐证了这一点。人权条约监督机构的解释是条约解释的重要参考。在 2010 年圭亚那诉刚果“迪亚洛案”中，国际法院通过 ICCPR 的一般性意见来解释它的相关条款。[46]经社文委员会是专门为监督 ICESCR 而设置的。2017 年，该机构发布了《第 24 号一般性意见》，专门规定国家对公司行为的域外义务，指出国家有域外的尊重、保护和实现人权的义务，且没有任何关于行使管辖的要求。[47]根据这一解释，ICESCR 的域外适用不以管辖为前提。

综上，根据条约解释规则，不包含管辖条款的 ICESCR 的域外适用不以个人受国家管辖为前提。但是一个现实困境是，该公约并没有像 ICCPR 那样设立类审判机构（quasi-tribunal）。且虽然公约的任择议定书授予了经社文委员会受

---

43 *Legal Consequences of the Construction of a Wall in the Occupied Palestinian Territory, Advisory Opinion, ICJ Reports 2004*, p. 180, para.112.

44 Ralph Wilde, “Human Rights Beyond Borders at the World Court: International Court of Justice's Jurisprudence on the Extraterritorial Application of International Human Rights Law Treaties,” *Chinese Journal of International Law*, Vol. 13, 2013, p. 668.

45 于亮：《国家在经济、社会和文化权利方面的域外义务》，《法制与社会发展》2016 年第 1 期，第 84 页。

46 *Ahmadou Sadio Diallo (Republic of Guinea v. Democratic Republic of the Congo), Merits, ICJ Reports 2010*, p. 664, para. 66.

47 *General Comment No. 24 (2017) on State Obligations under the International Covenant on Economic, Social and Cultural Rights in the Context of Business Activities*, CESCR, E/C.12/GC/24, 2017, p. 8, paras. 26-27.

理来文的权利，该议定书仍将来文限定在了于所声称侵害国“管辖下”的个人的来文。这将妨碍经社文委员会阐明公约域外适用范围的能力。[48]

（二）扩张解释管辖条款

对于包含明确管辖条款的人权公约，不应当将“管辖”的含义局限于一般国际公法下“管辖权”的定义中。联合国人权专家施凯宁教授（Martin Scheinin）提出了一种对“有效控制”标准更广义的解释方式。他认为衡量管辖权应当看国家是否对造成人权损害的行为实施了有效控制，而不是对具体的个人实施有效控制。[49] 这种观点与美洲国家间人权法院 2017 年“环境与人权”咨询意见相契合。法院认为，如果损害来源国可以对损害行为实施有效控制，并且该损害行为与人权损害有直接的因果关系，那么跨界环境损害的受害人便处于损害来源国的管辖之下，国家对其负有人权义务。[50] 这种解释方法的新颖之处在于，单纯对损害行为的有效控制就可以满足管辖条件。这看似与现有国际法冲突，但是其背后的逻辑链条仍然可以在国际法中找到依据。

首先，从“空间模式”到“个人模式”的发展体现了国际人权法趋向于承认 ICCPR 的普遍适用（universal application）。[51] 早在 1981 年，联合国人权理事会就作出了如下经典论述：在解释 ICCPR 第 2 条时，重要的不是国家与受害人所在的领土之间的关系，而是国家与个人之间的关系，因为该条被解释为允许一国在境外从事其在境内不被允许从事的违反人权的行为是不合理的。[52] 因此，只要能建立起一国与受害人个人之间的关系，便无须考虑该国是否能对被害人所在领土实施有效控制或者损害行为是否发生在该国领土上。在跨界环境损害

---

48 John Knox, “Diagonal Environmental Rights,” in Mark Gibney, Sigrun Skogly, eds., *Universal Human Rights and Extraterritorial Obligations* (University of Pennsylvania Press, 2010), p. 157.

49 Martin Scheinin, “*Extraterritorial Effect of the International Covenant on Civil and Political Rights,*” in F. Coomans, M. Kamminga, eds., *Extraterritorial Application of Human Rights Treaties* (Intersentia, 2004), pp. 73-75.

50 *Environment and Human Rights, Advisory Opinion OC-23/17 of 15 November 2017*, Requested by the Republic of Colombia, Inter-American Court of Human Rights (IACHR), paras. 101-103.

51 Denial Mogster, “Towards Universality: Activities Impacting the Enjoyment of the Right of Life and the Extraterritorial Application of the ICCPR,” EJIL Talk (27 November 2018), https://www.ejiltalk.org/towards-universality-activities-impacting-the-enjoyment-of-the-right-to-life-and-the-extraterritorial-application-of-the-iccpr/ (Last visited on 6 July 2020).

52 *Sergio Euben Lopez Burgos v. Uruguay* (1981), UNHRC, Communication No. R.12/52, para. 12.3.

中，虽然国家与受害人所在的领土之间不存在任何关系，但是与受害人之间有“行为 - 人权损害”上的联系。“个人模式”为跨界环境损害中人权条约的域外适用奠定了基础。

其次，“个人模式”中“权威和控制”的范围可被解释为比“国家代理人实施的权威与控制”更广泛。人权法并没有规定“管辖”或者“有效控制”的具体含义，因此，这种权威和控制并不一定是政治或者法律上的，也可以是事实上的。2018 年人权事务委员会在关于生命权的《第 36 号一般性意见》中提出了一种新的解释管辖的方式。该评论首先将 ICCPR 第 2 条的“境内并受其管辖之人”解释为“生命权处于一国的权威与有效控制之下的所有人”，将重点落在了国家与个人“权利”的关系上，而非国家与个人的关系上。接着，评论明确指出该条款中的“个人”包含所有生命权受到国家行为直接、可预见的影响的个人，即使他不处于该国有效控制的任何领土上。[53] 该评论将“权威与控制”广义地解释为“影响人权”。因此，只要国家的跨界环境损害行为足以影响境外的人权，便可使境外的受害人处于该国的“权威与控制”之下。联合国人权专家诺克斯指出，以全球变暖为例，海平面上升会导致小岛国家的人民流离失所，因此可以说他们处于那些高排放国家的控制之下。他们的命运与福祉都掌握在那些更发达的、实际造成了损害的国家手中。因此，这些国家需要承当相应的人权责任。[54] 在这样的扩张解释下，通过确立人权对环境的依赖，以及国家对该环境损害行为的控制这两个环节，便可建立起个人和损害来源国之间的联系。当一国实际上可以决定域外人权是否受到侵害时，就应当认定受害人处于该国的权威与控制之下。

以国家事实上对人权的损害作为管辖联系（jurisdiction link）解决了跨界环境损害中条约的域外适用问题。但是，这种方法也有一定的缺陷。一方面，有学者批判这种方法混淆了因果关系和域外适用条件，导致只要国家行为与损害之间存在因果关系，就可以建立国家与个人之间的管辖联系，从而使条约的管辖条款失去存在的意义，使国家负担过重的域外人权义务。[55] 另一方面，以因

---

53 *General Comment No. 36 (2018) on Article 6 of the International Covenant on Civil and Political Rights, on the Rights to Life*, Human Rights Committee, CCPR/C/GC/36, 2018, para. 63.

54 John Knox, “Climate Change and Human Rights Law,” *Virginia Journal of International Law*, Vol. 50, No. 1, 2009, p. 44.

55 Lorraine Aboagye, Giovanny Vega-Barbosa, “A Commentary on the Advisory Opinion of the Inter-American Court of Human Rights on the Environment and Human Rights,” *DPCE Online*, Vol. 34, No. 1, 2018, p. 296.

果关系作为管辖联系的方式也不能解决所有情况下的人权保护真空。美洲国家间人权法院强调，国家的域外义务是例外的，必须严格考察个案的法律与事实情况。[56]法院并没有明确这种管辖联系是适用于所有的人权，还是仅仅适用于诸如生存权这样最重要的权利。[57]诺克斯所举的例子也是一个极端情况。因此，对于单纯的经济文化权利受损是否能将受害人置于损害来源国的管辖下还有待于司法实践的进一步阐释。

（三）区分不同层次的国家义务

满足管辖条款只是承担国家责任的前提，并不等于承担国家责任。国家只有在不履行或者违反相应义务时才需要承担国家责任。国家的义务包含积极义务和消极义务，具体可以分为三层，即尊重义务（obligations to respect）、保护义务（obligations to protect）以及实现义务（obligations to fulfill）。[58]一国政府对其国民负有这三种完整的义务，但是对于外国政府来说，则需要分类讨论。

1. 尊重的义务

尊重的义务意味着国家不能自己或者通过可归责于自身的非国家行为者实施侵害人权的环境损害行为。[59]对于不包含管辖条款的ICESCR而言，国家无条件负有尊重域外人权的义务。对于含有管辖条款的ICCPR而言，“管辖”的连接点是国家有效控制下的行为造成直接和可预见的人权损害。也就是说，只要可以建立起人权损害与国家行为之间的因果关系，即使国家与受害人之间不存在传统意义上“空间模式”和“个人模式”下的管辖联系，也可以满足ICCPR第2条的管辖条款。因此，国家有义务不主动侵犯域外人权。[60]国家承担责任的前提是造成“可预见的损害”（foreseeable result），国家不需要对与自己行为联系相去甚远且不可预见的人权损害负责。[61]综上，在两大公约下，国家均不

56　*Environment and Human Rights*, *Advisory Opinion OC-23/17 of 15 November 2017*, Requested by the Republic of Colombia, IACHR, paras. 88, 104 (d).

57　Antal Berkes, “*A New Extraterritorial Jurisdictional Link Recognized by the IACtHR*,” EJIL Talk, 28 March 2018, https://www.ejiltalk.org/a-new-extraterritorial-jurisdictional-link-recognised-by-the-iacthr/ (Last visited on 6 July 2020).

58　孙世彦：《论国际人权法下的国家义务》，《法学评论》2013年第2期，第93页。

59　Maastricht Principles, Principles 19-21.

60　*Environment and Human Rights*, *Advisory Opinion OC-23/17 of 15 November 2017*, Requested by the Republic of Colombia, IACHR, para. 101.

61　Olivier De Schutter *et al*, “Commentary to the Maastricht Principles on Extraterritorial Obligations of States in the Area of Economic, Social and Cultural Rights,” *Human Rights*

能实施将造成可预见的域外人权损害的环境损害行为。

2. 保护的义务

保护的义务指国家需要采取立法、行政等规制措施，防止在其法律规制下的第三人侵犯域外人权，以及在损害发生后使违法者承担责任，为受害者提供有效的救济途径。[62] 两大公约下第三人的标准不同：对于含有管辖条款的公约来说，第三人的行为需要在该国的有效控制之下；[63] 对于不包含管辖条款的公约来说，第三人只需要与其有合理联系（reasonable link）即可。《马斯特里赫特原则》列举了以下几种情形：损害来源于该国领土；非国家行为者具有该国国籍；公司、母公司或实际控制公司的主要活动中心地、登记地或者主营业地在该国；国家和非国家行为者之间有合理联系，包括非国家实体行为的某些方面发生在该国领土上；损害经济、文化以及社会权利的行为违反了国际强行法。[64] 国家需要规制私人的行为不造成跨界环境损害，并且在发生了跨界环境损害之后，要追究相关人员的责任，为受害者提供有效救济。保护的义务是一种程序性义务，不要求最终结果的实现。

3. 实现的义务

实现的义务指国家需要单独或者共同促进人权的最终实现。通常认为，ICCPR 对国家施加了比 ICESCR 更加严格的义务。前者的表述是“确保……享受人权”，而后者的表述是“采取步骤……达到人权的充分实现”（take steps... to achieving the full realization of human rights...）。对于 ICCPR 而言，让国家履行实现的义务需要比较高的控制程度，通常需要对领土实施有效控制，比如持久的军事占领或者建立有权行使公权力的正式机构。[65] 因此，在单纯由跨界环境损害导致人权损害，且两国之间没有其他关系的时候，实现的义务是不成立的。与此相比，ICESCR 明确提及了国家的合作义务（international assistance and co-operation）。国家应当有单独或者通过国际合作建立促进经济、社会以及文化权利实现的国际环境。一方面，国家间须合作建立环境保护和人权保护的机制，

Quarterly, Vol. 34, No. 3, 2009, p. 1113.

62 Maastricht Principle, Principles 23, 24, 26.

63 *Environment and Human Rights*, *Advisory Opinion OC-23/17 of 15 November 2017*, Requested by the Republic of Colombia, IACHR, Official Summary Issued by the Inter-American Court, II (h).

64 Maastricht Principles, Principle 25.

65 胡钟月：《国际人权条约在缔约国域外之适用问题探究》，硕士学位论文，北京外国语大学研究生院国际组织项目，2015 年 5 月，第 35 页。

尤其是通过对多边、单边以及国际标准的制定、解释、运用和定期审查。[66] 例如，积极参与《巴黎协定》等国际环境公约的制定。另一方面，缔约国需要善意考虑外国提出的国际合作和援助请求。[67] 例如，向落后国家转移环保技术等。实现的义务是实体的积极义务，但是是一种较弱的义务，因为缔约国只需要尽己所能“采取步骤”“渐进”地实现人权。这通常被认为是国家的道德义务而非严格的法律义务。

综上，条约的域外适用需要区分不同层次的国家义务，不同层次的义务对应不同的控制内容和程度。这样既能实现人权的保障，防止人权保护出现真空，又可以避免国家承担过重的人权义务。

结论

环境与人权之间有着紧密的联系，国家有义务防止环境损害以保障人权。现存国际法实践已经承认了人权条约可以域外适用，但是无论条约是否包含管辖条款，均将国家承担义务的对象限于“受其管辖之人”。解决人权条约在跨界环境损害中域外适用的路径包括：首先，对于不含有管辖条款的条约，其适用不应当以管辖为前提；其次，对于含有管辖条款的条约，可以对“管辖”进行扩张解释，基于环境与人权之间的紧密联系，对造成人权损害的环境损害行为实施有效控制即可满足管辖条件；最后，应当区分讨论国家不同层次的义务，国家与个人的不同联系程度对应不同程度的人权义务，这样既可以更好地保障域外人权，也能防止一国承担过重的域外人权义务。

66　Maastricht Principles, Principle 29.

67　Maastricht Principles, Principles 32, 33.

《名古屋议定书》的实施问题

——以遗传资源相关传统知识利用为视角

叶欧仪

摘要：中国于2016年正式加入了《名古屋议定书》，这一举措意味着我国接受了遗传资源相关传统知识的惠益分享义务并承担了履约义务。由于《名古屋议定书》文本的模糊性，出现了条约不够明确和不易适用等问题。本文认为，《名古屋议定书》建立了传统知识的保护体系，将《生物多样性公约》提出的原则性目标落实为可以指引实践操作的具体规则，具有划时代的意义。但是，《名古屋议定书》的规定还需要细化和明确，特别是关于遗传资源相关传统知识的概念及其利用范围的界定。因此，中国应当尽早对上述重要概念作出界定，建立与《名古屋议定书》相配套的国内制度，从而加大对我国传统知识的保护力度。

关键词：《名古屋议定书》；遗传资源；传统知识；惠益分享

引言

1992年6月1日，《生物多样性公约》（以下简称《公约》）通过。截至2020年3月，共有196个国家签订了《公约》，使其成为国际社会广泛认可和遵守的国际条约。"公平合理分享由利用遗传资源而产生的惠益"（the fair and equitable sharing of the benefits arising from the utilization of genetic resources）（以下简称惠益分享）为《公约》最重要目标之一。为了达成该目标，缔约方大会开始构思并谈判一项相关的国际条约，即《关于获取遗传资源和公正公平分享其利用所产生惠益的名古屋议定书》（以下简称《名古屋议定书》）。《名古屋议定书》的一大制度突破是在《公约》的基础上建立了遗传资源相关传统知识（traditional knowledge associated with genetic resources）的保护制度，为传统知识的获取与利用提供了国际法依据，有利于规范相关实践。

《名古屋议定书》的谈判历时五年，经历了三届《公约》缔约方大会和九次特设工作组会议。起草过程中，由于在议定书适用范围和遵约两个关键领域无法达成共识，磋商小组明确表示不同意特设工作组提交的“议定书草案最终文本”，谈判破裂，议定书的制定进程几乎停滞。为了化解谈判僵局并尽早形成一定成果，“缔约方大会日本主席协调处”提出了一份妥协文本，将富有争议的条款全部删除，并对发展中国家和发达国家争论的关键条款进行了妥协处理，最终该妥协文本得以通过。[1]《名古屋议定书》的制定过程曲折冗长，充满了各国间的博弈、妥协，不可避免地导致在部分关键问题上存在立法空白或相当大的解释空间，进而在实践中产生种种适用问题。

特别是在传统知识保护这一创新领域，《名古屋议定书》的实施问题更为突出。《公约》通过第 8 条 j 款建立了遗传资源相关的传统知识和获取与惠益分享之间的联系；[2] 由此认可传统知识对于现代社会的价值；主张将传统知识的持有者纳入传统知识的广泛应用过程中，使其能够参与并享有提出建议的发言权；提倡国家将使用土著和地方社区的知识、创新和实践而获得的惠益进行公平分享。[3]《名古屋议定书》第 3 条覆盖《公约》第 8 条 j 款，规定其适用于与《公约》范围内的、与遗传资源相关的传统知识和利用此种知识所产生的惠益。[4] 但问题在于，由于议定书文本的模糊性且不存在其他相关国际条约，成员国对于条约条款有很大的自由解释空间，不可避免地导致了条约缺乏稳定性、可预期性和可操作性。例如，议定书中“遗传资源相关传统知识”的概念不清，传统知识的利用标准模糊，以及条约溯及力规定不明，均会造成上述问题。

中国于 1993 年批准加入《公约》，并于 2016 年成为《名古屋议定书》的缔约国，研究议定书的实施问题对保护我国权益具有重要意义。中国在传统知识保护领域具有双重角色，既是大量珍贵遗传资源的资源国和遗传资源相关传统知识的持有国，也逐渐有能力去获取外国的遗传资源，成为相关资源的获取

1　薛达元：《〈生物多样性公约〉新里程碑〈名古屋 ABS 议定书〉（上）》，《环境保护》2010 年第 23 期，第 70—72 页。

2 《生物多样性公约》第 8 条（就地保护）：“每一缔约国应尽可能并酌情：……（j）依照国家立法，尊重、保存和维持土著和地方社区体现传统生活方式而与生物多样性的保护和持久使用相关的知识、创新和做法并促进其广泛应用，由此等知识、创新和做法的拥有者认可和参与其事并鼓励公平地分享因利用此等知识、创新和做法而获得的惠益。”

3　托马斯 · 格雷伯：《遗传资源获取与惠益分享的〈名古屋议定书〉诠释》，薛达元等译，中国环境出版社，2013，第 16 页。

4 《名古屋议定书》第 3 条：“本议定书适用于《公约》第 15 条范围内的遗传资源和利用此种资源所产生的惠益。本议定书还适用于与《公约》范围内的与遗传资源相关的传统知识和利用此种知识所产生的惠益。”

国。[5]因此，《名古屋议定书》的实施情况和效果，对于我国遗传资源相关传统知识的保护具有影响。

一、“遗传资源相关的传统知识”的界定问题

由于《公约》和《名古屋议定书》没有对“遗传资源相关的传统知识”这一概念作出明确定义，实践中判断这一概念时需要同时考虑遗传资源、传统知识以及二者的相关性三个条件。

（一）遗传资源的概念

遗传资源的概念是整个《名古屋议定书》的核心所在，不论是来自动植物或微生物，它的用途广泛，普遍存在于基础科研或产品商业化中，在各行各业中都有巨大的社会经济效益。例如，2011 年制药业 20% 至 25% 的发展基于遗传资源；许多生物技术产品来自遗传资源，如酶、微生物等；农用种子的研究开发几乎全部来自遗传资源；此外，在个人护理以及食品饮料产业中，遗传资源的应用也贡献了大量市值。[6]由于产生于遗传资源获取与利用过程中的惠益数额如此显著，遗传资源范围的界定对确定缔约国的权利和义务意义重大。

1.《公约》及《名古屋议定书》中遗传资源的定义

目前关于遗传资源概念的绝大部分内涵较为清楚，《公约》及《名古屋议定书》对遗传资源采取相同的定义。根据《公约》第 2 条和《名古屋议定书》第 2 条，遗传资源为具有实际或潜在价值的遗传材料；遗传材料是指来自植物、动物、微生物或者其他来源的任何含有遗传功能单位（functional units of heredity）的材料。遗传功能单位也就是基因，即负责储存生物体遗传信息的 DNA 片段。[7]

由此可知，《公约》理论上要求遗传资源中含有基因序列。此外，《公约》所指的遗传资源，是指具有遗传材料属性的生物资源；如果对该生物资源的利用是基于其他属性，则不属于《公约》范围。例如，以获取木材为目的进入原始森林采伐不属于《公约》下惠益分享的范畴，但是如果试图利用该木材的遗

5 郭志勇：《〈名古屋议定书〉下我国的惠益分享权利与义务研究》，《南方论刊》2019 年第 6 期，第 57—59 页。

6 托马斯 · 格雷伯：《遗传资源获取与惠益分享的〈名古屋议定书〉诠释》，薛达元等译，中国环境出版社，2013，第 12 页。

7 齐凤军主编：《全息诊疗学》，湖北科学技术出版社，2009，第 2 页。

传材料，就会产生相关义务。[8] 为了种植而在市场上购买种子不属于惠益分享概念的范畴，但是为了植物育种而分析种子的基因组成则应当进行惠益分享。[9]

2. 衍生物是否属于遗传资源及相关争议

尽管《公约》和《名古屋议定书》明确定义了遗传资源，然而在部分重要领域仍存在争议，衍生物的定性问题便是其中之一。根据《名古屋议定书》第2条e款，衍生物是指由生物或遗传资源的遗传表达或新陈代谢产生的、自然生成的生物化学化合物，即使其不具备遗传功能单元。衍生物的形式广泛多样，具有极大的社会经济价值。衍生物主要包含：第一，自然界中的活细胞自发产生的蛋白质和酶等有遗传功能的自然生化化合物；第二，由人类干预（如使用物理方法提取）产生的，如香精油、香水、树脂、蛇毒、植物提取物等产品类的衍生物，普遍不含有遗传功能单位。[10] 这些化合物是药品、食品、化妆品成分等大量商业产品的研究、开发与商业化基础，从中产生的利润不可计数。例如，黄酮类化合物广泛应用于化妆品配方中，咖啡种子和巴西可可豆中发现的生物碱广泛应用于功能食品和饮料之中。[11]

首先需要明确的是，惠益分享义务是否适用于衍生物及衍生物是否属于遗传资源是两个不同层面的问题。后者不仅涉及衍生物相关的惠益分享义务，同时也会影响遗传资源相关传统知识这一概念的范围，以及遗传资源相关传统知识的惠益分享范围。如果认定遗传资源的概念范围包括衍生物，将会极大程度扩大传统知识的范围，从而扩大惠益分享对象的范围。因此，下文将对这两个问题进行区分讨论。

第一，《名古屋议定书》所规定的惠益分享义务适用于衍生物。如表1所示，《名古屋议定书》实际上通过“利用遗传资源”这一概念，把惠益分享的范围扩大到了衍生物领域，将自然产生的生物化学化合物纳入惠益分享的对象范围内，即使其中部分不具备遗传功能单元。

---

8 托马斯·格雷伯：《遗传资源获取与惠益分享的〈名古屋议定书〉诠释》，薛达元等译，中国环境出版社，2013，第14页。

9 “Frequently Asked Questions Declaration on the Rights of Indigenous Peoples,” Union for Ethical Bio-trade, https://www.culturalsurvival.org/news/frequently-asked-questions-about-un-declaration-rights-indigenous-peoples (Last visited on 22 June 2020).

10 托马斯·格雷伯：《遗传资源获取与惠益分享的〈名古屋议定书〉诠释》，薛达元等译，中国环境出版社，2013，第61页。

11 托马斯·格雷伯：《遗传资源获取与惠益分享的〈名古屋议定书〉诠释》，薛达元等译，中国环境出版社，2013，第60页。

表 1 《公约》和《名古屋议定书》中关于“遗传资源”定义的相关条款汇总

《名古屋议定书》第 3 条：本议定书适用于《公约》第 15 条范围内的遗传资源和（或）利用此种资源所产生的惠益。**本议定书还适用于与《公约》范围内的与遗传资源相关的传统知识和利用此种知识所产生的惠益。**
《公约》第 2 条：“遗传材料”是指来自植物、动物、微生物或其他来源的任何**含有遗传功能单位**的材料。“遗传资源”是指具有实际或潜在价值的遗传材料。
《名古屋议定书》第 2 条 c 款：“利用遗传资源”是指对遗传资源的遗传和（或）生物化学组成进行研究和开发（research and development），包括通过应用《公约》第 2 条定义的**生物技术**。
《公约》第 2 条：“生物技术”是指使用生物系统、生物体或其**衍生物**的任何技术应用，以制作或改变产品或过程以供特定用途。
《名古屋议定书》第 2 条 e 款：“衍生物”是指由生物或遗传资源的遗传表达或新陈代谢产生的、自然生成的生物化学化合物，**即使其不具备遗传功能单元。**

第二，衍生物不必然是遗传资源。根据上文所述，《名古屋议定书》的适用对象包括衍生物，即惠益分享责任涵盖衍生物，但并不能就因此认定议定书将衍生物认定为遗传资源的一类。如《公约》第 15 条仅限于遗传资源的利用，《名古屋议定书》第2条只是扩大了利用的范围，而非扩大了遗传资源的范围。[12] 具备遗传功能单元的衍生物如具有实际或潜在价值可能属于遗传资源，不具备遗传功能单元的衍生物则仍不在其概念范围内。

综上所述，缔约国在判断某一物质是否构成遗传资源并以获取该物质主张惠益分享的时候，需要将上述问题区分处理。从遗传资源使用国的视角判断，最有利的做法是严格采取“含有遗传功能单位”这一标准，尽可能将衍生物排除在外；从遗传资源原产国或提供国的视角判断，应在尽可能对遗传资源做扩大解释的基础上，同时主张依据利用衍生物产生的惠益分享义务。

（二）传统知识的含义

1.《公约》及《名古屋议定书》缺乏对传统知识的明确定义

《公约》没有对传统知识这一概念的内涵作出清晰的界定，第 8 条 j 款仅表明《公约》框架内应将传统知识理解为“体现传统生活方式而与生物多样性的

12　薛达元：《〈生物多样性公约〉新里程碑〈名古屋 ABS 议定书〉（上）》，《环境保护》2010 年第 23 期，第 70—72 页。

保护和持久使用相关的知识、创新和做法"。缔约方大会在后续通过的《阿格维古准则》（Akwé: Kon Guidelines）中延续了这一概念。[13]《名古屋议定书》虽然通过第 3 条将遗传资源相关传统知识纳入适用范围，但也没有对这一概念作出明确的定义。

国际自然保护联盟（International Union for Conservation of Nature）的《名古屋议定书》评注中对传统知识采取了广义的理解：传统知识可以存在的形式包括故事、歌曲、民歌、俗语、文化价值、信仰、习俗、社区法律、地方语言、农业实践等，通常是经过数百年的经验而形成的，根据当地文化及环境进行调整，通过口头形式代代相传并被集体拥有的。[14] 这种较为广义的理解方式有利于加强对传统知识的保护力度，与《公约》及《名古屋议定书》的立法意图相符合。然而，这种广义的理解在一定程度上可能增大实践适用的难度，会造成传统知识提供国和利用国的混淆。例如，可能出现一部分宗教信仰属于传统知识，而另一部分不属于的情况，这会导致通过知识产权法等法律工具进行管理变得更困难。

2. 世界知识产权组织（WIPO）对传统知识的定义

由于保护传统知识的相关规则或机制尚未建立，部分国际组织积极利用各自体系中的规则以配合达成《公约》目的。WIPO 作为职能最相关的国际组织，正在大力推进制度规则建设，希望利用现有的知识产权规则体系来保护传统知识。WIPO "知识产权和遗传资源、传统知识和民间文艺政府间委员会" 正在进行关于传统知识的谈判，并与成员国协商制定《世界知识产权组织传统知识文书草案》（The Protection of Traditional Knowledge: Draft Articles）。[15]

WIPO 对传统知识做了广义和狭义两种定义。广义的传统知识包含知识内容本身、传统文化表现形式、民间文艺表现形式，以及与传统知识相关的显著标志和符号。[16] 狭义的传统知识则指"因传统范畴的知识活动而产生的知识内容或实质性要素，其中包括构成传统知识体系的诀窍、技能、创新、做法和学

13　Art. II 6(h), *Akwé: Kon Guidelines*, CBD-COP 7, Decisions VII/16 F, UNEP/CBD/COP/7/21, 2004.

14　托马斯 · 格雷伯：《遗传资源获取与惠益分享的〈名古屋议定书〉诠释》，薛达元等译，中国环境出版社，2013，第 21 页。

15　*The Protection of Traditional Knowledge: Draft Articles*, World Intellectual Property Organization (WIPO), WIPO/GRTKF/IC/38/4, 2018.

16　世界知识产权组织：《传统知识：政策和法律备选方案》，WIPO/GRTKF/IC/6/4，第 28 页。

问，并包括体现土著和地方社区的传统生活方式的知识，或存在于经编纂的世代相传的知识体系中”的知识。[17] 在涉及遗传资源相关传统知识保护时，WIPO 相关委员会谈判和会议均采用狭义概念，不将传统及民间文化表现形式纳入考虑范围。该定义下的传统知识包括农业知识、环境知识、药学知识，以及遗传资源相关的传统知识，例如传统医药、传统捕猎技巧、动物迁徙和水源分布等知识。[18]

WIPO 所采用的狭义定义将传统及民间文化表现形式排除在外，并要求相关知识体现传统生活方式或世代相传，集中了保护的范围并增加了知识产权体系应用的可行性。这一定义使得其草案更有针对性，知识产权保护的力度更大，WIPO 缔约国的传统知识可能受到更好的保护。为实施《名古屋议定书》，各国制定国内法时，可以参考 WIPO 的定义，一方面更好地利用已有的知识产权制度，另一方面尽可能避免国内惠益分享制度与知识产权体系产生冲突。

（三）相关性的判定标准

主张对“遗传资源相关传统知识”享有权利时的常见问题之一是遗传资源和传统知识要相关到何种程度。关于相关性的标准存在分歧：如果按照遗传资源的定义来判断相关性，该传统知识应当能够指向来自植物、动物或者其他来源的遗传功能单位；[19] 而从传统知识持有者的角度出发，应当采取宽泛的标准，传统知识只要能够指向含有遗传功能单位的遗传材料即可。[20] 例如，当一个土著群体认为加入了红枣、人参炖的鸡汤能够预防感冒时，严格标准要求该土著群体知悉鸡汤中发挥药效的具体科学成分是什么，而根据宽泛标准该鸡汤配方本身就满足相关性要求。

关于与植物相关的传统知识，情况通常较容易判断。《公约》的资料清单表明传统知识是植物制剂业的基础，欧洲的传统医药、传统中药和印度草药都是

---

17 世界知识产权组织：《保护传统知识：经修订的目标和原则》，WIPO/GRTKF/IC/17/5，第 3 条。

18 *Traditional Knowledge and Traditional Cultural Expressions*, WIPO, WIPO/GRTKF/IC/22/INF/8, 2012, p. 14.

19 《生物多样性公约》第 2 条；Elisa Morgera *et al, Unraveling the Nagoya Protocol: A Commentary on the Nagoya Protocol on Access and Benefit-sharing to the Convention on Biological Diversity* (Brill, 2014), p. 60.

20 *Report of the Meeting of the Group of Technical and Legal Experts on Traditional Knowledge Associated with Genetic Resources in the Context of the International Regime on Access and Benefit-Sharing*, UN Environment Programme (UNEP), UNEP/CBD/WG-ABS/8/2, Annex, para.12.

很多新产品的来源。这不仅为长期的传统使用所证明，也为越来越多的深入研究所证明。[21]实践中，很多土著或地方社区对草药使用方法的权利主张得到了支持，有些甚至得到了知识产权保护，基本未出现质疑植物使用方法与遗传资源相关性的情况。例如，产于印度和中国的一种姜黄（*Curcuma longa*），能够消炎并促进伤口愈合，在东南亚及南亚用来治疗感冒发烧、肝脏病变、风湿病等已经上千年；两个美国学者以此在美国申请专利获批后，印度提出异议并举证其对该传统知识的权利后，美国专利局撤销了该专利。[22]由此可见，关于植物的传统医药知识受到的保护程度是较高的。

传统知识涉及动物时情况则较为复杂，是争议的集中点。与植物相比，动物体积较大、结构复杂。即使是同一种动物，各个部位在传统医药中的效用千差万别。大量的动物相关传统知识是以食疗药方形式存在的，大多非常笼统模糊，与遗传资源的相关性相对有限。例如，中医《金匮要略》中有一食疗药方为："寒疝腹中痛，及胁痛里急者，当归生姜羊肉汤主之。"这一传统知识将羊肉用以温补气血，但是未明确指明其所用部位或器官。在此类情况下，能否将药方认定为与遗传资源相关传统知识并以此要求惠益分享是存疑的。

除此之外，实践中还有一种争议情形：在医药领域，制药公司从笼统的传统知识中获得启发从而研发出特定药物是否需要惠益分享？以中医药膳为例，其功效并不指向治疗某一具体部位，而是通过使人体达到阴阳调和而康复，在整体上起到"养生"的作用。如果研究者因此受到启发，从该药方中找到一味药研究开发出能够治疗特定疾病的现代医学药物，是否构成对于该传统知识的利用而因此需要承担惠益分享责任？实践中还存在土著人及地方社区所持传统知识与宗教高度相关的情形，即土著人及地方社区认定服用某种植物会受到宗教的庇护从而延年益寿，对于他们的药用功能几乎没有认识。在这种情况下，对该植物进行研究并开发出药物，是否构成利用遗传资源相关传统知识？

以上问题的答案对传统知识持有者及药物开发者均会产生巨大影响，学界

21　Sarah Laird, Rachel Wynberg, "Bioscience at a Crossroads: Access and Benefit Sharing in a Time of Scientific, Technological and Industry Change: The Pharmaceutical Industry," Secretariat of the Convention on Biological Diversity, 2013, https://www.cbd.int/abs/resources/factsheets.shtml (Last visited on 22 June 2020).

22　Tobias Kiene, *The Legal Protection of Traditional Knowledge in the Pharmaceutical Field: An Intercultural on the International Agenda* (Waxmann, 2011), p.16.

和国家实践对此尚未形成确定的判断标准。但是从目前得到认可的部分对药物开发有价值的传统知识案例中，可总结一定的规则。例如，印度用蛇根草（*Rauwolfia serpentine*）来治疗高血压；南美洲用奎宁（*Cinchona spp.*）来治疗疟疾；马达加斯加用紫长春花属（*Catharanthus roseus*）来治疗癌症、糖尿病和疟疾；南非用蝴蝶亚仙人掌（*Hoodia gordonii*）抑制饥饿。[23] 通过分析可以发现，在以上得到认可的遗传资源相关传统知识中，传统知识持有者对于某一确定植物治疗某一特定疾病的功效存在清晰和明确认知。因此，应当参考此标准判断遗传资源与传统知识之间的相关性，从而较好地平衡传统知识持有者与利用者之间的权利义务关系，避免惠益分享的天平向某一方过度倾斜。

三、遗传资源相关传统知识的利用（utilization）问题

根据《名古屋议定书》第 3 条，议定书适用于与《公约》范围内的与遗传资源相关的传统知识和利用此种知识所产生的惠益。由此可知，对于传统知识的惠益分享义务的基础是对传统知识的利用。因此，利用遗传资源相关传统知识的定义和判断标准也成为重要议题，其概念内涵的范围大小将直接影响惠益分享的范围。

尽管《名古屋议定书》多个条款、前言和附件使用了“遗传资源相关传统知识的利用”的表述，[24] 但并没有对利用进行明确定义。《名古屋议定书》有目的地留下这一立法空白，实际是为了避免对与传统知识有关的若干用语作出定义或说明。由于与传统知识有关的概念和规定所涉及的影响范围广泛、情况复杂，对传统知识利用的理解需要为各个缔约国及其政府提供充分的灵活性，[25] 而不能一刀切地作出规定。由于没有其他国际条约涉及这一概念，如何理解这个立法上的空白变得至关重要。与《名古屋议定书》中任何其他与传统知识有关的术语或规定一样，解释“传统知识的利用”时需要依据相关的国际人权法规则，并将土著和地方社区的习惯法、规章制度和程序法等纳入考虑范围。

根据《维也纳条约法公约》第 31 条第 1 款，条约应依其用语按其上下文并参照条约之目的及宗旨所具有之通常意义，善意解释之。虽然未对“遗传资

23　薛达元、秦天宝、蔡蕾：《遗传资源相关传统知识获取与惠益分享制度研究》，中国环境科学出版社，2012，第 52 页；Tobias Kiene, *The Legal Protection of Traditional Knowledge in the Pharmaceutical Field: An Intercultural on the International Agenda* (Waxmann, 2011), p.16.

24　Art. 3, 5(5), 10, 12(2)-(4), 16(1), 18(1), Preamble and Annex, Nagoya Protocol.

25　*Report of the Expert Meeting on Traditional Knowledge*, UNEP, UNEP/CBD/WG-ABS/8/2, p. 10.

源相关传统知识的利用”进行概念界定，但《名古屋议定书》第 2 条 c 款对“遗传资源的利用”作出了定义：“利用遗传资源”是指对遗传资源的遗传和（或）生物化学组成进行研究和开发，包括通过应用《公约》第 2 条定义的生物技术。结合《名古屋议定书》上下文及其宗旨综合界定“利用遗传资源相关传统知识”这一概念时，[26]主流观点是通过体系解释，结合“利用遗传资源”的概念解释“利用遗传资源相关传统知识”，即将后者的利用同样解释为“研究和开发”。

尽管如此，《公约》或《名古屋议定书》均未对研究和开发作出明确定义。根据其通常意义，研究是指为发现和解释事实而进行的调查或实验；[27]在《名古屋议定书》语境下，研究和开发相联系使用时，是指旨在通过技术创新来创造新产品和给旧产品创造新形式这两个紧密相关的过程。[28]这可能包括为了发现物质潜在用途并为其实际应用，针对遗传资源的遗传或生物化学组成而进行的所有类型的系统工作。[29]在传统知识领域，则可能涉及以传统知识为基础或指引开展的上述工作。

四、《名古屋议定书》的溯及力问题

《公约》是首次规定“遗传资源相关的传统知识”保护规则的国际条约，《名古屋议定书》作出了进一步规定。[30]但实际情况是，在上述条约生效之前，大量与遗传资源相关的传统知识已被获取或利用，并进行研究、开发及商业化。以制药业为例，全球制药企业早已收集及持有足够丰富的遗传资源及相关传统知识；随着科技进步和新型研究工具的产生，制药业对于获取“新”遗传资源

26　Elisa Morgera *et al, Unraveling the Nagoya Protocol: A Commentary on the Nagoya Protocol on Access and Benefit-sharing to the Convention on Biological Diversity* (Brill, 2014), p. 74.

27　“A Search or Investigation Undertaken to Discover Facts and Reach New Conclusions by the Critical Study of A Subject or by A Course of Scientific Inquiry,” Oxford Dictionaries Online, http://oxforddictionaries.com/definition/english/research (Last visited on 22 June 2020).

28　“...two intimately related processes by which new products and new forms of old products are brought into being through technological innovation,” Encyclopedia Britannica Online, www.britannica.com/EBchecked/topic/499010/research-and-development (Last visited on 22 June 2020).

29　Elisa Morgera *et al, Unraveling the Nagoya Protocol: A Commentary on the Nagoya Protocol on Access and Benefit-sharing to the Convention on Biological Diversity* (Brill, 2014), p. 63.

30　托马斯 · 格雷伯：《遗传资源获取与惠益分享的〈名古屋议定书〉诠释》，薛达元等译，中国环境出版社，2013，第 16 页。

及传统知识的需求显著减少，现已集中转向对已有资源的多样研究和发展。[31]因此，缔约国是否可以主张《名古屋议定书》溯及既往地适用于其生效之前的情形并要求惠益分享是一个值得深入探讨的问题。

在召开《公约》第十次缔约方大会之前，"获取和惠益分享问题不限成员名额特设工作组"将《名古屋议定书草案》提交缔约方大会。[32]该草案第 3 条对《名古屋议定书》的时间范围给出了可溯及既往和不可溯及既往两种文本选择。[33]但是关于草案第 3 条的谈判未能达成一致意见，建议约文被摒弃，最终通过的《名古屋议定书》中不包含任何有关时间范围或条约溯及力的具体条款。[34]

因此，判断《名古屋议定书》适用的时间范围时，应当根据《维也纳条约法公约》中有关条约溯及力的默示条款进行解释。《维也纳条约法公约》第 28 条规定，除非缔约国赋予某一条约溯及力，否则该条约不具有溯及力。缔约国赋予条约溯及力的形式，通常体现为支持条约溯及既往的特殊条款或内容。[35]《名古屋议定书》不含有任何上述形式的条款，因此理论上无溯及力。

遗传资源相关传统知识惠益分享制度的发展阶段大致可以分为图 1 所示的三个阶段。《公约》对于获取遗传资源并公正和公平分享通过其利用所产生惠益的权利和义务首次作出了规定，上述权利义务只有在 1993 年《公约》生效之后才存在，其生效前发生的任何行为或事实，均不属于《公约》及《名古屋议定书》适用的时间范围，并且均不可被溯及既往地追究责任。因此，《名古屋议定书》必然不适用于《公约》生效前（第一阶段）的情形。但是，关于议定书在第二阶段和第三阶段的条约适用问题是存在争议的。

---

31 Sarah Laird, Rachel Wynberg, "Bioscience at a Crossroads: Access and Benefit Sharing in a Time of Scientific, Technological and Industry Change: The Pharmaceutical Industry," Secretariat of the Convention on Biological Diversity, 2013, https://www.cbd.int/abs/resources/factsheets.shtml (Last visited on 22 June 2020).

32 *Report of the Third Part of the Ninth Meeting of the ad hoc Open-Ended Working Group on Access and Benefit-sharing*, UNEP, UNEP/CBD/COP/10/5/Add.5, 2010, pp. 4-5.

33 *Report of the Third Part of the Ninth Meeting of the ad hoc Open-Ended Working Group on Access and Benefit-sharing*, UNEP, UNEP/CBD/COP/10/5/Add.5, 2010, pp. 9-10, Annex 1, Art. 3.

34 托马斯 · 格雷伯：《遗传资源获取与惠益分享的〈名古屋议定书〉诠释》，薛达元等译，中国环境出版社，2013，第 65 页。

35 Mark Villiger, *Commentary on the 1969 Vienna Convention on the Law of Treaties* (Leiden: Brill, 2009), p. 383. *Mavrommatis Palestine Concessions (Greece v. U.K.)*, 1924, P.C.I.J., Ser. B, No. 3, p. 34.

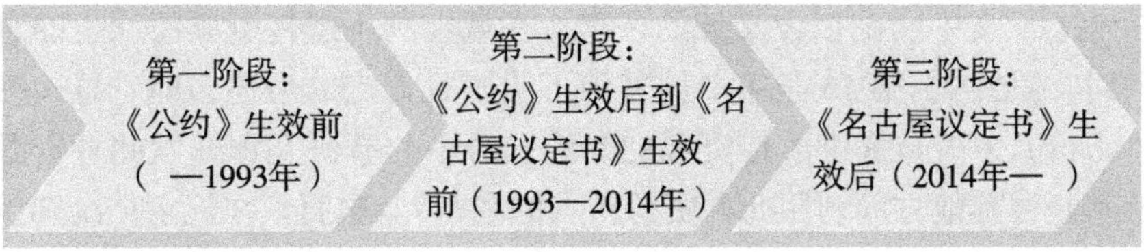

第一阶段：《公约》生效前（ —1993年）	第二阶段：《公约》生效后到《名古屋议定书》生效前（1993—2014年）	第三阶段：《名古屋议定书》生效后（2014年— ）

图 1　遗传资源相关传统知识惠益分享制度的发展阶段

（一）《公约》生效后到《名古屋议定书》生效前的情形

《名古屋议定书》在其第二阶段的适用问题上保持了缄默，所以缔约国在这一问题上产生了较大分歧。发展中国家作为遗传资源相关传统知识资源集中的国家，普遍主张《公约》生效时对因利用传统知识而产生的惠益分享义务作出规定，即使《名古屋议定书》尚未生效，惠益分享相关权利义务已经存在于《公约》，议定书应当溯及适用于这一阶段。[36] 这一主张遭到了绝大多数发达国家的强烈反对，它们拒绝对其已获得的大量惠益进行分享。[37]

解决上述争议的前提问题是《公约》是否创设了利用遗传资源相关传统知识的惠益分享义务。如果认为《公约》创设了该义务，那么缔约国在《公约》生效后《名古屋议定书》生效前确实应当承担惠益分享的责任；反之，则无须惠益分享。《维也纳条约法公约》第 31 条"解释之通则"规定："条约应依其用语按其上下文并参照条约之目的及宗旨所具有之通常意义，善意解释之。"下文将结合该解释规则对《公约》第 8 条 j 款进行解释。

从条约用语的通常意义来看，《公约》第 8 条 j 款所使用的措辞为"每一缔约国应尽可能并酌情""鼓励公平地分享因利用此等知识、创新和做法而获得的惠益"。这种表述，即"鼓励"（encourage）缔约国"尽可能"（as far as possible）对传统知识进行惠益分享，是否能够视为明确地为缔约国创设了因利用传统知识而产生的惠益分享义务，是存在质疑空间的。

36　*Collation of Operative Text Submitted by Parties, Governments, International Organizations, Indigenous and Local Communities and Relevant Stakeholders in respect of the Main Components of the International Regime on Access and Benefit-sharing Listed in Decision IX/12*, Submissions by Namibia on behalf of the African Group to the CBD Working Group on ABS, Annex I, UN Doc UNEP/CBD/WG-ABS/7/4, 2009, pp. 11-12.

37　*Report of the Second Part of the Ninth Meeting*, UNEP, UNEP/CBD/COP/10/5/ADD.4, 2010, p. 133.

参考上下文中明确创设义务的条款，在规定利用遗传资源而产生的惠益分享义务时，《公约》第 15 条第 7 款采用了明确且肯定的表述，即“每一缔约国应当（shall）……与提供遗传资源的缔约国公平分享研究和开发此种资源的成果以及商业和其他方面利用此种资源所获的利益”。然而，在规定传统知识的利用时，《公约》第 8 条 j 款则选用了相对缓和的用语，“鼓励”缔约国“尽可能”进行惠益分享。两者用语差别明显，因此，难以认定《公约》第 8 条 j 款为缔约国明确创设了传统知识惠益分享义务。在实践中，传统知识使用国可以利用这一解释空间，排除对于这一时间段的惠益分享义务。

此外，各缔约国立场的不同也造成了嗣后国内法对该问题的不同规定。例如，《欧盟执行名古屋议定书条例草案》明确规定，《名古屋议定书》只适用于其对欧盟生效之后获取的遗传资源，[38] 排除了欧盟对 2012 年之前利用遗传资源及相关传统知识所得惠益的分享义务。然而，纳米比亚等大部分发展中国家强烈主张更广泛的时间范围，将议定书适用于其生效前发生的事实。[39] 这些国家的国内立法或已经、或可预见地将与欧盟等发达国家或地区的立法相冲突，进而影响《名古屋议定书》适用范围的一致性。[40] 因此，其他缔约国在制定法律的过程中应当考虑上述冲突，以免给后期贸易或合作造成障碍。

（二）嗣后应用和商业化（subsequent applications and commercialization）的惠益分享

关于传统知识的惠益分享，还存在如下情形：对于传统知识的获取、研究与开发发生在《名古屋议定书》生效前（即图 1 中第一和第二阶段），但并未进行商业化，而在《名古屋议定书》生效之后（即图 1 中第三阶段）才开始大规模应用和商业化；或者《名古屋议定书》生效前已经将传统知识进行了应用和

38 *Proposal for a Regulation of the European Parliament and of the Council on Access to Genetic Resources and the Fair and Equitable Sharing of Benefits Arising from their Utilization in the Union*, European Commission, COM(2012) 576 Final, 2012, Draft Article 2.1.

39 *Collation of Operative Text Submitted by Parties, Governments, International Organizations, Indigenous and Local Communities and Relevant Stakeholders in respect of the Main Components of the International Regime on Access and Benefit-Sharing Listed in Decision IX/12*, Submissions by Namibia on behalf of the African Group to the CBD Working Group on ABS, Annex I, UN Doc UNEP/CBD/WG-ABS/7/4, 2009, pp. 11-12; *Report of the First Part of the Ninth Meeting,* UNEP, UNEP/CBD/WG-ABS/9/3, 2010, p. 119.

40 Elisa Morgera *et al*, *Unraveling the Nagoya Protocol: A Commentary on the Nagoya Protocol on Access and Benefit-sharing to the Convention on Biological Diversity* (Brill, 2014), pp. 79-80.

商业化。对于如上情形，该议定书生效之后产生的惠益是否需要开始分享。由于惠益实际上主要产生于嗣后的应用和商业化，上述情形是否属于《名古屋议定书》的适用范围成为值得讨论的问题。实践中，存在对这个问题的不同理解方式，有相当的解释空间。

根据《名古屋议定书》第3条，惠益分享的基础是对遗传资源和遗传资源相关传统知识的利用，即利用才是惠益分享的义务来源。如果嗣后的应用和商业化本身构成利用的一种形式，那么基于其产生的惠益必然属于《名古屋议定书》的适用范围。如上文所述，议定书语境下的利用指的是对传统知识的研究与开发。因此，问题的关键在于判断研究与开发是否包括嗣后的应用于商业化。

第一种观点认为，研究与开发所产生的惠益适用于从研发到商业化的整个商业链，包括研发过程中产生的信息和新知识。“开发”这一表述明确地将整个商业链纳入其中，即使后续进行应用和商业化的是第三方或国外公司。[41] 在这种情况下，即使某种基于传统知识研发出的药物早在1993年前就已上市商业化售卖，2014年后的应用及商业化行为也可以独立触发惠益分享机制，至少保证对《名古屋议定书》生效后所获惠益进行分享。

第二种观点认为，《名古屋议定书》第5条第1款将“利用”与“嗣后的应用和商业化”置于并列地位，[42] 可知两者之间并不存在包含关系，为两个不同的阶段，研究与开发并不覆盖整个商业链。在这种情况下，如果利用即研究与开发不受《名古屋议定书》规制，由于不存在能够触发惠益分享机制的利用行为，使用国对在嗣后应用和商业化过程中产生的惠益也没有分享义务。

由于《名古屋议定书》对这一问题规定模糊，各国在制定国内配套制度时，应当根据具体情况对这两个概念之间的关系进行明确。总体而言，传统知识提供国采用第一种解释更有利于加大保护力度，而使用国采用第二种解释则能够尽可能限缩惠益分享的范围。

41　薛达元、秦天宝、蔡蕾：《遗传资源相关传统知识获取与惠益分享制度研究》，中国环境科学出版社，2012，第69页。

42　《名古屋议定书》第5条第1款：“根据《公约》第15条第3款和第7款，应与提供遗传资源的缔约方——此种资源的原产国或根据《公约》已获得遗传资源的缔约方分享利用遗传资源以及嗣后的应用和商业化所产生的惠益。以公正和公平的方式分享时应遵循共同商定条件。”

结论

总体而言，《名古屋议定书》建立了对遗传资源相关传统知识的保护体系，将《公约》提出的原则性目标落实为可以指引实践操作的具体规则，具有划时代的意义。但是，《名古屋议定书》的规定还存在需要细化和明确的部分，特别是关于遗传资源相关的传统知识的利用，这是各国利益妥协的必然结果，也为各国实施《名古屋议定书》留下了自由裁量的空间。

我国历史源远流长，持有大量潜在价值很高的遗传资源相关传统知识，并有待开发利用。据估计，我国约有 80% 的人口以传统医药和治疗方法来维持健康。[43]从这个角度讲，我国是遗传资源及相关传统知识的提供国。另一方面，随着生物科学技术研究水平的快速提升，我国逐渐有能力，并开始去获取和利用外国的遗传资源和相关传统知识，成为遗传资源相关传统知识的获取国。我国于 2016 年成为《名古屋议定书》的缔约方，并正在逐步建立国内的惠益分享制度体系。关于遗传资源相关传统知识保护的规则零星地分布在《种子法》《畜牧法》和《中医药法》等部门法中，[44]尚未有一部专门立法将《名古屋议定书》中各项权利义务转化成国内法。

2017 年 4 月，原环境保护部发布《生物遗传资源获取与惠益分享管理条例（草案）》（征求意见稿）（以下简称《条例草案》）。[45]这是我国完善《名古屋议定书》国内法配套体系的重要一步，引发了社会各界的广泛关注。然而，《条例草案》主要集中在程序方面，对于实体问题规定不到位。比如，对生物遗传资源相关传统知识的定义仍然比较模糊，可操作性较低，基本是对于《公约》的重复。[46]国家基因库学者认为，这一定义对于我国履约来说仍然不够明晰，应当由专业学术机构作出更为细致全面的定义，否则在适用过程中将会面临大量问题。例如，无法判断近二三十年内随科技进步所产生的相关知识是否应受到

43 薛达元、秦天宝、蔡蕾：《遗传资源相关传统知识获取与惠益分享制度研究》，中国环境科学出版社，2012，第 57 页。

44 王镥权、赵富伟：《我国生物遗传资源立法模式路径选择》，《东北农业大学学报（社会科学版）》2016 年第 14 期，第 48—55 页。

45 《关于公开征求〈生物遗传资源获取与惠益分享管理条例（草案）〉（征求意见稿）意见的函》，环境保护部，2017 年 3 月 23 日（最后访问日期：2020 年 6 月 29 日）。

46 《生物遗传资源获取与惠益分享管理条例（草案）》（征求意见稿）第 2 条：本条例所称“生物遗传资源相关传统知识”，是指各族人民及地方社区在长期的传统生产生活实践中创造、传承和发展的，有利于生物遗传资源保护和可持续利用的知识、创新和做法。

保护和管理等。[47] 此外，《条例草案》未对利用标准和条约溯及力问题作出规定，显然不利于我国少数民族对 2016 年前他国利用中国传统知识的情形主张惠益分享。因此，《条例草案》仍存在较多需填补的制度漏洞。建议主管部门在后续的立法过程中，着重注意参考专业学术机构、少数民族、医药开发等各领域代表的意见，对遗传资源相关传统知识的利用作出界定。明确重要概念的范围对于切实地保护我国权利，以及维护《名古屋议定书》合作机制具有重大意义，建议尽早落实。

47　朱师达：《关于〈生物遗传资源获取与惠益分享管理条例（草案）〉（征求意见稿）的建议》，中国生物多样性保护与绿色发展基金会，2017 年 4 月 11 日，http://www.cbcgdf.org/NewsShow/4936/1962.html（最后访问日期：2020 年 6 月 22 日）。

国际法下自主武器系统的合法性及其规制

林泽宇

摘要：自主武器系统是新兴技术在武器系统中的运用，由于其使用机器或人工智能掌握人类的生杀予夺大权，众多团体或个人对这一新事物的合法性产生了怀疑和忧虑。然而，目前对自主武器系统的范围尚无公认界定，甚至在定义方法上也存在争议。本文基于对自主武器系统可以自主选择和攻击目标的宽泛界定，认为目前的国际法规则（主要是国际人道法规则）并未明确否认自主武器系统的合法性。在此基础上，讨论了国际法规则对自主武器系统提出的要求及其遵守此类规则的可能性。而对于自主武器系统造成的损害，由于人工智能或武器系统并不具有法律人格，因此相关责任最终应由使用人和国家承担。

关键词：自主武器系统；国际人道法；法律责任

几乎所有的重大科技进步都会被设想运用于军事领域，因此，当人工智能技术不断发展并成熟，各国都对这一技术在军事领域的应用给予了极大关注，并催生了“自主武器系统”（Autonomous Weapon System，AWS）这一概念的产生。与此同时，对 AWS 合法性的担忧也逐渐显现。为探讨 AWS 的合法性，国际红十字委员会（ICRC）进行了三次专家组会议；[1]联合国在《特定常规武器公约》（CCW）框架内也进行了三次非正式专家会议以及三次政府间专家会议。[2]但是，由于各国的意见分歧较大，这些国际会议除了对各国 AWS 发展中应当遵守的原则等问题达成部分共识外，对于 AWS 的合法性、规制措施、AWS 产生损害后的责任归属等问题并没有达成一致意见。因此，在国际层面，并没有特别规制 AWS 的国际法规则。

---

1 “Expert Meeting on Lethal Autonomous Weapons Systems,” International Committee of the Red Cross (ICRC) (15 November 2017), https://www.icrc.org/en/document/expert-meeting-lethal-autonomous-weapons-systems.

2 *Report of the 2019 session of the Group of Governmental Experts on Emerging Technologies in the Area of Lethal Autonomous Weapons Systems,* United Nations Office at Geneva (UNOG), CCW/GGE.1/2019/3, 25 September 2019, p. 7, para. 26.

长远地看，由于主要军事大国（包括美国、中国、俄罗斯）对 AWS 表现出极大的兴趣并投入大量资源进行研发，人工智能运用于武器已不可避免。[3] 因此，在国际法层面，研究的重点应关注现有规则对 AWS 的适用与空白，尤其是战争法对 AWS 的适用以及 AWS 造成损害的责任问题。

一、自主武器系统的概念与范围

在 2017 年 CCW 专家会议上，部分代表认为，现在开始研究 AWS 定义为时过早或无益。[4] 然而，如果不对这类武器系统的定义作出初步澄清，法律层面的讨论就缺乏明确的方向。因此，AWS 是否是一种新事物（如果答案是否定的，那么沿用既有规则即可）并界定其范围是讨论国际法能否规制、如何规制 AWS 的先决问题，这也是目前的共识。[5] 然而，目前不仅对 AWS 的定义尚未达成一致，甚至定义的方法也各有不同，主要可分为如下几类：特征式定义、分级式定义和“环”式定义。

（一）特征式定义

特征式定义的思考方式是通过提取 AWS 的几种离散特征以进行界定。如美国国防部第 3000.09 号指令性文件（DoDD 3000.09）中将 AWS 定义为“激活后可以选择和攻击目标而不需要操作员进一步干预的一种武器系统”，[6] 其特征包括：第一，是一种武器系统；第二，能够选择和攻击目标；第三，无人类干预。这也是被广泛接受的一种定义。[7]

但这种离散化的定义其实回避了对 AWS 核心特征的界定，即“自主”

---

3 “Artificial Intelligence and National Security,” *Congressional Research Service* (26 April 2018), https://crsreports.congress.gov/product/pdf/R/R45178/5.

4 *Report of the 2017 Group of Governmental Experts on Lethal Autonomous Weapons Systems,* UNOG, CCW/GGE.1/2017/CRP.1, 20 November 2017, p. 7, para. 2.

5 *Report of the 2017 Group of Governmental Experts on Lethal Autonomous Weapons Systems,* UNOG, CCW/GGE.1/2017/CRP.1, 20 November 2017, p. 7, para. 2.

6 *Directive 3000.09, Autonomy in Weapon Systems*, U.S. Department of Defense, 21 November 2012, p. 13.

7 See *Report of the Special Rapporteur on Extrajudicial, Summary or Arbitrary Executions, Christof Heyns,* Human Rights Council (HRC), A/HRC/23/47, 9 April 2013, p. 7, para. 38; *Perspectives on Lethal Autonomous Weapon System,* United Nations Office for Disarmament Office, UNODA Occasional Papers, No. 30, p. 5.

（autonomous）和“自动”（automatic）的区别问题，因此将一些已经被各国军队广泛应用的自动武器（例如车辆主动防护武器或密集阵等）也纳入了 AWS 的范围中。现有观点对自主和自动之间的区分可以归纳为两点。一是从系统的运行过程着眼，即自主系统可以不经人类干预而进行选择，而自动系统必须由人类为其选择目标。[8] 然而，问题在于，如果程序预先设定了数个具体的攻击目标（譬如使用无人机攻击几座已知坐标的建筑物），那么系统选择攻击其中一个目标的过程是否属于“选择”过程？因此，这一模糊之处表明，以能否自主选择目标区分“自主”与“自动”并不能表明两者之间的实质区别。二是从系统的运行环境着眼，2013 年联合国特别报告员克里斯多夫·海恩斯（Christof Heyns）在其报告中认为，自动系统只能在一个结构化和可预测的环境中运行，而自主系统可以在开放、非结构化和动态环境下工作。[9] 前者如家用电器，系统运行的环境是固定的，而后者没有预设的运行环境。但是，自动化系统也可以在开放和非结构化的环境下运行，如车辆自主防护系统会随着车辆的移动而变换运行环境，而理想的结构化和可预测的环境在现实中是少见的。[10] 因此，笔者认为，从运行结果着眼对二者进行区分更合适，即自动化系统只能按照人类预先编写的程序脚本运行，并完成预定的步骤，其运行结果也是可以预见的，譬如完成对某个具体目标的攻击；而自主系统则可以根据环境变化作出调整，且其运行结果也并不完全在设计者的预想之内，譬如对任何其遇到的配备敌军标识的对象进行攻击。而目前对自主武器的一大担忧就是其攻击目标可能并非人类本意，因而会导致平民伤亡或冲突升级，这种区分标准与该担忧相符合。[11]

（二）分级式定义

分级式定义将 AWS 看作一个具有层次性的概念，认为其与“自动系统”的区别并不显著。如 ICRC 认为，自主武器和自动武器的差别仅在于自主性程

8 Ozlem Ulgen, “Definition and Regulation of LAWS,” GGE Submission (5 April 2018), para. 7, https://autonomousweapons.org/definition-and-regulation-of-laws/.

9 *Report of the Special Rapporteur on Extrajudicial, Summary or Arbitrary Executions, Christof Heyns,* HRC, A/HRC/23/47, 9 April 2013, p. 14, para. 42.

10 Christopher Ford, “Autonomous Weapons and International Law,” *South Carolina Law Review*, Vol. 69, No. 2, 2017, p. 421.

11 Paul Scharre, “Autonomous Weapons and Operational Risk: Ethical Autonomy Project,” Center for a New American Security, 29 February 2016, p. 18.

度的差别。[12]这种分级式定义多被军事机构与军事科研机构所偏好。[13]例如，美国国防部关于 AWS 的描述中在自动系统和自主系统之间设立了“半自主系统”的概念，[14]一定程度上借鉴了分级式定义的方法。但是，该方法将不具有任何自主性的武器与理想中的人工智能按照自主程度进行分级，使如何界定 AWS 的范围成了纯粹的政策选择问题。其中，较为激进的观点甚至认为，从能够探测重量并据此决定是否引爆的地雷到具备人工智能的武器系统都属于自主武器。[15]

分级式定义虽然回避了自主与自动的区分问题，但法律层面的探讨仍然无法回避 AWS 的特殊性，因此，最终还是要回到“自主”概念的核心特征，否则，单纯对 AWS 进行分级式分类是没有意义的。

（三）“环”式定义

“环”式定义融合了军事理论中的“Boyd 循环”（Boyd loop）。Boyd 循环将军事行动分解为观察（observe）、定向（orient）、决策（decide）和行动（act）的循环程序（OODA），[16]人在这一循环中扮演的不同角色决定了武器的性质。“人在环中”（human-in-the-loop）是指武器只有在人的命令下才能进行攻击（如 MQ-1 捕食者无人机）；“人在环上”（human-on-the-loop）是指在人的监督下武器可以自行选择目标和攻击而人能介入其中（如密集阵）；而“人在环外”（human-out-of-the-loop）是指武器能够选择目标并在没有任何人工输入或交互作用的情况下进行攻击。[17]此时，AWS 被界定为“人在环外”或“人在环上”的、人为监督极为有限的武器系统。对这种定义的批评在于其区分标准过于简单。[18]随着武器发展得越来越复杂和精密，在武器系统的运行过程中可能

---

12 “Autonomous Weapon System: Technological, Military, Legal, and Humanitarian Aspects,” ICRC, May 26-28, 2014, p. 64, https://www.law.upenn.edu/live/files/4006-expert-meeting.

13 参见曹华阳等：《致命性自主武器系统的定义方法》，《装备学院学报》2017 年第 3 期，第 38 页。

14 *Directive 3000.09, Autonomy in Weapon Systems*, U.S. Department of Defense, 21 November 2012, p. 14.

15 Sparrow Robert, “Robots and Respect: Assessing the Case against Autonomous Weapon Systems,” *Ethics and International Affairs*, Vol. 30, No. 1, 2016, pp. 93-116.

16 John Boyd, “The Essence of Winning and Losing,” (August 2010), http://pogoarchives.org/m/dni/john_boyd_compendium/essence_of_winning_losing.pdf.

17 “Losing Humanity: The Case against Killer Robots,” Human Rights Watch (HRW) (19 November 2013), https://www.hrw.org/report/2012/11/19/losing-humanity/case-against-killer-robots.

18 William Marra, Sonia McNeil, “Understanding ‘The Loop’: Regulating the Next Generation of War Machines,” *Harvard Journal of Law and Public Policy*, Vol. 36, No. 3, 2012, p. 1179.

会具有众多独立的部分，人类可能在军事行动的某些部分（如观察）完全不介入，而在其他部分（如决策）有着较高程度的控制甚至完全控制。因此，这种方式并不一定可以准确评估系统的自主能力。

总结上述各种定义方式可以发现，无论何种定义都不能回避对自主程度和人机关系的描述，各方因其立场不同而希望适用于 AWS 的法律约束或严或松，因而在这两个方面的要求或宽或狭，由此成为引发争议的主要原因。事实上，在目前的讨论中，一方面，特征式定义（类于 DoDD 3000.09）被较多采纳，并以剩余两种定义作为辅助；另一方面，各国对 AWS 的发展与应用都还处在探索阶段，新兴技术与传统武器的结合还没有定型。因此，目前对 AWS 不宜作过分严格的定义。一个较宽泛的界定更适合国际社会在 AWS 发展初期进行监管。基于此，本文暂时采纳特征式定义。

二、AWS 对战争法规的影响

AWS 的主要用途在军事领域，因而对国际法的主要挑战也集中在战争法方面。战争法规包括了“诉诸战争的法”（*jus ad bellum*）和“战争中的法”（*jus in bello*），前者与战争或武装冲突的正义性或合法性问题有关，而后者涉及对敌对行动的管制。

（一）诉诸战争的法——AWS 更容易导致战争吗?

反对 AWS 的观点认为，AWS 会影响政治决策，因为 AWS 不需要有真正的人类投入战场，这种人力成本的优势使得国家在国际关系中更易于选择武力。并且，AWS 减少了武装冲突中实际人命的损失，社会公众可能因此而不反对甚至支持使用武力。[19]

然而，这些论述并不能推断出 AWS 的非法性。诉诸战争的法只讨论武力使用是否合法的问题以及战争的开始、结束及其法律后果。《联合国宪章》确认了自 20 世纪初形成的，在法律上不能把战争作为合法救济方法的观念，要求会员国避免使用武力或以武力进行威胁，[20]因此现代国家诉诸战争的权利已经受到

---

19 *Report of the Special Rapporteur on Extrajudicial, Summary or Arbitrary Executions, Christof Heyns,* HRC, A/HRC/23/47, 9 April 2013, p. 11, para. 58; *Special Rapporteur on Extrajudicial, Summary or Arbitrary Executions, Interim Report by Philip Alston,* United Nations, A/65/321, 23 August 2010, para. 44.

20 《联合国宪章》第 2 条第 4 款。

极大的限制。尽管如此，自卫和得到安理会授权的武力使用仍被认为是合法的行为。[21] 所以，作战武器的选择和使用问题与战争的合法性问题是分离的，武器的优势或最终造成的伤亡与战争合法性并不挂钩。事实上，如今许多武器都可进行跨境攻击，带来的优势和对战争形态的影响并不亚于 AWS，但这些武器的发展并没有显著地使国家更易于选择战争。

换言之，无论国家拥有何种武器，决定战争与和平的都是“人”。诉诸战争的法也只能在人的决策层面上进行调整，而不涉及武器审查和作战方法。所以，AWS 是否易于导致战争属于国际军备控制的问题，如一些学者指出，是属于法律之外的议题。[22] 甚至二战之后，人类战斗员的直接对抗锐减，但战争的爆发仍呈现逐渐减少的趋势，[23] 因此，AWS 使战争更可能发生的观点并不成立。

（二）战争中的法——AWS 能遵守国际法吗？

诉诸战争的法涉及开战正义，而战争中的法则涉及交战正义，包括对战争手段和方法的限制以及对战俘、伤病员和平民的保护。前者涉及 AWS 本身是否是一种合法武器的问题，后者涉及 AWS 在使用过程中应当遵守的规则问题。而在这两者之间，国家在研发和决定使用新武器时，尚有审查其合法性的义务。因此，下文从这三个方面进行讨论。

1. 马尔顿条款（Martens Clause）——AWS 是否是一种合法武器？

马尔顿条款于 1899 年第一次海牙和平会议期间由俄国代表弗里德里希·马尔顿（Friedrich Martens）提出，并被反映在嗣后历次制定的战争法条约中。纳入这一条款的目的在于防止部分国家主张凡是国际人道法未加禁止的行为即是可为的。[24]

马尔顿条款的一个反映是《日内瓦公约》的《第一附加议定书》第 1 条第 2 款，该条规定：“在本议定书或其他国际协议所未包括的情形下，平民和战斗员仍受来源于既定习惯（established custom）、人道原则（principles of humanity）和公众良心（public conscience）要求的国际法原则的保护和支配。”可以看到，因为承认了既定习惯、人道原则和公众良心对国家交战行为的约束

21 《联合国宪章》第 42 条、第 51 条第 1 款。

22 Marco Sassoli, “Autonomous Weapons and International Humanitarian Law: Advantages, Open Technical Questions and Legal Issues to Be Clarified,” *International Law Studies*, Vol. 90, No. 1, 2014, p. 313.

23 参见理查德·勒博:《国家为何而战》，陈定定等译，上海人民出版社，2014，第四章“数据集与发现”。

24 ICRC, *Commentaries on the Additional Protocols* (Leiden: Martinus Nijhoff Publishers, 1987), p. 39.

效力，所以国际人道法原则的范围远大于条约法的范围。

在 2019 年 CCW 专家会议上，各国代表仅仅原则性地承认了 AWS 的发展必须符合马尔顿条款，[25] 而正如这一条款本身的措辞一样，缺乏更为细致的解释。AWS 的反对者同样援引马尔顿条款，但也同样缺乏论证。[26] 在实践中，国际法院只是原则性地承认了马尔顿条款是解决科技迅速发展给国际人道法带来的挑战的有效途径，[27] 并没有对其内涵作过多释明。在 1996 年“威胁或使用核武器合法性咨询意见案”中，澳大利亚指出“人道”和“公众良心的要求”的概念都不是静态的，20 世纪初被国际社会认为可以接受的行为，现在可能被国际社会谴责为不人道。[28] 这一观点暗含着不能被国际社会接受的行为就是不符合人道原则和公众良心要求的行为的意思。另一部分学者则认为马尔顿条款并非是独立的法律规范，而只是提供了一个解释国际法规则的框架。也就是说，国际法院可以而且应该基于人道原则和公众良心对国际法规范进行解释，但不能仅凭人道原则和人道规范创造规则。[29]

到目前为止，尚未有国家或国际权威机构对公众关于 AWS 的态度进行过全面的调查。仅有部分学者在其研究过程中做过小范围的调研，而这几次调研均反映，对 AWS 持反对观点的占多数，[30] 但其样本总量较小，难以形成有力证据。相对而言，由“未来生活研究所”（Future of Life Institute）发起的《致命

25 *Report of the 2019 session of the Group of Governmental Experts on Emerging Technologies in the Area of Lethal Autonomous Weapons Systems,* UNOG, CCW/GGE.1/2019/3, 25 September 2019, p. 4, para. 17.

26 “Making the Case: The Dangers of Killer Robots and the Need for a Pre-emptive Ban,” HRW (9 December 2016), https://www.hrw.org/report/2016/12/09/making-case/dangers-killer-robots-and-need-preemptive-ban.

27 *Legality of the Threat or Use of Nuclear Weapons, Advisory Opinion, ICJ Reports 1996*, p. 257, para. 78.

28 *Legality of the Threat or Use of Nuclear Weapons, Verbatim Record 1995/22, ICJ Reports 1995*, p. 39, para. 10.

29 Michael Schmitt, “Autonomous Weapon Systems and International Humanitarian Law: A Reply to the Critics,” *Harvard National Security Journal*, Vol. 4, 2012, p. 32; Tyler Evans, “At War with the Robots: Autonomous Weapon Systems and the Martens Clause,” *Hofstra Law Review*, Vol. 41, No. 3, 2013, p. 718.

30 “Ethics and Autonomous Weapon Systems: An Ethical Basis for Human Control?” ICRC (3 April 2018), p. 19, https://www.icrc.org/en/document/ethics-and-autonomous-weapon-systems-ethical-basis-human-control.

自主武器宣言》更有代表性。签署宣言者承诺，出于道德原因，不会参与也不会支持致命自主武器系统的研发。迄今，已有超过 3000 名 AI 科技人员和 200 余科研机构和社会组织签字。[31] 联合国秘书长安东尼奥·古特雷斯（António Guterres）以及 28 个国家代表都明确表示，出于道德厌恶感，应当禁止致命性自主武器系统。[32]

然而，正如核武器合法性所遇到的窘境一样，即使有如此多的反对声音出现，能否判定 AWS 违反人道原则与公众良心呢？“允许机器拥有凌驾于人类之上的决定生与死的力量，是在贬低生命的价值”，[33] 这一判断可能恰当地反映了公众反对 AWS 的道德原因。但是，马尔顿条款的初衷不是为了将国际人道法与道德情感要求等同起来，而是为了避免条约规定力有不逮。因此，符合人道与公众良心要求的规则应当是那些已被认可为国际人道法规则但尚未被条约所表达出来的规则，而不是广泛的道德要求。否则，就是对国际人道法的误解（即认为国际人道法应以具有人道关怀的模样出现），但战争和武装冲突（在排除了政治色彩以后）一定是反人道的。即使核武器在大众的印象中总是与痛苦和恐惧相关联，但国际法院仅仅判定，只有使用核武器造成了不分皂白的攻击和不必要的痛苦时，其使用才是非法的，而国际法院对核武器本身的合法性并没有作出裁判。[34] 国际法院的回避态度也佐证了虽然马尔顿条款意义重大，但其实际效果可能并非如此显著。相较于 1899 年，在国际人道法规则充分而全面的今天，仅仅诉诸马尔顿条款可能无法否认 AWS 的合法性。

2.《第一附加议定书》第 36 条——使用 AWS 前的义务

1977 年《第一附加议定书》第 36 条要求，在研究、发展、取得或采用新的武器时，缔约一方有义务确认，在某些或所有情况下，该新武器是否为国际

---

31 “Lethal Autonomous Weapons Pledge,” Future of Life Institute (19 July 2018), https://www.lawfareblog.com/lethal-autonomous-weapons-systems-recent-developments.

32 “Country Views on Killer Robots,” Campaign to Stop Killer Robots (22 November 2018), https://www.lawfareblog.com/lethal-autonomous-weapons-systems-recent-developments; *UN Secretary General António Guterres' Address to the Paris Peace Forum*, United Nations, SG/SM/19338, 11 November 2018.

33 “Views of the ICRC on Autonomous Weapon Systems,” ICRC (11 April 2016), p. 3, https://www.icrc.org/en/document/views-icrc-autonomous-weapon-system.

34 *Legality of the Threat or Use of Nuclear Weapons, Advisory Opinion, ICJ Reports 1996*, p. 257, para. 78; *Legality of the Threat or Use of Nuclear Weapons, Separate Opinion of Judge Renjeva, ICJ Reports 1996*, p. 300.

法规则所禁止。由于 CCW 采用的是列举式方法规定被禁止的武器，因此，第 36 条填补了漏洞，重申了冲突方选择的作战方法和手段不是无限制的。

然而，出于国家安全和技术保密的原因，第 36 条所要求的“确认”是内部自省而非外部检查。[35] 因此，无论结论是某种新武器合法还是非法，国家都没有将调查结果公之于众的义务。因而，难以认为第 36 条为国家创设了“真正的义务”，而仅是在武器造成违反国际人道法的后果时，如果没有进行这种检查，将使国家为武器造成的损害承担责任。[36] 并且虽然有国家希望基于这一条款建立额外的机制进行监管和控制，但掌握 AWS 技术优势的国家坚决反对。[37]

就第 36 条的义务内容而言，国家主要检查新武器是否会造成不必要的痛苦。[38] 如上所述，除了由“机器人能决定生死”带来的道德厌恶感外，还没有国家或权威机构认定 AWS 会带来不必要的痛苦。与达姆弹、激光致盲武器等 CCW 禁止的武器相比，AWS 的创新之处是将新的驱动技术与既有武器结合，而不是一种新的杀伤手段，仅仅具有“自主”特征并不会使 AWS 造成额外的生理痛苦。相反，AWS 的支持者认为，机器人只按照程序行动，不具有人类所具有的一些缺点，反而比人类战斗员更能做到令行禁止，[39] 客观上可能保护战斗员免受非为军事目的而造成的伤害和痛苦，促使国际人道法的规则得到遵守。因此，使用 AWS 前的审查义务在目前可能难以构成国家决定使用 AWS 的重大障碍。

3. 国际人道法基本原则——使用 AWS 时必须遵守的原则

国际人道法对保护战俘、伤病员和平民的规定纷繁复杂，但贯穿其中的两个维度就是军事需要和人道保护，寻求两者之间的平衡催生了国际人道法的各项基本原则，如区分原则、比例原则等。其中，国际社会和国际人道法学者主要关心的是 AWS 能否遵守区分原则和比例原则。[40]

---

35 *Report of the Special Rapporteur on Extrajudicial, Summary or Arbitrary Executions, Christof Heyns,* HRC, A/HRC/23/47, 9 April 2013, p. 20, para. 107.

36 ICRC, *Commentaries on the Additional Protocols* (Leiden: Martinus Nijhoff Publishers, 1987), p. 423.

37 徐能武、龙坤：《联合国 CCW 框架下致命性自主武器系统军控辩争的焦点与趋势》，《国际安全研究》2019 年第 5 期，第 108 页。

38 *Protocol Additional to the Geneva Convention of 12 August 1949, and relating to the Protection of Victims of International Armed Conflict*, 1125 U.N.T.S. 3, 1977.

39 *Report of the Special Rapporteur on Extrajudicial, Summary or Arbitrary Executions, Christ of Heyns,* HRC, A/HRC/23/47, April 9, 2013, p. 10, para. 54.

40 张卫华：《人工智能武器对国际人道法的新挑战》，《政法论坛》2019 年第 4 期，第 144 页。

（1）区分原则

区分原则（principle of distinction）指武装冲突期间，冲突各方必须区分战斗员与非战斗员、武装部队与平民以及军事目标与非军事目标，包括了对人的区分和对物的区分。

第一，对人的区分。海牙公约体系要求战斗员佩戴有可从远处识别的标志且公开携带武器。[41] 从形式上看，只要训练数据足够且可靠，AWS 利用卷积神经网络等技术或许不难实现对战斗员与非战斗员的区分。然而，相较于海牙公约体系对战斗员的界定侧重于形式要件，日内瓦公约体系下对战斗员的界定更注重实质。《第一附加议定书》第 43 条将其定义为"由一个为其部下的行为向该方负责的司令部统率下的有组织的武装部队、团体和单位"的成员，而一个人隶属于某组织很难通过外部特征如服饰等进行判断。另外，介于战斗员和平民之间的一个中间概念是直接参加敌对行动的平民，这类平民在其参加敌对行动之外，享受平民待遇。[42] 如何判断直接参与敌对行动的身份仍是有争议的：ICRC 认为只有持续地作为某组织的战斗员才是合法的攻击目标，[43] 而反对观点认为该组织的一切人员，无论其作用如何，都可以被攻击。[44] 这种矛盾在非国际性武装冲突中更加显著，因为非国际性武装冲突（如内战）常常表现为政府武装和非政府武装之间的冲突，后者的重要支持者常常是直接参加敌对行动的平民。然而，一个平民在衣服中藏匿生活物资和藏匿炸药从外观和行迹上很难识别。所以，区分对象身份是保证 AWS 遵守区分原则的第一个困难。

AWS 面临的另一个困难是如何区分战斗员和失去战斗力的人（*hors de combat*）。明示投降意图和因伤病丧失知觉的人都属于失去战斗力的人，不能再作为合法的攻击目标。[45]"明示投降意图"的情况下，一个简便的解决途径是统

---

41 Annex, Article 1, *The Hague Convention Respecting the Laws and Customs of War on Land*, 18 October 1907.

42 Article 51, *Protocol Additional to the Geneva Convention of 12 August 1949, and relating to the Protection of Victims of International Armed Conflict*.

43 "Interpretive Guidance on the Notion of Direct Participation in Hostilities under International Humanitarian Law," ICRC (May 2009), http://www.icrc.org/Web/eng/siteeng0.nsf/htmlall/direct-participation-report_res/$File/direct-participation-guidance-2009-icrc.pdf.

44 Michael Schmitt, "Deconstructing Direct Participation in Hostilities: The Constitutive Elements," *New York Journal of International Law and Politics*, Vol. 42, 2010, p. 704.

45 Article 41, *Protocol Additional to the Geneva Convention of 12 August 1949, and relating to the Protection of Victims of International Armed Conflict*.

一表示投降意图的方式，但这毕竟只是理想情况，复杂的战争环境可能使得战斗员意欲投降而无法作出相应的表示，这便要求 AWS 能够理解人的意图和情绪，这也是目前的技术难点。[46] 因伤病丧失知觉的人和一个匍匐着的战斗员在外观上几乎难以区分，这需要联系当时的环境和各种因素加以确定，[47] 因此，能够独立行动的 AWS 需要具有理解环境状况的能力。

上述区分对于人类来说或许较为容易，但对于机器则并非如此。事实上，区分合法攻击目标和非法攻击目标的标准在国际人道法上尚未被完全概括出来。[48] 而且即使总结出部分特征后，仅凭这些特征判断目标是否可以攻击也未必符合国际人道法精神。[49] 譬如，美国曾使用无人机攻击任何位于恐怖分子营地中的适龄男性或与恐怖分子交往的人，[50] 但是仅凭这些特征并不足以证明其属于战斗员（可能只是被迫给战斗员做饭的平民）。而《第一附加议定书》第 57 条要求，在攻击对象的战斗员身份存疑时，对象应被认定为平民，因此，这种“特征攻击”可能违背国际人道法精神。所以，上述两个困难的根源除了目前技术水平不足外，更主要的是国际人道法规则固有的复杂性与模糊性。而后者的解决不仅需要法律研究的进步，还有赖于国家对国际法规则及其理解达成共识，因此需要更久的时间。所以，在复杂环境中确定攻击目标时，人类判断对 AWS 几乎必不可少，否则将可能违反区分原则。目前，国际社会达成的共识即是如此，[51] DoDD 3000.09 指令文件也要求针对人的攻击应当有人类监督（human-supervised）。[52]

---

46 *Report of the Special Rapporteur on Extrajudicial, Summary or Arbitrary Executions, Christof Heyns,* HRC, A/HRC/23/47, 9 April 2013, p. 13, para. 68.

47 “Interpretive Guidance on the Notion of Direct Participation in Hostilities under International Humanitarian Law,” ICRC (26 February 2009), p. 69, https://www.icrc.org/en/doc/assets/files/other/irrc-872-reports-documents.pdf.

48 *Prosecutor v. Galic*, Judgment ICTY, IT-98-29-T, 2003, p. 21, para. 50.

49 即所谓的特征攻击（signature strike），see Kevin Jon Heller, “One Hell of a Killing Machine: Signature Strikes and International Law,” *Journal of International Criminal Justice*, Vol. 11, No. 1, 2013, p. 1.

50 D. Filkins, “The Journalist and the Spies,” *New Yorker* (19 September 2011), http://www.newyorker.com/reporting/2011/09/19/110919fa_fact_filkins.

51 “Human judgment is essential,” see *Report of the 2019 session of the Group of Governmental Experts on Emerging Technologies in the Area of Lethal Autonomous Weapons Systems,* UNOG, CCW/GGE.1/2019/3, 25 September 2019, p. 4, para. 17.

52 *Directive 3000.09, Autonomy in Weapon Systems*, U.S. Department of Defense, 21 November 2012, p. 3.

第二，对物的区分。对物的区分即区分民用物体和军事目标。《第一附加议定书》第 52（1）条对军事目标的定义是“由于其性质、位置、目的或用途对军事行动有实际贡献，而且在当时情况下其全部或部分毁坏、缴获或失去效用提供明确的军事利益的物体”。

当物体因其性质和位置而对军事行动有实际贡献时，可以较容易地通过编程使 AWS 具有相应的区分能力。一方面，军事目标一般有显著的标志或特征，如迷彩外观、部队旗帜等，但另一方面，军事目标的标注常常属于军事情报的范围。如果处理好这两方面的信息，机器识别军事目标和民用物体或许并不困难。然而，当物体因为其目的或用途对军事行动有实际贡献而成为军事目标时，特别是民用物体转化为军事目标的情形（譬如民用机场被用于运输军用物资）时，对物的区分就较为复杂了。这需要 AWS 具备收集和分析情报从而识别敌人意图的能力，[53] 但是，情报也有可能是虚假的，或者并不充分，从而使 AWS 产生错误的判断。例如，二战时盟军就曾因为错误情报而将一座修道院误认为军事目标而进行了轰炸。[54]《第一附加议定书》第52条要求，当对某一物体是否属于军事目标有所怀疑时，应当推定其为民用物体。因此，对于因为目的或用途而成为军事目标的物体，除非 AWS 的程序能“肯定”其属于军事目标，否则，不应当允许 AWS 基于不充分的信息作出武断的判断。

（2）比例原则

比例原则（principle of proportionality）指在对军事目标进行攻击时应最大限度地减少对平民和民用物体造成的附带损害，对平民和民用物体造成的附带损害不应超过在军事行动中所要达到的预期的、具体的、直接的军事利益。[55]

比例原则较为模糊，是国际人道法中最复杂的原则之一。一个无辜的人的生命和一项军事利益之间可能难以轻易比较。[56] 所以，不同于区分原则，“合乎比例”完全是一项定性的判断，它能否通过定量分析达到可接受的结果特别值

53　Christopher Ford, “Autonomous Weapons and International Law,” *South Carolina Law Review*, Vol. 69, No. 2, 2017, p. 440.

54　Yoram Dinstein, *The Conduct of Hostilities under the Law of International Armed Conflict* (Cambridge University Press, 2004), p. 90.

55　*Prosecutor v. Kupreskic*, Judgment, ICTY, IT-95-16-T, 2000, p. 211, para. 524; *Prosecutor v. Martic*, Decision, ICTY, IT-95-11, 1996, p. 7, para. 18.

56　*Final Report to the Prosecutor by the Committee Established to Review the NATO Bombing Campaign against the Federal Republic of Yugoslavia*, International Criminal Tribunal for the Former Yugoslavia, June 2000.

得怀疑。[57] 这一点也可以从比例原则的标准看出。对于合乎比例，并没有形成统一的判断标准。前南刑庭（ICTY）采用了“理性指挥官标准”（reasonable commander standard），即一个消息相当灵通的人，合理地利用其所掌握的资料，是否可能预期这次攻击会造成过多的平民伤亡。[58] 不难发现，这种标准其实并没有给予任何攻击前的指导，而只是一种事后确定责任的规则。一个难以被量化的原则对于判断 AWS 是否遵循国际人道法来说是一个挑战。比例原则是一项国际条约与习惯国际法规则，[59] 如果当下技术无法使 AWS 符合比例原则的要求，那么，不应当减损比例原则的效力或者降低比例原则的要求，而只应当对 AWS 的使用作出更严格的限制。

从“理性指挥官标准”中，也能发现另一个对 AWS 的质疑，即“理性指挥官标准”是否意味着只有人才有资格来做这种判断呢？在 AWS 技术上具有优势的国家或许会反对这种观点：美国军方建议考虑武器系统的性质和破坏性、目标附近建筑物的组成和耐久性、基于以往的探测数据推断目标物属于民用的可能性等各项指标来评估附带损害。[60] 显然，这是为了方便计算机程序处理，然而，考虑这些方面只能判断武器造成的破坏是否会伤及平民及民用物体，例如一次轰炸是否会伤及居民区。但比例原则的内涵不止于此，还包括损害较小的平民利益而获取较大的军事利益，譬如破坏军民两用的发电厂和水厂，此时要评估目标物毁坏对平民利益造成的损失相比带来的军事利益是否过度。这种情况不仅要衡量伤及平民的可能性，而且要做“两利相权取其重”的取舍。有时，做这种取舍所要考虑的不仅仅是单纯的战场状况。譬如，二战时，考虑到将会造成的平民恐慌，美军放弃了对马尼拉的轰炸（日军和平民混杂其中）。[61] 可见，虽然有“理性指挥官标准”，但这一标准并没有提供可以公式化的规则，很多时候还依赖于人的主观判断。在面对复杂局面时，AWS 仍需要“人”作为最终的决策者与监督者。

---

57 Markus Wagner, “The Dehumanization of International Humanitarian Law: Legal, Ethical, and Political Implications of Autonomous Weapon Systems,” *Vanderbilt Journal of Transnational Law*, Vol. 47, 2014, p. 1397.

58 *Prosecutor v. Galic*, ICTY, IT-98-29-T, 2003, p. 24, para. 58.

59 Jean-Marie Henckaerts *et al*, *Customary International Humanitarian Law, Volume I: Rules* (Cambridge University Press, 2009), p. 46.

60 Joint Chiefs of Staffs, “No-Strike and the Collateral Damage Estimation Methodology,” CJCSI 3160.01 (February 13, 2009), https://www.aclu.org/files/dronefoia/dod/drone_dod_3160_01.pdf.

61 Gary Solis, *The Law of Armed Conflict* (Cambridge University Press, 2010), p. 276.

这种“两利相权取其重”的比例原则对 AWS 还有更大的挑战。军事利益的评估是动态的，不适合进行精确的数学计算，[62]而往往与武装冲突的全局状况相关。攻击一个军民两用的发电厂能带来一定的军事利益，但如果得到敌方已经完全退出该区域的情报后，攻击则不会带来任何军事利益。这只是一个简单的情形，真实战争的情况则会更复杂。这意味着能遵循比例原则的 AWS 不仅要有评估其所处环境的能力，还需要有理解和评估武装冲突全面形势的能力。因此，非军方机构与个人更倾向认为武力的种类和程度不能预先决定，必须根据有关情况加以决定。[63]

综上，尽管“理性指挥官标准”在语义上并不意味着必须有人做判断，但是由于比例原则的模糊性，AWS 可能缺乏符合比例原则要求的、对冲突局部或全局进行评估与理解的能力。因此，人类指挥官的判断必不可少，并且需要其能够随时中止 AWS 的运行。这种要求无疑阻止了 AWS 广泛应用的可能性，也是质疑 AWS 合法性最有力的论据。而 AWS 缺乏动态和全面理解战场情势能力的缺陷也限制了 AWS 的应用范围，即 AWS 只能在简单的环境和任务中使用。所以，AWS 只能是一种“战术性”武器，而不能是一种“战略性”武器。

三、AWS 的责任问题

当法律规则要求实施或抑制特定行为时，违法者因其行为应受到的惩罚就是责任。[64]没有责任，意味着违法者受不到制裁，规则也就流于具文，因此条约和习惯国际法都要求对严重违反国际人道法的行为负责。[65]例如，《罗马规约》将严重违反国际人道法的行为定义为战争罪。国际法上的责任承担模式包括了个人责任和国家责任。虽然有观点认为应当赋予机器人法律主体地位，但国际

62　Joint Chiefs of Staffs, “No-Strike and the Collateral Damage Estimation Methodology,” CJCSI 3160.01 (13 February 2009), https://www.aclu.org/files/dronefoia/dod/drone_dod_3160_01.pdf.

63　*Human Rights Implications of the Usage of Drones and Unmanned Robots in Warfare,* EXPO/B/DROI/2012/12, European Parliament, May 2003, p. 29; *Report of the Special Rapporteur on Extrajudicial, Summary or Arbitrary Executions, Christof Heyns,* HRC, A/HRC/23/47, 9 April 2013, p. 14, para. 74.

64　H. Hart, *Punishment and Responsibility* (Oxford University Press, 2008), 2nd ed., p. 196.

65　See 49, *Geneva Convention for the Amelioration of the Condition of the Wounded and Sick in Armed Forces in the Field*, 75 UNTS 31, 1949.

社会的共识仍然是由个人和国家承担最终的法律责任。[66]

（一）个人责任

国际社会对 AWS 违反国际法导致的个人责任的态度经历了一个逐步重视的转变过程。2017 年 CCW 第一次政府间专家会议上，最终结论是“在武装冲突中部署任何武器系统的责任仍然由国家承担”，并没有讨论个人责任的问题。[67] 在 2018 年的会议上，则认为责任不能转移给机器承担，要求保留决定使用武器系统的人的责任。[68] 而在 2019 年的报告中，要求国家、武装冲突各方和个人始终有责任遵守国际人道法，各国还必须确保使用 AWS 方面的个人责任。[69] 分析 AWS 的生产、制造和使用过程，主要有以下三种归责模式可以考虑：生产者责任、操作员责任和指挥官责任。

1. 生产者责任

生产者责任即将 AWS 造成的损害归责于 AWS 的设计者、生产者，要求其为设计、生产不符合国际人道法要求并造成损害的 AWS 负责。例如，程序设计者设计不能区分平民的程序，或者设计时根本没有考虑区分伤员和战斗员。这种归责方式是产品责任在人工智能中的延续。目前对于生产者责任的类型有两种看法：一是刑事责任，二是民事责任。[70]

就刑事责任而言，《罗马规约》（以下简称《规约》）对国际刑事法院（ICC）管辖的犯罪行为的构成要件做了具体的描述，而“开发武器”并不符合任何一条描述，因此，“生产”难以构成犯罪的实行行为，而一般被认为是帮助行为。[71] 然而，即使生产构成帮助行为，依据《规约》第 25 条 3（c）项使生产者承担刑事责任仍然面临两个理论难题：

---

66 *Report of the 2017 Group of Governmental Experts on Lethal Autonomous Weapons Systems,* UNOG, CCW/GGE.1/2017/CRP.1, 20 November 2017, p. 8.

67 *Report of the 2017 Group of Governmental Experts on Lethal Autonomous Weapons Systems,* UNOG, CCW/GGE.1/2017/CRP.1, 20 November 2017, p. 8.

68 *Report of the 2018 session of the Group of Governmental Experts on Emerging Technologies in the Area of Lethal Autonomous Weapons Systems,* UNOG, CCW/GGE.1/2018/3, 23 October 2018, p. 4.

69 *Report of the 2019 session of the Group of Governmental Experts on Emerging Technologies in the Area of Lethal Autonomous Weapons Systems,* UNOG, CCW/GGE.1/2019/3, 25 September 2019, p. 4.

70 美国内华达州的立法要求制造商为无人驾驶汽车承担民事责任和刑事责任，see *2017 Statutes of Nevada,* p. 4468, https://www.leg.state.nv.us/Statutes/79th2017/Stats201724.html#Stats201724page4468.

71 Tim McFarland, Tim McCormack, “Mind the Gap: Can Developers of Autonomous Weapons Systems be Liable for War Crimes?” *International Law Study*, Vol. 90, 2014, p. 376.

第一，就《规约》第 30 条规定的心理要件而言，要求行为人有意从事特定行为并有意造成某一结果，同时还需明知其行为会造成该结果。但是首先，《规约》要求的“明知”并非是一种“对可能产生结果视而不见”的心理状态，而是要确实知道其行为会必然地导致某一结果。[72] 但生产者生产设计时并不能预知使用者利用 AWS 从事战争罪行的事实，至多只能知道其行为可能会导致战争罪行发生的结果，更接近是一种“放任”的心理状态，并不符合“明知”的要求。而且，由于 AWS 的程序设计与生产工程浩大，往往需要整个团队进行协作，[73] 个人的工作结果也会受其他人工作的影响，因此也难以断定个人在设计和生产时明知其行为在日后会造成损害。其次，《规约》第 30 条要求的“故意”指的是帮助者有帮助犯罪的直接故意。[74] 因此，只有生产者故意设计不符合人道法要求的程序并且是出于帮助 AWS 使用者实施犯罪的意图，才可能构成“故意”，仅仅由于过失或者为了盈利而设计不严谨并不符合犯罪要件。

第二，AWS 可能在武装冲突前就已经进入军备序列，所以研发和生产很可能不在武装冲突期间进行。ICTY 在审判中并不支持在武装冲突之前即产生国际法上的刑事责任。在 1995 年“塔迪奇案”管辖权裁定中，法庭和检察方均认为，要违反国际人道法，就必须有武装冲突。[75] 而在 2004 年“伯拉斯季奇案”上诉判决中，上诉庭虽然承认帮助、教唆行为可以发生在主犯的犯罪行为之前，[76] 但上诉庭未认为帮助、教唆行为可以提前至武装冲突前，并且，这仅是法庭在论述过程中的一句附带说明（*obiter dicta*），法庭也没有以此作为刑事责任成立的基础。因此，如果 ICC 延续 ICTY 的审判法理，目前的实践并不足以认定武装冲突前的行为可以构成违反《规约》和国际人道法的犯罪行为。[77]

---

72 *Prosecutor v. Bemba*, Decision Pursuant to Article 61(7) (a) and (b) of the Rome Statute on the Charges of the Prosecutor against Jean-Pierre Bemba Gombo, ICC-01/05-01/08-424, 2009, p. 122, para. 362. 在《规约》的起草过程中，草案对“明知”的定义曾包含了“意识到某种情况很可能存在”的表述，但最终被删除，这一变化也可佐证“明知”要求的是“确实知道”。See *Report of the Preparatory Committee on the Establishment of an International Criminal Court,* Vol. 2, A/51/22, 1996, pp. 92-93.

73 Gary Marchant *et al*, “International Governance of Autonomous Military Robots,” *Columbia Science and Technology Law Review*, Vol. 12, 2011, p. 282.

74 *Prosecutor v. Labanga*, Judgment pursuant to Article 74 of the Statute, ICC, ICC-01/04-01/06, 2012, para.1011.

75 *Prosecutor v. Tadic*, Decision on Defence Motion forInterlocutory Appeal on Jurisdiction ICTY, IT-94-1-I, 1995, para. 67.

76 *Prosecutor v. Blaskic,* Appeal Judgment ICTY, IT-95-14-A, 2004, p. 18, para. 48.

77 Tim McFarland, Tim McCormack, “Mind the Gap: Can Developers of Autonomous Weapons Systems be Liable for War Crimes?” *International Law Study*, Vol. 90, 2014, p. 374.

综上所述，笔者认为，追究生产者的刑事责任是不现实的。

因此，多数学者探讨的其实是追究生产者的民事责任，使战争受损害者向生产者主张金钱赔偿，实质上属于侵权责任。侵权责任不需要审查生产商是否“故意”和“明知”，因此一些学者评价说，这种责任类型具有“直觉上的吸引力”，也可以促使生产商尽可能确保 AWS 的安全性。[78]但是，这一路径也存在操作困难。第一，对于国际性武装冲突而言，AWS 的生产者一般是外国企业，因此，战争受害者所在国法院可能不具有诉讼管辖权。[79]即使是在非国际性武装冲突中，或者受害者在生产者国籍国提起诉讼，受害者在时间、金钱和专业知识等方面也无法与生产者相对抗。[80]第二，按照各国实践，军事装备的生产者很少会为其生产有缺陷的产品而向受损害的平民负责。[81]如在 1988 年“波伊尔诉联合技术公司案”中，美国联邦最高法院判定，“不能对军事装备的设计缺陷追究责任”。[82]因此，追究生产者的侵权责任在现实层面存在一定困难。

2. 操作员责任

目前，可以被称之为 AWS 的武器都仍需要人类的操作，譬如，决定何时攻击或对目标进行筛选。类似于科幻电影中完全自主的 AWS 尚不存在，作为 AWS 的直接控制者，操作员也有可能成为相应的责任主体。美国 DoDD 3000.09 要求操作 AWS 的人应当“按照战争法规、相关条约、武器系统安全规则和交战规则，适当谨慎行事”。因此，在战场环境下，AWS 就相当于操作员的交战武器，操作员将为其利用 AWS 犯下的战争罪行承担刑事责任。譬如，某种 AWS 无法区分平民和战斗员，而操作员却在平民和战斗员混杂的地方选择使用这种 AWS。

如上文所述，AWS 在遵守人道法方面的主要困难在于能否符合比例原则

78 Daniel Hammond, “Autonomous Weapons and the Problem of State Accountability,” *Chicago Journal of International Law*, Vol. 15, No. 2, 2015, pp. 665-666.

79 美国最高法院曾裁定，如果国外制造商没有将产品销往美国，即使产品最终出现在美国并造成损害，美国法院也不对该国外制造商有管辖权。See J. McIntyre Machinery, *Ltd. v. Nicastro, 131 S. Ct. 2780.*

80 “Mind the Gap: The Lack of Accountability for Killer Robots,” HRW, International Human Rights Clinic (April, 2015) http://hrp.law.harvard.edu/wp-content/uploads/2015/04/arms0415_ForUpload_0.pdf.

81 Armin Krishnan, *Killer Robots: Legality and Ethicality of Autonomous Weapons* (Routledge, 2009), p. 104.

82 *Boyle v. United Technologies Corp.*, 487 U.S. 500, 1988, p. 512.

和区分原则的要求，因此，操作员可能利用 AWS 违反这两项规则。就比例原则而言，可能的情形是 AWS 不具有或欠缺对军事利益和攻击可能造成的损害进行权衡的能力，而操作员却放任 AWS 完全自主地进行攻击。这种情形符合《规约》犯罪要件第 8 条第 2（4）项的描述，可能构成战争罪。但是区分原则的情形却不同，操作员不太可能利用 AWS 对平民进行蓄意的直接攻击，而更可能是放任区分能力欠缺的 AWS 自主攻击，因此构成不分皂白的攻击。[83] 不分皂白的攻击没有被《规约》直接规定为犯罪，但是 ICTY 认为，不分皂白的攻击等同于对平民的攻击，[84] 且在各国的国内法中，不分皂白的攻击也被普遍规定为犯罪行为。[85] 因此，由于 ICC 可适用的法律包括了可予适用的条约、国际法原则和一般法律原则，[86] 利用 AWS 进行不分皂白的攻击也可以构成《规约》所制裁的国际罪行。

在心理要件上，使操作员承担刑事责任还需证明其存在“故意和明知”。在“明知”方面，需要证明操作员知道 AWS 无法区分战斗员和平民并且知道进行攻击会导致平民不成比例的伤亡。[87] 在“故意”方面，ICTY 的判例表明，使用可能伤害到平民的射击精度较低的武器即显示出攻击平民的意图。[88] 因此，操作员放任不具备区分能力或区分能力有欠缺的 AWS 自主攻击并造成平民过分伤亡的情形中，操作员有可能符合《规约》要求的心理要件。

3. 指挥官责任

指挥官为 AWS 承担责任的情形有两种：一是指挥官直接命令下级使用 AWS 犯罪；二是指挥官未能有效指挥和控制其部队而致使下级使用 AWS 犯罪。前者承担的是《规约》第 25 条规定的个人刑事责任，而后者才是承担第 28 条

83 Michael Schmitt, Jeffrey Thurnher, "'Out of the Loop': Autonomous Weapon Systems and the Law of Armed Conflict," *Harvard Natural Science Journal*, Vol. 4, 2013, p. 278.

84 *Prosecutor v. Galic*, Judgment ICTY, IT-98-29-T, 2003, p. 19, para. 52; *Prosecutor v. Martic*, Judgment, ICTY IT-95-11-T, 2007, p. 29, para. 69.

85 相关国家汇总见 Jean-Marie Henckaerts *et al*, *Customary International Humanitarian Law, Volume I: Rules* (Cambridge University Press, 2009), p. 589。

86 《国际刑事法院罗马规约》第 21 条。

87 *Prosecutor v. Galic*, Judgment ICTY, IT-98-29-T, 2003, pp. 20-21, paras. 58-61. 这里要求“不成比例”，是为了证明造成的平民伤亡并非军事行动中不可避免的附带伤害，see Jean-Marie Henckaerts *et al*, *Customary International Humanitarian Law, Volume I: Rules* (Cambridge University Press, 2009), pp. 589-560。

88 *Prosecutor v. Blaskic*, Judgment ICTY, IT-95-14-T, 2000, p. 174, para. 512.

规定的指挥官责任，即由上级对下级所犯的违反国际人道法的罪行负刑事责任，这在性质上是一种间接责任。[89]

根据国际法庭判例和《规约》，上级承担指挥官责任须满足以下构成要件：

第一，上下级关系的存在。《规约》区分了法律上的（*de jure*）指挥关系和事实上的（*de facto*）指挥关系，二者区别在于是否有官方授权。[90]但是，上下级关系的根本标准仍在于控制关系，对此，ICTY 的判断标准是上级能对下级的行为进行“有效控制”（effective control）。[91]ICC 则做了进一步的限缩，对控制的时间也做了要求，即指挥官的控制与犯罪行为之间存在时间上的重合。[92]

第二，指挥官知道犯罪即将被实施或已经被实施，这是成立指挥官责任的心理要件。对此，《规约》区分了两种情形：对于军事指挥官或具有军事指挥官身份的人来说，能够证明其“理应知道”就能满足这一心理要件；而对于并非军事指挥官但却能控制下级行动的人来说，证明标准更高，需得证明其“确实知道”或“故意不理会明确反映这一情况的情报”。[93]

第三，指挥官未能采取合理措施防止或惩罚这些行为。[94]这一要求表明，《规约》并非因指挥官未能阻止犯罪行为的发生，而是因其未尽到“控制责任”而对其进行追责，譬如在安排任务时未能考虑到下级的年龄、经验等因素。[95]因此，如果指挥官在安排战斗员操作 AWS 时，没有考虑到操作员的技术水平（譬如安排对 AWS 性能不了解的人进行操作），或者没有适时地进行视察，或者在操作员犯罪之后没有对其进行惩罚，那么就可以满足这一要件的要求。

上述讨论表明，指挥官责任并非是对 AWS 犯罪的直接控制，而是通过惩罚指挥官的不作为，间接控制操作员利用 AWS 从事犯罪的可能。因此，在归

89 K. Ambos, “Joint Criminal Enterprise and Command Responsibility,” *Journal of International Criminal Justice*, Vol. 5, No.1, 2007, p. 176.

90 Ilias Bantekas, “The Contemporary Law of Superior Responsibility,” *American Journal of International Law*, Vol. 93, No. 3, 1999, p. 578.

91 *Prosecutor v. Delalic*, Judgment, ICTY, IT-96-21-A, 2001, p. 58, para. 197.

92 *Prosecutor v. Bemba*, Decisionpursuant to Article 61(7)(a) and (b) of the Rome Statute on the charges of the prosecutor against Jean-Pierre Bemba Gombo, ICC-01/05-01/08-424, 2009, p. 147, para. 418.

93 《国际刑事法院罗马规约》第 28 条；朱文奇：《现代国际刑法》，商务印书馆，2015，第 429 页。

94 *Prosecutor v. Blaskic*, Appeal Judgment, ICTY IT-95-14-A, 2004, pp. 123-130, paras. 349-367;《国际刑事法院罗马规约》第 28 条。

95 *Canada v. Kurt Meyer*, Law Reports of Trials of War Criminals, Vol. 4, 1945, p. 98.

责方面，操作员应是归责的主体，指挥官责任只是一种辅助。

需要指出的是，部分学者所谓的指挥官责任实际上是将操作员和 AWS 的关系拟制为上下级关系，[96]认为操作员如同 AWS 的指挥官，一般可以控制 AWS 的行动。这一思路有两点不足。首先，它忽视了指挥官责任的间接责任性质，操作员承担指挥官责任的前提是 AWS 从事犯罪行为，而 AWS 无法具备《规约》所要求的心理要件，因而无法成立犯罪，更不会有指挥官责任。其次，对指挥官追责的前提是指挥官可以通过惩罚下级的行为而对下级进行控制，但是，操作员无法惩罚一个机器，[97]而由于操作员只负责操作，并非 AWS 的设计者，也不能期望操作员细致了解 AWS 的算法，因此操作员对 AWS 的控制能力要取决于 AWS 设计者设计的算法。[98]譬如，AWS 被设计成允许操作员筛选目标却不允许操作员中止 AWS 的攻击行为，因此操作员可以抗辩其不能有效地控制 AWS，从而减轻所应承担的控制责任，这不利于对犯罪的控制。所以，将操作员与 AWS 拟制为上下级的思路并不可取。

（二）国家责任

一国的国际不法行为将引起该国的国家责任。[99]一行为构成国际不法行为要求该行为依国际法归因于该国并且该行为构成对国际义务的违背。[100]《国家对国际不法行为的责任条款草案》对可归因于国家的情形做了详细的描述。因此，如果 AWS 由国家机关或者在国家指挥或控制下行动的实体操纵，这些机关的行为将会被归因于国家。

国家主要在两种情形下可能会对 AWS 造成的损害承担责任。第一种情形是其军队利用 AWS 违反人道法。《第一附加议定书》第 91 条申明，武装冲突一方应对组成其武装部队的人员所从事的一切行为负责。国家的正规军队成员，

96 "Mind the Gap: The Lack of Accountability for Killer Robots," HRW, International Human Rights Clinic (April 2015), p. 21, http://hrp.law.harvard.edu/wp-content/uploads/2015/04/arms0415_ForUpload_0.pdf.

97 惩罚的目的是“威慑”，但对于机器来说，威慑是不存在的。

98 Nehal Bhuta *et al,* eds., *Autonomous Weapons System* (Cambridge University Press, 2016), p. 332. 如计算机，用户可以控制计算机的程序运行，却未必有能力控制组成计算机的逻辑电路和连接线路。

99 *Responsibility of States for Internationally Wrongful Acts,* International Law Commission (ILC), A/56/83, 2001, Art. 1.

100 *Responsibility of States for Internationally Wrongful Acts,* ILC, A/56/83, 2001, Art. 2.

无论职位高低，都被视为国家的代理人，战斗员为其自己的行为承担个人责任并不影响国家在国际法上因战斗员的行为可归因于国家而承担国家责任。[101] 即使战斗员违反国家的指示或命令，国家也应承担责任，[102] 因为战斗员在此情形中借助了国家提供的便利条件和手段。[103] 因此，如果国家命令其军队利用 AWS 从事违反人道法的军事行动，或者战斗员违背命令或国家制定的操作规范而使用 AWS 进行不法行动，那么将这些行为归于国家是可能的。

第二种情形是，国家研发不能遵守人道法要求的 AWS 并予以军事化应用。《第一附加议定书》第 36 条要求，国家或者作为 AWS 研发、生产、装备的组织者与决定者，有义务确保 AWS 的设计符合人道法的要求，或者在 AWS 由私人主体研发的情况下作为装备的采购者，有义务对武器进行审查。如果国家故意生产使用不符合要求的 AWS 或未对 AWS 进行审查，可能会基于《第一附加议定书》第 36 条而承担相应的责任。但正如上文所说，国家对武器的审查并没有可供执行的统一标准，因此，中国代表在 2018 年 CCW 会议上指出，第 36 条无法从根本上解决 AWS 带来的责任归属问题。[104]

结论

AWS 作为新技术在战争中应用的产物，在技术成熟之前，一个确定的界定似乎并不容易得到。因此，保持法律对这一新事物的广泛规制能力，基于其核心功能的特征式定义更具优势。在这一定义下，AWS 并不具有先天的非法性，决定 AWS 合法性的关键在于其能否符合既有的战争法规则的要求。因此，不应当完全禁止 AWS 的发展（事实上也是不可能的）。目前，完全的自主武器系统在技术上尚未实现，而机器本身的容错性决定了即使其足够智能，也有违反国际人道法之虞。因此，有效的人类控制是 AWS 符合国际法的必不可少的要件。在这一前提下，国际人道法的各项规则可以通过人类控制和介入或算法实现。在 AWS 的归责方面，现有的国际法框架，即个人责任和国家责任的结合，在一定程度上可以解决利用 AWS 违反人道法规导致的责任问题。事实上，正

---

101 ICRC, *Commentaries on the Additional Protocols* (Martinus Nijhoff Publishers, 1987), p. 1093.

102 *Responsibility of States for Internationally Wrongful Acts,* ILC, A/56/83, 2001, Art. 7.

103 *Estate of Jean-Baptiste Caire (France) v. United Mexican States*, UNRIAA, 1929, Vol. V, p. 531.

104 *Position Paper Submitted by China,* CCW /GGE.1/2018/WP.7, April 11, 2018, p. 2, para. 4.

如技术中立原则所倡导的那样，技术本身不具有合法性，而是对技术的使用方式可能突破法律的底线。AWS 相关技术的领先者基本也是军事大国，因此，具有高自主性的 AWS 的出现几乎是一件必然的事。国际法无法阻止这一天的到来，而也正是这些引发人们思考、质疑甚至排斥的新事物的出现，一步步地推动着规则的逐步完善。正如前人所说，“战争是一把可怜的凿子，用来雕刻我们的未来”。

国际刑事法院逮捕令执行问题的最新发展

杨一梁

摘要：在“巴希尔案”中，国际刑事法院对时任苏丹总统巴希尔出具了逮捕令，但遭多国拒绝履行，由此引发了国家官员豁免权对国际刑事法院逮捕令执行影响的讨论。本文结合司法判例以及学者研究，认为该案在国家官员豁免权相关问题上实现了一定的突破。《国际刑事法院罗马规约》第 27 条在水平和垂直关系上限制了国家官员的豁免权。国际刑事法院可以按照其规约全部内容对安理会决议中所涉非缔约国情势行使管辖权，包括执行逮捕令。“巴希尔案”是国际刑事法院成立以来首次对非缔约国在任国家高级官员发布逮捕令的案件，相关问题仍需取决于后续的发展。

关键词：国际刑事法院；国家官员豁免权；逮捕令

引言

2005 年 3 月 31 日联合国安理会 1953 号决议将苏丹情势提交给国际刑事法院，[1]国际刑事法院检察官于同年6月1日决定接受。[2]国际刑事法院依据《国际刑事法院罗马规约》(后简称《罗马规约》) 第 13 条建立管辖权，[3]并由第一预审分庭于 2009 年 3 月 4 日和 2010 年 7 月 12 日以涉嫌战争罪、危害人类罪以及灭绝种族罪为由，对时任总统巴希尔签发逮捕令。[4]国际刑事法院依据《罗马规约》第九部分对缔约国发出逮捕和移交巴希尔的请求，但是部分缔约国以国家官员豁免权为由拒绝履行合作义务。为推进程序，国际刑事法院逐步出具

---

1 United Nation Security Council (UNSC) Resolution 1593, S/RES/1593 (2005), 31 March 2005.

2 *Report of the Prosecutor of the International Criminal Court to the UN Security Council Pursuant to UNSCR 1953,* 29 June 2005.

3 《罗马规约》第 13 条第 2 款：安全理事会根据《联合国宪章》第七章行事，向检察官提交显示一项或多项犯罪已经发生的情势。

4 *Warrant of Arrest for Omar Hassan Ahmad Al Bashir,* 4 March 2009, ICC-02/05-01/09; *Second Warrant of Arrest for Omar Hassan Ahmad Al Bashir,* 12 July 2010, ICC-02/05-01/09.

多份决定，认定乌干达[5]、吉布提[6]、南非[7]、约旦[8]等国家违反合作义务，要求缔约国执行逮捕令。

自国际刑事法院成立后，“巴希尔案”是第一个因联合国安理会提交情势确立管辖的案件，同时也是首次非缔约国在任国家高级官员被国际刑事法院发布逮捕令的案件。国际刑事法院如何突破国家官员豁免权，如何使逮捕令得到执行，这些问题都引起了国际社会的广泛讨论。

一、国家官员的豁免权

（一）国家官员的外国刑事管辖豁免权

国家官员拥有在外国免于民事或刑事起诉以及逮捕的豁免权作为习惯国际法规则已经得到了国际社会的广泛认可，[9]2002 年国际法院在刚果诉比利时的“逮捕令案”[10]中对此进行了明确认定。

习惯国际法中的国家官员豁免权是为了保证国家间相互尊重主权，并且保护代表一国的国家官员在外国免受可能滥用的权力影响。[11]当外国法庭行使管辖权时，实际上是在行使国家主权，因而应该尊重另一国国家主权，并相应地受到限制。但这并非意味着国家官员在任何情况下都享有豁免权。在“逮捕令案”中，国际法院认为，在四种例外情况下，相关对象不能因其作为国家高级官员

5　*Bashir-Uganda,* 11 July 2016, ICC-02/05-01/09-267.

6　*Bashir-Djibouti,* 11 July 2016, ICC-02/05-01/09-266.

7　*Bashir-South Africa,* 6 July 2017, ICC-02/05-01/09-302.

8　*Bashir-Jordan,* 11 December 2017, ICC-02/05-01/09-309.

9　*Gaddafi case,* General Prosecutor at the Court of Appeal of Paris, Appeal Judgment, Appeal No. 00-87215, Decision No. 64, 13 March 2001, (2001) 125 ILR 490; *Re Sharon and Yaron, HSA v. SA (Ariel Sharon) and YA (Amos Yaron)*, Final Appeal/Cassation, P.02.1139.F/2, 12th February 2003, Court of Cassation of Belgium; *Tachiona v. Mugabe,* United States District Court, S.D. New York, 169 F. Supp. 2d 259 (S.D.N.Y. 2001), October 30, 2001; *Seventh Report on Immunity of State Officials from Foreign Criminal Jurisdiction,* International Law Commission (ILC), A/CN.4/729, 2019.

10　*Case concerning the Arrest Warrant of 11 April 2000 (Democratic Republic of The Congo v. Belgium), Judgment, ICJ Reports 2002*, p. 21, para. 51.

11　Paola Gaeta, “Does President Al Bashir Enjoy Immunity from Arrest?” *Journal of International Criminal Justice*, Vol. 7, 2009, p. 320.

而免于刑事诉讼。[12]前三种均关乎一国国家官员与国内刑事法庭管辖，[13]而“巴希尔案”的争议有关国家官员与国际刑事法庭管辖，因此只有第四种例外情况与“巴希尔案”相关，即在任或曾任国家官方身份的人员在特定国际刑事法庭中受到刑事追诉。[14]

（二）国家官员在有管辖权的国际刑事法庭中的豁免权问题

为了审判二战战犯，1945 年 8 月 8 日，苏联、美国、英国以及法国签订《纽伦堡宪章》并建立了纽伦堡国际军事法庭。[15]《纽伦堡宪章》第 7 条表明：“无论被告人的官职是国家元首还是政府部门的负责人，都不构成免除其责任或减轻其处罚的理由。”联合国大会于 1946 年 12 月 11 日表明了它对纽伦堡军事法庭作出的判决以及坚持的国际原则的肯定，并指示国际法委员会将其确定为“纽伦堡原则”。[16]其中，原则三规定：“以国家元首或负有责任的政府官员身份行事，实施了违反国际法的犯罪行为的人，其官方身份不能作为免除国际法责任的理由。”[17]这一原则在《防止及惩治灭绝种族公约》第4条中得到重申，[18]并伴随国际刑事法院的建立由《罗马规约》第 27 条再一次确认。

联合国安理会于 1993 年通过了附有《前南国际法庭规约》（后简称《前南规约》）的第 827 号决议，设立前南斯拉夫问题国际刑事法庭（后简称前南刑庭）。[19]《前南规约》第 7 条第 2 款规定：“不因被告人拥有国家元首、政府首脑

---

12 *Case concerning the Arrest Warrant of 11 April 2000 (Democratic Republic of the Congo v. Belgium), Judgment, ICJ Reports 2002,*p. 25, para. 61.

13 前三种分别为：该国家官员在其本国内不享有国际法中的刑事豁免；该国家官员国籍国放弃了该国家官员对外国刑事管辖的豁免；该国家官员对其不再拥有官方身份之后的诉讼不享有豁免。

14 *Case concerning the Arrest Warrant of 11 April 2000 (Democratic Republic of the Congo v. Belgium), Judgment, ICJ Reports 2002*, p. 25, para. 61.

15 Charter of the International Military Tribunal, Annexed to the Agreement for the Prosecution and Punishment of the Major War Criminals of the European Axis, 82 UNTS 251, 1945.

16 *Affirmation of the Principles of International Law recognized by the Charter of the Nurnberg Tribunal*, United Nations General Assembly, UN Doc A/RES/95(1), 1946.

17 *Yearbook of the International Law Commission,* 1950, Vol. II, p. 375, paras. 103-104.

18 Convention on the Prevention and Punishment of the Crime of Genocide, 78 UNTS 22, 1948. 目前已有 152 个国家加入该条约。

19 7(2), Statute of the International Criminal Tribunal for the Former Yugoslavia (ICTY), Security Council Resolution 827 (1993), 25 May 1993, last amended by Security Council Resolution 1877 (2009), 7 July 2009.

或政府负责人的职务而免除其刑事责任，也不减轻其刑罚。”相似表述也出现在联合国安理会于 1994 年通过的第 955 号决议中的《卢旺达问题国际法庭规约》第 6 条第 2 款。[20] 在针对上述两个特设法庭规约作出的报告中，安理会明确强调国家官员豁免权不会构成辩护理由，也不会减轻惩罚。[21] 此外，塞拉利昂特别法庭作为一个根据安理会决议、由塞拉利昂政府和联合国秘书长通过协议建立的国际法庭,《塞拉利昂特别法庭规约》[22] 第 6 条第 2 款同样拒绝援引国家官员豁免权来阻却法庭管辖。

以上特设国际刑事法庭不仅具有否定国家高级官员豁免权的规定，也实际起诉了国家高级官员。例如，前南刑庭起诉斯洛博丹 · 米洛舍维奇（Slobodan Milosevic）、[23] 塞拉利昂特别法庭起诉和逮捕查尔斯 · 泰勒（Charles Ghankay Taylor）时，[24] 米洛舍维奇与泰勒分别时任南斯拉夫联盟共和国总统与利比里亚总统。不仅是《罗马规约》缔约国，在国际刑事法院成立后，安理会决议也两次将非缔约国情势提交给国际刑事法院以制裁国家官员。[25]

20　Statute of the International Criminal Tribunal for Rwanda (ICTR), Security Council Resolution 955 (1994), 8 November 1994, last amended by Security Council Resolution 1878 (2009), 7 July 2009. “The official position of any accused person, whether as head of state or government or as a responsible government official, shall not relieve such person of criminal responsibility nor mitigate punishment.”

21　*Report of the Secretary-General, Pursuant to Paragraph 2 of Security Council Resolution 808 (1993)*, UNSC, S/25704, 3 May 1993, p. 14; *Final Report of the Independent Commission of Experts Established in Accordance with Security Council Resolution 935 (1994), Annex to Letter Dated 9 December 1994 from the Secretary-General Addressed to the President of the Security Council,* UNSC, S/1994/1405, pp. 33-34, paras. 171, 173.

22　Statute of the Special Court for Sierra Leone (SCSL), Annexed to the Agreement between the United Nations and the Government of Sierra Leone Pursuant to Security Council Resolution 1315 (2000), 14 August 2000, 2178 UNTS 38342. “The official position of any accused persons, whether as head of state or government or as a responsible government official, shall not relieve such person of criminal responsibility nor mitigate punishment.”

23　*The Prosecutor of the Tribunal v. Slobodan Milosevic,* 22 May 1999, Case No. IT-99-37.

24　*The Prosecutor v. Charles Ghankay Taylor*, Decision Approving the Indictment and Order for Non-disclosure, 7 March 2003, SCSL-2003-01-I; *The Prosecutor v. Charles Ghankay Taylor*, Indictment, 7 March 2003, SCSL-2003-01-I; *The Prosecutor v. Charles Ghankay Taylorr*, Warrant of Arrest and Order for Transfer and Detention, 7 March 2003, SCSL-2003- 01-I.

25　安理会第 1593 号决议提交的苏丹情势，安理会第 1970 号决议提交的利比亚局势，see UNSC Resolution 1970 (2011)。

需要特别说明的是，国家官员豁免权不适用于国际刑事法庭的原因在于国际刑事法庭的管辖与国内刑事法庭的管辖来源不一样。正如上文所述，国家主权平等是国家官员外国刑事豁免权的根本原因。但是，国际刑事法庭并不代表某一特定国家，而是代表国际社会整体对国际刑事犯罪进行管辖。所以，“平等者之间无统治权”这一基于国家主权产生的原则不适用于国际刑事法庭，也不会阻碍国家官员被国际刑事法庭起诉。[26]

综上所述，目前已有实践表明，在对特定事项有管辖权的国际刑事法庭中，国家官员不享有豁免权。尽管如此，正如国际刑事法院在其“约旦违反义务决定”中提到的那样，[27]目前主要依据相关条约、公约以及国际刑事法庭的判决来证明习惯国际法。但通过“巴希尔案”可以看出，不少国家仍然对国际刑事法院逮捕非缔约国国家官员持有争议，[28]这无疑削弱了法院的上述观点。

二、《罗马规约》第 27 条对逮捕令执行的影响

《罗马规约》第 27 条规定了官方身份无关性，[29]对国际刑事法院产生了两方面的影响：第一是缔约国与国际刑事法院之间的垂直影响，即阻止以国家官员豁免权为由，拒绝逮捕或移交被法庭要求逮捕或移交的本国人；第二是缔约国之间的水平影响，即阻止以国家官员豁免权为由，拒绝履行国际刑事法院逮捕或移交另一国国家官员的请求。[30]作为司法机构，国际刑事法院没有自己的执法部门或警察部队，需要通过与各国进行合作来逮捕并将被捕者转移到海牙国际刑事法院拘留中心。[31]《罗马规约》第 27 条通过以上两方面的影响，保证缔

---

26 *The Prosecutor v. Charles Ghankay Taylor,* Decision on Immunity from Jurisdiction, 31 May 2004, SCSL-2003-01-I, para. 43; *Bashir-Jordan,* 6 May 2019, ICC-02/05-01/09 OA2, p. 58, para. 115.

27 *Bashir-Jordan,* 6 May 2019, ICC-02/05-01/09 OA2, p. 57, para. 113.

28 如前文所述，约旦、南非、尼日利亚等《罗马规约》缔约国家都拒绝履行逮捕令；非洲联盟委员会反对国际刑事法院对巴希尔出具逮捕令；中国也认为针对巴希尔的逮捕令存在不妥之处。

29 《罗马规约》第 27 条：“（一）本规约对任何人一律平等适用，不得因官方身份而差别适用。特别是作为国家元首或政府首脑、政府成员或议会议员、选任代表或政府官员的官方身份，在任何情况下都不得免除个人根据本规约所负的刑事责任，其本身也不得构成减轻刑罚的理由。（二）根据国内法或国际法可能赋予某人官方身份的豁免或特别程序规则，不妨碍本法院对该人行使管辖权。”

30 *Bashir-South Africa,* 6 July 2017, ICC-02/05-01/09-302, p. 28, para. 76.

31 “How the Court Works,” ICC, https://www.icc-cpi.int/about/how-the-court-works (Last visited on July 7, 2020).

约国能够尽到充分合作义务，促使逮捕令得到落实。

（一）垂直影响

第 27 条属于《罗马规约》第三部分“刑法的一般原则”，合作义务则出现在第九部分“国际合作与司法协助”。因此，有观点认为，第 27 条的规定只涉及法院行使管辖权的能力，条款本身并不为缔约国创造任何权利或强加任何义务，也不涉及缔约国逮捕或向法院移交人员的问题。[32] 然而，《罗马规约》第九部分包括了一般义务、移交、逮捕等合作、协作内容，[33] 这些都受第三部分一般原则的制约。因此，不应将两部分割裂来看，而应依据《维也纳条约法公约》第 31 条，[34] 结合《罗马规约》的目的及宗旨，进行整体解释。

从《罗马规约》目的及宗旨来看，设立国际刑事法院最重要的意义之一就是确保普遍尊重全世界个人的人权和基本自由。国际刑事法院只针对《罗马规约》第 5 条列出的犯罪拥有管辖权，涉及灭绝种族罪、危害人类罪、战争罪以及侵略罪。这些都是被国际社会关注的最严重的犯罪，也是严重违反国际人权法以及国际人道法的行为。[35] 国际刑事法院通过确立个人责任，填补国际法律体系中缺失的环节，旨在实现所有人的正义，结束有罪不罚的现状，增加结束冲突的可能性。[36] 想要实现以上目的，必须通过第 27 条承认官方身份无关性。由此看来，第 27 条当仁不让地在《罗马规约》中处于核心地位，自然需要贯穿《罗马规约》的全部内容，包括第九部分“国际合作与司法协助”。

同时，结合上下文考虑，第 27 条第 2 款特别表明不可援引国内法中的豁免。《罗马规约》第 21 条规定国际刑事法院本身不援引国内法作为法源，这一款的目的就是强调依据国内法享有豁免权的人不可援引国内法拒绝逮捕。[37] 国际刑事法院依赖于缔约国的合作以实施逮捕令，若位于第三部分的第 27 条与位于第九部分的合作义务无关，那么将导致国家官员在面对逮捕令时仍然享有豁

32 *Bashir-Jordan,* 12 March 2018, ICC-02/05-01/09-326, p. 10, para. 16.

33 参见《罗马规约》第 86 条、第 89 条、第 91 条和第 93 条。

34 《维也纳条约法公约》第 31 条第 1 款：“条约应依其用语按其上下文并参照条约目的及宗旨所具有的通常意义进行善意解释。”

35 “Core Crimes Defined in the Rome Statute of the International Criminal Court,” ICC, http://www.iccnow.org/documents/FS-CICC-CoreCrimesinRS.pdf (Last visited on 30 May 2020).

36 “Rome Statute Of The International Criminal Court-Overview,” ICC, https://legal.un.org/icc/general/overview.htm (Last visited on 30 May 2020).

37 *Bashir-Jordan,* 3 April 2018, ICC-02/05-01/09-331, p. 13, para. 25.

免权，则产生无法逮捕该国家官员的结果。

为了确保国际刑事法院有效行使管辖权并且有效惩治国际刑事犯罪，《罗马规约》第 27 条发挥的直接影响就是缔约国不可在国际刑事法院中通过援引国家官员豁免权拒绝逮捕或移交本国国家官员。

（二）水平影响

国际刑事法院需要通过其缔约国来行使自己的管辖权，除了向某一缔约国发出移交其国家官员这种受垂直影响约束的请求之外，也很有可能提出让某一缔约国去逮捕另一国国家官员这种涉及水平关系的请求，“巴希尔案”就属于这种情况。有观点认为，第 27 条并不存在水平影响，国家官员豁免权仍存在于一缔约国试图逮捕另一国国家官员的情形，并且《罗马规约》第 98 条[38]就是为了解决这一问题。[39]持该观点者认为，国际刑事法院正是因为意识到执行其请求可能与被请求国所负的国际法义务产生冲突，所以才利用第 98 条避免缔约国陷入违反国家官员豁免权的困境。[40]甚至有观点认为，该条款是对国家官员豁免权的保留。[41]

在评价这一观点之前，首先应当明确第 98 条中“第三国”一词的含义，讨论第三国所指代的对象。根据《维也纳条约法公约》第 2 条，第三国为非现有缔约国。但是，条约的起草者也可以赋予第三国其他含义，加之在《罗马规约》起草过程中并没有对第三国进行过多讨论，考虑到不应使条约出现起草者预料之外的状况，第 98 条第中的第三国应被解释为被请求国以外的国家。[42]因此，第三国可以分为缔约国和非缔约国。

对于国际刑事法院请求一缔约国逮捕另一缔约国国家官员的情形，第 98 条

38 《罗马规约》第 98 条第 1 款：“如果被请求国执行国际刑事法院的一项移交或协助请求，该国将违背对第三国的个人或财产的国家或外交豁免权所承担的国际法义务，则国际刑事法院不得提出该项请求，除非国际刑事法院能够首先取得该第三国的合作，由该第三国放弃豁免权。”

39 *Bashir-Jordan,* 12 March 2018, ICC-02/05-01/09-326, p. 11, para. 19.

40 喻贵英：《析个人国际豁免权对国际刑事法院逮捕令的制约——以苏丹总统巴希尔个案为考察对象》，《时代法学》2013 年第 2 期，第 91 页；Paola Gaeta, “Does President Al Bashir Enjoy Immunity from Arrest?” *Journal of International Criminal Justic*e, Vol. 7, 2009, p. 328.

41 *Bashir-Jordan,* 12 March 2018, ICC-02/05-01/09-326, p. 11, para. 20.

42 “Article 98-Third State,” ICC, https://www.casematrixnetwork.org/cmn-knowledge-hub/icc-commentary-clicc/commentary-rome-statute/commentary-rome-statute-part-9/#c2175 (Last visited on May 30, 2020).

并不能证明第 27 条不存在水平影响。首先，第九部分第 86 条要求缔约国与法院充分合作。根据上诉庭的解释，充分合作的义务包括缔约国对法院为了有效行使管辖权的所有义务。[43] 这里的管辖不仅指司法管辖，还有执行管辖，包括逮捕与移交。[44] 如果第 27 条只约束缔约国与法院的垂直关系，却在缔约国与缔约国的水平关系间承认国家官员豁免权，那么豁免权将阻碍逮捕，进而阻碍充分合作义务的履行，法院的管辖权也就无法有效行使。第 86 条规定的充分合作义务既需要以第 27 条为前提，也是对第 27 条水平影响的承认。其次，缔约国因应国际刑事法院要求进行合作而执行逮捕令时，并不是为了对另一国国家官员行使本国司法管辖权，而是作为国际刑事法院的工具，[45] 帮助其执行国际管辖权。[46] 最后，第 98 条文本本身并没有规定或是保留任何豁免权。结束犯罪、惩治犯罪的个人是国际刑事法院设立的初衷之一，缔约国加入《罗马规约》也就认同了国家官员豁免权不应阻碍法院管辖权。第 98 条实际上是一条规定法院在面对存在豁免的情况时应该如何操作的程序性规则，[47] 规范的对象是法院自身，而非国家。法院参考《罗马规约》第 21 条中适用的法律，[48] 判断豁免权是否存在；如果豁免权存在，法院才应当按照第 98 条的规定取得相应国家的放弃。[49]

对于国际刑事法院请求某一缔约国逮捕非缔约国国家官员的情形，尽管国际刑事法院在“巴希尔案”中要求逮捕非缔约国国家官员，但该非缔约国是安理会决议提交情势涉及的国家，该国因安理会决议负有与缔约国相同的义务而受到《罗马规约》第 27 条的限制。[50] 如上文所述，此时执行逮捕令不会受国家

43 *Bashir-Jordan,* 6 May 2019, ICC-02/05-01/09 OA2, p. 70, para. 143.

44 *Bashir-Jordan,* 6 May 2019, ICC-02/05-01/09 OA2, p. 63, para. 125.

45 *Bashir-Malawi,* 2001, ICC-02/05-01/09-139, p. 20, para. 46.

46 *Bashir-Jordan,* 6 May 2019, ICC-02/05-01/09 OA2, p. 64, para. 127.

47 *Bashir-Jordan,* 6 May 2019, ICC-02/05-01/09 OA2, p. 65, para. 130.

48 《罗马规约》第 21 条：“（一）本法院应适用的法律依次为：1. 首先，适用本规约、《犯罪要件》和本法院的《程序和证据规则》；2. 其次，视情况适用可予适用的条约及国际法原则和规则，包括武装冲突国际法规确定的原则；3. 无法适用上述法律时，适用本法院从世界各法系的国内法，包括适当时从通常对该犯罪行使管辖权的国家的国内法中得出的一般法律原则，但这些原则不得违反本规约、国际法和国际承认的规范和标准。（二）本法院可以适用其以前的裁判所阐释的法律原则和规则。”

49 *Bashir-Jordan,* 6 May 2019, ICC-02/05-01/09 OA2, p. 65, para. 130.

50 详见本文第三部分的论述。

官员豁免权的影响。此外，根据国际刑事法院的解释，即使是在极特殊情况下，法院在没有取得相应国家的放弃就发出了针对不在安理会提交情势内的非缔约国国家官员的逮捕令，被请求国也不能擅自拒绝履行逮捕令，因为第 98 条是一条针对法院的程序性规则，该条款并不赋予国家拒绝合作的权利。[51]

尽管如此，如果第 98 条仅是针对法庭的程序性规定，那么该条款似乎更应该被规定在《罗马规约》规定法院程序的第五部分调查与起诉中，而不是在规定国家合作义务的第九部分中。

三、安理会决议对逮捕令执行的影响

《罗马规约》于 1998 年 7 月 17 日至 12 月 31 日开放签署，此后向所有国家开放加入。根据《维也纳条约法公约》第 34 条，条约非经第三国同意，不为第三国创设权利或义务。作为条约，《罗马规约》的效力只及于缔约国。本文第二部分论证了，如果逮捕对象所在国与被请求执行国均为《罗马规约》缔约国，那么第 27 条可以保证逮捕令的执行。但是，“巴希尔案”的争议问题源于苏丹并非是《罗马规约》的缔约国。在这种情况下，逮捕令的执行是否会受到国家官员豁免权的影响?

在提交苏丹情势时，安理会第 1593 号决议第一段内容为：“决定于 2002 年 7 月 1 日起，将局势提交联合国安理会国际刑事法院检察官”；第二段内容为：“决定苏丹政府和冲突的所有其他各方应根据本决议与法院和检察官充分合作并提供任何必要的援助”。[52] 有观点认为，该决议至多确立了国际刑事法院的管辖权，不能表明《罗马规约》可适用于苏丹，因为《罗马规约》对合作义务已有规定，如果自动适用于苏丹，决议就无须在第二段特别规定苏丹的合作义务。[53] 但本文认为，正是因为决议的上述内容，国际刑事法院不仅可以根据《罗马规约》对苏丹情势行使管辖权，还使苏丹需要像缔约国一样与国际刑事法院合作，从而保证逮捕令的执行。

（一）安理会决议与国际刑事法院管辖权

根据《罗马规约》第 13 条，国际刑事法院可以在三种情况下行使管辖，其中包括联合国安理会根据《联合国宪章》第七章行事，向检察官提交犯罪或情

---

51 *Bashir-South Africa,* 6 July 2017, ICC-02/05-01/09-302, p. 37, para. 106.

52 United Nation Security Council Resolution 1593 (2005), S/RES/1593 (2005), 31 March 2005.

53 *Bashir-Jordan,* 12 March 2018, ICC-02/05-01/09-326, p. 27, para. 59.

势。[54]《罗马规约》第 1 条规定，国际刑事法院的管辖权和运作方式均根据《罗马规约》的条款；第 13 条的引言部分表明，无论因为何种理由拥有管辖权，国际刑事法院都需要按照《罗马规约》来行使。国际刑事法院由安理会决议第一段触发管辖权时，也被触发了最基本的法律框架——《罗马规约》，并且是《罗马规约》的全部内容。[55] 因此，尽管被提交国苏丹为非缔约国，国际刑事法院仍可以依据安理会决议按照《罗马规约》行使管辖权。[56]

尽管如此，仍然需要明确的是：国际刑事法院对非缔约国情势的管辖权因安理会决议建立，并不意味该非缔约国将成为《罗马规约》的缔约国；成为《罗马规约》的缔约国仍需国家明确表达受拘束的意图。

（二）安理会决议对被提交国义务的影响

因为国际刑事法院能够对苏丹所涉情势依据《罗马规约》整体进行管辖，因此，第九部分的合作义务具有可适用性。《罗马规约》第九部分规定了两种合作义务，分别为针对缔约国的第 86 条与针对非缔约国的第 87 条第 5 款。由此可见，尽管安理会可以附加给非缔约国与国际刑事法院合作的义务，但是《罗马规约》并没有特别规定针对安理会提交情势中非缔约国的合作义务。[57] 因此，在安理会决议缺少明确取代《罗马规约》合作方式的情况下，因安理会决议而与国际刑事法院合作的国家应当或依照缔约国的标准进行合作，或依照非缔约国的标准进行合作。[58]

缔约国根据《罗马规约》第 86 条应与国际刑事法院充分合作。非缔约国根据第 87 条第 5 款可以根据特别安排或是与国际刑事法院达成的协议以及其他适当基础，按规定提供协助。从表面上看，苏丹不是缔约国，所以应当适用非缔约国的合作义务，但由于苏丹没有接受任何特别安排或是与国际刑事法院达成

---

54 《罗马规约》第 13 条："在下列情况下，本法院可以依照本规约的规定，就第 5 条所述犯罪行使管辖权：（1）缔约国依照第十四条规定，向检察官提交显示一项或多项犯罪已经发生的情势；（2）安全理事会根据《联合国宪章》第七章行事，向检察官提交显示一项或多项犯罪已经发生的情势；或（3）检察官依照第十五条开始调查一项犯罪。"

55 *Bashir-South Africa,* 6 July 2017, ICC-02/05-01/09-302, p. 31, para. 86.

56 *The Prosecutor v. Saif Al-Islam Gaddafi and Abdullah Al-Senussi,* 1 June 2012, ICC-01/11-01/11-163, p. 11, paras. 28-29; *The Prosecutor v. Abdallah Banda Abakaer Nourain and Saleh Mohammed JerboJamus,* 1 July 2011, ICC-02/05-03/09-169, p. 11, para. 15.

57 *Bashir-Jordan,* 6 May 2019, ICC-02/05-01/09 OA2, p. 68, para. 137.

58 *Bashir-Jordan,* 6 May 2019, ICC-02/05-01/09 OA2, p. 68, para. 137.

任何协议，这将导致苏丹缺乏与法庭合作的依据以致无法合作。这一结果明显与安理会决议要求苏丹进行合作的意图相悖。对于这种情况，应当特别注意安理会决议的第二段内容，安理会要求苏丹与国际刑事法院“充分合作”，而充分合作正是适用于《罗马规约》缔约国的合作义务。

联合国成员根据《联合国宪章》第 25 条有义务接受并执行安理会决议。为了履行安理会决议，苏丹作为联合国成员，对国际刑事法院负有义务。[59] 根据第二部分的分析可以得知，《罗马规约》全文作为一个整体，第 86 条的充分合作义务以第 27 条为前提。苏丹在负有充分合作义务的同时，也将受到第 27 条的约束。由此可见，当安理会提交情势时，根据安理会决议，尽管被提交国不是缔约国，却实际上负有与缔约国相同的义务，不能再对法庭或是其他被请求执行逮捕令的国家以国家官员豁免权为由拒绝逮捕。同理，其他被请求国也不可因国家官员豁免权而拒绝执行逮捕令。

结语

巴希尔于 2019 年 4 月被罢免总统的职位，苏丹当局在 2020 年 2 月 11 日宣布将移送巴希尔至国际刑事法院，由“巴希尔案”引起的讨论也随之步入尾声。不过，该案仍在国际刑事法院逮捕令与国家官员豁免权相关问题上实现了一定的突破。“巴希尔案”通过对《罗马规约》第 27 条水平及垂直关系影响的讨论，明确了国家官员豁免权不得影响逮捕令的实施。国际刑事法院经由本案完善了联合国安理会提交情势中的管辖权问题，明确当存在特定安理会决议时，国际刑事法院可以按照《罗马规约》全部内容对决议所涉非缔约国情势行使管辖权。在取得一定突破的同时，本案也显露出有待解决的争议问题，包括：支持确立国际刑事法庭中不存在国家元首豁免权的国家实践不足；对《罗马规约》第 98 条的解释过于片面；对安理会提交情势下的非缔约国应承担与缔约国相同合作义务的理由尚未获得广泛的国家认可。但是无论如何，国际刑事法院应与国际社会将继续在秉承保障人权、维护和平以及惩治犯罪的宗旨下，逐步完善对于国家官员豁免的规范，为伸张正义提供更加公正可行的法律参考。

59 *Bashir-South Africa,* 6 July 2017, ICC-02/05-01/09-302, p. 32, para. 87.

《罗马规约》第 98 条第 1 款的解释和适用问题

余施语　严帅东

摘要:《罗马规约》第 98 条第 1 款的适用需要平衡国际刑事法院、被请求国与第三国在合作中的权利义务关系。实践中，缔约国对国际刑事法院的合作义务可能与其对第三国的豁免义务发生冲突，深层原因在于国际刑事法庭的官方身份无关性规则与基于国家主权平等的豁免规则的冲突。基于对《罗马规约》文本的分析，这种冲突只存在于被请求国对非缔约国履行合作义务的情形。鉴于官方身份无关性规则尚未构成一项习惯国际法规则，被请求国面临的潜在义务冲突可能长期存在。对此，国际刑事法院可以继续借助安理会提交情势的方式促使被请求国进行逮捕、移交方面的合作，同时也可以进一步发挥积极的补充性管辖权的作用。为了从根本上解决义务冲突的问题，则需明确合作义务的具体内容和冲突后的司法救济机制。

关键词:《罗马规约》第 98 条第 1 款；国际刑事法院；合作义务；国家官员豁免权

引言

国际刑事法院（以下简称为 ICC）自成立以来在追究个人刑事责任、保障被害人参与诉讼等方面取得了重大进展，国际影响力不断上升。然而，ICC 近年来在对非缔约国国家官员的执行问题上受到争议，争议焦点在于对《国际刑事法院罗马规约》(后简称《罗马规约》) 第 98 条第 1 款的解释与适用。2019 年“检察官诉巴希尔（Omar Hassan Ahmad Al-Bashir）案”（后简称“巴希尔案”）的判决再次掀起了对该问题的热议。在“巴希尔案”中，为了要求缔约国在未经非缔约国苏丹同意的情况下执行逮捕令，ICC 从习惯国际法论证路径逐渐转向安理会决议路径，态度摇摆不定。这表明需要进一步研究《罗马规约》中官方身份无关性规则的性质与 ICC 同被请求国之间的关系等问题。如何妥善解释和适用《罗马规约》第 98 条第 1 款是 ICC 发展所必须面临的问题，也对处理 ICC、缔约国与非缔约国三方关系意义重大。本文主要采用法条分析和实证研究的方法，结合《罗马规约》缔约历史、国家实践、学界观点探讨第 98 条第 1 款的解释与适用问题。

一、《罗马规约》第 98 条第 1 款概述

《罗马规约》第 98 条第 1 款规定："如果被请求国执行本法院的一项移交或协助请求，该国将违背对第三国的个人或财产的国家或外交豁免权所承担的国际法义务，则本法院不得提出该项请求，除非本法院能够首先取得该第三国的合作，由该第三国放弃豁免权。"此条款涉及被请求国履行合作义务与对第三国个人或财产的国家或外交豁免权所承担的国际法义务的冲突问题。

首先需要指出，在《罗马规约》谈判过程中，拟定第 98 条并未花费大量时间和精力。对比现行第 98 条与最初的草案可以发现，该条款绝大部分采纳了草案的内容，只进行了细微修改，[1]起草者也未对第 98 条予以重视。[2]但出乎意料的是，正是这一被忽视的条款在日后引起了国际社会的广泛讨论。

（一）第 98 条第 1 款中第三国的含义

根据《维也纳条约法公约》第 31 条，条约应依其用语按其上下文并参照条约之目的及宗旨所具有之通常意义，善意解释之。对于《罗马规约》第 98 条第 1 款中第三国含义的解释，可参照此方法。一般而言，第三国的通常含义指的是"非条约当事国之国家"。[3]而在《罗马规约》中，考虑上下文，即该条约的其他条款，例如第九部分中第 87 条第 5 款 b 项和第 94 条第 4 款提及非缔约国时采用"非本规约缔约国的国家"（a State not party to the Statute）的措辞，而非第三国（third party）。因此，第 98 条第 1 款中的第三国应解释为被请求国以外

1　1998 年 7 月 6 日，第 26 次联合国设立国际刑事法院全权代表外交会议通过了第 90 条之四《放弃豁免权》草案，该草案规定："如果被请求国遵守移交 / 合作的请求，该国将违背对第三国的个人或财产的国家或外交豁免权所承担的国际法义务，则法院应当根据本部分的规定取得该第三国的合作，由该第三国放弃豁免权。" *United Nations Diplomatic Conference of Plenipotentiaries on the Establishment of an International Criminal Court, Rolling Text of Articles 87, 90, 90 Ter and 90 Quater*, United Nations (UN), A/CONF183/C.1/WGIC/L.15, 6 July 1998, p. 5.

2　Claus Kreß, Kimberly Prost, "Article 98: Cooperation with Respect to Waiver of Immunity and Consent to Surrender," in Otto Triffterer ed, *Commentary on the Rome Statute of the International Criminal Court: Observers' Notes, Article by Article* (C.H. Beck · Hart · Nomos, 2008), 2nd edn, p. 1604.

3　参见 1969 年《维也纳条约法公约》第 2 条第 1 款。

的国家，[4]既可以是缔约国，也可以是非缔约国。

（二）第 98 条第 1 款中规定的豁免权类型

第 98 条第 1 款明确提到了两类豁免权，即个人或财产的国家豁免权以及外交豁免权。国家豁免权是指一国的行为和财产不受另一国的立法、司法和行政等方面的管辖，非经一国同意，该国的行为免受所在国法院的审判，其财产免受所在国法院扣押和强制执行。[5]外交豁免权指的是使馆和外交代表在接受国内应享有的豁免权，“外交代表不可侵犯”已然成为国际法中历史最悠久的规则之一。[6]由于“巴希尔案”的主要争议问题是缔约国合作义务与国家元首豁免权之间的冲突，那么本条款中提到的两类豁免权是否涵盖国家元首豁免权？

国家元首豁免权（immunity of the Head of State）仅限少数国家高级官员享有，如国家元首、政府首脑、外交部长。[7]不同于国家豁免权和外交豁免权，目前不存在多边条约直接规制国家元首豁免权问题，[8]尽管有条约间接涉及国家高级官员的地位，但通常只是采用“国际法给予的便利、特权和豁免”这类不具体的用语，语焉不详。[9]在 2002 年刚果民主共和国诉比利时“关于 2000 年 4 月 11 日逮捕令案”（后简称“逮捕令案”）中，国际法院确认了国家元首豁免权的习惯国际法地位，“在国际法中业已确立的是，诸如国家元首、政府首脑和外交部长，享有其他国家刑事管辖的豁免权”。[10]国内法院也曾多次将国家元首豁免

4　William Schabas, *The International Criminal Court: A Commentary on the Rome Statute* (Oxford University Press, 2010), p. 1041.

5　邵津主编《国际法》，北京大学出版社，2000，第 45 页。

6　Elieen Denza, *Diplomatic Law Diplomatic Law: Commentary on the Vienna Convention on Diplomatic Relations* (Oxford University Press, 2008), p. 256.

7　*Preliminary Report on Immunity of State Officials from Foreign Criminal Jurisdiction*, International Law Commission (ILC), A/CN.4/601, 2008, p. 187, para. 110.

8　Arthur Watts, “Heads of Governments and Other Senior Officials,” Max *Planck Encyclopedia of Public International Law* (October, 2010) https://opil.ouplaw.com/view/10.1093/law:epil/9780199231690/law- 9780199231690-e1417 (Last visited on 9 July 2020).

9　《联合国国家及其财产管辖豁免公约》第 3 条第 2 款；《特别使团公约》第 21 条。

10　*Case concerning the Arrest Warrant (Democratic Republic of the Congo/ Belgium), Judgment, ICJ Reports*, 2002, p. 21, para. 51;*Case concerning Certain Questions of Mutual Assistance in Criminal Matters (Djibouti/France), Judgment, ICJ Reports*, 2008, pp. 236-238, paras. 170-174.

权作为不予起诉现任国家元首的依据。[11]

只有少数学者认为应按照文本用语严格解释第 98 条第 1 款中的豁免权，也就是不包括国家元首豁免权，例如戴尔·特拉迪（Dire Tladi）认为不同种类豁免权龃龉互异。国家元首豁免权不同于外交豁免权：首先，两者的主体不同，外交豁免权针对外交代表，国家元首豁免权主要限于国家元首、政府首脑、外交部长；此外，两者的国际法渊源不同，外交豁免权的习惯国际法规则已被条约编纂，而国家元首豁免权仍停留于习惯法领域，尚未被系统编纂。而国家元首豁免权与国家豁免权之间的区别主要体现在 2004 年《联合国国家及其财产管辖豁免公约》第 3 条中，其规定国家豁免不妨碍外交以及国际法给予国家元首个人的特权和豁免，[12] 表明了两者属于不同概念。除此之外，倘若第 98 条的起草者意图囊括所有豁免权，则不必将条款局限于“国家或外交豁免权”，直接增加国家元首豁免权即可。最后，根据上下文和目的解释，将国家元首豁免权排除在保护范围之外可以避免《罗马规约》第 98 条与第 27 条的冲突，符合“终结有罪不罚，对罪大恶极者严惩不贷”的缔约宗旨。[13]

然而，通过分析第 98 条第 1 款的用语、目的和宗旨以及适用后果，应当认为该条款包含了国家元首豁免权。首先，由于第 98 条使用了“国际法义务”这一用语，因而应当涵盖习惯国际法、条约和一般法律原则产生的所有豁免权，既包括属事豁免，又包括属人豁免（属人豁免包含国家元首豁免权）。[14]《国家官员外国刑事管辖权豁免的初步报告》也表明“国家官员享有的外国刑事诉讼豁免”等同于“国家支持其官员享有属人豁免和属事豁免”。[15] 因此，应当将“个

---

11 *Re Honecker, Federal Supreme Court (Second Criminal Chamber) (Federal Republic of Germany), Judgment*, Case No. 2 ARs 252/84, 1984, International Law Report (ILR), Vol. 80, pp. 365-366; *Kadhafi, Court of Cassation (Criminal Division) (France)*, Judgment No. 1414, 2001, ILR, Vol. 125, pp. 508-510.

12 《联合国国家及其财产管辖豁免公约》第 3 条“1. 本公约不妨碍国家根据国际法所享有的有关行使下列职能的特权和豁免：(a) 其外交代表机构、领事机构、特别使团、驻国际组织代表团，或派往国际组织的机关或国际会议的代表团的职能；和 (b) 与上述机构有关联的人员的职能。2. 本公约不妨碍根据国际法给予国家元首个人的特权和豁免。”

13 Dire Tladi, “The ICC Decisions on Chad and Malawi:On Cooperation, Immunities, and Article 98,” *Journal of International Criminal Justice*, Vol. 11, No. 1, 2013, p. 218.

14 Camilla Lind, “Article 98 Cooperation with respect to Waiver of Immunity and Consent to Surrender,” in Mark Klamberg, Jonas Nilsson, eds., *Commentary on the Law of the International Criminal Court* (Torkel Opsahl Academic EPublisher, 2017), p. 665.

15 *Preliminary Report on Immunity of State Officials from Foreign Criminal Jurisdiction*, ILC, A/CN.4/601, 2008, p. 181, para. 94.

人的国家豁免权”解释为属事豁免和属人豁免的结合，以弥补立法之疏漏。

其次，如果不承认国家元首豁免权将会使第 98 条冗余且失去意义。缔约国与 ICC 合作很可能会违反国际义务，因为国家元首豁免权是最强有力的豁免权，最有可能触发合作义务和尊重豁免义务之间的冲突，倘若这一豁免权被排除在外，则与订立这一条款的初衷背道而驰。[16]

最后，即使因国家元首豁免权而导致 ICC 暂时无法管辖并不意味着永久性的有罪不罚。刑事管辖豁免和刑事责任是完全不同的概念，刑事管辖豁免是程序性问题，刑事责任则是实体问题。[17] 豁免权可能阻止在某一时期或对某些罪行提起诉讼，但不能免除享有豁免权的人的所有刑事责任。国家元首可以被国内法院起诉，并且在离职后将不再受国家元首豁免权荫庇，ICC 可继续追究其个人刑事责任。

（三）被请求国是否有权拒绝执行合作请求

被请求国的合作义务被规定在《罗马规约》第 86 条和《国际刑事法院程序与证据规则》[18]（后简称《程序与证据规则》）第195条中，是指“缔约国根据《罗马规约》规定与 ICC 在调查和起诉其管辖范围内的罪行时充分合作”。《罗马规约》第九编规定了合作义务的具体内容，以逮捕和移交被要求的人为主，同时还包括其他形式的合作，比如查明某人身份、送达文书、保护被害人等。然而实践中存在缔约国援引第 98 条第 1 款拒绝履行合作义务的问题，例如在“巴希尔案”中，非洲联盟提出不合作政策的原因是 ICC 未取得非缔约国苏丹同意而签发逮捕令并请求缔约国执行，而 ICC 认为被请求国无权拒绝执行合作请求。[19] 因此，争议的核心在于被请求国是否有权自行援引第 98 条第 1 款拒绝 ICC 的合作请求。结合条约解释的一般规则，应当认为该条款并未赋予缔约国

---

16 Claus Kreß, “The International Criminal Court and Immunities under International Law for States Not Party to the Court’s Statute”, in Bergsmo and Ling, eds., *State Sovereignty and International Criminal Law* (Brussels: Torkel Opsahl Academic EPublisher, 2012), pp. 237-238.

17 *Case concerning the Arrest Warrant (Democratic Republic of the Congo/ Belgium), Judgment, ICJ Reports*, 2002, p. 25, para. 60; *Jurisdictional Immunities of the State* (*Germany v. Italy: Greece Intervening*), *Judgment, ICJ Reports*, 2012, pp. 140-142, paras. 92-97.

18 *Rules of Procedure and Evidence*, Official Records of the Assembly of States Parties to the Rome Statute of the International Criminal Court, First session, New York, ICC-ASP/1/3 and Corr.1, 2002, part II.A.

19 *Bashir-South Africa*, 2017, ICC-02/05-01/09, p. 35, para. 99.

自行认为存在冲突并拒绝合作的权利，[20]ICC才是判断是否存在冲突的裁决者。[21]

第一，结合该条缔约历史及文本进行分析可以得出被请求国无权拒绝执行合作请求的结论。《罗马规约（草案）》第 87 条备选案文 2（e）的表述是："如果遵照【交出】【移送】【引渡】【请求】将使该国违反对另一国承担的一般国际法【条约】义务【的强制规范】所引起的现行义务，缔约国可以拒绝该项请求。"[22]（方括号中为可供选择的措辞，作者注）然而，《罗马规约》最终并未采用该表述，而是使用了"法院不得提出该请求"的用语，这是从 ICC 主导的角度出发，表明被请求国无权拒绝与 ICC 的合作义务。

第二，《程序与证据规则》的相关规定也支持上述结论。缔约国有权对逮捕令是否妥当签发提出质疑，但最终的判断权仍在ICC；[23]此外，被请求国应在执行逮捕令前向 ICC 提供关于可能违反对第三国义务的资料并提供协助。[24]然而，该条并未规定被请求国可以与 ICC 就补救措施进行磋商，因此最终应由 ICC 决定确认或撤回合作请求。

第三，应将第 98 条第 1 款置于整个《罗马规约》文本中理解。首先，第 59 条规定羁押国主管当局无权审议逮捕证是否适当发出的问题；其次，第 119 条第 1 款规定，"关于本法院司法职能的任何争端应由本法院的决定解决"。因此，缔约国无权依据对第 98 条第 1 款的自行理解而单方面决定不执行合作请求，即使存在豁免权也不能排除缔约国对法院的合作义务。同时，在"巴希尔案"中，ICC 进一步指出，一旦经过协商澄清并重申被请求国的义务，即使其对协商的方式不满意也应遵守。[25]

因此，虽然合作义务与尊重豁免权义务两者可能存在冲突，但处理这一问

---

20 *Bashir-Jordan*, 2017, ICC-02/05-01/09, p. 17, para. 43.

21 *Bashir-Malawi*, 2011, ICC-02/05-01/09-139, p.8, para. 11.

22 *United Nations Diplomatic Conference of Plenipotentiaries on the Establishmentof an International Criminal Court, Report of the Preparatory Committee on the Establishment of an International Criminal Court*, A/CONF183/2/Add.1, 1998, p. 134.

23 《程序与证据规则》第 117 条第 3 款："关于逮捕证是否依照第 58 条第 1 款第 1 项和第 2 项适当发出的质疑，应书面向预审分庭提出。申请书应列举提出质疑的根据。预审分庭在了解检察官的意见后，应从速对申请作出裁判。"

24 《程序与证据规则》第 195 条第 1 款："如果被请求国通知本法院，移交或协助请求引起第 98 条所述的执行问题，被请求国应提供一切有关资料协助本法院适用第 98 条。任何有关的第三国或派遣国都可以提供其他资料协助本法院。"

25 *Bashir-South Africa*, 2017, ICC-02/05-01/09, p. 16, para. 43.

题的责任（responsibility）[26]在于ICC而非缔约国。虽然部分缔约国指出，在未取得非缔约国放弃豁免权的情况下执行逮捕令相当于使被请求国承担因苏丹不遵守安理会决议内容而产生的责任。[27]该说法存在一定的合理性，但如前文所述，拒绝或无视合作义务显然不是解决冲突的正当救济措施，可采取的补救办法只能是司法性质的（例如上诉），这一问题最终必须由ICC以司法方式解决。

综上所述，第98条第1款主要涉及根据习惯国际法或国际条约享有豁免权的第三国的个人或实体，[28]结合对第三国的解释，就会产生两种不同的情形：其一，第三国是《罗马规约》缔约国，可能产生与《罗马规约》第27条第2款官方身份无关性规则的冲突；其二，第三国为非缔约国，根据条约不约束第三方的规则，可能产生合作义务与尊重第三国豁免权或其他条约义务的冲突。因此，本文将探讨上述两种情形下被请求国执行ICC移交或协助请求相关的问题。

二、被请求国对缔约国执行ICC移交或协助请求的问题

在“巴希尔案”中，ICC指出《罗马规约》第27条第2款和第98条第1款存在着内在的紧张关系。[29]部分学者也指出应慎重考虑第98条第1款与第27条第2款的关系，前者应限制后者的适用。[30]但该限制仅适用于被请求国执行合作义务与既有豁免义务（pre-existing obligation concerning immunity）之间的潜在冲突。[31]通过分析两条款的关系可以发现，缔约国国家官员在该情形中并不享有既有豁免权，因此被请求国履行合作义务时不存在尊重缔约国豁免权的义务。

首先，缔约国国家官员在ICC层面并不享有既有豁免权。在“巴希尔案”中，马拉维拒绝执行合作请求的理由之一是需要尊重非缔约国国家元首的豁免权。[32]但对于已批准《罗马规约》的第三国，接受第27条第2款意味着为了第

---

26 *Bashir-South Africa*, 2017, ICC-02/05-01/09, p. 35, para. 100.

27 *Bashir-South Africa*, 2017, ICC-02/05-01/09, p. 14, para. 34.

28 William Schabas, *The International Criminal Court: A Commentary on the Rome Statute* (Oxford University Press, 2010), p. 1041.

29 *Bashir-Malawi*, 2011, ICC-02/05-01/09-139, p. 18, para. 37.

30 Meghan Jakobsen, “Immunity versus Impunity? Reconciling Articles 27 (2) and 98 (1) of the Rome Statute,” paper delivered to “Riga Graduate School of Law (RGSL) Working Papers,” pp. 37-38.

31 *Bashir- Malawi*, 2011, ICC-02/05-01/09-139, p. 20, para. 54.

32 *Bashir- Malawi*, 2011, ICC-02/05-01/09-139, p. 11, para. 18.

98 条第 1 款的目的，放弃主张豁免权。因此，自批准加入《罗马规约》后，缔约国已放弃既有豁免权，自然不存在潜在的义务冲突。

其次，第 27 条第 2 款的效力在横向上适用于《罗马规约》缔约国之间的关系。正如缔约国不能援引豁免权拒绝 ICC 管辖一样，也不能在被请求国履行合作义务时援引同样的豁免权。[33] 因此，结合第 27 条第 2 款的上下文，在 ICC 提出合作请求时无须另行征得缔约国的同意，因为不存在需要放弃的豁免权。

最后，承认豁免权存在将使“官方身份无关性”规则失去意义。如果被请求国可以援引缔约国（第三国）国家官员的豁免权拒绝与 ICC 合作，那么 ICC 管辖权的行使将完全取决于被请求国是否执行合作请求，由此第 27 条将沦为纯粹的理论概念。[34] 尽管 ICC 承认逮捕和移交请求由被请求国国内相关机构实际执行，但这不能等同于国家机关所从事的纯粹国内行为。[35] 实际上，被请求国在代表 ICC 行事时实际上是作为 ICC 的延伸，并不涉及对其他缔约国豁免权的违反。若被请求国可以据此任意拒绝或无视合作义务，将使以 ICC 为核心的国际刑事司法合作体系陷于瘫痪，这完全违背了《罗马规约》的宗旨。

三、被请求国对非缔约国执行 ICC 移交或协助请求的问题

（一）“习惯国际法例外路径”的提出

针对缔约国执行移交或协助请求尚未产生较大争议，更多限于学理层面的讨论。而对非缔约国执行移交或协助请求的问题已上升至实践层面，成为近年来的矛盾焦点。首先必须说明的是，ICC 通常不会管辖非缔约国国民，除非涉及特定情形。例如，非缔约国通过声明主动接受 ICC 管辖；缔约国向检察官提交非缔约国国民在其境内犯罪的情势；以及联合国安理会提交情势等。[36] 确定 ICC 对非缔约国的管辖权之后，才会探讨对非缔约国执行的问题。

在“巴希尔案”中，由于非缔约国苏丹当时并未放弃巴希尔的国家元首豁免权，若 ICC 要求缔约国履行逮捕并移交巴希尔的合作义务，则需证明巴希尔在 ICC 中不享有国家元首豁免权。为实现此目的，存在两种在概念上截然不同

---

33 *Bashir-South Africa*, 2017, ICC-02/05-01/09, p. 28, para. 76.

34 *Bashir-South Africa*, 2017, ICC-02/05-01/09, p. 28, para. 75.

35 *Bashir- Malawi*, 2011, ICC-02/05-01/09-139, p. 20, para. 46.

36 参见《罗马规约》第 12 条第 2 款第 1 项、第 12 条第 3 款、第 13 条。

的路径：[37]一是根据安理会将苏丹情势提交给ICC决议的法律效力，预审分庭于2009年3月4日发布的逮捕令采用了“安理会决议路径”，认为安理会在1593号决议中援引《罗马规约》第86条一般合作义务，[38]其隐含意义是赋予苏丹类似缔约国的法律地位，以适用《罗马规约》第27条第2款，其他缔约国因此应当履行合作义务。[39]二是“习惯国际法例外路径”，即“当国际法庭希望逮捕实施国际罪行的国家元首时，习惯国际法为国家元首享有的豁免权创造了一项例外”。预审分庭在2011年“根据《罗马规约》第87条第7款作出的关于马拉维共和国未遵守ICC逮捕和移交巴希尔合作请求的决定”（后简称“马拉维不合作决定”）和同年“根据《罗马规约》第87条第7款作出的关于乍得共和国未遵守ICC逮捕和移交巴希尔合作请求的决定”中都采取了这种方法。[40]不同于“安理会决议路径”，“习惯国际法例外路径”无须安理会提交情势。ICC认为习惯国际法为国家元首豁免权在国际刑事诉讼层面创设了一项例外，因此缔约国的合作义务与其根据习惯国际法承担的义务之间不存在冲突，《罗马规约》第98条第1款并不适用。[41]

此种观点可追溯至其他国际法庭的更早实践。国际法院在“逮捕令案”中指出，“在国际刑事法庭有管辖权的情况下，现任或前任外交部长可受其刑事审判”。[42]塞拉利昂特别法庭在审判利比里亚前总统查尔斯·泰勒（Charles Taylor）时，根据纽伦堡法庭、远东国际军事法庭、特设国际刑事法庭和ICC的相关条款以及判例，认为“一种原则似乎已经建立了起来：国家间的主权平等不会阻碍国家元首在国际刑事法庭或法院中被起诉”。[43]“习惯国际法在国际刑事诉讼中创造了一项例外”进一步推进了上述判例的观点。该路径的开辟会对非缔约国产生影响，倘若阐论得当，甚至日后无须取得非缔约国合作即可审判其官员，

37　Claus Kreß, “The International Criminal Court and Immunities under International Law for States Not Party to the Court's Statute”, in Bergsmo and Ling, eds., *State Sovereignty and International Criminal Law* (Torkel Opsahl Academic EPublisher, 2012), p. 240.

38　UN Security Council Resolution 1593, 31 March 2005.

39　Dapo Akande, “The Legal Nature of Security Council Referrals to the ICC and its Impact on Al Bashir's Immunities,” *Journal of International Criminal Justice*, Vol. 7, No. 2, 2009, pp. 340-342.

40　*Bashir-Malawi*, 2011, ICC-02/05-01/09-139, p. 20, para. 43; p. 8, para. 13.

41　*Bashir-Malawi*, 2011, ICC-02/05-01/09-139, p. 20, para. 43.

42　*Case concerning the Arrest Warrant (Democratic Republic of the Congo/ Belgium)*, p. 26, para. 61.

43　*Prosecutor v. Charles Ghankay Taylor, Decision on Immunity from Jurisdiction*, SCSL-2003-01-I, 2004, p. 24, para. 52.

但证明这一路径的合法性并非易事。

（二）对“习惯国际法例外路径”的理论分析

对于ICC提出的“习惯国际法创造了一项例外”，国际刑法学界存在两种不同观点。

肯定派认为习惯国际法正处于发展历程之中，“在涉及国际犯罪时，不能主张国家元首豁免权”。[44] 首先，国际刑法属于现代习惯国际法（modern custom）范畴，与传统习惯国际法相较，“现代习惯国际法基于法律确信可以迅速确立”，[45] 国家实践不需要具有广泛性和一致性，“更为重要的是判断这一主张是否可以从广泛的法律演进或者一般国际法原则中推演出来”。[46] 习惯国际法例外这一主张源于惩戒违反国际强行法的国际罪行，根据《罗马规约》序言，ICC的核心目标便是终止核心罪行有罪不罚的局面，“对于整个国际社会关注的最严重犯罪，绝不能听之任之不予处罚”。其次，国家豁免以及外交豁免的权力源于法谚“平等者之间无统治权”（*par in parem imperium non habet*），是为平行国家间关系而创设的，因而这些豁免权不能在国际刑事诉讼中主张。[47] 还有部分学者主张“习惯国际法位阶论”，[48] 即强行法规范位阶高于一般习惯法，[49] 认为在苏丹情势中，防止违反强行法规范不被处罚的合作义务已然超越了尊重国家元首豁免权的一般习惯法义务。

另一方面，以达波·阿坎德（Dapo Akande）为代表的学者持反对观点。首先，由于缺乏“非缔约国国民不享有豁免”的国家实践，国家元首豁免权的例

44 Dapo Akande, “International Law Immunities and the International Criminal Court,” *American Journal of International Law*, Vol. 98, No. 3, 2004, p. 421.

45 Anthea Roberts, “Traditional and Modern Approaches to Customary International Law: A Reconciliation,” *American Journal of International Law*, Vol. 95, No. 4, 2001, p. 759.

46 Claus Kreß, Kimberly Prost, “Article 98: Cooperation with Respect to Waiver of Immunity and Consent to Surrender,” in Otto Triffterer, ed., *Commentary on the Rome Statute of the International Criminal Court: Observers' Notes, Article by Article* (C.H. Beck · Hart · Nomos, 2008), 2nd edn, p. 1611.

47 Paola Gaeta, “Official Capacity and Immunities,” in Cassese Antonio *et al*, *The Rome Statute of the International Criminal Court: A Commentary* (Oxford: Oxford University Press, 2002), p. 991.

48 Dire Tladi, “The ICC Decisions on Chad and Malawi:On Cooperation, Immunities,and Article 98,” *Journal of International Criminal Justice*, Vol.11, No. 1, 2013, p. 220.

49 *Prosecutor v. Furundzija, Judgment*, ICTY, IT-95-17/I-T, 1998, p.58, para.153; *Case concerning the Arrest Warrant (Democratic Republic of the Congo/ Belgium)*, Dissenting Opinion of Judge Van den Wyngaert, pp. 156-158, para. 28.

外尚未形成习惯国际法。[50]“预审法庭似乎认为这一规则得到了大量先例或条约佐证，能不证自明”，[51]但证明国家实践和法律确信绝非易事。[52]其次，虽然承认将犯罪人绳之以法是维护国际社会秩序的必要法律措施，是顺应人心的公正之举，但追求“终止有罪不罚”这一目标的重要性和合法性，本身并不构成 ICC 无视现任国家元首豁免权的合法性基础。[53]核心罪行不受惩罚，并不减损国家间业已确立的传统习惯国际法规则（即国家元首豁免权），如上文所述，豁免可能阻止在某一时期或对某些罪行提起诉讼，但不能免除享有豁免的人的刑事责任。最后，国际法院已明确否定“习惯国际法位阶论”，因为豁免规则是程序事项，而强行法规则属于实体事项，两者并不冲突。[54]国家元首能否享有豁免权是程序性问题，只有在确定法院具有管辖权后，方可判断涉案行为是否严重违反国际法。尽管部分国内法院在个案中承认强行法优于国家元首豁免权，[55]但并没有形成普遍的国家实践和法律确信，目前尚不能认为该规则已发展成为习惯国际法规则。

（三）对“马拉维不合作决定”中 ICC 论证理由的分析

ICC 在“马拉维不合作决定”中认为，习惯国际法为国家元首享有的豁免创造了一项例外，其论证依据有四：[56]其一，自一战以降，各国际刑事法庭一再驳回国家元首以享有豁免为由不接受审判的主张；其二，近十年来国际刑事法庭起诉国家元首的数量整体呈上升趋势；其三，在 ICC 成立后的 9 年间，多达 120 个国家成为《罗马规约》的缔约国，并且基于《罗马规约》第 27 条第 2 款

---

50 Dapo Akande, “International Law Immunities and the International Criminal Court”, *American Journal of International Law*, Vol. 98, No. 3, 2004; Yitiha Simbeye, *Immunity and International Criminal Law* (London: Routledge, 2004).

51 Konstantinos Magliveras, Gino Naldi, “The ICC Addresses Non-Cooperation by States Parties: The Malawi Decision,” *African Journal of Legal Studies*, Vol. 6, No. 1, 2013, p. 147.

52 本部分第三节将对此进行详细分析。

53 Paola Gaeta, “Does President Al Bashir Enjoy Immunity from Arrest,” *Journal of International Criminal Justice*, Vol. 7, No. 2, 2009, p. 323.

54 *Jurisdictional Immunities of the State* (*Germany v. Italy: Greece Intervening*), *Judgment, ICJ Reports, 2012,* p. 141, para. 95.

55 *Regina v. Street Metropolitan Stipendiary Magistrate, ex parte Pinochet Ugarte (No. 3)*, House of Lords, 1999, ILR, Vol. 119, p. 232; *Ferrini v. Federal Republic of Germany*, Italian Court of Cassation, Decision No 5044/2004, ILR, Vol. 128, pp. 668-669.

56 *Bashir-Malawi*, 2011, ICC-02/05-01/09-139, pp. 18-19, paras. 38-41.

同意放弃国家官员根据国际法享有的豁免权；其四，缔约国相继批准《罗马规约》或委托 ICC 对受到国际关注的最严重犯罪行使管辖权。然而，ICC 的论证依据存在部分问题。

首先，先前的国际刑事法庭建立途径异于 ICC，因此国家元首豁免权被排除的依据不同，不能认为习惯法已经完全支持国际法庭中的国家元首不享有豁免权。二战后，战败国通过签署投降书接受审判，因而战犯不享有豁免权；前南国际刑事法庭和卢旺达国际刑事法庭根据安理会决议而设，安理会依据其维持国际和平与安全的职能，设立国际性刑事法庭并据此排除所涉罪犯的豁免权；[57]塞拉利昂特别法庭根据塞拉利昂政府与联合国的协定而建立；[58]而ICC根据《罗马规约》建立，缔约国根据《罗马规约》第 27 条的规定自愿放弃本国国家官员所享有的豁免权。根据非经第三国同意，条约不拘束第三国原则以及 ICC 不允许缺席审判的规定，[59]需要非缔约国放弃豁免权的事实本身构成了对ICC行使管辖权的阻碍。

其次，ICC 提出的第三点和第四点主张均基于国家自愿放弃其官员豁免权。根据《罗马规约》第 87 条第 5 款及第 98 条第 1 款，只有在非缔约国自愿与 ICC 达成特别安排或协议时，才负有合作和司法协助义务。在本案中，非缔约国苏丹未曾自愿接受 ICC 管辖，也不曾放弃巴希尔享有的豁免权，正如达波 · 阿坎德所言，“如果允许国际法庭在非缔约国不同意放弃豁免权时也能起诉其高级官员，就是允许国际法庭颠覆作为国际法豁免基础的政策”。[60]尽管《罗马规约》缔约国数量达到 120 多个，的确可以反映国家实践和法律确信，[61]但习惯国际法要求国家实践必须普遍，即必须足够广泛和有代表性，还必须是一贯的。[62]而中国、美国、非盟国家等都不认为习惯国际法为国家元首豁免权创造

57 冯洁菡：《浅析〈罗马规约〉中的豁免规则——以巴希尔案为视角》，《法学评论》2010 年第 3 期，第 65 页。

58 *Prosecutor v. Morris Kallon and Brima Buzzy Kamara, Decision on Challenge to Jurisdiction: Lomé Accord Amnest*, SCSL-2004-15-AR72 (E) and SCSL-2004-16-AR72 (E), 2004, pp. 68, 70.

59 《罗马规约》第 63 条第 1 款：审判时被告人应当在场。

60 Dapo Akande, “International Law Immunities and the International Criminal Court,” *American Journal of International Law*, Vol. 98, No. 3, 2004, p. 417.

61 *Draft Conclusions on Identification of Customary International Law, with commentaries*, ILC, A/73/10, 2018, conclusion 6, 10.

62 *Draft Conclusions on Identification of Customary International Law, with commentaries*, ILC, A/73/10, 2018, conclusion 8.

例外，[63]说明这一规则缺乏实践上的一致性，尚未形成习惯国际法。

结合上述学者观点和分析可以发现，ICC 的四点论据仅可能证明存在该例外的发展趋势，不足以确定业已存在一项习惯国际法的例外。“习惯国际法例外路径”似乎并不可行，因此 ICC 应当选择“安理会决议路径”作为法律基础。在后续决定中 ICC 也确实放弃了“习惯国际法例外路径”，承认国家元首豁免权例外只局限于 ICC 缔约国。[64]

四、解决被请求国义务冲突的路径

（一）在提交情势阶段和执行阶段充分发挥安理会的作用

鉴于“官方身份无关性”规则尚未构成习惯国际法，执行移交或协助请求面临的困境在短期内无法解决。因此，若要在非缔约国拒绝放弃豁免的情况下完成对相关人员的逮捕、移交工作，则需要安理会介入。ICC 请求缔约国履行合作义务是合法的并不意味着某一国家的执行行为亦为合法。[65]尽管被请求国可以作为 ICC 的延伸执行合作请求，然而在执行过程中必然涉及国家间关系，没有安理会决议或未取得非缔约国放弃豁免的同意而执行 ICC 的合作请求，将必然违反对该国的义务从而构成国际不法行为。如果安理会根据《联合国宪章》（后简称《宪章》）第 25 条通过相关决议，那么根据《宪章》第 103 条，宪章义务要优先于其他义务。国家根据安理会决议的合作义务将优先于尊重豁免的义务。

ICC 认为，当安全理事会根据《罗马规约》第 13 条第 2 款授予管辖权时，它将凭借安理会根据《宪章》第七章的权力间接获得对非缔约国的管辖权，进而在职权范围内行使权力。[66]因此，实际中可以采用由安理会提交情势，并通过

63 *United Nations Diplomatic Conference of Plenipotentiaries on the Establishment of an International Criminal Court*, A/CONF183/SR.3, 1998, p. 6, paras. 35-38; Michael R. Pompeo, *U.S. Policy on the International Criminal Court Remains Unchanged* (October 9, 2019), https://www.state.gov/u-s-policy-on-the-international-criminal-court-remains-unchanged/ (Last visited on 10 June 2020).

64 *Bashir-Congo*, 2014, ICC-02/05-01/09, p.13, para. 26.

65 喻贵英：《析个人国际豁免权对国际刑事法院逮捕令的制约——以苏丹总统巴希尔个案为考察对象》，《时代法学》2013 年第 2 期，第 90 页。

66 *Joint Concurring Opinion of Judges Eboe-Osuji, Morrison, Hofmański and Bossa*, ICC-02/05-01/09-397-Anx1, 2019, p. 23, para. 53.

安理会决议的形式促使非缔约国与 ICC 合作，以解决被请求国履行合作义务时可能面临的义务冲突问题。尽管如此，有关“巴希尔案”的争议说明，在“官方身份无关性”规则尚未构成习惯国际法规则的情况下，安理会提交情势仍需明确要求非缔约国应在相关人员的逮捕与移交方面与 ICC 充分合作，以避免产生类似争议。

（二）进一步发展积极的补充性管辖权

可以从两个方面理解 ICC 的补充性管辖权：一是消极意义上的补充性管辖权，即在相关国家“不愿意”或“不能够”管辖的情形下，由 ICC 对犯有《罗马规约》规定罪行的人员行使管辖权；二是积极的补充性管辖权，即在国内法院行使管辖权的情况下，ICC 通过与相关国家的合作，对审判活动监督、审查、提供帮助等形式完善国内司法体系，完成对有关人员的审判工作。[67] 两种补充性管辖权都可以实现结束有罪不罚局面的目的。[68]

ICC 检察官路易斯·奥坎波（Luis Ocampo）认为应进一步推动 ICC 积极的补充性管辖权：“倘若有朝一日，各国能够管辖所有国际刑事案件，使得 ICC 无须对这些案件进行审理，这将会是一个重大胜利。”[69]2013 年检察官办公室《关于初步审查的政策文件》指出：“鉴于 ICC 的全球性质和互补性原则，检察官办公室在初步审查阶段的一个重要工作是鼓励各国履行其调查和起诉国际罪行的主要责任……并协助相关利益方确定尚未消除的有罪不罚漏洞和可能采取补救措施的范围。”[70]

由于被请求国面临的潜在义务冲突问题在短期内无法得到妥善解决，因此 ICC 可以转变思路，行使积极的补充性管辖权，推动一国国内司法机关有效运

---

67 Chandra Sriram, Stephen Brown, “Kenya in the Shadow of the ICC: Complementarity, Gravity and Impact,” *International Criminal Law Review*, Vol. 12, No. 2, 2012, p. 229.

68 William Burke-White, “Proactive Complementarity: The International Criminal Court and National Courts in the Rome System of International Justice,” *Harvard International Law Journal*, Vol. 49, No. 1, 2008, pp. 107-108.

69 Luis Moreno-Ocampo, *“Statement Made at the Ceremony for the Solemn Undertaking of the Chief Prosecutor of the ICC,”* (June 16, 2003), https://www.icc-cpi.int/NR/rdonlyres/D7572226-264A-4B6B-85E3-2673648B4896/143585/030616_moreno_ocampo_english.pdf (Last visited on 10 July 2020).

70 *Policy Paper on Preliminary Examinations*, Office of the Prosecutor (OTP), 2013, pp. 23-24, paras. 100-103.

作，自行调查和起诉在其管辖范围内的国际犯罪。[71]ICC 检察官在近日的报告中指出，巴希尔因腐败犯罪已在苏丹服刑，苏丹检察官还宣布了其与 1989 年政变有关的其他指控。同时，苏丹的反腐败机构没收了巴希尔及其家人等价值 40 亿美元的资产。[72]通过这一途径，ICC 无须请求缔约国履行合作义务，同时体现了 ICC 的补充性原则，有效减少了被请求国义务冲突的情形。因此，ICC 可以在之后涉及非缔约国的情形中加深此方面的合作，这也符合国际刑事司法制度的长远发展。

（三）修订《罗马规约》以确定义务冲突的司法救济方式

为了防止被请求国任意援引第 98 条第 1 款拒绝执行合作请求，有必要对与该条款的相关内容进行修订，明确被请求国是否有权拒绝合作请求以及相应的救济方式。就可行性而言，一方面，《罗马规约》第 51 条与第 121 条明确规定了《程序与证据规则》与规约的修改方式；另一方面，两文件的修订均有先例可遁，即有关侵略罪的修订。[73]由于部分缔约国拒绝履行合作义务的态度已严重威胁 ICC 的正常运作，因而有必要就涉及执行逮捕或移交合作请求的规则进行细化以防止 ICC 陷入瘫痪状态。从"巴希尔案"也可以看出，《罗马规约》和《程序与证据规则》对合作义务的规定语焉不详，且《程序与证据规则》缺乏对义务冲突产生后的补救机制。因此，可以进一步明确相关条款的内容，建立一套针对 ICC 和缔约国的双向约束机制以避免上述情况发生。

鉴于目前各方对第 98 条第 1 款的理解分歧较大，短期内修订《罗马规约》的可能性较小，且修订内容也需要各方充分磋商，因此本文仅探讨可能的修订思路。第一，为了维护 ICC 的权威，逮捕令是否恰当签发的判断权应当属于 ICC，且 ICC 的运作离不开缔约国执行各项请求，因此应当修改第 98 条第 1 款中"法院不得提出该项请求"的规定，进一步明确缔约国不得拒绝 ICC 的合作请求。第二，规定被请求国不得拒绝请求这一较为严格限制的同时，应在《程

71 William Burke-White, "Implementing A Policy of Positive Complementarity in the Rome System of Justice," *Criminal Law Forum*, Vol. 19, No. 1, 2008, p. 61.

72 "Statement to the United Nations Security Council on the Situation in Darfur, pursuant to UNSCR 1593 (2005)," OTP (10 June 2020), https://www.icc-cpi.int/Pages/item.aspx?name=200610-otp-statement-darfur (Last visited on 10 July 2020).

73 *Amendments to the Rome Statute of the International Criminal Court: Adoption of Amendments on the Crime of Aggression*, The Secretary-General of the United Nations, C.N.651.2010. TREATIES-8, 29 November 2010.

序与证据规则》中补充义务冲突后的补救机制，例如提供解决义务冲突的上诉机制。通过对被请求国不得拒绝合作请求的确认和补救机制的保障，可以免除被请求国执行合作请求时的“后顾之忧”，从而促进 ICC 执行机制的良性运作。

结语

《罗马规约》第 98 条第 1 款涉及关乎 ICC 发展的两大核心问题，一是被请求国执行逮捕、移交请求，二是尊重第三国国家官员的豁免权。对 ICC 而言，一方面，其承担着结束有罪不罚局面的重任；另一方面，其设立依据是《罗马规约》而非安理会决议，且国家元首豁免权的例外尚未构成一项习惯国际法。因此，被请求国执行移交或协助请求过程中可能面临义务冲突问题。对第 98 条第 1 款的解释与适用，有三点需要说明：第一，该条的第三国是指被请求国以外的国家，但因为缔约国根据《罗马规约》第 27 条已放弃援引豁免权，因此该条中的第三国实际只涉及非缔约国，并且结合《罗马规约》与《程序与证据规则》进行分析，被请求国无权拒绝或无视 ICC 的合作请求；第二，鉴于《罗马规约》第 27 条中的“官方身份无关性”规则尚未构成一项习惯国际法规则，对于非缔约国行使管辖权时仍应以国家同意为原则，因此在对非缔约国国家官员进行逮捕、移交前仍应事先取得该国放弃豁免权的同意；第三，为有效解决被请求国可能面临的义务冲突，ICC 可以基于现状在提交情势阶段和执行阶段充分发挥安理会的作用，并在实践中进一步发展积极的补充性管辖权。同时，可以通过修订《罗马规约》与《程序与证据规则》，尽可能避免被请求国面临的义务冲突并提供相应的司法救济机制，这是解决潜在义务冲突的根本途径。

—— 第三部分 ——

技 巧 分 析

指导杰赛普国际法模拟法庭竞赛的经验与思考

宋岩

传统的国际法教学模式较为单一，主要以教师讲授为主，学生更多是被动接受，缺乏有效参与；教学内容更重视基本概念、原则和理论，缺乏对实践的关注。这种模式难以帮助学生建立起对国际法全面正确的认识，导致学生缺乏学习和研究国际法的兴趣。为了解决上述问题，越来越多的国际法模拟法庭竞赛得到开展，给学生提供了一个全面参与诉讼活动的平台，学生在这里将静态的理论和法条转化成动态的专业行为和语言，而这个过程恰恰需要他们的创造性思考。[1] 近年来，多个国际法模拟法庭竞赛吸引了众多高校代表队参赛，例如杰赛普国际法模拟法庭竞赛（Philip C. Jessup International Law Moot Court Competition, 后简称杰赛普）、“贸仲杯”国际商事仲裁模拟仲裁庭辩论赛、国际刑事法院模拟法庭竞赛等。更多中国高校代表队参加了国际赛，与其他世界一流大学同台竞技，并且国际赛的成绩也越来越好，这反映了中国国际法教学和研究的进步。

作为教练，作者有幸指导了外交学院代表队参加 2017 年到 2020 年的杰赛普国际法模拟法庭竞赛，2017 年和 2019 年的海洋法模拟法庭竞赛。本文的主要目的是总结指导国际法模拟法庭竞赛的经验，归纳竞赛要求，分析外交学院代表队参赛的优势以及存在的问题。最后，因为国际法模拟法庭竞赛重点考察学生的国际公法专业水平，而本科阶段的国际公法教学为此奠定了基础，所以，本文还将结合存在的问题为完善国际公法教学提出建议。

一、杰赛普国际法模拟法庭竞赛的要求

杰赛普国际法模拟法庭竞赛是以知名国际法学家杰赛普（Philip C. Jessup）命名的全球性模拟法庭竞赛。[2] 自 1959 年开始，杰赛普已经举办了 60 多届，是

1　刘丹：《Jessup 模拟法庭结合国际法双语教学的探索与实践》，《云南大学学报法学版》2012 年第 5 期，第 116 页。

2　菲利普 · 杰赛普，1897 年出生于纽约，知名国际法学者、外交家、律师和教授，1961 年到 1970 年担任国际法院法官。

目前世界上规模最大、历史最悠久的专业性国际法模拟法庭比赛，被誉为国际法学界的“奥林匹克竞赛”。高规格的竞赛标准和高品质的竞赛内容使得此项赛事成为检验各大法学院校学生能力和教学水平的重要标准之一。比赛的核心和关键是对学生的选拔和训练，但前提是明确比赛的要求，因为只有这样才能使选拔和训练更加有的放矢。

（一）英语能力

杰赛普的比赛用语是英语，要求参赛学生用英语撰写双方书状、分析事实、提出主张并进行论证，在庭上陈述当事国主张，回答法官提出的各种问题，抗辩对方的主张等。在备赛过程中收集、阅读和研究的资料一般也是英文条约、文件和著作。训练和比赛过程中非常常见的问题是，虽然学生进行了大量研究，自己也比较熟悉研究题目，却词不达意，无法利用英语简洁、明确和直接地表达观点说服法官；不理解法官所提问题的侧重点，围着问题绕圈子，不能切中要害。因此，国际法模拟法庭竞赛要求参赛学生和教师能够熟练运用英语进行听、说、读、写，特别是具备一定的英语写作与表达能力。

（二）专业基础

作为专业性的模拟法庭竞赛，杰赛普要求参赛学生具备扎实的国际法基础知识和娴熟的知识运用能力。解决法律问题的前提是识别和检索法律规则，这涉及国际法渊源的问题。《国际法院规约》第 38 条反映了主要的国际法渊源，其中直接渊源包括国际条约、国际习惯、一般法律原则，而司法判例和公法学者学说一般作为确定法律规则的辅助方法；除此之外，部分国际组织的决议，例如联合国大会、安理会、国际法委员会，也可能帮助查找和确定国际法规则。[3] 为了获取上述国际法规则，需要教授学生法律检索的方法，训练他们这方面的能力，例如利用联合国条约数据库（UNTC）查找相关国际条约、利用国际司法和仲裁机构网站查找相关判例，以及利用法学数据库（例如 Heinonline、LexisNexis、马克斯 – 普朗特国际公法百科全书、Oxford）查找相关论文和著作。还要结合每年赛题的具体内容到相关国际组织的网站上检索信息，例如 2019 年赛题涉及与遗传资源相关传统知识利用产生的惠益分享制度，需要到《生物多样性公约》缔约国大会和世界知识产权组织（WIPO）的网页上查找相关国际法规则。

---

3 Malcolm N. Shaw, *International Law* (Cambridge University Press, 2008), 6th edn, pp. 70-71.

不同于国内法，国际法缺乏统一、系统的立法机关，国际法的制定主要取决于国家同意，[4]导致部分国际法规则过于抽象和模糊，甚至冲突。为了能够实际适用规则，必须重视解释方法的训练，具体方法包括根据解释规则（例如1969年《维也纳条约法公约》第31条和第32条）进行解释，或者参考国际法庭和学者的解释。[5]例如，2019年杰赛普赛题涉及国家责任中的可归因性问题（attribution），也就是判断实际行为人或机构的行为是否可以被视为国家的行为，从而应当由国家承担责任。[6]关于可归因性的基本国际法规则是：一国国家机关的行为应视为该国的行为。[7]但在具体适用该规则时，需要解释什么是国家机关。自治地方的政府部门、三权分立国家中司法机关的行为是否可以归因于国家？除了国内法中明确规定属于国家机关的部门之外，是否还应当包括实际行使政府职责的机关？为了回答这些问题，可以参考国际法委员会2001年《国际不法行为国家责任条款草案及其评注》，其中总结和归纳了各种国家实践、国际判例和学者观点。[8]

最后，因为每年的赛题都与时事热点相关，可能不存在系统全面的国际法规则，国家实践也较为有限，所以需要训练学生活学活用基本规则，类推适用已有规则并说明可适用性。例如，2017年赛题涉及难民接受国向难民来源地国求偿的问题，目前已有的国际难民条约都没有对此作出规定，国家实践也较为有限，这是正在发展的争议问题。为了解决该问题，可以考虑借鉴一项已经牢固确定的习惯国际法规则——一国不得故意允许利用其领土从事损害他国权利的行为，[9]为难民接受国的主张提供法律依据。

（三）灵活解释和利用事实

在备赛和训练过程中，需要自始至终向学生强调：对事实的适用与对规则

---

4 白桂梅编《国际法》（第三版），北京大学出版社，2015，第2—3页。

5 Anthony Aust, *Modern Treaty Law and Practice* (Cambridge University Press, 2013), 3nd edn, pp. 356-357.

6 *Case concerning the Kayleff Yak (Aurok/Rakkab), Special Agreement, 14 September 2018*, para. 49.

7 *Application of the Convention on the Prevention and Punishment of the Crime of Genocide (Bosnia and Herzegovina v. Serbia and Montenegro), Judgment, ICJ Reports 2007*, para. 385.

8 International Law Commission, "Draft Articles on Responsibility of States for Internationally Wrongful Acts, with Commentaries," *Yearbook of the International Law Commission*, Vol. II, Part Two, 2001, pp. 40-42.

9 *Corfu Channel case (United Kingdom v. Albania), Merits, Judgment, ICJ Reports 1949*, p. 22.

的解释同样重要。因为规则通常是确定的，而事实却可以从各个角度进行解读和利用。国际法模拟法庭竞赛的赛题提供了双方均认可的事实，要求学生在不增加、不曲解事实的前提下，结合法律规则合理解释和运用事实。具体适用规则时，不仅要注意到与问题直接相关的事实，还要灵活运用案件背景，特别是有关数量、时间、地理位置和行为方式的事实。以2017年赛题为例，如果认为双方已承诺公平、合理使用跨界水资源，对于后来发生的多年难遇的干旱，可以探讨是否能根据情势变迁规则终止之前的承诺。在情势变迁规则的构成要件中，该案最难以判断的要件就是：发生干旱的情况是否可以预见。结合案件背景事实，两国处于干旱地区，历史上曾多次发生过干旱，可以证明干旱并不是不可预见的；当然，另一方也可以主张本次发生了多年难遇的干旱，因而无法预见。因此，关键是训练学生如何灵活、全面地利用事实，合情合理地向法官讲述一个有利于己方的故事。特别是对于新的热点问题，更需要突破法律规定的局限性，通过合理解释和运用事实阐述主张以赢得法官的支持。

在指导学生组织和利用事实时还应当注意以下问题：第一，尽量使用中立和客观的语言，多使用“根据赛题事实”“根据双方均认可的事实”等表述，而不是“我方认为……”；第二，不要使用过于抽象的表述，例如“对方存在**重大**过失”“**严重**损害了我方利益”，而应当尽量列举客观事实，例如根据事实对方何时就已知损害发生、我方向对方主张权利的时间和次数、对方的反应，以及最终导致我方多少具体数量的财产和人身损失；第三，模拟法庭的事实适用需要联系现实情况，例如2019年的比赛需要判断赛题中的虚构药品是否获得了巨额利益，而赛题只给出了制药公司的收入情况，没有提供药品研发成本的信息，此时可以参考现实中开发类似药品的公司的财务数据，通过比较使论证说理更具说服力。

（四）团队配合

不同于个人竞赛，杰赛普是非常典型的团体竞赛。首先，它的赛题相对前沿和复杂，例如2020年赛题涉及条约继承、发展和使用自主武器的合法性、国际法庭管辖权的竞合、关税与国家安全，以及国家官员国际刑事法院管辖豁免，需要研究条约法、国际人道法、国际争端解决规则、WTO法律制度和国际刑法等众多问题，一个人根本无法完成，需要一个团队分工协作。杰赛普至少需要2名上场队员，一般情况下应当由4名上场队员和1名研究队员组成，针对赛题提出的4个研究题目，分别代表请求国和被告国陈述主张，这对团队协作提出了较高的要求。代表相同国家的队员需要互相配合，共同完成一国的主张；研究同一问题的双方队员需要互相借鉴，弥补主张中的弱点。比赛时，法官要为每一名陈述学生打分，每人的分数都会影响最终比赛的成绩。如果希望取得靠前的排名，任何一名参赛学生都不能掉链子，否则一损俱损。此外，受比赛注册队员人数限制（一支队伍有 5 名注册队员），并不是所有参与备赛的同学都有机会成为注册队员和上场队员，需要考虑个人特长进行内部协调。这些情况要求参赛学生具有团队精神，不仅要完成自己负责的部分，还要互相帮助、互相支持，有时要适当妥协，以实现团队利益的最大化。

（五）心理素质

与其他模拟法庭竞赛相比，杰赛普整个比赛时间跨度较大，从赛题发布到国际赛结束要持续 7 个多月的时间，跨越 2 个学期和 1 个寒假。这对参赛学生和指导教师的决心和毅力提出了挑战。备赛期间，基本每周都要集体讨论、分配任务、总结问题，特别是在寒假期间，参赛学生大部分时间都需要留在学校训练和练习，如果没有坚强的意志、团队的精神和崇高的荣誉感，很难坚持到底。高标准、高强度的专业比赛也带来了巨大的压力，要求参赛学生具备良好的心理素质和抗压能力。面对纷繁复杂的事实、存在冲突或空白的国际法规则和案例、漫长的备赛时间、法官各种刁钻古怪的问题，参赛学生必须保持积极乐观的精神，坚持研究，认真对待每一个问题，尽全力应对各种挑战。比赛主要取决于法官的裁量，最终也只有少数参赛队伍能够获得国际赛资格，因此，还必须保持平常心，淡然面对各种突发情况和最坏的可能性。在备赛过程中，指导教师需要重视参赛学生的心理建设，定期举行团建活动，多交流、多沟通、多鼓励、多陪伴。

二、外交学院的参赛优势

（一）英语优势

外交学院历来重视学生的英语学习。与其他高校相比，外交学院学生在本科阶段英语学习的课时量较多。以国际法系为例，要求英语必修课程修满 52 学分。相关课程涵盖听、说、读、写各个方面。同时，学院也聘请了外教，开设了多门双语专业课程。学生的大学英语四、六级考试成绩名列前茅。许多非英语专业的学生也能通过专业八级考试，在雅思、托福等考试中取得优异成绩。

这使得外交学院代表队队员英语基础扎实、口语能力突出、写作水平较高，为参加以英语为比赛语言的国际法模拟法庭竞赛奠定了良好的基础。这种优势在之前的比赛中非常突出，但随着对英语的重视和英语教育的普及，其他学校参赛队员的英语水平也很高，导致这种优势正在逐年减弱。

（二）比赛经验优势

外交学院国际法系致力于培养卓越涉外法治人才，历来鼓励学生参与模拟法庭竞赛。除杰赛普之外，每年学生都可以选择参加国际商事仲裁模拟仲裁庭比赛、国际刑事法院审判竞赛（英文）、红十字国际人道法模拟法庭竞赛、中国WTO模拟法庭比赛、知识产权模拟法庭竞赛、全国高校海洋法模拟法庭邀请赛以及北京市大学生模拟法庭竞赛等多项赛事。在参加杰赛普之前，学生一般已经参加过其他的一个或多个模拟法庭竞赛，有过撰写书状和口头陈述的经验。例如，2017年和2018年外交学院杰赛普代表队上场队员都有过参加多项国内赛，甚至国际赛的经验，之前的训练和经历使他们能够迅速投入比赛，避免出现常见问题。

（三）团队协作优势

由于学生数量较小，同一年级与不同年级学生之间更容易建立起密切的人际关系，共同学习、共同生活和共同活动的经历有助于团队精神的形成。杰赛普作为一项有着60多年历史的赛事，经验的传承和队伍风格的形成也必不可少。在这一方面，外交学院代表队优势突出。整个备赛的过程中，在选拔队员、分析事实、形成纲要、撰写书状和庭审练习等各个方面，上一年，甚至前几年的队员都会为当年参赛的队员提供建议并参与他们的训练。这形成了良好的传承，保证了外交学院代表队能够连续多年取得稳定的成绩。

三、外交学院代表队参赛中的问题

（一）满足比赛要求的学生数量有限

作为以培养一流外交外事人才的小规模、高层次、特色鲜明的外交部唯一直属高校，外交学院的招生规模有限，参加国际法模拟法庭竞赛的学生主要来自国际法系，本科一年招生约60余人。精英化的培养模式和小班化的教学模式，有助于强化教学效果，鼓励学生的课堂参与，使教师能够更关注学生的学习情况并因材施教。但同时也带来了一定的问题，学生基数的有限性导致了能够参与某项活动的人数有限，而该问题对杰赛普的影响格外突出。这也是小规模法学院面临的共同问题。

以外交学院国际法系为例，大一和大二学生没有系统学习国际公法，一般情况下难以参加专业要求相对较高的比赛；大四学生面临考研、出国和找工作的压力；研究生数量更为有限。因此，在这种情况下，参加杰赛普的主要是大三学生。但随着学院留学交流项目的增多，多数学生会选择在大三出国交流，一年比例接近 20%，导致基数进一步缩减，而且出国交流的学生往往是专业素质高、英语能力强的学生，导致外交学院代表队在比赛中的表现受到影响。受这些因素制约，报名参加杰赛普的学生数量有所下降，而且这种情况非常可能继续恶化，影响外交学院代表队的可持续发展。

在很大程度上，模拟法庭竞赛的成绩取决于参赛学生的素质和经验。但现实中满足比赛要求的学生有限，除了少数有比赛经验的学生外，多数学生从未独立写过书状和做过庭上陈述。此外，因为有多项模拟法庭赛事可供选择，会造成人员的进一步分散，这对在多数模拟法庭竞赛之后举办的杰赛普影响格外明显。最后，因为杰赛普备赛周期长达半年多，跨越寒假，并且提交书状的时间与期末考试时间重合，许多学生难以坚持到最后。以 2018 年外交学院代表队为例，最初选拔了 10 名同学准备比赛，有 5 人有参加模拟法庭的经验，但其中 2 人在第二学期出国交流，最终坚持下来的只有 4 名同学，人手严重不足。

为了缓解该问题的不利影响，目前已经开始采取部分措施。例如，由一名队员同时代表双方当事国，但学生负担较大；允许部分出国同学通过互联网参与比赛，但必须控制数量并要求学生保证持续参与；也接受外系同学参加比赛，但需要重点考核国际公法专业的学习情况。但这些措施的效果取决于众多因素。

（二）院内影响有限

杰赛普的竞赛历史悠久、专业性强、参与度高，是全球法学院中知名的赛事，许多国内和国际院校都非常重视这项赛事。在地区赛中赢得国际赛资格，在国际赛中取得前三十二强，都有助于提高学校的知名度。但在外交学院，该项赛事的影响力较为有限，基本局限于国际法系内部，远没有模拟联合国和英语类竞赛在学生中的知名度高，这主要是由于该项赛事的专业性太强。参加杰赛普的学生一般是大三、大四或者研一的学生，他们课业负担较大，对于杰赛普这样一个专业性强、耗时久、压力大的比赛，如果没有更多的鼓励和支持，将极大影响学生和教师参与的热情和积极性。在实践中，国际法作为国家之间的共同语言，熟练掌握和运用国际法可以更有效率地维护国家权利和减少争端，一位优秀的外交家应当掌握国际法。[10] 现实情况也使国家开始重视对复合型人才的培养，未来中国需要更多懂外交、外语好并精通国际法的实务型人才。[11] 参加杰赛普有助于培养学生运用国际法解决实际问题的能力，希望今后能提高宣传力度，鼓励更多的学生参与其中。

结语：完善本科生国际公法教学的建议

随着法律全球化的不断发展，对卓越涉外法治人才的需求越来越多，对法学教育也提出了更高的要求，有必要借鉴杰赛普的要求和模式，并结合外交学院参赛的优势及问题，对本科生国际公法教学进行完善，丰富教学方法和教学环节，提高国际公法教学水平。

第一，在开课时间方面，根据培养方案，国际法系学生在大二第二学期学习国际公法，辅修学生也是同一时间学习国际公法，国际公法同样是外交学系学生的必修课，学习时间是大二第一学期。大部分法学院都会将国际公法安排在大二第二学期或者大三第一学期。虽然国际公法并不必然要以国内法的学习为基础，但按照循序渐进的学习规律，一般先学习国内法再学习国际法，在法学基础教育中，国内法仍然是主要部分，并且国内法特别是民法和刑法等庞大的体系，需要大量的学时保证。因此，国际公法课程的开设不宜过早，可以继续保持原有的培养方案。

第二，在授课内容方面，虽然应当重视基本概念和理论，强调知识的体系性和完整性，但如果只是简单向学生讲授某一规则的构成要件，学生可能难以理解，最终只会死记硬背应付考试，无法活学活用。为了改变这种状况，有必要引入案例教学，在讲授规则的同时，通过生动形象的案例帮助学生理解规则、抓住要点。该方法的关键在于如何选取案例。选取案例可以借鉴杰赛普的相关经验。虽然每年杰赛普的赛题都不一样，但总有几个每年都会用到的案例，说明这些案例对于解决实际问题非常具有参考价值。例如，1949 年英国诉阿尔巴尼亚“科孚海峡案”、1951 年哥伦比亚诉秘鲁“庇护案”、1969 年“北海大陆架案”、1986 年尼加拉瓜诉美国“军事和准军事活动案”、1997 年匈牙利和斯洛文

10 Malcom N. Shaw, *International Law* (Cambridge University Press, 2014), 7th edn, p. 144.

11 2011 年《教育部、中央政法委员会关于实施卓越法律人才教育培养计划的若干意见》，教高〔2011〕10 号，http://old.moe.gov.cn//publicfiles/business/htmlfiles/moe/s3875/201204/134451.html（最后访问日期 2020 年 7 月 9 日）。

尼亚“加布奇科沃 - 大毛罗斯水坝案”，等等。当然，根据其内容，赛题也会涉及其他案件。可以在国际公法授课过程中，穿插介绍这些案件的相关事实、国际法庭的法律推理和裁判依据，这样做不仅有助于学生理解规则，还会为日后准备比赛积累论据。

第三，在授课形式方面，因为国际公法具有自身的特点，在主体、制定方式、实施机制和法律理念等方面与日常生活中更为熟悉的国内法相差甚远，对于本科生教学，仍然应当坚持发挥教师的主导作用。但是，也应当在教学过程中鼓励学生参与，引导学生分析问题、解决问题和独立思考。可以参考杰赛普的模式，与上文提到的案例教学相结合：首先学习国际法规则和理论，然后结合具体案例事实，引导学生思考如何利用规则和理论解决现实中的争端，并说明理由。这是一种参考英美国家案例教学的“IRAC”思维模式，即识别争议问题（issues）—查找法律规则（rules）—利用规则分析事实（analysis）—最终得出结论（conclusion），可以有效培养学生发现问题、解决问题和逻辑思维的能力。

第四，不同于国内法，国际法的通用语言是英语和法语，这也是国际法院的工作语言。与法语相比，英语的地位则更为重要，许多国际法文件、条约和经典著作都使用英语完成，杰赛普也要求学生用英语写书状和进行口头陈述。在这种情况下，有必要开展双语国际公法教学，使学生尽早接触专业英语，为日后查找资料、进行研究和交流奠定基础。同时，也应当坚持循序渐进的教学方法，不可操之过急，可以首先采取双语课件的方式，之后逐渐增加英文课件和英语讲授的比例，使学生慢慢适应，打好专业英语的基础。

第五，完善配套选修课的建设。国际公法是一门系统、全面的课程，包括国际法渊源、国家、个人、领土、海洋、条约、国际组织、外交关系和争端解决等各个部分，但本科生国际公法课程重点是向学生讲授基本理论和概念，所以不会对具体制度进行深入介绍，甚至因课时限制无法讲授所有部分，难以做到面面俱到。然而，实践中的争端经常与多个具体制度相关，如上文介绍的部分杰赛普赛题，不仅包括国际公法基本理论，也涉及各个分支部分中的具体制度。为了使学生更全面、更深入地学习国际公法，应当开设关于重要分支的选修课，例如海洋法、条约法和国际争端解决等课程。此外，为了更全面地学习国际公法专业英语，有必要开设国际公法经典著作课程，使学生能够熟练阅读英文国际公法资料，娴熟使用英语进行专业交流和写作。此外，解决国际法问题的前提是找到国际法规则。如何迅速查找到《国际法院规约》第 38（1）条规定的各种国际法渊源，不仅是国际法模拟法庭竞赛的考察重点，也是学生未来解决实际问题和进行学术研究的必需技能，所以有必要在讲授课程的同时向学生介绍法律文献检索方法，或者邀请图书馆或数据库专业技术人员定期举办讲座，向学生介绍各种数据库的使用方法。

法律研究与资料整理的经验与技巧

李子钰

法学院的每位学生在学习过程中都必须进行法律研究，但是对于中国学生来说，杰赛普的法律研究可能与国内法的学习方法有些许差别。对于这一耗时半年多的比赛来说，在法律研究的同时做好资料整理，能够帮助参赛者更好地回溯曾经做过的法律研究，形成更系统、更有逻辑的思路。本文以笔者对 2018 年赛题 R3 和 R4 问题的研究经历为基础，旨在分享备赛期间法律研究和资料整理的方法，希望能帮助参赛者更好地研究、整理和提高。

一、与赛题相关的法律研究

杰赛普的全称是“杰赛普国际法模拟法庭竞赛”，也就意味着其所依据的法律主要是国际法。与法学院传统学习的中国民法、刑法、民事诉讼法、刑事诉讼法不同，国际公法整体没有一个编纂完善的法典，这为法律研究带来了一些困难。

（一）识别赛题相关的国际法规则

杰赛普赛题的特点是简洁，相比于其他比赛长达数十页的赛题，杰赛普赛题的篇幅可以称得上短小精悍。以 2018 年赛题为例，第三个问题看似非常简单，探讨“Did A violate Article 16 of the bilateral treaty, *i.e.* nuclear disarmament obligation under international law, by commissioning and operating the sub-marine with nuclear weapons”的问题，也就是探讨请求国是否违反了两国之间的双边条约，即国际法上的核裁军义务。但是，正是由于问题很简洁，使得赛队在备赛时很可能出现思路偏差。

以此问题的备赛为例，关于国际法上的核裁军义务，《不扩散核武器条约》中的核裁军谈判义务自然是题中应有之义。除此之外，考虑到此问题要求论证请求国违反了双边条约中的义务，我们将第二个论点定为双边条约第 16 条创设的核裁军义务，从而将重点放在了条约解释和条约是否终止的论证上。尽管在研究和撰写书状第二个论点时遇到了重重困难，但是我们仍然坚持保留了这条思路，最终在比赛时却发现这一论点基本无法说服法官，也很少有其他赛队提及，而通常被主张的核裁军义务则来源于核裁军谈判义务以及赛题中的联合国安理会决议。然而，由于思路上的偏差，我们在比赛之前对安理会决议创设核裁军义务这一点未进行系统深入研究，只能白天比赛，晚上熬夜查资料查漏补缺，陷入被动。

通过赛队上述的经历可以发现：对于问题研究来说，确定可适用的国际法规则是非常重要的，一旦出现错误，就很有可能导致大篇幅的论证偏差。总结我们的经验，我认为寻找规则时，需要注意以下几点：

第一，着重分析问题中的用词。实际上，在讨论核裁军谈判义务以及赛题中的联合国安理会决议时，必须要注意国际法上的义务和违反双方条约义务之间的关系。如果只注意研究国际法上的核裁军义务，却忽略了请求国被指控的是违反条约义务，这一问题就根本无从谈起。

第二，着重分析赛题中的其他材料。如上文所述，如果能够更早注意到赛题中的联合国安理会决议不仅与第四个问题相关，也与第三个问题相关，也能建立核裁军义务，我们的备赛过程将会更顺畅。

第三，如果有很多个论点无法确定，与队友、教练讨论确定一个或几个论点用于书状写作。这样能够推进进程，但同时也需要记录下其他论点，在准备口头陈述（oral）的过程中继续进行研究，防止到了赛场才发现存在思路偏差且没有任何研究基础支撑的情况。

（二）检索国际法规则的方法

外交学院的国际法课程在大二开设，因此在比赛前，我们对于国际法的基础知识已经有了一定程度的掌握和了解。但比赛赛题通常需要对某一国际法最新热点问题进行深入探讨分析，已有的基础知识显然不足以应对深度研究，需要检索更多相关国际法规则。为了解决这一问题，我常用的检索方法大致有以下几种：

第一，在从马克斯普朗克国际公法百科全书（Max Planck Encyclopedia of Public International Law）中检索。马克斯普朗克国际公法百科全书可以通过举办方提供的牛津大学出版社（Oxford University Press）账号进入，因此无论学校是否购买，赛队都能检索使用。该数据库最大的好处在于，能够提供对某个研究问题的全面和概括的介绍，包括相关规则的构成要件、争议点、涉及的国际法案例等。可以通过这一渠道方便快捷地建立对研究问题的初步和整体印象。

第二，在谷歌和 Heinonline 上检索关键词，查找相关论文和报告或进一步研究。这一阶段就不只是检索一般性的介绍论文，而是特别地针对某个构成要件、某个争议点的论证文章，或者相关国际组织（例如国际法委员会）作出的研究报告。通过这些资料可以整理逻辑和思路，逐步建立起需要检索的基本问题清单，并逐个进行研究。

第三，对于需要系统研究的问题，再次利用牛津大学出版社账号检索专著进行研究。专著比论文更系统，研究也更为细致。例如，我在研究一贯反对者（persistent objector）问题时，在牛津大学出版社账号中找到了一本非常有用的著作，对于是否需要坚持反对（consistent objection）的问题进行了非常细致的论证。

第四，阅读国际法庭案例、判决的单独意见及案评也是非常必要的。尽管国际法庭的案例本身并不具有法律拘束力（legally binding force），但是在赛场上，相比于各种专著论文，国际法庭的案例可能是法官们最熟悉的材料，也更容易被法官接受。当然，在阅读国际法庭案例时，也要自己思考，不能仅仅因为是案例中的观点，就奉为金科玉律。可以说，对案例的理解程度很大一部分决定了比赛的结果。而如果遇到了对于己方主张非常不利的案例，更要学会做区分（distinction），避免对论证产生影响。区分的角度可以非常多样，案例中的事实与赛题的事实不同、所依据条约的目的和宗旨不同等，都可以成为建立区分的要点。但区分需要建立在对案例的熟悉程度和清楚认知之上。

（三）注重细节（即使是赛题的设定）

如果参加过其他的国际法模拟法庭，也会发现杰赛普和其他模拟法庭的侧重点有所不同。我在 2018 年参加完杰赛普后，2019 年参加了国际商事仲裁辩论赛（VIS EAST）。我对这两个比赛的体会是，国际商事仲裁辩论赛对于法律研究要求的深度要低于杰赛普，但对于当庭陈述的要求则略微高于杰赛普。我也是在国际商事仲裁辩论赛比赛的最后阶段才注意到两者的区别，正因为我在国际商事仲裁辩论赛备赛过程中过分依赖杰赛普的经验，导致比赛中出现一定的策略失误。

VIS EAST 的一个赛题是讨论仲裁庭是否有权修改合同（adaptation of contract），其中赛题设定是，D 国法律采用了示范法（Model Law），且判例法认为如果仲裁庭要行使修改合同的权利，必须要经过双方明示的同意。我研究该问题时却发现，在示范法中没有修改（adaptation）这一用语，最接近的用语是“*amiable compositeur*”。那么“adaption of contract”和“*amiable compositeur*”究竟有什么关系？对该问题的研究耗费了我大量的时间，然而在比赛中，仲裁庭基本没有对此提出任何疑问。出现这种情况非常有可能是因为当时我所在的赛队没有进入晋级赛，但如果在循环赛中都没有遇到该问题至少说明它并不特别重要。而我基于杰赛普的经验，在该问题上花费了大量精力，考虑到备赛时间的紧张，这的确是一种策略和判断失误。

这个例子能够说明杰赛普和 VIS EAST 之间的区别：

问题	我基于杰赛普的思路	VIS EAST 可能的思路
● Issue: Power of adaptation of the Arbitral Tribunal ● Rule: Article 28(3) of Model Law "The arbitral tribunal shall decide *ex aequo et bono* or as *amiable compositeur* only if the parties have expressly authorized it to do so."	●即使赛题中设定了 power of adaptation 就是 *amiable compositeur*，赛队仍旧会研究二者区别： 赛队会对 power of adaptation 和 *amiable compositeur* 之间的区别进行研究和讨论，从而发现其实二者并非一致：示范法在制定时有过几轮工作文件（Working Papers Submitted to the Working Group），在最开始工作文件中只有 *amiable compositeur* 的表述，但接下来的工作文件又引入了 adaptation of contract，并将 adaptation of contract 分为两类，最终版的工作文件认为 adaptation of contract 分歧巨大，不应当被纳入示范法中。 ●对被申请人的论点有帮助；另外，仲裁员也有很大可能问到。	●基本上赛队思路均会推定 power of adaptation 即 *amiable compositeur*，从而直接进入讨论。 ●双方以及仲裁员均不会对此讨论。

由此可见，我认为杰赛普的参与者（无论是法官还是参赛者）都非常关注赛题的细节，对于法律研究的要求非常高。

再举一例来说，2018 年赛题第三个问题与核武器相关，而赛题仅提到国际法中的核裁军义务。那么，这种义务是什么？我最开始时自然想到了《不扩散核武器条约》中的无核国家不扩散核武器的义务（non-proliferation），但是仔细想想，不扩散核武器义务与核裁军义务相同吗？从量上来说，两者的目的也许都是实质减少核武器，但从质上来说，核裁军义务是指核武器要从多到少，而核不扩散义务却是指核武器不能从无到有。这个关注点也许非常细微，但是却关系到第三个问题是围绕《不扩散核武器条约》的核不扩散义务展开，还是围绕《不扩散核武器条约》的核裁军谈判义务展开。这也是法律研究必须关注细节、关注用语之间细微差别的意义。

（四）利用其他学科基础知识

熟悉书状写作的人可能都知道“IRAC”结构，在检索到并研究规则后，接下来就是如何将规则适用于赛题的特定事实。这一步看似简单，但是实际上非常考验赛队的“脑洞”和基础知识。

以 2018 年赛题的第四个问题为例，也就是被告国使用 12 颗**巡航导弹**（cruise missile）攻击并击沉为核潜艇提供补给的**民用船只**（并未装备任何武器）是否合法。显然该问题依据的规则是比较容易辨别的：使用武力的合法性。但是作为被告国的辩手，仅了解该规则并不能很好地论证：第一，击沉一艘看似没有任何武力威胁的民用船只符合使用武力的必要且合比例的要求吗？第二，为什么要用巡航导弹攻击？

为了解决上述难题，不能仅关注必要且合比例的法律规则，同时也需要借助现实中的情况来适用规则。对于第一个问题，我们检索了核潜艇及补给船，得知现实中核潜艇的补给间隔时间较长，因此如果不能在此次及时阻止补给船，将更难寻觅得到补给后隐藏的核潜艇。对于第二个问题，我们检索了巡航导弹的特性，发现巡航导弹主要用于远距离打击。结合赛题中的特定事实，我们认为可以推断出被告国此时距离补给船的距离较远，如果不使用巡航导弹，将无法阻止补给船。我们同时着重强调了核武器的危害，以此来表达如果不抓住此次机会，将会给国际社会造成更大的危害。

当然，其实该问题的确为被告国造成了困难，即使找到上述佐证，仍然难以证明被告国的行为是必要且合比例的。但在赛场上，并非每个问题的论述都需要滴水不漏，只要能够建立自己的逻辑，表现出自己的研究和深度思考，就可能赢得法官的支持。在一场国内赛中，一名法官明显对我们的论点感兴趣，开始和我们探讨为什么赛题中攻击核潜艇使用的是深水炸弹（depth charge）而非鱼雷（torpedo）。当时这个问题显然超出了我们的研究范围，但是经他启发，我们在国际赛的陈述中融入了这一观点。

因此，在做研究时不能只关注法律规则的研究，不要忽略赛题中的一些特定事实。在“山重水复”时再次研究赛题，可能会“柳暗花明”。

二、资料整理

除法律研究以外，还有一个重点经常被忽略，那就是资料整理。长达六个月的备赛期，经常出现之前看过的文章已经忘记、进行过的研究无法想起这样的窘况；而重复研究、重复阅读会花费大量的时间，对于紧张的备赛来说无疑是不合适的。另外，资料整理还可以帮助我们整理思路。因此，资料整理非常重要。我简单分享下备赛时资料整理的方法：

首先，同一个问题下载的文章、报告、决议、案例等全部存储到一个文件夹，对看完的文章编号以区分看过和没看过的资料，并且摘录出资料中有用的部分，摘录的格式可以不必太过在意，但要写清出处，例如：

> ◆ ***(2) GA Resolution 53/101 of 8 December 1998 on Principles and Guidelines for International Negotiation***
> The resolution, *inter alia*, underlines that negotiations '**should be conducted in good faith**' [para. 2 (a)] as well as that 'States should endeavour to maintain a constructive atmosphere during negotiations and to **refrain from any conduct which might undermine the negotiations and their progress**' [para. 2 (e)].

在看完较多资料并有了一些想法后，可以开始着手整理思路。以谈判义务的要件为例，这些要件实际上源自 2016 年马绍尔群岛诉英国“停止核军备竞赛和核裁军谈判义务案”中马绍尔提交的诉状，经过后续阅读不断地被印证，最终整理下来。在整理过程中，可以不必关注自己是请求国还是被告国，而是基于客观公正的立场进行整理：

■ Element 1: entering into negotiations (from Marshall's MEMO)

- ***South West Africa Case***
  - ◆ The duty to pursue negotiations in good faith requires **first entering into negotiations**: "Nor should we overlook the psychological value of the opening of negotiations ... the opening of negotiations is often a decisive step toward the conclusion of an agreement." [*South West Africa (Ethiopia v. South Africa; Liberia v. South Africa), Preliminary Objections, Judgment, ICJ Reports 1962*, para. 188, Dissenting Opinion Judge De Visscher.]
- ***Mavrommatis Palestine Concessions***
  - ◆……（相关摘录，略）
  - ◆不只是进行谈判，而是要希望得到一个结果
- ***Railway Traffic between Lithuania and Poland, PCIJ***
  - ◆……（相关摘录，略）
- ***North Sea Continental Shelf***

◆ **that is the discussions must comprise more than merely going through a formal process;**

◆……（good faith-shafer p. 5）……（相关摘录，略）

- ***Lac Lanoux Arbitration***

◆……（相关摘录，略）

◆谈判要 meaningful

- ***North Sea Continental Shelf***

◆ **they are under an obligation so to conduct themselves that the negotiations are meaningful, which will not be the case when either of them insists upon its own position without contemplating any modification of it** [*North Sea Continental Shelf (Federal Republic of Germany/Denmark; Federal Republic of Germany/Netherlands), Judgment, ICJ Reports 1969*, p. 47, para. 85]

Claims arising out of Decisions of the Mixed Graeco-German Arbitral Tribunal Set Up under Article 304 in Part X of the Treaty of Versailles

◆……（相关摘录，略）

◆一直在 negotiation 中

- ***Arbitration between Kuwait and the American Independent Oil Company (AMINOIL) (1982)***

◆（good faith-shafer p.5）……（相关摘录，略）

- ***MAX PLANCK Agreement of the contracting out of the agreement on trade***

……

◆ Element 4: not defeat the object and purpose of future treaty

- ***Cassese, The Israel-PLO Agreement and Self-Determination, European Journal of International Law Vol. 567(4) (1993), http://www.ejil.org/pdfs/4/1/1219.pdf. Cf. Hisashi Owada, "Pactum decontrahendo, pactum de negotiando," Max Planck Encyclopedia of Public International Law (article last updated April 2008), para. 34, citing General Assembly Resolution A/RES/53/101, 8 December 1998, "Principles and guidelines for international negotiations".***

◆……（相关摘录，略）

◆ *pacta de contrahendo* vs. *pacta de negotiando*

资料整理并没有定式，我的整理方法也并不一定足够清晰合理。但是前期的资料整理帮助我建立了对 R3 和 R4 两个问题的理解，从而形成了自己的逻辑链条和思路，对研究帮助巨大。

备赛的半年可能是最痛苦但也最快乐的半年。看到自己的不足之多，也看到自己的成长之快。永远都会记得，最终在国际赛的闭幕现场，主持人历数国际法发展时的激动，那是一种难得的法律共同体的感觉。而备赛期间大家的眼泪和欢笑、互相督促和互相鼓励、一起早起查资料和练习口头陈述，点滴不敢忘。比赛有赢有输，但是在这段路程中共享的时光才最可贵。也祝大家能够在杰赛普备赛和比赛过程中收获很多，无论结果是好是坏，这都会是绝对不会后悔的经历。

事实分析的经验与技巧

叶欧仪

有幸连续参加了两年杰赛普之后，我获得了一些关于这一国际法赛事的个人思考和经验，现在进行部分梳理，并期待能为未来的参赛者们提供一些帮助。

需要明确的是，每个发言者（mooter）都有自己习惯的文字、语言、气场和风格。因此，在备赛和比赛的过程中，每个人也同样有个人的习惯和方法。模拟法庭的魅力之一就在于它只有相对的标准答案，没有绝对的标准答案：同样的研究材料，会随着不同的思维方式导向不同的论点；而相同的论证思路，也会随着表达方式的不同带来不同的结果。无论是指导老师、教练或是学长学姐，提供的经验都不免受到他们个人风格的影响。对于选手个人来说，很重要的一点就是不要被别人的经验束缚，提前给自己设限，要勇敢地去探索尝试，寻找适合自己的方式。因此，本文的目的不在于告诉大家什么是对的方法，而是总结个人经验，仅供大家参考和选择。

总体而言，与其他模拟法庭类似，杰赛普最重要的两个方面依然是法律研究（legal research）和事实分析（fact analysis）。具体形式类似打游戏，即所有人从同样的基础条件（facts）出发，通过进行法律研究升级自己，并争取最安全、高效地到达已知目的地（issue-conclusion）。想要较好地完成这场比赛，重点在于事实分析的精细度和法律研究的深度。关于法律研究的方法，其他同学已经做好了较为详细的技术总结，因此，本文将主要着眼于事实分析的方法。

一、做好事实梳理，重视初步思路

作为整个备赛阶段的第一步，事实梳理及在此过程中产生的初步思路，对于备赛有着不可小觑的作用。

由于赛题往往又长又复杂，经常多达二十几页，覆盖数个重大国际法问题，又存在大量与争议焦点相关度较低的信息，经常导致参赛选手们迷失在大量无关事实里。我们在开始正式的法律研究之前，要尽可能地杜绝对于某一事实有着“大概但模糊”的印象，因为这样的印象很有可能会在不经意间导致偏离研究方向。因此，为了找准研究的思路并为后期的书状写作打下坚实的基础，初期对于事实的清晰梳理和准确把握是极为重要的。以直观的形式将案件事实展现出来，对于后期查找和定位都有很大的帮助。

就我个人而言，初次阅读赛题之后，我会将自己负责问题相关的事实都挑出来，整理成一个表格并标明段落、中文概要、可能出现的争议焦点及可行的研究方向。这一步骤的要点在于尽量发散且全面地进行头脑风暴并记录下所有的想法，不要预设任何范围和限度。下表为 2020 年我所做的赛题整理片段，以此为例展示各列的目的和作用：首先，应列标明相关段落，方便后续以此表为目录或索引快速定位相关事实；其次，事实列摘出重点事实，可用中文总结加以辅助，方便能够迅速了解段落大意；再次，对事实的“使用方法”，也就是对证明目的做初步的判断；最后，列举出事实中存在的可能引起争议的问题，列下所有可能及可行的研究思路。这些想法不一定都能体现在最终的论证思路中，但是会指明研究方向，并且有很大的概率会在后期研究陷入瓶颈的时候提供新的思路和想法。

段落	事实 /Facts	证明目的	争议焦点及研究思路
34 35 36	1. “The border issue has fundamentally changed in its character. What were once disorganized gangs have become organized militias, and their crimes are no longer limited to opportunistic thievery.” 2. “These new militants are well armed and well-organized, and the police are simply unable to remove them.” 3. 请求国人袭击 9 个被告国边境警察局，杀死 21 名警官 目击者：the raiders were “heavily armed with military-grade weapons and equipment”, and that the attacks indicated “a high level of prior planning and training”.（证明犯罪有组织有纪律） 4. The report indicated that Adawan nationals had established permanent and well-defended encampments within Rasasan territory, which they were using as bases for international trafficking in illegal drugs.［即请求国人在被告国建立了贩毒基地；联合国毒品与犯罪办公室（UNDOC）认可贩毒基地的存在］	犯罪明显升级，有组织犯罪与被告国国家机构发生冲突。	被告国国内报道效力（低） UNODC 报道效力（高） 争议点： 1. 是否构成武装冲突？ a. 武装冲突定义 b. 如果构成，则日内瓦四公约可以适用，涉及平民保护，需研究人权保护到什么程度 2. 使用武力的合法性？非法使用武力越过边境，措施可以采取到什么程度？是否要求先用尽非致命性方法？ 3. 贩毒基地有什么用？打击跨国贩毒的手段可以到什么地步？能否使用武力？

此外，我建议大家重视初步阶段的原因是：这一阶段是选手们对赛题的想法与法官想法最接近的时期，也是思考过程最顺畅合理的时期。这一点要从模拟法庭的特性上去理解：事实上，大部分模拟法庭的法官对其所裁赛题都不会像选手一样深入研究，大多数情况下他们并不会过多地纠结某一前沿国际法问题的理论之争或规则异同，而是明显更重视选手们如何解释不利事实，而这些争议事实正是选手们初读赛题时标记出的那些明显不利于己方的事实。

研究进行到后期时，选手们很容易陷入的一个误区就是因为研究得太深入，过多地纠结于一些或前沿或艰深的规则和理论，忽视了对事实解释的完善。我们初读赛题时产生的那些疑问，正是赛场上法官会产生的那些疑问，也是最应当解决的问题；最直观想到的最粗略的论证思路实际上也是最为合理和自然的思路。

仍以上述 2020 年赛题整理表格为例，初步赛题整理阶段，我曾提出过“为什么可以使用武力”这个问题，然而后期研究过程中因为急于从相对不熟悉的人道法条约入手，很长一段时间忽视了对这一点的研究。最终在书状写作过程中返回来看，才发现逻辑链条上缺了最基础最重要的这一环：适用人道法条约的基本前提是存在正当的使用武力的理由。

综上，强烈建议选手们认真对待赛题阅读和整理的初步阶段，记录并利用好此阶段的思维过程。

二、利用好事实分析，突出有利信息

无论是在书状写作阶段还是口头陈述阶段，对于事实的解释和阐述方式是非常重要的。按照 IRAC 的思维逻辑，法律研究提供的仅仅是个前提，通过事实分析将其契合地套入规则之中才是决定论据强弱的关键。

这一阶段最容易产生的误区就是认为赛题中的表述是不能改动的，导致书状写作或口头陈述中完全照抄事实（facts）材料，无法突出自己想要表达的重点，与规则不够契合，大幅削弱了论点的强度。在此需要明确的是，忠于赛题并不等于忠于赛题的表述，对于案件事实做有利于己方的模糊或强调是合理且受到鼓励的。法律规则是客观准确的，对其扩大或限缩解释都不是易事，但对于事实的理解则是较为主观和容易改变的，而这一点正是我们应当加以利用的。

以 2020 年赛题为例简单展示：

请求国的目标：证明被告国安装的武器损害了其权利。
被告国的目标：证明自己安装的武器不损害请求国及其国民的任何权利。
赛题中的事实表述：Since the time of deployment, each tower that makes up the WALL has been situated within Rasasan territory, between six and 35 meters from the Rasasa-Adawa border, depending upon local terrain.
那么双方分别应当如何利用这一段话呢？这段话涉及该武器的安装位置。首先需要明确哪些事实是有解释空间的：6 至 35 米的数字是不能改变的，但对于距离远近的判断是一个相对主观的标准；请求国自然会主张武器已经非常逼近两国边界，而被告国则要主张无论如何，该武器都是安装在 R 国领土之上的。
在确定好目标之后，下一步就是要选用合适的措辞强调或者是模糊部分事实，突出己方想要表达的意思：对于请求国来说要突出 6 米这个数字之小，而对于被告国来说则要尽量模糊数字，例如：
请求国：Some parts of the WALL are deployed only 6 meters away from the border, covering a significant part of Adawan territory into its attack range and threatening the border security of Adawa.
被告国 : The WALL has been carefully deployed in a manner preventing any potential harm. All the towers that make up the WALL are situated within Rasasan territory, keeping adequate distance from the Rasasa-Adawa border.

通过上面的例子，我们可以感受到对同一事实采取不同的表述会传达出完全不同的主旨观点，并影响论点的说服力大小。建议大家反复打磨自己的事实表述，在可行限度之内采取最能支撑己方观点的行文方式。

三、积极利用“场外”事实信息

所谓“场外”事实信息，指的是赛题中并未提到，但存在于现实生活中的有效信息。备赛过程中，同学们紧跟赛题给的事实展开论证，生怕对事实做过度的曲解或扩张；而大家有时会在无形中被限制了思路，只重视寻找与规则相关的信息（比如联合国五大常任理事国对某一新规则的表态，或某一规则通过时的表决情况），而忽视对与事实相关的真实数据和信息的收集利用。事实上，这类“场外”事实信息的利用非常重要，能够显著增强论点的说服力和可信度，在医学及科技领域尤其如此。

以 2019 年的赛题为例，赛题中提到一种药物对糖尿病有出色的治疗效果，被告国主张这一药物是不可替代、不能停止生产的。这就需要论证糖尿病是一种相当严重的疾病。赛题中并未给出糖尿病相关的任何信息或诠释。实际上我们知道，糖尿病说严重也严重，说轻微也轻微，严重程度因人而异，相当模糊。

对于被告国来说，想要证明糖尿病不可忽视，现实中世界卫生组织对糖尿病做的数据调研是强有力的证据。通过对糖尿病进行深入学习和挖掘，我们了解到了它大致分为Ⅰ型和Ⅱ型，其中Ⅰ型糖尿病必须经过药物治疗患者才能生存下去。同时每年有相当数量的该数患者因不能及时且充分地获得相应的药物而面临生命危险，糖尿病治疗药物是他们生存下去的唯一希望。这可以在一定程度上有效证明题中药物的生产对于国际社会意义重大，不可轻易禁止。

以 2020 年的赛题为例，赛题中提到了自动化武器上配备了 0.50 口径的机关枪，被告方需要主张该自动化武器不违反国际人道法关于武器的基本原则。此处可以使用的场外信息就是 0.50 口径机关枪的杀伤力程度，从而据此判断其是否会引起不必要的痛苦。

赛题并非建立在百分之百的虚拟世界上，只要不是与赛题信息明显相悖，结合实际挖掘有效的“场外”信息不仅不是在钻赛题的空子，反而是大家应当积极尝试和利用的突破点。研究过程中，对规则的挖掘和对赛题事实的解释经常会陷入瓶颈，感觉缺少最直观有效、直指核心的一击。这时候大家就可考虑把视野放大一些，利用可靠且有力的“场外”数据增强观点的科学性和说服力。

以上三点为我在事实分析方面总结的一些小的技术建议，希望能够切实地帮助同学们。

杰赛普的旅程有苦有难，坚持到底并非易事，但正因为如此，才更加精彩纷呈。于人生而言，它绝非必需，但无疑是很有色彩的经历和体验。杰赛普不仅带给我们学识上、心灵上和思想上的成长，赋予我们前行的底气和动力，更为我们创造了时间不可磨灭的人与人之间的联结与感情。希望每一个有想法的你都勇敢地加入我们，相信你将不虚此行。

口头陈述的经验与技巧

刘燕彬

一、如何组织口头陈述稿?

(一)写稿方式

在备赛过程中,虽然我们的队员有过一些其他模拟法庭比赛的经验,但是杰赛普的难度和深度是其他模拟法庭比赛难以比拟的。因此,我们当时对于如何准备口头陈述也比较困惑。整体而言,准备口头陈述稿主要有两种方式:一种是先把稿子全文写出来,背下初稿,然后在模拟训练的过程中,结合队员、教练的反馈进行调整;另一种是只把论点和论据的关键点(bullet point)写出来,不写包含完整句子的陈述稿,而是通过不断练习,对于这些关键点做到"心里有数",自如表达。

参考示例:

Issue 1: Breach of obligations

Obligation A

Source: Customary International Law

- State practice:
  - √ Resolution:
  - √ Treaties:
  - √ Executive conduct:
    - ➢ Evidence Forms: [6 of Draft conclusions on identification of CIL, ILC]
- *Opinio Juris*:

  …

对比而言,第一种方式要做到脱稿会比较快速高效,背诵可能只要半天到一天的时间;但其缺点是,使用熟练背诵稿件的陈述方式,会容易使人觉得选手是在背诵稿件而不是在与法官"沟通"。因此,如果赛队想要采取这种方式,选手不能以"背"为目标,必须将书面稿仅作为一个参考,通过不断的练习脱离原来的稿件，尝试新的表达方式和新的论点呈现方式，并在反馈中不断调整，使自己最终能够灵活地重新组织语言、调整论点顺序。在过去的训练过程中，我们发现自己的陈述稿每一天都在变化修正，有时灵机一动，就会想到一个更好的陈述方式。有一个书面稿作为基础的另一个优点是，在练习过程中，队友对某些表述提出问题或是自己想到更好的陈述方式时，可以很快标注出来并进行修改。而采取第二种方式会显得速度较慢，容易卡壳。尽管如此，采用第二种方式虽然前期进展可能比较慢，但在长期的训练过程中，该方式对于提升选手的表达能力和对事实、依据的熟悉程度是很有帮助的，并且灵活性会更强。

（二）如何开头

关于杰赛普很重要的一点是，时间管理（time management）属于一项单独的评分要点。这一项考虑的因素包括：概括事实背景和论点顺序（roadmap）的时间、两个争议问题（issue）的时间分配、口头陈述与反驳的时间分配，以及口头陈述的时间总长等。即使认为自己有非常多精彩的论点，一旦陈述超时2—3 分钟，法官有可能不再关注陈述的内容，甚至很可能在这一项上打低分。因此，选手把控论点数量，并在规定时间内完成陈述的能力尤为重要。

为了能够预留后续论点的陈述时间，每场负责第一个陈述的选手有必要准备一下向法官概述事实背景的环节（brief the fact）。事实概述应当带有一定的本国立场色彩，与己方的论点相关联，并尽可能将事实背景压缩在两句话左右。此外，虽然法官比较希望听到论点顺序，了解陈述的顺序，但是在开头完整说一遍每个论点非常浪费时间，更简明的方式是用一些名词词组来概括将要论述的几个论点。

示例：I will spend [A] minutes on the pleadings concerning [X] and [Y], and [B] minutes on the rebuttal.

（三）筛选论点

另一个常常引起参赛选手困惑的问题是：书状中包含很多论点，如何在口头陈述中筛选论点。每一个争议问题可能包含多方面的内容：证明可适用的法律，例如，是否存在习惯国际法；如何解释法律，例如，细化规则的构成要件、选择条约解释的方法；如何适用法律，例如，将赛题相关事实与援引的案例进行比较；以及承担的国家责任形式，等等。这意味着在陈述时需要有所侧重，比如国家责任的形式问题，属于比较常规的问题，在预先准备答案时，应当尽量简短，而把时间留给前面的解释、适用这些难点部分。

由于陈述时间的限制，单个选手的陈述时间一般为 20 分钟左右（单场一方总发言时间为 45 分钟）。在这段时间内，考虑到法官还会不断提问，论点数量不宜过多。对于对手可能会攻击或法官可能会关注的部分，一旦有强力的论点回应，可以不必等到反驳的环节再提出，而是在陈述中提出先发制人的论点（preemptive argument）。此类有力论点应当在论点筛选中给予第一级别的优先性。其次，是对己方比较有力的论点，这些论点可能很多队伍都会提出，那么重要的是能否有一些更新、更相似或法院裁判更明确的案例可以适用，或者能否找到更好的融合事实、解释事实的方法，使得论点令人耳目一新。以 2017 年的第一个争议问题“地下含水层的公平使用”为例，在一场国际赛中，对方不知道国际法院在 2015 年“哥斯达黎加沿圣胡安河修建道路案”中明确了环境影响评价义务的习惯国际法性质和门槛标准，而仅援引了 2010 年“纸浆厂案”作为依据，向法官点出对方在法律依据上的不足，这也可以帮助己方加分。而对于没有把握的论点，可以尽量避免在陈述过程中直接提起。法官提问该问题之后再进行回应会比较保险。论点的筛选及呈现在很大程度上还是依赖于前期研究的成果。但是，在组织口头陈述稿的阶段，仍然要不断研究完善。

（四）事实解读

事实解读方面，可以每隔一段时间就开一个小会，在队内讨论一下个人对于争议问题相关事实的理解。非常重要的是对时间线的整理。例如，在准备比赛时，我们队长就以时间线作为间接证据来说明：虽然之前请求国对于被告国的行为不满，提出了抗议，但在被告国采取了相应措施后，在接下来的三年时间里，请求国都没有再提出抗议，以此来说明请求国的诉求已经得到了回应和解决，被告国并没有违反合作义务。因此，时间线不但可以帮助我们理解什么时间双方做了什么，还可以帮助我们发散去思考为什么一方在某个时间不作为。此外，对于部分事实，我们开始阅读赛题时并没有发现其用处，而随着研究的深入我们渐渐找到了它的用处。而且，在比赛过程中，法官的问题也会提示我们。

实际上，论述所能依赖的事实并不仅限于赛题本身，比如在讨论某国用水量是否过多时，可以将其与世界卫生组织公布的世界人均用水水平进行对比等。通过假设赛题中国家真实存在，并结合现实情况考虑赛题争议问题，这种方法将增加可以利用的数据以及法官的认可度。由于现在的赛题更加贴近时事热点问题，这一方法对于应对法官的提问也会很有帮助。

二、如何准备上场陈述稿?

在这里分享三种比赛时准备上场陈述稿（statement）的方式，供大家参考。

（一）方式一：陈述稿（左页）+ 依据（右页对应位置）

参考示例：

Statement	**Authorities**	**Statement**	**Authorities**
Opening Argument 1	 Argument 1 ● Element 1 ■ Legal basis: (binding: (persuasive: ■ Facts and Application:	Argument 2	Argument 2 ● Point 1 ■ Legal basis: (binding: (persuasive: ■ Facts and Application:
Page 1	Page 2	Page 3	Page 4

这种准备方式的优点在于：其一，左页的陈述稿可以帮助增加信心，不需要完全脱稿，即使处于比较紧张无法脱稿的状态，也能快速看一眼陈述稿，迅速串联到下一个论点；其二，尤其是对于被告国来说，可以在陈述稿上进行备注，依照对方论点调整发言顺序，还可以把法官提问的部分标注出来，强调并融入发言稿中，使法官认识到你有认真倾听对方的发言及法官的疑问，并且非常积极地回应；其三，因为每个论点都能有效回应对方的发言，法官也更容易接受你的论点；其四，在遇到法官提问时，也可以在右页中迅速找到对应论点的法律依据和事实依据，能够很大程度减少记忆负担及记错的风险。

（二）方式二：表格式（主要包括法律依据、相关事实的关键词、段落、页数等基本信息）

参考示例 1：

Points/Arguments	**Authorities/Evidences**
ISSUE 1: XXX	
Argument 1： **We submit that ...**	**Authorities:** (1) Article xx, XX Convention; (2) XXX case
Article xx, XX Convention	[quote key texts/elements] (Background Information: Date, Parties, Status etc.) Meaning of key concepts/elements Interpretation of the Article (1) Method (2) Evidence: Preparatory works, Commentaries, Cases etc.
XXX case	[Key rulings: XXX (para. x)] (Background Information: Parties, Date, Court etc.) Case Summary Case Analogy/Distinction
Facts and application	page. a, para. b of the Problem, [quote key sentences/phrases]

参考示例 2：

Defence Outline		
ISSUE 1:		
Argument 1	**Legal Basis**	**Factual Basis and Application**
	Applicant's legal basis: (Corresponding Rebuttal) Respondent's legal basis:	Applicant's application: (Rebuttal) Respondent's application:

第一种表格形式需要对陈述稿非常熟悉，无须再翻看原文［当然，原文还是应该备好一份放在文件夹（binder）中，主要作用是增强信心和安全感，即使无法脱稿也有 plan b］。表格式陈述稿的优点是，选手在准备时是按点进行的，即使在比赛过程中有法官提问打断，被迫转向另一个论点、案例或条约条款，由于前期已经着重于这方面的训练，选手借助表格式陈述稿能够迅速适应法官问题的跳跃性，灵活地予以回应。此外，这种方式也能在准备反驳环节时帮助选手快速找到陈述时遗漏的有力论点。

第二种表格形式非常适合被告国。被请求国可以将请求国可能使用的事实及法律依据列出，再一一列出反驳点，用于被告国陈述稿或每个论点的开篇；在临时组织陈述稿时，也方便选手快速标记勾选；组织成一份灵活且直击要点的陈述稿。

（三）方式三：陈述稿与法律依据、事实依据混合

参考示例：

We submit that based on Treaty/Case/Customary International law, to qualify a XXX, three elements must be established. They are A, B, and C.

Basis for conclusion of the elements: ■ Treaty/General Principle/Customary International law/Case etc.

Firstly, Element A could (not) be established in the present case.

Basis for interpretation of the element A： ■ Treaty/General Principle/Customary International law/Case etc. Application: Relevant facts: page. a, para. b of the Problem [quote key sentences/phrases] Analogy / Distinction (By abstracting the key elements/fact patterns in the case you quote, and showing the similarity/distinction of the two cases)

方式三的优点在于，在划分论点之后，都可以在相应位置附上相关的法律和事实依据，对应起来也比较快；缺点在于，这样会使得陈述稿非常长，在比赛时翻页会过多，并且相关内容不在一页时可能会使选手的陈述不够流畅。如果法律依据部分过长而陈述稿部分较短，选手在法官提问打断后重新定位到之前的内容会相对慢。因此，即使采用这种方式准备，也要避免罗列所有的法律依据和事实依据，要尽量精简内容，避免大段引用，法律依据部分可以尽量以

关键点的方式展现。

三、如何训练?

2017 年寒假，我们的队员在家待了不到十天就回到北京进行口头训练。练习采取的方式是每人每天完整地模拟一次，同时其他队员中途打断提出问题，由一人记录问题并整理给发言队员。下午则继续查资料整理，并将整理的国际法基础知识问题共享给队员。这样一来，每天都会有一个涉及案件争议点的问题清单以及一个一般国际法问题的清单。

每天训练的时候，都应该尽量模仿真实的比赛过程，做到起立，计时，提示所剩时间，保持仪态，调整语速语调，与“法官”进行眼神交流等。尤其重要的是，在训练中应当有意识地打断队员并转向另外一个问题，练习队员快速应对并返回到论点的能力。

四、如何准备问题?

初次参加模拟法庭的同学可能对在训练时准备什么问题比较困惑，不知道比赛过程中法官会问什么。我个人认为，最好的方法就是不要怕自己问得对不对，对于觉得疑惑、不清楚的部分，均可以提问。这是因为，在正式比赛中，法官的提问范围也是非常广泛的，包括条约中具体用语的定义、内涵，法律依据的完整条文、序号、缔约国数量、状态，援引案例的概要、争议当事方、裁判法院与时间；国际法的基础知识，例如习惯国际法的构成要件、证据；国际法的渊源，《国际法院规约》第 38 条不同法律渊源之间的关系，是否有层级（hierarchy）；等等。

如果实在没有头绪，建议参赛选手回顾下以往的法官备忘录（bench memo）。法官备忘录除了分析当年的争议问题外，在最后也会附上一个问题清单，主要涉及国际法渊源、国家责任等一般问题以及与当年赛题有关的问题。这些问题均可以在训练中穿插提问，还可以整理出一般性国际法问题的清单供全队使用，并传承给之后的队员。在训练后期，我们发现队员们已经很难再问出新问题，就邀请了一些以前参加过各种模拟法庭比赛的同学协助训练，接受一些新问题。

五、让法官觉得“亮眼”的技巧

总结国内赛和国际赛的经验，我认为有三个会让法官觉得眼前一亮的小技巧：

（一）讲好“故事”（Frame a story）

对于请求国第一个发言的选手来说，与其把诉求重复一遍，不如在开头讲好一个故事，这也是国内赛 8 进 4 时，法官对我们参加国际赛的建议。一开始，我们有讲故事的想法，但是我们认为讲故事需要把四个争议问题中对己方有利的内容都讲到，没有办法编出一个自然的故事就放弃了。在国际赛 32 进 16 时，对手智利天主教大学讲的故事才让我大概知道了故事应该怎么讲。当年的四个问题涉及跨界含水层的公平适用、文化遗产的保护、文化财产的非法转移及土著人权利、难民接收国的求偿问题等。智利选手从第一个问题开始，以 R 国（即被告国）没有合理利用水资源作为出发点，强调 R 国行为的不法性，强调水资源的珍贵，然后一句话带过 A 国（即请求国），之后表明第 2 到 4 个争议问题很大程度上都是因为 R 国的不法行为。当然中间的因果关系不能这样简单地阐述，但是这个故事的目的就是让法官知道大概发生了什么，而且尽力把法官的目光吸引到对己方有利的地方，然后在这样的氛围里进行后面的陈述。

在国内赛阶段，如果认为讲故事很难，那么还是应当将注意力放到主要的论点上。但如果对自己有信心，可以准备一个故事，作为锻炼。至于这个故事到底应该怎么讲，不同人有自己的风格，可以参考往年国际赛的视频多做练习。

（二）积极回应（Be responsive）

对于被告国一方来说，虽然法官不要求每一个被告律师都能积极回应对方的论点，但是如果做得好就一定是加分项。比如，我们队长每次的陈述稿都会调整论点的顺序，通过这种方式告诉法官，陈述顺序与请求国的论证顺序是对应的，并在开头就总结自己的几个论点，给法官一个很清楚的论点顺序。如果在陈述结尾，发现自己还有时间，则可以做一个简短的总结，有力地重申己方立场。这样做也能在陈述的结尾给法官留下逻辑清晰、叙述有条理的印象。

（三）强调差异或相似之处（Emphasize distinctions or similarities）

几乎每个参赛队都会引用主办方发放的第一批或第二批材料中的案例，如果想要突出研究成果，就要在法律适用（application）环节多花工夫。这就需要研究提供的案例是否与比赛案例相似。训练过程中常见的问题是，因为法律适用部分不充分，逻辑上给人一种直接依据某个规则和事实就得出了结论的跳跃感。所以建议大家要多问为什么，尽力去总结相关案件事实的模式（fact pattern），并强调案件的关键相似之处或关键差异。

举例来说，2017 年赛题中第一个争议问题涉及被告国的单方声明是否为其创设了义务，而请求国需要证明单方声明的作出者，即赛题中的水资源与农业部部长是否有资格代表该国家。关于这一点的论证，可以类比国际法院 2006 年刚果民主共和国诉卢旺达的“在刚果领土上的武装活动案”（Armed Activities on the Territory of the Congo）进行说明。该案提炼出来最重要的要件就是，国际法院认可了（1）卢旺达司法部部长（2）在其权限范围内的领域原则上有能力 / 资格代表卢旺达。通过类推适用，赛题中发表声明的是被告国的水资源与农业部部长，并且发言正是处于其负责的水资源利用与保护的权限范围内。因此，通过对这两个关键事实的比较，可以有效说服法官。

参考示例：

To prove A, we can make an analogy between Case XXX and the present one.

In case XXX, [element/pattern 1] and [element/pattern 2]. Similarly, in this case, we can find that firstly, ... and secondly, ... Therefore, it is reasonable for us to have a similar conclusion as in Case XXX. [Emphasize the conclusion in the end]

代表双方备赛的经验与技巧

李泽坤

法律的生命不在于逻辑，而在于经验。模拟法庭对于法学院学生来说，是一项性价比很高的综合素质拓展活动。不同学科的模拟法庭，虽然赛题内容和比赛规则有所不同，但一般来说都包括书状撰写和口头陈述等环节，选手既需要进行广而深的法律研究，还需要参与紧张的庭审对抗。与平时的课堂学习相比，模拟法庭能够在较短时间内快速提升选手的法律检索、文书写作、口头表达和批判思维等各项能力。

相较于其他模拟法庭，杰赛普在赛题难度和准备强度方面而言算得上首屈一指。我曾在 2015 年参加了第十三届比赛，准备过程着实艰辛，每当精疲力竭时也唠叨着以后再也不要参赛，结果三年后还是参加了第十六届比赛。第十六届比赛赛题难度丝毫不减当年，并且由于队伍成员的变动，我受命同时负责请求国（A 方，applicant）和被告国（R 方，responedent）双方书状的起草以及口头陈述，准备强度和难度陡增。当然，最后能够进入国际赛与其他国家及地区的选手切磋交流使我觉得一切努力都值得。

在与其他参赛小伙伴的交流过程中，我发现大家普遍认为同时准备双方的比赛大有裨益，例如对争议事实及法律规则的理解会更加透彻，能够更快地形成大局观并抓住核心问题；但也带来诸多挑战，例如正反方思维的转换，贯彻始终的观点对抗，以及备赛中的精力平衡等。本文将重点结合自己的经验谈谈如何代表双方备赛，当然，部分内容同样适用于单方准备。文中所述方法不一定具有普遍性，也不一定正确，如能对读者有些许帮助，都会令我感到欣慰。如有不当之处，请读者不吝指正。

一、事实及法律研究

法律研究是模拟法庭竞赛的重中之重，法律研究不扎实，书状撰写和口头陈述则犹如无根之木。杰赛普的法律研究兼具广度和深度，法律研究必须贯穿始终。以第十六届比赛第一个争议问题为例，该问题涉及国家间仲裁裁决的效力问题，法律检索的范围涵盖了国际法院、常设仲裁法院、国际海洋法法庭、国际投资争端解决中心等国际法庭判例、国内法院和仲裁机构的案例、联合国机构的决议、国际组织（如 ILC、ICCA、IBA）的报告及评述，以及论文和专著等。法律研究工作量巨大，通常情况下，一位选手需同时负责两个赛题争议问题，因此面对浩如烟海的检索资料，首先应当注重梳理案件事实和厘清研究内容和方向。

（一）事实梳理

赛题事实决定了法律研究的方向，并且对事实的不同解读将直接影响论述角度。每年的赛题大概都有近 20 页，可以说，每段内容都是干货，基本上每句话都有可以被选手利用的信息。因此需要常读、细读赛题事实，每读一遍都有可能在字里行间发现新线索。备赛时，应当先通读赛题了解案件背景，然后结合争议问题有针对性地梳理案件事实。

以当年赛题的第二个争议问题为例，大致的案件背景是，二战后原告国和被告国所在的地区武器泛滥，成为跨国军火走私的中心。为了维护地区的和平与稳定，保护商船免受海盗袭击或触礁，被告国长期收集周边海域的信息并共享给包括原告国在内的其他邻国。两国于 1947 年签订了《友好、通商、航行条约》(《FCN 条约》)，建立了良好的关系。但被告国 2015 年研发了一种水下无人潜航器（AUV），其体积不大，装有先进的视听声呐系统，能躲避物体、监测、识别，还能搬动小件物品。水下无人潜航器的程序设定是在领海之外自动航行。原告国认为该水下无人潜航器从事间谍活动，禁止进入其领海。之后原告国海军就在其领海 11 海里处捕获了水下无人潜航器。对此，被告国表示水下无人潜航器进入原告国领海原因不明，但目的是为了维护地区和平稳定，要求原告国返还。原告国认为水下无人潜航器正在非法窃取信息，因而拒绝返还。赛题中原告国的诉求是，被告国的行为违反了《FCN 条约》中关于尊重领土及领海的规定，原告国捕获水下无人潜航器没有违反条约中关于商业及航行自由的规定；被告国的诉求与原告国相反。

根据上述事实，可以初步判断原告国及被告国各自的立场以及可能需要进行的法律研究内容。例如，被告国的论点可能包括但不限于：第一，水下无人潜航器的程序设定是在 12 海里外自动航行，其进入原告国领海属于不可抗力；第二，水下无人潜航器进入原告国领海属于无害通过，行为完全合法；第三，原告国一直同意被告国在周边海域内部署海军收集信息，因此水下无人潜航器可以进入原告国领海。原告国的思路则与被告国完全相反，但本质上都是一个问题的正反面，需要研究的点基本一致。至此，研究方向已初步形成，不可抗力、无害通过、同意及禁止反言等内容可能是研究的重点。同时，《FCN 条约》中相关条款的解释也是重点关注的对象。

（二）法律研究

初期法律检索的概念宜大不宜小，例如先根据初步想到的论点查询不可抗力、无害通过的概念、内涵以及适用问题，至于水下无人潜航器的概念和间谍行为的认定等相对细节的问题，可以待研究主要概念后再深入检索。

赛题公布后一个月左右，举办方会发布第一批研究资料供各参赛队参考，如果前期研究扎实，那么前期研究基本能涵盖第一批研究材料。两个月后，将发布第二批研究资料。发布这两批研究材料的目的是引导法律研究，资料内容通常具有较高参考价值，可以起到查漏补缺和确认研究方向的作用。

在法律研究阶段，为避免后期研究资料过多而产生混乱，建议前期做好文件分类和管理，例如为每个争议问题单独建立文件夹，然后分别建立原告国和被告国的子文件夹，再按照条约、国际组织、案例、论文或其他类别对研究资料进行系统整理。分类的标准可以按照自己的习惯进行调整，主要是为了方便查询文件，提高查询效率。

法律研究中更重要的工作是梳理检索材料。阅读检索材料耗时却未必会有收获，看似与案件争议相关的材料，有时通篇读完也不一定有任何能够援引或参考的内容。梳理检索资料一方面有助于固定研究成果，步步为营，便于后续核实；另一方面也可以避免团队重复劳动，节省时间。梳理检索资料也可以遵循与整理文件类似的方法，即按照条约、习惯国际法、案例、论文著作等分类梳理支持双方主张的论据。梳理的过程本身就是理解和消化的过程，慢慢就会形成自己的观点以及论证框架，同时也会激发一些新的想法和思路，再通过法律检索进一步论证新的想法。如此循环检索梳理，基本上就是前期法律研究的主要内容。这项工作初期会比较耗时，但是将会为后期研究提供便利，特别是在同时准备双方研究的情况下。

二、书状写作

当法律研究形成初步成果并搭建起论述的逻辑框架后，就应当及时进入书状写作阶段。起草书状前，一定要注意比赛规则的相关要求，应当特别注意字数分配、格式、脚注等要求，否则后期再调整既麻烦又耗时。因为格式问题导致书状被扣分非常不值得。动笔之前不妨先阅读历年最佳书状（best memo），从目录到正文都通读一遍，内容看不懂没关系，但至少需要对优秀书状有感官上的认识。

书状的内容至少应当确保逻辑严谨、依据充分、论证周延，看目录就能清楚了解整个论证的思路，看脚注就可以知道论证的主要依据。至于语言措辞风格，则应当言简意赅、准确表达观点。如果时间或条件允许，也可以请英文母语者润色一下，以达到锦上添花的效果。

一篇优秀的书状在论证扎实的基础上还应当具有一定的故事性，对同一事实的不同解读以及组织事实的角度，都会影响整个故事所传达的信息和立场。对于同一个问题，原告国和被告国要讲的故事肯定完全不同，向法官呈现的立场也一定截然相反。讲好故事，必然要扎根于案件事实。因此，甄别对己方有利的事实并进行解读，也是起草书状的必备工作。

解读事实要忠于案件背景，不能推测、妄断，否则就是过分解读，背离案件事实。例如关于水下无人潜航器在原告国领海内是否在行使无害通过权的问题，《联合国海洋法公约》规定船舶（ships）可以行使无害通过权。那么原告国可能主张水下无人潜航器不是船舶，因此不能行使无害通过权；被告国必然持相反观点。赛题关于水下无人潜航器的原文表述是："They are programmed to navigate autonomously for one week, and then to return to the ship from which they were deployed."此外，原告国捕获水下无人潜航器时指出，可以轻易地辨别出水下无人潜航器属于被告国。法律研究时可以发现，潜航器行使无害通过权需要展示旗帜并浮出水面，也有的观点认为其上载有船员才能属于船舶。但从赛题的事实描述来看，并没有说水下无人潜航器上面有没有人、是否展示了旗帜，以及在穿过原告国领海时是否露出水面等。对于没有提及的事项，任何推测都与案件事实不符。结合已有事实，被告国可以主张，既然原告国能轻易识别水下无人潜航器属于被告国，说明水下无人潜航器上有易于识别的特征；但如果被告国坚持主张水下无人潜航器上有国旗，则背离了事实。

根据《国际法院规约》第 38 条的规定，国际法渊源主要包括条约、习惯国际法、一般法律原则以及判例和学说等。如果前期已经按照上文提到的分类梳理方法对检索资料做了整理，那么起草书状将可以直接使用前期的梳理结果，体会到分类梳理的便捷。有一点需要注意，关于习惯国际法，基本上每年赛题都会有某一规则是否构成习惯国际法的争议。习惯国际法的形成需要满足国家实践和法律确信两个要素。国际法院的有些判决会直接写明某个规则构成习惯国际法，可以直接援引，基本上没有问题。但如果要去证明某个规则构成了习惯国际法，将是极具挑战性的工作，并且对方必然会提出质疑，因为国家实践和法律确信到什么程度才能满足习惯国际法的标准，确实没有标准答案。那么，要不要证明某一规则构成了习惯国际法？我认为，在做足法律研究的前提下，完全可以大胆主张，即便法官最后没有采纳，至少可以展现出法律研究的扎实程度。

至于应该先起草哪一方书状，我认为没有定式，先考虑好哪一方的论证结构就先写哪一方。但是原告国和被告国的书状风格是有所不同的。通常情况下，原告国是立论的一方，观点站得住，基本就及格了。被告国在论证己方主张之外，还要对原告国大概率会抛出的论点做必要的回应。被告国的书状需要有针对性（responsive）一些，但也并不是所有潜在的论点都要一一回应，在篇幅允许的情况下回应原告国最可能提出的论点就可以了。

关于书状的脚注，有人认为每一句话后都应有脚注。这一说法有一定的夸张成分，但从某种程度上讲，脚注的数量体现了参赛队伍的态度。脚注数量过少可能让法官感觉研究不扎实、态度不认真，继而导致书状评分处于不利地位。但也不能单纯为了增加脚注数量而强行援引参考文献。根据对往年最佳书状的研究，两个争议问题的脚注数量大概在 100 到 130 个左右。如果书状中脚注数量过少，则应当思考法律研究是否充分。

三、口头陈述

书状提交之后，距离国内赛一般剩下 40 多天的准备时间，大家应该可以很快起草出口头陈述的框架或初稿。在同时代表双方备赛的情况下，口头陈述部分是最容易出现混乱的环节。准备过程大概要经历以下几个阶段：混乱—熟练—再混乱—再熟练。这非常符合“否定之否定规律”，一直在混乱和熟练之间徘徊。

通常情况下，口头陈述初稿基本是在书状的框架和论证内容的基础上略做调整，甚至可能是一个简化版的书状。这无可厚非，因为思维在开始阶段很大程度上还受书状的影响。但模拟练习几遍之后会发现，并不一定要讲书状的所有内容，否则要么时间不够用，要么容易淡化焦点。

根据比赛规则，每一方的陈述加上反驳的时间总共 45 分钟。每一个选手要负责陈述两个问题，可以分配到 20—22 分钟左右的时间，每个争议问题大概可以陈述 10 分钟。按照正常的语速，一分钟 120—130 个单词，在法官没有任何提问的情况下（但这是绝对不可能的），两个问题全部讲完，大概 2500 个左右的单词。考虑到“冷庭”和“热庭”等因素，两个问题的陈述稿字数在 1300—1800 词比较合理（相差的部分内容遇到“热庭”时可以选择不主动说）。此外，因为被告国的陈述要具有针对性，理论上陈述内容会比原告国多一些。因此，在陈述时间有限的情况下，口头陈述讲的都必须是核心内容，而书状中很多内容没有机会也没有必要讲。

模拟几次之后再调整修改的陈述稿，才是真正意义上的初稿，选手基本上将以此为蓝本开始熟悉论点并训练庭审问答。在初期准备双方陈述时，原告国和被告国的论点偶尔会搞混，尤其是在回答问题的时候，但这些都是正常现象，主要还是熟练度的问题。待思维逐渐适应之后，就会有很大改善。

需要注意的是，准备口头陈述并不意味着法律研究的结束，如前文所述，法律研究要贯穿始终。陈述稿也要随着法律研究的深入而做相应调整。之所以后来会进入“再混乱”阶段，很大程度上是因为对口头陈述的论证、表述等做了调整和补充。但经过多次训练，这种混乱的状态很快就会改善。

关于原告国和被告国的口头陈述准备，侧重点其实是不一样的。直观感受是：原告国基本上是在既有框架里演绎发挥，重点须关注法官的提问；被告国则须根据原告国的陈述，提出己方论点的同时有针对性地反驳原告国。但这并不代表原告国不需要考虑被告国可能提出的论点，无论是为了论证的周延还是为了准备反驳环节，原告国都有必要做相应准备。整体而言，被告国的工作量相对会多一些，一方面，被告国要预测原告国的论点并考虑好反驳的要点；另一方面，法官也有可能结合原告国的论点延伸提问。准备被告国的口头陈述时需要提前做好相应准备。

在比赛过程中，什么样风格的法官都有，关注事实的，关注法律渊源的，关注历史背景的，也有结合时事提问的。此外，也有法官为了综合考察选手会调整提问方式，如果选手陈述过多的法律规则，法官则会侧重提问案件事实；如果选手讲太多的事实，法官则会究问具体的法律依据。因此，庭审中什么情况都可能发生，不确定因素会很多，所以需要在准备阶段穷尽一切可能去假设问题并做相应准备。口头陈述更需要注重整体的平衡，包括时间把控、突出强点避开弱点、回避法官刁难式提问等，这需要在前期模拟训练中不断地总结。

四、其他注意事项

关于案卷整理，每个人的习惯都不同，可以完全按照自己的喜好做。我自己的整理顺序是，最上面放陈述稿，之后依次是赛题、法律研究、书状。其中，陈述稿翻开，右侧是陈述内容，左侧是对应的法律依据、法官在该部分可能的提问及相关回应要点等。陈述稿字号可以大一些，因为每一页的内容不是很多，所以页面还有部分的空余，可以临时做一些笔记。关于法律研究部分，主要是重点法条、案例摘要、重点文献的摘要等，但其实到了比赛的时候基本上没有时间去翻，主要还是起心理安慰的作用。

一般情况下，参赛队通常有四位上场队员，每人负责一方的两个争议问题，一人同时准备双方更多时候是颇为无奈的决定。准备双方的整个过程会面临较大的心理压力，所以状态的调整和精力的平衡是必要的。对于同时代表双方备赛的队员，剖析赛题、法律研究、撰写书状、庭审训练的过程会比较艰苦，因此一定注意劳逸结合。总体而言，得益于教练的指导和团队的协作，我们最终完成了比赛初期设定的目标。同时代表双方参加比赛虽然非常艰辛，但对于法律研究、英文写作、口语表达以及抗压能力的提升非常有帮助。

担任研究员的经验与技巧

李冰清

作为2019年杰赛普国际法模拟法庭比赛中的研究员（researcher），于我而言，备赛可以分为团队分工确定前和确定后两个阶段。前一阶段的经验主要与研读赛题和探索命题思路有关，具有一定的普遍性，因为研究员和口头陈述者都需要这些做基础。后一阶段的经验则关注研究员特有的任务，具有较强的针对性。

前一阶段从报名参赛到确定正式参赛队员和分工，历时大约两个月。因为此时距离正式比赛还有较长时间，而且不确定最终是否能够参加比赛，所以重点在于如何克服懒惰心理，高效地完成计划。解决这个问题的良方是定期召开组会，既可以互相监督，也可以交流想法、完善思路。在小组讨论时将自己想不明白的疑点、难点提出来进行讨论，经常会有意想不到的收获。

技术上，这一阶段的主要任务包括研读赛题和整理基本应对思路。个人建议从以下三个方面全方位、多层次解剖赛题，精细体会文字背后的内容。第一，分国别按时间顺序整理两个国家各自发生的事件，应尽量详细全面，暂时不用考虑单个事件与最终的诉求是否相关。第二，分主题整理，以2019年赛题为例，围绕Pivzao文明整理它的历史发展和传统习俗等。第三，也是最重要的，是在上述工作的基础上比较两国对同一事件的态度和反应。除了吃透赛题，在该阶段还需要确定基本思路。这要求深入了解事实，领悟命题者的意图，在明白各项诉求之后，以自己的知识储备为基础先形成一个大致的论证轮廓，然后确定查找文献的初步关键词，通过阅读文献进一步细化和完善论证思路。由于杰赛普命题的前沿性，个人建议以英文论文为主，关注脚注。搜索时，先用谷歌搜索，再用谷歌学术，且不能拘泥于简单的几个关键词，应该变换角度使用不同的关键词搜索。如此，方可为之后的工作铸成坚固基石，灵活处理接下来可能遇到的各种挑战。

后一阶段从确定正式参赛队员和分工到正式比赛结束，历时大约四个月。该阶段，作为一名研究员，要做到以下三个方面。首先，要明确自己的定位——辅助口头陈述者。既不能太过强势，干扰口头陈述者的研究思路，也不能毫无主见，要及时关注口头陈述者的需求，为其提供帮助。更重要的是能够提出问题，促使他们进一步完善提高。当然，最重要的是要有全局观念和整体意识，在团队最需要的位置发光发热，弥补团队的功能性缺失。其次，研究员的支持对象可能会有不同，有的专门对接一个口头陈述者，有的则负责整体对接。作为专门辅助人员，一定要和相应的口头陈述者保持沟通，确保为他 / 她提供强大的科研后盾。作为全队辅助人员，虽然总会有重点研究的一到两个诉求，但还是要尽力熟悉四个诉求，了解基本的思路和知识点，清楚正反方各自的宏观理论及逻辑。这样，在口头陈述者"当局者迷"的时候，可以作为旁观者进行提醒。最后，还要注意保持积极向上的心态。因为口头陈述者和研究员的分工肯定是根据团队每个人的特点作出的最佳安排，但不一定符合每个人的期待，这就要及时调整心态。不能因为做了研究员就放松对自己的要求，三天打鱼两天晒网。某种程度上，对研究员的要求比对口头陈述者还要高，如上所述，不仅有些时刻要两耳不闻窗外事地深入研究特定诉求，而且要高屋建瓴，掌握全队战略和动向。

技术上，这一阶段的主要任务包括撰写书状和一赛场逐鹿、舌战群雄（整个比赛最激动人心的时刻）。2019 年我负责了一个诉求的初稿撰写，以及和大家一起整理书状的格式与脚注。据个人经验，主要有三点建议。首先，为了方便添加脚注，建议动笔之前整个团队统一格式，然后每个人自己负责的部分最好能建一个参考文献的表格，分门别类标号。比如按案例、论文、国际组织决议等条目分类，每一类别包含做脚注用的基本信息。这样，即使最后脚注出了问题也可以及时查找修改。其次，建议每个人写自己负责的部分时先不带格式，合在一起之后再调整。虽然一份书状看似很多，但个人经验表明统一之后由一个人负责调整格式比两份带格式的文件合在一起再调整要节省时间。最后，除了以上两点外在形式，书状的灵魂还是内容。建议研究员敢写敢改，不要觉得思路不完善就不写，也不要不忍心大幅删减；还要多多请教前辈。

正式上场比赛之前主要是口头陈述者不断练习，完善思路，润色语言。但是研究员在练习的过程中并不是可有可无的，研究员作用的充分发挥对练习效率至关重要。因为每一遍练习，口头陈述者都需要全身心投入到自己的诉求和对方的观点之中，对自己比赛的语言习惯、手势动作和时间分配可能关注不够。这就需要研究员的陪练。然而，陪练并不是单纯的计时举牌，关键要做好两方面工作。一方面，应该记录每次提问的问题，标明哪些需要进一步研究，自己灵光一现的想法也要记录下来。这些内容要形成书面文件以方便保存和查阅。

但是口头陈述者后期准备的时间并不充裕，研究员最好能够在每次练习完成后，将自己的想法言简意赅地传达给他们。另一方面，应该在口头陈述者进行陈述时观察他们的神态、语言和手势，将一些不妥之处告诉他们。也要注意沟通技巧，争取准确表达自己的同时使他人易于接受。

最后就是万众瞩目的正式比赛阶段。此时研究员的主要任务有两个。第一个仍然是学术上的全力支持，最好能够在一些细节问题上快速回答口头陈述者的疑问，这样也有助于口头陈述者放松心情。当然，要做到这些离不开前期的认真备赛，所以前期各项任务一定要高质量地完成。第二个则是为口头陈述者提供高质量的后勤服务，确保他们可以没有后顾之忧地上战场，比如定好外卖、勘察好路线。此外，比赛过程中，口头陈述者的紧张和情绪波动不可避免，研究员最好能够做到暖心陪伴，满足他们的聊天谈心等心理需要。不过也要注意量力而行，不可起反作用。

时光飞逝，一年后再次想起那些人和事依然如此清晰。很幸运自己可以作为一名研究员参加比赛，知识的增长和能力的提升令我欣喜，而在比赛过程中角色的定位和心态的调整则令我明白：或许世间万物有各自的定规定法，但每个人的本心和努力可以超脱预定的框架，绘成独一份的景色。春日又至，百花深处虔诚地写下这篇小记，纪念师友相伴、并肩问道的幸福时光，也希望读到它的研究员可以有些许领悟。

国际法模拟法庭书状的引注格式及注意问题

宋岩　李奕慧　王姿月[1]

统一引注格式是书状写作中最为复杂的一项程序，需要队员们从一开始便确定格式并严格执行。引注的主要目的是，使读者根据引注能够准确定位论证依据的出处，因此，引注一般包括以下信息：文献名称、完成文献的单位或个人、日期、引用内容在文献中的具体页数或段落号。完整的引注信息不仅方便读者定位文献出处，更能体现论证的权威性和可靠性，给法官留下严谨认真的印象。本文主要依据《牛津法律依据引注标准》[*Oxford Standard for the Citation of Legal Authorities (OSCOLA)*]和《牛津法律依据引注标准：国际法分节》(*OSCOLA: Citing International Law Sources Section*)，按照不同国际法渊源分类举例讲解引注格式。需要说明的是，OSCOLA并非唯一的可参考格式，也可以参考其他格式，例如Blue Book等，或者内部协调统一的格式。

本文首先归纳适用于各种国际法渊源引注格式的一般规则，然后分别介绍各种渊源的引注格式。在各部分中，本文将首先总结引注的基本格式，然后示范说明首次引用和再次引用的格式。

一、一般规则

1. 引注的数字一般位于正文标点之后，使用上标。

2. 脚注中除介词与冠词外的单词首字母一般应大写，其他字母小写。

3. 标点注意问题：

(1)统一使用英文标点，避免中英文标点混用。

(2)OSCOLA尽量避免使用标点，特别是“.”和“,”。条约条款号不加点，例如art 12；年月日之间不加点，例如12 March 2020；姓名首字母缩写后的点去掉，例如M Shaw；缩写之间的点去掉，例如ICJ Rep，UNTS，UN Doc A/C6/56/L9等。该规则也较少使用“,”。“,”一般用于分隔数字，论文和著作作者姓名之后，但也无须过于严格，可根据具体情况选择是否使用“,”。

1　宋岩完成本文第一部分，审校和整理全文；李奕慧、王姿月完成本文第二至七部分。

（3）OSCOLA 不使用双引号，而使用单引号，例如 H Thirlway, 'The Law and Procedure of the International Court of Justice 1960 - 1989'。

4. 引用文献中有段号时，可以省略页码，直接援引段号，例如 *Military and Paramilitary Activities in and against Nicaragua* (Nicaragua v United States of America) (Judgment) [1986] ICJ Rep 14 [31]；如段号为 1.1 格式时，则需写为 para 1.1；如文献没有段号，特别是国际法院早期的判决、大部分论文和著作，则需援引页码，例如 *Corfu Channel case* (UK v Albania) (Merits) [1949] ICJ Rep 4, 22。

5. 援引段落一般用中括号加段号表示，例如只援引某一段 [31]，援引非连续多段 [31][35]，援引连续多段 [31]-[35]；援引页数一般直接用数字表示，例如 1 或者 1-2。

6. 案件名、书名、期刊名、*Compromis* 一般需斜体，其他部分一般无须斜体。

7. 再次引用注意问题：

（1）与上一条脚注的引注完全一致时，使用 ibid，例如 ibid [1]。

（2）条约一般在首次引用中增加条约缩写，再次引用直接写缩写，参见《联合国条约集》（UNTS）部分的范例。

（3）再次引用判例时，案名一般需简写，以简洁和便于识别为原则，例如 *Military and Paramilitary Activities in and against Nicaragua* 可以简写为 *Military and Paramilitary Activities*，然后在简写案名后加首次引用的脚注号，例如，该案在第 5 个脚注首次引用，再次引用则写为 *Military and Paramilitary Activities* (n 5)，详见本文判例部分的示范。

（4）再次引用国际组织文件，可以参考案例的写法，简写可以是文件名或者文件号。

（5）再次引用著作和论文时，简写仅保留作者姓氏，其余参考案例的写法，例如 Shaw (n 5)，详见本文著作和论文部分的示范。

（6）建议在书状定稿前，全文脚注应采取首次引用格式，待定稿后统一按照再次引用格式修改。

8. 本文未提及内容可参考 OSCOLA，其中规定更详细。如果 OSCOLA 没有规定，例如部分判例、国内法、国际组织文件，则可以参考一般标准和文中总结的基本格式，尽量全文统一。

二、国际条约

《国际法院规约》第 38 条第 1 款将国际条约列为第一项应当适用的国际法规则，可见其在国际法渊源中的重要地位。作为对缔约国有法律拘束力的明示协议，条约一般是法院裁判时首先考虑适用的渊源，也是书状写作中强有力的支撑。条约一般可以援引国际条约集，例如 UNTS (United Nations Treaty Series)，CTS (Consolidated Treaty Series) 或者 LNTS (League of Nations Treaty Series)；也可以援引各国官方条约集，例如 UKTS (UK Treaty Series)，ATS (Australian Treaty Series)；也可以援引 ILM (International Legal Materials) 等。

（一）联合国条约集（UNTS）

自联合国成立以来的主要国际条约一般可在 UNTC（United Nations Treaty Collection）官网检索。[2] 点击"Registration & Publication"选项，可以通过条约名称、通过时间等方式检索具体条约。

基本格式： 条约全称 |（通过时间，生效时间）| 卷号 |UNTS| 首页页码 |（条约缩写）| 具体条款 .

示例：首次引用

[5] International Covenant on Civil and Political Rights (adopted 16 December 1966, entered into force 23 March 1976) 999 UNTS 171 (ICCPR) art 1(2).

说明：

1. "999 UNTS 171" 表示该条约被编入 UNTS 第 999 卷，从该卷第 171 页开始，该编号可以在各条约页面确定。

2. 如下文将再次引用该条约，才需增加条约缩写，不再次引用则没有必要增加缩写。

示例：再次引用

[5] International Covenant on Civil and Political Rights (adopted 16 December 1966, entered into force 23 March 1976) 999 UNTS 171 (ICCPR) art 1(2).

……

[10] ICCPR art 5.

2　https://treaties.un.org/

（二）国际联盟条约

格式与联合国条约数据库基本一致，可在联合国条约集官网检索。[3] 如果检索不到条约的生效日期，则写明条约的签署或通过日期即可。

示例：

[5] Provisional Arrangement Concerning the Status of Refugees Coming from Germany (signed 4 July 1936) 3952 LNTS 77 art 1.

（三）双边条约

格式参照 UNTS，在条约名称后应写明双边条约的缔约方名称，并使用括号。

示例：

[5] Rehabilitation and Development Cooperation Agreement (Australia-Nauru) (5 May 1994) ATS 1994 15 art 1.

说明：

ATS 指代 *Australian Treaty Series*，即《澳大利亚条约集》。

三、判例

判例是模拟法庭中含金量较高的引注之一。尽管判例本身不是国际法的主要渊源，但法庭在判例中总结、解释和适用了国际法规则和概念，具有很高的借鉴价值。所以，无论是在书状中还是口头陈述中，都应熟练地引用和借鉴判例。

（一）国际法庭

1. 国际法院（ICJ）和常设国际法院（PCIJ）

常设国际法院（1922—1945 年）是国际法院的前身，其判决、年鉴等文件都被收录并公开在正式报告中，可以在国际法院官网检索。[4] 国际法院案件的判决、书状和庭审等相关文件也可在其官网检索到。[5]

---

3 https://treaties.un.org/Pages/LONOnline.aspx?clang=_en

4 http://www.icj-cij.org/icjwww/idecisions/icpi

5 http://www.icj-cij.org

基本格式：*案件名称（斜体）*|（当事方）|（判决类型）|[判决年份]|ICJ Rep| 判决于报告中的起始页码	引用页码 /[引用段落号].

示例：首次引用：

[5]*Corfu Channel case* (UK v Albania) (Merits) [1949] ICJ Rep 4, 22.

说明：

1. 需标明 ICJ 判决的类型，因为同一案件可能作出多个判决，例如 Preliminary Objections, Merits 等。

2. "ICJ Rep 4" 指的是该判决被收录于 ICJ Reports 中，判决从该报告的第 4 页开始。

3. ICJ 早期判决没有标注段号，所以引用时写页码。

4. 牛津引注标准避免使用标点符号，本脚注援引了该判决第 22 页的内容，但 "22" 前必须加 ","，属于例外情形，因为要与前面的起始页码 "4" 分开，否则会造成混淆。

[6]*Military and Paramilitary Activities in and against Nicaragua* (Nicaragua v USA) (Judgment) [1986] ICJ Rep 14 [31].

说明：

ICJ 后期判决标有段号，则页码可以省略，必须写清段落号，并使用中括号；如果段号为 1.1 形式时，则使用 para 1.1 格式。

[7]*Case Concerning the Factory at Chorzów* (Germany v Poland) (Merits) [1927] PCIJ Rep Series A No 17, 21.

示例：再次引用

[5]*Corfu Channel case* (UK v Albania) (Merits) [1949] ICJ Rep 4, 22.

[6]*Military and Paramilitary Activities in and against Nicaragua* (Nicaragua v United States of America) (Judgment) [1986] ICJ Rep 14 [31].

[7]*Case Concerning the Factory at Chorzów* (Germany v Poland) (Merits) [1927] PCIJ Rep Series A No 17, 21.

[8] ibid 22.

……

[10]*Corfu Channel* (n 5) 25.

[11]*Military and Paramilitary Activities* (n 6) [35].

[13]*Chorzów Factory* (n 7) 23.

2. 常设仲裁法院（PCA）

常设仲裁法院于 1899 年成立于荷兰海牙，为国际社会提供争端解决服务。它所处理的案件涉及领土、海洋边界、主权、国际投资以及国际贸易等一系列法律问题，具有参考价值，案件裁决等材料可在其官方网站上进行检索。[6]

基本格式： *案件名称（斜体）*|（当事方）|[裁决年份]| 案号 | 引用页码 /[引用段落号].

示例：首次引用

[5] *Arctic Sunrise Arbitration* (Kingdom of the Netherlands v Russian Federation) (Award on the Merits) [2015] PCA Case No 2014-02 [10].

示例：再次引用

[10] *Arctic Sunrise* (n 5) [20].

3. 联合国国际仲裁裁决报告（RIAA）

在国际法的渊源方面，仲裁裁决也属于《国际法院规约》第 38 条中的“司法判例”，作为“确定法律规则的辅助手段”，对于解释和适用国际法规则也具有参考价值。RIAA 即 *United Nations Reports of International Arbitration Awards*，是对国际仲裁裁决的汇编，裁决的电子版可以在其官网上检索。[7]

基本格式： *案件名称（斜体）*|（当事方）|[裁决年份]| 引用卷号 |RIAA| 裁决于报告中的起始页码 | 引用页码 /[引用段落号].

示例：首次引用

[5]*Tinoco Arbitration* (Great Britain v Costa Rica) [1923] 1 RIAA 369, 370.

[6]*Territorial Sovereignty and Scope of the Dispute* (Eritrea and Yemen) [1998] 22 RIAA 209 [10].

6 https://pca-cpa.org/en/cases/

7 https://legal.un.org/riaa/

示例：再次引用

[10]*Tinoco Arbitration* (n 5) 371.

[11]*Eritrea and Yemen case* (n 6) [20].

4. 国际投资争端解决中心（ICSID）

国际投资争端解决中心是专门解决国际投资争议的仲裁机构，ICSID 的判例主要被用于向法院阐释国际经济法领域的具体问题，有时也可用于论述程序问题，相关裁决可以在其官网数据库中检索。[8]

基本格式： *案件名称（斜体）* |（裁决类型）|[裁决年份]| 案号 |[引用段落号].

示例：首次引用

[5]*ADC v Hungary* (Award) [2006] ICSID Case No ARB/03/16[10].

[6]*The Rompetrol Group N.V. v The Republic of Romania* (Preliminary Objections on Jurisdiction and Admissibility) [2008] ICSID Case No ARB/06/3 [10].

示例：再次引用

[10]*ADC v Hungary* (n 5) [20].

[11]*Rompetrol Group N.V.* (n 6) [20].

5. 国际海洋法法庭（ITLOS）

国际海洋法法庭是依据 1982 年《联合国海洋法公约》设立的特别法庭，其判决、咨询意见汇编于 ITLOS Report 中，与案件相关的所有资料可于其官方网站检索。[9]

基本格式： *案件名称（斜体）* |（当事方）|（判决类型）|ITLOS Reports 判决年份	引用页码 /[引用段落号].

示例：首次引用

[5]*The 'Arctic Sunrise' case* (Netherlands v Russian Federation) (Provisional Measures) ITLOS Reports 2013 [10].

8　https://icsid.worldbank.org/en/Pages/cases/AdvancedSearch.aspx

9　http://www.itlos.org

示例：再次引用

[10]*Arctic Sunrise* (n 5) [20].

6. 国际刑事法庭（ICTY/ICTR/ICC）

前南斯拉夫国际刑事法庭（ICTY）[10]、卢旺达国际刑事法庭（ICTR）[11]、国际刑事法院（ICC）[12]的判例对于国际刑法和国际人道法问题具有参考价值，可以在各自官方网站上检索。

基本格式： *案件名称（斜体）*|（判决类型）|[判决年份]| 案号 |[引用段落号].

示例：首次引用

[5]*Prosecutor v DuškoTadić* (Judgment) [1997] ICTY IT-94-1-T [10].

[6]*Prosecutor v Akayesu* (Judgment) [1998] ICTR-96-4-T [10].

[7]*The Prosecutor v Omar Hassan Ahmad Al Bashir* (Judgment in the Jordan Referral re Al-Bashir Appeal) [2019] ICC-02/05-01/09-397-Corr [10].

示例：再次引用

[10]*Tadić* (n 5) [20].

[11]*Akayesu* (n 6) [20].

[12]*Bashir Jordan Appeal* (n 7) [20].

7. 国际法报告（ILR）

《国际法报告》是系统汇编国际法庭判决、国际仲裁裁决以及涉及国际法问题国内判决的英文报告集，涵盖了从 1919 年至今所有重要国际公法案件，涉及范围非常广泛，是书状写作中常见的论据。自 1929 年以来，该报告多次出版，但名称有所变化，其中第 1–16 卷名为《国际公法案件年度摘要》(*Annual Digest of Public International Law Cases*)；自第 17 卷起，开始以《国际法报告》为名出版。

基本格式： *案件名称（斜体）*|（当事方）|[判决年份]| 卷号 |ILR| 判决于报告中的起始页码 | 引用页码 /[引用段落号].

10 https://www.icty.org/en/cases

11 https://unictr.irmct.org/en/cases

12 https://www.icc-cpi.int/pages/cases.aspx

示例：首次引用

[5]*Delimitation of the Continental Shelf* (United Kingdom v France) [1979] 54 ILR 6, 10.

示例：再次引用

[10] *Delimitation of the Continental Shelf* (n 5) 20.

（二）区域法庭

1. 欧洲法院（ECJ）

欧洲法院是欧盟的最高法院，其首要任务是审查欧盟措施的合法性，确保欧盟法律的统一解释和适用。欧洲法院的案件判决、报告等相关文件可在其官网检索。[13]

基本格式：案号 | *案件名称（斜体）*|[判决年份]| 报告缩写 | 引用页码 /[引用段落号].

示例：首次引用

[5]Case C－176/03 *Commission v Council* [2005] ECR I–7879 [47]–[48].

说明：

该案的案号为 C－176/03，当事方为欧盟委员会和欧盟理事会，判决在 2005 年作出，被收录于 *European Court Report*（ECR）中（收录于 *Common Market Law Reports* 的则记为 CMIR）卷 I 中的第 7879 页，脚注援引了第 47 和 48 段。

示例：再次引用

[10]*Commission* (n 5) [47]–[48].

2. 欧洲人权法院

欧洲人权法院是根据《欧洲人权公约》第 19 条设立的常设机构，旨在维护 1948 年《世界人权宣言》中提及的部分权利。欧洲人权法院的判决、报告等可在其官网上检索。[14]

13　https://curia.europa.eu/jcms/jcms/j_6/en/

14　https://www.echr.coe.int/Pages/home.aspx?p=home

基本格式：*案件名称（斜体）*| 案号 | 引用页码 /[引用段落号].

示例：首次引用

[5]*Osman v UK* ECHR 1998-VIII 3124 [10].

[6]*Omojudi v UK* [2010] 51 EHRR 10 [10].

说明：

脚注 5 中该案的当事方为 Osman 和英国，被收录于 1998 年 *Reports of Judgments and Decisions*（ECHR）第 VIII 卷第 3124 页，该脚注援引了判决第 10 段；脚注 6 中该案的当事方为 Omojudi 和英国，判决在 2010 年作出，被收录于 *European Human Rights Reports*（EHRR）中第 10 页，该脚注援引了判决第 10 段。

示例：再次引用

[10]*Osman* (n 5) [20].

[11]*Omojudi* (n 6) [20].

3. 中美洲人权法院[15]

基本格式：*案件名称（斜体）*|[判决年份]|IACHR| 案号 | 引用页码 /[引用段落号].

示例：首次引用

[5]*Case of González et al v Mexico* [2009] IACHR Series C No 205 [10].

示例：再次引用

[10]*González case* (n 5) [20].

（三）国内法院

1. 英国法院

基本格式：*案件名称（斜体）*|[判决年份]| 引用卷号 | 案例集缩写 | 判决的起始页码 |（法院缩写）| 引用页码 /[引用段落号].

15 http://www.corteidh.or.cr/cf/Jurisprudencia2/busqueda_casos_contenciosos.cfm?lang=en

示例：首次引用

[5]*Barrett v Enfield LBC* [2001] 2 AC 550 (HL) [10].

说明：

该案的当事方是 Barrett 和 Enfield LBC，由 House of Lord（HL）在 2001 年作出裁决，裁决被收录于 *Appeal Cases*（AC）案例集第 2 卷，起始页码是第 550 页，脚注援引了第 10 段。

示例：再次引用

[10]*Barrett* (n 5) [20].

2. 美国法院

基本格式：*案件名称（斜体）* | 引用卷号 | 案例集缩写 | 判决的起始页码 |（年份）| 引用页码 /[引用段落号].

示例：首次引用

[5] *Miranda v Arizona* 384 US 436 (1996) 437.

说明：

本案的当事方是米兰达和美国亚利桑那州，判决被收录在美国最高法院（US Supreme Court）案例集（US）第 384 卷，起始页码是 436 页，判决作出的时间是 1996 年，脚注援引了第 437 页。

示例：再次引用

[10]*Miranda* (n 5) 440.

四、国际组织文件

国际组织文件并不属于《国际法院规约》第 38 条明确列明的国际法渊源。《联合国宪章》并未明确指出联合国决议对其会员国有法律拘束力，而在第 14 条、第 20 条和第 25 条中使用了“建议”一词。然而，一些重要的国际组织文件可能会总结或引导国家实践，并在一定程度上体现了各国的法律确信。这些文件也时常被国际法院援引，是书状的重要借鉴材料，尤其是在缺乏相关国际条约和案例时。文件一般可以在相关国际组织的官网上检索。[16]

16　联合国文件：https://www.un.org/zh/sections/general/documents/index.html 或 https://digitallibrary.un.org/；国际法委员会：https://legal.un.org/ilc/site_index.shtml。

基本格式： 机构名称（如之后将再次引用，括号需注明简称）|' 文件名 '（没有则可省略；如文件已被汇编成书，则需斜体）|（通过时间）| 文件号 | 引用页码 /[引用段落号].

1. **联合国大会** (UNGA)

示例：首次引用

[5] United Nations General Assembly (UNGA) 'Declaration on the Granting of Independence to Colonial Countries and Peoples'(14 December 1960) UN DocA/RES/1514 (XV).

示例：再次引用

[10] UN Doc A/RES/1514 (XV) (n 5).

或者，简写文件名

[10] Declaration on the Granting of Independence to Colonial Countries and Peoples (n 5).

2. **联合国安理会**（UNSC）

示例：首次引用

[5] United Nations Security Council (UNSC) UN Doc S/RES/2083 (17 December 2012).

示例：再次引用

[10] UN Doc S/RES/2083 (n 5).

3. **联合国第六委员会**（UN Six Committee）

联合国第六委员会是联合国大会处理法律问题的主要机构。

示例：首次引用

[5] United Nations General Assembly (UNGA) Sixth Committee 'Report of the Working Group on Measures to Eliminate International Terrorism' (29 October 2001) UN Doc A/C6/56/L9.

示例：再次引用

[10] UN Doc A/C6/56/L9 (n 5).

4. 联合国人权委员会（UNCHR）

联合国人权委员会是联合国审议人权问题的主要机构之一。

示例：首次引用

[5] United Nations Commission on Human Rights (UNCHR) UN Doc E/CN4/RES/2001/37 (2001).

示例：再次引用

[10] UN Doc E/CN4/RES/2001/37 (n 5).

5. 国际法委员会（ILC）

国际法委员会是联合国的国际法研究机构，其宗旨是促进国际法的发展和编纂。国际法委员会的条款草案具有重要参考价值，特别是对习惯国际法识别、国家责任等问题。

示例：首次引用

[5] International Law Commission (ILC) 'Draft Articles on Responsibility of States for Internationally Wrongful Acts, with Commentaries' (2001) UN Doc A/56/10 art 5, 43.

[6] ILC 'Draft Articles on Succession of States in respect of Treaties with Commentaries' *Yearbook of the International Law Commission* (1974) UN Doc A/CN4/SERA/1974/Addl (Part I) 200.

示例：再次引用

[10] ARSIWA (n 5) art 6, 44.

[11] Draft Articles on Succession of States in respect of Treaties (n 6) 205.

五、论文和著作

（一）论文

基本格式：作者名 ,|' 论文题目 '|（发表年份）| 卷数 | 期刊名全称或缩写 | 论文起始页码 | 引用页码 .

示例：首次引用

[5] Jeremy Waldron, 'The Core of the Case against Judicial Review' (2006) 115 Yale LJ 1346, 1372.

说明：

先名后姓，姓名缩写无须加标点，该论文发表于 *Yale Law Journal* 杂志 2006 年第 115 卷，首页页码为第 1346 页，脚注援引了论文的第 1372 页。

示例：再次引用

[10] Waldron (n 5) 1373.

说明：

只保留作者姓氏即可，无须加“,”。

（二）著作

基本格式：作者名 ,| *书名（斜体）*|（其他信息 , 版本 ,| 出版社 | 年份）| 引用页码 /[引用段落号].

1. 专著

示例：首次引用

[5] Malcom Shaw, *International Law* (6th edn, CUP 2008) 100.

说明：

书名需斜体。部分知名出版社可用缩写，例如 Cambridge University Press 可缩写为 CUP，Oxford University Press 可缩写为 OUP。

示例：再次引用

[10] Shaw (n 5) 102.

2. 编著或译著

示例：

[5] Jeremy Horder (ed.), *Oxford Essays in Jurisprudence: Fourth Series* (OUP 2000) 100.

[6] Peter Birks and Grant McLeod (trs.), *The Institutes of Justinian* (Duckworth 1987), 100.

说明：

编著或译著作者后加（ed.）或者（tr.），多人则加（eds.）或（trs.）。

3. 编著中的论文或章节

示例：

[5]Justine Pila, ‘The Value of Authorship in the Digital Environment’ in William H Dutton and Paul W Jeffreys (eds.), *World Wide Research: Reshaping the Sciences and Humanities in the Century of Information* (MIT Press 2010) 100.

六、网络资源

网络文献的效力相对有限，因此引用时务必慎重，频率不宜过高。

基本格式：作者名 ,|‘ 文章题目 ’|（发表日期）| 卷数（没有则忽略）| 期刊名或其他机构名称 |< 网址 >| 访问日期 .

示例：

[5]Graham Greenleaf, ‘The Global Development of Free Access to Legal Information’ (2010) 1(1) EJLT <http://ejlt.org/article/view/17> accessed 27 July 2010.

七、赛题事实

基本格式：*案件名称（斜体）*|（当事方）|（文件类型）|[年份]|（文件名缩写）|[引用段落号]/[序号].

示例：首次引用

[5]*Case concerning the Sisters of the Sun* (Atania v Rahad) (Special Agreement) [2016] (*Compromis*) [10].

[6]*Case concerning the Helian Hyacinth* (Adawa v Rasasa) (Statement of Agreed Facts) [2019] (*Facts*) [10].

[7]*Case concerning the Helian Hyacinth* (Adawa v Rasasa) (Clarifications) [2019] (*Clarifications*) [10].

说明：

如赛题是 Special Agreement 形式，则缩写为 *Compromis*；如赛题是 Statement

of Agreed Facts 形式，则缩写为 *Facts*。

示例：再次引用

[10] *Compromis* [20].

[11] *Facts* [20].

[12] *Clarifications* [20].